731 Rapid Recipes For Busy Cooks

SINCE the first issue of *Quick Cooking* magazine was published in 1998, folks across the country have come to enjoy its fast food full of "from scratch" flavor.

This *2002 Quick Cooking Annual Recipes* cookbook conveniently gathers every fast-to-fix recipe published in *Quick Cooking* during the year 2001—that's 731 recipes in all—into one reader-friendly collection. This recipe-packed book is filled with hundreds of mouth-watering photos, so you can see what many of the dishes look like before you prepare them.

Here's what else you'll find inside:

Chapters That Meet Your Needs. With 20 chapters that correspond to popular features in *Quick Cooking* magazine, it's a snap to find a recipe that matches your family's taste and your timetable. (A complete list of chapters can be found on page 3.)

For example, when your family is eyeing the table and *you're* eyeing the clock, see the "30 Minutes to Mealtime" chapter for 12 complete meals, all of which go from start to finish in less than half an hour.

Or when you have a mere 10 minutes to spare in the kitchen, rely on Basil Chicken Strips, Honey-Garlic Angel Hair, Lemon Blueberry Dessert or any of the 19 other timeless recipes in the "10 Minutes to the Table" chapter.

Award-Winning Recipes. You'll get all the palate-pleasing, quick-to-prepare foods that earned top honors in the six national contests we held last year: Flavorful Freezer Favorites, 30-Minute Side Dishes, Foods with Five Ingredients or Fewer, Swift 'n' Thrifty Recipes, Bake Sale Goodies and Delicious Company Dishes.

Easy-to-Use Indexes. To make all 731 recipes easy to find, we've listed them in two indexes. (See page 334.) The general index lists every recipe by food category and/or major ingredient. The alphabetical listing is great for folks who are looking for a specific family favorite. In both indexes, you'll find a bold red checkmark (✓) in front of all recipes that use less fat, sugar or salt and include Nutritional Analysis and Diabetic Exchanges.

What's on the Menu? To make meal planning simple, our food editors grouped several recipes from various chapters to create a host of around-the-clock suggested menus. (This time-saving tool appears on page 4.)

Every rapid recipe and helpful hint in this *2002 Quick Cooking Annual Recipes* cookbook was specifically selected with the busy cook in mind. You're sure to enjoy this timeless treasury for years to come...and you'll be able to treat your loved ones to comforting, wholesome home cooking without spending all of your precious time in the kitchen.

2002 Quick Cooking Annual Recipes

Editor: Julie Schnittka

Art Director: Kristin Bork

Food Editor: Janaan Cunningham

Associate Editors: Heidi Reuter Lloyd,
Jean Steiner, Susan Uphill

Production: Ellen Lloyd, Catherine Fletcher

Cover Photography: Rob Hagen

Food Photography Artist:
Stephanie Marchese

Taste of Home Books
©2001 Reiman Publications, LLC
5400 S. 60th St., Greendale WI 53129

International Standard Book Number:
0-89821-327-4
International Standard Serial Number:
1522-6603

PICTURED ON THE COVER: Creamy Lemonade Pie
(p. 201) and Almond Chicken Stir-Fry (p. 154).

To order additional copies of this book or any other Reiman Publications books, write: *Taste of Home* Books, P.O. Box 908, Greendale WI 53129; call toll-free 1-800/344-2560 to order with a credit card or visit our Web site at **www.reimanpub.com**.

Taste of Home's
QUICK COOKING

Executive Editor: Kathy Pohl
Editor: Julie Kastello
Food Editor: Janaan Cunningham
Associate Food Editor: Coleen Martin
Senior Recipe Editor: Sue A. Jurack
Recipe Editor: Janet Briggs
Associate Editors: Mark Hagen, Kristine Krueger
Test Kitchen Director: Karen Johnson
Test Kitchen Home Economists: Karen Wright, Julie Herzfeldt, Sue Draheim, Peggy Fleming, Joylyn Jans, Kristin Koepnick, Mark Morgan, Pat Schmeling, Wendy Stenman
Test Kitchen Assistants: Rita Krajcir, Megan Taylor
Editorial Assistant: Ursula Maurer
Design Director: Jim Sibilski
Art Director: Brian Sienko
Food Photography: Rob Hagen, Dan Roberts
Food Photography Artists: Stephanie Marchese, Vicky Marie Moseley
Photo Studio Manager: Anne Schimmel
Production: Ellen Lloyd, Catherine Fletcher
Publisher: Roy Reiman

⏱ Contents

What's on The Menu?

GRAB A MENU from the best "fast food" place in town—your kitchen! The price is right, the atmosphere is relaxing, and the service couldn't be friendlier nor the guests more appreciative. And with the *2002 Quick Cooking Annual Recipes* book in your hands, you've already given yourself a generous tip!

Here's how to use the menu ideas featured here: Our food editors screened all the recipes that appear in this book, then "grouped" several from various chapters to make up menus for everyday and special-occasion family meals. Plus, you can mix and match recipes to make up menus of your own.

For even more complete meals, turn to the following chapters: The Busiest Cooks in the Country (p. 6), 30 Minutes to Mealtime (p. 20), Thinking Up a Theme (p. 38) and Company's Coming! (p. 298).

Six Breakfast Choices

Eighteen Lunch Choices

Thirty-One Dinner Choices

FOR MOST FOLKS across the country, the day begins early in the morning and ends late in the evening. Between work, school and a slew of other activities, you probably pack more than possible into a typical day.

It's no wonder you think there's little extra time to prepare a wholesome, hearty dinner for your hungry brood. But this chapter pleasantly proves that even everyday menus can feature unforgettable fare.

Six fellow frenzied cooks from across the country share their family's most treasured recipes, time-saving tips and menu-planning pointers that are guaranteed to put you on the fast track for making marvelous meals your entire clan will clamor for.

MEMORABLE MEAL. Clockwise from upper left: Raspberry Sorbet, Green Rice, Dressed-Up Salad and Breaded Chicken Breasts (all recipes on pp. 14 and 15).

This Artist Designs Fast Food

HARDWORKING artist Christine Panzarella of Buena Park, California is so busy with her own home business, you would think she'd "bearly" have time for cooking.

"I just started designing a collectible line of bear jewelry that I call Heartfelt Teddies," Christine says of the cute items she molds, paints and sells on the Internet. "Although this keeps my hands full, I couldn't give up cooking. It's my favorite way to relax.

"Actually, I think preparing food is a lot like art. The key ingredient for both is imagination," she adds. "Because my studio is in our home, I can whip up a recipe between steps in my jewelry projects."

Her husband's schedule could easily paint Christine into a corner at mealtime. "Paul works in commercial refrigeration, and when he's on call, he can sometimes get home at 11 p.m.," she explains.

"That's why quick make-ahead dishes that can be reheated are a must for us. The busier we are, the more important sit-down dinners become. It's our time to spend together and talk about highlights of our day," Christine says.

The conversation might include her volunteer experience painting faces at hospitals or special events.

Other hobbies include swimming, gardening, reading and drawing upon her creativity with food. "I enjoy inventing original recipes," she says. "Then I letter each one onto a recipe card illustrated with my own watercolor picture of the dish.

"My sister Priscilla and I are currently working on mini cookbooks, complete with drawings, to give to family and friends. We can't think of a better way to show how much we care."

Those books may well be dedicated to the woman who stirred their interest in cooking—their mother, Kathy. "Mom always taught us the best time-saver is a clean, well-organized kitchen," Christine advises.

"I use airtight storage containers to keep cereal, crackers and nuts fresh. This also eliminates open boxes and clutter. And before I start a recipe, I make sure I have all of the ingredients and utensils close at hand," she notes.

Christine's grocery shopping strategy is equally streamlined. "Before my once-a-week trips to the store, I make a list of needed items and try to stick to it," she offers.

"I gather nonperishable items first, then go to the produce department and on to dairy, meats and frozen foods. That way everything stays cool until I get home.

"I purchase most of our meats in bulk," she says. "Later, I divide them into storage bags labeled with the type of meat and date. I keep them with other freezer essentials like vegetables, fruit and juice."

Flair for Fast Fare

Among Christine's made-in-minutes mainstays is her Heartwarming Chili. "Loaded with both beef and pork, it's extra meaty," she says. "I keep it mild so it's easy on sensitive stomachs and for children who can't handle hot spices.

"Prep time and cleanup are minimal, because I make it in one pot with convenient chili seasoning mix and canned tomatoes and beans. It's a meaty meal in one.

"This chili recipe is very versatile, too. Sometimes, I make the chili without beans and serve it on hot dogs, as a meat base for burritos or over white rice for a main dish," she notes.

Confetti Salad is a colorful accompaniment. "My mother-in-law shared this recipe," Christine recalls. "The red and yellow peppers add to its flavor and eye-appeal. To speed it to the table, I often use a package of mixed greens.

"I like to dress it with a bottled vinaigrette or ranch dressing," she adds.

For dessert, she assembles Crunchy Banana Splits, a hurried-up version of fried ice cream. Coated with buttery crushed cereal and nuts, they're a heavenly treat for drop-in company.

"When kids visit, I let them make their own sundaes with their favorite ice cream and extra toppings like toasted coconut and candies," she says. "Everyone has fun assembling these treats."

Christine's Color Cues

- In planning parties with family and friends, I often ask those attending to bring their favorite appetizer, side dish or dessert. That way, I spend more time with my guests than I do in the kitchen.

- I enjoy dressing up the table for dinner. Something as simple as a bouquet of fresh flowers, pretty napkins or candles can add to the atmosphere. If youngsters are on my guest list, I might use a stuffed animal or special toy and a sprinkling of colorful confetti as a centerpiece.

- When I'm feeling artistic, I love to add a full palette of fruits and veggies to my meals. I avoid overcooking produce to make sure it doesn't lose its vibrant colors.
  —*Christine Panzarella*

Heartwarming Chili

Ready in 1 hour or less

1 pound ground beef
1 pound ground pork
1 medium onion, chopped
1/2 cup chopped green pepper
1-1/2 to 2 cups water
1 can (15 ounces) tomato sauce
1 can (15 ounces) pinto beans, rinsed and drained
1 can (14-1/2 ounces) diced tomatoes, undrained
1 envelope chili seasoning mix
1/4 teaspoon garlic salt
Shredded cheddar cheese, sour cream, chopped green onions *and/or* hot pepper slices, optional

In a large saucepan or Dutch oven, cook beef, pork, onion and green pepper over medium heat until meat is no longer pink and vegetables are tender; drain. Add the water, tomato sauce, beans, tomatoes, chili seasoning and garlic salt. Bring to a boil. Reduce heat; simmer, uncovered, until heated through. Garnish with cheese, sour cream, green onions and/or hot peppers if desired. **Yield:** 8-10 servings.

Confetti Salad

Ready in 15 minutes or less

✓ Uses less fat, sugar or salt. Includes Nutritional Analysis and Diabetic Exchanges.

6 cups torn salad greens

1 can (2-1/4 ounces) sliced ripe olives, drained
1 small red onion, halved and sliced
1/2 cup chopped sweet red pepper
1/2 cup chopped sweet yellow pepper
1/2 cup shredded red cabbage
1 cup (4 ounces) shredded mozzarella cheese
1 to 2 cups Italian salad dressing *or* dressing of your choice

In a bowl, toss greens, olives, onion, peppers, cabbage and cheese. Serve with dressing. **Yield:** 8-10 servings.
Nutritional Analysis: One 3/4-cup serving (prepared with part-skim mozzarella and 1 cup fat-free Italian dressing) equals 77 calories, 3 g fat (2 g saturated fat), 8 mg cholesterol, 441 mg sodium, 7 g carbohydrate, 2 g fiber, 5 g protein. **Diabetic Exchanges:** 1-1/2 vegetable, 1/2 meat.

Crunchy Banana Splits

Ready in 30 minutes or less

2-1/2 cups crushed cornflakes
5 teaspoons butter *or* margarine, melted
4 teaspoons finely chopped pecans
5 cups vanilla ice cream, softened
5 medium ripe bananas, quartered
1/2 cup chocolate syrup
Whipped topping and maraschino cherries

In a bowl, combine the cornflakes, butter and pecans. Drop ice cream by 1/2 cupfuls into cornflake mixture and roll into a ball. Place two banana quarters in each dessert dish. Top with an ice cream ball, chocolate syrup, whipped topping and a cherry. **Yield:** 10 servings.

Fashioning a Fine Feast In a Flash

WHEN the weather becomes warmer, Cindy Reams is ready to spring ahead into a brand-new season. To begin, the energetic wife and mother from rural Philipsburg, Pennsylvania gets a jump on cooking.

"I'm an avid gardener, so my mind's more on starting seeds and plotting out my vegetable patch than on making elaborate dinners," Cindy says with a smile. "I grow everything from beets, beans and celery to peppers, sweet corn and tomatoes."

Raising two fast-sprouting daughters is also a priority for this down-to-earth mother. With help from her husband, Tim, she keeps pace with daughters Ashley and Hailey...and their paper routes and karate lessons as well.

To defend against mealtime mix-ups, Cindy's learned some effective moves of her own. "Tim alternates between day and night shifts as a corrections officer, so our menus are flexible enough to serve as lunch or dinner," she says.

"For us, restaurant meals are rare, so 'eating out' means a backyard barbecue," Cindy adds. "We make a point of eating together at least once a day. The dinner table is the place where we reconnect—the hub of our busy lives."

Between bites, her girls might ask, "What did you do in class today, Mom?" Cindy's a volunteer room mother and reading tutor at her daughters' school. She also enjoys quilting, crocheting, designing stationery on her computer and introducing her family to nature.

"As the weather warms up, we take long bike rides in the country," Cindy says. "In spring and summer, we gather wild fruit as it ripens, including raspberries and blackberries.

"When I was growing up, my mother passed on to me the basics of home canning and freezing. She also taught me the fastest, most efficient way to shop for produce: Go out to the garden and start picking! Homegrown flavor is the best."

Cindy picked up another insight as a girl. "My enjoyment of cooking declines as the stack of dirty dishes rises," she chuckles. "Now, after I finish using a utensil or dish, I put it directly into the dishwasher. In addition, I rework recipes so they can be prepared and served in one pan. That way, I don't spend all night scrubbing."

You'd have to get up pretty early to appreciate Cindy's trick for stocking up on groceries. "I shop first thing in the morning when it's not so crowded," she notes. "Not only is it easier to look around and check out quickly, the shelves have usually been restocked overnight.

"Along with cereals, soups and mixes, my favorite staples are instant rice, potatoes and couscous," she continues.

To whet her daughters' appetites for cooking, Cindy has made her kitchen kid-friendly. "I keep peeled bananas in our freezer. The girls enjoy blending them with milk and yogurt to make smoothies," she says.

"When I buy a watermelon, I remove the fruit with an ice cream scoop and keep it in an airtight container. The melon doesn't take up much refrigerator space, and the girls can easily serve themselves," she adds.

Adding special touches to food does not have to be tedious, Cindy explains, using her Herbed Chicken and Rice as an example. "A little bit of seasoning makes this entree smell and taste like Thanksgiving. Guests especially like the nice surprise of chopped walnuts.

"For an even nuttier texture, I sometimes substitute brown rice. Without the chicken, it makes a versatile side dish," she suggests.

To complement this speedy skillet supper, Cindy tosses together refreshing Salad with Vinaigrette. "This dressing is so popular in our house that I always keep a bottle in the fridge. Besides drizzling it on greens, I use it to top off my cold pasta salads," she notes.

Her final course is as easy as pie, Cindy reports. "Caramel Apple Burritos are such fun to experiment with. I've made them with different varieties of apples and have substituted applesauce or pie filling.

"Topped with ice cream, caramel or chocolate sauce, they make a memorable dessert. The girls and I even like fixing them for a snack."

Herbed Chicken and Rice

Ready in 30 minutes or less

✓ Uses less fat, sugar or salt. Includes Nutritional Analysis and Diabetic Exchanges.

- 1/2 **pound boneless skinless chicken breasts, cut into 1-inch strips**
- 1 **tablespoon butter** *or* **stick margarine**
- 2 **large carrots, shredded**
- 1 **small onion, chopped**
- 2 **cups water**
- 1/4 **teaspoon dried marjoram**
- 1/4 **teaspoon dried thyme**

1/8 teaspoon dried rosemary, crushed
1/8 teaspoon rubbed sage
   2 cups instant rice
1/2 cup chopped walnuts

In a skillet, saute the chicken in butter for 3-4 minutes. Add the carrots and onion; saute until tender. Add water and seasonings; bring to a boil. Stir in the rice. Cover and remove from the heat; let stand for 5 minutes. Sprinkle with walnuts. **Yield:** 5 servings.

Nutritional Analysis: One serving equals 299 calories, 11 g fat (2 g saturated fat), 31 mg cholesterol, 66 mg sodium, 35 g carbohydrate, 3 g fiber, 16 g protein. **Diabetic Exchanges:** 2 starch, 1 meat, 1 vegetable, 1 fat.

Salad with Vinaigrette

Ready in 15 minutes

   5 cups mixed salad greens
   1 small tomato, cut into wedges
   1 cup sliced cucumber
   1 small red onion, sliced and separated into rings
1/3 cup vegetable oil
   2 tablespoons plus 1-1/2 teaspoons red wine vinegar *or* cider vinegar
1-1/2 teaspoons sugar
1/2 teaspoon Italian seasoning
1/2 teaspoon lemon juice
   1 garlic clove, minced
Salt and pepper to taste

In a salad bowl, toss the greens, tomato, cucumber and onion. In a jar with a tight-fitting lid, combine the remaining ingredients; shake well. Drizzle dressing over salad just before serving. **Yield:** 5 servings.

Caramel Apple Burritos

Ready in 15 minutes or less

✓ Uses less fat, sugar or salt. Includes Nutritional Analysis and Diabetic Exchanges.

   3 large tart apples, peeled and sliced
10 caramels*
   5 flour tortillas (8 inches), warmed

Place apple slices in a saucepan; cover and cook over medium heat for 3-4 minutes or until tender. Reduce heat. Add caramels; cook and stir until caramels are melted. Spoon apple mixture off center on each tortilla; fold sides and ends over filling and roll up. **Yield:** 5 servings.

Nutritional Analysis: One serving equals 251 calories, 1 g fat (1 g saturated fat), 1 mg cholesterol, 294 mg sodium, 48 g carbohydrate, 2 g fiber, 5 g protein. **Diabetic Exchanges:** 2 starch, 1 fruit, 1/2 fat.

***Editor's Note:** This recipe was tested with Hershey brand caramels.

Cindy's Tips for Quick Creativity

- Try at least three new recipes a week. Your family won't sing those "same-old-thing" blues.
- Keep a log of the dishes you'd like to try. For easy reference, note the name of the recipe, the cookbook and page number where it's found.
- Record each day's main meal on a large calendar or computer file. You'll see at a glance when you last had a specific dish. Plus, it's fun to keep track of all the recipes you've tried.
- To increase feedback on new recipes, I make a little extra and deliver a "Taste-Testers' Special" to my parents.
  —Cindy Reams

Shorten Time Spent In Kitchen

IF LIFE followed a recipe, her family's would be filled with all sorts of interesting ingredients, confirms Lorna Nault from Chesterton, Indiana. At any given time, something fun and satisfying is cooking on all burners.

"We live a mile from Lake Michigan," Lorna says. "In summer, my husband, Tom, our sons and I enjoy picnicking, hiking and swimming. Our meals emphasize easy eating and quick cleanup so we can get out and savor all that the country has to offer."

This energetic mother has no problem keeping pace with sons Kevin and Adam, who are active in baseball, bowling and Cub Scouts. Tom stays on the go as a civil engineer designing roads, while Lorna puts her cooking know-how into words.

"I write a weekly food column for our local newspaper," she explains. "Luckily, I work at home, so I can take a break to sizzle up a stir-fry or make a casserole between deadlines.

"I prepare sit-down meals as often as possible," she continues. "The dinner table is a great place to catch up on each other's day.

"We volunteer together as a family for a cause that's very close to our hearts," Lorna shares. "Kevin has muscular dystrophy, and we participate in fund-raising events to help fight neuromuscular diseases."

A slow cooker is one of Lorna's recipe secrets. "When I need to be away for the day, I put it to work making soups, roasts, chili and more," she says. "I also depend on my microwave to defrost and heat food, and to cook instant potatoes or ramen noodles. Plus, it allows me to prepare, serve and store a dish all in one container."

Convenience foods do show up on her shopping list, Lorna acknowledges. "It's amazing the number of ways you can dress up boneless chicken breasts, sirloin steak, ground chuck and canned vegetables. They're among my staples along with pork chops, tuna, rice, soups and mixes for side dishes."

To appeal to her sons' sometimes finicky taste buds, Lorna regularly relies on kid-friendly cuisine.

"I look for basic recipes with steps that can be done in assembly-line fashion. Our sons enjoy make-it-yourself anything," she affirms. "To carry the lesson further, Tom and I let the boys play a part in the cleanup, too—as well as the menu planning."

A frequent entry on her men's meal request list is Fabulous Beef Fajitas. "It's a breeze to make with the no-fuss Italian dressing marinade and fast-cooking sirloin steak," Lorna says.

Red and green peppers add garden-fresh color and crispness to this tasty mixture. "If you prefer, pork tenderloin or chicken is a delicious replacement for the beef," she recommends.

Partner this Mexican main dish with Salsa Pinto Beans, a zippy alternative to refried beans. "This easy side dish is so homey and hearty," Lorna observes. "Sometimes I top it off with a sprinkling of shredded cheese or a dollop of sour cream."

A refreshing finale to this flavorful feast is "berry" simple, Lorna guarantees. "The only thing difficult about my Creamy Raspberry Pie is letting it chill. We can't wait for that first light, fluffy slice!"

Fabulous Beef Fajitas

Ready in 1 hour or less

✓ Uses less fat, sugar or salt. Includes Nutritional Analysis and Diabetic Exchanges.

- 1/2 **cup prepared Italian salad dressing,** *divided*
- 1/2 **teaspoon chili powder**
- 1 **pound boneless beef sirloin steak, cut into 1/4-inch strips**
- 1 **medium sweet red pepper, sliced**
- 1 **medium green pepper, sliced**
- 1 **medium onion, sliced and separated into rings**
- 6 **flour tortillas (8 inches), warmed**

In a large resealable plastic bag, combine 1/4 cup salad dressing and chili powder; add steak. Seal and turn to coat; refrigerate for 30 minutes. In a skillet, saute peppers and onion in remaining salad dressing until crisp-tender. Remove and keep warm. Drain steak, discarding marinade. In the skillet, saute steak for 6-8 minutes or until no longer pink. Return vegetables to pan; heat through. Spoon meat and vegetables down the center of tortillas; fold in sides. **Yield:** 6 servings.

Nutritional Analysis: One serving (prepared with fat-free Italian dressing) equals 289 calories, 8 g fat (2 g saturated fat), 45 mg cholesterol, 584 mg sodium, 33 g carbohydrate, 1 g fiber, 22 g protein. **Diabetic Exchanges:** 3 lean meat, 1-1/2 starch.

Salsa Pinto Beans

Ready in 15 minutes or less

- 1 **small onion, chopped**
- 1 **garlic clove, minced**

2 teaspoons minced fresh cilantro *or* parsley
1 tablespoon vegetable oil
2 cans (15 ounces *each*) pinto beans, rinsed
   and drained
2/3 cup salsa

In a large skillet or saucepan, saute onion, garlic and cilantro in oil until tender. Stir in the beans and salsa; heat through. **Yield:** 6 servings.

Lorna's Tips on Grocery Lists

- Keep your shopping list handy so you can jot down items as you run out of them.
- Pick out a few recipes you'd like to make in the coming week. Read them thoroughly and add ingredients you need to your grocery list.
- Arrange your grocery list to correspond to the store's layout. That saves you from revisiting aisles.
- Go through your store flyers and coupons and place stars on your grocery list beside sale items.
- Purchase large packages of meat when they're on special. Then wrap meal-size portions in plastic and foil, label with the contents and store in the freezer.
  —*Lorna Nault*

Creamy Raspberry Pie
Plan ahead...needs to chill

✓ Uses less fat, sugar or salt. Includes Nutritional Analysis and Diabetic Exchanges.

   1 package (3 ounces) raspberry gelatin
1/2 cup boiling water
   1 cup frozen vanilla yogurt
   1 cup fresh *or* frozen unsweetened raspberries
1/4 cup lime juice
   2 cups whipped topping
   1 graham cracker crust (9 inches)
Lime slices and additional raspberries and whipped topping, optional

In a bowl, dissolve the gelatin in boiling water. Stir in frozen yogurt until melted. Add raspberries and lime juice. Fold in whipped topping. Spoon into crust. Refrigerate for 3 hours or until firm. Garnish with lime, raspberries and whipped topping if desired. **Yield:** 8 servings.

Nutritional Analysis: One slice (prepared with sugar-free gelatin, reduced-fat frozen yogurt, reduced-fat whipped topping and reduced-fat graham cracker crust; calculated without garnish) equals 112 calories, 2 g fat (2 g saturated fat), 1 mg cholesterol, 259 mg sodium, 12 g carbohydrate, 1 g fiber, 7 g protein. **Diabetic Exchanges:** 1/2 starch, 1/2 lean meat, 1/2 fruit.

Family Time Around the Table

KARIN BAILEY hasn't forgotten that families used to gather at the supper table every night and enjoy a home-cooked meal with one another.

"My mom and dad made sure we ate dinner together as a family," recalls this Golden, Colorado cook. "That was very important to them—and to me, too."

But between managing the office at her church, volunteering at an elementary school and participating in an investment club, Karin was constantly racing against the clock.

Fortunately, she found ways to decrease her time in the kitchen and increase the time spent with her husband, Dick, and their sons, Derek and Kyle.

With some planning, Karin can assemble sit-down dinners at least five times a week. "Even when Dick is out of town, my boys and I sit at the table with real dishes and silverware and have a meal together," she says. "The trick is being organized and knowing what you're going to cook in advance."

One important lesson Karin says her mother taught her was to cook with fresh ingredients. To do that, Karin tends a large garden.

"I like to wash and cut several vegetables at one time," she shares. "Then I store them in the refrigerator for easy access. This really saves time when I need to throw a salad together.

Karin relies on recipes that are short on time but long on flavor. "My father used to serve spectacular dinners every Sunday," she says. "But he spent several hours cooking them.

"I want to give my family similar meals on Sunday nights, but without spending that much time in the kitchen. With a few basic ingredients, some fresh produce and a little planning, I can make Sunday suppers my family asks for time and again."

Karin's menu frequently features golden Breaded Chicken Breasts. "A friend and I created this recipe, and it's been a hit with my family ever since," she says. "We love the chicken's light lemon flavor and the moist breading." Green onions and parsley give Green Rice its name, but the appealing flavor is what makes it memorable.

Dressed-Up Salad is an attractive medley that works well with most main courses. "My mother served us this salad nearly every day," Karin recalls.

With an abundant crop of fresh raspberries from the backyard, it's no wonder Karin relies on Raspberry Sorbet for a tasty, no-fuss frozen dessert.

Breaded Chicken Breasts

Ready in 1 hour or less

- 3/4 cup dry bread crumbs
- 1/2 cup grated Parmesan cheese
- 4-1/2 teaspoons minced fresh parsley
- 3/4 teaspoon salt
- 1/4 teaspoon pepper
- 1/3 cup butter *or* margarine, melted
- 3 tablespoons lemon juice
- 2 garlic cloves, minced
- 6 boneless skinless chicken breast halves

Dash paprika

In a shallow bowl, combine the bread crumbs, Parmesan cheese, parsley, salt and pepper. In another bowl, combine the butter, lemon juice and garlic. Dip chicken in butter mixture, then roll in crumbs. Roll-up chicken jelly-roll style; place seam side down in a greased 11-in. x 7-in. x 2-in. baking dish. Drizzle with any remaining butter mixture; sprinkle with paprika. Bake, uncovered, at 350° for 35 minutes or until juices run clear. **Yield:** 6 servings.

Green Rice

Ready in 1 hour or less

- 1 cup chopped green onions
- 1 cup minced fresh parsley
- 4-1/2 teaspoons olive *or* vegetable oil
- 4-1/2 teaspoons butter *or* margarine
- 1-1/2 cups uncooked long grain rice
- 3 cups chicken broth
- 1/8 teaspoon cayenne pepper
- 1 bay leaf

Karin's Time-Saving Secrets

- I keep ingredients for a few favorite main dishes on hand. That way I can fall back on one of these recipes if something keeps me from making what I originally planned.

- Since I often use fresh lemon juice, I squeeze several lemons at one time and freeze the juice. When I need a few tablespoons for a recipe, I thaw the juice in the microwave in a jiffy.

- I plan for leftovers by cooking a large roast or grilling additional chicken breasts. Then I freeze the extras for nights when we need a quick meal.

—*Karin Bailey*

In a saucepan, saute onions and parsley in oil and butter for 1 minute or until tender. Add rice; cook over medium heat until rice is coated with oil and translucent, about 3 minutes. Stir in the broth, cayenne and bay leaf. Bring to a boil. Reduce heat; cover tightly and simmer for 18-20 minutes or until liquid is absorbed and rice is tender. Discard bay leaf. **Yield:** 6 servings.

Dressed-Up Salad

Ready in 15 minutes or less

- 1 package (8 ounces) ready-to-serve salad greens
- 1 cup sliced cucumber
- 1 cup julienned sweet red pepper
- 1 cup julienned green pepper
- 1/2 cup sliced radishes
- 1/3 cup sliced green onions
- 1/4 cup minced fresh parsley

DIJON VINAIGRETTE:
- 1/4 cup olive or vegetable oil
- 1/3 cup red wine vinegar or cider vinegar

- 1 teaspoon sugar
- 1 teaspoon minced fresh tarragon *or* 1/4 teaspoon dried tarragon
- 1 teaspoon Dijon mustard
- 1/4 teaspoon salt
- 1/8 teaspoon pepper

In a large salad bowl, combine the greens, cucumber, peppers, radishes, onions and parsley. In a jar with a tight-fitting lid, combine the vinaigrette ingredients; shake well. Drizzle over salad just before serving. **Yield:** 6 servings.

Raspberry Sorbet

Plan ahead...needs to freeze

- 1/4 cup plus 1-1/2 teaspoons lemon juice
- 3-3/4 cups unsweetened raspberries
- 2-1/4 cups confectioners' sugar

In a blender or food processor, combine all ingredients; cover and process until smooth. Pour into six dessert dishes. Cover; freeze for 1 hour or until set. Remove from freezer 15 minutes before serving. **Yield:** 6 servings.

Meat Pies Star in This Supper

WHEN Suzie Salle got married, she decided the kitchen would be her domain. And as she and husband Tom started their family, she found heartwarming value in preparing home-cooked dinners each night.

"I love cooking for my family," she says. "Preparing nutritious meals is a necessary part of everyday life, but I gladly do it. I make the time to prepare homemade meals every day—regardless of our busy schedules."

When not busy with the couple's four children—Nicholas, Jessica, Sophia and Isabella—Suzie is tending to the family home in Renton, Washington.

Keeping up and staying organized helps her run the household. "Being organized is a tremendous time-saver in the kitchen," she notes. "For example, I keep an ongoing grocery list so I'm aware of what ingredients I need. The list saves time in the long run because I never make a trip to the grocery store for just one item.

"I also keep the kitchen clean and organized while I'm cooking," Suzie shares. "If I feel overwhelmed, I stop, clean the area where I'm working and then go back to preparing the meal. It may not seem like it at first, but cooking becomes much speedier when things are neat and organized."

In addition, Suzie creates weekly dinner plans, making notes about each entree. "If grilled chicken is on my plan, I'll write myself a note to prepare and refrigerate a bit extra. This way, I'm able to eliminate a few steps when making chicken enchiladas later in the week.

"My notes highlight which dinners are a snap to reheat, too," she says. "As part-owner and butcher at his family's Italian grocery store, Tom works a varied schedule. There are many instances when he's not home for dinner, so I simply make a plate for him that he can pop in the microwave."

Suzie believes that growing produce at home is a great way to get kids involved in cooking. "Our children like picking veggies and fruit and then using them to help me prepare dinner," she notes. "I try to relate cooking to what the kids learn in school—subjects like reading, math and science.

"And there's nothing like having a few extra sets of hands in the kitchen," she says.

Cooks of all ages will be eager to fix dinner when it starts with golden Turkey 'n' Swiss Calzones. "These savory stuffed sandwiches are great when you're short on time," Suzie suggests.

Even though the dough is made from scratch, quick-rise yeast speeds up the preparation. "As the dough rises, you can prepare the simple filling and tend to other parts of your meal," she says. Leftovers freeze well, so the handheld pockets are perfect for last-minute lunches.

For a fast and flawless side dish, you'll need just three ingredients to fix colorful Green Beans with Tomatoes.

An impressive yet effortless dessert tops off meals at Suzie's house. Microwave Apple Crisp can be assembled in a snap and cooks up in minutes, making it a delectable dessert for unexpected guests.

For a sweeter sensation, use cinnamon graham crackers instead of the regular variety. "You'll love it served with a scoop of vanilla ice cream or whipped topping," she promises.

Turkey 'n' Swiss Calzones

    4 cups all-purpose flour
4-1/2 teaspoons quick-rise yeast
    2 teaspoons brown sugar
  1/4 teaspoon salt
1-1/2 cups water
    3 tablespoons olive *or* vegetable oil
3-1/2 cups cubed cooked turkey
1-1/2 cups (6 ounces) shredded Swiss cheese
    3 tablespoons Dijon mustard
    1 egg, beaten

In a mixing bowl, combine 3 cups flour, yeast, brown sugar and salt. In a saucepan, heat the water and oil to 120°-130°. Add to dry ingredients and beat until smooth. Stir in enough remaining flour to make a soft dough. Turn onto a floured surface; knead until smooth and elastic, about 4 minutes. Cover and let rest in a warm place for 15 minutes.

Meanwhile, in a bowl, combine the turkey, cheese and mustard. Divide dough into eight pieces. On a floured surface, roll each piece into a 7-in. circle. Place filling on half of each circle. Fold dough over filling; pinch seams to seal. Place on greased baking sheets. Brush with egg. Bake at 375° for 25-30 minutes or until golden brown. **Yield:** 8 servings.

Green Beans with Tomatoes

Ready in 15 minutes or less

2 pounds fresh *or* frozen cut green beans
4 large tomatoes, seeded and chopped
1 cup Italian salad dressing

Suzie's Kid-Friendly Kitchen

- It's fun to have little helpers in the kitchen, but be sure to supervise them. Choose tasks that are appropriate for their age, and only allow them to use kitchen tools that are safe for them to handle. For example, younger children can stir ingredients while older ones can use the microwave.
- If you grow your own produce, incorporate it into your meal preparation. Our kids love picking vegetables and fruits from our garden, washing berries and tearing lettuce for salads.
- Children will jump at the chance to help prepare foods they are familiar with and enjoy eating, such as desserts, snacks, cold sandwiches and salads.
- Teach your youngsters basic kitchen cleanup tasks. They'll learn valuable skills and get a great sense of accomplishment from helping out. —*Suzie Salle*

Place beans in a saucepan and cover with water; bring to a boil. Cook, uncovered, for 8-10 minutes or until crisp-tender; drain. Add the tomatoes and salad dressing; toss to coat. **Yield:** 8 servings.

Microwave Apple Crisp

Ready in 30 minutes or less

    1 cup graham cracker crumbs (about 16 squares)
1/2 cup all-purpose flour
1/2 cup packed brown sugar
    1 teaspoon ground cinnamon
1/2 teaspoon ground nutmeg
1/2 cup butter *or* margarine, melted
    8 medium tart apples, peeled and sliced
Whipped topping *or* ice cream

In a bowl, combine the cracker crumbs, flour, brown sugar, cinnamon, nutmeg and butter; mix well. Place apples in a greased microwave-safe 2-1/2-qt. baking dish. Top with crumb mixture. Microwave, uncovered, on high for 12 minutes or until apples are tender. Serve warm with whipped topping or ice cream. **Yield:** 8 servings.

Editor's Note: This recipe was tested in an 850-watt microwave.

Make the Grade with a Simple Supper

SUBTRACTING time from kitchen work is elementary for Lori Blevins. "My husband, Robert, and I are both teachers," explains the Douglasville, Georgia cook. "But because we work at different grade schools, we are racing between two calendars of extracurricular activities."

After the final bell rings, Lori helps out with school projects, grades papers and volunteers with the parent-teacher organization. Then she dashes home to take care of her two favorite teacher's pets—daughter Elizabeth and son Will.

"Even though Robert and I have complicated schedules with ever-changing hours, I make sure we sit down to dinner as a family five or six times each week," she shares.

"I can't allow complicated meal preparations to interfere with that, so I fix as much of the meal as possible the night before," she says. "After the children go to sleep, I brown meat, slice veggies and complete whatever steps I can for the following night's dinner.

"Sometimes, I'll have dinner completely ready the night before, particularly if it's a casserole," she continues. "Then, as soon as we get home, we just pop it in the oven."

Another of Lori's time-saving secrets is creating weekly dinner plans that take leftovers into consideration. "For example, I'll serve a roast for supper, planning to turn what's left into Italian beef sandwiches the next day," she says. "Other times, I'll prepare a little extra, freezing the leftovers for a night that I know will be particularly busy."

When she needs to throw together a side dish or two, Lori turns to pantry staples. "Instant rice and quick-cooking pasta are great ways to round out meals when you're pressed for time," she suggests. "I depend on convenience products like minced garlic in a jar and dried minced onion to quickly season sides and get them on the table fast.

"I also keep packages of frozen vegetables on hand," she continues. "And when I'm chopping peppers, I freeze a handful or two in a resealable bag. This saves time when I want to add them to soups, stews or whatever I'm making in the slow cooker."

Lori uses her slow cooker often, especially on the weekends. "My mom cooked this way quite a bit, and it rubbed off on me," she says.

"When I come home from volunteering at our church's Sunday school program, I put a few ingredients in the slow cooker. We have a meal that night and I don't spend my Sunday in the kitchen. Instead, I can read, cross-stitch and, most importantly, spend time with my children and husband.

"While I want to provide great meals for my family, I don't want to spend a lot of time fixing them," Lori says. "Keeping the preparation simple leaves plenty of time to play with the kids, give them baths, read them stories and all of the other things that make having children so wonderful."

Lori says she and Robert are constantly on the lookout for good food that's ready in a jiffy. And since Basil Orange Chops require only one pan and little work, both teachers give this flavorful dish high marks. An easy-to-prepare orange sauce nicely dresses up the tender chops.

"It's a delicious main course that comes together easily when time is short," Lori comments. "It's special enough for company and wonderful when served with Zucchini Rice Pilaf.

"I created the colorful rice and veggie side dish one night by combining a few ingredients I had on hand," she explains. "Robert loved it, and I've been making it ever since." If your family's not big on zucchini, Lori suggests yellow squash or mushrooms instead.

"While the pilaf is simmering, I mix up the filling for Pecan Chocolate Pie, pour it into a prepared pastry crust and pop it in the oven," she adds. Chock-full of nuts and chocolate chips, the sweet treat is the perfect ending to the meal.

"For a change of pace, replace the chocolate chips with the butterscotch variety," recommends Lori. "No matter which you use, guests are bound to ask for the recipe...and a second slice."

Basil Orange Chops

Ready in 30 minutes or less

    4 boneless butterflied pork chops (1/2 inch thick)
    1 green onion, sliced
    1 tablespoon vegetable oil
    1 cup orange juice
    1 tablespoon grated orange peel
    2 teaspoons dried basil
    2 teaspoons cornstarch
    2 teaspoons water

In a large skillet, brown pork chops and onion in oil. Add the orange juice, peel and basil. Cover and cook until meat juices run clear. Remove chops and keep warm. In a small bowl, combine the cornstarch and water until smooth; add to the skillet. Cook and stir for 2 minutes or until thickened. Serve over the chops. **Yield:** 4 servings.

Zucchini Rice Pilaf

Ready in 30 minutes or less

✓ Uses less fat, sugar or salt. Includes Nutritional Analysis and Diabetic Exchanges.

1/2 teaspoon dried basil
2 tablespoons butter *or* stick margarine
2-1/4 cups water
1-1/4 teaspoons chicken bouillon granules
1 cup uncooked long grain rice
1/2 cup shredded carrot
1 small zucchini, halved and thinly sliced

In a skillet, saute basil in butter for 1 minute. Add water and bouillon; bring to a boil. Stir in the rice and carrot. Reduce heat; cover and simmer for 10 minutes. Add zucchini; simmer 10 minutes longer or until vegetables are tender. **Yield:** 4 servings.

Nutritional Analysis: One serving (1 cup) equals 235 calories, 6 g fat (4 g saturated fat), 16 mg cholesterol, 427 mg sodium, 40 g carbohydrate, 2 g fiber, 4 g protein. **Diabetic Exchanges:** 2 starch, 2 vegetable, 1/2 fat.

Pecan Chocolate Pie

1 cup sugar
1/2 cup all-purpose flour
2 eggs
1/2 cup butter *or* margarine, melted
3/4 cup semisweet chocolate chips
1/2 cup chopped pecans
1 unbaked pastry shell (9 inches)
3/4 cup whipping cream, whipped
2 tablespoons miniature semisweet chocolate chips

In a mixing bowl, combine sugar, flour and eggs. Add butter; mix well. Fold in chocolate chips and pecans. Pour into pastry shell. Bake at 350° for 35-40 minutes or until a toothpick inserted near the center comes out with moist crumbs and edges begin to crack. Cool on a wire rack. Garnish with whipped cream and miniature chips. Store in refrigerator. **Yield:** 6-8 servings.

Grocery Shopping Made Simple

- Create your shopping list based on a weekly dinner plan. Ideally, you'll have to go to the grocery store only once a week, avoiding additional trips for one or two ingredients.
- Keep the list on the refrigerator or in the kitchen in clear view. If you see it regularly, you're more likely to remember to add items to it.
- Add staples to the list as soon as you run low. Even if your weekly dinner plan doesn't call for a particular staple, add it to the list so you have it on hand when you need it.

—Lori Blevins

BUSY weekdays call for made-in-minutes menus that can be prepared in a flash and fill up your family fast.

So when your hectic schedule doesn't allow you to spend hours in the kitchen, rely on these 12 complete meals that you can put together in a half hour or less.

In addition to the appealing assortment of full menus, you'll find 12 savory side dishes that also go from start to finish in a mere 30 minutes.

Each and every fast-to-fix favorite comes from the recipe file of a fellow busy cook. So your family is sure to give each delicious dish rave reviews.

SPEEDY SIDES. Clockwise from upper left: Southwestern Spuds (p. 36), Garbanzo Gazpacho (p. 34), Creamy Fruit Salad (p. 37) and Creole Green Beans (p. 35)

FEEDING THE MINDS of young students and the stomachs of family and friends gives lots of satisfaction to Traci Maloney of Toms River, New Jersey.

Traci, a busy wife, mother and high school English teacher, is an avid recipe collector and cook. Still, there are days when she has little time in her kitchen.

"I leave the house at 6 a.m. on weekdays and must come up with meals for my husband, Michael, an attorney who works late several nights a week, and our daughter, Diane.

"My mom, brother and sister-in-law live within walking distance, so they join us frequently for supper," she adds.

Traci is the dinner coordinator for her church's midweek children's program. "I plan, shop for and help prepare a meal for 80 children and volunteers once a week," she says. She also periodically provides food for a local group that helps those in need.

When cooking for her own family, Traci often fixes a big batch of soup on the weekend and a special Sunday dinner, so there are leftovers on hand for quick meals during the week.

"Other weeknights, I rely on easy dishes that taste impressive but save time by using convenience items," she shares. The rapid recipes in this satisfying supper are good examples.

To start, Traci works backward and makes dessert first. "White Chocolate Tarts are scrumptious but really no fuss, because they call for prepared tart shells, instant pudding and whipped topping," she explains.

While the tarts chill, she makes Turkey Noodle Stew, a mixture of turkey, vegetables and noodles.

For a quick complement to the effortless main dish, Traci bakes Crunchy Biscuits. Convenient refrigerated biscuits get a tasty treatment when topped with crushed corn chips. "They couldn't be easier," she promises.

Turkey Noodle Stew

2 turkey breast tenderloins (about 1/2 pound *each*), cut into 1/4-inch slices
1 medium onion, chopped
1 tablespoon vegetable oil
1 can (14-1/2 ounces) chicken broth
1 can (10-3/4 ounces) condensed cream of celery soup, undiluted
2 cups frozen mixed vegetables
1/2 to 1 teaspoon lemon-pepper seasoning
3 cups uncooked extra wide egg noodles

In a large skillet, cook turkey and onion in oil until turkey is no longer pink, about 6 minutes; drain. Combine the broth, soup, vegetables and lemon-pepper. Add to the skillet; bring to a boil. Stir in noodles. Reduce heat; cover and simmer for 10 minutes or until noodles and vegetables are tender. **Yield:** 6 servings.

Crunchy Biscuits

1 tube (7-1/2 ounces) refrigerated home-style biscuits, separated into 10 biscuits
1 tablespoon butter *or* margarine, melted
1/3 cup crushed corn chips

Arrange biscuits in a greased 8-in. round baking pan. Brush with butter. Sprinkle with corn chips; gently press into dough. Bake at 400° for 14-16 minutes or until golden brown. **Yield:** 10 biscuits.

White Chocolate Tarts

1 can (14 ounces) sweetened condensed milk
1 cup cold water
1 package (3.4 ounces) instant white chocolate pudding mix
2 cups whipped topping
2 packages (6 count *each*) individual graham cracker tart shells

In a mixing bowl, combine milk, water and pudding mix. Beat on low speed for 2 minutes. Cover and refrigerate for 10 minutes. Fold in whipped topping. Spoon about 1/3 cup into each tart shell. Refrigerate until serving. **Yield:** 12 servings.

To round out the meal, she serves glasses of Frosty Fruit Drink. "Since you just toss everything into the blender, these smooth thick shakes are ready in minutes," Jo assures.

Cheesy Broccoli Soup

2 cups water
1 teaspoon chicken bouillon granules
1 package (16 ounces) frozen chopped broccoli, thawed
1 medium onion, chopped
1/4 cup butter *or* margarine
3 tablespoons all-purpose flour
1 cup milk
1 pound process American cheese, cubed

In a large saucepan, bring water and bouillon to a boil. Add broccoli. Reduce heat; cover and simmer for 3-4 minutes or until crisp-tender. Drain, reserving 3/4 cup liquid. In another large saucepan, saute onion in butter until tender. Whisk in flour until blended. Add the milk and cheese. Cook over medium-low heat until cheese is melted, stirring frequently. Stir in broccoli and reserved cooking liquid. **Yield:** 4 servings.

Speedy Supper Is a Science

ALL THE ELEMENTS are in place for Jo Maasberg, a high school science teacher and farm wife in Farson, Wyoming, to make fast no-fuss meals a priority. Both she and her husband, Bob, have busy schedules.

"I teach a variety of classes, including biology, chemistry and physical science," Jo explains. "When I get home, I correct students' papers, then help Bob outside on our grain farm.

"He also works part-time as an electrician, so dinners are often hurried or eaten late in the evening," she continues.

Jo's life is the textbook description of busy. She sponsors school activities, helps prepare meals for church gatherings, sells cosmetics out of her home, belongs to reading and writing groups and stays in touch with daughters Jennifer and Billie Jo on the West Coast.

When time is short, Jo doesn't experiment in the kitchen. What's her secret for eating well and still beating the clock? She chooses proven recipes that can be prepared quickly and easily.

That's why she often serves Cheesy Broccoli Soup. "This creamy and flavorful soup goes together in a flash because it uses frozen chopped broccoli and process American cheese," she explains. Plus, it's easy to warm up if Bob works late.

While the soup simmers, Jo assembles tasty Mozzarella Tuna Melts. "Our daughter's home economics teacher shared the recipe for these all-American favorites," she notes.

Mozzarella Tuna Melts

✓ Uses less fat, sugar or salt. Includes Nutritional Analysis and Diabetic Exchanges.

1 can (6 ounces) water-packed tuna, drained and flaked
1/4 cup finely chopped celery
1/4 cup finely chopped onion
1/4 cup mayonnaise
4 hamburger buns, split
4 mozzarella cheese slices
4 tomato slices
4 lettuce leaves

In a bowl, combine the tuna, celery, onion and mayonnaise. Spread on bottom of buns; set bun tops aside. Top tuna mixture with a slice of cheese and tomato. Place on an ungreased baking sheet. Bake, uncovered, at 350° for 12-15 minutes or until heated through and cheese is melted. Top each with a lettuce leaf; replace bun tops. **Yield:** 4 servings.

Nutritional Analysis: One serving (prepared with fat-free mayonnaise and part-skim mozzarella) equals 272 calories, 8 g fat (4 g saturated fat), 28 mg cholesterol, 648 mg sodium, 27 g carbohydrate, 2 g fiber, 23 g protein. **Diabetic Exchanges:** 2 starch, 2 lean meat.

Frosty Fruit Drink

1 cup unsweetened raspberries
2 medium ripe bananas
1-1/2 cups frozen vanilla yogurt
1 1/2 cups raspberry-blend juice, chilled

In a blender, combine all ingredients. Cover and process until smooth. Pour into glasses; serve immediately. **Yield:** 4 servings.

moist and mildly flavored," she says. "They can be broiled in the oven, but I often cook them on our outdoor grill instead to reduce kitchen cleanup.

"While the fish is marinating, I toss together a big bowl of Italian Spinach Salad," Judy continues. "Prepared Italian dressing makes this twist on traditional wilted spinach salad simple to fix."

Her fast finale, Pound Cake with Sherbet, is easy to assemble and sure to get compliments. "It's lusciously light and refreshing. Feel free to vary the fruit to suit what's in season," Judy adds.

Broiled Orange Roughy

✓ Uses less fat, sugar or salt. Includes Nutritional Analysis and Diabetic Exchanges.

1-1/2 pounds fresh *or* frozen orange roughy, red snapper *or* haddock fillets, thawed
1 teaspoon garlic powder
1/4 cup butter *or* stick margarine, melted
1/4 cup lemon juice
1/4 cup soy sauce
Paprika

Place the fillets in a shallow dish; sprinkle with garlic powder. Combine the butter, lemon juice and soy sauce; pour over fish and turn. Marinate for 10 minutes. Drain and discard marinade. Place fillets on a broiler pan. Broil 3-4 in. from the heat for 10 minutes or until the fish flakes easily with a fork, turning once. Sprinkle with paprika. **Yield:** 4 servings.

Nutritional Analysis: One serving (prepared with orange roughy and reduced-sodium soy sauce) equals 189 calories, 7 g fat (4 g saturated fat), 50 mg cholesterol, 489 mg sodium, 5 g carbohydrate, trace fiber, 26 g protein. **Diabetic Exchanges:** 4 very lean meat, 1 fat.

Italian Spinach Salad

1 package (6 ounces) fresh baby spinach
1 green onion, thinly sliced
1 hard-cooked egg, chopped
3 bacon strips, cooked and crumbled
3 tablespoons Italian salad dressing
2 tablespoons shredded Parmesan cheese

In a large salad bowl, toss spinach, onion, egg and bacon. In a microwave-safe bowl, heat salad dressing on high for 30-45 seconds or until warm. Pour over the salad and toss to coat. Sprinkle with Parmesan cheese. Serve immediately. **Yield:** 4 servings.

Pound Cake with Sherbet

4 slices pound cake (3/4 inch thick)
1 pint raspberry sherbet *or* flavor of your choice
1 cup fresh raspberries *or* fruit of your choice

Place pound cake on dessert plates. Top each slice with a scoop of sherbet and raspberries. **Yield:** 4 servings.

Savor These Time-Savers

ONCE upon a time, Judy Bernacki spent a good part of most days preparing meals. Luckily, she learned to make a short story of her long hours in the kitchen.

"For years, I made daily meals for my husband, Gene, and our two children. We often had dinner guests besides," the Las Vegas, Nevada native states. "Now that our children are adults, my interests have grown beyond the kitchen."

An avid reader and recipe collector, Judy is also active in her church. Currently, she volunteers as a hospital chaplain, offering patients prayers and words of encouragement.

As an empty nester, she's ready to spread her culinary wings. "Since I've found ways of doing things more efficiently, I like cooking more than ever," Judy shares.

"A slow cooker or bread machine can give new life to an old recipe. And I'm always eager for other cooks to share their ideas and suggestions," she notes.

"I figure no matter our age, interests or family situation, we all have to eat," she laughs. "So we may as well make meal planning and preparation as enjoyable as we can."

One entree Judy guarantees will catch diners' fancy is her Broiled Orange Roughy. "The fillets are flaky,

Rapid Recipes Drive Dinner

WITH a full-time job, a teenage daughter and a husband who's a truck driver, Chris Rentmeister of Ripon, Wisconsin is accustomed to life in the fast lane.

Even with a schedule that's bursting at the seams, Chris fits in plenty of time for her family. "My husband, Horst, our daughter, Carrie, and I try to share a sit-down meal every day," she says.

To steer clear of mealtime roadblocks, Chris plans menus a week ahead. "I write down each dish and create a grocery list at the same time," she reports.

On weekends, work demands simmer down—and the oven heats up. "I do most of my baking on Saturday and Sunday, often with Carrie's help," Chris says. "It's fun to experiment with cookie recipes and tuck our successes into Horst's lunches."

A main dish that's always a family favorite is tender and savory Dijon Pork Chops. "They only take minutes to prepare, but they taste like you've fussed for hours," she affirms.

While the chops bake, Chris speeds nicely seasoned Garlic Carrots to her skillet. She uses bite-size carrots that don't need to be cut or peeled and keeps a jar of prepared minced garlic on hand to save time.

"To complete the meal, I pass a basket of Mini Cheese Biscuits," Chris notes. "We're garlic lovers, so we enjoy the flavor of these easy biscuits.

"Friends and family tell me these treats are best warm from the oven," Chris adds. "But then, they never last long enough to cool off!"

Dijon Pork Chops

✓ Uses less fat, sugar or salt. Includes Nutritional Analysis and Diabetic Exchanges.

      3 tablespoons Dijon mustard
      6 boneless pork loin chops (1-1/2 pounds
        and 3/4 inch thick)
    1/3 cup seasoned bread crumbs
Dash pepper

Spread mustard on both sides of pork chops. Place in a greased shallow 2-qt. baking dish. Combine crumbs and pepper; press onto top and sides of chops. Bake, uncovered, at 375° for 20-25 minutes or until meat juices run clear and topping is lightly browned. **Yield:** 6 servings.

Nutritional Analysis: One serving equals 179 calories, 6 g fat (2 g saturated fat), 72 mg cholesterol, 424 mg sodium, 6 g carbohydrate, trace fiber, 25 g protein. **Diabetic Exchange:** 3 lean meat.

Garlic Carrots

✓ Uses less fat, sugar or salt. Includes Nutritional Analysis and Diabetic Exchanges.

      1 pound baby carrots
      2 garlic cloves, minced
      1 to 2 tablespoons olive *or* canola oil
    1/4 cup hot water
    1/2 teaspoon salt
    1/4 teaspoon dried thyme
Dash pepper

In a skillet, saute carrots and garlic in oil for 5 minutes. Add water, salt, thyme and pepper. Bring to a boil. Reduce heat; cover and cook for 8-12 minutes or until carrots are tender. **Yield:** 6 servings.

Nutritional Analysis: One 2/3-cup serving (prepared with 1 tablespoon oil) equals 50 calories, 3 g fat (trace saturated fat), 0 cholesterol, 222 mg sodium, 7 g carbohydrate, 1 g fiber, 1 g protein. **Diabetic Exchange:** 2 vegetable.

Mini Cheese Biscuits

      2 cups biscuit/baking mix
    1/2 cup shredded cheddar cheese
      2 garlic cloves, minced
    2/3 cup milk
      2 tablespoons butter *or* margarine, melted
    1/4 teaspoon garlic powder

In a bowl, combine biscuit mix, cheese and garlic. With a fork, stir in milk just until moistened. Drop by rounded tablespoonfuls onto a lightly greased baking sheet. Bake at 450° for 9-11 minutes or until golden brown. Combine butter and garlic powder; brush over biscuits. **Yield:** about 1 dozen.

Make Haste In Kitchen

A TASTE for anything homemade explains Lorri Speer's appetite for crafting and her short-on-time creativity in the kitchen.

"As a buyer, designer and events planner for my parents' craft store, I cook up some pretty interesting projects," says the Centralia, Washington mom. "We publish a monthly crafters' newsletter, and I often include favorite recipes along with fun packaging ideas."

Lorri is wrapped up in family life, too. Her husband, Jeff, is a detective with the state patrol, and daughter Jacki and son Steven are active in all sorts of sports. "Our schedules are never the same twice," she reports.

"I also teach part-time as a clinical nursing instructor at our community college," Lorri continues. "Often, I go from work...to a basketball, soccer or volleyball game...and then home, within minutes of mealtime."

With such a demanding game plan, Lorri raises a cheer for her slow cooker. "Opening the front door to the aroma of a supper that's ready to eat is so comforting," she says.

"In my spare time, I page through my cookbook collection looking for recipes I can shorten. The crafty side of me is always dreaming up ways to modify a pattern, with a nip here or a tuck there," Lorri shares. "I do the same with recipes—altering them to fit our busy family."

For example, she took the concept for the fast-food chicken snacks her children love and turned out home-cooked Sesame Chicken Strips. "I start with chicken that is partially frozen, because it's easier to cut," Lorri notes. "Then I cover it with an easy crushed cracker coating. A hint of ginger really jazzes up the flavor."

While the chicken bakes, she tosses together Crisp 'n' Crunchy Salad. "I always have the easy ingredients for this fun combination on hand," she says. "Plus, kids don't mind eating their fruits and veggies when they're glazed with sweet honey."

To complete the meal, Lorri whips up a pan of Chocolate Peanut Butter Bars. "These chewy cereal treats are the perfect no-fuss contribution to a potluck or bake sale," she adds. "I've discovered a few minutes in the refrigerator helps the bars' frosting set faster. Of course, the trick is getting them in there before they disappear!"

Sesame Chicken Strips

    3 tablespoons butter *or* margarine, melted
    1 tablespoon soy sauce
    1 cup crushed sesame snack crackers (about 30 crackers)
    1 teaspoon ground ginger
  1/4 teaspoon salt
    1 pound boneless skinless chicken breasts, cut into 1-inch strips

In a bowl, combine the butter and soy sauce. In another bowl, combine the cracker crumbs, ginger and salt. Dip chicken strips in butter mixture, then roll in crumbs until coated on all sides. Place in a single layer on a greased baking sheet. Bake at 450° for 10 minutes or until juices run clear. **Yield:** 6 servings.

Crisp 'n' Crunchy Salad

    1 medium Golden Delicious apple, chopped
    1 medium red apple, chopped
    2 celery ribs, thinly sliced
  1/2 cup chopped walnuts
  1/2 cup golden raisins
  1/4 cup honey

In a bowl, combine the first five ingredients. Add honey; mix well. Serve immediately. **Yield:** 6 servings.

Chocolate Peanut Butter Bars

    1 cup sugar
    1 cup light corn syrup
    1 cup peanut butter
    6 cups crisp rice cereal
    2 cups (12 ounces) semisweet chocolate chips, melted

In a large saucepan, combine the sugar, corn syrup and peanut butter. Cook over medium-low heat until the sugar is dissolved. Remove from the heat; add cereal and stir until coated. Spread into a greased 13-in. x 9-in. x 2-in. pan; press lightly. Spread melted chocolate over bars. Chill. **Yield:** 1-1/2 to 2 dozen.

Trot Out Brisk Dinners

AFTER horsing around on the job all day, Sherri Parks finds it can be a race to mealtime.

"Living in the heart of Florida's horse country, I show Thorough-breds at local breeders' sales," Sherri shares from her home in Silver Springs.

"My husband, Charles Goosmann, and I try to have at least one sit-down meal together every day," Sherri says. "That's a challenge, since his schedule is as action-packed as mine.

"As the technical director for our local civic theater, he's busy building sets or making sure the production runs smoothly," she says.

"We enjoy inviting people over for dinner. Traditionally, I plan menus that allow me to spend time with our guests. I also rely on recipes I can start before they arrive," Sherri continues.

One exceptional entree Sherri gets cracking on in advance is her Tuna Cheese Omelet. "I try to keep chopped mushrooms, olives and onions in the refrigerator to cut down on prep time," she says.

Precut ingredients also take the effort out of Fiesta Mixed Greens. "It's a colorful and refreshing side dish," Sherri says.

Guests always save room for fun and frosty Watermelon Sundaes.

Tuna Cheese Omelet

    3 fresh mushrooms, chopped
    2 tablespoons chopped ripe olives
    1 green onion, chopped
    2 garlic cloves, minced
    1 teaspoon butter or margarine
    6 eggs
 1/4 cup milk
 1/4 cup canned tuna, drained and flaked
    1 teaspoon Italian seasoning
 1/2 teaspoon salt
 1/4 teaspoon pepper
    1 cup (4 ounces) shredded cheddar cheese

In a large skillet, saute the mushrooms, olives, onion and garlic in butter. In a bowl, lightly beat the eggs and milk; pour over vegetables. Cook over medium heat; as eggs set, lift edges, letting uncooked portion flow underneath. When the eggs are nearly set, sprinkle with tuna, seasonings and cheese. Remove from the heat; let stand for 1-2 minutes or until cheese is melted. Cut into wedges. **Yield:** 4 servings.

Fiesta Mixed Greens

    4 cups torn mixed salad greens
    1 large tomato, chopped
    1 medium sweet yellow pepper, chopped
 3/4 cup stuffed olives
    1 celery rib, chopped
    1 green onion, chopped
 1/4 cup olive or vegetable oil
    2 tablespoons plus 1-1/2 teaspoons white wine
      vinegar or cider vinegar
    1 tablespoon salsa
 1/8 teaspoon garlic salt
 1/8 teaspoon dried oregano
 1/8 teaspoon dried cilantro or parsley flakes
 1/8 teaspoon ground cumin
 1/8 teaspoon pepper

In a salad bowl, combine the greens, tomato, yellow pepper, olives, celery and onion. In a jar with a tight-fitting lid, combine the remaining ingredients; shake well. Just before serving, drizzle over salad and toss to coat. **Yield:** 4 servings.

Watermelon Sundaes

    1 cup cubed watermelon, seeds removed
    1 teaspoon honey
 1/4 teaspoon ground cinnamon
Vanilla ice cream

In a blender or food processor, combine the watermelon, honey and cinnamon; cover and process until chunky. Serve over ice cream. **Yield:** 4 servings.

Easy Fare for Company

ENTERTAINING is not a chore for Marilou Robinson of Portland, Oregon. While she often invites family and friends for delectable dinners, she never frets over stressful setups.

A retired librarian, Marilou usually cooks for one. Her love of hosting dinners, however, keeps her on the lookout for meals that are simple to assemble, but memorable to serve. "I love to cook, but I stay away from courses that involve a lot of difficult preparation.

"When I'm planning the menu for a get-together, I look for dishes I can make ahead of time," Marilou explains. "I read through cookbooks, highlighting recipes that can be changed into quick fixes and items that can be frozen until the day of the event."

Marilou notes there are several tools that can help any host or hostess spend less time in the kitchen and more time with guests. "I rely on appliances like my microwave, bread machine, food processor and blender," she says. "These devices do all of the work that I don't like to do.

"I also think of convenience foods as 'extra sets of hands' in the kitchen. Today, many prepared crusts, canned fruits and bottled dressings are of such high quality that guests will think you fussed and made everything from scratch."

Such is the case with her favorite 30-minute meal. "I start by preparing Ambrosia Tarts," says Marilou. "I created this dessert for my niece who loves the tangy combination of fruit and marshmallows. Once the tarts are in the refrigerator, I begin the salad."

Marilou's Three-Pepper Salad is a five-ingredient time-saver that serves as an attractive and welcome variation on veggies. "After topping the peppers and onion with bottled vinaigrette, I focus on my entree," she shares.

"It's hard to find fun main dishes that don't scare away the meat-and-potatoes crowd," Marilou says. "My Curried Chicken Pitas are a nice change of pace that pack a satisfying punch."

Chicken, pecans and touches of honey and curry make this festive favorite just as tasty when wrapped in tortillas or served over crispy greens. Perfect for any gathering, this dish is a flavorful addition to your menu plan.

Ambrosia Tarts

  1 can (11 ounces) mandarin oranges, drained
  1 can (8 ounces) crushed pineapple, drained
1/2 cup miniature marshmallows
1/4 cup flaked coconut
  1 cup whipped topping
  4 individual graham cracker shells

In a bowl, combine the oranges, pineapple, marshmallows and coconut. Fold in whipped topping. Spoon into shells. Refrigerate until serving. **Yield:** 4 servings.

Three-Pepper Salad

 Uses less fat, sugar or salt. Includes Nutritional Analysis and Diabetic Exchanges.

  1 *each* medium sweet red, yellow and green pepper, thinly sliced
  1 small onion, cut into 1/4-inch wedges
1/3 cup prepared vinaigrette salad dressing

In a bowl, combine the peppers and onion. Add dressing and toss to coat. Refrigerate until serving. **Yield:** 4 servings.

Nutritional Analysis: One 3/4-cup serving (prepared with fat-free Italian salad dressing) equals 58 calories, trace fat (trace saturated fat), 0 cholesterol, 187 mg sodium, 14 g carbohydrate, 2 g fiber, 1 g protein. **Diabetic Exchange:** 2 vegetable.

Curried Chicken Pitas

1/2 cup mayonnaise
  1 tablespoon honey
  1 teaspoon curry powder
  2 cups cubed cooked chicken
  1 cup halved green grapes
1/2 cup chopped pecans
  4 green onions, chopped
  4 pita breads, halved, warmed
  8 lettuce leaves

In a bowl, combine mayonnaise, honey and curry powder. Stir in the chicken, grapes, pecans and onions. Line pita halves with lettuce; spoon 1/2 cup chicken mixture into each. **Yield:** 4 servings.

The Secret to Speedy Suppers

IF THERE'S ONE thing people share, it's secrets. And according to Deborah Elliott, the best secrets are recipes! "Everyone has to eat every day, so we should all share our recipes with one another," suggests this energetic housewife.

"Someday, I hope to put together a cookbook of all the terrific recipes I've gotten from family and friends over the years," says Deborah.

A chapter in that book will likely be devoted to time-saving specialties and no-fuss fare. Even though their three children are grown and on their own, this Ridge Spring, South Carolina cook and her husband, Walter, continue to whip up quick dinners.

"We depend on meals that can be prepared in a flash because Walter's work hours change daily," Deborah explains. Once Walter finishes his day working for a computer storage company, the couple enjoys getting out of the kitchen and into the great outdoors. "We can't wait to get outside and take in all the beauty and fresh air that summer brings," she says.

When Deborah's not tending to the couple's two horses or playing with their five dogs, she can usually be found in the garden. "I plant many vegetables to use in cooking," she shares. "Tomatoes, cucumbers and zucchini are among our favorites."

Perhaps that's why Stir-Fried Zucchini is so popular at her house. "Italian seasoning, garlic and olive oil give this snappy side dish its zip.

"A friend gave me the recipe for Chili Beef Noodle Skillet," Deborah continues. "Walter likes this entree's hearty blend of beef, onions and tomatoes. I like it because I can get it to the table so quickly."

To cap off the meal, Deborah prepares Creamy Lemonade Cups. "Our daughters took my mother's lemon pie recipe and adapted it for individual dessert dishes," she says.

Chili Beef Noodle Skillet

- 1 package (8 ounces) egg noodles
- 2 pounds ground beef
- 1 medium onion, chopped
- 1/4 cup chopped celery
- 2 garlic cloves, minced
- 1 can (28 ounces) diced tomatoes, undrained
- 1 tablespoon chili powder
- 1/4 to 1/2 teaspoon salt
- 1/8 teaspoon pepper
- 1/2 to 1 cup shredded cheddar cheese

Cook noodles according to package directions. Meanwhile, in a large skillet, cook beef, onion, celery and garlic over medium heat until meat is no longer pink and vegetables are tender; drain. Add tomatoes, chili powder, salt and pepper; mix well. Cook and stir for 2 minutes. Drain noodles; stir into beef mixture and heat through. Remove from the heat. Sprinkle with cheese; cover and let stand for 5 minutes or until cheese is melted. **Yield:** 8 servings.

Stir-Fried Zucchini

- 2 pounds zucchini, sliced
- 2 garlic cloves, minced
- 1/4 cup olive or vegetable oil
- 1 teaspoon salt
- 1/2 teaspoon Italian seasoning
- 1/4 teaspoon pepper

In a large skillet, saute the zucchini and garlic in oil until zucchini is crisp-tender, about 5 minutes. Sprinkle with seasonings. Serve immediately. **Yield:** 8 servings.

Creamy Lemonade Cups

- 1-1/4 cups graham cracker crumbs (about 20 squares)
- 1/4 cup butter or margarine, melted
- 2 tablespoons sugar
- 1/2 cup finely chopped nuts
- 1 can (14 ounces) sweetened condensed milk
- 3/4 cup lemonade concentrate
- 1 carton (8 ounces) frozen whipped topping, thawed

In a bowl, combine the crumbs, butter and sugar. Stir in the nuts. Set aside 1/4 cup for topping; press the remaining mixture onto the bottom of eight dessert dishes. In another bowl, combine the milk and lemonade concentrate; fold in the whipped topping. Spoon into prepared dishes. Sprinkle with reserved crumbs. Chill until serving. **Yield:** 8 servings.

Serve a Salad And Sandwich

WHEN time is tight, busy cooks look for complete meals they can put on the table in a jiffy. This time, our food editors pulled together three tasty recipes from readers to create this made-in-minutes menu that's perfect for a hearty lunch or light dinner any time of year.

From Orleans, Ontario, Maya Whittier shares Salmon Dill Croissants. "The original recipe made a cheese ball that my parents served only at Christmas parties," she recalls. "It was so delicious on crackers that I decided to try it as a filling inside croissants.

"These smoky salmon sandwiches taste so wonderfully rich that everyone assumes they're gourmet," Maya says. "No one needs to know they're so fast and easy to prepare by using canned salmon."

To accompany the sandwiches, serve Tricolor Pasta Salad from Lorraine Darocha of Berkshire, Massachusetts. Pretty pasta spirals and convenient frozen veggies are tossed with a light dressing to make this colorful medley.

"For vegetarians, you can add protein-rich chickpeas or beans to make it a main dish," Lorraine recommends.

Cap off this speedy supper with Chocolate Cream Fruit Dip created by Debbie Bond of Richwood, West Virginia. The thick, sweet mixture has a mild chocolate flavor that's especially good on strawberries.

"This recipe is truly an accident," Debbie says. "While hosting a graduation party, I realized I'd forgotten the fruit dip. So I raided my cabinets and slapped this combination together. It was a surprising success and has since become one of our family's favorites."

Salmon Dill Croissants

- 1 package (8 ounces) cream cheese, softened
- 1 can (7-1/2 ounces) salmon, drained, bones and skin removed
- 1/4 cup mayonnaise
- 1 tablespoon lemon juice
- 1 tablespoon grated onion
- 1 teaspoon prepared horseradish
- 1/2 teaspoon dill weed
- 1/4 teaspoon salt
- 1/4 teaspoon garlic powder
- 1/4 teaspoon liquid smoke, optional
- 6 croissants, split
- 1 cup shredded lettuce

In a mixing bowl, beat the cream cheese until smooth. Stir in the salmon, mayonnaise, lemon juice, onion, horseradish, dill, salt, garlic powder and liquid smoke if desired. Spread over croissants; top with lettuce. **Yield:** 6 servings.

Tricolor Pasta Salad

- 1 package (16 ounces) tricolor spiral pasta
- 1 package (16 ounces) frozen California-blend vegetables (broccoli, cauliflower and carrots)
- 1 can (2-1/4 ounces) sliced ripe olives, drained
- 1 to 1-1/3 cups Italian salad dressing
- 1/4 to 1/2 teaspoon garlic salt, optional

Cook the pasta according to package directions. Meanwhile, place vegetables in a microwave-safe dish. Cover and microwave at 50% power for 7-8 minutes or until thawed; drain. Drain pasta and rinse in cold water. In a bowl, combine the pasta, vegetables and olives. Combine salad dressing and garlic salt if desired; pour over salad and toss to coat. Refrigerate until serving. **Yield:** 6-8 servings.

Editor's Note: This recipe was tested in an 850-watt microwave.

Chocolate Cream Fruit Dip

- 1 package (8 ounces) cream cheese, softened
- 1/4 cup chocolate syrup
- 1 jar (7 ounces) marshmallow creme
- Apple wedges, fresh strawberries and banana chunks

In a small mixing bowl, beat the cream cheese and chocolate syrup. Fold in the marshmallow creme. Cover and refrigerate until serving. Serve with assorted fruit. **Yield:** about 2 cups.

Breaded Dijon Pork Chops

3/4 cup crushed saltines (about 20 crackers)
1/2 teaspoon dried thyme
1/4 teaspoon pepper
1/8 to 1/4 teaspoon rubbed sage
3 tablespoons Dijon mustard
4 boneless pork loin chops (1/2 inch thick)
1/4 cup vegetable oil

In a bowl, combine the cracker crumbs, thyme, pepper and sage. Spread mustard on both sides of pork chops; coat with crumb mixture. In a skillet, cook pork chops in oil over medium-high heat for 4-5 minutes on each side or until golden brown and juices run clear. **Yield:** 4 servings.

Corn Bread Dressing

1 package (6 ounces) corn bread stuffing cubes
1 medium onion, finely chopped
1 celery rib, finely chopped
1 can (8-1/4 ounces) cream-style corn
1 cup water
1 tablespoon butter *or* margarine, melted
1 tablespoon spicy brown mustard

In a large bowl, combine the stuffing, onion, celery, corn and water. Spoon into a greased 8-in. square baking dish. Combine the butter and mustard; drizzle over stuffing. Bake, uncovered, at 375° for 20 minutes or until heated through. **Yield:** 4-6 servings.

Marvelous Homespun Meal

SEARCHING for quick-to-fix fare that has old-fashioned appeal? Look no further than this mouth-watering meal compiled by our food editors. They combined three hearty home-cooked dishes that feature speed as the key ingredient, so you can have dinner on the table in less than a half hour.

Start your supper with Breaded Dijon Pork Chops shared by Shannon Gerardi from Dayton, Ohio. "This treatment for pork chops is so delicious that even my dad and my husband, who aren't fond of pork, love it," she says.

The golden breading that coats these tender chops is moist and subtly seasoned with Dijon mustard. "While the recipe calls for pork chops, I sometimes make it with pork tenderloin instead," Shannon adds.

Marybeth Thompson of Thurmont, Maryland uses convenient pantry items to create Corn Bread Dressing, a swift side dish that complements the chops.

"I revised a main-dish casserole recipe to make this unique stuffing side dish," Marybeth explains. "I've often delivered it, along with pork or chicken, to friends who are just out of the hospital. It always receives rave reviews."

The heavenly aroma of Cinnamon Baked Apples from Margaret McNeil of Memphis, Tennessee is sure to bring your family to the table without you even asking. "To save time, after I peel the apples, I use an apple corer/wedger to core and cut the fruit into pieces," she notes.

The warm spiced side dish is nice with pork chops but also can be served with a scoop of vanilla ice cream or whipped cream for dessert.

Cinnamon Baked Apples

3 large tart apples, peeled, cored and cut into wedges
2 tablespoons lemon juice
2/3 cup apple juice
2/3 cup packed brown sugar
2 tablespoons butter *or* margarine
1/4 teaspoon ground cinnamon
4 cinnamon sticks (3 inches), optional
Whipped topping, optional

Place apples in an ungreased 11-in. x 7-in. x 2-in. baking dish. Drizzle with lemon juice; toss to coat. Set aside. In a small saucepan, combine the apple juice, brown sugar, butter and cinnamon. Cook and stir over medium heat until sugar is dissolved and butter is melted. Pour over apples. Add cinnamon sticks if desired. Bake, uncovered, at 375° for 20 minutes or until apples are tender. Discard cinnamon. Serve warm with whipped topping if desired. **Yield:** 4 servings.

Creamy Tomato Chicken

    6 boneless skinless chicken
      breast halves
    2 tablespoons vegetable oil
    1 can (14-1/2 ounces) Italian
      diced tomatoes, undrained
    1 can (10-3/4 ounces)
      condensed cream of chicken
      soup, undiluted
  1/8 teaspoon ground cinnamon
    6 slices mozzarella cheese
Hot cooked noodles

In a large skillet, cook the chicken in oil over medium heat until juices run clear. Remove and keep warm. Combine the tomatoes, soup and cinnamon; add to the skillet. Cook and stir until heated through. Return the chicken to the skillet; top with the cheese. Cover and heat until the cheese is melted. Serve over noodles. **Yield:** 6 servings.

Favorites Stand Test of Time

Cinnamon Carrots

✓ Uses less fat, sugar or salt. Includes Nutritional Analysis and Diabetic Exchanges.

    1 package (16 ounces) frozen sliced carrots
  1/4 cup honey
    1 to 2 tablespoons butter *or* stick margarine
  1/2 to 1 teaspoon ground cinnamon

Cook carrots according to package directions. Meanwhile, in a saucepan, heat the honey, butter and cinnamon until butter is melted; stir to blend. Drain carrots; place in a serving bowl. Drizzle with honey mixture. **Yield:** 6 servings.
  Nutritional Analysis: One 1/2-cup serving (prepared with 1 tablespoon butter) equals 90 calories, 2 g fat (1 g saturated fat), 5 mg cholesterol, 65 mg sodium, 19 g carbohydrate, 3 g fiber, 1 g protein. **Diabetic Exchanges:** 1 vegetable, 1 fruit.

EVEN AFTER Charlene Kalb leaves her job at the local high school cafeteria, she can't escape student life.
  "My husband, David, and our daughter, Anna, both take night classes at a community college," Charlene says from her Catonsville, Maryland home. "So I make a point to get a good dinner on the table fast, giving them plenty of time to eat before they head out.
  "I like the three of us to eat together as often as possible. But Anna's work at a theater sometimes causes her to miss dinner, so it's important that the recipes I prepare reheat well," she says.
  "I love coming up with different ways to fix the foods my family likes. I'm always experimenting with new ways to cook chicken," she explains.
  And Charlene found a surefire success in Creamy Tomato Chicken. Served over noodles, the effortless entree is great for weeknight meals yet tastes special enough for weekend company.
  Frozen vegetables make for a fast and fabulous side dish in Charlene's Cinnamon Carrots.
  Charlene likes to top off meals with a time-tested treat. "After Sunday dinners, my grandmother served her special Hot Fudge Sundaes," remembers Charlene. "The thick fudgy sauce comes together in no time and is terrific over ice cream. My whole family looks forward to this delicious dessert."

Hot Fudge Sundaes

  3/4 cup sugar
    6 tablespoons baking cocoa
    1 can (5 ounces) evaporated milk
  1/3 cup butter *or* margarine
  3/4 cup miniature marshmallows
    1 teaspoon vanilla extract
Vanilla ice cream
Nuts and maraschino cherries, optional

In a saucepan, combine the sugar and cocoa; stir in milk. Add butter. Bring to a boil over medium heat; cook and stir until sugar is dissolved. Add marshmallows; cook until melted. Remove from the heat; stir in vanilla. Serve over ice cream. Top with nuts and cherries if desired. **Yield:** 2 cups.

Find Time for Family Dinner

VOLUNTEER work is a way of life at the Crosby home. Just ask Bissy Crosby from Columbia, Missouri. When this busy mother of three isn't working as a teacher, she's running charity programs or helping various youth groups.

Similarly, her husband, John, manager of a furniture store, dedicates much of his free time to teaching in an adult-learning program and coaching their children's baseball and soccer teams.

"John and I understand the value of doing things as a family," Bissy says. "Volunteer work is a wonderful way to accomplish that. For instance, we take the kids (Daniel, Karis Ann and Margie) along when we work at a local soup kitchen. It's a great way to spend time together, and it's rewarding, too.

"With the help of a few speedy recipes, I'm able to put together a delicious meal for all of us at least five times a week," she states.

"White Bean 'n' Ham Soup is economical, quick and yummy," she says.

Ramen noodles, broccoli and nuts get a unique treatment in Crunchy Romaine Toss from a sweet-tart dressing.

To complete the meal, Bissy assembles festive Candy Cane Parfaits. "No one ever guesses that five ingredients are all it takes to make these layered holiday desserts," she shares.

White Bean 'n' Ham Soup

2 cans (15-1/2 ounces *each*) great northern beans, rinsed and drained
2 medium carrots, diced
1 small onion, chopped
2 tablespoons butter *or* margarine
2-1/4 cups water
1-1/2 cups cubed fully cooked ham
1/2 teaspoon salt
1/8 to 1/4 teaspoon white pepper
1 bay leaf

Mash one can of beans; set aside. In a large saucepan, saute the carrots and onion in butter. Stir in the water, ham, seasonings, and whole and mashed beans; cook over medium heat until heated through. Discard bay leaf before serving. **Yield:** 6 servings.

Crunchy Romaine Toss

1/2 cup sugar
1/2 cup vegetable oil
1/4 cup cider vinegar
2 teaspoons soy sauce
Salt and pepper to taste
1 package (3 ounces) ramen noodles, broken
2 tablespoons butter *or* margarine
1-1/2 cups chopped broccoli
1 small bunch romaine, torn
4 green onions, chopped
1/2 cup chopped walnuts

In a jar with a tight-fitting lid, combine the sugar, oil, vinegar, soy sauce, salt and pepper; shake well. Discard seasoning packet from noodles or save for another use. In a skillet, saute noodles in butter until golden. In a large bowl, combine noodles, broccoli, romaine and onions. Just before serving, toss with dressing and walnuts. **Yield:** 6-8 servings.

Candy Cane Parfaits

2 cups cold milk
1 package (3.9 ounces) instant chocolate pudding mix
24 chocolate cream-filled sandwich cookies, crushed
1 carton (8 ounces) frozen whipped topping, thawed
3 candy canes, crushed

In a mixing bowl, beat the milk and pudding mix on low speed for 2 minutes. Divide half of the cookie crumbs among six parfait glasses. Layer with half of the pudding and whipped topping. Repeat cookie and pudding layers. Dollop with the remaining whipped topping and sprinkle with candy canes. **Yield:** 6 servings.

30-Minute Side Dishes

WHEN you're looking to round out family meals in a flash, these 12 speedy side dishes that can be completed in half an hour or less are especially helpful.

Spinach Parmesan Linguine

(Pictured above)

If you want a tasty change from plain buttered noodles, serve this pleasing pasta toss as a streamlined side dish. Frozen spinach and Parmesan cheese add lively flavor to linguine. —Mary Curran, Sandwich, Illinois

  1 package (16 ounces) linguine
  1 cup chicken broth
  1 small onion, chopped
  2 garlic cloves, minced
  1 package (10 ounces) frozen chopped
     spinach, thawed and well drained
1/3 cup milk
  2 tablespoons cream cheese
Salt and pepper to taste
  1 cup (4 ounces) shredded Parmesan cheese
1/2 cup shredded mozzarella cheese

Cook the linguine according to package directions. Meanwhile, in a saucepan over medium-high heat, bring broth to a boil. Add onion and garlic. Reduce heat; cook, uncovered, for 5 minutes. Stir in spinach; cook for 2 minutes. Add milk, cream cheese, salt and pepper; stir until cheese is melted. Drain linguine and place in a serving bowl. Add sauce and toss to coat. Sprinkle with Parmesan and mozzarella cheeses; toss to coat. **Yield:** 10 servings.

Garbanzo Gazpacho

(Pictured on page 21)

This chunky chilled soup is terrific in warm weather, but our family loves it so much I often prepare it in winter, too. I made some slight changes to the original recipe to suit our tastes, and the fresh flavorful combination has been a favorite ever since. —Mary Ann Gomez
Lombard, Illinois

✓ Uses less fat, sugar or salt. Includes Nutritional Analysis and Diabetic Exchanges.

  1 can (15 ounces) garbanzo beans *or*
     chickpeas, rinsed and drained
  1 can (14-1/2 ounces) Italian diced tomatoes,
     undrained
1-1/4 cups V8 juice
  1 cup beef broth
  1 cup quartered cherry tomatoes
1/2 cup chopped seeded cucumber
1/4 cup chopped red onion
1/4 cup minced fresh cilantro *or* parsley
  3 tablespoons lime juice
  1 garlic clove, minced
1/2 teaspoon salt
1/4 teaspoon hot pepper sauce

In a large bowl, combine all ingredients; cover and refrigerate until serving. **Yield:** 6 servings.

Nutritional Analysis: One serving (1 cup) equals 126 calories, 1 g fat (trace saturated fat), trace cholesterol, 993 mg sodium, 23 g carbohydrate, 4 g fiber, 6 g protein. **Diabetic Exchange:** 1-1/2 starch.

Zucchini Pancakes

In place of potato pancakes, try these cute rounds that are very simple to prepare with on-hand ingredients. Not only are they tasty, they're pretty, too. To eliminate some of the fat, I use a nonstick griddle coated with butter-flavored cooking spray. —Teressa Eastman
El Dorado, Kansas

1/3 cup biscuit/baking mix
1/4 cup grated Parmesan cheese
1/8 teaspoon pepper
  2 eggs, lightly beaten
  2 cups shredded zucchini
  2 tablespoons butter *or* margarine

In a bowl, combine the biscuit mix, Parmesan cheese, pepper and eggs just until blended. Add the zucchini; mix well. In a large skillet, melt butter. Drop batter by about 1/3 cupfuls into skillet; press lightly to flatten. Fry until golden brown, about 3 minutes on each side. **Yield:** 5 pancakes.

1 tablespoon Worcestershire sauce
1 teaspoon salt
1/2 teaspoon pepper
1/2 teaspoon ground mustard
1 can (14-1/2 ounces) diced tomatoes, undrained

Cook beans according to package directions. Meanwhile, in a skillet, cook bacon, onion and green pepper over medium heat until bacon is crisp and vegetables are tender. Remove with a slotted spoon. Stir the flour, brown sugar, Worcestershire sauce, salt, pepper and mustard into the drippings until blended. Stir in tomatoes. Bring to a boil; cook and stir for 2 minutes or until thickened. Drain beans and add to skillet. Stir in bacon mixture. **Yield:** 6 servings.

Swiss Tossed Salad

(Pictured below)

This simple green salad requires just a few ingredients, yet its blend of flavors and combination of textures make it seem special. You can toss all the ingredients with the basic dressing or dollop it over individual servings.
—Sherian Peterson, High Ridge, Missouri

12 bacon strips, diced
1 bunch red leaf lettuce, torn (about 10 cups)
1 small red onion, julienned
1 block (8 ounces) Swiss cheese, cubed
1/4 cup sliced ripe olives
1/3 cup mayonnaise
1/3 cup sour cream

In a skillet over medium heat, cook bacon until crisp. Remove to paper towels to drain. In a large bowl, combine lettuce, onion, cheese, olives and bacon. In a small bowl, combine mayonnaise and sour cream. Serve with the salad. **Yield:** 8-10 servings.

Mandarin Glazed Beets

(Pictured above)

Mandarin oranges and a warm glaze transform canned beets into a super side dish. Lemon juice provides a bit of tartness. If your family doesn't like the tart flavor, I suggest adding a little more sugar.
—Shirley Dehler, Columbus, Wisconsin

1/4 cup sugar
2 teaspoons cornstarch
1/4 cup lemon juice
2 tablespoons butter *or* margarine
2 cans (15 ounces *each*) sliced beets, drained
1 can (11 ounces) mandarin oranges, drained

In a large saucepan, combine the sugar and cornstarch. Add lemon juice and butter. Bring to a boil; cook and stir for 2 minutes or until thickened. Stir in beets; heat through. Gently stir in oranges; heat through. **Yield:** 4 servings.

Creole Green Beans

(Pictured on page 20)

Even though our children are grown, my husband and I remain busy. So we rely on speedy recipes that call for everyday ingredients. This peppery treatment really wakes up green beans. It makes enough that we have leftovers, which is helpful since our schedules sometimes keep us from eating together. —Sue Kuhn, Dublin, Ohio

1 package (16 ounces) frozen cut green beans
5 bacon strips, diced
1 medium onion, chopped
1/2 cup chopped green pepper
2 tablespoons all-purpose flour
2 tablespoons brown sugar

Dilly Veggie Pasta Salad

(Pictured below)

My sister shared the recipe for this fresh crunchy salad seasoned with dill. It's handy because you can assemble and eat it right away…or cover and refrigerate it to take to a picnic or potluck the next day. The longer it chills, the more tangy it is.
—Anna Emory-Royal
Murfreesboro, Tennessee

2-3/4 cups uncooked medium shell pasta
   1 cup halved cherry tomatoes
   1 cup sliced green pepper
   1 cup (4 ounces) shredded cheddar cheese
1/2 cup chopped green onions
1/2 cup sliced ripe olives
DRESSING:
  1/4 cup olive *or* vegetable oil
   2 tablespoons lemon juice
   2 tablespoons white wine vinegar *or*
     cider vinegar
   1 teaspoon dill weed
   1 teaspoon dried oregano
   1 teaspoon salt
  1/8 teaspoon pepper

Cook pasta according to package directions; drain and rinse in cold water. Place in a large bowl. Add tomatoes, green pepper, cheese, onions and olives. In a small bowl, whisk together the dressing ingredients. Pour over salad and toss to coat. Cover and refrigerate until serving. **Yield:** 8 servings.

Orange Candied Carrots

(Pictured above)

My son always asks for these glazed carrot coins at Thanksgiving. The orange flavor in the sweet mild sauce really comes through. This pleasant side dish is a great way to dress up a meal of holiday leftovers.
—Lori Lockrey, West Hill, Ontario

   1 pound carrots, cut into 1/2-inch slices
  1/4 cup butter *or* margarine, softened, cubed
  1/4 cup jellied cranberry sauce
   1 orange peel strip (1 to 3 inches)
   2 tablespoons brown sugar
  1/2 teaspoon salt

Place 1 in. of water and carrots in a skillet; bring to a boil. Reduce heat; cover and simmer for 15-20 minutes or until crisp-tender. Meanwhile, in a blender, combine the butter, cranberry sauce, orange peel, brown sugar and salt. Cover and process until blended. Drain carrots; drizzle with cranberry mixture. **Yield:** 3 servings.

Southwestern Spuds

(Pictured on page 20)

I came up with this attractive side dish when my best friend unexpectedly stayed for dinner. While my husband grilled pork chops, I perked up potatoes with tasty taco fixings. The results received rave reviews. This recipe is even quicker to fix with leftover baked potatoes.
—Penny Dykstra, Porterville, California

   3 medium potatoes
Salt and pepper to taste
   1 cup (4 ounces) shredded cheddar cheese

1 cup (4 ounces) shredded pepper Jack cheese
3 green onions, chopped
1 can (2-1/4 ounces) sliced ripe olives, drained
Sour cream and salsa, optional

Pierce potatoes; place on a microwave-safe plate. Microwave on high for 8-10 minutes or until almost tender. Cool slightly; peel and cut into 1/8-in. slices. Arrange half of the potatoes in a greased microwave-safe 9-in. pie plate. Season with salt and pepper. Sprinkle with half of the cheeses. Repeat layers. Top with onions and olives. Microwave, uncovered, for 10 minutes or until cheese is melted and potatoes are tender. Serve with sour cream and salsa if desired. **Yield:** 4-6 servings.

Editor's Note: This recipe was tested in an 850-watt microwave.

Molly's Mexicorn

(Pictured below)

I jazzed up a corn recipe with some spicy seasonings to create this offering for a Mexican potluck. Everyone liked it so much that now it's all I'm ever asked to bring.
—Molly, Mason, Denver, Colorado

6 cups fresh *or* frozen corn
2 jars (4 ounces *each*) sliced pimientos, drained
1/3 cup sliced green onions
1 small green pepper, diced
2 tablespoons butter *or* margarine
1 tablespoon chili powder
1 tablespoon ground cumin
1/2 teaspoon salt

In a large saucepan, combine all the ingredients. Cover and cook over medium heat for 10 minutes or until vegetables are tender. **Yield:** 8 servings.

Caramelized Onions

(Pictured above)

These lightly golden onions have a delicate taste that complements green beans, peas and almost any type of meat. Try them over steaks, on burgers and with pork chops.
—Melba Lowery, Rockwell, North Carolina

4 large onions, thinly sliced
1/4 cup vegetable oil
3 tablespoons cider vinegar
2 tablespoons brown sugar

In a large skillet, saute onions in oil over medium heat until tender, about 15 minutes. Stir in vinegar and brown sugar. Cook 10 minutes longer or until onions are golden. **Yield:** 4-6 servings.

Creamy Fruit Salad

(Pictured on page 21)

Cream cheese and yogurt form the light dressing that coats this fast fruit medley. The salad is a snap to assemble because it takes advantage of canned peaches, pineapple chunks and mandarin oranges you likely keep in your pantry. Miniature marshmallows add a sweet touch.
—Brittany Tyrrell, Manchester, Iowa

1 can (11 ounces) mandarin oranges, drained
1 can (8-1/4 ounces) sliced peaches, drained
1 can (8 ounces) pineapple chunks, drained
1 cup miniature marshmallows
4 ounces cream cheese, softened
1/2 cup plain yogurt
1/4 cup sugar

In a bowl, combine the oranges, peaches, pineapple and marshmallows. In a small mixing bowl, beat the cream cheese, yogurt and sugar until smooth. Pour over the fruit and toss to coat. Refrigerate for 15 minutes. **Yield:** 4 servings.

Chapter 3

38

WHY NOT add a fun and festive touch to your ordinary get-togethers the next time you're entertaining family and friends?

You don't have to panic at the thought of hosting a fun and festive theme party. Our Quick Cooking kitchen staff has done the planning for you by creating six easy menus that celebrate events throughout the year.

From an effortless Easter buffet, a grand-slam baseball bash and a wonderful watermelon-themed picnic to a "spook-tac-ular" Halloween spread, a feast fit for Santa and playful fare that's all in good fun, you can easily create long-remembered occasions for your relatives and friends with just a short time spent in the kitchen.

ARE YOU GAME? Clockwise from top: Dartboard Pizza, Scrabble Brownies, Gelatin Game Chips and Cheese Spread Dice (all recipes on p. 51)

Easter Buffet Is a Hopping Success

PREPARING an effortless Easter buffet doesn't have to seem as impossible as pulling a rabbit out of a hat. In fact, success is just a hop, skip and jump away with this memorable menu.

Mushroom Spinach Dip

Plan ahead...needs to chill

This thick, creamy mixture is easy to stir up and gets its fresh flavor from mushrooms, spinach and green onions. Serve it in the fun Easter Bunny Bread (below) or in a bowl with a platter of crackers or crunchy vegetables.

    1 package (10 ounces) frozen chopped
       spinach, thawed and squeezed dry
1-1/2 cups (12 ounces) sour cream
    1 cup mayonnaise
    1 package vegetable soup mix
    1 cup chopped fresh mushrooms
    3 green onions, finely chopped
Raw vegetables *or* crackers

In a bowl, combine the spinach, sour cream, mayonnaise, soup mix, mushrooms and onions; mix well. Cover and refrigerate for 2 hours. Serve with vegetables or crackers. **Yield:** 3 cups.

Easter Bunny Bread

With its toothy grin, lovely golden crust and tummy that's perfect for serving dip, this charming rabbit is sure to bring a smile to guests young and old.

    2 loaves (1 pound *each*) frozen bread dough,
       thawed
    2 raisins
    2 sliced almonds
    1 egg, lightly beaten
Lettuce leaves
Mushroom Spinach Dip (recipe above) *or* dip of
    your choice

Cut a fourth off of one loaf of dough; shape into a pear to form head. For body, flatten remaining portion into a 7-in. x 6-in. oval; place on a greased baking sheet. Place head above body. Make narrow cuts, about 3/4 in. deep, on each side of head for whiskers. Cut second loaf into four equal portions. For ears, shape two portions into 16-in. ropes; fold ropes in half. Arrange ears with open ends touching head. Cut a third portion of dough in half; shape each into a 3-1/2-in. oval for back paws. Cut two 1-in. slits on top edge for toes. Position on each side of body.

Divide the fourth portion of dough into three pieces. Shape two pieces into 2-1/2-in. balls for front paws; shape the remaining piece into two 1-in. balls for cheeks and one 1/2-in. ball for nose. Place paws on each side of body; cut two 1-in. slits for toes. Place cheeks and nose on face. Add raisins for eyes and almonds for teeth. Brush dough with egg. Cover and let rise in a warm place until doubled, about 30-45 minutes.

Bake at 350° for 25-30 minutes or until golden brown.

Remove to a wire rack to cool. Place bread on a lettuce-lined 16-in. x 13-in. serving tray. Cut a 5-in. x 4-in. oval in center of body. Hollow out bread, leaving a 1/2-in. shell (discard removed bread or save for another use). Line with lettuce and fill with dip. **Yield:** 1 loaf.

Holiday Ham Kabobs

Ready in 1 hour or less

A little sugar and spice make these ham-stacked skewers oh-so-nice as an Easter entree. The colorful kabobs are simple to broil in the oven...or grill them outdoors if the weather allows.

    1 can (20 ounces) unsweetened pineapple
       chunks
    6 tablespoons butter *or* margarine
  1/3 cup packed brown sugar
  1/2 teaspoon ground cinnamon
    2 medium sweet potatoes, peeled and cut into
       3/4-inch slices
    1 medium green pepper, cut into chunks
1-1/2 cups cubed fully cooked ham (1-inch cubes)

Drain pineapple, reserving 2 tablespoons juice; set pineapple aside (discard remaining juice or save for another use). In a saucepan, combine juice, butter, brown sugar and cinnamon; cook and stir over medium heat until sugar is dissolved. Set aside. Place sweet potatoes in another saucepan and cover with water; bring to a boil. Reduce heat. Simmer, uncovered, for 10-12 minutes or until potatoes are tender; drain.

On metal or soaked bamboo skewers, alternately thread sweet potatoes, green pepper, ham and pineapple. Brush with brown sugar mixture. Broil 4 in. from heat for 4-6 minutes on each side or until heated through and peppers are tender, basting occasionally. **Yield:** 4 servings.

Carrot-Topped Cupcakes

A handy spice cake mix gets a tasty treatment when dressed up with shredded carrots and chopped walnuts. The mini carrot cakes are eye-catching, too.

    1 package (18-1/4 ounces) spice cake mix
1-1/2 cups shredded carrots
  1/2 cup chopped walnuts
    1 teaspoon ground cinnamon
    1 can (16 ounces) cream cheese frosting
Orange paste food coloring
Fresh parsley sprigs

Prepare cake batter according to package directions. Fold in carrots, walnuts and cinnamon. Fill paper-lined muffin cups half full. Bake at 350° for 18-23 minutes or until a toothpick comes out clean. Remove from pans to wire racks to cool completely. Frost cupcakes with 1-1/4 cups frosting. Place remaining frosting in a small resealable plastic bag, tint with orange food coloring. Cut a small hole in the corner of bag; pipe a carrot on the top of each cupcake. Add a parsley sprig for greens. **Yield:** 2 dozen.

Fare Scores a Grand Slam

BATTER UP! Our home economists were good sports about fielding easy recipes for a baseball-themed bash that will have your hungry team feeling like all-stars. You'll make a great impression right off the bat when you step up to the plate with this lip-smacking lineup of sandwiches, salad, snack mix and cookies.

Pop Fly Popcorn

Pecans and almonds add nutty goodness to this crisp chewy mix. The way this tasty treat attracts snackers, you may need an umpire for the bowl.

      10 to 12 cups popped popcorn
       1 cup pecan halves
       1 cup slivered almonds
   1-1/3 cups sugar
       1 cup butter (no substitutes)
     1/2 cup light corn syrup
       1 teaspoon vanilla extract
     1/2 teaspoon cream of tartar
     1/2 teaspoon baking soda

In a large bowl, combine popcorn and nuts; set aside. In a large saucepan, bring sugar, butter and corn syrup to a boil. Boil for 5 minutes, stirring occasionally. Remove from the heat; add vanilla, cream of tartar and baking soda. Drizzle over popcorn mixture; stir to coat. Immediately spread onto two greased baking sheets; let dry for about 1 hour. Store in an airtight container. **Yield:** 10-12 servings.

Home Run Hoagies

Ready in 15 minutes or less

Kids can pitch in with assembling these colorful sandwiches stacked with chicken, cheese, lettuce and tomatoes. To score with big appetites, try adding extra slices of meat or offer a few varieties of sliced cheese.

     3/4 cup mayonnaise
     1/2 cup prepared Italian salad dressing
      12 hoagie buns, split
      24 slices deli chicken (about 2-1/2 pounds)
      12 slices cheddar cheese, halved
      12 lettuce leaves
       8 medium tomatoes, sliced

In a small bowl, combine mayonnaise and salad dressing. Spread on cut side of buns. On bun bottoms, layer chicken, cheese, lettuce and tomatoes. Replace bun tops. **Yield:** 12 servings.

Strikeout Salad

Ready in 30 minutes or less

This medley of garden-fresh vegetables, tender pasta and a homemade vinaigrette is sure to execute a triple play on your taste buds. The tubular noodles and round olives will likely remind your crew of bats and balls.

       1 package (16 ounces) tube pasta
       2 cups halved cherry tomatoes

       1 block (4 ounces) provolone cheese, cubed
       1 cup chopped sweet red pepper
     1/2 cup chopped green pepper
       1 medium onion, chopped
       1 can (14 ounces) pitted ripe olives, drained
DRESSING:
     2/3 cup vegetable oil
     1/3 cup red wine vinegar *or* cider vinegar
       3 tablespoons minced fresh basil *or* 3
           teaspoons dried basil
       1 garlic clove, minced
       1 tablespoon Dijon mustard
   1-1/2 teaspoons salt
       1 teaspoon sugar
       1 teaspoon onion powder

Cook pasta according to package directions; drain and rinse with cold water. Place in a salad bowl; add tomatoes, cheese, peppers, onion and olives. In a blender, combine the dressing ingredients; cover and process until blended. Pour over pasta mixture and toss to coat. Refrigerate until serving. **Yield:** 12 servings.

Cap and Ball Cookies

Ready in 1 hour or less

The cook will have a ball decorating plain packaged cookies to create these clever confections that look like baseballs and team caps.

       2 cups vanilla *or* white chips
       1 tablespoon shortening
      16 cream-filled chocolate sandwich cookies
       1 tube red decorating frosting
       1 package (12 ounces) chocolate and
           marshmallow cookies*
      12 chocolate wafer cookies
      12 red M&M's

In a microwave or heavy saucepan, melt chips and shortening; stir until smooth. Dip sandwich cookies into mixture and allow excess to drip off; place on waxed paper to harden. Meanwhile, spread red frosting over half of the bottom of each marshmallow cookie; press off-center onto a chocolate wafer, creating a cap. (See photo at right.) Pipe a line of frosting where the cookies meet. Pipe stitching lines down sides of marshmallow cookies. Attach an M&M on top with a dab of frosting. On dipped sandwich cookies, pipe stitch marks to create baseballs. **Yield:** 12 caps and 16 baseballs.

   *Editor's Note: This recipe was tested with Nabisco Pinwheels.

Melon Makes Perfect Picnics

THE MELON PATCH was a refreshing retreat for the home economists in our Test Kitchen as they planned this pleasing picnic. They added the delightful flavor of watermelon to all kinds of fast-to-fix outdoor dishes.

Pork with Watermelon Salsa

Ready in 30 minutes or less

A colorful combination of watermelon, strawberries, kiwifruit and peaches makes a sweet salsa that's ideal to serve alongside grilled pork basted with peach preserves.

        1 cup seeded chopped watermelon
    1/2 cup chopped strawberries
    1/2 cup chopped kiwifruit
    1/4 cup chopped peaches
        3 tablespoons lime juice
        4 teaspoons honey
    1/2 teaspoon grated lime peel
        1 to 2 mint leaves, chopped
    1/2 cup peach preserves
        3 pork tenderloins (3/4 pound *each*)

For salsa, combine the first eight ingredients in a bowl; set aside. In a saucepan or microwave, heat the preserves for 1 minute. Grill pork, covered, over indirect medium heat for 5 minutes. Turn; brush with some of the preserves. Grill 8-9 minutes longer or until juices run clear and a meat thermometer reads 160°, basting occasionally with preserves. Serve with salsa. **Yield:** 6-8 servings (1-1/4 cups salsa).

Watermelon Spinach Salad

Ready in 30 minutes or less

Dark green spinach leaves provide a rich backdrop for brilliant raspberries, cubed watermelon and sliced almonds in this eye-appealing salad. The light vinaigrette is the perfect way to dress up summer's finest produce.

POPPY SEED VINAIGRETTE:
    1/2 cup white wine vinegar *or* cider vinegar
    1/2 cup sugar
    1/2 teaspoon ground mustard
    1/4 teaspoon onion powder
    1/2 teaspoon salt
    1/2 cup vegetable oil
    1/4 cup chopped onion
        1 teaspoon poppy seeds
SALAD:
        1 package (6 ounces) fresh baby spinach, torn
        2 cups seeded cubed watermelon
        1 cup halved green grapes
        1 cup fresh raspberries
    1/4 cup sliced almonds

In a blender or food processor, combine the vinegar, sugar, mustard, onion powder and salt. Cover and process until sugar is dissolved. Continue processing while adding oil in a steady stream. Add onion and poppy seeds; process until combined. In a salad bowl, combine the spinach, watermelon, grapes and raspberries; sprin-

kle with almonds. Serve with vinaigrette. **Yield:** 8 servings (about 1 cup vinaigrette).

Watermelon Gelatin Cups

Plan ahead...needs to chill

Let these delightful watermelon wannabes add a bit of fun to your next picnic spread. Limes are halved and hollowed to hold pretty pink gelatin, while mini chocolate chips serve as seeds in the cute cups.

        1 package (3 ounces) watermelon gelatin
        1 cup boiling water
        1 cup cold water
        4 large limes
    1/4 cup miniature chocolate chips

In a bowl, dissolve gelatin in boiling water. Stir in cold water. Refrigerate for 1 hour or until slightly thickened. Meanwhile, slice limes in half lengthwise. With a small scissors or sharp knife, cut the membrane at each end to loosen pulp from shell. Using fingertips, pull membrane and pulp away from shell (discard pulp or save for another use). Fold chocolate chips into gelatin; spoon into lime shells. Refrigerate for 2 hours or until completely set. **Yield:** 8 servings.

Watermelon Cake

No one will ever guess how simple this make-ahead melon is to assemble. After one bite of the showstopping cake, kids of all ages will be lining up for a second slice of the sweet sensation.

        1 package (18-1/4 ounces) white cake mix
        1 package (3 ounces) watermelon gelatin
        2 eggs
    1-1/4 cups water
    1/4 cup vegetable oil
    2-1/2 cups prepared vanilla or cream cheese
            frosting, *divided*
    Red and green gel food coloring
    Chocolate chips

In a mixing bowl, combine dry cake mix, gelatin, eggs, water and oil. Beat on low speed just until moistened. Beat on high for 2 minutes or until well blended. Pour into two greased and floured 9-in. round baking pans. Bake at 350° for 30-35 minutes or until a toothpick inserted near the center comes out clean. Cool for 10 minutes; remove from pans to wire racks to cool completely.

Set aside 2 tablespoons frosting for decorating. Place 1-1/4 cups frosting in a bowl; tint red. Tint remaining frosting green. Place one cake layer on a serving plate; spread with 1/2 cup red frosting to within 1/4 in. of edges. Top with second cake. Frost top with remaining red frosting to within 3/4 in. of edges. Frost sides and top edge with green frosting. Place reserved white frosting in a small heavy-duty resealable plastic bag; cut a 1/4-in. hole in one corner. Pipe around top edge of cake where green and pink frosting meets. For seeds, insert chocolate chips upside down into cake top. **Yield:** 12 servings.

Scare Up This Fun Feast

SURPRISE your favorite goblins with a boo-tiful buffet of eerie edibles at a Halloween celebration.

Boo Beverage

Silly spooks garnish glasses of this smooth fruity drink.

    2 cups orange juice
    2 cups milk
    2 pints orange sherbet
    4 medium ripe bananas
    2 cups whipped topping
    18 miniature chocolate chips

In four batches, process the orange juice, milk, sherbet and bananas in a blender until smooth. Pour into glasses. Cut a hole in the corner of a pastry or plastic bag; fill with whipped topping. Pipe a ghost shape on top of each beverage. Position chocolate chips for eyes. **Yield:** 9 servings.

Monster Munchies

Magically transform squash or pumpkin seeds into a spellbinding snack with ranch salad dressing mix.

    1 cup seeds from freshly cut squash *or*
      pumpkin, washed and dried
    2 tablespoons vegetable oil
    1 to 2 tablespoons ranch salad dressing mix

In a skillet, saute seeds in oil for 5 minutes or until lightly browned. Using a slotted spoon, transfer seeds to an ungreased 15-in. x 10 in. x 1-in. baking pan. Sprinkle with salad dressing mix; stir to coat. Spread in a single layer. Bake at 325° for 10-15 minutes or until crisp. Store in an airtight container for up to 3 weeks. **Yield:** 1 cup.

Bewitching Chili

Ready in 30 minutes or less

Anne Mitchell of Lynchburg, Ohio lends a hearty homespun chili to our menu.

1-1/2 pounds ground beef
  1/2 cup chopped sweet red pepper
  1/2 cup chopped green pepper
    1 medium onion, chopped
    1 garlic clove, minced
    1 can (32 ounces) tomato juice
    1 can (15-1/2 ounces) hot chili beans,
      undrained
    1 can (14-1/2 ounces) diced tomatoes,
      undrained
    1 can (10-1/2 ounces) condensed beef broth,
      undiluted
    1 can (6 ounces) tomato paste
    2 tablespoons chili powder
1-1/2 teaspoons ground cumin
    1 teaspoon salt
    1 teaspoon sugar
  1/4 teaspoon pepper
Sour cream

In a Dutch oven, cook beef, peppers, onion and garlic over medium heat until meat is no longer pink; drain.

Stir in tomato juice, beans, tomatoes, broth, tomato paste and seasonings; bring to a boil. Reduce heat; cover and simmer for 15 minutes. Serve in Cauldron Bread Bowls (recipe below) if desired. Garnish with sour cream. **Yield:** 8-10 servings.

Cauldron Bread Bowls

Quick-rise yeast cuts the preparation time of this make-ahead bread.

    4 to 5 cups all-purpose flour
    1 cup rye flour
    3 teaspoons quick-rise yeast
    3 teaspoons salt
    2 teaspoons baking cocoa
    2 cups water
  1/3 cup molasses
  1/4 cup vegetable oil

In a mixing bowl, combine 4 cups all-purpose flour, rye flour, yeast, salt and cocoa. Heat water, molasses and oil to 120°-130°. Add to dry ingredients; beat until smooth. Stir in enough remaining all-purpose flour to form a soft dough. Turn onto a floured surface; knead until smooth and elastic, about 6-8 minutes. Cover and let rest for 10 minutes.

Divide dough into eight portions; shape each into a ball. Place on greased baking sheets. Cover and let rise in a warm place until doubled, about 20 minutes. Bake at 375° for 20 minutes or until golden brown. Cut the top fourth off each roll; carefully hollow out bottom, leaving a 1/4-in. shell (discard removed bread or save for another use). Fill each bowl with 1/2 cup chili. Serve bread tops on the side if desired. **Yield:** 8 bread bowls.

Candy Corn Cookies

Plan ahead...needs to chill

Get a head start on these buttery cookies by shaping and chilling the homemade dough ahead of time.

1-1/2 cups butter (no substitutes), softened
1-1/2 cups sugar
  1/2 teaspoon vanilla extract
    3 cups all-purpose flour
    1 teaspoon baking soda
  1/2 teaspoon salt
Yellow and orange paste food coloring

In a mixing bowl, cream butter and sugar. Beat in vanilla. Combine flour, baking soda and salt; gradually add to creamed mixture. Divide dough in half. Tint one portion yellow. Divide remaining dough into two-third and one-third portions. Color the larger portion orange; leave smaller portion white.

Shape each portion of dough into two 8-in. logs. Flatten top and push sides in at a slight angle. Place orange logs on yellow logs; push the sides in at a slight angle. Top with white logs; form a rounded top. Wrap in plastic wrap. Chill for 4 hours or until firm. Unwrap and cut into 1/4-in. slices. Place 2 in. apart on ungreased baking sheets. Bake at 350° for 10-12 minutes or until set. Remove to wire racks to cool. **Yield:** about 5 dozen.

DOES the thought of hosting a gathering during the hectic holidays leave you cold? You're sure to warm up to the notion with this below-zero buffet.

Penguin Veggie Platter

Ready in 1 hour or less

An eye-catching eggplant penguin is sure to encourage guests to sample this colorful appetizer. The dapper fellow watches over a platter of fresh vegetables and a creamy dip flecked with bits of green and sweet red pepper.

    1 large sweet red pepper
    1 cup (8 ounces) sour cream
    1 cup mayonnaise
    1 envelope Italian salad dressing mix
    1/4 cup chopped green pepper
    1 medium eggplant
    1 medium sweet yellow pepper
    3 tablespoons whipped cream cheese
    2 raisins
Broccoli florets, cherry tomatoes, sliced cucumbers
    and carrots *or* vegetables of your choice

Chop a fourth of the red pepper; set aside. Cut a piece of red pepper into a bow tie shape; slice remaining pepper and set aside. In a bowl, combine the sour cream, mayonnaise, salad dressing mix and chopped red and green peppers; mix well. Refrigerate until serving.

Cut a thin slice off the bottom of the eggplant to make a flat surface. Cut the removed section into two slices for flippers. Break a wooden toothpick in half; press one piece into each side of whole eggplant and gently press flippers onto toothpicks. Cut yellow pepper in half, cut one piece into two feet. Place at base of eggplant. From remaining yellow pepper, cut out a 1-in. x 3/4-in. triangle for beak; attach to eggplant with a toothpick.

Place cream cheese in a pastry or plastic bag; cut a small hole in a corner. Pipe two 1-in. ovals for eyes and a 2-1/2-in. x 2-1/4-in. oval for belly. Press a raisin into the center of each eye. Attach red pepper bow tie below the beak with a toothpick; pipe a small amount of cream cheese in the center of the tie.

Arrange sliced red pepper and other vegetables around the penguin. Serve with dip. **Yield:** 1 penguin (2 cups dip).

Mitten Sandwiches

Plan ahead...uses a slow cooker

Although you don't wear them, these cute mitten-shaped sandwiches are sure to warm you up. Frozen bread dough is formed into mitten buns, then filled with a barbecue beef filling. —Charm Holman, Springfield, Missouri

    1 boneless beef chuck roast (about 2 pounds)
    1 loaf (1 pound) frozen bread dough, thawed
Red liquid food coloring
    1 egg
    1 tablespoon water
    1 cup barbecue sauce
    1/2 cup packed brown sugar
    1/2 cup ketchup
    1/2 cup grape jelly

Place the roast in a slow cooker. Cover and cook on low for 8 hours or until the meat is tender. Meanwhile, divide bread dough into eighths. Tint two portions with red food coloring; divide red portions into thirds. Roll each into a 3-in. rope; set aside. For each mitten, flatten one white portion into a 4-in. oval. Place on a greased baking sheet. With a sharp knife or kitchen shears, make a 1-1/2-in. diagonal cut into side of oval toward the center for the thumb. Tuck tip under to form a round thumb; spread thumb and mitten apart.

For cuff, place a colored rope below each mitten; pinch edges together and flatten slightly. In a small bowl, beat egg and water; brush over dough (dough does not need to rise). Bake at 350° for 15-20 minutes or until golden brown. Cool on a wire rack.

Remove roast from slow cooker; discard juices. Shred beef with a fork and return to slow cooker. Add the barbecue sauce, brown sugar, ketchup and jelly; heat through. Split mitten rolls; fill with shredded beef. **Yield:** 6 sandwiches.

Igloo Salad

Ready in 30 minutes or less

Miniature marshmallows cover this fluffy fruit salad that's fashioned into an Eskimo igloo.

    1 can (15-1/4 ounces) fruit cocktail, drained
    1 can (11 ounces) mandarin oranges, drained
    1/2 cup flaked coconut
    1-3/4 cups whipped topping, *divided*
    2-1/2 cups miniature marshmallows, *divided*

In a bowl, combine the fruit cocktail, oranges, coconut, 1 cup whipped topping and 1/2 cup marshmallows. Spoon into two balls, one 5-1/2 in. and one 3-1/2 in., on a serving plate, with smaller ball in front of larger ball. Spoon out some salad from small ball to make a doorway. Cover with remaining whipped topping and marshmallows. **Yield:** 6 servings.

Snowshoe Cookies

Ready in 1 hour or less

Store-bought peanut butter sandwich cookies create these sweet snowshoes. Pretzel sticks threaded with mini marshmallows make accompanying poles.

    12 Nutter Butter peanut butter sandwich
        cookies
    1/3 cup semisweet chocolate chips, melted
    12 miniature marshmallows
    12 pretzel sticks

Place cookies on a wire rack over a large piece of waxed paper. Drizzle chocolate over cookies in a crisscross pattern to form snowshoes. Let stand until chocolate has hardened. For ski poles, thread a marshmallow on one end of each pretzel stick. Serve a set of poles with a pair of snowshoes. **Yield:** 6 servings.

Playful Fare Is in Good Fun

THE NEXT TIME you're shuffling through ideas for a card club luncheon or game night with family and friends, try your luck at this winning spread.

Dartboard Pizza

Ready in 30 minutes or less

This fast-to-fix entree aims to please as a saucy takeoff on a popular game. With its zesty combination of pepperoni, green pepper and cheese, this pizza will have guests darting to the table.

    1 tube (10 ounces) refrigerated pizza crust
    1 can (8 ounces) pizza sauce
    2 cups (8 ounces) shredded mozzarella cheese
    1 package (3-1/2 ounces) sliced pepperoni
1-1/2 cups (6 ounces) shredded cheddar cheese
    1 cup chopped green pepper

Unroll pizza crust onto an ungreased 14-in. pizza pan; flatten dough and build up edges slightly. Prick dough several times with a fork. Bake at 425° for 7 minutes or until lightly browned. Cool on a wire rack. Spread pizza sauce over the crust; sprinkle with mozzarella cheese.

Place one pepperoni slice in the center of the pizza; chop remaining pepperoni. Sprinkle some chopped pepperoni around outer edge of pizza, leaving 1/2 in. of crust. Sprinkle remaining pepperoni in a circle between center slice and outer edge. Arrange cheddar cheese and green pepper alternately in a spoke pattern. Bake at 425° for 12 minutes or until cheese is melted and pizza is heated through. **Yield:** 1 pizza (8 slices).

Cheese Spread Dice

Plan ahead...needs to chill

This novel cube of seasoned cream cheese with ripe olives is easily spotted.

✓ Uses less fat, sugar or salt. Includes Nutritional Analysis and Diabetic Exchanges.

    3 packages (8 ounces *each*) cream cheese,
        softened, *divided*
    2 cups (8 ounces) shredded Italian-blend *or*
        mozzarella cheese
    1 small onion, finely chopped
    1 tablespoon Worcestershire sauce
    1 tablespoon minced fresh parsley
    1 teaspoon milk
    8 medium pitted ripe olives
Assorted crackers

In a mixing bowl, combine two packages of cream cheese, shredded cheese, onion, Worcestershire sauce and parsley. Press into a plastic wrap-lined 8-in. x 4-in. x 2-in. loaf pan. Cover and refrigerate overnight. Remove from pan; cut in half widthwise. Stack one on top of the other on a serving plate. In a mixing bowl, beat milk and remaining cream cheese until smooth. Spread over cube. Cut olives in half; arrange on top and sides of dice. Serve with crackers. **Yield:** 3 cups.

Nutritional Analysis: One 2-tablespoon serving (prepared with reduced-fat cream cheese and part-skim mozzarella cheese; calculated without crackers) equals 69 calories, 4 g fat (2 g saturated fat), 15 mg cholesterol, 169 mg sodium, 2 g carbohydrate, trace fiber, 5 g protein. **Diabetic Exchanges:** 1 fat, 1/2 lean meat.

Gelatin Game Chips

Plan ahead...needs to chill

It's a safe bet these gelatin gems will delight a full house of friends. The white ones have a creamy vanilla taste while the others are sweet and fruity.

    1/2 cup milk
    1/2 cup sugar
      3 envelopes unflavored gelatin
    3/4 cup cold water
1-1/2 teaspoons vanilla extract
      2 cups (16 ounces) sour cream
      5 cups lemon-lime soda
      4 packages (3 ounces *each*) berry blue gelatin
      4 packages (3 ounces *each*) raspberry gelatin

In a saucepan, heat milk and sugar over low heat until sugar is dissolved. Soften unflavored gelatin in water; stir into the milk mixture until dissolved. Remove from the heat; add vanilla. Cool to lukewarm; blend in sour cream. Pour into a 13-in. x 9-in. x 2-in. dish. Chill until set.

In a saucepan, bring the soda to a boil. Place blue gelatin in a bowl; stir in 2-1/2 cups of soda until gelatin is dissolved. Pour into another 13-in. x 9-in. x 2-in. dish. Repeat with raspberry gelatin and remaining soda. Refrigerate until set. Using a 1-1/2-in. round cookie cutter, cut white, blue and red gelatin into rounds. Stack or scatter on a serving plate. **Yield:** 9 dozen.

Scrabble Brownies

One bite will send snackers scrambling for their dictionaries to describe these unbeatable blond brownies.

    1 cup butter *or* margarine, softened
    3 cups packed brown sugar
    4 eggs
    2 teaspoons vanilla extract
    3 cups all-purpose flour
    1 teaspoon baking powder
    1 teaspoon salt
    1 cup chopped nuts
    1 can (16 ounces) chocolate frosting
    1 cup vanilla frosting

In a mixing bowl, cream the butter and brown sugar. Add eggs, one at a time, beating well after each addition. Beat in vanilla. Combine the flour, baking powder and salt; add to the creamed mixture and mix well. Fold in the nuts. Spread into a greased 15-in. x 10-in. x 1-in. baking pan.

Bake at 350° for 25-30 minutes or until a toothpick comes out clean. Cool. Frost brownies with chocolate frosting. Cut into 1-1/2-in. squares. Place vanilla frosting in a small heavy-duty resealable plastic bag; cut an 1/8-in. hole in one corner. Pipe letters on brownies and arrange on a serving platter to form words. **Yield:** 5 dozen.

Chapter 4

Give Me 5 or Fewer

IT'S NOT hard to figure. Recipes that call for fewer ingredients usually take less time to prepare.

So it's no wonder that time-pressed cooks with spirited schedules often rely on recipes that feature few ingredients and lots of convenience.

With just five ingredients—or fewer—per recipe, each delicious dish in this chapter is so simple to assemble.

But while these tasty entrees, side dishes, soups, salads and desserts are short on ingredients, they're long on flavor. So you can offer wholesome foods your whole family will favor.

THE BEST FOR LESS. Clockwise from top: Bacon-Tomato Bagel Melts (p. 61), Broccoli Waldorf Salad (p. 64), No-Bake Cheesecake Pie (p. 67) and Pork Chops with Apples and Stuffing (p. 67)

Glazed Pork Chops

(Pictured below)

Ready in 30 minutes or less

I'm a new mom and need good healthy meals that are fast to fix. These moist chops fit the bill perfectly. Since this entree requires a single pan, cleanup's quick, too.
— *Kristin Tanis, Hatfield, Pennsylvania*

  4 bone-in pork loin chops (3/4 inch thick)
1/3 cup plus 1 tablespoon cider vinegar, *divided*
  3 tablespoons soy sauce
  3 garlic cloves, minced
1-1/2 teaspoons cornstarch

In a nonstick skillet over medium heat, brown pork chops on both sides. In a bowl, combine 1/3 cup vinegar, soy sauce and garlic; pour over the chops. Cover and simmer for 8-10 minutes or until the meat is no longer pink. In a bowl, combine the cornstarch and remaining vinegar until smooth; stir into the skillet. Bring to a boil; cook and stir for 1 minute or until thickened. **Yield:** 4 servings.

Chunky Applesauce

(Pictured below)

Plan ahead...uses slow cooker

My mother gave me the recipe for this warm and cinnamony apple dish. Simmering it in a slow cooker fills the house with a wonderful aroma. You can also serve it with cream for dessert.
— *Lisa Roessner*
Ft. Recovery, Ohio

✓ Uses less fat, sugar or salt. Includes Nutritional Analysis and Diabetic Exchanges.

  8 to 10 large tart apples, peeled and cut into chunks
1/2 to 1 cup sugar
1/2 cup water
  1 teaspoon ground cinnamon

Combine apples, sugar, water and cinnamon in a slow cooker; stir gently. Cover and cook on low for 6-8 hours or until apples are tender. **Yield:** 5 cups.
  Nutritional Analysis: One 3/4-cup serving (prepared with sugar substitute equivalent to 1/2 cup sugar) equals 93 calories, 0 fat (0 saturated fat), 0 cholesterol, 77 mg sodium, 25 g carbohydrate, 4 g fiber, 1 g protein. **Diabetic Exchanges:** 2-1/2 fruit, 1 meat.

Creamy Italian Noodles

(Pictured below)

Ready in 30 minutes or less

Here's an easy recipe for no-fail noodles that are a flavorful accompaniment to most any meat. Rich and creamy, they're special enough for company, too.
— *Linda Hendrix, Moundville, Missouri*

  1 package (8 ounces) wide egg noodles
1/4 cup butter *or* margarine, softened
1/2 cup whipping cream, half-and-half cream *or* evaporated milk
1/4 cup grated Parmesan cheese
2-1/4 teaspoons Italian salad dressing mix

Chunky Applesauce
Glazed Pork Chops
Creamy Italian Noodles

Cook the noodles according to package directions; drain and place in a bowl. Toss with the butter. Add the remaining ingredients and mix well. Serve immediately. **Yield:** 4-6 servings.

Cordon Bleu Stromboli

I get the taste of chicken cordon bleu without all the work. I roll Swiss cheese and deli meats into a swirled sandwich loaf that bakes to a golden brown. My entire gang looks forward to this dinner. —Diane Schuelke Madison, Minnesota

> 1 loaf (1 pound) frozen bread dough, thawed
> 2 tablespoons butter *or* margarine, softened
> 8 ounces thinly sliced deli ham
> 1/2 cup shredded Swiss cheese
> 5 ounces thinly sliced deli chicken

On a lightly floured surface, roll dough into a 10-in. x 8-in. rectangle; spread with butter. Top with ham, cheese and chicken. Roll up jelly-roll style, starting with a long side; pinch seam to seal and tuck ends under. Place seam side down on a greased baking sheet. Cover and let rise for 20 minutes. Bake at 350° for 25-30 minutes or until golden brown. Refrigerate leftovers. **Yield:** 6 servings.

Potato Sloppy Joe Bake

Ready in 1 hour or less

I created this speedy sensation while racing against the clock one day. I needed a quick meal that was low on ingredients but high on taste, so I came up with this hearty casserole featuring ground beef and potatoes.
—Ruth Chiarenza, Cumberland, Maryland

> 1 pound ground beef
> 1 can (15-1/2 ounces) sloppy joe sauce
> 1 can (10-3/4 ounces) condensed cream of potato soup, undiluted
> 1 package (32 ounces) frozen cubed hash brown potatoes, thawed
> 1 cup (4 ounces) shredded cheddar cheese

In a skillet, cook beef over medium heat until no longer pink; drain. Add sloppy joe sauce and soup. Place hash browns in a greased 13-in. x 9-in. x 2-in. baking dish. Top with beef mixture. Cover and bake at 450° for 20 minutes. Uncover; bake 10 minutes more or until heated through. Sprinkle with cheese. **Yield:** 6-8 servings.

Strawberry Rhubarb Gelatin

Plan ahead...needs to chill

Rhubarb lends a hint of natural tartness to this sweet salad. As a fruity side dish, its vibrant color is sure to add eye-opening appeal to almost any meal.
—Opal Schmidt, Battle Creek, Iowa

> 2 cups diced fresh *or* frozen rhubarb
> 1/2 to 3/4 cup sugar

Baked Bean Chili

> 1/4 cup water
> 1 package (3 ounces) strawberry gelatin
> 1-1/2 cups whipped topping

In a saucepan, bring rhubarb, sugar and water to a boil. Reduce heat; simmer, uncovered, for 3-5 minutes or until the rhubarb is softened. Remove from the heat; stir in gelatin until dissolved. Pour into a bowl. Refrigerate for 20 minutes or until partially set. Fold in whipped topping. Chill until firm. **Yield:** 4 servings.

Baked Bean Chili

(Pictured above)

Ready in 30 minutes or less

Who says a good chili has to simmer all day? This zippy chili—with a touch of sweetness from the baked beans— can be made on the spur of the moment. It's an excellent standby when unexpected guests drop in. Served with bread and a salad, it's a hearty dinner everyone raves about. —Nancy Wall, Bakersfield, California

> 2 pounds ground beef
> 3 cans (28 ounces *each*) baked beans
> 1 can (46 ounces) tomato juice
> 1 can (11-1/2 ounces) V8 juice
> 1 envelope chili seasoning

In a Dutch oven, cook beef over medium heat until no longer pink; drain. Stir in the remaining ingredients. Bring to a boil. Reduce heat; simmer, uncovered, for 10 minutes. **Yield:** 24 servings.

Beef Noodle Soup
Banana-Nut Corn Bread
Chocolate Chip Cheese Bars

Banana-Nut Corn Bread

(Pictured above)

A boxed corn bread mix gets a tasty treatment when dressed up with bananas and chopped walnuts. The moist golden loaves are a great addition to a brunch buffet or bake sale. —Janice France, Depauw, Indiana

  2 packages (8-1/2 ounces *each*) corn bread/muffin mix
  1 cup mashed ripe bananas (about 2 medium)
  1 cup chopped walnuts
  1 cup milk

In a bowl, combine all ingredients just until blended. Spoon into two greased 8-in. x 4-in. x 2-in. loaf pans. Bake at 350° for 35-40 minutes or until a toothpick inserted near the center comes out clean. Cool for 10 minutes before removing from pans to wire racks to cool completely. **Yield:** 2 loaves.

Chocolate Chip Cheese Bars

(Pictured above)

This is my most requested dessert recipe. Everyone loves these yummy bars with their soft cream cheese filling... and they couldn't be easier. —Teri Lindquist, Gurnee, Illinois

  1 tube (18 ounces) refrigerated chocolate chip cookie dough*
  1 package (8 ounces) cream cheese, softened
  1/2 cup sugar
  1 egg

Cut cookie dough in half. For crust, press half of the dough onto the bottom of a greased 8-in. square baking pan. In a mixing bowl, beat cream cheese, sugar and egg until smooth. Spread over crust. Crumble remaining dough over top. Bake at 350° for 35-40 minutes or until a toothpick inserted near the center comes out clean. Cool on a wire rack. Refrigerate leftovers. **Yield:** 12-16 servings.

  *Editor's Note: 2 cups of your favorite chocolate chip cookie dough can be substituted for the refrigerated dough.

Beef Noodle Soup

(Pictured above)

Ready in 30 minutes or less

Bowls of this chunky mixture are chock-full of ground beef, noodles and vegetables. —Arlene Lynn, Lincoln, Nebraska

  1 pound ground beef
  1 can (46 ounces) V8 juice
  1 envelope onion soup mix

1 package (3 ounces) beef ramen noodles
1 package (16 ounces) frozen mixed vegetables

In a large saucepan, cook beef over medium heat until no longer pink; drain. Stir in the V8 juice, soup mix, contents of noodle seasoning packet and mixed vegetables. Bring to a boil. Reduce heat; simmer, uncovered, for 6 minutes or until vegetables are tender. Return to a boil; stir in noodles. Cook for 3 minutes or until noodles are tender. **Yield:** 8 servings.

Pizza Spread

Ready in 15 minutes or less

For a satisfying snack, spread slices of French bread with this thick cheesy mixture. It's a very adaptable recipe. It would also be good with Italian sausage instead of ground beef. —Beverly Mons, Middletown, New York

1 pound ground beef
1 jar (26 ounces) marinara *or* spaghetti sauce
1 teaspoon dried oregano
4 cups (16 ounces) shredded mozzarella cheese
1 loaf Italian *or* French bread, cubed *or* sliced

In a saucepan, cook beef over medium heat until no longer pink; drain. Stir in marinara sauce and oregano. Gradually stir in cheese until melted. Pour into a fondue pot or small slow cooker to keep warm. Serve with bread. **Yield:** 8-10 servings.

Last-Minute Cranberry Relish

Ready in 15 minutes or less

Feature this no-fuss relish alongside your bird or roast and just wait for the compliments. One year I brought this to a church Thanksgiving dinner, and several people asked what spices I used to make it so terrific. —Cathy Rogers Asheville, North Carolina

1 can (16 ounces) whole-berry cranberry sauce
1 can (8 ounces) crushed pineapple, drained
1/4 teaspoon apple pie spice
Pinch ground cloves
1/4 cup chopped pecans

In a bowl, combine the cranberry sauce, pineapple, apple pie spice and cloves. Stir in pecans. Serve immediately. **Yield:** about 2 cups.

Onion-Topped Chicken

I throw together this saucy combination of tender chicken and potatoes when family or friends come to visit. French-fried onions add golden crunch to the casserole. — Kay Faust, Deerwood, Minnesota

4 boneless skinless chicken breast halves
4 medium potatoes, peeled and halved

1 can (10-3/4 ounces) condensed cream of chicken soup, undiluted
1 cup (8 ounces) sour cream
1 can (2.8 ounces) french-fried onions

Place chicken in a greased 9-in. square baking dish. Arrange potatoes around chicken. Combine soup and sour cream; spread over chicken and potatoes. Bake, uncovered, at 350° for 1-1/4 hours. Sprinkle with onions; bake 10 minutes longer. **Yield:** 4 servings.

Pull-Apart Bacon Bread

(Pictured below)

I stumbled across this recipe while looking for something different to take to a brunch. Boy, am I glad I did! Everyone asked for the recipe and could not believe it only called for five ingredients. It's the perfect item to bake for an informal meal. —Traci Collins, Cheyenne, Wyoming

12 bacon strips, diced
1 loaf (1 pound) frozen bread dough, thawed
2 tablespoons olive *or* vegetable oil, *divided*
1 cup (4 ounces) shredded mozzarella cheese
1 envelope (1 ounce) ranch salad dressing mix

In a skillet, cook bacon over medium heat for 5 minutes or until partially cooked; drain on paper towels. Roll out dough to 1/2-in. thickness; brush with 1 tablespoon of oil. Cut into 1-in. pieces; place in a large bowl. Add the bacon, cheese, dressing mix and remaining oil; toss to coat. Arrange pieces in a 9-in. x 5-in. oval on a greased baking sheet, layering as needed. Cover and let rise in a warm place for 30 minutes or until doubled. Bake at 350° for 15 minutes. Cover with foil; bake 5-10 minutes longer or until golden brown. **Yield:** 1 loaf.

Pull-Apart Bacon Bread

Gooey Chip Bars

Ready in 1 hour or less

You can satisfy a sweet tooth in a jiffy with these chewy chocolaty bars. You'll never believe how easy they are to assemble. —Beatriz Boggs, Delray Beach, Florida

> 2 cups graham cracker crumbs (about 32 squares)
> 1 can (14 ounces) sweetened condensed milk
> 1 cup (6 ounces) semisweet chocolate chips, *divided*
> 1/2 cup chopped walnuts *or* pecans, optional

In a bowl, combine cracker crumbs and milk. Stir in 1/2 cup chocolate chips and nuts if desired (batter will be very thick). Pat into a well-greased 8-in. square baking pan. Sprinkle with remaining chocolate chips. Bake at 350° for 20-25 minutes or until golden brown. Cool; cut into bars. **Yield:** 1-1/2 dozen.

Picante Chicken

(Pictured below)

Ready in 1 hour or less

My husband used to claim this entree as his specialty until I made it and discovered how quick and easy it is. Our two sons love the juicy chicken, while my husband and I enjoy the twist that brown sugar and mustard give the picante sauce. —Karen Stattelman, Effingham, Kansas

 Uses less fat, sugar or salt. Includes Nutritional Analysis and Diabetic Exchanges.

> 4 boneless skinless chicken breast halves (1 pound)
> 1 jar (16 ounces) picante sauce
> 3 tablespoons brown sugar

Picante Chicken

> 1 tablespoon prepared mustard
> Hot cooked rice, optional

Place chicken in a greased shallow 2-qt. baking dish. In a small bowl, combine the picante sauce, brown sugar and mustard; pour over chicken. Bake, uncovered, at 400° for 30-35 minutes or until chicken juices run clear. Serve over rice if desired. **Yield:** 4 servings.
  Nutritional Analysis: One serving (calculated without rice) equals 209 calories, 2 g fat (trace saturated fat), 66 mg cholesterol, 1,009 mg sodium, 19 g carbohydrate, trace fiber, 26 g protein. **Diabetic Exchanges:** 3 lean meat, 1/2 starch.

Tortellini Soup

Ready in 30 minutes or less

This soup is fast, flavorful and good for you. Packaged cheese tortellini meets colorful summer squash, fresh spinach and shredded carrots in every eye-appealing bowl. —Chris Snyder, Boulder, Colorado

✓ Uses less fat, sugar or salt. Includes Nutritional Analysis and Diabetic Exchanges.

> 5 cups chicken broth
> 3-1/2 cups shredded carrots (about 10 ounces)
> 1 cup chopped yellow summer squash
> 3 cups torn fresh spinach
> 1 package (9 ounces) refrigerated cheese tortellini

In a large saucepan, combine the broth, carrots and squash. Bring to a boil. Reduce heat; simmer, uncovered, for 3 minutes. Stir in spinach and tortellini. Cover and cook for 5 minutes or until tortellini is heated through. **Yield:** 7 servings.
  Nutritional Analysis: One serving (1 cup) equals 160 calories, 3 g fat (2 g saturated fat), 14 mg cholesterol, 806 mg sodium, 24 g carbohydrate, 3 g fiber, 8 g protein. **Diabetic Exchanges:** 2 vegetable, 1 starch.

Spaghetti Carbonara

Ready in 30 minutes or less

This is a swift and yummy recipe that I received from a dear friend. My family asks for it often. —Roni Goodell, Spanish Fork, Utah

> 1 package (7 ounces) thin spaghetti
> 10 bacon strips, diced
> 1/3 cup butter *or* margarine
> 2 eggs, lightly beaten
> 3/4 cup grated Parmesan cheese

Cook spaghetti according to package directions. Meanwhile, in a skillet, cook bacon over medium heat until crisp; drain on paper towels. Add butter to drippings; heat until melted. Drain spaghetti; toss with eggs and Parmesan cheese. Add to skillet; cook and stir over medium heat for 3-4 minutes or until eggs are set. Sprinkle with bacon. **Yield:** 3-4 servings.

Seasoned Cube Steaks

Plan ahead…needs to marinate

Soy sauce really wakes up the flavor of these nicely browned cube steaks. I serve this meaty main dish with mixed vegetables and rice or baked potatoes. My family loves this meal.
—Cathee Bethel
Lebanon, Oregon

1 cup soy sauce
1 teaspoon dried minced garlic
1 teaspoon dried minced onion
4 cube steaks (about 1-1/4 pounds)

In a large resealable plastic bag, combine the soy sauce, garlic and onion; add cube steaks. Seal bag; turn to coat. Refrigerate for 30-45 minutes, turning once. Drain and discard marinade. Place steaks on a greased broiler pan. Broil 4 in. from the heat for about 4 minutes on each side or until meat reaches desired doneness. **Yield:** 4 servings.

Corn 'n' Bean Bake

Ready in 1 hour or less

Surprise your family when you put this green bean dish with a twist on the table. I add whole kernel corn and buttery crackers to the creamy casserole, bringing a new taste to a time-honored tradition.
—Nellie Perdue
Summer Shade, Kentucky

1 package (16 ounces) frozen cut green beans
1 can (15-1/4 ounces) whole kernel corn, drained
1 can (10-3/4 ounces) condensed cream of mushroom soup, undiluted
1 cup (4 ounces) shredded cheddar cheese, *divided*
1/2 cup crushed butter-flavored crackers (about 12)

In a bowl, combine the beans, corn, soup and 1/2 cup cheese. Spoon into a greased 1-1/2-qt. baking dish. Top with crackers and remaining cheese. Bake, uncovered, at 350° for 35 minutes or until heated through. **Yield:** 4 servings.

Chicken Broccoli Skillet

Ready in 30 minutes or less

When you're looking for a good way to use up leftover chicken, consider this simple stovetop supper. The creamy combination is fast and filling when served over helpings of hot rice. —Marlene Harguth, Maynard, Minnesota

2-1/2 cups cubed cooked chicken
1 package (10 ounces) frozen broccoli florets *or* 1-2/3 cups fresh broccoli florets
8 ounces process American cheese, cubed
1/2 cup mayonnaise *or* salad dressing
Hot cooked rice

In a skillet, combine the chicken, broccoli and cheese. Cover and cook over medium heat until broccoli is crisp-tender and cheese is melted. Stir in mayonnaise; heat through (do not boil). Serve over rice. **Yield:** 4 servings.

Horseradish Crab Dip

Horseradish Crab Dip

(Pictured above)

Ready in 15 minutes or less

I depend on this mildly seasoned crab dip when hosting parties. It's a terrific time-saver when accompanied by celery sticks or your favorite raw veggie. It's so simple to prepare that it gives me time to get other appetizers ready or mingle with guests.
—Kathleen Snead
Lynchburg, Virginia

✓ Uses less fat, sugar or salt. Includes Nutritional Analysis and Diabetic Exchanges.

1 package (8 ounces) cream cheese, softened
2 to 3 tablespoons picante sauce
1 to 2 tablespoons prepared horseradish
1 can (6 ounces) crabmeat, drained, flaked and cartilage removed
Celery sticks

In a mixing bowl, beat cream cheese, picante sauce and horseradish; mix well. Stir in the crab. Serve with celery. **Yield:** about 1-1/2 cups.

Nutritional Analysis: One 1/4-cup serving of dip (prepared with reduced-fat cream cheese and 2 tablespoons picante sauce) equals 119 calories, 7 g fat (4 g saturated fat), 46 mg cholesterol, 257 mg sodium, 4 g carbohydrate, trace fiber, 10 g protein. **Diabetic Exchanges:** 1-1/2 fat, 1 lean meat.

Chicken Potato Bake
Roasted Green Beans
Lemonade Fruit Dressing

Chicken Potato Bake

(Pictured above)

Ready in 1 hour or less

In the evenings, I'm busy helping our two kids with homework and don't have time to spend in the kitchen. Italian dressing gives fast flavor to juicy chicken and tender potatoes in this satisfying supper. —Debbi Mullins
Canoga Park, California

   1 broiler/fryer chicken (about 3 pounds), cut up
   1 pound red potatoes, cut into chunks
1/2 to 3/4 cup prepared Italian salad dressing
   1 tablespoon Italian seasoning
1/2 to 3/4 cup grated Parmesan cheese

Place chicken in a greased 13-in. x 9-in. x 2-in. baking dish. Arrange potatoes around chicken. Drizzle with dressing; sprinkle with Italian seasoning and Parmesan cheese. Cover and bake at 400° for 20 minutes. Uncover; bake 20-30 minutes longer or until potatoes are tender and chicken juices run clear. **Yield:** 4 servings.

Roasted Green Beans

(Pictured above)

Ready in 30 minutes or less

Red wine vinegar really perks up everyday green beans in this simple side dish. Season with salt and pepper to suit your taste.
—LaVonne Hegland, St. Michael, Minnesota

3/4 pound fresh green beans
   1 small onion, thinly sliced and separated into rings
   2 garlic cloves, thinly sliced
   1 tablespoon red wine vinegar *or* cider vinegar
   2 teaspoons olive *or* vegetable oil

Place beans in a saucepan and cover with water; bring to a boil. Cook, uncovered, for 8-10 minutes or until crisp-tender. Drain and place in a greased 11-in. x 7-in. x 2-in. baking dish. Top with onion and garlic. Drizzle with vinegar and oil; toss to coat. Bake, uncovered, at 450° for 10 minutes. Stir; bake 5 minutes longer. **Yield:** 4 servings.

Lemonade Fruit Dressing

(Pictured at left)

Ready in 30 minutes or less

I like to dollop this tart yet rich dressing over an assortment of seasonal fruit. It makes a very colorful and refreshing dessert that helps beat the summer heat.
—Emma Magielda, Amsterdam, New York

   2 eggs
3/4 cup lemonade concentrate
1/3 cup sugar
   1 cup whipping cream, whipped
Assorted fresh fruit

In a heavy saucepan, combine eggs, lemonade concentrate and sugar. Cook and stir over low heat just until mixture comes to a boil. Cool to room temperature, stirring several times. Fold in the whipped cream. Serve over fruit. Refrigerate leftovers. **Yield: about 3 cups.**

Hot Ham 'n' Swiss

Ready in 30 minutes or less

I've been preparing these versatile open-faced sandwiches for more than 20 years for different occasions and mealtimes. They're a special beginning to a cozy Sunday brunch. —Debbie Petrun, Smithfield, Pennsylvania

   5 eggs
   8 slices Italian bread (3/4 inch thick)
   1 pound thinly sliced deli ham
   8 slices Swiss cheese

In a shallow bowl, beat eggs. Dip both sides of bread in eggs. Cook on a greased hot griddle until lightly browned on both sides. Transfer to a baking sheet; top each slice with ham and cheese. Broil 4 in. from the heat for 5 minutes or until cheese melts. **Yield: 8 servings.**

Cheddar Sausage Muffins

Ready in 1 hour or less

Handy biscuit mix and cheese soup hurry along these hearty muffins. These golden treats are great at breakfast, brunch or a soup lunch. —Melissa Vannoy, Childress, Texas

   1 pound bulk pork sausage
   1 can (10-3/4 ounces) condensed cheddar
     cheese soup, undiluted
   1 cup (4 ounces) shredded cheddar cheese
2/3 cup water
   3 cups biscuit/baking mix

In a skillet over medium heat, cook sausage until no longer pink; drain. In a bowl, combine soup, cheese and water. Stir in biscuit mix until blended. Add sausage. Fill greased muffin cups three-fourths full. Bake at 350° for 20-25 minutes or until a toothpick comes out clean. Cool for 5 minutes before removing from pans to wire racks. Serve warm. **Yield: about 1-1/2 dozen.**

Peanut Butter Drops

Ready in 30 minutes or less

These simple saucepan cookies are a snap to make. In fact, I can whip them up in 10 minutes for school lunches. The little treats are a big hit with any crowd.
—Marg Mitro, Grafton, Ontario

   1 cup light corn syrup
1/2 cup sugar
   1 cup peanut butter*
   1 teaspoon vanilla extract
   4 to 5 cups cornflakes

In a large saucepan, bring the corn syrup and sugar to a boil. Add the peanut butter. Remove from the heat; stir in vanilla and cornflakes. Drop by heaping teaspoonfuls onto waxed paper. Store in an airtight container. **Yield: about 6-1/2 dozen.**
  ***Editor's Note:** Reduced-fat or generic brands of peanut butter are not recommended for this recipe.

Chili Casserole

Ready in 1 hour or less

I threw together this main dish when my husband unexpectedly invited his hunting buddies for dinner. It was on the table by the time they'd unpacked their gear and washed up. —Karen Bruggman, Edmonds, Washington

   1 can (40 ounces) chili with beans
   1 can (4 ounces) chopped green chilies
   1 can (2-1/4 ounces) sliced ripe olives, drained
   2 cups (8 ounces) shredded cheddar cheese
   2 cups ranch-flavored tortilla chips, crushed

In a bowl, combine all ingredients. Transfer to a greased 2-1/2-qt. baking dish. Bake, uncovered, at 350° for 30-35 minutes or until bubbly. **Yield: 6 servings.**

Bacon-Tomato Bagel Melts

(Pictured on page 52)

Ready in 15 minutes or less

My husband introduced me to this open-faced sandwich shortly after we got married, and it quickly became an all-time favorite. It's good made with plain or onion bagels. Have fun experimenting with various toppings and dressings, too.
—Lindsay Orwig, Grand Terrace, California

   2 bagels, split and toasted
   8 tomato slices
   8 bacon strips, cooked
   1 cup (4 ounces) shredded mozzarella cheese
Prepared ranch salad dressing

Place bagel halves cut side up on a baking sheet. Top each with two tomato slices and two bacon strips. Sprinkle with cheese. Broil 5 in. from the heat for 1-2 minutes or until cheese begins to brown. Serve with ranch dressing. **Yield: 4 sandwiches.**

Sweet and Savory Brisket

Sweet and Savory Brisket

(Pictured above)

Plan ahead...uses slow cooker

I like this recipe not only because it makes such tender and flavorful beef, but because it takes advantage of a slow cooker. It's wonderful to come home from work and have this mouth-watering main dish waiting for you.
—Chris Snyder, Boulder, Colorado

        1 beef brisket (3 to 3-1/2 pounds)*, cut in half
        1 cup ketchup
    1/4 cup grape jelly
        1 envelope onion soup mix
    1/2 teaspoon pepper

Place half of the brisket in a slow cooker. In a bowl, combine the ketchup, jelly, soup mix and pepper; spread half over meat. Top with the remaining meat and ketchup mixture. Cover and cook on low for 8-10 hours or until meat is tender. Slice brisket; serve with cooking juices. **Yield:** 8-10 servings.
   *Editor's Note: This is a fresh beef brisket, not corned beef.

Bacon Cabbage Stir-Fry

Ready in 15 minutes or less

If you like cabbage, you'll enjoy this stir-fried side dish. It's not only delicious, but fast to fix when you need to get dinner on the table quickly.
—Lori Thompson
New London, Texas

        6 bacon strips, diced
        1 small head cabbage, chopped
        1 teaspoon garlic powder
    3/4 teaspoon salt
    1/2 teaspoon ground mustard

In a large skillet, cook bacon over medium heat until crisp. Remove to paper towels; drain, reserving 1 tablespoon drippings. Stir-fry cabbage in drippings for 5 minutes. Add garlic powder, salt, mustard and bacon; cook and stir until heated through. **Yield:** 6 servings.

Perch Fillets

Ready in 30 minutes or less

Guests will never guess that lemon-lime soda and pancake mix are the secret ingredients behind these tasty perch fillets in a golden coating. If perch isn't available, try substituting haddock. —Connie Tibbetts, Wilton, Maine

    1-1/2 cups lemon-lime soda
        1 pound perch fillets
        2 cups pancake mix
    1/4 teaspoon pepper
Oil for frying

Pour soda into a shallow bowl; add fish fillets and let stand for 15 minutes. In another shallow bowl, combine pancake mix and pepper. Remove fish from soda and coat with pancake mix. In a large skillet, heat 1/4 in. of oil over medium-high heat. Fry fish for 2-3 minutes on each side or until fish flakes with a fork. Drain on paper towels. **Yield:** 4 servings.

Flavorful Fryer Chicken

This tender chicken with its full-flavored sauce is a lifesaver on busy nights. This entree is quick to prepare and uses ingredients I always have on hand. It has become a family favorite. —Marsha Murray, Niverville, Manitoba

        1 broiler/fryer chicken (3 to 4 pounds), cut up
        1 can (10-3/4 ounces) condensed cream of mushroom soup, undiluted
        1 cup orange juice
        2 tablespoons onion soup mix
Hot mashed potatoes *or* cooked rice

Place the chicken in a greased 13-in. x 9-in. x 2-in. baking dish. Combine the soup, orange juice and soup mix; pour over chicken. Cover and bake at 350° for 45 minutes. Uncover; bake 15-20 minutes longer or until the chicken juices run clear. Serve over potatoes or rice. **Yield:** 6 servings.

Cashew Apple Salad

Ready in 15 minutes or less

My sister-in-law brought this crunchy salad to a potluck, and it's been a favorite ever since. It goes with any entree because the sweet dressing is so light.
—Tammy Burnham, Hamilton, Montana

1/2 cup confectioners' sugar
1/4 cup mayonnaise *or* salad dressing
4 celery ribs, sliced
2 small apples, chopped
1 can (10 ounces) salted cashews

In a bowl, combine confectioners' sugar and mayonnaise until smooth. Stir in the celery, apples and cashews. Serve immediately. **Yield:** 8-10 servings.

Black Bean Quesadillas

Ready in 30 minutes or less

When I get home late from work as an operating room nurse, I often rely on this handy recipe. Topped with salsa and sour cream, the crisp wedges are always a hit. When I have extra time, I add chopped onion, black olives and green chilies to the beans. —Jane Epping
Iowa City, Iowa

2 cans (15 ounces *each*) black beans, rinsed and drained
1 jar (8 ounces) salsa, *divided*
10 flour tortillas (8 inches)
2 cups (8 ounces) shredded Colby-Monterey Jack cheese
Sour cream

In a bowl, mash the beans; add 1 cup salsa. Place five tortillas on ungreased baking sheets; spread with bean mixture. Sprinkle with cheese; top with the remaining tortillas. Bake at 350° for 15-18 minutes or until crisp and heated through. Cut into wedges. Serve with sour cream and remaining salsa. **Yield:** 5 servings.

Frozen Cherry Cream Pie

Plan ahead...needs to freeze

This pretty pink pie is a cool and tangy treat. It's convenient to make and freeze ahead of time. To serve, just cut it and top slices with whipped cream. —Kristyn Hall
Mt. Clemens, Michigan

✓ Uses less fat, sugar or salt. Includes Nutritional Analysis and Diabetic Exchanges.

4 ounces cream cheese, softened
1-1/2 cups cherry pie filling
2 cups whipped topping
1 graham cracker crust (9 inches)

In a mixing bowl, beat cream cheese until smooth. Fold in the pie filling and whipped topping until blended. Spoon into crust. Cover and freeze for 8 hours or overnight. Remove from the freezer 15 minutes before serving. **Yield:** 8 servings.
Nutritional Analysis: One piece (prepared with fat-free cream cheese, reduced-sugar pie filling, reduced-fat whipped topping and reduced-fat graham cracker crust) equals 114 calories, 5 g fat (4 g saturated fat), 0 mg cholesterol, 48 mg sodium, 15 g carbohydrate, trace fiber, 2 g protein. **Diabetic Exchanges:** 1 starch, 1/2 fat.

Reuben Dogs

Ready in 30 minutes or less

My husband and children enjoy Reuben sandwiches, and this quick casserole is as close as you can get without the mess. —Colleen Hawkins, Monrovia, Maryland

1 can (27 ounces) sauerkraut, rinsed and drained
1 to 2 teaspoons caraway seeds
8 hot dogs, halved lengthwise
1 cup (4 ounces) shredded Swiss cheese
Thousand Island salad dressing

Place sauerkraut in a greased 2-qt. baking dish. Sprinkle with caraway seeds. Top with hot dogs. Bake, uncovered, at 350° for 15-20 minutes or until heated through. Sprinkle with the cheese. Bake 3-5 minutes longer or until cheese is melted. Serve with the salad dressing. **Yield:** 4-6 servings.

Ham 'n' Cheese Mashed Potatoes

(Pictured below)

Ready in 30 minutes or less

The way I dress up leftover ham and mashed potatoes is a surefire success in my house! Cheddar cheese and cream add richness to this casserole, while garlic seasons it nicely. It's something my family looks forward to having on a regular basis. —Debra Herlihy
Swedesboro, New Jersey

2 cups mashed potatoes
3/4 teaspoon garlic salt
1 cup diced fully cooked ham
1 cup (4 ounces) shredded cheddar cheese
1/2 cup whipping cream, whipped

In a bowl, combine the potatoes and garlic salt. Spread into a greased 1-1/2-qt. baking dish. Sprinkle with ham. Fold cheese into whipped cream; spoon over ham. Bake, uncovered, at 450° for 15 minutes or until golden brown. **Yield:** 4-6 servings.

Ham 'n' Cheese Mashed Potatoes

Blueberry Angel Dessert

6 cups broccoli florets
1 large red apple, chopped
1/2 cup raisins
1/4 cup chopped pecans
1/2 cup prepared coleslaw dressing

In a large serving bowl, combine the first four ingredients. Drizzle with dressing; toss to coat. Refrigerate leftovers. **Yield:** 10 servings.
Nutritional Analysis: One 3/4-cup serving (prepared with reduced-fat coleslaw dressing) equals 87 calories, 4 g fat (trace saturated fat), 3 mg cholesterol, 133 mg sodium, 14 g carbohydrate, 2 g fiber, 2 g protein. **Diabetic Exchanges:** 1 vegetable, 1 fruit.

Blueberry Angel Dessert

(Pictured above)

Plan ahead...needs to chill

Make the most of angel food cake, pie filling and whipped topping by creating this light impressive dessert that doesn't keep you in the kitchen for hours. It's the perfect way to end a summer meal. I frequently get requests for the recipe. —Carol Johnson, Tyler, Texas

1 package (8 ounces) cream cheese, softened
1 cup confectioners' sugar
1 carton (8 ounces) frozen whipped topping, thawed
1 prepared angel food cake (14 ounces), cut into 1-inch cubes
2 cans (21 ounces *each*) blueberry pie filling

In a large mixing bowl, beat the cream cheese and sugar; fold in whipped topping and cake cubes. Spread evenly into an ungreased 13-in. x 9-in. x 2-in. dish; top with pie filling. Cover and refrigerate for at least 2 hours before cutting into squares. **Yield:** 12-15 servings.

Broccoli Waldorf Salad

(Pictured on page 53)

Ready in 15 minutes or less

This salad is as easy to prepare as it is to eat! A colorful combination of apples, raisins and pecans jazzes up broccoli florets in this side dish. Its tangy-sweet flavor makes it a standout at company picnics and church potlucks. —Vicki Roehrick, Chubbuck, Idaho

Cream of Carrot Soup

Ready in 1 hour or less

I came up with this rich yummy soup when I was in a hurry one day, and we needed something hot to eat. It's versatile, too. You can substitute most any vegetable with excellent results.
—Ruth Andrewson, Peck, Idaho

4 cups chicken broth
4 large carrots, cut into chunks
1/2 cup whipping cream
1 teaspoon sugar

In a saucepan, bring the broth and carrots to a boil. Reduce heat; simmer, uncovered, until the carrots are tender, about 15 minutes. Cool slightly. In a blender, cover and process the soup in small batches until smooth; return to the pan. Stir in cream and sugar; heat through. **Yield:** 5 servings.

Swiss Onion Crescents

(Pictured at right)

Ready in 30 minutes or less

I put a special spin on these golden crescents by filling them with Swiss cheese, green onions and Dijon mustard. They're a snap to prepare because I use refrigerated dough. —Joy McMillan, The Woodlands, Texas

1 tube (8 ounces) refrigerated crescent rolls
3 tablespoons shredded Swiss cheese, *divided*
2 tablespoons chopped green onion
1-1/2 teaspoons Dijon mustard

Unroll crescent dough and separate into eight triangles. Combine 2 tablespoons cheese, green onion and mustard; spread about 1 teaspoon over each triangle. Roll up from the short side. Place point side down on an ungreased baking sheet and curve into a crescent shape. Sprinkle with the remaining cheese. Bake at 375° for 11-13 minutes or until golden brown. Serve warm. **Yield:** 8 rolls.

Garlic Potatoes and Ham

Ready in 1 hour or less

(Pictured below)

Not even my finicky little eaters can resist the veggies in this main dish when they're seasoned with soup mix. I sometimes replace the ham with cooked kielbasa or smoked sausage for a change of pace.

—Melody Williamson, Blaine, Washington

8 small red potatoes, cut into wedges
1 tablespoon vegetable oil
1 package (16 ounces) frozen broccoli cuts, partially thawed
1 cup cubed fully cooked ham
1 envelope herb with garlic soup mix*

In a large skillet, cook the potatoes in oil over medium-high heat for 10 minutes or until lightly browned. Stir in the broccoli, ham and dry soup mix. Reduce heat; cover and cook for 25 minutes or until the potatoes are tender. **Yield:** 4 servings.

*Editor's Note: This recipe was tested with Lipton Recipe Secrets Savory Herb with Garlic soup mix.

Apple German Chocolate Cake

(Pictured below)

This delectable dessert is perfect to bake when unexpected guests stop by. A boxed cake mix and canned pie filling make the moist snack cake a cinch to put together, while chocolate chips and nuts create the quick-and-easy topping.

—Shirley Weaver, Zeeland, Michigan

1 can (21 ounces) apple pie filling
1 package (18-1/4 ounces) German chocolate cake mix
3 eggs
3/4 cup coarsely chopped walnuts
1/2 cup miniature semisweet chocolate chips

Place pie filling in a blender; cover and process until the apples are in 1/4-in. chunks. Pour into a mixing bowl; add dry cake mix and eggs. Beat on medium speed for 5 minutes. Pour into a greased 13-in. x 9-in. x 2-in. baking pan. Sprinkle with nuts and chocolate chips. Bake at 350° for 40-45 minutes or until a toothpick inserted near the center comes out clean. Cool completely on a wire rack before cutting. **Yield:** 12-15 servings.

Garlic Potatoes and Ham
Swiss Onion Crescents
Apple German Chocolate Cake

Pineapple Coconut Snowballs

(Pictured below)

Plan ahead...needs to chill

Canned pineapple adds refreshing taste to these frosty-looking finger foods. —*Marlene Rhodes*
Colorado Springs, Colorado

✓ Uses less fat, sugar or salt. Includes Nutritional Analysis and Diabetic Exchanges.

> 1 package (8 ounces) cream cheese, softened
> 1 can (8 ounces) crushed pineapple, well drained
> 2-1/2 cups flaked coconut

In a small mixing bowl, beat cream cheese and pineapple until combined. Cover and refrigerate for 30 minutes. Roll into 1-in. balls; roll in coconut. Refrigerate for 6 hours or overnight. **Yield:** about 2 dozen.

Nutritional Analysis: One snowball (prepared with fat-free cream cheese) equals 67 calories, 5 g fat (5 g saturated fat), 1 mg cholesterol, 55 mg sodium, 4 g carbohydrate, 1 g fiber, 2 g protein. **Diabetic Exchanges:** 1 fat, 1/2 fruit.

Coated Cookie Drops

(Pictured below)

It's a good thing these no-bake drops are simple, because I like to serve them throughout the year. Their moist, cake-like center and sweet coating satisfy the chocolate lover in everyone. —*Amanda Reid, Oakville, Iowa*

> 1 package (20 ounces) chocolate cream-filled sandwich cookies
> 1 package (8 ounces) cream cheese, softened

> 15 ounces white candy coating
> 12 ounces chocolate candy coating
> Red *and/or* green candy coating, optional

Place the cookies in a blender or food processor; cover and process until finely crushed. In a small mixing bowl, beat cream cheese and crushed cookies until blended. Roll into 3/4-in. balls. Cover and refrigerate for at least 1 hour.

In a small saucepan over low heat, melt white candy coating, stirring until smooth; dip half of the balls to completely coat. Melt chocolate candy coating and dip remaining balls. Place on waxed paper until hardened.

Drizzle white candies with remaining chocolate coating and chocolate candies with remaining white coating. Or melt red or green coating and drizzle over balls. Store in the refrigerator. **Yield:** about 7-1/2 dozen.

Christmas Village Houses

(Pictured below)

Bring some holiday magic to your home with these cute creations from our Test Kitchen. The edible establishments are so easy to assemble and decorate.

> 19 whole graham crackers (about 5 inches x 2-1/2 inches)*
> 1 can (16 ounces) vanilla frosting
> Life Savers, M&M's and Cake Mate snowflake decors

Using a serrated knife, cut 10 graham crackers in half, forming 20 squares; set remaining whole crackers aside. Diagonally cut four squares in half, forming eight triangles. Fill a pastry or plastic bag two-thirds full with frosting; cut a small hole in a corner of the bag. Insert a round #4 pastry tip if desired.

Pineapple Coconut Snowballs
Coated Cookie Drops
Christmas Village Houses

For each roof (make four), pipe a strip of frosting on the short edges of two triangles. Pipe a strip of frosting on three sides of two graham cracker squares. Join the frosted edges of the triangles and squares to form roof. Let stand until set (about 1 hour). Frost roofs and decorate with candies as desired.

For each short house (make two), pipe frosting on two opposite edges of four graham cracker squares; press frosted edges together to form house. For each tall house (make two), pipe frosting on two opposite long edges of four reserved whole crackers; press frosted edges together to form house. Let stand until set.

For doors, cut the remaining whole cracker into two 2-1/2-in. x 1-1/8-in. rectangles and two 1-1/2-in. x 1-1/4-in. rectangles (discard remaining pieces or save for another use). With frosting, attach large rectangles on the front of tall houses and small rectangles on short houses. Pipe frosting around outer edge of each door.

Attach roofs to houses with a thin strip of frosting. Pipe eaves and doorknobs, using a star #24 pastry tip if desired. Pipe windows on sides of houses and above doors. For wreaths, pipe frosting into a circle; attach snowflake decors. Let stand until set. **Yield:** 4 houses (2 tall and 2 short).

*Editor's Note: This recipe was tested with Nabisco graham crackers.

Pork Chops with Apples and Stuffing

(Pictured on page 52)

Ready in 1 hour or less

The heartwarming taste of cinnamon and apples is the perfect accompaniment to these tender pork chops. This dish is always a winner with my family. It's a main course I can serve with little preparation. —Joan Hamilton Worcester, Massachusetts

  6 **boneless pork loin chops (1 inch thick)**
  1 **tablespoon vegetable oil**
  1 **package (6 ounces) crushed stuffing mix**
  1 **can (21 ounces) apple pie filling with cinnamon**

In a skillet, brown pork chops in oil over medium-high heat. Meanwhile, prepare stuffing according to package directions. Spread pie filling into a greased 13-in. x 9-in. x 2-in. baking dish. Place the pork chops on top; spoon stuffing over chops. Cover and bake at 350° for 35 minutes. Uncover; bake 10 minutes longer or until a meat thermometer reads 160°. **Yield:** 6 servings.

No-Bake Cheesecake Pie

(Pictured on page 52)

Plan ahead...needs to chill

I came up with this creamy white chocolate cheesecake after remembering one evening that I needed to bring a treat to the office the next day. It was a tremendous hit. It's quick to fix yet tastes like you fussed.
—Geneva Mayer, Olney, Illinois

Creamy Vegetable Casserole

  1 **cup vanilla *or* white chips**
  2 **packages (8 ounces *each*) cream cheese, cubed**
  1 **carton (8 ounces) frozen whipped topping, thawed**
  1 **graham cracker crust (9 inches)**
1/3 **cup English toffee bits *or* almond brickle chips**

In a heavy saucepan, melt chips over medium-low heat; stir until smooth. Remove from the heat; stir in cream cheese until smooth. Fold in whipped topping. Pour into the crust. Cover and refrigerate overnight or until set. Just before serving, sprinkle with toffee bits. **Yield:** 6-8 servings.

Creamy Vegetable Casserole

(Pictured above)

Ready in 1 hour or less

Searching for a different way to prepare vegetables? Look no further. I have a fussy eater in my house who absolutely loves this medley. It can be assembled in a snap, leaving time to fix the main course, set the table or just sit back and relax. —Tami Kratzer, West Jordan, Utah

  1 **package (16 ounces) frozen broccoli, carrots and cauliflower**
  1 **can (10-3/4 ounces) condensed cream of mushroom soup, undiluted**
  1 **carton (8 ounces) spreadable garden vegetable cream cheese**
1/2 **to 1 cup seasoned croutons**

Prepare vegetables according to package directions; drain and place in a large bowl. Stir in soup and cream cheese. Transfer to a greased 1-qt. baking dish. Sprinkle with croutons. Bake, uncovered, at 375° for 25 minutes or until bubbly. **Yield:** 6 servings.

Chapter 5

68

⏱ *10 Minutes to the Table*

ON THOSE DAYS when you're running behind schedule, a mere 10 minutes is just about all the time you have to prepare great-tasting food.

So if you're hungry and truly "down to the wire" on putting a homemade meal on the table for your famished family, take a deep breath and count to 10.

Then turn to this time-saving chapter for a flavorful assortment of main dishes, sandwiches, side dishes, snacks, desserts and more. Each fantastic dish goes from start to finish in just about 10 minutes...but tastes like you spent hours in the kitchen.

FAST, FUSS-FREE FARE. Club Quesadillas (p. 74).

Angel Food Torte

Turkey Salad Tortillas

With a little mixing and a little fixing, you can put together these spicy burritos in a hurry. Zap them in the microwave and put a family-pleasing dinner on the table in no time. —*Pauline Hershberger, Lott, Texas*

☑ Uses less fat, sugar or salt. Includes Nutritional Analysis and Diabetic Exchanges.

    2 cups cubed cooked turkey
    1 cup (4 ounces) shredded cheddar cheese
  3/4 cup finely chopped celery
  1/2 cup finely chopped onion
    1 can (2-1/4 ounces) sliced ripe olives, drained
  1/2 cup mayonnaise
  1/4 cup picante sauce
  1/2 teaspoon salt, optional
    6 flour tortillas (7 inches)

In a bowl, combine the first eight ingredients; mix well. Spoon about 1/2 cup filling off center on each tortilla. Fold sides and ends over filling, then roll up. Place in a shallow microwave-safe dish. Cover and microwave on high for 2-3 minutes or until cheese is melted and filling is hot. **Yield:** 6 servings.

    Nutritional Analysis: One serving (prepared with reduced-fat cheese, reduced-fat mayonnaise and fat-free tortillas and without salt) equals 255 calories, 7 g fat (2 g saturated fat), 37 mg cholesterol, 736 mg sodium, 31 g carbohydrate, 2 g fiber, 15 g protein. **Diabetic Exchanges:** 1-1/2 starch, 1-1/2 meat, 1 vegetable.

    Editor's Note: This recipe was tested in an 850-watt microwave.

Angel Food Torte

(Pictured above)

This impressive dessert can be whipped up in 10 minutes and adds a festive look to your table. —*Jane Lynn Duncansville, Pennsylvania*

☑ Uses less fat, sugar or salt. Includes Nutritional Analysis and Diabetic Exchanges.

1/2 cup cold milk
  1 package (3.4 ounces) instant vanilla pudding mix
  1 can (8 ounces) unsweetened crushed pineapple
  1 carton (8 ounces) frozen whipped topping, thawed
  1 prepared angel food cake (10 inches)
1/2 cup flaked coconut, optional
Maraschino cherries, optional

In a bowl, combine milk, pudding mix and pineapple; mix well. Fold in the whipped topping. Cut cake horizontally into three layers. Place the bottom layer on a serving plate; spread with 1-1/3 cups pineapple mixture. Repeat. Place top layer on cake; spread with remaining pineapple mixture. If desired, sprinkle with coconut and garnish with cherries. **Yield:** 12 servings.

    Nutritional Analysis: One serving (prepared with fat-free milk, sugar-free pudding and reduced-fat whipped topping) equals 210 calories, 3 g fat (3 g saturated fat), trace cholesterol, 590 mg sodium, 42 g carbohydrate, trace fiber, 3 g protein. **Diabetic Exchanges:** 1-1/2 starch, 1 fruit, 1/2 fat.

Prairie Fire Dip

This flavorful dip for crunchy corn chips goes fast at get-togethers, so be sure to make enough. For a bit more zip, increase the amount of chili powder. —*Jo Johnson Park City, Montana*

☑ Uses less fat, sugar or salt. Includes Nutritional Analysis and Diabetic Exchanges.

    1 can (16 ounces) refried beans
  1/2 cup shredded provolone cheese
    2 tablespoons butter *or* margarine, optional
    1 tablespoon finely chopped onion
    1 garlic clove, minced
    2 to 3 teaspoons chili powder
Dash hot pepper sauce
Large corn chips

In a saucepan, combine the beans, cheese, butter if desired, onion, garlic, chili powder and hot pepper sauce. Cook over low heat until the cheese is melted and dip is heated through. Serve with the corn chips. **Yield:** 1-3/4 cups.

    Nutritional Analysis: One 2-tablespoon serving (prepared with fat-free refried beans and without butter; calculated without corn chips) equals 56 calories, 2 g fat (1 g saturated fat), 6 mg cholesterol, 200 mg sodium, 5 g carbohydrate, 2 g fiber, 4 g protein. **Diabetic Exchanges:** 1/2 starch, 1/2 fat.

Lemon Broccoli Pasta

This pleasant pasta toss is delicious, simple to make and uses just one saucepan. My family and friends really like it, so I serve it often. —Margaret Fuhrman
Erie, Pennsylvania

✓ Uses less fat, sugar or salt. Includes Nutritional Analysis and Diabetic Exchanges

    2 cans (14-1/2 ounces *each*) chicken broth
    1 teaspoon lemon juice
    1 teaspoon grated lemon peel
    1/4 teaspoon garlic powder
    1/4 teaspoon pepper
    6 ounces uncooked angel hair pasta
    3 cups broccoli florets
    3/4 cup sour cream
    2 tablespoons grated Parmesan cheese

In a saucepan, combine the broth, lemon juice and peel, garlic powder and pepper. Bring to a boil. Add pasta and broccoli. Reduce heat; simmer, uncovered, for 3-4 minutes or until pasta is tender. Drain; stir in sour cream. Sprinkle with cheese. **Yield:** 4 servings.

Nutritional Analysis: One 1-cup serving (prepared with reduced-fat sour cream) equals 238 calories, 6 g fat (4 g saturated fat), 17 mg cholesterol, 393 mg sodium, 30 g carbohydrate, 2 g fiber, 16 g protein. **Diabetic Exchanges:** 2 vegetable, 1-1/2 starch, 1 meat.

Tropical Ambrosia

I add whipped topping to convenient pantry items to create this light and fluffy dessert. Toasted coconut and sweet pineapple give the creamy combination its tropical taste. —Marguerite Widrick
Adams, New York

    1 can (20 ounces)
      pineapple tidbits
    1 package (3.4 ounces)
      instant coconut cream
      or vanilla pudding mix
    1 carton (8 ounces)
      frozen whipped
      topping, thawed
    4 tablespoons flaked
      coconut, toasted,
      divided
Maraschino cherries, optional
    1 teaspoon maraschino
      cherry juice, optional

Drain the pineapple, reserving the juice; set pineapple aside. In a mixing bowl, combine the pineapple juice and pudding mix; beat on low speed for 2 minutes or until thickened. Fold in the whipped topping. Stir in pineapple and 3 tablespoons coconut. Transfer to a serving bowl. Garnish with the remaining coconut, cherries and cherry juice if desired. Chill until serving. **Yield:** 6 servings.

Easy Cheesy Nachos

(Pictured below)

There's no need to brown ground beef when fixing this satisfying snack. Top crunchy chips with warm chili and melted cheese, then sprinkle it all with chopped tomato and onion. —Laura Jirasek, White Lake, Michigan

    1 package (14-1/2 ounces) tortilla chips
    2 cans (15 ounces *each*) chili without beans
    1 pound process American cheese, cubed
    4 green onions, sliced
    1 medium tomato, chopped

Divide chips between six plates; set aside. In a saucepan, warm chili until heated through. Meanwhile, in another saucepan, heat the cheese over medium-low heat until melted, stirring frequently. Spoon the chili over chips; drizzle with cheese. Sprinkle with onions and tomato. **Yield:** 6 servings.

Easy Cheesy Nachos

Tropical Tuna Melts

Bring the taste of the Caribbean to your kitchen with these open-faced sandwiches. Consider replacing the English muffins with bagels.
—Renée Sagmoe
Champlin, Minnesota

> 1 can (6 ounces) tuna, drained and flaked
> 1 to 2 tablespoons mayonnaise
> 1 to 2 tablespoons finely chopped celery
> 1/4 to 1/2 teaspoon salt
> 1/8 to 1/4 teaspoon lemon-pepper seasoning
> 2 English muffins, split and toasted
> 1 can (8 ounces) sliced pineapple, drained
> 4 slices process American cheese

Combine tuna, mayonnaise, celery, salt and lemon-pepper; spread over muffin halves. Top each with a slice of pineapple and cheese. Broil 6 in. from the heat for 2 minutes or until cheese is melted and lightly browned. Serve immediately. **Yield:** 2-4 servings.

Peachy Pork

(Pictured below)

Who says you can't make a hearty dinner when you're racing against the clock? This unique combination of peach preserves and salsa makes a heartwarming main dish your family will ask for time and time again.
—Marilyn Monroe, Erie, Michigan

> 1 pound pork tenderloin, cut into 1/8- to 1/4-inch slices
> 1 to 2 tablespoons vegetable oil
> 3 to 4 garlic cloves, minced
> 1 jar (16 ounces) salsa
> 1/4 cup peach preserves
> Hot cooked rice

Peachy Pork

In a large skillet, saute pork in oil for 4 minutes. Add garlic; cook and stir 1 minute longer. Stir in salsa and preserves; bring to a boil. Reduce heat; cover and simmer for 2 minutes or until meat is no longer pink. Serve over rice. **Yield:** 3-4 servings.

Quick Clam Chowder

Dressing up canned soups allows you to enjoy the comfort of clam chowder with a fraction of the work.
—Judy Jungwirth, Athol, South Dakota

> 1 can (10-3/4 ounces) condensed cream of celery soup, undiluted
> 1 can (10-3/4 ounces) condensed cream of potato soup, undiluted
> 2 cups half-and-half cream
> 2 cans (6 1/2 ounces *each*) minced clams, drained
> 1/2 teaspoon ground nutmeg
> Pepper to taste

In a large saucepan, combine all ingredients. Cook and stir over medium heat until heated through. **Yield:** 5 servings.

Lemon Blueberry Dessert

Fresh blueberries (and only two other ingredients) star in this light and luscious treat.
—Nykii Chouteau
Clermont, Florida

☑ Uses less fat, sugar or salt. Includes Nutritional Analysis and Diabetic Exchanges.

> 1 carton (8 ounces) frozen whipped topping, thawed
> 1 cup fresh blueberries
> 1 carton (8 ounces) lemon yogurt

Fold the whipped topping and blueberries into the yogurt. Spoon mixture into a serving bowl or individual dishes. Serve immediately or refrigerate. **Yield:** 6 servings.
   Nutritional Analysis: One 1/2-cup serving (prepared with reduced-fat whipped topping and reduced-fat yogurt) equals 140 calories, 5 g fat (5 g saturated fat), 2 mg cholesterol, 26 mg sodium, 18 g carbohydrate, 1 g fiber, 2 g protein. **Diabetic Exchanges:** 1 starch, 1 fruit.

Pecan Pineapple Fluff

Pineapple, cream cheese, marshmallows and pecans make it an ideal no-bake alternative when you're short on time. —Susan Barlow, Hayden, Indiana

> 1 can (20 ounces) crushed pineapple

2 packages (8 ounces *each*) cream cheese, softened
1/2 cup butter *or* margarine, softened
1/3 cup sugar
1-1/2 cups miniature marshmallows
1/2 cup chopped pecans

Drain pineapple, reserving 1/3 cup juice. In a mixing bowl, beat cream cheese, butter, sugar and reserved juice. Stir in pineapple, marshmallows and pecans. Serve immediately. **Yield:** 8 servings.

Zippy Zucchini Pasta

Creamed Crab On Toast

This is a great ready-in-a-jiffy luncheon dish or Sunday supper. Marjoram and lemon juice in the sauce complement the flavor of the crab quite nicely. It's quickly and conveniently made in the microwave.   —Nina DeWitt, Aurora, Ohio

1 can (10-3/4 ounces) condensed cream of mushroom soup, undiluted
1 can (6 ounces) crabmeat, rinsed, drained and cartilage removed
1 tablespoon lemon juice
1/4 teaspoon dried marjoram
Dash cayenne pepper
Toast *or* biscuits

In a 1-qt. microwave-safe dish, combine the first five ingredients. Cover and microwave on high for 3-1/2 to 4-1/2 minutes or until heated through, stirring once. Serve on toast or biscuits. **Yield:** 4 servings.

Editor's Note: This recipe was tested in an 850-watt microwave.

Feta Cucumber Salad

If you like the distinctive taste of feta cheese, you'll enjoy this crisp and refreshing cucumber medley. Even our twin daughters ask me to make this speedy salad.
—Connie Lasko, Mistatim, Saskatchewan

2 medium cucumbers
1/2 teaspoon salt
1/4 cup chopped green onions
1 cup (4 ounces) feta *or* blue cheese, crumbled
2 tablespoons lemon juice
1 tablespoon olive *or* vegetable oil
1/8 to 1/4 teaspoon coarsely ground pepper

Cut the cucumbers in half lengthwise. Using a spoon, remove the seeds and discard. Cut the cucumbers into 1/2-in. cubes; place in a bowl. Sprinkle with salt. Stir in the onions. Combine cheese, lemon juice, oil and pep-

per; add to the cucumber mixture and stir gently. **Yield:** 4-5 servings.

Zippy Zucchini Pasta

(Pictured above)

A colorful combination of zucchini and canned tomatoes is delicious over quick-cooking angel hair pasta.
—Kathleen Timberlake, Dearborn Heights, Michigan

1 package (7 ounces) angel hair pasta *or* thin spaghetti
2 small zucchini, sliced 1/4 inch thick
2 garlic cloves, minced
3 tablespoons olive *or* vegetable oil
1 can (16 ounces) Mexican diced tomatoes, undrained
1/4 cup minced fresh parsley
1 teaspoon dried oregano
1/8 to 1/2 teaspoon crushed red pepper flakes

Cook pasta according to package directions. Meanwhile, in a skillet, saute zucchini and garlic in oil until zucchini is crisp-tender. Add the tomatoes, parsley, oregano and red pepper flakes; heat through. Drain pasta; top with zucchini mixture. **Yield:** 3 servings.

No More Boil-Overs

Before boiling water to cook pasta, I rub a bit of butter on the rim and 1/4 inch down the inside of the pot. This keeps the water from boiling over.
—Lou Ann Ryhal, Shelby, Indiana

Club Quesadillas

Club Quesadillas

(Pictured above and on page 68)

A traditional club sandwich gets a fun change of pace when the bread is replaced with soft flour tortillas. It's easy to get the children to help assemble these. I serve salsa and corn chips on the side. —Victoria Hahn
Northampton, Pennsylvania

    1/2 cup mayonnaise *or* salad dressing
      8 flour tortillas (8 inches)
      4 lettuce leaves
      2 medium tomatoes, sliced
      8 slices deli turkey
      8 slices deli ham
      8 slices provolone cheese
      8 bacon strips, cooked
Salsa

Spread mayonnaise on each tortilla. On four tortillas, layer lettuce, tomatoes, turkey, ham, cheese and bacon; top with remaining tortillas. Cut into quarters. Serve with salsa. **Yield:** 4 servings.

Broiled Parsley Tomatoes

I get loads of compliments on this tomato side dish. My mother shared the quick recipe with me. She loved to make great-tasting meals but preferred spending time with us rather than in the kitchen. —Howie Wiener
Spring Hill, Florida

      4 large plum tomatoes, halved lengthwise
      3 tablespoons butter *or* margarine, melted
      2 teaspoons minced fresh parsley
    1/4 teaspoon salt
    1/4 teaspoon pepper

With a knife, make deep cuts in the cut surface of each tomato. Place tomatoes cut side up on a greased baking sheet. In a small bowl, combine the remaining ingredients; spoon over tomatoes. Broil 3-4 in. from the heat for 3-4 minutes or until tops are lightly browned. **Yield:** 4 servings.

Nutty Apple Dip

For a tempting after-school snack or anytime treat, serve this delightful dip with fresh apple slices. I need just five ingredients to blend together the sweet nutty mixture. —Jean Morgan, Roscoe, Illinois

      1 package (8 ounces) cream cheese, softened
    3/4 cup packed brown sugar
    1/4 cup sugar
      1 teaspoon vanilla extract
      1 cup chopped pecans
Apple slices *or* wedges

In a small mixing bowl, combine cream cheese, sugars and vanilla; beat until smooth. Stir in pecans. Serve with apples. **Yield:** about 2 cups.

Basil Chicken Strips

I'm an attorney and my husband is an architect, so our careers keep our schedules busy. This easy chicken entree seasoned with basil is great for the weeknight rush. I serve it with broccoli and Parmesan noodles. —Barbara Rokow
Geneva, New York

    1/2 pound boneless skinless chicken breasts, cut
        into strips
      2 tablespoons all-purpose flour
      3 tablespoons butter *or* margarine
      2 tablespoons red wine vinegar *or* cider
        vinegar
    1/2 teaspoon dried basil

In a large resealable plastic bag, shake chicken strips and flour until coated. In a large skillet over medium-high heat, melt butter. Add the chicken; saute for 5 minutes. Stir in the vinegar and basil; cook until chicken juices run clear. **Yield:** 2 servings.

Honey-Garlic Angel Hair

(Pictured below)

I got this recipe from the captain of our fire department. The speedy side dish is nicely seasoned with garlic and basil and has a subtle sweetness from honey.
—*Terri Frabotta, Sterling Heights, Michigan*

- 1 package (16 ounces) angel hair pasta
- 2 to 3 garlic cloves, minced
- 1/2 cup butter *or* margarine
- 1/4 cup honey
- 1 teaspoon dried basil
- 1 teaspoon dried thyme
- 1/4 cup grated Parmesan cheese

Cook pasta according to package directions. Meanwhile, in a skillet, saute the garlic in butter. Stir in the honey, basil and thyme. Drain pasta; add to garlic mixture and toss to coat. Sprinkle with Parmesan cheese. **Yield:** 8 servings.

Spiced Ham Steak

(Pictured below)

Orange marmalade, mustard and a hint of ginger become a fast-to-fix glaze for ham. The mouth-watering entree may be short on time, but it's long on flavor.
—*Connie Moore, Medway, Ohio*

- 1 bone-in fully cooked ham steak (about 1 pound)
- 1/4 cup orange marmalade
- 2 tablespoons water
- 1 tablespoon butter *or* margarine
- 1 tablespoon prepared mustard
- 1 teaspoon corn syrup
- 1/8 to 1/4 teaspoon ground ginger

In a large skillet coated with nonstick cooking spray, cook ham for 4 minutes on each side or until lightly browned; drain. Meanwhile, combine the remaining ingredients in a saucepan; bring to a boil. Spoon over ham. Cover and cook for 1-2 minutes or until heated through. **Yield:** 4 servings.

Texas Toast Turkey Melts

Strips of bacon and warm cheese sauce turn these open-faced sandwiches into a lip-smacking lunch. Serve with a bowl of soup for a speedy meal. They're just as good when the turkey is replaced with ham.   —*Karen Gentry Somerset, Kentucky*

- 6 tablespoons butter *or* margarine, softened
- 6 thick slices fresh white bread
- 1/2 pound thinly sliced deli turkey
- 18 bacon strips, cooked
- 1 cup process cheese sauce

Butter one side of each slice of bread; place buttered side up on a baking sheet. Broil 5 in. from the heat for 3 minutes or until lightly toasted. Top with turkey; broil for 2 minutes or until heated through. Top each with three strips of bacon.

Place the cheese sauce in a microwave-safe dish. Microwave on high for 1 minute; stir. Microwave for 1 minute longer or until heated through. Pour over the sandwiches. **Yield:** 6 servings.

Editor's Note: This recipe was tested in an 850-watt microwave.

Honey-Garlic Angel Hair
Spiced Ham Steak

Five-Can Chili

Who says a thick hearty chili has to simmer all day on the stove? With five canned goods and zero prep time, a warm pot of this zesty specialty is a snap to whip up. Kids can also help make it.
—*Jo Mann Westover, Alabama*

- 1 can (15 ounces) chili with beans
- 1 can (15 ounces) mixed vegetables, drained
- 1 can (11 ounces) whole kernel corn, drained
- 1 can (10-3/4 ounces) condensed tomato soup, undiluted
- 1 can (10 ounces) diced tomatoes and green chilies

In a saucepan, combine all the ingredients; heat through. **Yield:** 6 servings.

Chapter 6

WHEN the clock starts ticking closer to dinnertime and you're at a loss for what to prepare, just take a peek into your pantry and put together a mouth-watering meal pronto!

It can be as simple as beefing up pasta and canned goods to make a comforting casserole, jazzing up a potato mix to make an effortless entree, using a cake mix to create quick cookies, or using fruit-flavored gelatin to whip up a pleasing pie—just a few of the speedy strategies you'll learn about here.

Or save yourself the shopping time—and money, too—by making your own homemade mixes. The appealing assortment in this chapter is easy to assemble in advance and will give you a handy head start on menu planning.

MIX MAGIC. Left to right, Fruit Cobbler and Blueberry Quick Bread (both recipes on p. 97).

Fast Fixes With Mixes

GOOD EATING doesn't require a lot of effort or running around. With the wide range of packaged convenience foods available today, you can have a tasty home-prepared meal ready in minutes.

Chicken Fried Rice

Ready in 30 minutes or less

I rely on a fried rice mix to start this speedy skillet supper. It makes the most of leftover cooked chicken and a can of crunchy water chestnuts.
—Kathy Hoyt
Maplecrest, New York

1 package (6.2 ounces) fried rice mix
2 cups cubed cooked chicken
1-1/2 cups cooked broccoli florets
1 can (8 ounces) sliced water chestnuts, drained
1 cup (4 ounces) shredded mozzarella cheese

Cook rice according to package directions. Stir in chicken, broccoli and water chestnuts; heat through. Sprinkle with cheese. **Yield:** 4 servings.

Impossible Pumpkin Pie

Because you don't need to fuss with a crust, this twist on the classic Thanksgiving standby may be the easiest pie you've ever prepared. I'm a working mother and rely on this moist dessert every year for the holidays.
—Linda Cummings, Atoka, Tennessee

✓ Uses less fat, sugar or salt. Includes Nutritional Analysis and Diabetic Exchanges.

2 eggs
1 can (12 ounces) evaporated milk
1 can (15 ounces) solid-pack pumpkin
3/4 cup sugar
1/2 cup biscuit/baking mix
2 tablespoons butter *or* stick margarine, melted
2-1/2 teaspoons ground allspice
2 teaspoons vanilla extract
Whipped topping, optional

In a blender, combine the eggs, milk, pumpkin, sugar, biscuit mix, butter, allspice and vanilla. Cover and process until smooth. Pour into a greased 9-in. pie plate (dish will be full). Bake at 350° for 50-55 minutes or until a knife inserted near the center comes out clean. Serve with whipped topping if desired. **Yield:** 8 servings.

Nutritional Analysis: One piece (prepared with 1/2 cup egg substitute, fat-free evaporated milk and reduced-fat baking mix; calculated without whipped topping) equals 193 calories, 4 g fat (2 g saturated fat), 11 mg cholesterol, 203 mg sodium, 34 g carbohydrate, 2 g fiber, 6 g protein. **Diabetic Exchanges:** 2 starch, 1/2 fat-free milk.

French Onion Mashed Potatoes

Ready in 1 hour or less

I dress up instant potato flakes with cream cheese, French onion dip and garlic salt. I'm always elected to bring these rich potatoes to family get-togethers.
—Lori Piatt
Danville, Illinois

3 cups water
1-1/2 cups milk
1/3 cup plus 1 tablespoon butter *or* margarine, *divided*
1 teaspoon salt
4 cups mashed potato flakes
1 package (8 ounces) cream cheese, softened
1 carton (8 ounces) French onion dip
1-1/2 teaspoons garlic salt
1/4 teaspoon paprika

In a large saucepan, bring the water, milk, 1/3 cup butter and salt to a boil. Remove from the heat; gradually stir in potato flakes. In a mixing bowl, combine the cream cheese and onion dip. Stir into the potatoes. Add garlic salt.

Transfer to an ungreased 13-in. x 9-in. x 2-in. baking dish. Melt remaining butter; drizzle over the top. Sprinkle with paprika. Bake, uncovered, at 350° for 30-35 minutes or until heated through. Let stand for 5-10 minutes before serving. **Yield:** 8-10 servings.

Shrimp Curry Rice

Ready in 30 minutes or less

There aren't any leftovers when I serve my family this fast and easy dish. Convenient canned or frozen shrimp rounds out the flavors of this quick but classic entree.
—Sandi Rush, Athens, Texas

2-1/3 cups water
1 tablespoon butter *or* margarine
1 package (6 ounces) long grain and wild rice mix
1/2 teaspoon curry powder
1 can (6 ounces) small shrimp, rinsed and drained *or* 1 cup frozen cooked salad shrimp
4 bacon strips, cooked and crumbled

Place water and butter in a large saucepan; stir in rice, contents of rice seasoning packet and curry powder. Bring to a boil. Reduce heat; cover and simmer for 15 minutes. Add shrimp and bacon. Cover and simmer 10 minutes longer or until liquid is absorbed and rice is tender. **Yield:** 2-3 servings.

Pear-Cranberry Coffee Cake

(Pictured below)

Ready in 1 hour or less

My daughter and I enjoy this tender cake for brunch on the Saturday mornings we spend at home. A delightful hint of orange from the quick bread mix blends nicely with the other fruit flavors in this simple treat. —Patricia Clark
Lake Forest, California

- 1 package (15.6 ounces) cranberry-orange quick bread mix
- 1 can (15 ounces) sliced pears, drained and halved
- 1 teaspoon lemon juice
- 1/3 cup all-purpose flour
- 1/3 cup sugar
- 1/2 teaspoon ground cinnamon
- 2 to 3 tablespoons butter *or* margarine, melted

Prepare bread mix according to package directions; pour batter into a greased 9-in. square baking pan. Sprinkle pears with lemon juice; arrange over batter.

In a bowl, combine flour, sugar and cinnamon; stir in butter until crumbly. Sprinkle over pears. Bake at 375° for 35-40 minutes or until a toothpick inserted near the center comes out clean. **Yield:** 9 servings.

Creamy Hot Chocolate

(Pictured below)

Ready in 15 minutes or less

You need just a few basic ingredients to stir up this spirit-warming sipper. The comforting beverage is smooth and not too sweet, making it right for cozy winter days. —Flo Snodderly, North Vernon, Indiana

- 1/2 cup baking cocoa
- 1 can (14 ounces) sweetened condensed milk
- 1/8 teaspoon salt
- 6-1/2 cups water
- 1-1/2 teaspoons vanilla extract
- Miniature marshmallows, optional

In a large saucepan, combine cocoa, milk and salt. Cook and stir over medium heat. Gradually add water; cook and stir until heated through. Stir in vanilla. Top with marshmallows if desired. **Yield:** 8 servings.

Pear-Cranberry Coffee Cake
Creamy Hot Chocolate

Ham Macaroni Salad

(Pictured below)

Plan ahead...needs to chill

I made some changes to the original recipe by adding extra tomatoes for more color, celery for crunch, relish for a hint of sweetness and ham to make it more filling. It's great for picnics and potlucks or as a side dish for any meal. It's also handy because you make it ahead of time. —*Karen Ballance, Wolf Lake, Illinois*

    1 package (7-1/2 ounces) macaroni and cheese
  1/2 cup mayonnaise
    2 tablespoons Dijon mustard
    3 medium tomatoes, seeded and chopped
    1 medium cucumber, peeled and chopped
    1 cup diced fully cooked ham
    4 hard-cooked eggs, chopped
  1/2 cup chopped celery
  1/4 cup sweet pickle relish
    2 tablespoons chopped onion
  1/2 teaspoon salt
  1/8 teaspoon pepper

Prepare macaroni and cheese according to package directions; cool for 20 minutes. Stir in the mayonnaise and mustard. Fold in the remaining ingredients. Refrigerate for 2 hours or until chilled. **Yield:** 8 servings.

Ham Macaroni Salad

Beefy Hash Brown Bake

Ready in 1 hour or less

A topping of french-fried onions provides a little crunch to this meaty main dish. Since this casserole is practically a meal in itself, I simply accompany it with a fruit salad and dessert. —*Rochelle Boucher, Brooklyn, Wisconsin*

    4 cups frozen shredded hash brown potatoes
    3 tablespoons vegetable oil
  1/8 teaspoon pepper
    1 pound ground beef
    1 cup water
    1 envelope brown gravy mix
  1/2 teaspoon garlic salt
    2 cups frozen mixed vegetables
    1 can (2.8 ounces) french-fried onions, *divided*
    1 cup (4 ounces) shredded cheddar cheese, *divided*

In a bowl, combine the potatoes, oil and pepper. Press into a greased 8-in. square baking dish. Bake, uncovered, at 350° for 15-20 minutes or until potatoes are thawed and set.

Meanwhile, in a saucepan over medium heat, cook the beef until no longer pink; drain. Stir in water, gravy mix and garlic salt. Bring to a boil; cook and stir for 2 minutes. Add vegetables; cook and stir for 5 minutes. Stir in half of the onions and cheese.

Pour over potatoes. Bake for 5-10 minutes. Sprinkle with remaining onions and cheese; bake 5 minutes longer or until cheese is melted. **Yield:** 4 servings.

Sweet-Sour Chicken Nuggets

(Pictured above right)

Ready in 30 minutes or less

Frozen breaded chicken and canned pineapple make this dish a snap to prepare, and its sweet tangy taste keeps them asking for more. —*Arlene Best, East Ridge, Tennessee*

    1 medium green pepper, cut into chunks
    1 large onion, cut into wedges

Peanut Butter Brownie Pizza
Sweet-Sour Chicken Nuggets

1 to 2 tablespoons vegetable oil
1 can (14-1/2 ounces) chicken broth
1/2 cup pancake syrup
1/4 cup cider vinegar
1 tablespoon soy sauce
1 can (8 ounces) pineapple chunks
2 to 3 tablespoons cornstarch
2-1/2 cups frozen chicken nuggets, thawed
Hot cooked rice

In a skillet, saute green pepper and onion in oil until crisp-tender; remove and keep warm. Add broth, syrup, vinegar and soy sauce to the skillet; bring to a boil.

Drain pineapple, reserving juice; set pineapple aside. Combine cornstarch and juice until smooth; gradually add to broth mixture. Bring to a boil; cook and stir for 2 minutes or until thickened. Add chicken nuggets; cook for 2 minutes. Stir in the pineapple and sauteed vegetables; heat through. Serve over rice. **Yield:** 4 servings.

Peanut Butter Brownie Pizza

(Pictured above)

I constantly had cravings for peanut butter while I was pregnant with our second child. This unusual dessert pizza satisfied me, and using a brownie mix meant I could throw it together in no time.
—Karen Jagger
Columbia City, Indiana

1 package brownie mix (8-inch square pan size)
1 package (8 ounces) cream cheese, softened
1/3 cup peanut butter
1/4 cup sugar
3 large ripe bananas, cut into 1/4-inch slices
1/2 cup orange *or* lemon juice
1/4 cup chopped peanuts
2 squares (1 ounce *each*) semisweet chocolate
2 teaspoons butter (no substitutes)

Prepare brownie batter according to package directions and spread into a greased 12-in. pizza pan. Bake at 375° for 15-20 minutes or until a toothpick inserted near the center comes out clean. Cool completely on a wire rack.

In a mixing bowl, beat the cream cheese, peanut butter and sugar until smooth. Spread over crust. Toss bananas with juice; drain well. Arrange bananas over cream cheese mixture. Sprinkle with peanuts.

In a microwave, melt chocolate and butter. Drizzle over bananas. Refrigerate until chocolate is set. **Yield:** 12 servings.

Orange Cream Cake

Orange Cream Cake

(Pictured above)

Kids of all ages will enjoy the old-fashioned flavor of this super-moist cake topped with a soft light frosting. This dessert reminds me of the frozen Creamsicles I enjoyed as a child. —Star Pooley, Paradise, California

      1 package (18-1/4 ounces) lemon cake mix
      1 envelope unsweetened orange soft drink mix
      3 eggs
      1 cup water
  1/3 cup vegetable oil
      2 packages (3 ounces *each*) orange gelatin, *divided*
      1 cup boiling water
      1 cup cold water
      1 cup cold milk
      1 teaspoon vanilla extract
      1 package (3.4 ounces) instant vanilla pudding mix
      1 carton (8 ounces) frozen whipped topping, thawed

In a mixing bowl, combine cake and drink mixes, eggs, water and oil. Beat on medium speed for 2 minutes. Pour into an ungreased 13-in. x 9-in. x 2-in. baking pan. Bake at 350° for 25-30 minutes or until a toothpick inserted near the center comes out clean. Using a meat fork, poke holes in cake. Cool on a wire rack for 30 minutes. Meanwhile, in a bowl, dissolve one package of gelatin in boiling water. Stir in cold water. Pour over cake. Cover and refrigerate for 2 hours. In a mixing bowl, combine milk, vanilla, pudding mix and remaining gelatin; beat on low for 2 minutes. Let stand for 5 minutes; fold in whipped topping. Frost cake. Refrigerate leftovers. **Yield:** 12-15 servings.

Nacho Chicken

Ready in 1 hour or less

I have been serving this rich and zippy chicken casserole for several years, and it's a favorite of my family and friends. It's sure to disappear quickly at potluck suppers, too. —Thom Britton, Three Rivers, Michigan

      4 cups cubed cooked chicken
      1 pound process American cheese, cubed
      2 cans (10-3/4 ounces *each*) condensed cream of chicken soup, undiluted
      1 can (10 ounces) diced tomatoes and green chilies, undrained
      1 cup chopped onion
  1/2 teaspoon garlic salt
  1/4 teaspoon pepper
      1 package (14-1/2 ounces) nacho cheese tortilla chips

In a large bowl, combine the first seven ingredients; mix well. Crush chips; set aside 1 cup for topping. Add remaining chips to chicken mixture. Spoon into a greased 13-in. x 9-in. x 2-in. baking dish; sprinkle with reserved chips. Bake, uncovered, at 350° for 30 minutes or until cheese is melted and edges are bubbly. **Yield:** 8-10 servings.

Sausage Potatoes Au Gratin

Ready in 1 hour or less

A packaged potato mix gets special treatment when jazzed up with sausage and vegetables. I enjoy serving this cheesy casserole with warm bread.
—Mary Akker
Ellsworth, Minnesota

  1 pound fully cooked smoked sausage, halved lengthwise and sliced
  1 medium onion, chopped
  1 tablespoon vegetable oil
  4 medium carrots, julienned
  1 package (5-1/4 ounces) au gratin potatoes
2-2/3 cups water
  1/4 teaspoon pepper
  1 package (10 ounces) frozen broccoli cuts, thawed and drained
  1 cup (4 ounces) shredded cheddar cheese

In a large saucepan or Dutch oven, cook sausage and onion in oil until lightly browned; drain. Stir in carrots, potatoes with contents of sauce mix, water and pep-per. Bring to a boil. Reduce heat; cover and simmer for 10-20 minutes or until vegetables are tender. Stir in broccoli; cover and cook 5 minutes longer or until heated through. Sprinkle with cheese; cover and let stand until cheese is melted. **Yield:** 4 servings.

Easy-to-Make Crepes

My husband combines a fruit-flavored muffin mix, two eggs and milk to create a special pancake batter. When the pancakes are done, he spreads canned pie filling over each and rolls them up like crepes. He tops them with cinnamon or confectioners' sugar.
—Dolly Larsen, Webster, Wisconsin

Turkey-Berry Stuffing Balls

(Pictured below)

Ready in 1 hour or less

You'll spend less time in the kitchen when you prepare this quick side dish that takes advantage of stuffing mix. This is terrific to take to potlucks and holiday dinners. The recipe can easily be dou-bled for large gatherings.
—Bernadine Dirmeyer
Harpster, Ohio

    1 pound ground turkey
    1 celery rib, finely chopped
  1/4 cup finely chopped onion
    2 eggs, beaten
1-1/4 cups chicken broth
    4 cups seasoned stuffing croutons
  3/4 cup fresh *or* frozen cranberries, halved

In a large skillet, cook turkey, celery and onion over medium heat until meat is no longer pink; drain. In a large bowl, combine eggs, broth and stuffing; let stand for 5 minutes. Stir in turkey mixture and cranberries. Shape into 12 balls and place in a greased 11-in. x 7-in. x 2-in. baking dish. Bake, uncovered, at 325° for 35-40 minutes or until heated through. **Yield:** 4-6 servings.

Turkey-Berry Stuffing Balls

Chicken-Pesto Pan Pizza

(Pictured below)

Ready in 30 minutes or less

A packaged pesto mix tastefully replaces traditional tomato sauce in this tempting pizza. Served alongside a tossed green salad, this is one of my husband's favorite meals.
—Juanita Fleck, Bullhead City, Arizona

- 1 tube (10 ounces) refrigerated pizza crust
- 1/2 cup water
- 3 tablespoons olive *or* vegetable oil
- 1 envelope pesto sauce mix
- 1 package (10 ounces) frozen chopped spinach, thawed and squeezed dry
- 1/2 cup ricotta cheese
- 1/4 cup chopped onion
- 2 cups shredded cooked chicken
- 1 jar (4-1/2 ounces) sliced mushrooms, drained
- 4 plum tomatoes, sliced
- 1 cup (4 ounces) shredded Swiss cheese
- 1/4 cup grated Romano cheese

Unroll pizza crust into an ungreased 15-in. x 10-in. x 1-in. baking pan; flatten dough and build up edges slightly. Prick dough several times with a fork. Bake at 425° for 7 minutes or until lightly browned.

Meanwhile, combine the water, oil and pesto sauce mix in a saucepan. Cook until heated through (do not boil). Add the spinach, ricotta and onion; mix well. Spread over crust. Top with chicken, mushrooms, tomatoes and Swiss and Romano cheeses. Bake at 425° for 7 minutes or until crust is golden and cheese is melted. **Yield:** 6-8 servings.

Ricotta Pepperoni Dip

(Pictured below)

Ready in 30 minutes or less

This warm appetizer dip gets its flavor from an herb soup mix. Crispy golden pizza dough strips are perfect for digging into the thick cheesy mixture. —Barbara Carlucci
Orange Park, Florida

PIZZA STICKS:
- 1 tube (10 ounces) refrigerated pizza crust
- 1 tablespoon olive *or* vegetable oil
- 2 tablespoons grated Parmesan cheese
- 1 tablespoon Italian seasoning
- 1/4 teaspoon garlic powder
- 1/8 teaspoon pepper

DIP:
- 1 cup (8 ounces) sour cream
- 1 cup ricotta cheese
- 1 tablespoon savory herb with garlic soup mix
- 1/4 cup chopped pepperoni
- 1 cup (4 ounces) shredded mozzarella cheese
- 1 tablespoon grated Parmesan cheese

On a lightly floured surface, roll out pizza crust to a 12-in. x 8-in. rectangle. Brush with oil. Combine the Parme-

Chicken-Pesto Pan Pizza
Ricotta Pepperoni Dip

san cheese, Italian seasoning, garlic powder and pepper; sprinkle over dough. Cut into 3-in. x 1-in. strips; place on a greased baking sheet. Bake at 425° for 6-9 minutes or until golden brown.

Meanwhile, combine the sour cream, ricotta, soup mix and pepperoni in a saucepan; heat through. Stir in mozzarella and Parmesan cheeses just until melted. Serve warm with pizza sticks. **Yield:** about 2-1/2 dozen pizza sticks and 2 cups dip.

Corn in the Cobbler

Ready in 1 hour or less

Canned goods and corn bread mix combine in this golden brunch bake. When I served it to my parents, they loved it. It makes a lot, so I often freeze half. —Judith Taylor
North Attleboro, Massachusetts

  1 can (15 ounces) corned beef hash
  2 cans (8 ounces *each*) tomato sauce
1/2 cup diced green pepper
  2 tablespoons plus 1 teaspoon dried minced onion, *divided*
  2 tablespoons Worcestershire sauce
1/2 teaspoon salt
1/4 teaspoon pepper
  1 package (8-1/2 ounces) corn bread/muffin mix
  1 cup all-purpose flour
  1 cup milk
  2 eggs, beaten
  2 cups (8 ounces) shredded cheddar cheese, *divided*

In a large bowl, combine hash, tomato sauce, green pepper, 2 tablespoons onion, Worcestershire sauce, salt and pepper; set aside. In another bowl, combine the corn bread mix, flour, milk and eggs just until moistened. Add 1 cup cheese and remaining onion.

Spread the batter into a greased 13-in. x 9-in. x 2-in. baking dish. Spread the hash mixture evenly over top. Sprinkle with the remaining cheese. Bake, uncovered, at 375° for 35 minutes or until corn bread layer is golden brown and pulls away from the sides of the pan. **Yield:** 12-16 servings.

Super Soups

- To liven up a can of tomato soup, I add half-and-half, a can of stewed tomatoes and 2 teaspoons dill weed.
  —*Paula Myers, Readlyn, Iowa*
- I can make a meal out of canned vegetable soup by combining it with a drained can of mixed vegetables. This works just as well if you want to increase one ingredient, such as mushrooms or corn.
  —*Stacey Aldridge, Miamisburg, Ohio*
- For a great pot of chili, try browning some Italian sausage with the beef. I also like to stir in a jar of picante sauce for extra zip.
  —*Mary Shull
  Mountain City, Tennessee*

Raisin Pound Cake

Raisin Pound Cake

(Pictured above)

Yellow cake mix, applesauce and raisins make this moist pleasantly spiced loaf a no-fuss favorite. I turn to this recipe when unexpected guests drop by because I usually have the ingredients in the cupboard. For a special occasion, top slices with fresh fruit. —LuEllen Spaulding
Caro, Michigan

  1 package (18-1/4 ounces) yellow cake mix
  1 cup applesauce
1/2 cup water
1/4 cup vegetable oil
  3 eggs
1/2 teaspoon ground cinnamon
1/4 teaspoon ground nutmeg
1/4 teaspoon ground allspice
1/2 cup raisins

In a mixing bowl, combine dry cake mix, applesauce, water, oil, eggs, cinnamon, nutmeg and allspice. Beat on medium speed for 2 minutes. Stir in raisins. Pour into two greased 8-in. x 4-in. x 2-in. loaf pans.

Bake at 350° for 45-50 minutes or until a toothpick inserted near the center comes out clean. Cool for 5-10 minutes before removing from pans to wire racks. **Yield:** 2 loaves.

Broccoli Ham Ring

Pepperoni Cheese Ravioli

Ready in 30 minutes or less

This nicely spiced pasta toss is a wonderful last-minute main dish. —Lisa Mouton
Orlando, Florida

  1 package (25 ounces) frozen cheese ravioli
1/2 pound fresh mushrooms, sliced
  1 package (3-1/2 ounces) sliced pepperoni, diced
  1 small onion, cut into wedges
  1 tablespoon butter *or* margarine
  1 can (8 ounces) tomato sauce
1/4 cup grated Parmesan cheese
1/2 teaspoon garlic powder
1/2 teaspoon dried basil
1/2 teaspoon dried oregano
1/8 teaspoon cayenne pepper
1/2 cup sour cream

Cook ravioli according to package directions. Meanwhile, in a large saucepan, saute mushrooms, pepperoni and onion in butter until onion is tender. Stir in tomato sauce, Parmesan cheese, garlic powder, basil, oregano and cayenne; heat through. Remove from the heat; stir in sour cream. Drain ravioli; toss with cream sauce. **Yield:** 4-6 servings.

Broccoli Ham Ring

(Pictured above)

Ready in 1 hour or less

Since this sandwich ring uses convenient crescent rolls, it takes little fuss to prepare. I like to fix it for a Sunday evening meal when our son comes to visit. It makes a great appetizer for a party, too. —Janet Dishong
Manheim, Pennsylvania

  2 tubes (8 ounces *each*) refrigerated crescent roll dough
1-1/2 cups (6 ounces) shredded Swiss cheese
1/4 pound fully cooked ham, diced (about 1/2 cup)
2-1/4 cups chopped fresh broccoli
  1 small onion, chopped
1/4 cup minced fresh parsley
  2 tablespoons Dijon mustard
  1 teaspoon lemon juice

Unroll crescent roll dough and place triangles on a 12-in. pizza pan, forming a ring with pointed ends facing outer edge of pan and wide ends overlapping. Lightly press wide ends together.

Combine the remaining ingredients; spoon over wide ends of rolls. Fold points over filling and tuck under wide ends (filling will be visible). Bake at 375° for 20-25 minutes or until golden brown. **Yield:** 6-8 servings.

Savory Side Dishes

- For a delightful change to plain homemade macaroni and cheese, add a heaping tablespoon of French onion dip to the mixture after the cheese melts. If you're using a boxed macaroni and cheese mix, also add two slices of American cheese for better flavor. —*Carol Johnson, Maud, Oklahoma*

- I jazz up a jar of plain applesauce by mixing in a teaspoon of vanilla or sprinkling servings with apple pie spice instead of cinnamon. —*Donna Smith Outlook, Montana*

- My family really likes potato pancakes. To make them in a hurry, I thaw Tater Tots and mash them rather than grate raw potatoes. I add seasonings, an egg and a little flour to hold the mixture together, then cook the pancakes in a skillet coated with nonstick cooking spray until browned. They're fast and easy. —*Alice Kaspar, Houston, Texas*

Enchilada-Style Burritos

(Pictured below)

Ready in 1 hour or less

Our family loves Mexican food, but I couldn't find a recipe for homemade burritos that we liked as much as the frozen varieties. So I came up with a not-too-spicy sauce that dresses them up. —Terry Ann Christensen, Roy, Utah

6 frozen prepared bean and cheese burritos
2 tablespoons butter *or* margarine
3 tablespoons all-purpose flour
1-3/4 cups water
1 can (8 ounces) tomato sauce
1-1/2 teaspoons chili powder
1 teaspoon beef bouillon granules
3/4 teaspoon ground cumin
1/2 teaspoon salt
2 cups (8 ounces) shredded Mexican cheese blend *or* cheddar cheese
1 can (2-1/4 ounces) sliced ripe olives, drained, optional
1/3 cup chopped green onions

Place frozen burritos in a greased 13-in. x 9-in. x 2-in. baking dish; set aside. In a saucepan, melt butter. Stir in flour until smooth; gradually stir in water. Bring to a boil; cook and stir for 2 minutes or until thickened. Add the tomato sauce, chili powder, bouillon, cumin and salt. Simmer, uncovered, for 5 minutes or until thickened.

Pour over the burritos. Sprinkle with cheese, olives if desired and onions. Bake, uncovered, at 350° for 35-40 minutes or until heated through. **Yield:** 6 servings.

Beefy Jalapeno Corn Bake

(Pictured below)

You'll want a fork to dig into hearty squares of this beefed-up corn bread. Chock-full of ground beef, corn, cheese and jalapeno peppers, it's so filling, it can be served as an entree. —James Coleman, Charlotte, North Carolina

1 pound ground beef
2 eggs
1 can (14-3/4 ounces) cream-style corn
1 cup milk
1/2 cup vegetable oil
1 cup cornmeal
3 tablespoons all-purpose flour
1-1/2 teaspoons baking powder
3/4 teaspoon salt
4 cups (16 ounces) shredded cheddar cheese, *divided*
1 medium onion, chopped
4 jalapeno peppers, seeded and chopped

In a skillet, cook beef over medium heat until no longer pink; drain and set aside. In a bowl, beat eggs, corn, milk and oil. Combine the cornmeal, flour, baking powder and salt; add to egg mixture and mix well.

Pour half of the batter into a greased 13-in. x 9-in. x 2-in. baking dish. Sprinkle with 2 cups cheese; top with the beef, onion and jalapenos. Sprinkle with remaining cheese; top with remaining batter.

Bake, uncovered, at 350° for 55-60 minutes or until a toothpick inserted into corn bread topping comes out clean. Serve warm. Refrigerate any leftovers. **Yield:** 12 servings.

Enchilada-Style Burritos
Beefy Jalapeno Corn Bake

Cinnamon Nut Cake

(Pictured below)

This moist bundt cake is an easy-to-assemble treat for brunch or dessert. Top with a dollop of whipped cream and you're ready to enjoy.
—*Margaret Wilson*
Hemet, California

    1 package (18-1/4 ounces) yellow cake mix
    3 eggs
1-1/3 cups water
  1/4 cup vegetable oil
1-1/4 cups finely chopped walnuts
7-1/2 teaspoons sugar
4-1/2 teaspoons ground cinnamon

In a mixing bowl, combine the cake mix, eggs, water and oil. Beat on medium speed for 2 minutes. Combine walnuts, sugar and cinnamon. Sprinkle a third of the nut mixture into a greased 10-in. fluted tube pan. Top with half of the batter and another third of the nut mixture. Repeat layers.

Bake at 350° for 35-40 minutes or until a toothpick inserted near the center comes out clean. Cool for 10 minutes before removing from pan to a wire rack to cool completely. **Yield:** 12-14 servings.

Cinnamon Nut Cake
Giant Spice Cookies

Giant Spice Cookies

(Pictured at left)

Ready in 1 hour or less

I heard this cookie recipe over the radio about 1950—shortly after my husband and I married. The big spicy treats are so nice and chewy, they remain my favorite to this day. —*Sandy Pyeatt, Tacoma, Washington*

    1 package (18-1/4 ounces) spice cake mix
  1/2 teaspoon ground ginger
  1/4 teaspoon baking soda
  1/4 cup water
  1/4 cup molasses
    6 teaspoons vanilla extract

In a bowl, combine the cake mix, ginger and baking soda. Stir in water, molasses and vanilla; mix well. With floured hands, roll into 10 balls. Place 3 in. apart on greased baking sheets; flatten slightly.

Bake at 375° for 13-15 minutes or until surface cracks and cookies are firm. Remove to wire racks to cool. **Yield:** 10 cookies.

Garden Crescent Rolls

(Pictured above right)

I adapted an old family recipe to take advantage of the handy roll mixes that are available these days. These sa-

Garden Crescent Rolls
Cheesy Beef Spirals

vory crescents are a must at holiday get-togethers and special occasions. —Dawn Conlan, Woodbridge, Virginia

- 1 package (16 ounces) hot roll mix
- 1/2 cup warm tomato juice (120° to 130°)
- 1/2 cup warm water (120° to 130°)
- 1 egg, lightly beaten
- 3 tablespoons butter *or* margarine, melted, *divided*
- 1 tablespoon grated carrot
- 1 tablespoon minced celery
- 1 tablespoon grated onion
- 1 cup grated Parmesan cheese
- 1 teaspoon garlic powder

In a bowl, combine roll mix and contents of yeast packet; mix well. Stir in tomato juice, water, egg and 2 tablespoons of butter. Add carrot, celery and onion; stir until dough pulls away from the sides of the bowl. Turn onto a lightly floured surface; knead for 5 minutes. Cover and let rest for 5 minutes.

Divide dough in half; roll each portion into a 12-in. circle. Brush with remaining butter. Combine Parmesan cheese and garlic powder; sprinkle over dough. Cut each circle into eight wedges; roll up wedges from the wide end. Place, point side down, 2 in. apart on lightly greased baking sheets.

Cover and let rise in a warm place until doubled, about 25 minutes. Bake at 375° for 15-20 minutes or until golden brown. Remove to wire racks to cool. **Yield:** 16 rolls.

Cheesy Beef Spirals

(Pictured above)

My mom shared this easy-to-assemble casserole years ago. It's very good with garlic toast. Large shell macaroni or ziti noodles can be used instead of spiral pasta.
—Brenda Marschall, Poplar Bluff, Missouri

- 2 cups uncooked spiral pasta
- 2 pounds ground beef
- 2 small onions, chopped
- 1 garlic clove, minced
- 1 jar (26 ounces) spaghetti sauce
- 1 jar (4-1/2 ounces) sliced mushrooms, drained
- 1/2 cup sour cream
- 1/2 pound process American cheese, cubed
- 2 cups (8 ounces) shredded mozzarella cheese

Cook pasta according to package directions. Meanwhile, in a large saucepan, cook the beef, onions and garlic over medium heat until meat is no longer pink; drain. Stir in spaghetti sauce and mushrooms; bring to a boil. Reduce heat; cover and simmer for 20 minutes.

Place 1/2 cup meat sauce in a greased shallow 2-1/2-qt. baking dish. Drain pasta; place half over sauce. Top with half the remaining meat sauce; spread with sour cream. Top with American cheese and remaining pasta and meat sauce. Sprinkle with mozzarella cheese. Cover and bake at 350° for 25-30 minutes. Uncover; bake 5-10 minutes longer or until bubbly. **Yield:** 8-10 servings.

Streusel Strawberry Pizza

Streusel Strawberry Pizza

(Pictured above)

Ready in 1 hour or less

This is the best dessert pizza I've ever tasted. The fruity treat is easy to put together, too, because it uses convenient cake mix and any flavor of canned pie filling. It's great for children's parties. —Karen Ann Bland, Gove, Kansas

  1 package (18-1/4 ounces) white cake mix
1-1/4 cups quick-cooking oats
  1/3 cup butter *or* margarine, softened
  1 egg
  1 can (21 ounces) strawberry pie filling *or* flavor of your choice
  1/2 cup chopped nuts
  1/4 cup packed brown sugar
  1/8 teaspoon ground cinnamon

In a mixing bowl, combine the dry cake mix, oats and butter until blended; set aside 3/4 cup for topping. Add egg to the remaining crumb mixture and mix well. Press into a greased 12-in. pizza pan. Build up edges and flute if desired. Bake at 350° for 12 minutes.

Spread pie filling over crust to within 1 in. of edges. Combine the nuts, brown sugar, cinnamon and reserved crumb mixture; sprinkle over filling. Bake for 15-20 minutes or until lightly browned. Cool on a wire rack. Refrigerate any leftovers. **Yield: 8-10 servings.**

Blackberry Breeze Pie

Plan ahead...needs to chill

Making a dessert doesn't necessarily require heating my kitchen. This fluffy no-bake treat is simple to fix with gelatin, whipped topping and fresh berries.
—Gail Toepfer, Iron Ridge, Wisconsin

☑ Uses less fat, sugar or salt. Includes Nutritional Analysis and Diabetic Exchanges.

  1 package (3 ounces) black cherry *or* cherry gelatin
  1 cup boiling water
  1 cup cold water
1-1/2 cups fresh blackberries
  1 carton (8 ounces) frozen whipped topping, thawed
  1 graham cracker crust (8 to 10 inches)

In a bowl, dissolve gelatin in boiling water. Stir in cold water. Refrigerate for 1 hour or until thickened. Gently fold in blackberries and whipped topping. Pour into crust. Chill 2 hours or until serving. **Yield: 8 servings.**

Nutritional Analysis: One piece (prepared with sugar-free cherry gelatin, reduced-fat whipped topping and reduced-fat graham cracker crust) equals 130 calories, 4 g fat (4 g saturated fat), 0 cholesterol, 300 mg sodium, 11 g carbohydrate, 1 g fiber, 4 g protein. **Diabetic Exchanges: 1-1/2 fruit, 1/2 starch.**

Hearty Hamburger Soup

Ready in 1 hour or less

This thick soup, chock-full of veggies and noodles, satisfies my husband's appetite after a busy day on the farm. It's especially handy for us to make because we raise our own beef. —Julie Green, Hull, Iowa

    2 pounds ground beef
1/2 cup chopped onion
    6 cups water
    1 package (10 ounces) frozen mixed
      vegetables
    1 can (14-1/2 ounces) diced tomatoes,
      undrained
    1 package (6-3/4 ounces) beef pasta dinner
      mix
    1 bay leaf
1/4 to 1/2 teaspoon salt
1/4 teaspoon pepper

In a Dutch oven or soup kettle, cook the beef and onion over medium heat until meat is no longer pink; drain. Stir in the remaining ingredients; bring to a boil. Reduce heat; cover and simmer until pasta is tender. Discard bay leaf before serving. **Yield:** 12 servings.

Taco Quiche

Ready in 1 hour or less

Chock-full of ground beef, cheddar cheese, onion and green pepper, this swift south-of-the-border bake is guaranteed to liven up any meal. We enjoy it for dinner as well as for brunch. —Mary Johnston, Wasilla, Alaska

    1 pound ground beef
1/4 cup chopped onion
1/4 cup chopped green pepper
    1 envelope taco seasoning
    1 cup (4 ounces) shredded cheddar cheese
1/2 cup biscuit/baking mix
    2 eggs, beaten
    1 cup milk

In a large skillet, cook the beef, onion, green pepper and taco seasoning over medium heat until meat is no longer pink; drain. Spread into a 9-in. greased pie plate. Sprinkle with cheese. In a bowl, combine the biscuit mix, eggs and milk; mix well. Pour over the cheese. Bake at 400° for 20-25 minutes or until a knife inserted near the center comes out clean. **Yield:** 4-6 servings.

Crisp Walnut Cookies

This is a terrific way to bake fresh cookies in minutes. Easy one-bowl preparation results in yummy treats that are crisp and chewy at the same time. —Alice Walcher, North Fairfield, Ohio

    1 package (18-1/4 ounces) yellow cake mix
    2 cups quick-cooking oats

1/2 cup sugar
    1 cup vegetable oil
    3 eggs
1-1/2 teaspoons vanilla extract
    1 cup finely chopped walnuts

In a mixing bowl, combine cake mix, oats and sugar. Beat in oil, eggs and vanilla. Stir in walnuts. Drop by rounded teaspoonfuls 2 in. apart onto ungreased baking sheets. Bake at 350° for 12-14 minutes or until lightly browned. Remove to wire racks to cool. **Yield:** 6 dozen.

Sausage Stroganoff Soup

I start this rich soup with handy scalloped potato mix and brown-and-serve breakfast sausages. It's not your ordinary potato soup. —Helen Haviland, Greenfield, Illinois

    1 package (12 ounces) brown-and-serve
      sausage links, cut into 1/2-inch slices
    1 garlic clove, minced
    1 package (5 ounces) scalloped potatoes
    3 cups water
    1 can (14-1/2 ounces) chicken broth
    1 jar (4-1/2 ounces) sliced mushrooms, drained
    1 cup half-and-half cream
    1 cup (8 ounces) sour cream
    2 tablespoons Dijon mustard
Paprika, optional

In a large saucepan, cook sausage and garlic until sausage is lightly browned, about 6 minutes. Stir in the contents of the potato and sauce packets. Add water, broth and mushrooms. Bring to a boil. Reduce heat; simmer, uncovered, for 14-16 minutes or until potatoes are tender. Stir in the cream, sour cream and mustard; heat through (do not boil). Sprinkle with paprika if desired. **Yield:** 6-8 servings.

Desserts in a Dash

- To make better tasting brownies from a boxed mix, I swirl chocolate syrup over the top of the batter after spreading it in the pan. The brownies come out so fudgy, they don't need icing. My husband's friends gobble them up as fast as I can make them!
  —Stacey Shannon, Muncie, Indiana
- When stirring up a batch of fudge, I use 1/2 teaspoon of vanilla and 1/2 teaspoon of almond extract in place of 1 teaspoon vanilla called for in the recipe. It gives the fudge a wonderful flavor that has people asking for my secret ingredient.
  —Peggy-Jo Thompson, Lebanon, Tennessee
- When our kids were little, I substituted mint extract for vanilla in my chocolate chip cookies. Now, 30 years later, my son's friend still comments on them.
  —Dolores Point, Bismarck, North Dakota
- When I make a cake from a boxed mix, I prefer to use 1/2 cup of mayonnaise where the directions call for 1/2 cup vegetable oil or shortening. The mayonnaise gives the cake a homemade flavor.
  —Jennifer McKinney, Washington, Illinois

Homemade Mixes

STORE-BOUGHT mixes can be convenient, but these homemade cookie, pancake, beverage, soup and seasoning mixes deliver all the great taste of the popular specialty products—but for far less cost.

Editor's Note: The contents of mixes may settle during storage. When preparing the recipe, spoon the mix into a measuring cup.

Master Cookie Mix

I only use a few ingredients in my sweet and simple cookie mix. Throw the mix together yourself and you'll have enough to bake all of the taste-tempting cookies on this page...and still have extra for the months ahead.
—Ruth Kloss, Two Rivers, Wisconsin

    4-1/2 cups all-purpose flour
    1-1/2 cups sugar
    1-1/2 cups packed brown sugar
        2 teaspoons salt
        2 teaspoons baking soda
    1-1/2 cups shortening

In a large bowl, combine the flour, sugars, salt and baking soda. Cut in shortening until crumbly. Store in an airtight container in a cool dry place for up to 6 months. **Yield:** about 10 cups.

Peanut Butter Cookies
Cinnamon Raisin Cookies

Peanut Butter Cookies

(Pictured below left)

Everyone loves homemade peanut butter cookies...and with a little help from my cookie mix, you can whip up a batch in no time. Imagine the smiles you'll receive when you bring out these tender treats for an after-school snack.
—Ruth Kloss

    1/2 cup peanut butter*
      2 eggs
      1 teaspoon vanilla extract
      2 cups Master Cookie Mix (recipe on this page)

In a mixing bowl, combine all ingredients; mix well. Drop by rounded tablespoonfuls 2 in. apart onto ungreased baking sheets. Flatten slightly with a glass dipped in sugar if desired. Bake at 350° for 10-12 minutes or until set and edges are lightly browned. Cool for 1-2 minutes before removing to wire racks. **Yield:** about 2-1/2 dozen.
    *Editor's Note: Reduced-fat or generic brands of peanut butter are not recommended for this recipe.

Cinnamon Raisin Cookies

(Pictured below left)

The master mix shaves much of the prep time off these cinnamon delights that are chock-full of raisins and walnuts. The cookie jar won't be full for long once your family samples these mouth-watering morsels. *—Ruth Kloss*

        2 eggs
    1/2 teaspoon ground cinnamon
    1/2 teaspoon almond extract
    2-1/2 cups Master Cookie Mix (recipe on this page)
    1/2 cup raisins
    1/2 cup chopped walnuts

In a mixing bowl, combine eggs, cinnamon, extract and cookie mix; mix well. Stir in raisins and nuts. Drop by rounded tablespoonfuls 2 in. apart onto lightly greased baking sheets. Bake at 350° for 10-12 minutes or until set and edges are lightly browned. Cool for 1-2 minutes before removing to wire racks. **Yield:** about 2-1/2 dozen.

Banana Cookies

The down-home flavor of banana bread comes to a cookie in these soft sweet snacks. They can be stirred up in seconds, thanks to my handy mix. *—Ruth Kloss*

        2 eggs
    1/2 cup mashed ripe bananas
    1/4 cup all-purpose flour
      1 teaspoon vanilla extract
    2-1/2 cups Master Cookie Mix (recipe on this page)
    1/2 cup chopped pecans

In a mixing bowl, combine the first five ingredients; mix well. Stir in the pecans. Drop by rounded tablespoonfuls 2 in. apart onto lightly greased baking sheets. Bake at 350° for 10-11 minutes or until set and edges are lightly browned. Cool for 1-2 minutes before removing to wire racks. **Yield:** about 3 dozen.

Chicken Crumb Coating

A crunchy cornflake coating made with sesame seeds, oregano and Parmesan cheese complements this chicken. I love serving it to company because it always turns out wonderfully.
—Joan Laurenzo
Johnstown, Ohio

    2 cups crushed cornflakes
    1 cup grated Parmesan cheese
    1/4 cup sesame seeds
    1 teaspoon paprika
    1/2 teaspoon ground oregano
ADDITIONAL INGREDIENTS:
    1 broiler/fryer chicken (3 to 4 pounds), cut up
    1/3 to 1/2 cup milk

In a bowl, combine the first five ingredients. Cover and refrigerate for up to 4 months. **Yield:** 2 batches (about 3 cups total).

To prepare chicken: Dip chicken pieces in milk, then roll in about 1-1/4 cups coating mix. Place in a greased 13-in. x 9-in. x 2-in. baking pan. Bake, uncovered, at 350° for 45-50 minutes or until chicken juices run clear. **Yield:** 4-6 servings per batch.

Spiced Tea Mix

(Pictured above right)

For years, my family has relied on this homespun mix to make hot spiced tea and a heartwarming punch. My parents always served steaming mugs of this punch at Thanksgiving. It was everyone's favorite.
—Deb McKinney, Cedar Falls, Iowa

    1 jar (21.1 ounces) orange breakfast drink mix
    1 jar (6 ounces) sugar-free instant lemon iced tea mix
    2/3 cup sweetened lemonade drink mix
    2 teaspoons ground cinnamon
    1 teaspoon ground cloves
ADDITIONAL INGREDIENTS FOR HOT SPICED TEA:
    1 cup boiling water
ADDITIONAL INGREDIENTS FOR HOT SPICED PUNCH:
    2 quarts apple juice *or* cider
1-1/2 cups cranberry juice
    3 cinnamon sticks (3-1/2 inches)

In an airtight container, combine the first five ingredients. Store in a cool dry place for up to 6 months. **Yield:** about 7-1/2 cups total.

To prepare tea: Dissolve about 1 tablespoon tea mix in boiling water; stir well. **Yield:** 1 serving.

To prepare punch: In a slow cooker, combine the juices, 1/4 to 1/3 cup tea mix and cinnamon sticks. Cover and cook on low for 4 hours. **Yield:** about 12 servings (6 ounces each).

Cranberry Muffin Mix
Spiced Tea Mix

Cranberry Muffin Mix

(Pictured above)

We enjoy muffins so much that I created this quick and simple mix. Cranberries give these golden treats a burst of color and just a bit of tartness that will keep friends and family asking for the recipe.
—Ruth Andrewson
Peck, Idaho

8-1/4 cups all-purpose flour
    3 cups sugar
1/3 cup baking powder
    1 tablespoon salt
    1 cup shortening
ADDITIONAL INGREDIENTS:
    1 egg
    1 cup evaporated milk
    1 tablespoon butter *or* margarine, melted
    1 cup fresh *or* frozen cranberries

In a large bowl, combine the flour, sugar, baking powder and salt. Cut in shortening until the mixture resembles coarse crumbs. Store in an airtight container in a cool dry place for up to 6 months. **Yield:** about 4 batches (11-1/2 cups total).

To prepare muffins: Place 2-3/4 cups muffin mix in a bowl. Combine the egg, milk and butter; stir into mix just until moistened. Fold in cranberries. Fill greased or paper-lined muffin cups three-fourths full. Bake at 400° for 15-18 minutes or until a toothpick comes out clean. Cool for 5 minutes before removing from pan to a wire rack. Serve warm. **Yield:** 1 dozen.

Oatmeal Raisin Cookie Mix
Hot Cocoa Mix

Hot Cocoa Mix

(Pictured above)

I first tasted this warming beverage on a camping trip in the mountains. It was a wonderful treat on those crisp mornings. —Ruby Gibson, Newton, North Carolina

6-2/3 cups nonfat dry milk powder
   1 cup instant chocolate drink mix
   1 package (5 ounces) cook-and-serve chocolate pudding mix
1/2 cup confectioners' sugar
1/2 cup powdered nondairy creamer
1/2 cup baking cocoa
ADDITIONAL INGREDIENTS:
   1 cup boiling water
Miniature marshmallows, optional

In a bowl, combine the first six ingredients. Store in an airtight container in a cool dry place for up to 3 months. **Yield:** 21 batches (about 7 cups total).

   To prepare hot cocoa: Dissolve 1/3 cup cocoa mix in boiling water. Top with miniature marshmallows if desired. **Yield:** 1 serving per batch.

Oatmeal Raisin Cookie Mix

(Pictured above)

You'll love the old-fashioned taste of these chewy raisin-studded cookies. I tie a jar of this layered mix with a pretty ribbon and give it as a housewarming gift. —Merwyn Garbini, Tucson, Arizona

   1 cup all-purpose flour
   1 teaspoon baking soda
   1 teaspoon ground cinnamon
1/2 teaspoon ground nutmeg
1/2 teaspoon salt
3/4 cup packed brown sugar
1/2 cup sugar
3/4 cup raisins
   2 cups quick-cooking oats
ADDITIONAL INGREDIENTS:
3/4 cup butter *or* margarine, softened
   1 egg
   1 teaspoon vanilla extract

In a bowl, combine the first five ingredients; set aside. In a 1-qt. glass container, layer brown sugar, sugar, raisins and oats, packing well between each layer. Top with flour mixture. Cover; store in a cool dry place up for to 6 months. **Yield:** 1 batch (about 4 cups total).

   To prepare cookies: In a mixing bowl, cream the butter. Beat in egg and vanilla. Add cookie mix and mix well. Drop by rounded teaspoonfuls 2 in. apart onto greased baking sheets. Bake at 350° for 9-11 minutes or until golden brown. Cool for 2 minutes before removing to wire racks. **Yield:** about 5 dozen per batch.

Parmesan Macaroni Mix

This creamy macaroni and cheese mix is better than the kind you buy at the store. The sauce is smooth, rich and so yummy! —Iola Egle, McCook, Nebraska

      2 cups nonfat dry milk powder
1-3/4 cups freshly grated Parmesan cheese
   1/2 cup all-purpose flour
      1 teaspoon paprika
   1/2 teaspoon ground mustard
   1/4 teaspoon pepper
   1/2 cup cold butter *or* margarine

ADDITIONAL INGREDIENTS:
1-1/2 cups uncooked elbow macaroni
1/2 cup milk
1/2 cup water
1/4 to 1/2 teaspoon salt

In a large bowl, combine the first six ingredients. Cut in butter until crumbly. Cover and refrigerate for up to 2 months. **Yield:** 5 batches (about 5 cups total).

To prepare macaroni: Cook macaroni according to package directions. Meanwhile, combine 1 cup mix, milk, water and salt in a saucepan. Cook and stir until mixture comes to a boil. Cook and stir for 2 minutes or until thick and bubbly. Drain macaroni; stir into sauce until evenly coated. **Yield:** 2-3 servings per batch.

Mocha Cooler

Why go to a coffee shop for an iced mocha drink when you can easily whip up a refreshing glass at home? I created this mocha mix from a few basic ingredients. Now I can enjoy this cool beverage whenever I want. —Susan Beck
Napa, California

1/4 cup instant coffee granules
1 cup sugar
1 cup nonfat dry milk powder
1 cup powdered nondairy creamer
1/3 cup baking cocoa
1/4 teaspoon salt
ADDITIONAL INGREDIENTS:
1-1/2 cups crushed ice
1/2 cup milk
Whipped topping, optional

With a rolling pin, crush coffee granules into a fine powder between sheets of waxed paper. Place in an airtight container. Add the sugar, milk powder, creamer, cocoa and salt; mix well. Store in a cool dry place for up to 1 year. **Yield:** 7 batches (3-1/2 cups total).

To prepare cooler: In a blender, combine the ice, milk and 1/2 cup of mocha mix; cover and process on high until smooth. Pour into glasses. Top with whipped topping if desired. **Yield:** 2 servings per batch.

Seasoning for Tacos

Ground beef tacos and taco salads are nicely enhanced by this mixture. It's so easy to mix up a batch and keep it in the pantry. It's convenient and saves money, too.
—Sue Gronholz, Beaver Dam, Wisconsin

2 tablespoons chili powder
5 teaspoons paprika
4-1/2 teaspoons ground cumin
3 teaspoons onion powder
3 teaspoons salt
2-1/2 teaspoons garlic powder
1/8 teaspoon cayenne pepper
ADDITIONAL INGREDIENTS:
1 pound ground beef
2/3 to 3/4 cup water

In a bowl, combine the first seven ingredients. Store in an airtight container in a cool dry place for up to 6 months. **Yield:** 3 batches (about 1/2 cup total).

To prepare taco meat: In a saucepan, cook beef over medium heat until no longer pink; drain. Add water and 8 teaspoons seasoning mix. Bring to a boil. Reduce heat; simmer, uncovered, for 10 minutes. **Yield:** 4 servings per batch.

Homemade Pancake Mix

(Pictured below)

I use whole wheat flour to bring extra flavor to the flapjacks at my breakfast table. My family particularly likes the blueberry banana variation. —Wendy Mink
Huntington, Indiana

4 cups all-purpose flour
2 cups whole wheat flour
2/3 cup sugar
2 tablespoons baking powder
1 tablespoon baking soda
ADDITIONAL INGREDIENTS FOR PANCAKES:
1 egg
3/4 cup milk
ADDITIONAL INGREDIENTS FOR BLUEBERRY BANANA PANCAKES:
1 egg
3/4 cup milk
1 medium ripe banana, mashed
3/4 cup blueberries

In a bowl, combine the first five ingredients. Store in an airtight container in a cool dry place for up to 6 months. **Yield:** 6-7 batches of pancakes (about 6-3/4 cups total).

To prepare pancakes: In a bowl, combine egg and milk. Whisk in 1 cup pancake mix. Pour batter by 1/4 cupfuls onto a lightly greased hot griddle; turn when bubbles form on top of pancakes. Cook until second side is golden brown. **Yield:** about 6 pancakes per batch.

To prepare blueberry banana pancakes: In a bowl, combine egg, milk and banana. Whisk in 1 cup pancake mix. Fold in blueberries. Cook as directed above. **Yield:** about 8 pancakes per batch.

Homemade Pancake Mix

Hush Puppy Mix

(Pictured below)

I add garlic powder and red pepper flakes to the cornmeal mix that creates these golden hush puppies. You'll win rave reviews for the crunchy crust and spicy flavor of these corn-filled bites. —Edna Bullett, Wilburton, Oklahoma

4-1/3 cups cornmeal
3/4 cup all-purpose flour
6-1/2 teaspoons baking powder
2 tablespoons sugar
2 tablespoons garlic powder
1 tablespoon pepper
1 tablespoon salt
1/2 teaspoon crushed red pepper flakes
ADDITIONAL INGREDIENTS:
1 can (8-1/2 ounces) cream-style corn
1/2 cup chopped onion
1 egg
Oil for deep-fat frying

In a bowl, combine the first eight ingredients; mix well. Store in an airtight container in a cool dry place for up to 6 months. **Yield:** 3 batches (4-1/2 cups total).

To prepare hush puppies: In a bowl, combine 1-1/2 cups mix, corn, onion and egg; stir just until moistened. In an electric skillet or deep-fat fryer, heat 1-1/2 in. of oil to 375°. Drop batter by teaspoonfuls into oil; fry until golden brown. Drain on paper towels. Serve warm. **Yield:** about 4 dozen per batch.

Hush Puppy Mix

Jambalaya Mix

If you keep this zippy jambalaya mix on hand, a full-flavored meal is never far away. I add shrimp, smoked sausage and a few other easy ingredients to the nicely seasoned rice mix to create a speedy skillet sensation. You can make all three batches when cooking for a crowd. —Sybil Brown, Highland, California

3 cups uncooked long grain rice
3 tablespoons dried minced onion
3 tablespoons dried parsley flakes
4 teaspoons beef bouillon granules
1 tablespoon dried minced chives
1 tablespoon dried celery flakes
1-1/2 teaspoons pepper
3/4 teaspoon cayenne pepper
3/4 teaspoon garlic powder
3/4 teaspoon dried thyme
ADDITIONAL INGREDIENTS:
2 cups water
1/2 cup chopped green pepper
1 can (8 ounces) tomato sauce
1 pound fully cooked smoked sausage, cut into 1/4-inch slices
1 pound uncooked medium shrimp, peeled and deveined

In an airtight container, combine the first 10 ingredients. Store in a cool dry place for up to 6 months. **Yield:** about 3 batches (about 3-1/3 cups total).

To prepare jambalaya: In a saucepan, bring water and green pepper to a boil. Stir in 1 cup of the jambalaya mix; return to a boil. Reduce heat; cover and simmer for 18-20 minutes or until the rice is tender. In another saucepan, heat the tomato sauce and sausage. Cook the shrimp in boiling water until pink; drain. Stir into sausage mixture. Serve over rice mixture. **Yield:** 4-6 servings.

Chicken Rice Soup Mix

This quick combination produces bowls of steaming soup that are sure to warm up your family. The mix calls for brown rice instead of white rice and is subtly seasoned with tarragon and pepper. —Iola Egle
McCook, Nebraska

2 cups uncooked long grain brown rice
1/2 cup chicken bouillon granules
4 teaspoons dried tarragon
4 teaspoons dried parsley flakes
1 teaspoon white pepper
ADDITIONAL INGREDIENTS:
3 cups water
1 tablespoon butter *or* margarine

In a bowl, combine the first five ingredients. Cover and store in a cool dry place for up to 6 months. **Yield:** 4 batches (about 2-2/3 cups).

To prepare soup: In a saucepan, bring water, butter and 2/3 cup soup mix to a boil. Reduce heat; cover and simmer for 30-35 minutes or until the rice is tender. **Yield:** 2-3 servings per batch.

Master Baking Mix

One batch of this mix is enough to bake all of the goodies on this page...and more! I always keep this versatile mix handy.
—*Ruby Love*
Deer Island, Oregon

    8 cups all-purpose flour
    2 cups nonfat dry milk powder
1/3 cup baking powder
1/4 cup sugar
    1 tablespoon salt
    2 cups shortening

In a large bowl, combine the flour, milk powder, baking powder, sugar and salt. Cut in shortening until mixture resembles coarse crumbs. Store in an airtight container in a cool dry place or freeze for up to 6 months. **Yield:** 14-1/2 cups.

Fruit Cobbler
Blueberry Quick Bread

Yellow Cake

Put the supermarket cake mix back on the shelf (and the money it costs back in your wallet) because baking a cake from scratch just got easier! Top off squares with your favorite frosting or a fruity sauce. —*Ruby Love*

    3 cups Master Baking Mix (recipe on this page)
1-1/4 cups sugar
    2 eggs
    1 cup water
    1 teaspoon vanilla extract

In a mixing bowl, combine baking mix and sugar. Add eggs, water and vanilla; beat on medium speed for 2 minutes. Pour into a greased 13-in. x 9-in. x 2-in. baking pan. Bake at 350° for 25-30 minutes or until a toothpick inserted near the center comes out clean. Cool on a wire rack. **Yield:** 12-15 servings.

Fruit Cobbler

(Pictured above and on page 76)

Let the aroma of this cobbler waft through your home the next time you entertain. Its golden crust and tender fruit make it ideal to serve with ice cream. —*Ruby Love*

2-1/2 cups fresh *or* frozen unsweetened raspberries *or* fruit of your choice
1-1/4 cups water, *divided*
1-1/3 cups sugar, *divided*
    4 tablespoons butter *or* margarine, *divided*
    1 cup Master Baking Mix (recipe on this page)

Thaw and chop fruit if necessary. In a saucepan, combine the fruit, 3/4 cup water, 1 cup sugar and 2 tablespoons butter. Cook and stir over medium heat just until mix-

ture begins to simmer and butter is melted. Remove from the heat; set aside.

In a bowl, combine baking mix and remaining sugar. Melt remaining butter. Stir butter and remaining water into dry ingredients until smooth. Transfer to a greased 2-qt. baking dish. Spoon fruit mixture over batter. Bake at 375° for 35 minutes or until cake tests done. Serve warm. **Yield:** 6-8 servings.

Blueberry Quick Bread

(Pictured above and on page 76)

The down-home goodness of this loaf makes it the perfect snack...morning, noon or night. Chock-full of blueberries, this moist bread also has a hint of orange that will have your family asking for seconds. —*Ruby Love*

    3 cups Master Baking Mix (recipe on this page)
2/3 cup sugar
3/4 cup fresh *or* frozen blueberries*
    1 tablespoon grated orange peel
    1 egg
3/4 cup orange juice
1/4 cup water

In a bowl, combine baking mix, sugar, blueberries and orange peel. In another bowl, whisk egg, orange juice and water; stir into the dry ingredients. Pour into a greased 9-in. x 5-in. x 3-in. loaf pan. Bake at 350° for 50-55 minutes or until a toothpick inserted near the center comes out clean. Cool for 10 minutes before removing from pan to a wire rack. **Yield:** 1 loaf.

*Editor's Note: If using frozen blueberries, do not thaw.

Chapter 7

LEFTOVERS can make for quick-and-easy meals—without looking or tasting the same the second or even third time around.

Cooking up a little extra on weekends and then having "planned" leftovers can be the key to made-in-minutes meals during the rest of the week.

For example, start by offering your family Mom's Meatballs pictured at left and featured on page 106. (Like all the weekend dishes that supply the main ingredient for the weekday recipes, its title is highlighted in a colored box.) Later, surprise them with such lively leftovers as Meatball Minestrone and Meatball Lasagna.

Your family will never again turn up their noses at leftovers when you dress up the food in a deliciously different disguise!

SECOND-TIME-AROUND SUCCESS. Clockwise from top: Meatball Minestrone, Mom's Meatballs and Meatball Lasagna (all recipes on page 106).

Roast Beef with Gravy

Plan ahead...uses slow cooker

Start this simple roast in the morning, and you'll have savory slices of meat and gravy ready at suppertime. The tender beef is loaded with homemade taste and leaves plenty for main dishes later in the week.
—Tracy Ashbeck, Wisconsin Rapids, Wisconsin

    1 boneless beef sirloin tip roast (about 4
      pounds)
1/2 cup all-purpose flour, *divided*
    1 envelope onion soup mix
    1 envelope brown gravy mix
    2 cups cold water
Hot mashed potatoes

Cut roast in half; rub with 1/4 cup flour. Place in a 5-qt. slow cooker. In a bowl, combine soup and gravy mixes and remaining flour; stir in water until blended. Pour over roast. Cover and cook on low for 6-8 hours or until meat is tender. Slice roast; serve with mashed potatoes and gravy. **Yield:** 16 servings.

Roast Beef Stew

Ready in 1 hour or less

I serve this hearty stew with corn bread and chocolate pie for dessert. I've never had a complaint. —Annice Brewer
Meridian, Mississippi

    2 cups cubed cooked roast beef
    4 cups tomato juice
    2 cans (14-1/2 ounces *each*) diced tomatoes,
      undrained
    2 cups water
    3 large red potatoes, diced
    2 cups frozen lima beans
    1 large onion, diced
    1 cup diced celery
    1 tablespoon beef bouillon granules
    1 to 2 teaspoons sugar, optional
Salt and pepper to taste
    1 bay leaf

In a Dutch oven or soup kettle, combine all of the ingredients. Bring to a boil. Reduce heat; cover and cook until vegetables are tender, about 30 minutes. Discard bay leaf before serving. **Yield:** 12 servings.

Speedy Stroganoff

Ready in 30 minutes or less

I have tried many different ways to use up leftover roast beef, but my husband says this is the best! I experimented until I came up with all the right ingredients.
—Emma Magielda, Amsterdam, New York

    2 to 3 cups julienned cooked roast beef
    1 small onion, chopped

    2 garlic cloves, minced
    1 teaspoon vegetable oil
    1 can (10-3/4 ounces) condensed cream of
      mushroom soup, undiluted
    1 cup milk
    1 jar (4-1/2 ounces) sliced mushrooms, drained
    2 tablespoons ketchup
    1 teaspoon beef bouillon granules
1/4 to 1/2 teaspoon salt
1/4 teaspoon pepper
Hot cooked noodles

In a saucepan over medium heat, cook and stir beef, onion and garlic in oil until onion is tender. Stir in soup and milk until blended. Add mushrooms, ketchup, bouillon, salt and pepper; mix well. Bring to a boil. Reduce heat; simmer, uncovered, for 8-10 minutes or until heated through. Serve over noodles. **Yield:** 3-4 servings.

Peanut Butter Maple Cookies

(Pictured at right)

I bake these crispy yet chewy peanut butter cookies often. My grandchildren can't wait to dig into the cookie jar. The recipe makes a big batch.
—Lois Bowman
Swanton, Maryland

    1 cup butter *or* margarine, softened
1/2 cup peanut butter*
    1 cup sugar
    1 cup packed brown sugar
    2 eggs
    1 tablespoon maple syrup
    2 teaspoons vanilla extract
    2 cups all-purpose flour
3/4 cup quick-cooking oats
1-1/2 teaspoons baking powder
    1 teaspoon baking soda
    1 teaspoon salt
    1 package (10 ounces) peanut butter chips

In a mixing bowl, cream the butter, peanut butter and sugars. Add the eggs, one at a time, beating well after each addition. Beat in syrup and vanilla. Combine the flour, oats, baking powder, baking soda and salt; add to the creamed mixture and mix well. Stir in peanut butter chips. Drop by heaping tablespoonfuls 2 in. apart onto ungreased baking sheets. Bake at 325° for 15-18 minutes or until golden brown. Cool for 1 minute before removing to wire racks. **Yield:** about 5 dozen.

*Editor's Note: Reduced-fat or generic brands of peanut butter are not recommended for this recipe.

Peanut Butter Icebox Dessert

(Pictured above right)

Plan ahead...needs to chill

Leftover crushed cookies create the yummy crust for this crowd-pleasing dessert. It's covered with a smooth cream

Peanut Butter Maple Cookies
Peanut Butter Icebox Dessert
Peanut Butter Cookie Parfait

cheese mixture, chocolate pudding and whipped topping for a lovely layered look. —Nancy Mueller
Bloomington, Minnesota

2-1/4 cups crushed peanut butter cookies (about 11 cookies)
1/4 cup sugar
1/4 cup butter *or* margarine, melted
2 packages (3 ounces *each*) cream cheese, softened
1 cup confectioners' sugar
1 carton (8 ounces) frozen whipped topping, thawed, *divided*
2-1/2 cups cold milk
2 packages (3.9 ounces *each*) instant chocolate pudding mix
Additional peanut butter cookies, crushed

In a bowl, combine the crushed cookies, sugar and butter; press into an ungreased 13-in. x 9-in. x 2-in. baking dish. Bake at 350° for 6-8 minutes or until golden brown; cool on a wire rack.

In a mixing bowl, beat the cream cheese and confectioners' sugar; fold in 1 cup whipped topping. Spread over cooled crust. In another mixing bowl, beat milk and pudding mix on low speed for 2 minutes or until thickened. Spread over cream cheese layer. Top with remaining whipped topping; sprinkle with cookie pieces. Refrigerate for at least 1 hour before serving. **Yield:** 12-15 servings.

Peanut Butter Cookie Parfait

(Pictured above)

Ready in 15 minutes or less

You'll need just three ingredients to assemble the cool, creamy and crunchy dessert. This single-serving sundae is a perfect way to treat yourself...or someone special. —Jamie Wright, Kalamazoo, Michigan

3 peanut butter cookies, coarsely chopped
2/3 cup vanilla ice cream
3 tablespoons hot fudge ice cream topping, warmed

Set aside one large cookie piece. Sprinkle half of the chopped cookies in a parfait glass; top with half of the ice cream and hot fudge topping. Repeat. Garnish with reserved cookie piece. **Yield:** 1 serving.

Basic Beef Stew

When I make pot roast, I always add extra carrots, potatoes and celery. Then later in the week, I thicken a can of beef broth with flour and add the leftover meat and extra vegetables for a quick beef stew.

—Judy Studebaker, Berne, Indiana

Ginger Pork Over Spaghetti

Ready in 1 hour or less

I first tasted this speedy skillet dish when my daughter and son-in-law prepared it for us. With a salad and French bread, it makes a wonderful meal. —Linda Stone
Dothan, Alabama

    2 pounds uncooked spaghetti
    2 pounds ground pork
    2 garlic cloves, minced
  1/2 teaspoon ground ginger *or* 2 teaspoons
      minced fresh gingerroot
  1/2 teaspoon crushed red pepper flakes
7-1/2 teaspoons cornstarch
    2 cups water
  1/2 cup soy sauce
  1/4 cup white wine *or* chicken broth
    1 cup sliced green onions

Cook spaghetti according to package directions. Meanwhile, in a skillet, cook the pork, garlic, ginger and pepper flakes over medium heat until meat is no longer pink; drain. In a bowl, combine the cornstarch, water, soy sauce and wine or broth until smooth. Add to pork mixture with onions. Bring to a boil; cook and stir for 2 minutes or until thickened.

Drain spaghetti; place 6 cups in a large serving bowl. Add pork mixture and toss to coat. Refrigerate remaining spaghetti. **Yield:** 6-8 servings.

Spaghetti Crab Quiche

This light, flavorful quiche will get rave reviews when you serve it at your next brunch. It's easy to prepare, yet the addition of crab makes it taste special.
—Delores Broz, Lincoln, Nebraska

1-1/2 cups cooked spaghetti
    2 tablespoons butter *or* margarine, melted
    5 eggs
  1/3 cup grated Parmesan cheese
1-1/4 cups chopped imitation crabmeat (about 4
      ounces)
    1 cup (4 ounces) shredded Swiss cheese
  1/3 cup finely chopped onion
1-1/2 cups half-and-half cream
    1 teaspoon salt
  1/4 teaspoon pepper
  1/8 teaspoon cayenne pepper, optional

Place spaghetti in a bowl; drizzle with butter. In another bowl, combine 2 eggs and Parmesan cheese. Pour over the spaghetti and toss to coat. Press onto the bottom and up the sides of a greased 9-in. pie plate. Sprinkle with crab, Swiss cheese and onion.

In a bowl, lightly beat remaining eggs. Whisk in the cream, salt, pepper and cayenne if desired. Slowly pour into crust. Bake, uncovered, at 350° for 25 minutes. Cover and bake 15-20 minutes longer or until a knife inserted near the center comes out clean. Let stand for 10 minutes before cutting. **Yield:** 6 servings.

Spaghetti Pizza

Ready in 1 hour or less

I have five children who are finicky eaters, but they all like this fun variation on traditional pizza. Spaghetti noodles form the crust while the delicious sauce and spicy Italian sausage give it authentic flavor. —Helen Van Norman
Maplewood, Minnesota

    6 cups cooked spaghetti
    2 eggs, lightly beaten
  1/3 cup milk
    1 jar (28 ounces) spaghetti sauce
    1 pound bulk Italian sausage, cooked and
      drained
    1 jar (6 ounces) sliced mushrooms, drained
    1 can (2-1/4 ounces) sliced ripe olives, drained
2-1/2 cups (10 ounces) shredded mozzarella
      cheese

In a bowl, combine spaghetti, eggs and milk. Spread into a greased 15-in. x 10-in. x 1-in. baking pan. Top with spaghetti sauce, sausage, mushrooms, olives and cheese. Bake at 350° for 30 minutes or until cheese melts and pizza is heated through. **Yield:** 6-8 servings.

Garlic Lime Salmon

(Pictured at right)

Ready in 30 minutes or less

This moist tender fish, which I prepare on the grill, is mildly seasoned, so the leftovers work well in other recipes.
—Gail Uchwat, Sand Springs, Oklahoma

  1/2 cup vegetable oil
    1 medium onion, diced
    2 tablespoons lime juice
    1 teaspoon grated lime peel
    1 garlic clove, minced
    2 salmon fillets (about 1-1/2 pounds *each*)
Lime slices, optional

In a jar with a tight-fitting lid, combine the first five ingredients; shake well. Broil salmon, skin side down, 4-6 in. from the heat for 20 minutes or until fish flakes easily with a fork, basting every 5 minutes with lime mixture. Garnish with lime slices if desired. **Yield:** 6 servings.

Salmon Chowder

(Pictured at right)

Ready in 1 hour or less

When you live near some of the best salmon fishing in the world, you're always searching for imaginative ways to serve it. I came up with this creamy chowder that uses salmon in place of shellfish. We love it.
—Mary Lou Pearce, Victoria, British Columbia

    2 cups diced peeled potatoes
1-1/2 cups fresh *or* frozen mixed vegetables

1 large onion, chopped
1/2 teaspoon celery seed
2 cups water
6 plum tomatoes, peeled, seeded and chopped
3 tablespoons butter *or* margarine
3 tablespoons all-purpose flour
1/4 teaspoon salt
Dash pepper
2 cups milk
2 cups cubed cooked salmon

In a Dutch oven or soup kettle, combine the potatoes, vegetables, onion, celery seed and water. Bring to a boil. Reduce heat; cover and simmer for 20 minutes or until vegetables are tender. Add the tomatoes; simmer 5 minutes longer. In a saucepan, melt butter. Stir in the flour, salt and pepper until smooth. Gradually add milk. Bring to a boil; cook and stir for 2 minutes or until thickened. Add to vegetable mixture with salmon; heat through. **Yield:** 8 servings.

Salmon Pasta Primavera

(Pictured below)

Ready in 30 minutes or less

*I created this recipe one Sunday afternoon to use up in-*gredients I had on hand. My husband and a guest loved the combination of salmon, vegetables and noodles.
—Jenny Kimberlin, Overland Park, Kansas

8 ounces uncooked spinach fettuccine, broken in half
1-1/2 cups fresh *or* frozen broccoli florets
1/4 cup chopped red onion
2 tablespoons chopped green pepper
2 garlic cloves, minced
4 tablespoons butter *or* margarine, *divided*
1 envelope Alfredo sauce mix
1/2 cup evaporated milk
1/2 cup water
Salt and pepper to taste
1 cup cubed cooked salmon
Crumbled cooked bacon, optional

Cook fettuccine according to package directions. Meanwhile, in a large skillet, saute the broccoli, onion, green pepper and garlic in 2 tablespoons butter until vegetables are tender. In a large saucepan, combine the sauce mix, milk, water, salt, pepper and remaining butter. Cook over medium heat until thickened. Add the salmon and heat through. Drain pasta; add to vegetable mixture. Top with sauce and gently toss to coat. Sprinkle with bacon if desired. **Yield:** 4 servings.

Garlic Lime Salmon
Salmon Pasta Primavera
Salmon Chowder

Italian Sausage Sandwiches
Italian Sausage Spaghetti
Sausage French Bread Pizza

Italian Sausage Sandwiches

(Pictured above)

Ready in 30 minutes or less

There's no need for other condiments when you jazz up sausages with zippy peppers. This is a favorite of mine in the summer, when peppers are at their peak.
—Bonnie Jost, Manitowoc, Wisconsin

 16 uncooked Italian sausage links
  4 large sweet peppers (1 *each* red, yellow, orange and green), julienned
  1 banana pepper, julienned, optional
  1 onion, halved and sliced
  2 tablespoons vegetable oil
  8 brat *or* hot dog buns

In a large skillet, cook sausages over medium heat until no longer pink. Meanwhile, in another skillet, saute the peppers and onion in oil. Drain sausages; place eight in buns. Top each with about 1/3 cup pepper mixture. Refrigerate remaining sausages. **Yield:** 8 sandwiches plus 8 extra sausages.

Italian Sausage Spaghetti

(Pictured above)

Ready in 30 minutes or less

Spicy slices of leftover sausage and Italian seasoning lend plenty of flavor to this speedy spaghetti sauce. The chunky mixture turns a plate of ordinary pasta into a satisfying second-day supper, which no one can resist.
—Joyce Hostetler, Midway, Arkansas

 1 small onion, chopped
 1 small green pepper, chopped
 3 garlic cloves, minced
 2 teaspoons olive *or* vegetable oil
 5 cooked Italian sausage links, cut into 1/4-inch slices

1 can (28 ounces) diced tomatoes, undrained
1 can (6 ounces) tomato paste
1/4 cup water
1 tablespoon Italian seasoning
1 teaspoon sugar
1/2 teaspoon salt
1/2 teaspoon pepper
Hot cooked spaghetti

In a large saucepan, saute the onion, green pepper and garlic in oil until tender. Stir in the sausage, tomatoes, tomato paste, water and seasonings. Bring to a boil. Reduce heat; cover and simmer for 15 minutes. Serve over spaghetti. **Yield:** 5 servings.

Sausage French Bread Pizza

(Pictured at left)

Ready in 30 minutes or less

I never have pizza dough on hand, but that doesn't stop our family from enjoying pizza. I top crusty French bread with creamy Alfredo sauce, sausage and veggies. It's great to serve at a party for children or teens.
—Cherie Sweet, Evansville, Indiana

1 loaf (1 pound) unsliced French bread
1-1/3 cups prepared Alfredo sauce
3 cooked Italian sausage links, chopped
1 can (2-1/4 ounces) sliced ripe olives, drained
1 small sweet red pepper, chopped
1 small onion, chopped
1/2 cup chopped broccoli
1/2 cup chopped cauliflower
2-1/4 cups sliced fresh mushrooms
1-1/2 cups (6 ounces) shredded pizza cheese

Cut bread in half horizontally; place on a baking sheet. Spread cut sides with Alfredo sauce. Sprinkle with sausage, olives, red pepper, onion, broccoli, cauliflower, mushrooms and cheese. Bake at 350° for 15-20 minutes or until heated through. Cut into serving-size pieces. **Yield:** 8 servings.

Rich Chocolate Sauce

Ready in 30 minutes or less

I use just six ingredients to whip up a big batch of this thick chocolate sauce. It's delicious draped over scoops of ice cream. The extra sauce also can be used in other recipes.
—Carolyn Pinckney
Wilmington, North Carolina

1 cup butter (no substitutes)
4 squares (1 ounce *each*) unsweetened chocolate
3 cups sugar
1 cup baking cocoa
2 cups whipping cream
2 teaspoons vanilla extract
Ice cream

In a heavy saucepan over low heat, melt butter and chocolate. Stir in the sugar and cocoa until smooth. Gradually add cream; mix well. Cook for 10 minutes or until sugar is dissolved, stirring frequently. Remove from the heat; stir in vanilla. Serve over ice cream. Store leftover sauce in the refrigerator. **Yield:** 5 cups.

Chocolate Sauce Brownies

These moist cake-like brownies are loaded with crunchy nuts and topped with sweet frosting. If you don't have leftover chocolate sauce, substitute purchased chocolate syrup for equally tasty results.
—Vickie Overby
Wahpeton, North Dakota

1/2 cup butter *or* margarine, softened
1 cup sugar
4 eggs
1-1/2 cups Rich Chocolate Sauce (recipe on this page) *or* 1 can (16 ounces) chocolate syrup
1 teaspoon vanilla extract
1 cup plus 1 tablespoon all-purpose flour
1/2 teaspoon baking powder
1 cup chopped pecans *or* walnuts
FROSTING:
1 cup sugar
6 tablespoons milk
6 tablespoons butter *or* margarine
1/2 cup semisweet chocolate chips

In a mixing bowl, cream butter and sugar. Add the eggs, one at a time, beating well after each addition. Stir in chocolate sauce and vanilla. Combine flour and baking powder; add to the creamed mixture and mix well. Stir in nuts. Pour into a greased 15-in. x 10-in. x 1-in. baking pan. Bake at 350° for 20-25 minutes or until a toothpick inserted near the center comes out clean. Cool on a wire rack.

For frosting, combine the sugar, milk and butter in a heavy saucepan. Bring to a boil over medium heat; boil for 1 minute. Remove from the heat. Add chocolate chips; stir or whisk for 5 minutes or until smooth. Spread over brownies. **Yield:** 5 dozen.

Chocolate-Topped Fruit Cups

Ready in 15 minutes or less

The addition of orange extract gives a special taste to leftover chocolate sauce when drizzled over colorful summery fruit. I like to toss together this tropical medley, but any fruit will do. —Nancy Hill, Macomb, Illinois

3 to 4 cups sliced kiwifruit, pineapple, strawberries, banana *or* other fruit
2 to 3 tablespoons orange juice
2/3 cup Rich Chocolate Sauce (recipe on this page) *or* chocolate syrup
1/4 teaspoon orange extract

Toss fruit with orange juice; spoon into dessert dishes. In a small bowl, combine chocolate sauce and orange extract; drizzle over fruit. **Yield:** 4 servings.

Mom's Meatballs

(Pictured below and on page 99)

When I bake a large batch of these moist meatballs, I serve some for dinner and freeze the extras. —Dorothy Smith El Dorado, Arkansas

1-1/2 cups chopped onion
1/3 cup ketchup
3 tablespoons lemon juice
1 tablespoon Worcestershire sauce
3/4 cup crushed saltines (about 24 crackers)
3 pounds ground beef

In a bowl, combine the onion, ketchup, lemon juice, Worcestershire sauce and crackers. Crumble beef over mixture and mix well. Shape into 1-in. balls. Place in ungreased 15-in. x 10-in. x 1-in. baking pans. Bake, uncovered, at 400° for 10 minutes or until meat is no longer pink. Serve meatballs immediately, or refrigerate or freeze for use in other recipes. **Yield:** 7 dozen.

Meatball Minestrone

(Pictured below and on page 98)

Ready in 30 minutes or less

You don't have to thaw the frozen meatballs before adding them to this satisfying soup, so you can have it on the table in minutes. My husband and I appreciate quick meals like this. —Linda de Beaudrap, Calgary, Alberta

6 cups water
1 can (16 ounces) kidney beans, rinsed and drained
1 package (16 ounces) frozen mixed vegetables
2 tablespoons beef bouillon granules
1 tablespoon dried minced onion
1 bay leaf
1 teaspoon dried basil
1 teaspoon salt
1/2 teaspoon pepper
4 ounces spaghetti, broken into 2-inch pieces
24 cooked meatballs
1 can (14-1/2 ounces) stewed tomatoes

In a Dutch oven or soup kettle, combine the first nine ingredients. Bring to a boil; add spaghetti. Reduce heat; cover and simmer for 10 minutes or until spaghetti is tender. Add the meatballs and tomatoes; heat through. Discard bay leaf. **Yield:** 10-12 servings.

Meatball Lasagna

(Pictured below and on page 98)

My family requests that I make this savory casserole all the time. —Addella Thomas, Mt. Sterling, Illinois

2 cans (14-1/2 ounces *each*) diced tomatoes, undrained
1 can (8 ounces) tomato sauce
1 cup water
1 can (6 ounces) tomato paste
1 medium onion, chopped

Mom's Meatballs
Meatball Lasagna
Meatball Minestrone

1 garlic clove, minced
1 tablespoon dried basil
4 teaspoons dried parsley flakes
2 teaspoons sugar
Garlic salt to taste
8 uncooked lasagna noodles
24 cooked meatballs
1 egg
1 cup ricotta cheese
2 cups (8 ounces) shredded mozzarella cheese
3/4 cup grated Parmesan cheese

In a large saucepan, combine the first 10 ingredients. Bring to a boil. Reduce heat; cover and simmer for 20 minutes. Meanwhile, cook lasagna noodles according to package directions; drain. Crumble meatballs into the sauce.

In a small bowl, combine egg and ricotta cheese. Spoon 1 cup of the meat sauce into a greased 13-in. x 9-in. x 2-in. baking dish. Layer with half of the noodles, ricotta mixture, meat sauce, mozzarella and Parmesan cheeses. Repeat layers. Cover and bake at 350° for 45 minutes. Uncover; bake 5-10 minutes longer or until golden brown. Let stand for 15 minutes before cutting. **Yield:** 8-10 servings.

Basic Boiled Potatoes

Ready in 1 hour or less

Cook a big pot of red potatoes, and you'll not only have a fuss-free side dish, but a head start on other meals. Add butter and parsley to the portion you're serving immediately, then refrigerate the rest for the recipes that follow.

5 pounds medium red potatoes (about 24)
Melted butter and minced fresh parsley, optional

Place potatoes in a Dutch oven or stockpot and cover with water. Cover and bring to a boil over medium-high heat; cook for 15-30 minutes or until tender. Drain well. Serve eight potatoes with butter and parsley if desired. Refrigerate remaining potatoes. **Yield:** 4 servings plus 16 leftover potatoes.

Western Potatoes

Ready in 1 hour or less

I love to fix this saucy casserole for potluck dinners or when I need to feed a crowd. The zippy potatoes go well with grilled foods.   —Janice Thompson, Martin, Michigan

1/2 cup chopped sweet red pepper
1/2 cup chopped onion
2 tablespoons butter *or* margarine
1 can (10-3/4 ounces) condensed cream of celery soup, undiluted
1/4 cup milk
1 can (4 ounces) chopped green chilies
1/4 teaspoon salt
1/8 teaspoon cayenne pepper, optional
1/8 teaspoon hot pepper sauce

1 cup (4 ounces) shredded cheddar cheese, *divided*
8 cooked medium red potatoes, cubed

In a large saucepan or Dutch oven, saute red pepper and onion in butter until tender. Stir in the soup, milk, chilies, salt, cayenne if desired and hot pepper sauce; heat through. Stir in 3/4 cup cheese until melted. Add potatoes; stir to coat.

Transfer to a greased 11-in. x 7-in. x 2-in. baking dish. Bake, uncovered, at 350° for 20-25 minutes or until bubbly. Sprinkle with remaining cheese. Bake 5 minutes longer or until cheese is melted. Let stand for 10 minutes before serving. **Yield:** 6-8 servings.

Red Potato Salad

Ready in 30 minutes or less

I created this recipe while trying to find an alternative to the usual potato salad. Its flavor might remind you of a baked potato with all the toppings.   —Susan Martin Hollis, New Hampshire

7 cooked medium red potatoes, cubed
1/4 cup sour cream
1/4 cup mayonnaise
1/4 cup shredded cheddar cheese
2 tablespoons chopped red onion
1 bacon strip, cooked and crumbled
1-1/2 teaspoons snipped chives
Salt and pepper to taste

In a bowl, combine all of the ingredients; mix well. Refrigerate until serving. **Yield:** 4-6 servings.

Potato Omelet

Ready in 30 minutes or less

This hearty omelet is a weekend favorite, because there always seems to be that one leftover potato from Friday's dinner. —Nancy Harris, Prince George, British Columbia

1 cooked medium red potato, cubed
1/2 cup chopped fresh broccoli
2 tablespoons chopped onion
1 small tomato, seeded and chopped
1/2 teaspoon dill weed
2 tablespoons butter *or* margarine, *divided*
4 eggs
1 tablespoon water
Salt and pepper to taste
3/4 cup shredded cheddar *or* Swiss cheese

In a saucepan, saute the potato, broccoli, onion, tomato and dill in 1 tablespoon butter until tender; keep warm. In a bowl, beat the eggs, water, salt and pepper. In a skillet, melt the remaining butter; add egg mixture. As the eggs set, lift edges, letting uncooked portion flow underneath. When the eggs are completely set, remove skillet from the heat. Spoon vegetable mixture and cheese over half of the eggs; fold in half. Serve immediately. **Yield:** 2 servings.

Honey-Spice Acorn Squash

I've made this simple side dish for more than 35 years. Cinnamon and ginger give a nice spiced flavor to the moist, tender squash halves. —Alpha Wilson
Roswell, New Mexico

   1/3 cup honey
   1/4 cup butter *or* margarine, melted
   1/2 teaspoon salt
   1/4 teaspoon ground cinnamon
   1/4 teaspoon ground ginger
      4 medium acorn squash

In a bowl, combine the honey, butter, salt, cinnamon and ginger. Cut squash in half; discard the seeds. Fill squash halves with butter mixture. Place in a greased 15-in. x 10-in. x 1-in. baking pan. Cover and bake at 375° for 1 hour or until squash is tender. Uncover; bake 10 minutes longer.

Serve four squash halves. Drain and discard butter mixture from remaining squash; mash. Refrigerate squash for another use. **Yield:** 4 servings plus about 4 cups mashed squash.

Squash Waffles

Ready in 15 minutes or less

Mashed acorn squash provides the moistness in these soft golden waffles. They are a good way to sneak veggies into your family's meals without them noticing. Our kids love these, so I always make a double batch.
—Sue Gronholz, Beaver Dam, Wisconsin

      2 cups all-purpose flour
   1/4 cup sugar
      4 teaspoons baking powder
      1 teaspoon salt
   1/4 teaspoon ground cinnamon
      3 eggs
 1-1/2 cups milk
   1/2 cup mashed cooked acorn squash
      2 tablespoons butter *or* margarine, melted
Maple syrup

In a bowl, combine the flour, sugar, baking powder, salt and cinnamon. Combine the eggs, milk, squash and butter; stir into dry ingredients just until combined. Bake in a preheated waffle iron according to manufacturer's directions until golden brown. Serve with syrup. **Yield:** 10 waffles.

Acorn Squash Soup

Ready in 30 minutes or less

The recipe for this thick and creamy soup was given to me by a fellow squash lover. The attractive, rich yellow soup is especially enjoyable during the cool nights of Indian summer and gets a head start from leftover cooked squash. —Dorrene Butterfield, Chadron, Nebraska

      1 small onion, chopped
   1/4 cup chopped celery

      2 tablespoons butter *or* margarine
      2 tablespoons all-purpose flour
      1 teaspoon chicken bouillon granules
   1/2 teaspoon dill weed
   1/4 teaspoon curry powder
Dash cayenne pepper
      2 cups chicken broth
      1 can (12 ounces) evaporated milk
      3 cups mashed cooked acorn squash
Salt and pepper to taste
      5 bacon strips, cooked and crumbled

In a large saucepan, saute the onion and celery in butter. Stir in flour, bouillon, dill, curry and cayenne until blended. Gradually add broth and milk. Bring to a boil; cook and stir for 2 minutes. Add the squash, salt and pepper; heat through. In a blender, process the soup in batches until smooth. Pour into bowls; garnish with bacon. **Yield:** 6 servings.

Pork with Apricot Sauce

(Pictured at right)

Ready in 1 hour or less

To dress up pork tenderloin, I create a sweet apricot sauce mildly seasoned with ginger. It makes an impressive entree, yet leaves plenty of extra pork for meals later in the week. The sauce is also good on baked ham.
—Kris Wells, Hereford, Arizona

      4 pounds pork tenderloin
      1 jar (12 ounces) apricot preserves
   1/3 cup lemon juice
   1/3 cup ketchup
   1/4 cup sherry *or* chicken broth
      3 tablespoons honey
      1 tablespoon soy sauce
   1/8 to 1/4 teaspoon ground ginger

Place tenderloins on a rack in a shallow roasting pan. Bake, uncovered, at 450° for 30-35 minutes or until a meat thermometer reads 160°. Meanwhile, in a saucepan, combine the remaining ingredients. Cook and stir until heated through.

Slice the pork; serve 1-1/2 pounds with the apricot sauce. Refrigerate remaining pork for another use. **Yield:** 4-6 servings (2 cups sauce) plus 2-1/2 pounds leftover pork.

Chili Verde

(Pictured above right)

Ready in 15 minutes or less

Leftover pork adds heartiness to this zippy chil. It's great on a cool night with a stack of tortillas. I've taken it to many gatherings and it's always gone when the party's over. —Jo Oliverius, Alpine, California

      2 cups cubed cooked pork (about 1 pound)
      1 can (16 ounces) kidney beans, rinsed and drained

Barbecued Pork Sandwiches
Chili Verde
Pork with Apricot Sauce

1 can (15 ounces) pinto beans, rinsed and
  drained
1 can (15 ounces) chili with beans, undrained
1 can (14-1/2 ounces) stewed tomatoes
1-1/2 to 2 cups green salsa
1 large onion, chopped
2 cans (4 ounces *each*) chopped green chilies
2 garlic cloves, minced
1 tablespoon minced fresh cilantro *or* parsley
2 teaspoons ground cumin

In a large saucepan, combine all ingredients. Bring to a
boil. Reduce heat; simmer, uncovered, for 10 minutes.
Yield: 8 servings.

Barbecued Pork Sandwiches

(Pictured above)

Ready in 15 minutes or less

*I found this recipe in one of my great-aunt's cookbooks.
The original recipe called for beef, but I used leftover pork
roast I had on hand. My family loves these tangy sandwiches.* —Melissa Norris, Churubusco, Indiana

1/4 cup sugar
4 teaspoons cornstarch
1-1/2 teaspoons dried minced onion
1 teaspoon salt
1/4 teaspoon pepper
1-1/2 cups ketchup
3/4 cup water
1/4 cup cider vinegar
1/4 cup butter *or* margarine, cubed
3 tablespoons Worcestershire sauce
2 tablespoons lemon juice
1 tablespoon prepared mustard
3 cups sliced cooked pork (about 1-1/2
  pounds)
8 sandwich buns, split

In a large saucepan, combine the first 12 ingredients; stir
until blended. Bring to a boil; cook and stir for 2 minutes
or until thickened. Add pork; heat through. Serve on
buns. **Yield:** 8 servings.

Corny Corn Bread

(Pictured below)

Ready in 1 hour or less

I bake a big pan of this golden corn bread for my growing family. Each moist square is chock-full of sweet kernels. Since the recipe makes a lot, it's handy for large gatherings...or use the leftovers in the two recipes that follow.
—Diana Leskauskas, Chatham, New Jersey

- 2 cups cornmeal
- 2/3 cup all-purpose flour
- 1/4 cup sugar
- 4 teaspoons baking powder
- 1-1/2 teaspoons salt
- 1 teaspoon baking soda
- 4 eggs, beaten
- 2 cups milk
- 1 cup vegetable oil
- 1 small onion, finely chopped
- 2 cans (14-1/2 ounces *each*) whole kernel corn, drained

In a bowl, combine the cornmeal, flour, sugar, baking powder, salt and baking soda. Stir in the eggs, milk, oil and onion just until blended. Fold in the corn. Pour into a greased 13-in. x 9-in. x 2-in. baking dish. Bake at 400° for 25-30 minutes or until a toothpick inserted near the center comes out clean. Serve warm. **Yield:** 12-15 servings.

Corn Bread Salad

Plan ahead...needs to chill

My family loves this cool, crisp medley. You can fix this ahead of time and vary the vegetables to suit your tastes.
—Martha Spears, Lenoir, North Carolina

- 1 cup coarsely crumbled corn bread
- 1 can (8-3/4 ounces) whole kernel corn, drained
- 1/2 cup *each* chopped onion, cucumber, broccoli, green pepper, sweet red pepper and seeded tomato
- 1/2 cup peppercorn ranch salad dressing
- Salt and pepper to taste
- Lettuce leaves, optional

Corn Bread Chicken Bake
Corny Corn Bread
Corn Bread Salad

In a bowl, combine the corn bread, vegetables, salad dressing, salt and pepper; mix well. Cover and refrigerate for 4 hours. Serve on a lettuce-lined plate if desired. **Yield:** 6 servings.

Corn Bread Chicken Bake

To make the most of leftover corn bread, try this hearty main-dish casserole. It's moist, delicious and good on any occasion. —Madge Britton, Afton, Tennessee

1-1/4 pounds boneless skinless chicken breasts
   6 cups cubed corn bread
   8 bread slices, cubed
   1 medium onion, chopped
   2 cans (10-3/4 ounces *each*) condensed cream
      of chicken soup, undiluted
   1 cup chicken broth
   2 tablespoons butter *or* margarine, melted
1-1/2 to 2 teaspoons rubbed sage
   1 teaspoon salt
 1/2 to 1 teaspoon pepper

Place chicken in a large skillet and cover with water; bring to a boil. Reduce heat; cover and simmer for 12-14 minutes or until juices run clear. Drain and cut into cubes. In a large bowl, combine the remaining ingredients. Add chicken. Transfer to a greased 13-in. x 9-in. x 2-in. baking dish. Bake, uncovered, at 350° for 45 minutes or until heated through. **Yield:** 8-10 minutes.

Turkey with Cranberry Sauce

Plan ahead...uses slow cooker

This is a very tasty and easy way to cook a turkey breast in the slow cooker. To complete the meal, I just cook some vegetables and whip up mashed potatoes. The sweet cranberry sauce complements the turkey nicely. I like to save some cooked turkey for quick meals later in the week. —Marie Ramsden, Fairgrove, Michigan

   2 boneless skinless turkey breast halves (about
      4 pounds *each*)
   1 can (14 ounces) jellied cranberry sauce
 1/2 cup plus 2 tablespoons water, *divided*
   1 envelope onion soup mix
   2 tablespoons cornstarch

Cut each turkey breast in half; place in a 5-qt. slow cooker. In a bowl, combine the cranberry sauce, 1/2 cup water and soup mix; mix well. Pour over turkey. Cover and cook on low for 4-6 hours or until turkey is no longer pink and a meat thermometer reads 170°. Remove turkey and keep warm.

Transfer cranberry mixture to a small saucepan. In a bowl, combine the cornstarch and remaining water until smooth. Bring cranberry mixture to a boil, stir in cornstarch mixture. Cook and stir for 2 minutes or until thickened. Slice turkey; serve with cranberry sauce. **Yield:** 20-25 servings.

Crunchy Turkey Casserole

Ready in 1 hour or less

This comforting second-time-around casserole is perfect for a family supper or potluck. With its appealing crunch from water chestnuts, almonds and chow mein noodles, this economical main dish is enjoyed by all. —Lois Koogler Sidney, Ohio

   2 cans (10-3/4 ounces *each*) condensed cream
      of mushroom soup, undiluted
 1/2 cup milk *or* chicken broth
   4 cups cubed cooked turkey
   2 celery ribs, thinly sliced
   1 small onion, chopped
   1 can (8 ounces) sliced water chestnuts,
      drained and halved
   1 tablespoon soy sauce
   1 can (3 ounces) chow mein noodles
 1/2 cup slivered almonds

In a large bowl, combine soup and milk. Stir in turkey, celery, onion, water chestnuts and soy sauce. Transfer to a greased shallow 2-qt. baking dish. Sprinkle with noodles and almonds. Bake, uncovered, at 350° for 30 minutes or until heated through. **Yield:** 6-8 servings.

Curried Turkey Salad

Plan ahead...needs to chill

I blend leftover turkey with grapes, peanuts and celery, then tie it together with a creamy curry dressing. The colorful combination is great for lunch or dinner. —Jo Crouch, East Alton, Illinois

   3 cups cubed cooked turkey
1-1/2 cups seedless red grapes, halved
   4 celery ribs, chopped
 2/3 cup mayonnaise
   2 tablespoons lemon juice
   1 to 2 teaspoons curry powder
 1/2 to 1 teaspoon salt
   1 to 2 teaspoons sugar, optional
 1/2 cup salted peanuts

In a large bowl, combine the turkey, grapes and celery. In a small bowl, combine the mayonnaise, lemon juice, curry powder, salt and sugar if desired. Pour over turkey mixture and toss to coat. Cover and refrigerate for 1 hour. Just before serving, stir in the peanuts. **Yield:** 6-8 servings.

Quick Casserole

I cube leftover turkey or chicken and put a layer in a baking dish. I cover it with a box of prepared stuffing mix, then pour undiluted cream of chicken or cream of mushroom soup over it. I bake this casserole until it's warmed through. My family never complains because it doesn't taste like leftovers. —Minnie Riley Portsmouth, Virginia

Chapter 8

MAKE-AHEAD MEALS stored in the freezer can be a real convenience to cooks on action-packed weeknights.

By doing a lot of the prep work on more leisurely days, it's easy to pop an already assembled entree in the oven after a long day. Soon you have a hot and homemade dinner on the table without a lot of fuss—and all the while keeping your cool in the kitchen.

In addition to main dishes, this chapter features time-easing and appetite-appeasing recipes for soups, salads and desserts that also hurriedly give hunger the cold shoulder.

FAST FREEZER FARE. Clockwise from upper left: Flavorful Swedish Meatballs (p. 123), Italian Chicken Roll-Ups (p. 110), Breakfast Bake (p. 115) and Taco-Filled Pasta Shells (p. 127).

Tex-Mex Chicken Starter

I developed this seasoned chicken mixture to reduce meal preparation time. It's handy to keep in the freezer for a head start on three different meals. —Nancy Pease
Lafayette Hill, Pennsylvania

      1/2 cup lemon juice
      1/2 cup vegetable oil
        3 tablespoons chili powder
    1-1/2 teaspoons *each* garlic powder, ground
          cumin, dried coriander and dried oregano
      3/4 teaspoon salt
      3/4 teaspoon pepper
      1/4 to 1/2 teaspoon cayenne pepper, optional
        3 pounds boneless skinless chicken breasts,
          cut into 1-inch strips
        3 medium onions, halved and sliced into rings
        4 garlic cloves, minced

In a large resealable plastic bag, combine lemon juice, oil and seasonings. Add chicken. Seal bag and turn to coat; refrigerate for 1 hour.

In a large skillet or Dutch oven over medium-high heat, bring chicken and marinade to a boil in batches. Reduce heat; cook and stir for 6 minutes or until juices run clear. Remove chicken with tongs to a large bowl.

In the drippings, saute onions and garlic until onions are crisp-tender. Pour over chicken and mix well. Cool for 30 minutes. Divide mixture between three freezer containers; cover and freeze for up to 3 months. Thaw before using. **Yield:** 6 cups.

Tex-Mex Chicken Salad

(Pictured below)

I top packaged greens with a warm chicken and onion combo, then I toss in tomato, red pepper and shredded cheese to create this colorful salad. An easy dressing of zippy salsa and bottled vinaigrette adds the final flavorful touch. —Nancy Pease

        1 medium sweet red pepper, julienned
        2 teaspoons vegetable oil
        2 cups Tex-Mex Chicken Starter (recipe on this
          page)
        1 package (10 ounces) ready-to-serve salad
          greens
        1 medium tomato, chopped
        1 medium onion, chopped
        1 cup (4 ounces) shredded Monterey Jack
          cheese
    1-1/2 cups salsa
      1/3 cup prepared vinaigrette salad dressing

Creamy Peanut Dessert
Tex-Mex Chicken Salad

In a skillet, saute red pepper in oil until crisp-tender. Add chicken starter; heat through. In a salad bowl, combine the greens, tomato, onion and cheese. Top with chicken mixture. In a bowl, whisk salsa and dressing until blended. Serve over salad. **Yield:** 6 servings.

Tex-Mex Chicken Pasta

For a very different treatment, the spicy chicken mixture is coated with a cream sauce and served over hot cooked linguine. Sometimes I garnish this dish with fresh cilantro and crunchy fried tortilla strips. —Nancy Pease

        1 package (1 pound) linguine
        1 medium sweet red pepper, chopped
        2 teaspoons vegetable oil
        2 cups Tex-Mex Chicken Starter (recipe on
            opposite page)
        1 cup fresh *or* frozen corn
        1 cup whipping cream
    1/2 cup shredded Monterey Jack cheese
Minced fresh cilantro *or* parsley, optional

Cook the linguine according to package directions. Meanwhile, in a skillet, saute the red pepper in oil until crisp-tender. Add the chicken starter and corn; heat through. Stir in the cream and cheese. Cook and stir over medium-low heat until the cheese is melted and the sauce is thickened. Drain linguine; top with the chicken mixture. Sprinkle with cilantro if desired. **Yield:** 4-6 servings.

Tex-Mex Chicken Fajitas

To make this satisfying main dish, I simply fold the zesty chicken starter into warm flour tortillas. Then I top them with fresh tomatoes, lettuce and sour cream.
—Nancy Pease

        1 medium sweet red pepper, thinly sliced
        2 teaspoons vegetable oil
        2 cups Tex-Mex Chicken Starter (recipe on
            opposite page)
        2 tablespoons water
        8 flour tortillas (7 inches), warmed
Shredded Monterey Jack cheese, shredded lettuce,
    chopped tomato, sour cream and salsa, optional

In a skillet, saute red pepper in oil until crisp-tender. Add chicken starter and water; heat through. Spoon filling down the center of tortillas; fold in half. Serve with cheese, lettuce, tomato, sour cream and salsa if desired. **Yield:** 4 servings.

Creamy Peanut Dessert

(Pictured at left)

Anyone who tries a piece of this sweet peanut butter-flavored dessert asks for the recipe...and a second helping. We make enough to serve the 76 people who live on our grain farm, so it has to be good. —Judy Hofer
Grande Prairie, Alberta

    1-1/2 cups graham cracker crumbs (about 24
            squares)
      1/2 cup chopped salted peanuts
      1/4 cup butter *or* margarine, melted
        2 tablespoons peanut butter
FILLING:
        1 package (8 ounces) cream cheese, softened
      1/2 cup peanut butter
      1/2 cup sugar
        2 teaspoons vanilla extract
        1 carton (16 ounces) frozen whipped topping,
            thawed
        3 to 4 tablespoons chocolate syrup

In a bowl, combine cracker crumbs and peanuts. Stir in butter and peanut butter; mix well. Set aside 1/2 cup for topping. Press the remaining crumb mixture into a greased 13-in. x 9-in. x 2-in. dish. Cover and refrigerate for 30 minutes.

Meanwhile, in a mixing bowl, beat the cream cheese and peanut butter until smooth. Beat in sugar and vanilla. Fold in whipped topping; spoon over crust. Drizzle with chocolate syrup; sprinkle with reserved crumb mixture. Cover and freeze for up to 3 months. Remove from the freezer 15 minutes before serving. **Yield:** 15-20 servings.

Breakfast Bake

(Pictured on page 113)

This light fluffy egg casserole, sprinkled with tasty bacon, retains its fresh flavor after freezing. While it's great for breakfast, it's an easy-to-reheat meal for lunch or dinner, too. The recipe makes two casseroles, so you can serve one right away and freeze the second one for later.
—Kim Weaver, Olathe, Kansas

    4-1/2 cups seasoned croutons
        2 cups (8 ounces) shredded cheddar cheese
        1 medium onion, chopped
      1/4 cup chopped sweet red pepper
      1/4 cup chopped green pepper
        1 jar (4-1/2 ounces) sliced mushrooms, drained
        8 eggs
        4 cups milk
        1 teaspoon salt
        1 teaspoon ground mustard
      1/8 teaspoon pepper
        8 bacon strips, cooked and crumbled

Sprinkle croutons, cheese, onion, peppers and mushrooms into two greased 8-in. square baking dishes. In a bowl, combine the eggs, milk, salt, mustard and pepper. Slowly pour over vegetables. Sprinkle with bacon.

Cover and freeze one casserole for up to 3 months. Bake the second casserole, uncovered, at 350° for 45-50 minutes or until a knife inserted near the center comes out clean.

To use frozen casserole: Completely thaw in the refrigerator for 24-36 hours. Remove from refrigerator 30 minutes before baking. Bake, uncovered, at 350° for 50-60 minutes or until a knife inserted near center comes out clean. **Yield:** 2 casseroles (6-8 servings each).

Pasta Crab Casserole

(Pictured below)

This is an easy dish to freeze ahead for company. A yummy combination of spiral pasta, crab and sauteed veggies is coated with a buttery sauce, then covered with cheddar cheese. All that's needed to complete the meal is warm garlic bread and a tossed green salad. —Georgia Mountain
Tampa, Florida

      8 ounces uncooked spiral pasta
      2 large onions, chopped
  1/2 pound fresh mushrooms, sliced
  1/2 cup chopped green pepper
      2 garlic cloves, minced
  1/2 cup butter *or* margarine
      2 packages (8 ounces *each*) imitation
          crabmeat, chopped
  1/2 cup sour cream
      2 teaspoons salt
1-1/2 teaspoons dried basil
1-1/2 cups (6 ounces) shredded cheddar cheese

Cook pasta according to package directions. Meanwhile, in a skillet, saute onions, mushrooms, green pepper and garlic in butter until crisp-tender. Remove from the heat. Drain pasta; add to vegetable mixture. Stir in the crab, sour cream, salt and basil.

Transfer to two greased 8-in. square baking dishes. Sprinkle with the cheese. Cover and freeze one casserole for up to 1 month. Cover and bake the second casserole at 350° for 20 minutes. Uncover and bake 5 minutes longer.

To use frozen casserole: Thaw in the refrigerator for 24 hours. Remove from the refrigerator 30 minutes before baking. Cover and bake at 350° for 55-60 minutes or until heated through. **Yield:** 2 casseroles (4-6 servings each).

Pasta Crab Casserole

Chicken Broccoli Spaghetti

I serve one casserole for supper the night I make it and freeze the other for a quick dinner later.
—Jeanette Fuehring
Concordia, Missouri

1-1/2 pounds boneless skinless chicken breasts
      1 package (1 pound) spaghetti
      2 cups fresh broccoli florets
      1 can (10-3/4 ounces) condensed cream of
          chicken soup, undiluted
      1 can (10-3/4 ounces) condensed cream of
          mushroom soup, undiluted
1-1/4 cups water
      1 pound process cheese (Velveeta), cubed
  1/4 teaspoon pepper

Place chicken in a large skillet and cover with water; bring to a boil. Reduce heat; cover and simmer for 12-14 minutes or until juices run clear. Meanwhile, cook spaghetti according to package directions; drain. Drain chicken and cut into cubes; set aside.

In a saucepan, cook broccoli in a small amount of water for 5-8 minutes or until crisp-tender. Drain and set aside. In the same pan, combine soups and water. Stir in cheese; cook and stir until cheese is melted. Add the chicken, broccoli and pepper; heat through. Stir in spaghetti; mix well.

Transfer to two greased 8-in. square baking dishes. Cover and freeze for up to 3 months. Or bake, uncovered, at 350° for 30-40 minutes or until lightly browned and edges are bubbly.

To bake frozen casserole: Completely thaw in the refrigerator. Cover and bake at 350° for 45-50 minutes or until heated through. **Yield:** 2 casseroles (4-6 servings each).

Italian Chicken Roll-Ups

(Pictured on page 113)

Because I have a busy schedule, I like to keep a batch of these tender chicken rolls in the freezer. Coated with golden crumbs, they seem fancy enough for company. I've substituted mozzarella cheese for the provolone and pastrami for the ham with equally delicious results.
—Barbara Wobser, Sandusky, Ohio

☑ Uses less fat, sugar or salt. Includes Nutritional Analysis and Diabetic Exchanges.

      8 boneless skinless chicken breast halves
          (2 pounds)
      4 slices provolone cheese, halved
      8 thin slices (4 ounces) deli ham
  2/3 cup seasoned bread crumbs
  1/2 cup grated Romano *or* Parmesan cheese
  1/4 cup minced fresh parsley
  1/2 cup milk

Flatten chicken to 1/4-in. thickness. Place a slice of cheese and ham on each piece of chicken. Roll up from a short side and tuck in ends; secure with a toothpick.

In a shallow bowl, combine bread crumbs, grated cheese and parsley. Pour milk into another bowl. Dip chicken rolls in milk, then roll in crumb mixture.

Wrap and freeze four chicken roll-ups for up to 2 months. Place the remaining roll-ups, seam side down, on a greased baking sheet. Spritz chicken with nonstick cooking spray. Bake, uncovered, at 425° for 25 minutes or until juices run clear. Remove toothpicks.

To use frozen chicken: Completely thaw in the refrigerator. Unwrap roll-ups and place on a greased baking sheet. Spritz with nonstick cooking spray. Bake, uncovered, at 425° for 30 minutes or until juices run clear. **Yield:** 8 servings.

Nutritional Analysis: One serving (prepared with reduced-fat provolone cheese, lean ham and fat-free milk) equals 254 calories, 8 g fat (4 g saturated fat), 84 mg cholesterol, 772 mg sodium, 9 g carbohydrate, trace fiber, 36 g protein. **Diabetic Exchanges:** 5 very lean meat, 1 fat, 1/2 starch.

Sloppy Joes

I simmer up a big batch of this tangy sandwich filling, then freeze the extras. Just thaw and reheat it for a quick dinner. It's also good for larger gatherings.
—*Sandra Castillo, Sun Prairie, Wisconsin*

> 2 pounds ground beef
> 2 medium onions, chopped
> 2 to 3 garlic cloves, minced
> 2 cups ketchup
> 1 cup barbecue sauce
> 1/4 cup packed brown sugar
> 1/4 cup cider vinegar
> 2 tablespoons prepared mustard
> 1 teaspoon Italian seasoning
> 1 teaspoon onion powder
> 1/2 teaspoon pepper
> Hamburger buns, split

In a large skillet, cook beef, onions and garlic over medium heat until the meat is no longer pink; drain. Stir in the ketchup, barbecue sauce, brown sugar, vinegar, mustard, Italian seasoning, onion powder and pepper. Bring to a boil. Reduce heat; simmer, uncovered, for 20 minutes.

Serve about 1/2 cup meat mixture on each bun. Or cool and freeze in freezer containers for up to 3 months.

To use frozen sloppy joes: Thaw in the refrigerator; place in a saucepan and heat through. Serve on buns. **Yield:** 12 servings (about 6 cups).

Sloppy No More

A friend and I discovered a neat trick for eating sloppy joe sandwiches. We ran out of hamburger buns, so we used hot dog buns instead. To our surprise, they held the mixture better, so eating them was less messy. In fact, that's all we use now when serving sloppy joes.
—*Mary Withey, Cass City, Michigan*

Meat Loaf Miniatures

Meat Loaf Miniatures

(Pictured above)

I do not usually like meat loaf, but my family and I can't get enough of these little muffins topped with a sweet ketchup sauce. They are the perfect portion size. This recipe requires no chopping, so it's quick and easy to make a double batch and have extras for another day. They're great to give to new moms, too.
—*Joyce Wegmann
Burlington, Iowa*

> 1 cup ketchup
> 3 to 4 tablespoons packed brown sugar
> 1 teaspoon ground mustard
> 2 eggs, beaten
> 4 teaspoons Worcestershire sauce
> 3 cups Crispix cereal, crushed
> 3 teaspoons onion powder
> 1/2 to 1 teaspoon seasoned salt
> 1/2 teaspoon garlic powder
> 1/2 teaspoon pepper
> 3 pounds lean ground beef

In a large bowl, combine ketchup, brown sugar and mustard. Remove 1/2 cup for topping; set aside. Add eggs, Worcestershire sauce, cereal and seasonings to remaining ketchup mixture; mix well. Let stand for 5 minutes. Crumble beef over cereal mixture and mix well.

Press meat mixture into 18 muffin cups (about 1/3 cup each). Bake at 375° for 18-20 minutes. Drizzle with reserved ketchup mixture; bake 10 minutes longer or until meat is no longer pink and a meat thermometer reads 160°. Serve desired number of meat loaves. Cool remaining loaves; freeze. Transfer to freezer bags; freeze for up to 3 months.

To use frozen meat loaves: Completely thaw in the refrigerator. Place loaves in a greased baking dish. Bake at 350° for 30 minutes or until heated through, or cover and microwave on high for 1 minute or until heated through. **Yield:** 1-1/2 dozen.

Mocha Ice Cream Pie
Sherbet Cookie Delight

Sherbet Cookie Delight

(Pictured above)

Looking to save some time when preparing for a party? Throw together this creamy crowd-pleaser and freeze it a day or two before the event. The combination of raspberry and chocolate in this dessert is delightful, but it's also good made with lime sherbet, vanilla sandwich cookies and walnuts. —Donna Carper, South Jordan, Utah

  1/2 gallon raspberry sherbet, softened
    2 cups whipping cream
  1/3 cup confectioners' sugar
   15 chocolate cream-filled sandwich cookies
  3/4 to 1 cup chopped slivered almonds, toasted
Additional chocolate cream-filled sandwich cookies, optional

Place sherbet in a 13-in. x 9-in. x 2-in. dish. Freeze for 10 minutes. In a mixing bowl, beat cream and confectioners' sugar until stiff. Break each cookie into six pieces; fold into cream mixture with almonds. Spoon over sherbet. Cover and freeze for up to 2 months.

Remove from the freezer 15 minutes before serving. Cut into squares. Garnish with additional cookies if desired. **Yield:** 16-20 servings.

Mocha Ice Cream Pie

(Pictured above)

Topped with a crushed candy bar, this easy-to-assemble ice cream pie includes all of my husband's favorite flavors. —Ruth Turner, Aloha, Oregon

    3 cups butter pecan ice cream, softened
  1/3 cup strong brewed coffee, cooled
    1 package (3 ounces) cream cheese, softened
  1/2 cup chocolate syrup
    1 to 2 tablespoons sugar
    1 cup whipped topping
    1 graham cracker crust (9 inches)
    1 Heath candy bar (1.4 ounces), crushed

In a large mixing bowl, beat the ice cream and coffee until blended; set aside. In a small mixing bowl, beat the cream cheese, chocolate syrup and sugar. Fold in whipped topping. Remove 1/4 cup; cover and refrigerate. Add remaining chocolate mixture to ice cream mixture. Pour into crust; freeze until firm.

Pour the reserved chocolate mixture over the top and swirl gently. Cover and freeze for up to 2 months. Just before serving, sprinkle with the crushed candy bar. **Yield:** 6-8 servings.

Rhubarb Coffee Cake

I adapted several coffee cake recipes to come up with this tender treat. It's so moist and yummy that even people who usually don't care for rhubarb (like me!) ask for seconds. —Deb Quest, Saskatoon, Saskatchewan

  1/2 cup shortening
1-1/2 cups packed brown sugar
    1 egg
    2 cups all-purpose flour
    1 teaspoon baking soda
  1/2 teaspoon salt
    1 cup (8 ounces) sour cream

2 cups diced fresh *or* frozen rhubarb, thawed
TOPPING:
  1/2 cup packed brown sugar
  1/2 cup chopped walnuts
    1 tablespoon butter *or* margarine, melted
    1 teaspoon ground cinnamon

In a mixing bowl, cream shortening and brown sugar. Beat in the egg. Combine flour, baking soda and salt; add to the creamed mixture alternately with sour cream. Fold in rhubarb. Pour into two greased 8-in. square baking dishes.

    Combine the topping ingredients; sprinkle over batter. Bake at 350° for 40-45 minutes or until a toothpick inserted near the center comes out clean. Cool on wire racks. May be frozen for up to 6 months. **Yield:** 2 coffee cakes (9 servings each).

Cheese Frenchy Sandwiches

I remember enjoying these crispy golden sandwiches at a restaurant when I was a teenager. After it closed, I came up with this recipe. Now I make a batch and keep them in the freezer, ready to fry at any time. —Darlene Markel
Salem, Oregon

    1/4 cup mayonnaise
      8 slices bread
      8 slices process American cheese
      1 egg
    1/2 cup milk
    1/4 teaspoon salt
      1 cup crushed saltines (about 25 crackers)
Vegetable oil for frying

Spread mayonnaise on one side of each slice of bread. Top four slices with two cheese slices. Top with remaining bread, mayonnaise side down. Cut each sandwich into four triangles.

    In a bowl, beat the egg, milk and salt. Dip sandwiches into egg mixture, then roll in cracker crumbs. Wrap in foil and freeze for up to 1 month.

    In a skillet, heat 1 in. of oil to 375°. Fry a few frozen sandwiches at a time for 2 minutes on each side or until golden brown. **Yield:** 4 servings.

Organizing Your Freezer

- When I'm preparing recipes to freeze and enjoy later, I line my baking dish with foil. When the food is frozen, I use the foil to lift it out of the dish. Then I wrap the food or place it in a freezer bag and return it to the freezer. Not only does this save space in the freezer, it allows me to use my baking dish in the meantime. —*Tina Jacobs, Sussex, New Jersey*
- Did you ever forget you put extra chili or other leftovers in your freezer? To avoid that, I attach a list to my freezer door with the type of leftovers and the date. This way I can see at a glance what should be used or sounds good for a quick meal.
—*Di Petrick, Hoquiam, Washington*

Enchilada Casserole

(Pictured below)

This zippy Mexican casserole is a real winner at our house. It's so flavorful and filling, we usually just accompany it with rice and black beans. If your family has spicier tastes, increase the chili powder and use a medium or hot salsa.
    —*Julie Huffman, New Lebanon, Ohio*

1-1/2 pounds ground beef
    1 large onion, chopped
    1 cup water
    2 to 3 tablespoons chili powder
1-1/2 teaspoons salt
    1/2 teaspoon pepper
    1/4 teaspoon garlic powder
    2 cups salsa, *divided*
   10 flour tortillas (7 inches) cut into 3/4-inch strips, *divided*
    1 cup (8 ounces) sour cream
    2 cans (15-1/4 ounces *each*) whole kernel corn, drained
    4 cups (16 ounces) shredded mozzarella cheese

In a skillet, cook beef and onion over medium heat until meat is no longer pink; drain. Stir in water, chili powder, salt, pepper and garlic powder. Bring to a boil. Reduce heat; simmer, uncovered, for 10 minutes. Place 1/4 cup salsa each in two greased 8-in. square baking dishes. Layer each dish with a fourth of the tortillas and 1/4 cup salsa. Divide meat mixture, sour cream and corn between the two casseroles. Top with remaining tortillas, salsa and cheese.

    Cover and freeze one casserole for up to 1 month. Cover and bake the second casserole at 350° for 35 minutes. Uncover; bake 5-10 minutes longer or until heated through.

    To use frozen casserole: Thaw in the refrigerator for 24 hours. Remove from the refrigerator 30 minutes before baking. Bake as directed above. **Yield:** 2 casseroles (4-6 servings each).

Enchilada Casserole

Honey-Dijon Chicken

(Pictured below)

These moist tender chicken breasts are nicely browned, then covered in a flavorful sauce that gets its sweetness from honey and pineapple juice. It's delicious served over egg noodles. Even kids are sure to like it.

—Barbara Leventhal, Hauppauge, New York

☑ Uses less fat, sugar or salt. Includes Nutritional Analysis and Diabetic Exchanges.

   12 boneless skinless chicken breast halves
      (3 pounds)
    4 garlic cloves, minced
    2 teaspoons dried thyme
Salt and pepper to taste
    1 tablespoon vegetable oil
    2 tablespoons cornstarch
1-1/2 cups unsweetened pineapple juice
  1/2 cup water
  1/2 cup Dijon mustard
  1/3 cup honey
Hot cooked rice *or* noodles

Rub chicken with garlic and thyme. Sprinkle with salt and pepper. In a skillet, cook chicken in oil until no longer pink. In a bowl, combine cornstarch, pineapple juice and water until smooth. Stir in mustard and honey. Add to the skillet. Bring to a boil; cook and stir for 2 minutes or until thickened. Spoon half of the chicken and sauce into a greased 11-in. x 7-in. x 2-in. baking dish; cool. Cover and freeze for up to 3 months. Serve remaining chicken and sauce over rice or noodles.

To use frozen chicken: Completely thaw in refrigerator. Remove from refrigerator 30 minutes before baking. Cover and bake at 350° for 35 minutes or until heated through. **Yield:** 2 casseroles (6 servings each).

Nutritional Analysis: One serving (prepared without salt; calculated without rice) equals 198 calories, 5 g fat (1 g saturated fat), 63 mg cholesterol, 308 mg sodium, 15 g carbohydrate, trace fiber, 24 g protein. **Diabetic Exchanges:** 3-1/2 very lean meat, 1 fruit.

Honey-Dijon Chicken

Tomato Ground Beef Mix

After more than 50 years of cooking, I'm happy to find recipes like this one that help put a variety of meals on the table. The mixture is handy to keep in the freezer to jump-start three favorite main dishes.

—Lorraine Caland, Thunder Bay, Ontario

    4 pounds ground beef
    4 medium onions, chopped
    4 garlic cloves, minced
    3 cans (28 ounces *each*) diced tomatoes,
      drained
    2 cans (6 ounces *each*) tomato paste
    1 pound fresh mushrooms, sliced
    4 celery ribs, chopped
    2 tablespoons minced fresh parsley
    1 tablespoon salt
    1 tablespoon Italian seasoning
    2 to 3 teaspoons dried rosemary, crushed
    1 teaspoon pepper

In a Dutch oven or soup kettle, cook beef, onions and garlic over medium heat until meat is no longer pink; drain. Add the remaining ingredients; mix well. Bring to a boil. Reduce heat; cover and simmer for 15 minutes. Uncover; simmer 15 minutes longer. Cool.

   Freeze mixture in 2-cup portions in freezer containers. May be frozen for up to 3 months. Thaw in the refrigerator before using. **Yield:** about 16 cups.

Shepherd's Pie

(Pictured above right)

My chunky beef mix adds heartiness to this comforting supper. To give this flavorful shepherd's pie a pretty look, pipe on the mashed potatoes using a large star tip.

—Lorraine Caland

    3 cups warm mashed potatoes (prepared with
      milk and butter), *divided*
    2 medium carrots, grated
  1/4 pound fresh mushrooms, chopped
    1 tablespoon onion soup mix
    2 cups Tomato Ground Beef Mix (recipe on
      this page)
    2 tablespoons grated Parmesan cheese

In a bowl, combine 1 cup potatoes, carrots, mushrooms and soup mix. Spread in a greased 2-qt. baking dish. Top with beef mix and remaining potatoes. Sprinkle with Parmesan cheese. Bake, uncovered, at 350° for 40-50 minutes or until potatoes are lightly browned. **Yield:** 4-6 servings.

Beefy Vegetable Soup

(Pictured above right)

For a satisfying lunch or dinner, I serve bowls of this thick soup with fresh-baked bread. Brimming with colorful potatoes, celery, carrots and peas, it's easy to stir together.

—Lorraine Caland

Tangy Beef Salad
Shepherd's Pie
Beefy Vegetable Soup

2 cups Tomato Ground Beef Mix (recipe on opposite page)
3 cups tomato juice
2 cans (10-1/2 ounces *each*) condensed beef consomme, undiluted
2 medium potatoes, peeled and cubed
2 celery ribs, thinly sliced
2 large carrots, grated
1 cup fresh *or* frozen peas
1 teaspoon sugar
1/4 cup uncooked long grain rice

In a large saucepan, combine the beef mix, tomato juice, consomme, potatoes, celery, carrots, peas and sugar. Bring to a boil. Stir in rice. Reduce heat; cover and simmer for 20-25 minutes or until vegetables and rice are tender. **Yield:** 8-10 servings (about 2-1/2 quarts).

Tangy Beef Salad

(Pictured above)

Prepared Catalina dressing adds tangy-sweet flavor to this fast, fresh-tasting salad chock-full of good stuff.
—Lorraine Caland

2 cups Tomato Ground Beef Mix (recipe on opposite page)
6 cups torn iceberg lettuce
1 medium green pepper, diced
1 small onion, chopped
1 large tomato, cut into wedges

1 can (16 ounces) kidney beans, rinsed and drained
1 cup (4 ounces) shredded cheddar cheese
1 bottle (8 ounces) Catalina salad dressing
1/2 to 1 cup coarsely crushed corn chips

In a saucepan, heat beef mix. In a large bowl, combine the lettuce, green pepper, onion, tomato, beans and cheese. Add beef mix. Drizzle with dressing. Sprinkle with corn chips. Serve immediately. **Yield:** 6-8 servings.

Chocolate Sundae Pie

I keep one of these cool and creamy chocolate desserts in my freezer at all times. I've taken it to church suppers and family get-togethers. It's always a hit.
—Barbara Soyars, Danville, Virginia

4 ounces cream cheese, softened
1/2 cup sweetened condensed milk
4 teaspoons baking cocoa
1 carton (8 ounces) frozen whipped topping, thawed
1 chocolate crumb crust (9 inches)
1/2 cup chocolate syrup
1/2 cup chopped pecans

In a mixing bowl, beat the cream cheese until smooth. Add the milk and cocoa; beat until smooth. Fold in the whipped topping. Spoon into crust. Drizzle with the chocolate syrup and pecans. Cover and freeze overnight. **Yield:** 6-8 servings.

Green Bean Chicken Casserole

(Pictured below)

My husband, who claims to be strictly a meat-and-potatoes man, asked for seconds the first time I threw together this comforting all-in-one meal. My daughter and several guests raved about it, too. It's easy to assemble with cooked chicken, frozen green beans and convenient pantry items. —DeLissa Mingee, Warr Acres, Oklahoma

1 package (6 ounces) long grain and wild rice mix
4 cups cubed cooked chicken
1-3/4 cups frozen French-style green beans
1 can (10-3/4 ounces) condensed cream of mushroom soup, undiluted
1 can (10-3/4 ounces) condensed cream of chicken and broccoli soup, undiluted
1 can (4 ounces) mushroom stems and pieces, drained
2/3 cup chopped onion
2/3 cup chopped green pepper
1 envelope onion soup mix
3/4 cup shredded Colby cheese
ADDITIONAL INGREDIENT (for each casserole):
2/3 cup french-fried onions

Prepare the wild rice according to package directions. Stir in the chicken, beans, soups, mushrooms, onion, green pepper and soup mix. Spoon into two greased 1-1/2-qt. baking dishes. Sprinkle with the cheese. Cover and freeze one casserole for up to 3 months. Cover and bake the second casserole at 350° for 25-30 minutes or until heated through. Uncover and sprinkle with french-fried onions; bake 5 minutes longer or until the onions are golden.

To use frozen casserole: Completely thaw in the refrigerator. Remove from the refrigerator 30 minutes before baking. Cover and bake at 350° for 60-65 minutes or until heated through. Uncover and sprinkle with french-fried onions; bake 5 minutes longer. **Yield:** 2 casseroles (4-6 servings each).

Pizzawiches

Kids of all ages will love these pizza-flavored sandwiches. And because the meat-filled buns don't need to thaw before baking, they make an ideal after-school snack.
—Jennifer Short, Omaha, Nebraska

2 pounds ground beef
1 medium onion, chopped
2 cans (10-3/4 ounces *each*) condensed tomato soup, undiluted
1 teaspoon dried oregano
1 teaspoon chili powder
1/2 teaspoon garlic salt
1 cup (4 ounces) shredded cheddar cheese
1 cup (4 ounces) shredded mozzarella cheese
12 hamburger buns, split
3 to 4 tablespoons butter *or* margarine, melted

In a large skillet, cook beef and onion over medium heat until meat is no longer pink; drain. Stir in the soup, oregano, chili powder and garlic salt. Bring to a boil. Remove from the heat; stir in cheeses. Place about 1/3 cup meat mixture on each bun. Brush tops of buns with butter. Place on an ungreased baking sheet. Bake at 375° for 7-9 minutes or until cheese is melted. Or wrap sandwiches in foil and freeze for up to 3 months.

To bake frozen sandwiches: Place foil-wrapped buns on an ungreased baking sheet. Bake at 375° for 35-40 minutes or until heated through. **Yield:** 12 sandwiches.

Wild Rice Mushroom Chicken

I use a wild rice mix to put a tasty spin on a traditional chicken and rice bake. It's simple and delicious. It's also yummy made with leftover chicken or turkey. This casserole doesn't lose any flavor in the freezer.
—Jacqueline Thompson Graves, Lawrenceville, Georgia

2 packages (6 ounces *each*) long grain and wild rice mix
8 boneless skinless chicken breast halves
5 tablespoons butter *or* margarine, *divided*
1 large sweet red pepper, chopped
2 jars (4-1/2 ounces *each*) sliced mushrooms, drained

Prepare rice according to package directions. Meanwhile, in a large skillet, cook chicken in 3 tablespoons

Green Bean Chicken Casserole

butter for 10 minutes on each side or until browned and juices run clear. Remove chicken and keep warm.

Add remaining butter to pan drippings; saute red pepper until tender. Stir in mushrooms; heat through. Add to rice. Serve four chicken breasts with half of the rice mixture. Place remaining chicken in a greased 11-in. x 7-in. x 2-in. baking dish; top with remaining rice mixture. Cool. Cover and freeze for up to 3 months.

To use frozen dish: Thaw in the refrigerator. Cover and bake at 350° for 35-40 minutes or until heated through. **Yield:** 2 casseroles (4 servings each).

Flavorful Swedish Meatballs

(Pictured on page 112)

Our son and daughter both love to roll the ground beef and pork mixture into these moist meatballs. We enjoy them prepared in a creamy gravy. But the frozen meatballs also are great additions to soups and stews, or to stir into spaghetti sauce and serve over pasta.
—Stacy Thomas
Anchorage, Alaska

 Uses less fat, sugar or salt. Includes Nutritional Analysis and Diabetic Exchanges.

  2 eggs, lightly beaten
1/4 cup ketchup
3/4 cup dry bread crumbs
  2 tablespoons dried parsley flakes
  2 tablespoons Worcestershire sauce
  1 teaspoon onion powder
  1 teaspoon garlic powder
  1 teaspoon pepper
1/2 teaspoon salt
1/2 teaspoon chili powder
  2 pounds ground beef
  1 pound ground pork *or* turkey breast
ADDITIONAL INGREDIENTS (for *each* batch):
  1 envelope brown gravy mix
1/2 cup sour cream
Dash *each* nutmeg and pepper
Hot cooked noodles

In a bowl, combine the first 10 ingredients. Crumble meat over mixture and mix well. Shape into 1-in. balls (about 6 dozen). Place in a single layer in ungreased 15-in. x 10-in. x 1-in. baking pans. Bake at 400° for 20 minutes or until no longer pink, turning often. Cool.

Place about 35 meatballs each into freezer containers. May be frozen for up to 3 months. **Yield:** 2 batches (35 meatballs per batch).

To prepare Swedish meatballs: Completely thaw in the refrigerator. In a large skillet, prepare gravy according to package directions. Add meatballs; cover and cook for 10 minutes or until heated through. Remove from the heat; stir in sour cream, nutmeg and pepper. Serve over noodles. **Yield:** 7 servings.

Nutritional Analysis: Five Swedish meatballs (prepared with 1/2 cup egg substitute, lean ground beef, turkey breast and reduced-fat sour cream) equals 198 calories, 8 g fat (3 g saturated fat), 36 mg cholesterol, 375 mg sodium, 8 g carbohydrate, trace fiber, 23 g protein. **Diabetic Exchanges:** 3 lean meat, 1/2 starch.

Slow-Cooked Chunky Chili

Slow-Cooked Chunky Chili

(Pictured above)

Pork sausage, ground beef and plenty of beans make this chili a hearty meal-starter. I keep the versatile mixture in serving-size containers in my freezer at all times. I can quickly warm up bowls of it on cold days—or use it to fix chili dogs, chili tacos and more.
—Margie Shaw
Greenbrier, Arkansas

  1 pound ground beef
  1 pound bulk pork sausage
  4 cans (16 ounces *each*) kidney beans, rinsed and drained
  2 cans (14-1/2 ounces *each*) diced tomatoes, undrained
  2 cans (10 ounces *each*) diced tomatoes and green chilies, undrained
  1 large onion, chopped
  1 medium green pepper, chopped
  1 envelope taco seasoning
1/2 teaspoon salt
1/4 teaspoon pepper

In a skillet, cook beef and sausage over medium heat until meat is no longer pink; drain. Transfer to a 5-qt. slow cooker. Stir in the remaining ingredients. Cover and cook on high for 4-5 hours or until vegetables are tender. Serve desired amount. Cool the remaining chili; transfer to freezer bags or containers. Freeze for up to 3 months.

To use frozen chili: Thaw in the refrigerator; place in a saucepan and heat through. Add water if desired. **Yield:** 3 quarts (12 servings).

German Chocolate Cream Pie
Chicken Neapolitan

Chicken Neapolitan

(Pictured above)

I often prepare a week's worth of recipes on the weekend and freeze them so I can quickly have dinner ready for our hungry teenage boys after one of their many sports activities. Served over noodles, this moist chicken with a flavorful sauce is a favorite.
—*Joan Williams*
Baltimore, Maryland

    8 boneless skinless chicken breast halves
    2 teaspoons salt
    1 teaspoon pepper
    3 tablespoons olive *or* vegetable oil
    1 cup chopped onion
    4 garlic cloves, minced
    1 pound fresh mushrooms, quartered
    2 cans (10-3/4 ounces *each*) condensed
       tomato bisque soup, undiluted
    3/4 cup red wine *or* beef broth
    1 teaspoon dried basil
    1 teaspoon dried oregano
Hot cooked noodles *or* rice
Sliced ripe olives and minced fresh parsley,
    optional

Sprinkle chicken with salt and pepper. In a large electric skillet, heat oil over medium-high heat. Cook chicken for 8 minutes. Turn chicken; add the onion, garlic and mushrooms. Cook 8 minutes longer or until chicken juices run clear. Using a slotted spoon, remove four chicken breast halves and half of the vegetables to a greased 2-1/2-qt. baking dish. Cool.

In a bowl, whisk together the soup, wine or broth, basil and oregano; pour half over chicken in skillet. Cover and simmer for 5-10 minutes or until heated through. Serve over noodles or rice. Garnish with olives and parsley if desired.

Pour remaining soup mixture over chicken in baking dish. Cover and freeze for up to 3 months.

To use frozen chicken: Thaw in the refrigerator overnight. Cover and bake at 350° for 35-40 minutes or until heated through. Serve over noodles or rice. Garnish with olives and parsley if desired. **Yield:** 2 casseroles (4 servings each).

German Chocolate Cream Pie

(Pictured above)

This lovely light-textured pie is simple to whip up ahead of time, yet looks and tastes like you fussed. —*Genise Krause*
Sturgeon Bay, Wisconsin

    1 package (4 ounces) German sweet chocolate
1/3 cup milk
    1 package (3 ounces) cream cheese, softened
    2 tablespoons sugar
    1 carton (8 ounces) frozen whipped topping,
       thawed
    1 graham cracker crust (9 inches)
Whipped topping, fresh mint and chocolate dessert
    decorations, optional

In a saucepan over low heat, cook the chocolate and milk until chocolate is melted; stir until smooth. In a mixing bowl, beat cream cheese and sugar until smooth. Stir in chocolate mixture. Fold in whipped topping. Spoon into crust. Freeze until firm. May be frozen for up to 3 months.

Remove from the freezer 10 minutes before serving. Garnish with whipped topping, mint and chocolate dessert decorations if desired. **Yield:** 6-8 servings.

Sweet-Sour Ham Balls

Pineapple, brown sugar and mustard combine to create a tangy sauce for these savory ham and pork appetizers. I like to keep a batch on hand for card parties and other occasions. —Dorothy Pritchett, Wills Point, Texas

    4 eggs, lightly beaten
1/4 cup chopped onion
1-1/2 cups soft bread crumbs
    2 pounds ground ham
    1 pound ground pork
    2 cans (8 ounces *each*) crushed pineapple, undrained
    1 cup packed brown sugar
1/4 cup prepared mustard
    2 tablespoons cider vinegar

In a bowl, combine the eggs, onion and bread crumbs. Crumble meat over mixture and mix well. Shape into 1-1/2-in. balls. Place in two greased 13-in. x 9-in. x 2-in. baking dishes. In a blender, combine the pineapple, brown sugar, mustard and vinegar; cover and process until smooth. Pour over ham balls. Cover and freeze for up to 2 months. Or bake, uncovered, at 350° for 45-50 minutes or until a meat thermometer reads 160°, basting occasionally with sauce.

To bake frozen ham balls: Completely thaw in the refrigerator. Bake as directed. **Yield:** 2 batches (about 30 ham balls each).

Frosty Blueberry Dessert

If you're looking for a different way to showcase blueberries, try this quick-to-assemble recipe. The sweet squares make a refreshing dessert. —Evelyn Pedersen Shoreview, Minnesota

    1 can (21 ounces) blueberry pie filling
    1 can (12 ounces) evaporated milk
1/4 cup lemon juice
1/4 teaspoon almond extract
    1 carton (8 ounces) frozen whipped topping, thawed
Additional whipped topping, optional

In a bowl, combine the pie filling, milk, lemon juice and extract. Fold in the whipped topping. Spread in a greased 11-in. x 7-in. x 2-in. dish. Cover and freeze for up to 2 months.

Remove from the freezer 20 minutes before serving. Cut into squares. Garnish with additional whipped topping if desired. **Yield:** 12-15 servings.

Sausage Spaghetti Pie

(Pictured below)

I have made freezer meals for years now, and this is by far my most requested. In fact, I like to make several of these Italian pies at one time, so we can have one every week for more than a month! With its lasagna-like flavor, this dish is very tasty when it's hot from the oven.
—Linda Remillard, Bonaire, Georgia

    1 package (1 pound) spaghetti
    4 eggs, beaten
2/3 cup grated Parmesan cheese
    1 cup chopped onion
1/4 cup butter *or* margarine
    2 cups (16 ounces) sour cream
    2 teaspoons Italian seasoning
    2 pounds bulk pork sausage
    2 cups water
    1 can (12 ounces) tomato paste
    1 cup (4 ounces) shredded mozzarella cheese
1/2 cup shredded cheddar cheese

Cook spaghetti according to package directions; drain and place in a large bowl. Add eggs and Parmesan cheese. Transfer to three greased 9-in. pie plates; press mixture onto the bottom and up the sides to form a crust. Set aside.

In a saucepan, saute onion in butter until tender. Remove from the heat; stir in sour cream and Italian seasoning. Spoon into the crusts. In a skillet, cook the sausage over medium heat until no longer pink; drain. Stir in water and tomato paste. Simmer, uncovered, for 5-10 minutes or until thickened. Spoon over sour cream mixture. Sprinkle with mozzarella and cheddar cheeses. Cover and freeze two pies for up to 1 month. Cover and bake third pie at 350° for 35-40 minutes or until heated through.

To use frozen pies: Completely thaw in refrigerator. Remove from refrigerator 30 minutes before baking. Bake as directed. **Yield:** 3 pies (6 servings each).

Sausage Spaghetti Pie

Southwestern Casserole

(Pictured below)

I've been making this pleasing casserole for years. It makes a second one to freeze and enjoy later. —Joan Hallford
North Richland Hills, Texas

    1 package (7 ounces) elbow macaroni
    2 pounds ground beef
    1 large onion, chopped
    2 garlic cloves, minced
    2 cans (14-1/2 ounces *each*) diced tomatoes, undrained
    1 can (16 ounces) kidney beans, rinsed and drained
    1 can (6 ounces) tomato paste
    1 can (4 ounces) chopped green chilies, drained
1-1/2 teaspoons salt
    1 teaspoon chili powder
  1/2 teaspoon ground cumin
  1/2 teaspoon pepper
    2 cups (8 ounces) shredded Monterey Jack cheese
    2 jalapeno peppers, seeded and chopped*

Cook macaroni according to package directions. Meanwhile, in a large saucepan or Dutch oven, cook beef, onion and garlic over medium heat until meat is no longer pink; drain. Stir in the tomatoes, beans, tomato paste, chilies and seasonings. Bring to a boil. Reduce heat; simmer, uncovered, for 10 minutes. Drain macaroni; stir into beef mixture.Transfer to two greased 2-qt. baking dishes. Top with cheese and jalapenos. Cover and bake at 375° for 30 minutes. Uncover; bake 10 minutes longer or until bubbly and heated through. Serve one casserole. Cool the second casserole; cover and freeze for up to 3 months.

To use frozen casserole: Thaw in the refrigerator for 8 hours. Cover and bake at 375° for 20-25 minutes or until heated through. **Yield:** 2 casseroles (6 servings each).

*Editor's Note: When cutting or seeding hot peppers, use rubber or plastic gloves to protect your hands. Avoid touching your face.

Pumpkin Chocolate Loaf

(Pictured below)

These moist chocolate loaves, with a hint of pumpkin and spice, have been a favorite for years. They can be sliced to serve as snacks or dessert. —Kathy Gardner
Rockville, Maryland

3-1/2 cups sugar
1-1/4 cups vegetable oil
    3 eggs
    1 can (29 ounces) solid-pack pumpkin
    3 squares (1 ounce *each*) unsweetened chocolate, melted and cooled
1-1/2 teaspoons vanilla extract
3-3/4 cups all-purpose flour
1-1/2 teaspoons salt
1-1/2 teaspoons baking powder
1-1/4 teaspoons baking soda
1-1/4 teaspoons ground cinnamon
    1 to 1-1/4 teaspoons ground cloves

Southwestern Casserole
Pumpkin Chocolate Loaf

1/2 teaspoon ground nutmeg
2 cups (12 ounces) semisweet chocolate chips

In a large bowl, combine sugar and oil. Add eggs; mix well. Stir in the pumpkin, chocolate and vanilla; mix well. Combine the dry ingredients; stir into pumpkin mixture just until blended. Stir in chips.

Transfer to three greased 9-in. x 5-in. x 3-in. loaf pans. Bake at 350° for 55-65 minutes or until a toothpick inserted near the center comes out clean. Cool for 10 minutes before removing from pans to wire racks. Wrap and freeze for up to 6 months. **Yield:** 3 loaves.

Taco-Filled Pasta Shells

(Pictured on page 112)

I've been stuffing pasta shells with different fillings for years, but my family enjoys this version with taco-seasoned meat the most. The frozen shells are so convenient, because you can take out only the number you need for a single-serving lunch or family dinner.

—Marge Hodel, Roanoke, Illinois

  2 pounds ground beef
  2 envelopes taco seasoning
  1 package (8 ounces) cream cheese, cubed
24 uncooked jumbo pasta shells
1/4 cup butter *or* margarine, melted
ADDITIONAL INGREDIENTS (for each casserole):
  1 cup salsa
  1 cup taco sauce
  1 cup (4 ounces) shredded cheddar cheese
  1 cup (4 ounces) shredded Monterey Jack *or* mozzarella cheese
1-1/2 cups crushed tortilla chips
  1 cup (8 ounces) sour cream
  3 green onions, chopped

In a skillet, cook beef over medium heat until no longer pink; drain. Add taco seasoning and prepare according to package directions. Add cream cheese; cover and simmer for 5-10 minutes or until melted, stirring occasionally. Transfer to a bowl; refrigerate for 1 hour.

Cook pasta according to package directions; drain and gently toss with butter. Fill each shell with about 3 tablespoons of the meat mixture. Place 12 shells in a greased 9-in. square baking dish. Cover and freeze for up to 3 months.

To prepare remaining shells, spoon salsa into a greased 9-in. square baking dish. Top with stuffed shells and taco sauce. Cover and bake at 350° for 30 minutes. Uncover; sprinkle with cheeses and chips. Bake 15 minutes longer or until cheese is melted. Serve with sour cream and onions.

To use frozen pasta shells: Thaw in the refrigerator for 24 hours (shells will be partially frozen). Remove from baking dish. Spoon salsa into dish; arrange shells over salsa. Top with taco sauce. Cover and bake at 350° for 10 minutes. Uncover; sprinkle with cheeses and chips. Bake 15 minutes longer or until heated through and cheese is melted. Serve with sour cream and onions. **Yield:** 2 casseroles (6 servings each).

Pizza Hoagies

Pizza Hoagies

(Pictured above)

My husband and three sons love these crispy sandwiches filled with a moist pizza-flavored mixture. They're so popular, I often make them on a weekend and double the recipe. On weeknights when I'm busy or helping my son with homework, I pop the sandwiches in the oven and have a family-pleasing dinner on the table without a lot of effort. —Barbara Mery, Bothell, Washington

  1 pound ground beef
1/2 cup chopped onion
  1 can (15 ounces) pizza sauce
1/4 cup chopped ripe olives
  2 teaspoons dried basil
  1 teaspoon dried oregano
  8 hoagie *or* submarine sandwich buns *or* French rolls
  2 cups (8 ounces) shredded mozzarella cheese

In a skillet, cook beef and onion over medium heat until meat is no longer pink; drain. Stir in pizza sauce, olives, basil and oregano. Cook for 10 minutes or until heated through. Cut 1/4 in. off the top of each roll; set aside. Carefully hollow out bottom of roll, leaving a 1/4-in. shell (discard removed bread or save for another use). Sprinkle 2 tablespoons cheese inside each shell. Fill each with about 1/2 cup meat mixture. Sprinkle with remaining cheese, gently pressing down to flatten. Replace bread tops.

Individually wrap four sandwiches tightly in foil; freeze for up to 3 months. Place remaining sandwiches on a baking sheet. Bake at 375° for 15 minutes or until heated through.

To use frozen hoagies: Place foil-wrapped sandwiches on a baking sheet. Bake at 375° for 60-70 minutes or until heated through. **Yield:** 8 servings.

Chapter 9

⏱ *Easy Morning Eye-Openers*

FOR MOST families, the mad rush to get ready and out the front door for work, school and other activities starts at the crack of dawn, often leaving little time to prepare and enjoy a satisfying breakfast.

Too many times, folks either head to their nearest fast-food drive-thru or, even worse, forgo a morning meal altogether.

This chapter steers you to quick and tasty recipes that will help get your family's day off to a delicious, nutritious start in short order.

Families on the go will make time for these fast-to-fix egg dishes, beverages, French toast, fruit salads and more.

FAST RISING. Clockwise from upper left. Green 'n' Gold Egg Bake, Cranberry Brunch Punch and Apple Ham Puffs (all recipes on p. 141).

Maple French Toast Bake

(Pictured at right)

Plan ahead...start the night before

This yummy French toast casserole is a breeze to whip up the night before a busy morning. —Cindy Steffen
Cedarburg, Wisconsin

  12 slices bread, cubed
   1 package (8 ounces) cream cheese, cubed
   8 eggs
   1 cup milk
 1/2 cup maple syrup
Additional maple syrup

Arrange half of the bread cubes in a greased shallow 2-qt. baking dish. Top with the cream cheese and remaining bread. In a bowl, whisk eggs, milk and syrup; pour over bread. Cover and refrigerate overnight. Remove from the refrigerator 30 minutes before baking. Cover and bake at 350° for 30 minutes. Uncover; bake 20-25 minutes longer or until golden brown. Serve with additional syrup. **Yield:** 8 servings.

Smoky Bacon Wraps

(Pictured at right)

Ready in 1 hour or less

These cute little sausage and bacon bites are finger-licking good. They have a sweet and salty taste. —Cara Flora
Kokomo, Indiana

   1 pound sliced bacon
   1 package (16 ounces) miniature smoked
     sausage links
   1 cup packed brown sugar

Cut each bacon strip in half widthwise. Wrap one piece of bacon around each sausage. Place in a foil-lined 15-in. x 10-in. x 1-in. baking pan. Sprinkle with brown sugar. Bake, uncovered, at 400° for 30-40 minutes or until bacon is crisp and sausage is heated through. **Yield:** about 3-1/2 dozen.

Strawberry Orange Shakes

(Pictured at right)

Ready in 15 minutes or less

I found the recipe for this refreshing shake more than a dozen years ago. —Ann Smith, Weatherford, Texas

   2 cups orange juice
 1/2 cup milk
   1 package (10 ounces) frozen sweetened sliced
     strawberries, partially thawed
   1 to 3 teaspoons sugar
   1 cup ice cubes
Whole strawberries, orange wedges and mint
   sprigs, optional

In a blender, combine orange juice, milk, strawberries and sugar. Cover and process until smooth. Add the ice cubes; cover and process until mixture reaches desired consistency. Pour into glasses; garnish with a strawberry, orange wedge and mint sprig if desired. Serve immediately. **Yield:** 4 servings.

Ham 'n' Cheese Pie

Ready in 1 hour or less

One of my 4-H students entered this family-pleasing fare in a local contest. The recipe makes two easy-to-assemble pies. —Mary Anderson, De Valls Bluff, Arkansas

   2 cups cubed fully cooked ham
   2 cups (8 ounces) shredded cheddar cheese
   1 cup chopped onion
   4 eggs
   2 cups milk
   1 cup biscuit/baking mix
Dash pepper

Sprinkle ham, cheese and onion into two greased 9-in. pie plates. In a bowl, combine eggs, milk, biscuit mix and pepper until blended; pour over ham mixture. Bake at 400° for 35-40 minutes or until a knife inserted near the center comes out clean. Let stand for 5 minutes before cutting. **Yield:** 2 pies (4-6 servings each).

Applesauce Quesadillas

Ready in 15 minutes or less

Family and friends really enjoy these applesauce- and cheese-filled wedges. They're delicious with plain yogurt. —Sharon Triplett, Hendersonville, Tennessee

☑ Uses less fat, sugar or salt. Includes Nutritional Analysis and Diabetic Exchanges.

   4 flour tortillas (7 inches)
 2/3 cup unsweetened applesauce
 2/3 cup shredded cheddar cheese
Cinnamon-sugar, optional
   1 tablespoon butter *or* margarine, melted

Place two tortillas on an ungreased baking sheet. Spread each with applesauce; sprinkle with cheese and cinnamon-sugar if desired. Top with remaining tortillas. Brush tops with butter. Sprinkle with cinnamon-sugar. Bake at 400° for 7-8 minutes or until lightly browned. Cut each into eight wedges. **Yield:** 16 wedges.

Nutritional Analysis: One wedge (prepared with reduced-fat cheese and stick margarine, without cinnamon-sugar) equals 38 calories, 1 g fat (trace saturated fat), 1 mg cholesterol, 48 mg sodium, 5 g carbohydrate, trace fiber, 2 g protein. **Diabetic Exchange:** 1/2 starch.

Cooking Bacon with Little Mess

I space bacon strips on a rack in a baking pan, then bake for about 10 minutes at 400°. It cooks perfectly!
—*Julie Klein, Brooklyn, Iowa*

Maple French Toast Bake
Strawberry Orange Shakes
Smoky Bacon Wraps

Cheese Sausage Strata
Dutch Honey Syrup
Waffle Sandwiches

Cheese Sausage Strata

(Pictured at left)

Plan ahead...start the night before

Sausage provides plenty of flavor in this hearty morning casserole. It's a great addition to a brunch buffet, because it's assembled the night before to cut down on last-minute fuss. —Teresa Marchese, New Berlin, Wisconsin

```
1-1/2 pounds bulk pork sausage
    9 eggs, lightly beaten
    3 cups milk
    9 slices bread, cubed
1-1/2 cups (6 ounces) shredded cheddar cheese
  1/2 pound sliced bacon, cooked and crumbled
1-1/2 teaspoons ground mustard
```

In a large skillet, cook the sausage over medium heat until no longer pink; drain. Add the eggs, milk, bread, cheese, bacon and mustard. Transfer to a greased shallow 3-qt. baking dish. Cover and refrigerate 8 hours or overnight. Remove from the refrigerator 30 minutes before baking. Cover and bake at 350° for 60-65 minutes or until a knife inserted near the center comes out clean. **Yield:** 12-15 servings.

Dutch Honey Syrup

(Pictured at left)

Ready in 15 minutes or less

I grew up on a farm where a big breakfast was an everyday occurrence. Still, it was a special treat when Mom served this scrumptious syrup with our pancakes.
—Kathy Scott, Hemingford, Nebraska

```
1 cup sugar
1 cup corn syrup
1 cup whipping cream
1 teaspoon vanilla extract
```

In a saucepan, combine sugar, corn syrup and cream. Bring to a boil over medium heat; boil for 5 minutes or until slightly thickened, stirring occasionally. Stir in vanilla. Serve warm over pancakes, waffles or French toast. **Yield:** 2 cups.

Waffle Sandwiches

(Pictured at left)

Ready in 30 minutes or less

I start the day off right by combining three favorite breakfast foods into one. These sandwiches are delicious with regular maple syrup or homemade Dutch Honey Syrup (above). —Robyn Parrish, Daly City, California

```
    8 eggs
  1/4 teaspoon salt
Dash pepper
    1 tablespoon butter or margarine
    8 frozen waffles
    8 bacon strips, cooked and drained
Maple syrup
```

In a bowl, beat the eggs, salt and pepper. In a 9-in. skillet over medium heat, melt butter; add the egg mixture. As the eggs set, lift the edges, letting the uncooked portion flow underneath. When the eggs are completely set, cut into four wedges. Meanwhile, prepare the waffles according to package directions. For each sandwich, place one waffle on a plate. Top with an omelet wedge, two bacon strips and another waffle. Serve with syrup. **Yield:** 4 servings.

Baked Omelet

Ready in 1 hour or less

There's lots of stuff to like in these tasty baked egg squares. The family-size dish is loaded with green chilies, ham, mushrooms, green pepper and onion. —Bill Tucker Chattanooga, Tennessee

✓ Uses less fat, sugar or salt. Includes Nutritional Analysis and Diabetic Exchanges.

```
    2 cups (8 ounces) shredded Monterey Jack
      cheese
    1 medium green pepper, chopped
    1 can (4 ounces) chopped green chilies
    1 can (4 ounces) mushroom stems and pieces,
      drained or 1 cup sliced fresh mushrooms
    1 medium onion, chopped
  1/2 cup cubed fully cooked ham
   12 eggs or 3 cups egg substitute
  1/2 cup milk
    1 teaspoon hot pepper sauce
  1/4 teaspoon salt
Dash pepper
```

In a greased 13-in. x 9-in. x 2-in. baking dish, layer half of the cheese, green pepper, chilies, mushrooms, onion and ham. Repeat layers. In a bowl, beat the eggs, milk, hot pepper sauce, salt and pepper; pour over vegetable mixture. Bake, uncovered, at 350° for 25-30 minutes or until a knife inserted near the center comes out clean. **Yield:** 8 servings.

Nutritional Analysis: One serving (prepared with reduced-fat cheese, fresh mushrooms, lean ham and egg substitute) equals 193 calories, 9 g fat (4 g saturated fat), 25 mg cholesterol, 644 mg sodium, 5 g carbohydrate, 1 g fiber, 23 g protein. **Diabetic Exchanges:** 3 lean meat, 1 vegetable.

Hard-Boiled Hint

If you're planning to hard-cook eggs for breakfast, the American Egg Board suggests you follow this cooking method:

Place eggs in a single layer in a saucepan. Add water until it's at least 1 inch above the eggs. Cover the pan and bring the water to a boil. Remove from the heat and let stand, covered, for 15 minutes for large eggs. (Adjust the time up or down 3 minutes for eggs each size larger or smaller.) Immediately run cold water over eggs or place in ice water until completely cooled before using.

Sunny-Side-Up Pizza

(Pictured at right)

Ready in 30 minutes or less

Preparing this recipe is the best way I know to make sure my family takes time for breakfast. I just call out "pizza's ready!" and amazingly everyone comes to the table.
—Rose Koren, Brookfield, Illinois

> 1 prebaked thin Italian bread shell crust (10 ounces)
> 6 eggs
> 1-1/2 cups shredded mozzarella cheese
> 8 bacon strips, cooked and crumbled
> 1/2 cup chopped sweet red pepper
> 1/2 cup chopped green pepper
> 1 small onion, chopped

Place crust on a greased pizza pan. Using a 2-1/2-in. biscuit cutter, cut out six circles from crust, evenly spaced and about 1 in. from edge. (Remove circles and save for another use.) Break an egg into each hole. Sprinkle with cheese, bacon, peppers and onion. Bake at 450° for 8-10 minutes or until the eggs are completely set. **Yield:** 6 servings.

Blackberry Banana Smoothies

(Pictured at right)

Ready in 15 minutes or less

I originally began blending up this simple beverage when our young girls shied away from berries. Now they're thrilled whenever I serve it. The thick fruity drink is a refreshing treat no matter what kind of berries you use.
—Heidi Butts, Streetsboro, Ohio

✓ Uses less fat, sugar or salt. Includes Nutritional Analysis and Diabetic Exchanges.

> 2 cups orange juice
> 1/3 cup vanilla yogurt
> 2 medium ripe bananas, cut into thirds and frozen
> 1/2 cup fresh *or* frozen blackberries

In a blender, combine all ingredients. Cover and process until blended. Serve immediately. **Yield:** 4 servings.

Nutritional Analysis: One 3/4-cup serving (prepared with reduced-fat yogurt) equals 136 calories, 1 g fat (trace saturated fat), 1 mg cholesterol, 14 mg sodium, 32 g carbohydrate, 2 g fiber, 2 g protein. **Diabetic Exchanges:** 1 starch, 1 fruit.

Hash Brown Potatoes

(Pictured at right)

Ready in 1 hour or less

My mother-in-law served these buttery potatoes at brunch a while ago, and I wouldn't leave until I had the recipe. Chopped red pepper provides this stovetop side dish with a bit of color. —*Holly VeDepo, West Liberty, Iowa*

> 4 medium baking potatoes
> 1/4 cup finely chopped onion

> 1/2 medium sweet red pepper, cut into 1-inch strips, optional
> 2 tablespoons all-purpose flour
> 1/4 cup milk
> 1/4 teaspoon salt
> Pepper to taste
> 1/4 cup butter *or* margarine

Pierce the potatoes; place on a microwave-safe plate. Microwave, uncovered, on high for 12-14 minutes or until tender, turning once. Cool slightly; peel and cube. Place potatoes in a bowl; add onion and red pepper if desired. In another bowl, combine the flour, milk, salt and pepper until smooth. Pour over potato mixture and toss. In a large skillet, melt butter. Add potato mixture. Cook over medium heat for 15 minutes or until potatoes are golden brown, stirring occasionally. **Yield:** 6 servings.

Editor's Note: This recipe was tested in an 850-watt microwave.

Apple Sausage Pitas

Ready in 15 minutes or less

This is such a simple recipe, but it's my favorite breakfast for family or company. Filled with sausage and apple slices, the meal-in-hand sandwiches are great to munch on the way to work or school. —*Michelle Komaroski Pueblo, Colorado*

> 1 package (8 ounces) brown-and-serve sausage links, sliced
> 4 medium tart apples, peeled and thinly sliced
> 1/4 cup maple syrup
> 4 pita breads (6 inches), halved

In a skillet, cook the sausage and apples until sausage is heated through and the apples are tender. Add syrup and heat through. In a microwave, warm pitas on high for about 20 seconds. Fill with the sausage mixture. **Yield:** 4 servings.

Bacon Quiche

Ready in 1 hour or less

Enjoy the traditional flavor of a bacon quiche without the effort by preparing this quick version. Using baking mix means there's no need to fuss over a pastry crust.
—Helen Hoppes, Wabash, Indiana

> 3 eggs
> 1-1/2 cups milk
> 1/4 cup butter *or* margarine, melted
> 1/2 cup biscuit/baking mix
> Dash pepper
> 8 bacon strips, cooked and crumbled
> 3/4 cup shredded cheddar cheese

In a blender, combine the eggs, milk and butter. Add the biscuit mix and pepper; cover and process for 15 seconds. Pour into a greased 9-in. pie plate. Top with bacon and cheese. Bake at 350° for 30-35 minutes or until a knife inserted near the center comes out clean. Let stand for 10 minutes before cutting. **Yield:** 6-8 servings.

Blackberry Banana Smoothies
Hash Brown Potatoes
Sunny-Side-Up Pizza

Maple Cream Fruit Topping
Sausage Mushroom Quiche
Peach French Toast

Sausage Mushroom Quiche

(Pictured at left)

Ready in 1 hour or less

I created this tasty pie to get our family to eat a filling breakfast. A prepared pastry crust, Italian sausage and vegetables make this all-in-one meal a great way to start any day.   —*Shirley Biel, Tallahassee, Florida*

- 1/2 pound bulk Italian sausage, cooked and drained
- 1 cup (4 ounces) shredded Swiss cheese
- 1 can (4 ounces) mushroom stems and pieces, drained
- 1/4 cup finely chopped green pepper
- 1 tablespoon dried minced onion
- 1 frozen deep-dish pastry shell (9 inches)
- 5 eggs
- 3/4 cup half-and-half cream
- 1/2 teaspoon ground mustard
- 1/4 teaspoon salt
- 1/8 teaspoon pepper

In a bowl, combine the sausage, cheese, mushrooms, green pepper and onion; sprinkle into pastry shell. Combine the eggs, cream, mustard, salt and pepper; pour over sausage mixture.

Bake at 375° for 35-40 minutes or until a knife inserted near the center comes out clean. Let stand for 10 minutes before cutting. **Yield:** 6-8 servings.

Maple Cream Fruit Topping

(Pictured at left)

Plan ahead...needs to chill

Transform plain fruit salad into a special brunch treat with a dollop of this rich and creamy topping. The topping can be served with a variety of fruit...we think it's wonderful over sliced melons.   —*Bethel Walters*
Willow River, Minnesota

- 1 tablespoon all-purpose flour
- 3/4 cup maple syrup
- 1 egg
- 1 tablespoon butter (no substitutes)
- 1 cup whipping cream, whipped

Assorted fresh fruit

In a saucepan, combine flour, syrup and egg until smooth. Add butter. Bring to a boil; boil and stir for 2 minutes or until thickened and bubbly. Cover and refrigerate until completely cooled. Fold in whipped cream. Serve over fruit. **Yield:** about 2 cups.

Peach French Toast

(Pictured at left)

Plan ahead...start the night before

Let the aroma of baked peaches, brown sugar and cinnamon wake up your clan when you prepare this homespun

dish. Drizzle the golden syrup that bakes at the bottom of this casserole over the tender slices of French toast.
—*Geraldine Casey, Anderson, Indiana*

- 1 cup packed brown sugar
- 1/2 cup butter *or* margarine
- 2 tablespoons water
- 1 can (29 ounces) sliced peaches, drained
- 12 slices day-old French bread (3/4 inch thick)
- 5 eggs
- 1-1/2 cups milk
- 1 tablespoon vanilla extract

Ground cinnamon

In a saucepan, bring brown sugar, butter and water to a boil. Reduce heat; simmer for 10 minutes, stirring frequently. Pour into a greased 13-in. x 9-in. x 2-in. baking dish; top with peaches. Arrange bread over peaches. In a bowl, whisk the eggs, milk and vanilla; slowly pour over the bread. Cover and refrigerate for 8 hours or overnight.

Remove from the refrigerator 30 minutes before baking. Sprinkle with cinnamon. Cover and bake at 350° for 20 minutes. Uncover; bake 25-30 minutes longer or until the bread is golden brown. Serve with a spoon. **Yield:** 6-8 servings.

Breakfast Bars

I like to stash these satisfying squares in the freezer. When I need a quick breakfast or anytime snack, I simply microwave the not-too-sweet bars until they're thawed.
— *Candace Jenks, Minot, North Dakota*

- 1 cup butter *or* margarine, softened
- 1 cup packed brown sugar
- 1 cup quick-cooking oats
- 1 cup all-purpose flour
- 1 cup whole wheat flour
- 1/2 cup toasted wheat germ
- 4 eggs
- 2 cups chopped pecans
- 1 cup flaked coconut
- 1 cup (6 ounces) semisweet chocolate chips

In a mixing bowl, cream the butter and brown sugar. Combine oats, flours and wheat germ; gradually add to creamed mixture. Press into a greased 13-in. x 9-in. x 2-in. baking pan. In a small bowl, beat eggs until foamy. Stir in pecans, coconut and chocolate chips. Spread evenly over crust. Bake at 350° for 30-35 minutes or until edges are golden brown. Cool on a wire rack. Cut into bars. Store in the refrigerator. **Yield:** about 2 dozen.

Toasting Trick

I use my electric waffle iron to make French toast. A nonstick coating makes cleanup a breeze, and the pretty waffle pattern adds lots of eye appeal.
—*Sheila Shipston, Eleanor, West Virginia*

Breakfast Fruit Salad

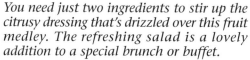

(Pictured at right)

Ready in 15 minutes or less

You need just two ingredients to stir up the citrusy dressing that's drizzled over this fruit medley. The refreshing salad is a lovely addition to a special brunch or buffet.
—Teri Albrecht, Mt. Airy, Maryland

2 cups cubed cantaloupe
2 large red apples, chopped
1 cup red *or* green grapes
1 medium firm banana, sliced
1/2 cup lemon yogurt
1 tablespoon orange juice concentrate

In a serving bowl, combine the fruit. Combine the yogurt and orange juice concentrate; drizzle over fruit. **Yield:** 6 servings.

Pineapple Orange Drink

(Pictured at right)

Ready in 15 minutes or less

Pineapple and cinnamon complement each other in this warm beverage. With pretty orange slices, this drink is a favorite at holidays. —Roxanna Colon, Norco, Louisiana

6 cups water
3 cups orange juice
1/2 cup pineapple juice
3 tablespoons lemon juice
3/4 cup sugar
1 cinnamon stick (3 inches)
1 medium navel orange, sliced, optional
Additional cinnamon sticks, optional

In a large saucepan, combine the water, juices and sugar until sugar is dissolved; add the cinnamon stick. Heat through. Serve warm or transfer to a pitcher and chill until serving. Garnish with orange slices and cinnamon sticks if desired. **Yield:** about 2-1/4 quarts.

Apple Sausage Pancakes

(Pictured at right)

Ready in 30 minutes or less

Our family enjoys these unique pancakes as often as possible. Loaded with sausage and apple, the filling flapjacks are yummy with the spiced cider syrup. —Kathi Duerr
Fulda, Minnesota

1/2 pound bulk pork sausage
1 egg
2/3 cup milk
2 tablespoons vegetable oil
1 cup pancake mix
1/2 teaspoon ground cinnamon
1/2 cup shredded peeled apple
CIDER SYRUP:
1/2 cup sugar
1 tablespoon cornstarch

1/8 teaspoon pumpkin pie spice
1 cup apple cider
1 tablespoon lemon juice
2 tablespoons butter *or* margarine

In a skillet, cook sausage over medium heat until no longer pink; drain and set aside. In a bowl, beat egg, milk and oil. Stir in pancake mix and cinnamon just until moistened. Fold in apple and sausage. Pour batter by 1/4 cupfuls onto a lightly greased hot griddle; turn when bubbles from on top. Cook until second side is golden brown. For syrup, combine the sugar, cornstarch and pumpkin pie spice in a saucepan. Gradually stir in cider and lemon juice until smooth. Bring to a boil; cook and stir for 2 minutes or until thickened. Remove from the heat; stir in butter until melted. Serve warm with the pancakes. **Yield:** 8 pancakes (1-1/3 cups syrup).

Ham 'n' Egg Skillet

Ready in 30 minutes or less

This is great for a weekend brunch or as a spur-of-the-moment supper served with toast and juice. The nicely seasoned skillet dish is hearty with ham, cheese and potatoes.
—LuEllen Spaulding, Caro, Michigan

3 medium uncooked potatoes, peeled and diced
1 tablespoon butter *or* margarine
1/4 cup chopped onion
1/4 cup chopped green pepper
1 cup cubed fully cooked ham
3 eggs, beaten
1 cup (4 ounces) shredded cheddar cheese
Salt and pepper to taste

In a skillet, saute potatoes in butter until tender and golden brown. Add the onion and green pepper; saute until crisp-tender. Add ham, eggs, cheese, salt and pepper. Cook until the eggs are completely set, stirring occasionally. **Yield:** 4 servings.

Bacon Cheese Stromboli

Ready in 30 minutes or less

Use refrigerated pizza dough to speed up preparation of this bacon-filled breakfast stromboli. Our kids love the cheesy slices with salsa and sour cream. —Abby Thompson
Madison Heights, Virginia

1 tube (10 ounces) refrigerated pizza dough
3/4 cup shredded cheddar cheese
3/4 cup shredded mozzarella cheese
5 bacon strips, cooked and crumbled
1 jar (12 ounces) salsa
Sour cream, optional

On an ungreased baking sheet, roll the dough into a 12-in. circle. On one half of dough, sprinkle cheeses and bacon to within 1/2 in. of edges. Fold dough over filling; pinch edges to seal. Bake at 425° for 9-11 minutes or until golden brown. Serve with salsa and sour cream if desired. **Yield:** 4 servings.

Breakfast Fruit Salad
Pineapple Orange Drink
Apple Sausage Pancakes

Green 'n' Gold Egg Bake
Cranberry Brunch Punch
Apple Ham Puffs

Green 'n' Gold Egg Bake

(Pictured at left and on page 128)

Ready in 1 hour or less

I need just five ingredients to assemble this pretty casserole. The firm squares have a delicious spinach flavor that's welcome at breakfast or dinner.
—*Muriel Paceleo, Montgomery, New York*

✓ Uses less fat, sugar or salt. Includes Nutritional Analysis and Diabetic Exchanges.

    1 cup seasoned bread crumbs, *divided*
    2 packages (10 ounces *each*) frozen chopped
      spinach, thawed and squeezed dry
    3 cups (24 ounces) small-curd cottage cheese
    1/2 cup grated Romano *or* Parmesan cheese
    5 eggs

Sprinkle 1/4 cup bread crumbs into a greased 8-in. square baking dish. Bake at 350° for 3-5 minutes or until golden brown. In a bowl, combine the spinach, cottage cheese, Romano cheese, three eggs and remaining crumbs. Spread over the baked crumbs. Beat remaining eggs; pour over spinach mixture.

Bake, uncovered, at 350° for 45 minutes or until a knife inserted near the center comes out clean. Let stand for 5-10 minutes before serving. **Yield:** 9 servings.

Nutritional Analysis: One 1/2-cup serving (prepared with fat-free cottage cheese and egg substitute) equals 181 calories, 6 g fat (2 g saturated fat), 127 mg cholesterol, 808 mg sodium, 15 g carbohydrate, 2 g fiber, 18 g protein. **Diabetic Exchanges:** 2 lean meat, 1 starch.

Apple Ham Puffs

(Pictured at left and on page 128)

Ready in 30 minute or less

The recipe for these individual apple-topped puffs is on a well-worn index card. For our family, it's a must for special occasions like Easter and Christmas morning.
—*Suzanne Sebaste, Lake Wylie, South Carolina*

    2 tablespoons plus 2 teaspoons all-purpose
      flour
    1/2 teaspoon salt
    8 eggs
    1 cup whipping cream
    2 cups diced fully cooked ham
    4 medium tart apples, peeled and thinly sliced
    1/4 cup butter *or* margarine
    1/4 cup sugar
    1 teaspoon ground cinnamon

In a mixing bowl, combine the flour and salt. Beat in the eggs and cream until smooth. Divide the ham among six greased 10-oz. custard cups. Top with egg mixture. Bake at 450° for 15 minutes or until a knife inserted near the center comes out clean.

Meanwhile, in a skillet, saute the apples in butter. Sprinkle with sugar and cinnamon; cook until sugar is dissolved. Spoon into the center of each puff. **Yield:** 6 servings.

Cranberry Brunch Punch

(Pictured at left and on page 129)

Ready in 15 minutes or less

For a festive party punch, you can't miss with this refreshing beverage. It's excellent served warm or cold.
—*Edie DeSpain, Logan, Utah*

    4 cups cranberry juice
    2 cups orange juice
    1 cup pineapple juice
    1/2 cup lemon juice
    1/2 cup water
    1/3 cup sugar
    1 teaspoon almond extract

In a large container, combine all ingredients; stir until sugar is dissolved. Refrigerate until serving. **Yield:** 2 quarts.

Smoked Sausage Pockets

Ready in 1 hour or less

These sausage-and-egg sandwiches are always a hit. The golden crust has a complete meal hidden inside.
—*Jan Badovinac, Harrison, Arkansas*

    2 packages (3 ounces *each*) cream cheese,
      softened
 1-1/2 teaspoons minced fresh parsley
    3/4 teaspoon seasoned salt
    1/4 teaspoon pepper
    2/3 cup shredded cheddar cheese
    2 tablespoons butter *or* margarine
    5 eggs, beaten
    1 tube (17.3 ounces) large refrigerated biscuits
    1 egg white
    1 teaspoon water
   16 miniature smoked sausage links

In a mixing bowl, combine first four ingredients. Stir in cheddar cheese; set aside. In a skillet, melt butter over medium heat. Add eggs; cook and stir until completely set. Separate biscuits into eight pieces. On a lightly floured surface, roll each piece into a 5-in. circle. On each circle, spread about 2 tablespoons cream cheese mixture to within 1/2 in. of edges.

Beat egg white and water; brush some over edges of dough. Top with scrambled eggs and two sausage links. Fold dough over; seal edges and press together with a fork. Place on an ungreased baking sheet. Brush with remaining egg white mixture. Bake at 375° for 14-16 minutes or until golden brown. **Yield:** 8 servings.

Fast Breakfast

When I make oatmeal, I prepare a double batch for two breakfasts. I put the oatmeal in bowls, cover them with plastic wrap, stack them in the refrigerator and microwave when needed on another morning.
—*June Dearman, Canton, Ohio*

Chapter 10

Casseroles and Skillet Suppers

CONVENIENCE is often the key to success in the kitchen for cooks who don't have much time on their hands.

That's what makes all-in-one casseroles so appealing. This "comfort" food is packed with a blend of meat, vegetables, pasta, rice and sauces and can be tossed together in a matter of minutes. In no time, you'll be dishing out hearty helpings of a scrumptious main course or side dish.

For even faster preparation, turn to this chapter's assortment of skillet suppers that require just a single pan and only a few minutes to make. You'll surely file these in-a-dash dinners under "F" for filling, flavorful...and flat-out fast!

CLASSIC CASSEROLE. Colorful Vegetable Bake (p. 146).

Catchall Casseroles

THE COMFORTING CASSEROLES highlighted here are long on convenience—many can be easily assembled while you're waiting for the oven to preheat.

Pepperoni Macaroni

(Pictured below)

Ready in 1 hour or less

This hearty pasta bake is jazzed up with pepperoni, sausage and olives for pizza-like flavor. It can be assembled ahead of time, then baked right before serving.
—Marlene Mohr, Cincinnati, Ohio

2-1/2 cups uncooked elbow macaroni
   1 pound bulk Italian sausage
   1 large onion, chopped
   1 can (15 ounces) pizza sauce
   1 can (8 ounces) tomato sauce
1/3 cup milk
   1 package (3-1/2 ounces) sliced pepperoni, halved
   1 jar (4-1/2 ounces) sliced mushrooms, drained
   1 can (2-1/4 ounces) sliced ripe olives, drained
   1 cup (4 ounces) shredded mozzarella cheese

Cook macaroni according to package directions. Meanwhile, in a skillet over medium heat, cook sausage and onion until meat is no longer pink; drain. Drain macaroni. In a large bowl, combine pizza sauce, tomato sauce and milk. Stir in sausage mixture, macaroni, pepperoni, mushrooms and olives.

Transfer to a greased 13-in. x 9-in. x 2-in. baking dish. Cover and bake at 350° for 30 minutes. Uncover; sprinkle with cheese. Bake 10-15 minutes longer or until bubbly and cheese is melted. **Yield:** 8-10 servings.

Chicken Potato Delight

I make the most of leftover chicken and convenience items to create this hearty casserole. It's quick to prepare and comforting. —Nicki Ussery, Mt. Sterling, Illinois

   1 can (10-3/4 ounces) condensed cream of chicken soup, undiluted
3/4 cup sour cream
1/4 cup milk
   1 cup cubed cooked chicken
2-1/2 cups (10 ounces) shredded cheddar cheese, *divided*
2-1/2 cups frozen shredded hash brown potatoes, thawed
   1 can (2.8 ounces) french-fried onions
   1 cup crushed sour cream and onion potato chips

In a bowl, combine soup, sour cream, milk, chicken and 1-1/4 cups cheese. Spread three-fourths of the mixture in a greased 2-qt. baking dish. Sprinkle hash browns over the top and press down lightly. Spread with the remaining soup mixture.

Sprinkle with onions, potato chips and remaining cheese. Bake, uncovered, at 350° for 1 hour or until bubbly. Let stand for 5-10 minutes before serving. **Yield:** 6 servings.

Busy Day Ham Bake

Ready in 1 hour or less

This eye-catching casserole conveniently calls for just a few everyday ingredients. It's great with crusty rolls and fruit salad. Sometimes I replace the ham with cooked turkey for a change of pace. —Brenda Daugherty
Lake City, Florida

   1 can (10-3/4 ounces) condensed cheddar cheese soup, undiluted
   1 package (10 ounces) frozen chopped broccoli, thawed
   1 cup cooked rice
   1 cup cubed fully cooked ham
1/4 cup sour cream
1/4 cup mayonnaise
1/4 cup dry bread crumbs
   1 tablespoon butter *or* margarine, melted

In a large bowl, combine the first six ingredients. Transfer to a greased 1-1/2-qt. baking dish. Toss bread crumbs and butter; sprinkle over the top. Bake, uncovered, at 350° for 30 minutes or until heated through. **Yield:** 4 servings.

Pepperoni Macaroni

Creamy Chow Mein Chicken

Ready in 1 hour or less

Looking for something different to take to potlucks? Look no further. This tasty alternative turns basic pantry items into a tempting Oriental delight. —Mary Edwards
Vacaville, California

1 package (6 ounces) chow mein noodles, *divided*
2 cups cubed cooked chicken
4 celery ribs, chopped
1 large onion, chopped
1 can (10-3/4 ounces) condensed cream of mushroom soup, undiluted
1 can (10-3/4 ounces) condensed cream of chicken soup, undiluted
1 cup milk
1 can (8 ounces) sliced water chestnuts, undrained
1 jar (4-1/2 ounces) sliced mushrooms, undrained
1/2 cup cashews

Creamy Corned Beef Bake

Sprinkle half of the chow mein noodles into a greased 13-in. x 9-in. x 2-in. baking dish. In a bowl, combine the chicken, celery, onion, soups, milk, water chestnuts, mushrooms and cashews. Spoon over the noodles; top with remaining noodles. Bake, uncovered, at 325° for 35-40 minutes or until heated through. **Yield:** 6-8 servings.

Chicken and Rice

Are you often crunched for time? Consider this fast-to-fix chicken and rice bake. After popping it in the oven, you can toss together a salad and have dinner on the table in no time.
—Doris Barb
El Dorado, Kansas

6 boneless skinless chicken breast halves
1-1/2 cups uncooked instant rice
1/2 cup boiling water
1 can (10-3/4 ounces) condensed cream of chicken soup, undiluted
1 can (10-3/4 ounces) condensed cream of celery soup, undiluted
2 tablespoons onion soup mix
1 package (10 ounces) frozen peas, thawed
1/2 cup minced fresh parsley

Place chicken in a greased 13-in. x 9-in. x 2-in. baking dish. In a bowl, combine the rice and water. In another bowl, combine the soups, soup mix and peas; stir into rice mixture. Spread over the chicken. Cover and bake at 350° for 40 minutes. Uncover; sprinkle with parsley. Bake 10-15 minutes longer or until the chicken juices run clear. **Yield:** 6 servings.

Creamy Corned Beef Bake

(Pictured above)

I remember my grandmother making this comforting casserole when my family visited her. Now that I'm married, I fix it for my husband and me as an easy meal.
—Brenda Myers, Overland Park, Kansas

1-1/2 cups cubed cooked corned beef *or* 1 can (12 ounces) cooked corned beef
1 can (10-3/4 ounces) condensed cream of chicken soup, undiluted
8 ounces cheddar cheese, cubed
1 package (7 ounces) small shell pasta, cooked and drained
1 cup milk
1/2 cup chopped onion
2 bread slices, cubed
2 tablespoons butter *or* margarine, melted

In a bowl, combine the first six ingredients. Transfer to a greased 2-qt. baking dish. Toss bread cubes with butter; sprinkle over top. Bake, uncovered, at 350° for 40-45 minutes or until golden brown. Let stand for 10 minutes before serving. **Yield:** 4 servings.

Quick Casserole

When preparing pasta casseroles that call for onions and celery, add the chopped vegetables to the boiling water along with the noodles. This technique only uses one pan. —Barb Weimer, Valparaiso, Indiana

Colorful Vegetable Bake

Cheesy Beef Tetrazzini

Ready in 1 hour or less

If your family is anything like mine, it won't be long before this hearty casserole becomes a favorite. My gang loves it for the flavor. I love it because it's simple to make and can be assembled the night before serving. —Gladys Van Beek
Lynden, Washington

1-1/2 pounds ground beef
  1 small onion, chopped
  1 can (15 ounces) tomato sauce
  1/2 to 1 teaspoon salt
  1/4 teaspoon pepper
  1 package (8 ounces) cream cheese, softened
  1 cup small-curd cottage cheese
  1 cup (8 ounces) sour cream
  1/4 cup chopped green pepper
  1/4 cup thinly sliced green onions
  1 package (7 ounces) thin spaghetti, cooked and drained
  1/4 cup grated Parmesan cheese

In a large skillet over medium heat, cook beef and onion until meat is no longer pink; drain. Stir in tomato sauce, salt and pepper; bring to a boil. Reduce heat; simmer, uncovered, for 5 minutes.

In a mixing bowl, beat cream cheese, cottage cheese and sour cream until blended. Stir in green pepper, onions and spaghetti. Transfer to a greased 2-1/2-qt. baking dish. Top with beef mixture. Sprinkle with Parmesan cheese. Bake, uncovered, at 350° for 30-35 minutes or until bubbly. **Yield:** 6 servings.

Colorful Vegetable Bake

(Pictured above and on page 142)

My sister gave me the recipe for this side dish years ago, and it's become a favorite in our household. Chock-full of colorful veggies, it's delicious and feeds a crowd.
—Betty Brown, Buckley, Washington

✓ Uses less fat, sugar or salt. Includes Nutritional Analysis and Diabetic Exchanges.

  3 cups frozen cut green beans, thawed and drained
  2 medium green peppers, chopped
  6 plum tomatoes, chopped and seeded
  2 to 3 cups (8 to 12 ounces) shredded cheddar cheese
  3 cups chopped zucchini
  1 cup biscuit/baking mix
  1/2 teaspoon salt
  1/2 teaspoon cayenne pepper
  6 eggs
  1 cup milk

Place beans and peppers in a greased 13-in. x 9-in. x 2-in. baking dish. Top with tomatoes, cheese and zucchini. In a bowl, combine the biscuit mix, salt, cayenne, eggs and milk just until moistened. Pour over the vegetables.

Bake, uncovered, at 350° for 55-60 minutes or until puffed and a knife inserted near the center comes out clean. Let stand for 10 minutes before serving. **Yield:** 12 servings.

Nutritional Analysis: One serving (prepared with 2 cups reduced-fat cheese, reduced-fat biscuit/baking mix, 1-1/2 cups egg substitute and fat-free milk) equals 146 calories, 5 g fat (2 g saturated fat), 11 mg cholesterol, 400 mg sodium, 15 g carbohydrate, 2 g fiber, 12 g protein. **Diabetic Exchanges:** 2 vegetable, 1 lean meat, 1 fat.

Classic Crunchy Chicken

I keep 2-cup portions of cooked wild rice in the freezer so I always have the ingredients for this casserole on hand for "emergency" dinners. It gets its crunch from water chestnuts, almonds and a sprinkling of french-fried onions.
—Barbara Wagener, Waconia, Minnesota

✓ Uses less fat, sugar or salt. Includes Nutritional Analysis and Diabetic Exchanges.

  1 can (10-3/4 ounces) condensed cream of chicken soup, undiluted
  1 can (10 ounces) chunk white chicken,* drained
  1 can (8 ounces) sliced water chestnuts, drained
  2 cups cooked wild rice
3/4 cup milk
  2 to 4 tablespoons slivered almonds
  1/2 teaspoon dried thyme
  1/4 teaspoon pepper
  1/2 cup french-fried onions, optional

In a bowl, combine the first eight ingredients; mix well. Pour into a greased shallow 1-1/2-qt. baking dish. Cover and bake at 350° for 30 minutes. Uncover; top with onions if desired. Bake 5-10 minutes longer or until bubbly. **Yield:** 4 servings.

Nutritional Analysis: One 1-cup serving (prepared with reduced-fat soup and 2 tablespoons almonds and without onions) equals 276 calories, 5 g fat (1 g saturated fat), 38 mg cholesterol, 615 mg sodium, 36 g carbohydrate, 5 g fiber, 21 g protein. **Diabetic Exchanges:** 2 starch, 2 lean meat, 1 vegetable.

*Editor's Note: 2 cups cubed cooked chicken may be substituted for the canned chicken.

Easy Chicken Divan

Ready in 1 hour or less

I got this recipe from a co-worker and then made a few changes to it to suit my family's tastes. It's excellent with corn bread. —Violet Englert, Leicester, New York

    3 cups cubed cooked chicken
    1/2 teaspoon salt
    1/4 teaspoon pepper
    1 package (10 ounces) frozen broccoli florets, thawed
    2 cans (10-3/4 ounces *each*) condensed cream of chicken soup, undiluted
    1/3 cup mayonnaise*
    1/4 cup milk
    2 cups (8 ounces) shredded taco *or* Mexican cheese blend *or* cheddar cheese, *divided*

In a greased shallow 2-1/2-qt. baking dish, combine the chicken, salt and pepper. Top with the broccoli. In a bowl, combine the soup, mayonnaise, milk and 1-1/2 cups cheese; pour over broccoli. Sprinkle with the remaining cheese. Bake, uncovered, at 375° for 20-25 minutes or until heated through. **Yield:** 4-6 servings.

*Editor's Note: Reduced-fat or fat-free mayonnaise may not be substituted for the regular mayonnaise.

Pineapple Ham and Rice

Ready in 1 hour or less

As a parent of two teens with completely different tastes in food, it's always a challenge to cook something that they'll both enjoy. I created this casserole to use up leftovers, and it turned out to be one of their favorites. —Donald Courtney Farmington Hills, Michigan

    2 cups cooked rice
    2 cups cubed fully cooked ham
    1 can (20 ounces) crushed pineapple, undrained
    1/2 cup packed brown sugar
    1 tablespoon lemon juice
    1 teaspoon ground mustard

In a bowl, combine all of the ingredients. Spoon into a greased 1-1/2-qt. baking dish. Bake, uncovered, at 350° for 25-30 minutes or until heated through. **Yield:** 4 servings.

Zucchini Tomato Casserole

(Pictured below)

Ready in 1 hour or less

Even people who don't like zucchini can't seem to get enough of this full-flavored side dish. I always bring it to family gatherings and potlucks because it goes well with any entree. —Cathy Johnston, Ranchester, Wyoming

    6 medium zucchini, diced (about 6 cups)
    4 tablespoons butter *or* margarine, melted, *divided*
    2 medium tomatoes, diced
    1 cup (4 ounces) shredded cheddar cheese
    1 cup cubed process cheese (Velveeta)
    1 cup soft bread crumbs
    2 eggs, beaten
    2 tablespoons dried minced onion
    1 tablespoon dried parsley flakes
    1 teaspoon dried basil
    1/2 teaspoon garlic powder
    1/2 teaspoon salt
    1/2 teaspoon pepper

In a large skillet, saute zucchini in 2 tablespoons butter until crisp-tender; drain well. In a bowl, combine the remaining ingredients. Stir in the zucchini and remaining butter. Transfer to an ungreased 2-qt. baking dish. Bake, uncovered, at 350° for 25-30 minutes or until bubbly. Let stand for 10 minutes before serving. **Yield:** 8 servings.

Zucchini Tomato Casserole

Grandma's Rice Dish

(Pictured below)

Ready in 1 hour or less

My grandmother often made this casserole when I was young. I forgot about it until I found myself adding the same ingredients to leftover rice one day. The memories came flooding back, and I've made this recipe regularly since then. —Lorna Moore, Glendora, California

   1 pound ground beef
   1 small onion, chopped
1/2 cup chopped green pepper
   2 cups cooked long grain rice
   1 can (14-1/2 ounces) diced tomatoes, undrained
   1 can (11 ounces) whole kernel corn, drained
   1 can (2-1/4 ounces) sliced ripe olives, drained
   6 bacon strips, cooked and crumbled
   2 teaspoons chili powder
   1 teaspoon garlic powder
   1 teaspoon salt
1-1/2 cups (6 ounces) shredded cheddar cheese, *divided*
1/2 cup dry bread crumbs
   1 tablespoon butter *or* margarine, melted

In a skillet, cook beef, onion and green pepper over medium heat until meat is no longer pink; drain. Stir in the rice, tomatoes, corn, olives, bacon, chili powder, garlic powder and salt. Bring to a boil; remove from the heat. Add 1 cup of cheese; stir until melted.

Transfer to a greased 11-in. x 7-in. x 2-in. baking dish. Sprinkle with remaining cheese. Toss bread crumbs with butter; sprinkle over cheese. Bake, uncovered, at 350° for 15-20 minutes or until cheese is melted. **Yield:** 4-6 servings.

Grandma's Rice Dish

Tasty Hamburger Casserole

Just a few ingredients are needed to pack a lot of flavor into this hearty ground beef bake. My daughter received this recipe from a missionary when they were both serving in Zambia. —Faith Richards, Tampa, Florida

5 medium potatoes, peeled and sliced
1 small onion, chopped
1 pound lean ground beef
1 can (10-3/4 ounces) condensed cream of mushroom soup, undiluted
1 can (10-1/2 ounces) condensed vegetarian vegetable soup, undiluted
1 cup crushed potato chips

In a greased 13-in. x 9-in. x 2-in. baking dish, layer potatoes and onion. Crumble beef over onion. Spread soups over beef. Cover and bake at 350° for 55 minutes. Uncover; sprinkle with chips. Bake 20 minutes more or until meat is no longer pink. **Yield:** 4-6 servings.

Chicken Celery Casserole

Ready in 1 hour or less

When time is short and I have many guests, this is the recipe I reach for. The comforting dish has a crunchy topping and can be on the table in under an hour. —Ruth Andrewson, Peck, Idaho

4 cups cubed cooked chicken
8 celery ribs, thinly sliced
1 cup chopped pecans
1 small onion, diced
2 cups mayonnaise*
1 tablespoon lemon juice
1 teaspoon garlic salt
1 cup crushed potato chips
1 cup crushed french-fried onions
1/2 cup shredded cheddar cheese

In a bowl, combine the chicken, celery, pecans and diced onion. Combine the mayonnaise, lemon juice and garlic salt; add to chicken mixture and mix well. Transfer to a greased 13-in. x 9-in. x 2-in. baking dish. Bake, uncovered, at 350° for 20 minutes. Top with potato chips, french-fried onions and cheese. Bake 5-10 minutes longer or until chips are crisp and cheese is melted. **Yield:** 8 servings.

*Editor's Note: Light or fat-free mayonnaise may not be substituted for regular mayonnaise.

Pour-a-Pan Pizza

Ready in 1 hour or less

This main dish is great on Friday nights when the kids want pizza and I don't have much time to make a homemade crust. —Sally Seidel, Banner, Wyoming

1 cup all-purpose flour
1 teaspoon salt
1/2 teaspoon garlic powder
1/8 teaspoon pepper

2/3 cup milk
2 eggs, beaten
1 pound bulk Italian sausage
1 package (3-1/2 ounces) sliced pepperoni
2 tablespoons chopped onion
2 tablespoons chopped green pepper
1 cup pizza sauce
2 cups (8 ounces) shredded mozzarella cheese

In a bowl, combine the flour, salt, garlic powder and pepper; stir in milk and eggs. Pour into a greased 13-in. x 9-in. x 2-in. baking pan. In a skillet, cook sausage over medium heat until no longer pink; drain. Sprinkle over the crust. Top with pepperoni, onion and green pepper.

Bake, uncovered, at 425° for 15 minutes or until a toothpick inserted near the center comes out clean. Spread with the pizza sauce and sprinkle with the cheese. Bake 5 minutes longer or until cheese is melted. Let stand for 5 minutes before cutting. **Yield:** 6-8 servings.

Broccoli Cauliflower Bake

Butter Baked Carrots

Ready in 1 hour or less

If you're looking for a quick-to-fix side dish, look no further. I cover colorful carrots in a rich cream sauce before finishing the casserole with a crispy and golden bread crumb topping. —Gladys De Boer Castleford, Idaho

1-1/2 pounds carrots, cut into 3-inch julienne strips
1/4 cup chopped celery
2 tablespoons chopped onion
6 tablespoons butter *or* margarine, *divided*
3 tablespoons all-purpose flour
1/2 teaspoon salt
1/8 teaspoon pepper
1-1/2 cups milk
1/2 cup dry bread crumbs

Place 1 in. of water in a saucepan; add carrots. Cover and bring to a boil. Reduce heat; cook for 8-10 minutes or until crisp-tender.

Meanwhile, in another saucepan, saute celery and onion in 3 tablespoons butter until tender. Stir in flour, salt and pepper until blended. Gradually whisk in milk. Bring to a boil; cook and stir for 2 minutes or until thickened.

Drain carrots; place in a greased 8-in. square baking dish. Top with the white sauce. Melt the remaining butter and toss with bread crumbs. Sprinkle over the top. Bake, uncovered, at 350° for 25-30 minutes or until mixture is bubbly and topping is golden brown. **Yield:** 6-8 servings.

Broccoli Cauliflower Bake

(Pictured above)

Ready in 1 hour or less

Guests always ask for the recipe whenever I serve these vegetables. And because this dish is so easy to prepare, I have plenty of time to finish up the rest of our dinner. —Erika Anderson, Wausau, Wisconsin

1 medium head cauliflower, broken into small florets
1 pound fresh broccoli, broken into small florets
1-1/2 cups shredded Monterey Jack cheese
1 cup (8 ounces) sour cream
1 can (4 ounces) chopped green chilies, drained
4 tablespoons butter *or* margarine, melted, *divided*
1 teaspoon salt
1/4 teaspoon pepper
3/4 cup crushed seasoned stuffing

Add 1 in. of water to a Dutch oven; add cauliflower and broccoli. Bring to a boil. Reduce heat; cover and cook for 7 minutes or until tender. Meanwhile, in a bowl, combine the cheese, sour cream, chilies, 2 tablespoons butter, salt and pepper. Drain vegetables well; gently fold in cheese mixture.

Transfer to a greased 2-1/2 qt. baking dish. Toss stuffing and remaining butter; sprinkle over vegetables. Bake, uncovered, at 350° for 20-25 minutes or until heated through. **Yield:** 6-8 servings.

Dash in the Pan

YOU'VE come to the right place if "going steady" with your stove doesn't fit your active lifestyle. These mouth-watering main dish recipes take less than an hour to put on the table.

Chicken Rice Skillet

(Pictured below)

Ready in 1 hour or less

Pleasant seasonings and plenty of vegetables highlight this traditional chicken and rice pairing. Leftovers are great re-heated in the microwave. —Jan Balata
Kilkenny, Minnesota

      4 boneless skinless chicken breast halves
          (1 pound)
      2 tablespoons olive *or* vegetable oil
      2 celery ribs, chopped
      4 green onions, thinly sliced
  1/2 cup chopped sweet red pepper
  1/2 cup chopped sweet yellow pepper
      2 cups frozen green beans, thawed
      1 jar (4-1/2 ounces) sliced mushrooms, drained
      1 can (14-1/2 ounces) chicken broth
  1/4 cup water
      3 garlic cloves, minced
  1/2 teaspoon salt
  1/4 teaspoon lemon-pepper seasoning
  1/8 teaspoon garlic powder
  1/8 teaspoon pepper
      2 cups uncooked instant rice

In a large skillet over medium heat, brown chicken in oil for about 4 minutes on each side or until almost tender. Add celery, onions and peppers; cook until vegetables are crisp-tender. Stir in the beans and mushrooms;

Chicken Rice Skillet

cook until chicken juices run clear.

Stir in the broth, water and seasonings. Bring to a boil. Stir in rice; cover and remove from the heat. Let stand for 5 minutes or until rice is tender; fluff rice with a fork. **Yield:** 4 servings.

Spicy Jambalaya

Ready in 30 minutes or less

Just the right amount of seasonings spice up this memorable main dish. It's loaded with zesty sausage, tender chicken and tasty shrimp, too. —Amy Chop
Eufaula, Alabama

      1 package (4.4 ounces) chicken-flavored rice
          and sauce mix
  1/2 pound boneless skinless chicken breasts,
          cubed
  1/4 pound bulk Italian sausage
      2 garlic cloves, minced
      2 tablespoons butter *or* margarine
      1 medium green pepper, chopped
      1 celery rib, thinly sliced
      1 small onion, chopped
      1 medium tomato, chopped
  1/2 to 1 teaspoon ground cumin
  1/2 teaspoon dried oregano
  1/2 teaspoon salt
  1/2 teaspoon pepper
  1/8 teaspoon hot pepper sauce
  1/4 pound uncooked medium shrimp, peeled,
          deveined and chopped

Prepare rice mix according to package directions. Meanwhile, in a large skillet, cook chicken, sausage and garlic in butter for 5 minutes. Add the green pepper, celery and onion; cook and stir until meat is no longer pink and vegetables are tender.

Stir in tomato and seasonings; heat through. Add the shrimp; cook and stir for 3-4 minutes or until shrimp turn pink. Serve with the prepared rice. **Yield:** 4 servings.

Pantry Skillet

Ready in 30 minutes or less

An envelope of soup mix gives fast flavor to this beefy stovetop supper. I came up with this all-in-one dish by using whatever ingredients I had on hand. —Susie Smith
Sauk Village, Illinois

      1 pound ground beef
      1 can (10-3/4 ounces) condensed tomato soup,
          undiluted
1-1/2 cups water
      1 envelope onion mushroom soup mix
  1/2 pound fresh mushrooms, sliced
1-1/2 cups frozen cut green beans
      3 medium carrots, grated
      1 cup cooked rice
      2 slices process American cheese, cut into
          strips

In a large skillet over medium heat, cook beef until no longer pink; drain. Stir in soup, water and soup mix; mix well. Stir in mushrooms, beans, carrots and rice. Bring to a boil. Reduce heat; cover and simmer for 5-7 minutes or until beans are tender. Top with cheese; cover and let stand until cheese melts. **Yield:** 6 servings.

Chicken with Blueberry Sauce

Ready in 1 hour or less

This is one of my best recipes. Blueberries are mixed with apricot jam and mustard to create a sweet tangy sauce for tender chicken. —*Thomas Jewell Sr. Avenel, New Jersey*

☑ Uses less fat, sugar or salt. Includes Nutritional Analysis and Diabetic Exchanges.

> 4 boneless skinless chicken breast halves (1 pound)
> 1 tablespoon vegetable oil
> 1/2 cup apricot preserves *or* fruit spread
> 3 tablespoons Dijon mustard
> 1/3 cup white wine vinegar *or* cider vinegar
> 1/2 cup fresh *or* frozen blueberries
> Hot cooked rice, optional

In a large skillet over medium heat, cook chicken in oil for about 4 minutes on each side or until lightly browned. Combine preserves and mustard; spoon over chicken. Reduce heat; cover and simmer for 15 minutes or until chicken juices run clear.

With a slotted spoon, remove chicken and keep warm. Add vinegar to skillet; bring to a boil. Reduce heat; simmer, uncovered, for 3 minutes or until sauce is reduced by one-third, stirring occasionally. Stir in blueberries. Serve over chicken and rice if desired. **Yield:** 4 servings.

Nutritional Analysis: One serving (prepared with 100% apricot fruit spread; calculated without rice) equals 264 calories, 6 g fat (1 g saturated fat), 66 mg cholesterol, 360 mg sodium, 26 g carbohydrate, 1 g fiber, 27 g protein. **Diabetic Exchanges:** 3 lean meat, 1-1/2 fruit.

Zucchini Mexicali

Ready in 30 minutes or less

Try this swift skillet sensation when you're strapped for time. This vegetable side dish goes with practically any meal. For more south-of-the-border flavor, simply increase the taco sauce. —*Pauletta Bushnell, Lebanon, Oregon*

> 1/4 cup vegetable oil
> 1 medium zucchini, thinly sliced
> 1 large onion, chopped
> 1 large carrot, coarsely shredded
> 3/4 cup chopped celery
> 1/2 cup julienned green pepper
> 1/2 teaspoon garlic salt
> 1/4 teaspoon dried basil
> 1/3 cup taco sauce
> 2 teaspoons prepared mustard
> 2 medium tomatoes, cut into wedges

Asparagus Beef Stroganoff

In a large skillet, combine the first eight ingredients. Cover and cook over medium-high heat for 5 minutes. Stir in the taco sauce and mustard; top with tomato wedges. Cook, uncovered, for 5 minutes or until heated through. **Yield:** 6 servings.

Asparagus Beef Stroganoff

(Pictured above)

I prepare this tasty all-in-one dish for the presentation and flavor it offers. It's a great way to incorporate vegetables into a meal. —*Becky Upchurch, Waco, Texas*

> 1 pound boneless beef round steak, cut into 3-inch strips
> 1 medium onion, chopped
> 2 to 3 tablespoons butter *or* margarine
> 1 jar (4-1/2 ounces) sliced mushrooms, drained
> 1/2 teaspoon salt
> 1/4 teaspoon pepper
> 1/4 teaspoon ground mustard
> 1 package (8 ounces) cream cheese, cubed
> 2/3 cup milk
> 1-1/2 pounds fresh asparagus spears, trimmed
> Hot cooked noodles
> Paprika

In a large skillet over medium heat, cook beef and onion in butter until meat is no longer pink. Add the mushrooms, salt, pepper and mustard. Reduce heat; cover and simmer for 1 hour or until meat is tender. Add cream cheese and milk; cook and stir until cream cheese is melted.

In another skillet, cook asparagus in a small amount of water for 4 minutes or until crisp-tender; drain. On a serving platter, arrange asparagus over noodles; top with beef mixture. Sprinkle with paprika. **Yield:** 5 servings.

Spicy Pepper Penne

Spicy Pepper Penne

(Pictured above)

Ready in 30 minutes or less

I sure know how to bring a bit of Sicily to the supper table! My combination of pepperoni, pasta and peppers adds a little kick to your dinner lineup. —*Candace Greene Columbiana, Ohio*

  1 package (16 ounces) penne *or* tube pasta
1/2 teaspoon minced fresh rosemary *or*
      1/8 teaspoon dried rosemary, crushed
  2 packages (3-1/2 ounces *each*) sliced
      pepperoni, halved
1/2 cup sliced pepperoncinis*
  1 jar (7 ounces) roasted sweet red peppers,
      drained and chopped
3-1/2 cups boiling water
1/2 cup whipping cream
1/2 cup grated Parmesan cheese

In a large skillet, layer the pasta, rosemary, pepperoni, pepperoncinis and red peppers. Add water; bring to a boil. Reduce heat; cover and simmer for 12 minutes or until pasta is tender. Add cream and Parmesan cheese; toss to coat. **Yield:** 8 servings.

  *Editor's Note: Look for pepperoncinis (pickled peppers) in the pickle and olive section of your grocery store.

Dilled Ham on Rice

Ready in 30 minutes or less

When expecting company, I fix this main dish featuring ham in a comforting sauce seasoned with mustard and dill. It makes a nice presentation with a tossed green salad, corn and dinner rolls. —*Debby Cole Wolf Creek, Oregon*

  4 cups julienned fully cooked ham
  2 tablespoons butter *or* margarine
  2 celery ribs, thinly sliced
  1 medium onion, chopped
  1 cup sliced fresh mushrooms
  1 can (10-3/4 ounces) condensed cream of
      chicken soup, undiluted
1/4 to 1/2 cup milk
  2 teaspoons prepared mustard
1/4 to 1/2 teaspoon dill weed
1/2 cup sour cream
Hot cooked rice

In a large skillet, cook the ham in butter until lightly browned. Add celery, onion and mushrooms; saute until tender. Combine the soup, milk, mustard and dill; add to the ham mixture. Bring to a boil; reduce heat. Stir in sour cream; heat through. Serve over the rice. **Yield:** 6 servings.

Mexicana Skillet Stew

Ready in 1 hour or less

I bring the Southwest to my table with this super supper. I sometimes serve this hearty mixture in warm flour tortillas. Add some scrambled eggs, and you have a terrific breakfast burrito. —*Bobby Walker Lake Isabella, California*

☑ Uses less fat, sugar or salt. Includes Nutritional Analysis and Diabetic Exchanges.

  1 pound ground beef
  2 large potatoes, peeled and cut into 1/2-inch
      cubes
  1 large onion, chopped
  1 large green pepper, chopped
  1 can (4 ounces) mushroom stems and pieces,
      undrained
3/4 cup picante sauce
Garlic salt *or* powder and pepper to taste

In a skillet, cook beef, potatoes, onion, green pepper and mushrooms over medium heat until meat is no longer pink; drain. Reduce heat; cover and simmer for 20 minutes or until potatoes are tender, stirring occasionally. Add picante sauce, garlic salt and pepper. Cook 5 minutes longer or until heated through. **Yield:** 4 servings.

  Nutritional Analysis: One 1-cup serving (prepared with lean ground beef and garlic powder) equals 344 calories, 11 g fat (4 g saturated fat), 41 mg cholesterol, 527 mg sodium, 35 g carbohydrate, 4 g fiber, 27 g protein. **Diabetic Exchanges:** 3-1/2 meat, 1-1/2 starch, 1 vegetable.

Chicken with Veggies

Ready in 30 minutes or less

Tender chicken and bright vegetables combine deliciously in this blend. I sometimes serve it over wild rice for an interesting change. —*Frankie Allen Mann Warrior, Alabama*

2 tablespoons all-purpose flour
2 teaspoons garlic powder, *divided*
3/4 teaspoon salt, *divided*
1/2 teaspoon pepper, *divided*
1 pound boneless skinless chicken breasts, cubed
2 tablespoons olive *or* vegetable oil
1/4 cup white wine *or* chicken broth
1/4 cup prepared Italian salad dressing
1 large green pepper, julienned
2 large carrots, thinly sliced
1 cup sliced fresh mushrooms
1 small onion, chopped
1 tablespoon butter *or* stick margarine, optional
Hot cooked rice

In a large resealable plastic bag, combine the flour, 1 teaspoon garlic powder, 1/4 teaspoon salt and 1/4 teaspoon pepper. Add chicken and shake to coat. In a skillet, saute chicken in oil until browned. Add wine or broth, salad dressing, green pepper, carrots, mushrooms, onion, butter if desired and remaining garlic powder, salt and pepper. Cover and cook until vegetables are tender. Serve over rice. **Yield:** 4 servings.

Nutritional Analysis: One serving (prepared with fat-free salad dressing; calculated without butter and rice) equals 265 calories, 10 g fat (2 g saturated fat), 63 mg cholesterol, 730 mg sodium, 16 g carbohydrate, 3 g fiber, 26 g protein. **Diabetic Exchanges:** 3 lean meat, 1 starch, 1 vegetable.

Honey Pork and Carrots

Ready in 30 minutes or less

This tangy island-inspired entree is both smoky and sweet. Since everything cooks together, there's little to clean up, which gives me more time to do other things. The serving size is perfect for folks who cook for one or two people, but the recipe can easily be doubled.
—Susan Morrissey, St. Croix, Virgin Islands

1 pound pork tenderloin, thinly sliced
4 medium carrots, thinly sliced
3 tablespoons butter *or* margarine
3 celery ribs, thinly sliced
1 small onion, thinly sliced
3 tablespoons honey
1 to 2 teaspoons liquid smoke, optional
1 garlic clove, minced
1/4 to 1/2 teaspoon ground ginger
1/4 teaspoon rubbed sage
1/4 teaspoon salt
1/4 teaspoon pepper

In a skillet or wok, stir-fry pork and carrots in butter for 3-5 minutes. Stir in the remaining ingredients. Cover and simmer for 10-12 minutes or until the pork is no longer pink and the vegetables are tender, stirring occasionally. **Yield:** 3-4 servings.

Polynesian Sausage Supper

(Pictured below)

Ready in 30 minutes or less

When my sister first served us this unusual medley, I couldn't believe how good it was because she had thrown it together so quickly. Sweet pineapple really adds to the taste.
—Laura McCarthy, Butte, Montana

1 pound fully cooked smoked sausage, cut into 1/2-inch slices
1 medium onion, chopped
1 medium green pepper, cut into 1-inch chunks
1 can (14-1/2 ounces) diced tomatoes, undrained
1/2 cup beef broth
1 tablespoon brown sugar
1/4 teaspoon garlic powder
1/4 teaspoon pepper
1 can (20 ounces) unsweetened pineapple chunks
2 tablespoons cornstarch
Hot cooked rice

In a skillet, cook the sausage, onion and green pepper until the sausage is lightly browned; drain. Add tomatoes, broth, brown sugar, garlic powder and pepper. Drain pineapple, reserving juice. Stir pineapple into sausage mixture. Bring to a boil; cook, uncovered, for 5 minutes.

Combine cornstarch and reserved pineapple juice until smooth; gradually add to sausage mixture. Bring to a boil; cook and stir for 2 minutes or until thickened. Serve over rice. **Yield:** 6 servings.

Nutritional Analysis: One 1-cup serving (prepared with reduced-fat turkey sausage; calculated without rice) equals 201 calories, 7 g fat (2 g saturated fat), 48 mg cholesterol, 851 mg sodium, 22 g carbohydrate, 3 g fiber, 13 g protein. **Diabetic Exchanges:** 2 lean meat, 1 vegetable, 1 fruit.

Polynesian Sausage Supper

Almond Chicken Stir-Fry

(Pictured below and on cover)

Ready in 30 minutes or less

Almonds and water chestnuts add crunch to this speedy supper. It's great with frozen stir-fry vegetables, too.
—Denise Uhlenhake, Ossian, Iowa

✓ Uses less fat, sugar or salt. Includes Nutritional Analysis and Diabetic Exchanges.

1-1/2 pounds boneless skinless chicken breasts, cut into strips
   3 tablespoons canola oil
1-1/2 cups cauliflowerets
1-1/2 cups broccoli florets
  3/4 cup julienned carrots
  1/2 cup chopped celery
  1/4 cup chopped sweet red pepper
   1 can (8 ounces) sliced water chestnuts, drained
   3 cups chicken broth
   3 tablespoons soy sauce
  1/3 cup cornstarch
  1/2 cup cold water
Hot cooked rice, optional
  1/3 to 1/2 cup slivered almonds, toasted

In a skillet or wok, stir-fry chicken in oil until no longer pink. Stir in the vegetables, broth and soy sauce. Bring to a boil. Reduce heat to low; cover and cook until vegetables are crisp-tender. Combine cornstarch and water until smooth; stir into chicken mixture. Bring to a boil; cook and stir for 2 minutes or until thickened. Serve over rice if desired. Sprinkle with almonds. **Yield:** 6 servings.

Nutritional Analysis: One 1-cup serving (prepared with reduced-sodium soy sauce and 1/3 cup almonds; calculated without rice) equals 331 calories, 15 g fat (2 g saturated fat), 66 mg cholesterol, 843 mg sodium, 19 g carbohydrate, 5 g fiber, 29 g protein. **Diabetic Exchanges:** 3-1/2 lean meat, 1 starch, 1 vegetable, 1 fat.

Almond Chicken Stir-Fry

Taco Noodle Dinner

Ready in 1 hour or less

Taco seasoning provides the family-appealing flavor in this speedy skillet supper. The sour cream topping enhances this combination nicely. —Marcy Cella, L'Anse, Michigan

   1 pound ground beef
  1/4 cup chopped onion
  3/4 cup water
   1 envelope taco seasoning
  1/2 teaspoon salt
   1 can (4 ounces) mushroom stems and pieces, drained
   3 cups uncooked fine egg noodles
2-1/2 to 3 cups tomato juice
   1 cup (8 ounces) sour cream
   1 tablespoon minced fresh parsley

In a large skillet over medium heat, cook the beef and onion until meat is no longer pink; drain. Stir in the water, taco seasoning and salt. Reduce heat; simmer for 2-3 minutes. Add the mushrooms. Sprinkle noodles over the top. Pour tomato juice over the noodles and stir gently. Cover and simmer for 20-25 minutes or until noodles are tender.

Remove from the heat. Combine the sour cream and parsley; spread over the top. Cover and let stand for 5 minutes. **Yield:** 6 servings.

Crab Rice Primavera

Ready in 30 minutes or less

I try to take a lunch to work as often as possible. This colorful tasty entree reheats so well that its leftovers have become one of my all-time brown-bag favorites.
—Michelle Armistead, Marlboro, New Jersey

✓ Uses less fat, sugar or salt. Includes Nutritional Analysis and Diabetic Exchanges.

1-1/2 cups frozen vegetable blend (broccoli, red pepper, onions and mushrooms)
  1/4 cup water
1-1/2 cups milk
  1/2 cup grated Parmesan cheese
   2 tablespoons butter *or* stick margarine
   1 teaspoon dried basil
  1/2 teaspoon garlic powder
  3/4 pound flaked imitation crabmeat
1-1/2 cups uncooked instant rice

In a large saucepan, bring vegetables and water to a boil. Reduce heat; cover and simmer for 3 minutes. Stir in milk, Parmesan cheese, butter, basil, garlic powder and crab. Bring to a boil. Stir in rice. Remove from the heat; cover and let stand for 5 minutes. Fluff with a fork. Serve immediately. **Yield:** 5 servings.

Nutritional Analysis: One 1-cup serving (prepared with fat-free milk) equals 325 calories, 9 g fat (5 g saturated fat), 55 mg cholesterol, 483 mg sodium, 41 g carbohydrate, 1 g fiber, 19 g protein. **Diabetic Exchanges:** 2 starch, 2 lean meat, 1 vegetable, 1/2 fat.

Meaty Zucchini Stew

Ready in 1 hour or less

If you're going to a potluck, make sure to take along this savory stew. Slices of zucchini are mixed with ground beef, pork sausage and an assortment of other vegetables to create this one-dish wonder.
—*Phyllis Bertin*
Thunder Bay, Ontario

✓ Uses less fat, sugar or salt. Includes Nutritional Analysis and Diabetic Exchanges.

- 1 pound ground beef
- 1 pound bulk pork sausage
- 2 cans (14-1/2 ounces *each*) diced tomatoes
- 2 medium green peppers, cut into 1/2-inch pieces
- 2 cups thinly sliced celery
- 1 cup chopped onion
- 6 medium zucchini, halved and cut into 1/2-inch slices
- 1 cup tomato juice
- 1 teaspoon salt
- 1 teaspoon Italian seasoning
- 1 teaspoon dried oregano
- Grated Parmesan cheese, optional

In a Dutch oven or large saucepan over medium heat, cook beef and sausage until no longer pink; drain and set aside. Drain tomatoes, reserving the juice; set tomatoes aside. In the same pan, combine the peppers, celery, onion and reserved juice. Cover and cook over medium heat for 10 minutes.

Add the meat, tomatoes, zucchini, tomato juice and seasonings. Cover and cook for 15 minutes or until zucchini is tender, stirring occasionally. Garnish with cheese if desired. **Yield:** 12 servings.

Nutritional Analysis: One 1-cup serving (prepared with lean ground beef and turkey sausage; calculated without Parmesan cheese) equals 175 calories, 8 g fat (3 g saturated fat), 45 mg cholesterol, 630 mg sodium, 10 g carbohydrate, 3 g fiber, 17 g protein. **Diabetic Exchanges:** 2 lean meat, 2 vegetable.

Cranberry Chicken

Ready in 30 minutes or less

If you're looking for something fast but different for dinner, try this unique entree. I combine chili sauce, brown sugar and cranberry sauce to give the tender chicken a welcome zip.
—*Brigitte Schaller, Flemington, Missouri*

- 1-1/4 pounds boneless skinless chicken breasts, cut into strips
- 1 large onion, chopped
- 3 tablespoons butter *or* margarine
- 1-1/3 cups chili sauce
- 3/4 cup whole-berry cranberry sauce
- 1/3 cup packed brown sugar
- 3 tablespoons cider vinegar
- 4-1/2 teaspoons Worcestershire sauce
- 4-1/2 teaspoons prepared mustard
- Hot cooked rice *or* noodles

In a large skillet, saute the chicken and onion in butter until chicken is no longer pink. Add the chili sauce, cranberry sauce, brown sugar, vinegar, Worcestershire sauce and mustard. Simmer, uncovered, for 5 minutes. Serve over rice or noodles. **Yield:** 6 servings.

Pork Chop Supper

Pork Chop Supper

(Pictured above)

Ready in 1 hour or less

My husband, Clark, and I reserve this recipe for Sundays after the grandkids have gone home and we're too tired to prepare a big meal. It's comforting and quick.
—*Kathy Thompson, Port Orange, Florida*

- 1 tablespoon butter *or* margarine
- 4 pork loin chops (1/2 inch thick)
- 3 medium red potatoes, cut into small wedges
- 2 cups baby carrots *or* 3 medium carrots, sliced 1/2 inch thick
- 1 medium onion, quartered
- 1 can (10-3/4 ounces) condensed cream of mushroom soup, undiluted
- 1/4 cup water

In a skillet over medium heat, melt butter. Brown chops for 3 minutes on each side. Add the potatoes, carrots and onion. Combine soup and water; pour over the top. Cover and simmer for 15-20 minutes or until the vegetables are tender. **Yield:** 4 servings.

Don't Burn the Butter

Here's a little trick to prevent butter from burning in a skillet when frying or browning foods: Add a teaspoon of oil to the skillet along with the butter. It works perfectly every time.
—*Anna Reich*
Albuquerque, New Mexico

 Breads in a Jiffy

FLUFFY rolls...savory loaves...fruit-filled muffins...sweet coffee cakes. Cooks agree breads make great accompaniments to a delicious breakfast, hearty lunch or speedy supper.

You can enjoy home-baked items such as these without spending hours in the kitchen.

The quick breads featured here promise oven-fresh flavor without the work traditional yeast breads require. Just mix the batter, fill the pan and pop it in the oven.

Don't think you have time to make old-fashioned home-made bread from scratch? Think again!

Thanks to today's bread machines, yummy yeast breads can be quick and easy, too.

A BOUNTY OF BREAD. Top to bottom: Swiss Onion Drop Biscuits and Herb Biscuit Loaf (both recipes on p. 164).

157

Oven-Fresh Quick Breads

WITH NO kneading or rising times required, quick breads are a boon to busy cooks. Whether you want sweet or savory, you're sure to find a recipe to suit your taste and time.

Angel Rolls

(Pictured at right)

Ready in 1 hour or less

Delight family and friends with these soft tender yeast rolls that are done in a jiffy, thanks to quick-rise yeast. My family especially likes them with sausage gravy.
—Debbie Graber, Eureka, Nevada

3-1/2 cups bread flour
    2 tablespoons sugar
    1 package (1/4 ounce) quick-rise yeast
1-1/4 teaspoons salt
    1 teaspoon baking powder
    1/2 teaspoon baking soda
    1 cup warm buttermilk* (120° to 130°)
    1/2 cup vegetable oil
    1/3 cup warm water (120° to 130°)
Melted butter *or* margarine

In a mixing bowl, combine 1-1/2 cups flour, sugar, yeast, salt, baking powder and baking soda. Add the buttermilk, oil and water; beat until moistened. Stir in enough remaining flour to form a soft dough. Turn onto a floured surface and knead until smooth and elastic, about 4-6 minutes. Cover and let rest for 10 minutes.

Roll out to 1/2-in. thickness; cut with a 2-1/2-in. biscuit cutter. Place on a greased baking sheet. Bake at 400° for 15-18 minutes or until golden brown. Brush tops with butter. **Yield:** 14 rolls.

*Editor's Note: Warm buttermilk will appear curdled.

Provolone Corn Loaf

(Pictured above right)

The flavors of cheese, pepper and sage come through in slices of this zippy corn bread that's best served right out of the oven. Warm slices are great with a simple soup.
—Norma Pederson, Colman, South Dakota

✓ Uses less fat, sugar or salt. Includes Nutritional Analysis and Diabetic Exchanges.

    2 teaspoons plus 1 cup cornmeal, *divided*
1-1/2 cups all-purpose flour
    1 tablespoon minced fresh sage *or* 1 teaspoon rubbed sage
    2 teaspoons baking powder
    1 teaspoon salt
    3/4 teaspoon coarsely ground pepper
    1/2 teaspoon baking soda
    1/8 teaspoon cayenne pepper, optional
    2 eggs
1-1/4 cups buttermilk
    1/4 cup olive *or* vegetable oil
    1 cup (4 ounces) shredded provolone *or* mozzarella cheese

Sprinkle 2 teaspoons of cornmeal on the bottom and sides of a greased 8-in. x 4-in. x 2-in. loaf pan; set aside. In a large bowl, combine the flour, sage, baking powder, salt, pepper, baking soda, cayenne if desired and remaining cornmeal. In another bowl, beat the eggs, buttermilk and oil. Stir into dry ingredients just until moistened. Fold in cheese.

Pour into prepared pan. Bake at 350° for 40-50 minutes or until a toothpick inserted near the center comes out clean. Cool for 10 minutes before removing from pan to a wire rack. Refrigerate leftovers. **Yield:** 1 loaf (16 slices).

Nutritional Analysis: One slice (prepared with part-skim mozzarella cheese) equals 138 calories, 6 g fat (2 g saturated fat), 31 mg cholesterol, 275 mg sodium, 16 g carbohydrate, 1 g fiber, 5 g protein. **Diabetic Exchanges:** 1 starch, 1/2 meat, 1/2 fat.

Cinnamon Cheese Roll-Ups

Ready in 30 minutes or less

Basic white bread is spread with a sweet creamy filling to make these scrumptious roll-ups. They're very easy to assemble yet taste extra special.
—Marie Delffs
Shelbyville, Tennessee

    1 loaf (16 ounces) thinly sliced white bread, crusts removed
    1 package (8 ounces) cream cheese, softened
    1 egg yolk
    3/4 cup confectioners' sugar
    1 cup sugar
1-1/2 teaspoons ground cinnamon
    3/4 cup butter *or* margarine, melted

Flatten bread with a rolling pin. In a mixing bowl, combine cream cheese, egg yolk and confectioners' sugar. In another bowl, combine sugar and cinnamon; set aside. Spread about 1 tablespoon of cheese mixture on each slice of bread. Roll up, jelly-roll style. Dip in melted butter, then in cinnamon-sugar. Place on an ungreased baking sheet. Bake at 350° for 20 minutes or until golden brown. **Yield:** 16 roll-ups.

Morning Glory Muffins

Ready in 1 hour or less

These moist muffins are chock-full of goodies like coconut, apple, pineapple, carrots and nuts. They're delicious for breakfast or lunch. I get many requests for the recipe.
—Evelyn Winchester, Hilton, New York

Angel Rolls
Provolone Corn Loaf

2-1/2 cups all-purpose flour
1-1/4 cups sugar
    3 teaspoons ground cinnamon
    2 teaspoons baking soda
1/2 teaspoon salt
    3 eggs
3/4 cup applesauce
1/2 cup vegetable oil
    1 teaspoon vanilla extract
    2 cups grated carrots
    1 medium tart apple, peeled and grated
    1 can (8 ounces) crushed pineapple, drained
1/2 cup flaked coconut
1/2 cup raisins
1/2 cup chopped walnuts

In a large bowl, combine the first five ingredients. In another bowl, combine the eggs, applesauce, oil and vanilla. Stir into the dry ingredients just until moistened (batter will be thick). Stir in the carrots, apple, pineapple, coconut, raisins and nuts. Fill greased or paper-lined muffin cups two-thirds full. Bake at 350° for 20-24 minutes or until a toothpick comes out clean. Cool for 5 minutes before removing from pans to wire racks. **Yield:** 2 dozen.

Chocolate Banana Bread

Nothing tops old-fashioned banana bread, except maybe this chocolate version. Each slice is studded with nuts.
—Connie Deke, DeWitt, Nebraska

1/2 cup butter *or* margarine, softened
    1 cup sugar
    2 eggs
    1 cup mashed ripe bananas (about 2 medium)
1/4 cup milk
    1 teaspoon vanilla extract
    2 cups all-purpose flour
1/4 cup baking cocoa
    1 teaspoon baking soda
    1 teaspoon salt
1/2 cup chopped nuts, optional

In a mixing bowl, cream butter and sugar. Add eggs, bananas, milk and vanilla. Combine the flour, cocoa, baking soda and salt; add to the banana mixture and mix just until combined. Fold in nuts if desired. Spoon into a greased 9-in. x 5-in. x 3-in. loaf pan. Bake at 350° for 60-65 minutes or until a toothpick inserted near the center comes out clean. Cool for 10 minutes before removing from pan to a wire rack. **Yield:** 1 loaf.

Easy Dumplings

Looking for a fuss-free way to make delicious dumplings? Try using a package of refrigerated biscuits. There are usually 10 biscuits to a tube, so you may want to drop five into your simmering kettle of soup or stew, and bake the rest into biscuits to serve alongside.
—Tom Scott, Clearlake, California

Chocolate Banana Muffins

(Pictured below)

Ready in 1 hour or less

I serve these tender muffins with jam for breakfast or with ice cream and chocolate syrup for dessert.
—Stephanie Kienzle, North Miami Beach, Florida

  1/2 cup butter *or* margarine, softened
  1/2 cup sugar
  1/2 cup packed brown sugar
    2 eggs
1-1/2 cups mashed ripe bananas (about 3 large)
    3 teaspoons vanilla extract
    2 cups all-purpose flour
    3 teaspoons baking soda
    1 cup chopped walnuts
    1 cup (6 ounces) semisweet chocolate chips

In a mixing bowl, cream butter and sugars. Beat in eggs, bananas and vanilla. Combine flour and baking soda; add to creamed mixture just until combined. Stir in the walnuts and chocolate chips. Fill greased or paper-lined muffin cups half full. Bake at 350° for 15-20 minutes or until a toothpick comes out clean. Cool for 5 minutes before removing from pans to wire racks. **Yield:** 2 dozen.

Cinnamon Sticky Buns

(Pictured below)

Ready in 1 hour or less

I enjoy giving these sweet treats to friends for a "just because" gift. They reheat in the microwave very well.   —Jean Edwards
Indianapolis, Indiana

    1 cup packed brown sugar
  1/2 cup corn syrup
  1/2 cup butter *or* margarine
    1 cup coarsely chopped pecans
  1/2 cup sugar
    2 tablespoons ground cinnamon
    2 tubes (17.3 ounces *each*) large refrigerated biscuits

In a saucepan, combine the brown sugar, corn syrup and butter; cook and stir until sugar is dissolved. Add the pecans. Spoon into a greased 13-in. x 9-in. x 2-in. baking pan. In a shallow bowl, combine sugar and cinnamon. Cut each biscuit in half; dip in cinnamon-sugar. Place, cut side down, over brown sugar mixture. Bake at 375° for 25-30 minutes or until golden brown. Invert onto a serving plate; serve warm. **Yield:** 12-16 servings.

Chocolate Banana Muffins
Cinnamon Sticky Buns

Apple Yogurt Muffins

Ready in 1 hour or less

Even if you're like me and don't care for yogurt, you'll love these apple muffins. I sometimes individually wrap them in colored plastic wrap, and tie them with a ribbon to sell at bake sales or share with others. —Cheri Huff
Litchfield, Michigan

✓ Uses less fat, sugar or salt. Includes Nutritional Analysis and Diabetic Exchanges.

2 cups all-purpose flour
1/2 cup sugar
3 teaspoons baking powder
1/2 teaspoon salt
1/4 teaspoon ground cinnamon
1 carton (8 ounces) vanilla yogurt
1 egg
1/4 cup vegetable oil
2 tablespoons milk
1 small tart apple, peeled and chopped
1/3 cup raisins, optional
TOPPING:
2 tablespoons all-purpose flour
2 tablespoons sugar
1/2 teaspoon ground cinnamon
1 tablespoon cold butter *or* stick margarine

In a bowl, combine the flour, sugar, baking powder, salt and cinnamon. Combine the yogurt, egg, oil and milk; stir into dry ingredients just until moistened. Stir in apple and raisins if desired (batter will be thick). Fill greased or paper-lined muffin cups two-thirds full.

For topping, combine flour, sugar and cinnamon in a bowl; cut in butter until crumbly. Sprinkle over batter. Bake at 400° for 20-24 minutes or until a toothpick comes out clean. Cool for 5 minutes before removing from pan to a wire rack. **Yield:** 1 dozen.

Nutritional Analysis: One muffin (prepared with reduced-fat vanilla yogurt and fat-free milk and without raisins) equals 201 calories, 6 g fat (1 g saturated fat), 22 mg cholesterol, 247 mg sodium, 32 g carbohydrate, 1 g fiber, 4 g protein. **Diabetic Exchanges:** 2 starch, 1 fat.

Nutty Quick Bread

Ready in 1 hour or less

Grape-Nuts cereal gives these fast-to-fix loaves their nutty flavor and chewy texture. The bread is a family favorite because it's so unusual. Warm slices are delicious with butter. —Melissa Walworth, Boise, Idaho

✓ Uses less fat, sugar or salt. Includes Nutritional Analysis and Diabetic Exchanges.

2 cups 1% buttermilk
1 cup Grape-Nuts
1 egg, lightly beaten
3 cups all-purpose flour
1 cup sugar
1 teaspoon baking powder
1 teaspoon baking soda
1/2 teaspoon salt

In a bowl, combine the buttermilk and cereal; let stand for 10 minutes. Add egg. Combine the dry ingredients; stir into cereal mixture just until moistened. Spoon into two greased 8-in. x 4-in. x 2-in. loaf pans. Bake at 375° for 30-35 minutes or until a toothpick inserted near the center comes out clean. Cool for 10 minutes before removing from pans to wire racks. **Yield:** 2 loaves (12 slices each).

Nutritional Analysis: One slice equals 110 calories, 1 g fat (trace saturated fat), 10 mg cholesterol, 162 mg sodium, 25 g carbohydrate, 1 g fiber, 3 g protein. **Diabetic Exchange:** 1-1/2 starch.

Streusel Rhubarb Bread

This tender bread has a sweet crunchy topping and great rhubarb taste. My family asks me to make it time and time again, and I'll happily oblige. —Irene Sankey
Stevens Point, Wisconsin

1-1/2 cups packed brown sugar
1/2 cup vegetable oil
1 egg
1 cup buttermilk
1 teaspoon vanilla extract
2-1/2 cups all-purpose flour
1 teaspoon baking soda
1 teaspoon salt
1-1/2 cups chopped fresh *or* frozen rhubarb
1/2 cup chopped walnuts *or* pecans
TOPPING:
1/2 cup sugar
1/4 teaspoon ground cinnamon
1 tablespoon cold butter *or* margarine

In a mixing bowl, combine brown sugar and oil. Add egg; mix well. Beat in buttermilk and vanilla. Combine the flour, baking soda and salt; stir into brown sugar mixture just until combined. Fold in the rhubarb and nuts. Pour into two greased 8-in. x 4-in. x 2-in. loaf pans.

For topping, in a bowl, combine sugar, cinnamon and butter until crumbly; sprinkle over batter. Bake at 350° for 60-65 minutes or until a toothpick inserted near the center comes out clean. Cool for 10 minutes before removing from pans to wire racks. Cut with a serrated knife. **Yield:** 2 loaves.

Breads in Brief

- Do you have recipes for baked goods that call for fresh chopped apple? Since I don't always have apples on hand, I keep my pantry stocked with jars of diced apples from the baby food section of the grocery store. I drain them and use them in apple bread with great results. And there's no waste—you can drink the apple juice that's drained off.
  —Darlene Clark, Laughlin, Nevada
- When baking, I use my pastry blender to mix together the dry ingredients called for in a recipe. It works in a snap. —JoAnn Baker, Lexington, Kentucky

Southern Buttermilk Biscuits

Ready in 30 minutes or less

The recipe for these four-ingredient biscuits has been handed down for many generations. —Fran Thompson Tarboro, North Carolina

1/2 cup cold butter *or* margarine
2 cups self-rising flour*
3/4 cup buttermilk
Melted butter *or* margarine

In a bowl, cut butter into flour until mixture resembles coarse crumbs. Stir in buttermilk just until moistened. Turn onto a lightly floured surface; knead 3-4 times. Pat or lightly roll to 3/4-in. thickness. Cut with a floured 2-1/2-in. biscuit cutter. Place on a greased baking sheet. Bake at 425° for 11-13 minutes or until golden brown. Brush tops with butter. Serve warm. **Yield:** 9 biscuits.

Editor's Note: As a substitute for each cup of self-rising flour, place 1-1/2 teaspoons baking powder and 1/2 teaspoon salt in a measuring cup. Add all-purpose flour to measure 1 cup.

Broccoli Corn Muffins

Ready in 1 hour or less

I dress up convenient corn bread mix with broccoli and cheese to make these savory muffins. —Dona Hamilton Cabazon, California

1 package (8-1/2 ounces) corn bread/muffin mix
1 package (10 ounces) frozen chopped broccoli, thawed and well drained
4 eggs, beaten
1 cup (4 ounces) shredded cheddar cheese
1 small onion, chopped
1/4 cup butter *or* margarine, melted

In a bowl, stir all ingredients just until combined. Fill greased muffin cups three-fourths full. Bake at 350° for 20-25 minutes or until a toothpick comes out clean. Cool for 5 minutes before removing from pans. Serve warm. **Yield:** 1-1/2 dozen.

Chocolate Coffee Cake

My mom often prepared this yummy cinnamon and nutmeg spiced treat while I was growing up. —Lauren Heyn Oak Creek, Wisconsin

3 cups all-purpose flour
2 cups sugar
1 cup cold butter *or* margarine
4 teaspoons baking cocoa
3 teaspoons ground cinnamon
1 teaspoon baking soda
1/2 teaspoon baking powder
1/2 teaspoon ground nutmeg
1/8 teaspoon salt
1/8 teaspoon ground cloves
1 cup raisins

1/2 cup chopped nuts
2 cups buttermilk

In a large bowl, combine the flour and sugar; cut in butter until crumbly. Set aside 1-1/4 cups for topping. To the remaining mixture, add cocoa, cinnamon, baking soda, baking powder, nutmeg, salt and cloves; mix well. Stir in raisins and nuts. Make a well in the center; pour in buttermilk and stir just until moistened. Transfer to a greased 13-in. x 9-in. x 2-in. baking pan. Sprinkle with reserved crumb mixture. Bake at 350° for 35-40 minutes or until a toothpick inserted near the center comes out clean. Cool on a wire rack. **Yield:** 12-16 servings.

Pineapple Banana Bread

Our four kids like this tropical-tasting banana bread for breakfast. —Mary Watkins, Chaska, Minnesota

3 cups all-purpose flour
2 cups sugar
1 teaspoon salt
1 teaspoon baking soda
1 teaspoon ground cinnamon
3 eggs
1-1/4 cups vegetable oil
2 teaspoons vanilla extract
1 can (8 ounces) crushed pineapple, drained
2 cups mashed ripe bananas (4 to 5 medium)

In a large bowl, combine the first five ingredients. In another bowl, beat eggs, oil and vanilla; add pineapple and bananas. Stir into dry ingredients just until moistened. Pour into two greased 8-in. x 4-in. x 2-in. loaf pans. Bake at 350° for 60-65 minutes or until a toothpick comes out clean. Cool for 10 minutes before removing from pans to wire racks. **Yield:** 2 loaves.

Apple Custard Coffee Cake

Once you try this luscious coffee cake, your mouth will water just thinking about it. —Vickie Tinsley Boonville, Missouri

2 cups biscuit/baking mix
1 cup sugar, *divided*
3/4 cup milk
1 teaspoon vanilla extract
1 cup chopped pecans
2 medium tart apples, peeled and chopped
1 teaspoon ground cinnamon, *divided*
3 eggs
1 cup whipping cream

In a bowl, combine biscuit mix, 1/4 cup sugar, milk and vanilla; mix well. Stir in pecans. Pour into a greased 9-in. square baking dish. Toss apples with 1/4 cup sugar and 1/2 teaspoon of cinnamon. Sprinkle over batter. In a bowl, combine eggs, cream and remaining sugar. Pour over the apples; sprinkle with remaining cinnamon. Bake, uncovered, at 350° for 40-45 minutes or until a knife inserted near the center comes out clean. Serve warm. Refrigerate leftovers. **Yield:** 9 servings.

Featherlight Scones

(Pictured below)

Ready in 30 minutes or less

Scones fit into just about every meal. This dough bakes up beautifully into fluffy golden wedges. We love the tender triangles fresh from the oven with butter and cinnamon-sugar.
—Stephanie Moon, Nampa, Idaho

3 cups all-purpose flour
3 teaspoons baking powder
1/2 teaspoon baking soda
1/2 teaspoon salt
1 cup cold butter *or* margarine
1 egg
1 cup vanilla yogurt
1/2 teaspoon vanilla extract
2 teaspoons milk
Sugar

In a bowl, combine flour, baking powder, baking soda and salt; cut in butter until mixture resembles coarse crumbs. Stir in egg, yogurt and vanilla just until combined. Turn onto a floured surface; knead 6-8 times. Roll into a 9-in. circle; cut into eight wedges. Place on an ungreased baking sheet. Brush tops with milk; sprinkle with sugar. Bake at 425° for 12-15 minutes or until golden brown. Serve warm. **Yield:** 8 servings.

Lemon Yogurt Loaf

(Pictured below)

This delicate tea bread is perfect for a light dessert or Sunday treats table. —Angela Biggin, Lyons, Illinois

3/4 cup plus 2 teaspoons lemon yogurt, *divided*
1/2 cup dried apricots
1/2 cup butter *or* margarine, softened
3/4 cup plus 2 tablespoons confectioners' sugar, *divided*
3 eggs
1 tablespoon grated lemon peel
2 cups self-rising flour*

In a blender, combine 3/4 cup yogurt and apricots; cover and process until smooth. In a mixing bowl, cream butter and 3/4 cup confectioners' sugar. Beat in eggs, lemon peel and yogurt mixture; mix well. Add flour just until combined. Spoon into a greased 8-in. x 4-in. x 2-in. loaf pan. Bake at 325° for 60-65 minutes or until a toothpick comes out clean. Cool for 10 minutes before removing from pan to a wire rack to cool completely. Combine remaining yogurt and confectioners' sugar; drizzle over loaf. **Yield:** 1 loaf.

   *Editor's Note: As a substitute for each cup of self-rising flour, place 1-1/2 teaspoons baking powder and 1/2 teaspoon salt in a measuring cup. Add all-purpose flour to measure 1 cup.

Featherlight Scones
Lemon Yogurt Loaf

Swiss Onion Drop Biscuits
Herb Biscuit Loaf

Herb Biscuit Loaf

(Pictured above and on page 156)

Ready in 1 hour or less

These buttery golden rolls are a sure way to make any meal special—from Thanksgiving dinner to a weekday supper. Their great herb flavor makes my husband think I fussed.
—Amy Smith, Maplewood, Minnesota

   1/4 cup butter *or* margarine, melted
   1/2 teaspoon dried minced onion
   1/2 teaspoon dried basil
   1/4 to 1/2 teaspoon caraway seeds
   1/8 teaspoon garlic powder
     2 tubes (12 ounces *each*) buttermilk biscuits

In a shallow bowl, combine the first five ingredients. Dip biscuits in butter mixture; fold in half and place in rows in a greased 9-in. square baking pan. Drizzle with remaining butter mixture. Bake at 350° for 27-30 minutes or until golden brown. **Yield:** 8-10 servings.

Swiss Onion Drop Biscuits

(Pictured above and on page 157)

Ready in 30 minutes or less

I stir up a big batch of these tender drop biscuits made with whole wheat flour. They're yummy spread with butter alongside a bowl of soup or a luncheon salad.
—Edna Hoffman, Hebron, Indiana

    2 cups all-purpose flour
  3/4 cup whole wheat flour
    1 tablespoon sugar
    3 teaspoons baking powder
  3/4 teaspoon onion salt
  1/2 teaspoon baking soda
  1/2 cup cold butter *or* margarine
    1 cup (4 ounces) shredded Swiss cheese
  1/3 cup thinly sliced green onions
    2 eggs
  3/4 cup plus 2 tablespoons buttermilk

In a bowl, combine the dry ingredients. Cut in butter until mixture resembles coarse crumbs. Stir in the cheese and onions. Combine eggs and buttermilk; stir into cheese mixture just until moistened. Drop by tablespoonfuls 2 in. apart onto greased baking sheets. Bake at 425° for 12-15 minutes or until golden brown. **Yield:** 2 dozen.

Blueberry Spice Muffins

Ready in 1 hour or less

These nicely spiced blueberry muffins are a pleasant complement to an informal brunch or as a special treat for breakfast. I know you'll love them. —Faye Hintz
Duarte, California

1-3/4 cups all-purpose flour
1/2 cup sugar
2-1/2 teaspoons baking powder
3/4 teaspoon ground cinnamon
1/2 teaspoon salt
1/4 teaspoon ground nutmeg
1 egg, lightly beaten
3/4 cup milk
1/3 cup butter *or* margarine, melted
1-1/4 cups fresh *or* frozen blueberries*
TOPPING:
1 tablespoon sugar
1/4 teaspoon ground cinnamon

In a bowl, combine the dry ingredients. Combine egg and milk. Add egg mixture and butter to dry ingredients; stir just until moistened. Fold in blueberries. Fill greased or paper-lined muffin cups two-thirds full. Combine the topping ingredients; sprinkle over batter. Bake at 400° for 16-20 minutes or until a toothpick comes out clean. Cool for 5 minutes before removing from pan to a wire rack. **Yield:** 1 dozen.

Editor's Note: If using frozen blueberries, do not thaw before adding to batter.

Cantaloupe Nut Bread

Slices of this unusual melon-flavored loaf are good plain, served with cantaloupe wedges or garnished with whipped cream for dessert. While it looks like ordinary bread, its terrific taste sets it apart. —Lorie McGuire
St. Paul, Kansas

1/3 cup shortening
2/3 cup sugar
1 egg
1-3/4 cups all-purpose flour
2 teaspoons baking powder
1/4 teaspoon baking soda
1/4 teaspoon salt
1 cup mashed ripe cantaloupe, drained
1/2 cup chopped nuts

In a mixing bowl, cream shortening and sugar. Beat in egg. Combine flour, baking powder, baking soda and salt; add to creamed mixture alternately with cantaloupe

until blended (mixture will appear curdled). Fold in nuts. Transfer to a greased 8-in. x 4-in. x 2-in. loaf pan. Bake at 350° for 55-60 minutes or until a toothpick inserted near the center comes out clean. Cool for 10 minutes before removing from pan to a wire rack. **Yield:** 1 loaf.

Tropical Coffee Cake

My aunt gave me this appealing recipe she often doubles for large groups. Lightly sweetened with pineapple and topped with coconut, it was an instant winner in my household. —Alisha Juhnke, Lebanon, Oregon

1 cup sugar
1/2 cup vegetable oil
2 eggs
1 cup (8 ounces) sour cream
1-1/2 cups all-purpose flour
2 teaspoons baking powder
1/2 teaspoon salt
1 can (8 ounces) crushed pineapple, drained
TOPPING:
1/2 cup flaked coconut
3 tablespoons sugar
1/2 teaspoon ground cinnamon

In a mixing bowl, blend the sugar and oil. Add eggs, one at a time, beating well after each addition. Beat in the sour cream. Combine the flour, baking powder and salt; add to the sour cream mixture. Stir in the pineapple. Spoon batter into a greased 9-in. square baking dish. Combine the topping ingredients; sprinkle over batter. Bake at 350° for 35-40 minutes or until a toothpick inserted near the center comes out clean. Cool on a wire rack. **Yield:** 9 servings.

Golden Peach Muffins

Ready in 1 hour or less

As soon as you try these moist and flavorful peach muffins, you'll know why they are a family favorite. I'm always happy to make them because they're so fast and easy to prepare. —Jody Borowski
Sheppard Air Force Base, Texas

1-1/2 cups all-purpose flour
1 cup sugar
3/4 teaspoon salt
1/2 teaspoon baking soda
1/8 teaspoon ground cinnamon
2 eggs
1/2 cup vegetable oil
1/2 teaspoon vanilla extract
1 can (15-1/4 ounces) sliced peaches, drained and finely chopped

In a bowl, combine the first five ingredients. In another bowl, combine the eggs, oil and vanilla; stir into dry ingredients just until moistened (batter will be thick). Fold in peaches. Fill paper-lined muffin cups two-thirds full. Bake at 350° for 25-30 minutes or until a toothpick comes out clean. Cool for 5 minutes before removing from pan to a wire rack. **Yield:** 1 dozen.

Pear Zucchini Bread

Put a subtle spin on traditional zucchini bread by adding chopped fresh pears. The ingredients are simple to assemble and yield two wonderfully moist loaves.
—*Gwynne Fleener, Coeur d'Alene, Idaho*

2 cups all-purpose flour
1 cup whole wheat flour
3/4 cup sugar
3/4 cup packed brown sugar
2 teaspoons pumpkin pie spice
1 teaspoon baking soda
1/2 teaspoon baking powder
1/2 teaspoon salt
3 eggs
3/4 cup vegetable oil
3 teaspoons vanilla extract
2 cups finely chopped peeled ripe pears (about 3 medium)
1 cup shredded zucchini
1/2 cup chopped pecans *or* walnuts

In a large bowl, combine the first eight ingredients. In another bowl, beat eggs, oil and vanilla. Add the pears and zucchini. Stir into dry ingredients just until moistened. Fold in nuts. Pour into two greased 9-in. x 5-in. x 3-in. loaf pans. Bake at 350° for 50-60 minutes or until a toothpick inserted near the center comes out clean. Cool for 10 minutes before removing from pans to wire racks. **Yield:** 2 loaves.

Easy Biscuit Squares

Ready in 30 minutes or less

With just three ingredients, you can bake these short-cake-like biscuits that are perfect topped with strawberries and cream. The cake mix makes them light, fluffy and slightly sweet. —*Marilou Robinson, Portland, Oregon*

3 cups biscuit/baking mix
1 cup yellow cake mix*
3/4 cup water

In a bowl, combine biscuit and cake mixes. Stir in water just until moistened. Turn onto a floured surface; knead 10-12 times. Pat into a greased 9-in. square baking pan. Score the surface, making nine squares. Bake at 425° for 12-15 minutes or until golden brown. Break biscuits apart at score marks. **Yield:** 9 biscuits.
*Editor's Note: This recipe was tested with Pillsbury yellow cake mix.

Cheddar Casserole Bread

Ready in 1 hour or less

Whether served on a brunch buffet or alongside a bowl of soup, one wedge of this rugged round loaf won't be enough. You'll only need a few items to create this savory sensation that keeps guests asking for more.
—*Marillyn Miner, Santa Margarita, California*

2-1/2 cups all-purpose flour
1 tablespoon baking powder

1/4 teaspoon salt
3/4 cup milk
1/2 cup mayonnaise*
1 egg, beaten
2 cups (8 ounces) shredded cheddar cheese
1/2 cup chopped green onions

In a bowl, combine the flour, baking powder and salt. Add the milk, mayonnaise and egg; mix just until combined. Fold in the cheese and onions. Spoon into a greased 9-in. round baking pan. Bake at 425° for 20-25 minutes or until a toothpick inserted near the center comes out clean. Cool for 5 minutes before removing from pan to a wire rack. Refrigerate any leftovers. **Yield:** 6-8 servings.
*Editor's Note: Reduced-fat or fat-free mayonnaise may not be substituted for regular mayonnaise.

Poppy Seed Plum Muffins

Ready in 1 hour or less

Bring the harvest-fresh taste of ripe plums to the breakfast table with these change-of-pace muffins. I don't mind making an extra batch because they freeze so well.
—*Carol Twardzik, Spy Hill, Saskatchewan*

✓ Uses less fat, sugar or salt. Includes Nutritional Analysis and Diabetic Exchanges.

2 cups all-purpose flour
2/3 cup sugar
1 tablespoon baking powder
1 tablespoon poppy seeds
1/2 teaspoon salt
1/2 teaspoon ground cinnamon
1 egg
3/4 cup milk
1/4 cup butter *or* stick margarine, melted
1/2 cup finely chopped peeled fresh plums

In a bowl, combine flour, sugar, baking powder, poppy seeds, salt and cinnamon. In another bowl, beat the egg, milk and butter; stir into dry ingredients just until moistened. Fold in plums. Fill greased or paper-lined muffin cups two-thirds full.
Bake at 425° for 18-22 minutes or until a toothpick comes out clean and muffins are golden brown. Cool for 5 minutes before removing from pan to a wire rack. Serve warm. **Yield:** 1 dozen.
Nutritional Analysis: One muffin equals 175 calories, 5 g fat (3 g saturated fat), 28 mg cholesterol, 209 mg sodium, 29 g carbohydrate, 1 g fiber, 3 g protein. **Diabetic Exchange:** 2 starch.

Wheatstraw Photo

Pecan Cherry Bread

(Pictured above right)

My mom made this delicious bread for special occasions. Full of sweet cherries and nuts, the taste and appearance of this golden loaf makes it ideal for autumn.
—*Pat Habiger, Spearville, Kansas*

Sweet Raisin Roll-Ups
Pecan Cherry Bread

1/2 cup butter *or* margarine, softened
3/4 cup sugar
2 eggs
2 cups all-purpose flour
1 teaspoon baking soda
1/2 teaspoon salt
1 cup buttermilk
1 cup chopped pecans
1 jar (10 ounces) maraschino cherries, drained and chopped
1 teaspoon vanilla extract

In a mixing bowl, cream the butter and sugar. Add eggs, one at a time, beating well after each addition. Combine the flour, baking soda and salt; add to the creamed mixture alternately with buttermilk. Stir in the pecans, cherries and vanilla. Pour into a greased and floured 8-in. x 4-in. x 2-in. loaf pan. Bake at 350° for 65-75 minutes or until a toothpick inserted near the center comes out clean. Cool for 10 minutes before removing from the pan to a wire rack. **Yield:** 1 loaf.

Sweet Raisin Roll-Ups

(Pictured above)

Ready in 1 hour or less

Refrigerated buttermilk biscuits help me prepare these standout sweets in minutes. Drizzled with a simple homemade glaze, the warm-from-the-oven roll-ups offer cinnamon, raisins and walnuts in every mouth-watering bite. —Linda Devine, Eminence, Missouri

3/4 cup raisins
1/3 cup chopped walnuts
1/4 cup sour cream
2 tablespoons honey
3 tablespoons butter *or* margarine, softened, *divided*
1 teaspoon ground cinnamon
1 teaspoon grated lemon peel
1 tube (12 ounces) refrigerated buttermilk biscuits
GLAZE:
3/4 cup confectioners' sugar
1/2 teaspoon vanilla extract
1 to 2 tablespoons milk

In a bowl, combine the raisins, nuts, sour cream, honey, 2 tablespoons butter, cinnamon and lemon peel; set aside. Separate the biscuit dough into 10 pieces. On a lightly floured surface, roll each piece into a 6-in. oval. Place a rounded tablespoonful of raisin mixture on each. Roll up jelly-roll style, starting with a short side; seal seam. Place roll-ups seam side down on an ungreased baking sheet.

Melt remaining butter; brush over dough. Bake at 375° for 12-14 minutes or until golden brown. Cool for 2 minutes. Combine confectioners' sugar, vanilla and enough milk to achieve drizzling consistency; drizzle over rolls. Serve warm. **Yield:** 10 servings.

Orange Breakfast Ring

(Pictured below)

Ready in 1 hour or less

This beautiful breakfast ring is perfect for a special occasion. Whether formed into a festive wreath or shaped into two rectangles, it's so yummy that no one will ever suspect the sweet treat starts with convenient crescent rolls.
—Wendy Fitzgerald, Eau Claire, Michigan

    1 package (8 ounces) cream cheese, softened
1/2 cup sugar
    1 tablespoon grated orange peel
    2 tubes (8 ounces *each*) refrigerated crescent rolls
1/3 cup chopped almonds, toasted
1/2 cup confectioners' sugar
    1 tablespoon orange juice
Sliced almonds

In a small mixing bowl, beat the cream cheese, sugar and orange peel until blended; set aside. Unroll both tubes of dough; press perforations and seams together to form two rectangles. Overlap rectangles at one end and press the seam to seal. Spread cream cheese mixture over dough to within 1/2 in. of edges. Sprinkle with the chopped almonds.

Roll up jelly-roll style, starting with a long side; pinch seam to seal. Place seam side down on a greased baking sheet; pinch ends together to form a ring. With scissors, cut from outside edge two-thirds of the way toward center of ring at 1-in. intervals. Separate strips slightly; twist to allow filling to show.

Bake at 350° for 15-18 minutes or until golden brown. Cool for 10 minutes before carefully removing from pan to a wire rack. Combine confectioners' sugar and or-ange juice; drizzle over warm coffee cake. Garnish with sliced almonds. **Yield:** 1 coffee cake.

Paradise Buns

(Pictured below)

These flavorful knots are delicious with soup...or use them for sandwiches or burgers.
—Liz Lazenby
Victoria, British Columbia

☑ Uses less fat, sugar or salt. Includes Nutritional Analysis and Diabetic Exchanges.

    1 loaf (1 pound) frozen bread dough, thawed
    1 cup (4 ounces) shredded cheddar cheese
1/4 cup *each* diced mushrooms, broccoli and sweet red and yellow pepper
    1 tablespoon chopped green onion
    1 garlic clove, minced
1/2 teaspoon garlic powder

Divide bread dough into eight pieces. In a bowl, combine the cheese, vegetables, garlic and garlic powder. Roll each piece of dough into an 8-in. rope. Roll in cheese mixture, pressing mixture into dough. Tie into a knot and press vegetables into dough; tuck ends under.

Place 2 in. apart on greased baking sheets. Cover and let rise until doubled, about 30 minutes. Bake at 375° for 15-20 minutes or until golden brown. **Yield:** 8 servings.

Nutritional Analysis: One bun (prepared with reduced-fat cheddar cheese) equals 198 calories, 5 g fat (2 g saturated fat), 8 mg cholesterol, 403 mg sodium, 31 g carbohydrate, 2 g fiber, 10 g protein. **Diabetic Exchanges:** 2 starch, 1 fat.

Paradise Buns
Orange Breakfast Ring

Carrot Raisin Muffins

Ready in 1 hour or less

These moist muffins are full of raisins and carrots. My husband likes them at breakfast along with his cereal.
—Patti Wolfe Bailey, Chanute, Kansas

✓ Uses less fat, sugar or salt. Includes Nutritional Analysis and Diabetic Exchanges.

- 2 cups whole wheat flour
- 2 teaspoons baking soda
- 2 teaspoons ground cinnamon
- 1/2 teaspoon salt
- 2 eggs
- 1 cup honey
- 1 carton (8 ounces) plain yogurt
- 1/2 cup canola oil
- 2 teaspoons lemon juice
- 2 teaspoons vanilla extract
- 1-1/2 cups shredded carrots
- 1/2 cup raisins
- 1/2 cup chopped walnuts, optional

In a bowl, combine the dry ingredients. In another bowl, combine the eggs, honey, yogurt, oil, lemon juice and vanilla. Stir into the dry ingredients just until blended. Fold in the carrots, raisins and nuts if desired. Fill greased or paper-lined muffin cups two-thirds full. Bake at 350° for 20-25 minutes or until a toothpick comes out clean. Cool for 5 minutes before removing from pans to wire racks. **Yield:** 1-1/2 dozen.
Nutritional Analysis: One muffin (prepared without nuts) equals 189 calories, 7 g fat (1 g saturated fat), 24 mg cholesterol, 226 mg sodium, 31 g carbohydrate, 2 g fiber, 3 g protein. **Diabetic Exchanges:** 1 starch, 1 fruit, 1 fat.

Sweet Potato Biscuits

Ready in 30 minutes or less

The recipe for these mild-tasting biscuits was my grandmother's. They're a family favorite that we always serve at Thanksgiving. *—Nancy Daugherty, Cortland, Ohio*

✓ Uses less fat, sugar or salt. Includes Nutritional Analysis and Diabetic Exchanges.

- 2-1/2 cups all-purpose flour
- 1 tablespoon baking powder
- 1 teaspoon salt
- 1/3 cup shortening
- 1 can (15 ounces) sweet potatoes, drained
- 3/4 cup milk

In a bowl, combine the flour, baking powder and salt. Cut in shortening until mixture resembles coarse crumbs. In another bowl, mash the sweet potatoes and milk. Add to the crumb mixture just until combined. Turn onto a floured surface; knead 8-10 times. Roll to 1/2-in. thickness; cut with a 2-1/2-in. biscuit cutter. Place on ungreased baking sheets. Bake at 425° for 8-10 minutes or until golden brown. Remove to wire racks. Serve warm. **Yield:** 1-1/2 dozen.

Nutritional Analysis: One biscuit (prepared with fat-free milk) equals 124 calories, 4 g fat (1 g saturated fat), trace cholesterol, 192 mg sodium, 19 g carbohydrate, 1 g fiber, 3 g protein. **Diabetic Exchanges:** 1 starch, 1 fat.

Fruitcake Bran Muffins

Ready in 1 hour or less

We've been trying to get more fiber in our diet, but we don't like the cardboard taste of regular bran muffins. So I jazzed these up, and now they taste almost like Christmas fruitcake! *—Norene Stead, Salt Lake City, Utah*

- 1-1/2 cups All-Bran
- 1-1/2 cups milk
- 1/2 cup vegetable oil
- 1-1/4 cups all-purpose flour
- 3/4 cup sugar
- 1 tablespoon baking powder
- 1/2 teaspoon salt
- 2 eggs, beaten
- 1/2 cup chopped red and green candied cherries
- 1/2 cup chopped candied pineapple
- 1/2 cup chopped citron

In a bowl, combine the bran, milk and oil; let stand for 5 minutes. Meanwhile, combine the dry ingredients in a large bowl. Stir in eggs and bran mixture. Fold in the cherries, pineapple and citron. Fill greased or paper-lined muffin cups three-fourths full. Bake at 400° for 20-25 minutes or until a toothpick comes out clean. Cool for 5 minutes before removing from pans to wire racks. **Yield:** 1-1/2 dozen.

Pistachio Mini Loaves

I bake up this green-hued bread for any occasion, but it's especially appropriate for Christmas or St. Patrick's Day. The little loaves have a pistachio flavor, light cake-like texture and crunchy topping. *—Joanne Loefgren Carmel, Indiana*

- 1 package (18-1/4 ounces) yellow cake mix
- 1 package (3.4 ounces) instant pistachio pudding mix
- 1 cup (8 ounces) sour cream
- 4 eggs
- 1/4 cup vegetable oil
- 1/4 cup water
- 3/4 cup finely chopped pecans
- 3 tablespoons brown sugar
- 2-1/2 teaspoons ground cinnamon

In a mixing bowl, combine cake and pudding mixes. Add sour cream, eggs, oil and water; beat until blended. Pour into five greased 5-3/4-in. x 3-in. x 2-in. loaf pans. Combine the pecans, brown sugar and cinnamon; sprinkle over batter.
Bake at 350° for 35-40 minutes or until a toothpick inserted near the center comes out clean. Cool for 10 minutes before removing from pans to wire racks. **Yield:** 5 loaves.

Sunflower Oatmeal Bread

1/2 cup quick-cooking oats
3 cups bread flour
2 tablespoons nonfat dry
   milk powder
2-1/4 teaspoons active dry yeast
1/2 cup salted sunflower
   kernels, toasted

In bread machine pan, place all ingredients in order suggested by manufacturer. Select basic bread setting. Choose crust color and loaf size if available. Bake according to bread machine directions (check dough after 5 minutes of mixing; add 1 to 2 tablespoons water or flour if needed). **Yield:** 1 loaf (about 1-1/2 pounds, 16 slices).

   Nutritional Analysis: One slice equals 157 calories, 4 g fat (1 g saturated fat), 4 mg cholesterol, 243 mg sodium, 25 g carbohydrate, 1 g fiber, 4 g protein. **Diabetic Exchange:** 2 starch.

Ranch Hamburger Buns

The dough setting on my bread machine makes it easy to prepare fresh rolls in a variety of shapes. We especially like these hamburger buns that are golden, tender and flavorful.
—*Nancy Whitney, Seattle, Washington*

✓ Uses less fat, sugar or salt. Includes Nutritional Analysis and Diabetic Exchanges.

1/2 cup water (70° to 80°)
1/2 cup plain yogurt
   1 egg
3/4 cup shredded cheddar cheese
   2 tablespoons nonfat dry milk powder
4-1/2 teaspoons sugar
   1 tablespoon ranch salad dressing mix
1-1/2 teaspoons salt
   3 cups bread flour
2-1/4 teaspoons active dry yeast
EGG WASH:
   1 egg
   2 tablespoons water
Poppy seeds *or* **sesame seeds, optional**

In bread machine pan, place the first 10 ingredients in order suggested by manufacturer. Select dough setting (check dough after 5 minutes of mixing; add 1 to 2 tablespoons of water or flour if needed).

   When the cycle is completed, turn dough onto a lightly greased surface. Cut into 12 pieces; shape each into a round ball. Place in greased jumbo muffin cups or 4-1/2-in. disposable aluminum foil pans. (If using foil pans, place on two baking sheets.)

   Cover and let rise in a warm place until doubled, about 45 minutes. Meanwhile, whisk together egg and water. Brush over buns; sprinkle with poppy or sesame seeds if desired. Bake at 400° for 8-12 minutes or until lightly

Bread at The Touch Of a Button

BREAD MACHINES make it convenient to bake bread at home. It takes only a few minutes to put your ingredients in the pan and flick a few switches. Soon, the aroma of just-baked bread will fill your kitchen!

Editor's Note: All recipes were tested in a Regal brand bread machine and in a West Bend or Black & Decker bread machine.

Sunflower Oatmeal Bread

(Pictured above)

Sunflower kernels give an interesting nutty flavor and crunch to this moist bread. It's good plain or toasted.
—*Elvera Dallman, Franklin, Nebraska*

✓ Uses less fat, sugar or salt. Includes Nutritional Analysis and Diabetic Exchanges.

   1 cup plus 2 tablespoons water (70° to 80°)
1/4 cup honey
   2 tablespoons butter *or* stick margarine, softened
1-1/2 teaspoons salt

browned. Remove from pans to wire racks to cool. **Yield:** 1 dozen.

Nutritional Analysis: One bun (prepared with reduced-fat cheddar cheese) equals 137 calories, 1 g fat (1 g saturated fat), 20 mg cholesterol, 397 mg sodium, 25 g carbohydrate, 1 g fiber, 7 g protein. **Diabetic Exchange:** 2 starch.

Editor's Note: If your bread machine has a time-delay feature, we recommend you do not use it for this recipe.

Ham 'n' Swiss Bread

My bread machine saves me a lot of time. I often use it to bake this flavorful loaf that includes diced ham and cheese. It's especially good warm. —Betty Bergman
East Jordan, Michigan

1-1/3 cups water (70° to 80°)
   2 tablespoons butter *or* margarine, softened
   3 tablespoons mashed potato flakes
   1 tablespoon nonfat dry milk powder
   2 tablespoons cornmeal
1-1/2 teaspoons salt
   4 cups bread flour
   1 tablespoon active dry yeast
 1/2 cup diced fully cooked ham
 1/2 cup diced Swiss cheese

In bread machine pan, place the first eight ingredients in order suggested by manufacturer. Select basic bread setting. Choose crust color and loaf size if available. Bake according to bread machine directions (check dough after 5 minutes of mixing; add 1 to 2 tablespoons of water or flour if needed). Just before final kneading (your machine may audibly signal this), add ham and cheese. Refrigerate leftovers. **Yield:** 1 loaf (2 pounds).

Editor's Note: If your bread machine has a time-delay feature, we recommend you do not use it for this recipe.

Herb Garlic Loaf

Everyone who tastes this savory bread immediately asks me for the recipe. With its mild garlic seasoning, slices of it are excellent with spaghetti, chili, stew or soup. —Juanita Patterson
Quartzsite, Arizona

☑ Uses less fat, sugar or salt. Includes Nutritional Analysis and Diabetic Exchanges.

   1 cup plus 2 tablespoons water (70° to 80°)
4-1/2 teaspoons butter *or* stick margarine, softened
 1/2 teaspoon salt
   3 cups bread flour
   1 envelope savory herb with garlic soup mix
4-1/2 teaspoons nonfat dry milk powder
   1 tablespoon sugar
2-1/4 teaspoons active dry yeast

In a bread machine pan, place all ingredients in order suggested by manufacturer. Select basic bread setting. Choose crust color and loaf size if available. Bake according to bread machine directions (check dough after 5 minutes of mixing; add 1 to 2 tablespoons of water or flour if needed). **Yield:** 1 loaf (1-1/2 pounds, 16 slices).

Nutritional Analysis: One slice equals 93 calories, 1 g fat (1 g saturated fat), 3 mg cholesterol, 116 mg sodium, 18 g carbohydrate, 1 g fiber, 3 g protein. **Diabetic Exchange:** 1 starch.

Golden Egg Bread

(Pictured below)

Cut this lovely loaf into thick slices to fix excellent French toast. It also makes good sandwiches. —Sybil Brown, Highland, California

 3/4 cup water (70° to 80°)
   3 tablespoons sugar
   3 tablespoons vegetable oil
   2 eggs
1-1/2 teaspoons salt
3-1/2 cups bread flour
2-1/4 teaspoons active dry yeast

In bread machine pan, place all ingredients in order suggested by manufacturer. Select basic bread setting. Choose crust color and loaf size if available. Bake according to bread machine directions (check dough after 5 minutes of mixing; add 1 to 2 tablespoons of water or flour if needed). **Yield:** 1 loaf (about 1-1/2 pounds).

Editor's Note: If your bread machine has a time-delay feature, we recommend you do not use it for this recipe.

Golden Egg Bread

Sour Cream Chive Bread

(Pictured below)

This savory loaf mildly flavored with chives is delicious when served warm with a meal, soup, salad or stew. It also tastes wonderful toasted the next day for breakfast.
—Deborah Plank, West Salem, Ohio

        2/3 cup warm milk (70° to 80°)
        1/4 cup water (70° to 80°)
        1/4 cup sour cream
          2 tablespoons butter *or* margarine
    1-1/2 teaspoons sugar
    1-1/2 teaspoons salt
          3 cups bread flour
        1/8 teaspoon baking soda
        1/4 cup minced chives
    2-1/4 teaspoons active dry yeast

In bread machine pan, place all ingredients in the order suggested by manufacturer. Select basic bread setting. Choose crust color and loaf size if available. Bake according to bread machine directions (check dough after 5 minutes of mixing; add 1 to 2 tablespoons of water or flour if needed). **Yield:** 1 loaf (1-1/2 pounds).

Editor's Note: If your bread machine has a time-delay feature, we recommend you do not use it for this recipe.

Greek Loaf

My father and I love Greek food, so we developed this recipe that features feta cheese and olives. Zesty slices dress up any meal, and leftovers make great salad croutons.
—Melanie Parker, Gloucester, Ontario

✓ Uses less fat, sugar or salt. Includes Nutritional Analysis and Diabetic Exchanges.

          1 cup milk (70° to 80°)
          1 tablespoon olive *or* vegetable oil
        1/2 to 1-1/2 teaspoons salt
        3/4 cup crumbled feta cheese *or* shredded
              mozzarella cheese
          3 cups bread flour
          1 tablespoon sugar
    2-1/4 teaspoons active dry yeast
        1/4 cup sliced ripe olives

In bread machine pan, place the first seven ingredients in order suggested by manufacturer. Select basic bread setting. Choose crust color and loaf size if available. Bake according to bread machine directions (check dough after 5 minutes of mixing; add 1 to 2 tablespoons of water or flour if needed). Just before the final kneading (your machine may audibly signal this), add the olives. **Yield:** 1 loaf (1-1/2 pounds, 16 slices).

Nutritional Analysis: One slice (prepared with fat-free milk, 1/2 teaspoon salt and feta cheese) equals 114 calories, 3 g fat (1 g saturated fat), 7 mg cholesterol, 179 mg sodium, 19 g carbohydrate, 1 g fiber, 5 g protein. **Diabetic Exchanges:** 1 starch, 1/2 fat.

Editor's Note: If your bread machine has a time-delay feature, we recommend you do not use it for this recipe.

Buttery Rolls

I use my bread machine to stir up the dough for these lovely golden dinner rolls. They're tender, fluffy and delicious when eaten warm from the oven.
—Debbie Leonard
Roseburg, Oregon

          1 cup warm milk (70° to 80°)
        1/2 cup butter *or* margarine, softened
        1/4 cup sugar
          2 eggs
    1-1/2 teaspoons salt
          4 cups bread flour
    2-1/4 teaspoons
              active dry yeast

In bread machine pan, place all ingredients in the order suggested by manufacturer. Select the dough setting (check dough after 5 minutes of mixing; add 1 to 2 tablespoons of water or flour if needed).

When the cycle is completed, turn dough onto a lightly floured surface. Divide into 24 portions; shape into balls. Place in a greased 13-in. x 9-in. x 2-in. baking pan. Cover and let rise in a warm place for 15 minutes. Bake at 375° for

Sour Cream Chive Bread

Garden Vegetable Bread

13-16 minutes or until golden brown. **Yield:** 2 dozen.

Editor's Note: If your bread machine has a time-delay feature, we recommend you do not use it for this recipe.

Garden Vegetable Bread

(Pictured above)

Red pepper, zucchini and green onions provide the attractive color and pleasant flavor in this moist loaf.
—Jean Moore, Pliny, West Virginia

✓ Uses less fat, sugar or salt. Includes Nutritional Analysis and Diabetic Exchanges.

    1/2 cup warm buttermilk (70° to 80°)
    3 tablespoons water (70° to 80°)
    1 tablespoon canola oil
    2/3 cup shredded zucchini
    1/4 cup chopped red sweet pepper
    2 tablespoons chopped green onions
    2 tablespoons grated Romano *or* Parmesan
       cheese
    2 tablespoons sugar
    1 teaspoon salt
    1/2 teaspoon lemon-pepper seasoning
    1/2 cup old-fashioned oats
    2-1/2 cups bread flour
    1-1/2 teaspoons active dry yeast

In bread machine pan, place all ingredients in order suggested by manufacturer. Select basic bread setting. Choose crust color and loaf size if available. Bake according to bread machine directions (check dough after 5 minutes of mixing; add 1 to 2 tablespoons of water or flour if needed). **Yield:** 1 loaf (1-1/2 pounds, 16 slices).

Nutritional Analysis: One slice (prepared with 1% buttermilk and salt-free lemon-pepper seasoning) equals 94 calories, 1 g fat (trace saturated fat), 1 mg cholesterol, 165 mg sodium, 18 g carbohydrate, 1 g fiber, 4 g protein. **Diabetic Exchange:** 1 starch.

Editor's Note: If your bread machine has a time-delay feature, we recommend you do not use it for this recipe.

Italian Seasoned Bread

When I didn't have the onion soup mix called for in the original recipe, I used Italian salad dressing mix instead.
—Jill Dickinson, Aurora, Minnesota

    1 cup plus 3 tablespoons water (70° to 80°)
    4-1/2 teaspoons butter *or* margarine
    1/2 teaspoon salt
    1 envelope zesty Italian salad dressing mix
    1 tablespoon sugar
    3 cups bread flour
    4-1/2 teaspoons nonfat dry milk powder
    2-1/4 teaspoons active dry yeast

In bread machine pan, place all ingredients in order suggested by manufacturer. Select basic bread setting. Choose crust color and loaf size if available. Bake according to bread machine directions (check dough after 5 minutes of mixing; add 1 to 2 tablespoons of water or flour if needed). **Yield:** 1 loaf (1-1/2 pounds).

Bran Knot Rolls

8 g fat (2 g saturated fat), 15 mg cholesterol, 134 mg sodium, 25 g carbohydrate, 2 g fiber, 4 g protein. **Diabetic Exchanges:** 1-1/2 starch, 1 fat.

Pecan Oatmeal Loaf

I add chopped pecans to this oatmeal bread, giving it a wonderful nutty flavor. It's good toasted, too.
—Gertrude Stoegbauer
Menasha, Wisconsin

  1-1/4 cups water (70° to 80°)
      2 tablespoons butter *or* margarine, softened
    1/2 cup old fashioned oats
      3 tablespoons sugar
      2 tablespoons nonfat dry milk powder
  1-1/4 teaspoons salt
      3 cups all-purpose flour
      2 teaspoons active dry yeast
    1/2 cup chopped pecans

In bread machine pan, place the first eight ingredients in order suggested by manufacturer. Select basic bread setting. Choose crust color and loaf size if available. Bake according to bread machine directions (check dough after 5 minutes of mixing; add 1 to 2 tablespoons of water or flour if needed). Just before the final kneading (your machine may audibly signal this), add the pecans. **Yield:** 1 loaf (1-1/2 pounds).

Bran Knot Rolls

(Pictured above)

I save time by using my bread machine to mix the dough for these rolls. Full of bran flavor, they come out of the oven with a tender crust every time. —Rosalea Hoeft
Kimball, Minnesota

✓ Uses less fat, sugar or salt. Includes Nutritional Analysis and Diabetic Exchanges.

    1 cup water (70° to 80°)
 1/2 cup butter-flavored shortening
    1 egg
 1/3 cup sugar
 3/4 teaspoon salt
 1/2 cup bran flakes
 1-1/2 cups bread flour
 1-1/2 cups whole wheat flour
 2-1/4 teaspoons active dry yeast
    1 egg white, lightly beaten

In bread machine pan, place all ingredients in order suggested by manufacturer. Select dough setting (check dough after 5 minutes of mixing; add 1 to 2 tablespoons water or flour if needed).

When cycle is completed, turn dough onto a lightly floured surface. Punch down. Cover and let rest for 10 minutes. Divide into 14 pieces; roll each into a rope. Tie into a knot; pinch ends and tuck under. Place on greased baking sheets. Cover and let rise in a warm place until doubled, about 45 minutes. Brush with egg white. Bake at 375° for 15-20 minutes or until golden brown. **Yield:** 14 rolls.

Nutritional Analysis: One roll equals 181 calories,

Triple Apple Bread

Apples, applesauce and apple juice are a winning combination. This flavorful loaf is a big hit. —Diane Marino
New Castle, Delaware

✓ Uses less fat, sugar or salt. Includes Nutritional Analysis and Diabetic Exchanges.

  3/4 cup finely chopped peeled apples
  3/4 cup warm apple juice (70° to 80°)
  1/4 cup warm applesauce (70° to 80°)
    1 tablespoon butter *or* stick margarine
    2 tablespoons brown sugar
 1-1/2 teaspoons salt
    1 teaspoon ground cinnamon
  1/8 teaspoon ground nutmeg
    2 cups bread flour
    1 cup whole wheat flour
 2-1/4 teaspoons active dry yeast

In bread machine pan, place all ingredients in order suggested by manufacturer. Select basic bread setting. Choose crust and loaf size if available. Bake according to bread machine directions (check dough after 5 minutes of mixing; add 1 to 2 tablespoons of water or flour if needed). **Yield:** 1 loaf (1-1/2 pounds, 16 slices).

Nutritional Analysis: One slice equals 99 calories, 1 g fat (trace saturated fat), 2 mg cholesterol, 229 mg sodium, 21 g carbohydrate, 2 g fiber, 3 g protein. **Diabetic Exchanges:** 1 fruit, 1/2 starch.

Raisin Rye Bread

Satisfying slices of this moist dark brown bread get plenty of flavor from aniseed, caraway and fennel, along with bursts of sweetness from the raisins.
—Audrey Lanier, Amite, Louisiana

  1 cup warm milk (70° to 80°)
  1/4 cup water (70° to 80°)
  1/4 cup vegetable oil
  1/4 cup molasses
  1/4 cup packed brown sugar
1-1/2 teaspoons salt
  1 teaspoon grated orange peel
  1/4 cup quick-cooking oats
  3/4 cup rye flour
2-3/4 cups bread flour
2-1/4 teaspoons active dry yeast
  1/2 cup raisins
  1/2 teaspoon aniseed
  1/2 teaspoon caraway seeds
  1/4 teaspoon fennel seed, crushed

In bread machine pan, place the first 11 ingredients in order suggested by manufacturer. Select basic bread setting. Choose light crust color and loaf size if available. Bake according to bread machine directions (check dough after 5 minutes of mixing; add 1 to 2 tablespoons of water or flour if needed). Just before the final kneading (your machine may audibly signal this), add the raisins, aniseed, caraway and fennel. **Yield:** 1 loaf (2 pounds).

   Editor's Note: If your bread machine has a time-delay feature, we recommend you do not use it for this recipe.

Harvest Fruit Bread

(Pictured below)

My sister is raising two little girls but always makes time to bake homemade bread. They like this loaf best. It's studded with fruit and nuts.
—Sandy Vias
San Leandro, California

✓ Uses less fat, sugar or salt. Includes Nutritional Analysis and Diabetic Exchanges.

  1 cup plus 2 tablespoons water (70° to 80°)
  1 egg
  3 tablespoons butter *or* stick margarine, softened
  1/4 cup packed brown sugar
1-1/2 teaspoons salt
  1/4 teaspoon ground nutmeg
Dash allspice
3-3/4 cups plus 1 tablespoon bread flour
  2 teaspoons active dry yeast
  1 cup dried fruit (dried cherries, cranberries *and/or* raisins)
  1/3 cup chopped pecans

In bread machine pan, place the first nine ingredients in order suggested by manufacturer. Select basic bread setting. Choose crust color and loaf size if available. Bake according to bread machine directions (check dough after 5 minutes of mixing; add 1 to 2 tablespoons water or flour if needed). Just before final kneading (your machine may audibly signal this), add fruit and pecans. **Yield:** 1 loaf (2 pounds, 12 slices).

   Nutritional Analysis: One slice equals 214 calories, 6 g fat (2 g saturated fat), 25 mg cholesterol, 330 mg sodium, 36 g carbohydrate, 2 g fiber, 6 g protein. **Diabetic Exchanges:** 2 starch, 1/2 fruit.

   Editor's Note: If your bread machine has a time-delay feature, we recommend you do not use it for this recipe.

Harvest Fruit Bread

Chapter 12

⏱ *Snappy Soups, Salads & Sandwiches*

FOR time-pressed cooks, minutes really matter, especially around mealtime. So it's no wonder fast-to-fix soups, salads and sandwiches are mouth-watering mainstays for lunch, dinner or snacks in between.

Your family won't have to wait long to hear "Soup's on!" when you add one or more of these easy-to-prepare items to your menu.

And they'll like what they see on the table—simple-to-make soups, speedy salads and short-cut sandwiches that are undeniably delicious and surprisingly filling.

SAVORY SPREAD. Clockwise from upper left: Broccoli Turkey Salad, Giant Sandwich and Onion Cheese Soup (all recipes on p. 181).

177

Oriental Chicken Salad

(Pictured at right)

Ready in 1 hour or less

This satisfying salad is crunchy, nutty and sweet all at the same time. To speed up preparation, I use chow mein noodles instead of fried wonton wrappers called for in the original recipe. —Barb Mickelson, Glenwood, Iowa

  1/2 cup sugar
    1 tablespoon cornstarch
  1/4 cup water
  1/4 cup vegetable oil
  1/4 cup ketchup
    3 tablespoons cider vinegar
    1 tablespoon soy sauce
    1 medium head iceberg lettuce, torn
    2 cups cubed cooked chicken
    1 cup salted cashews
    1 can (8 ounces) sliced water chestnuts, drained
    1 package (6 ounces) frozen snow peas, thawed
    1 can (3 ounces) chow mein noodles
  1/4 cup chopped green onions

In a small saucepan, combine the first seven ingredients. Bring to a boil; cook and stir for 2 minutes or until thickened. Cool. In a large salad bowl, combine the remaining ingredients; add dressing and toss to coat. Serve immediately. **Yield:** 8-10 servings.

Teriyaki Steak Subs

(Pictured at right)

Ready in 30 minutes or less

I layer submarine sandwich rolls with a seasoned mixture of sirloin strips, sliced peppers and pineapple rings. The interesting flavors in these meaty sandwiches blend quite nicely. —Sandra Burgess, Birch Tree, Missouri

  1/4 cup steak sauce
    1 tablespoon brown sugar
    1 tablespoon soy sauce
  1/2 teaspoon ground ginger
    1 pound boneless beef sirloin steak, cut into 1/2-inch strips
    1 medium sweet red pepper, thinly sliced
    1 medium green pepper, thinly sliced
    1 medium onion, thinly sliced
    2 garlic cloves, minced
    1 tablespoon vegetable oil
    8 pineapple slices
    4 hoagie buns, split and toasted

In a bowl, combine steak sauce, brown sugar, soy sauce and ginger; set aside. In a skillet or wok, stir-fry steak, peppers, onion and garlic in oil for 5 minutes. Stir in reserved sauce; top with pineapple. Cover and simmer for 5 minutes or until heated through. Spoon meat mixture onto rolls; top each with two pineapple slices. **Yield:** 4 servings.

Curried Chicken Rice Soup

(Pictured at right)

Ready in 30 minutes or less

With its mild curry flavor and colorful chunks of carrot and celery, this thick soup draws rave reviews every time I fix it. —Judie Anglen, Riverton, Wyoming

    2 large carrots, diced
    2 celery ribs, diced
    1 small onion, chopped
  3/4 cup butter *or* margarine
  3/4 cup all-purpose flour
    1 teaspoon seasoned salt
  1/2 to 1 teaspoon curry powder
    3 cans (12 ounces *each*) evaporated milk
    4 cups chicken broth
    2 to 3 cups cubed cooked chicken
    2 cups cooked long grain rice

In a large saucepan, saute carrots, celery and onion in butter for 2 minutes. Stir in flour, seasoned salt and curry until smooth. Gradually add milk. Bring to a boil; cook and stir for 2 minutes or until thickened. Gradually add broth. Stir in chicken and rice. Return to a boil. Reduce heat; simmer, uncovered, for 10 minutes or until vegetables are tender. **Yield:** 10-12 servings.

Rhubarb Soup

Ready in 1 hour or less

Served warm or chilled, this thick fruit soup makes an interesting first course. —Linda Murray, Allenstown, New Hampshire

    4 cups diced fresh *or* frozen rhubarb
    1 cup plus 2 tablespoons water, *divided*
  1/2 cup sugar
    1 cinnamon stick (2 inches)
    1 tablespoon cornstarch
    1 cup white grape juice *or* white wine
Toasted sliced almonds, optional

In a 3-qt. saucepan, combine the rhubarb, 1 cup of water, sugar and cinnamon; bring to a boil. Reduce heat; simmer, uncovered, for 15-20 minutes or until rhubarb is tender. Combine cornstarch and remaining water until smooth; stir into rhubarb mixture. Bring to a boil; cook and stir for 2 minutes or until thickened. Remove from the heat and discard cinnamon stick. Stir in grape juice. Serve warm or cover and refrigerate overnight. Garnish with almonds if desired. **Yield:** 4 servings.

Try a Tortilla

I keep flour tortillas in the fridge for those times when I run out of bread. When I need a quick sandwich, I put the sandwich fixings on a tortilla and roll it up. It's a fun change of pace and makes the sandwich easier to eat when you're in the car or on the run.

—Stacey Aldridge, Miamisburg, Ohio

Oriental Chicken Salad
Curried Chicken Rice Soup
Teriyaki Steak Subs

Broccoli Turkey Salad
Giant Sandwich
Onion Cheese Soup

Onion Cheese Soup

(Pictured at left and on page 176)

Ready in 30 minutes or less

I made a few adjustments to this savory soup recipe I came across in a community cookbook. It's rich, buttery and cheesy. —Janice Pogozelski, Cleveland, Ohio

- 1 large onion, chopped
- 3 tablespoons butter *or* margarine
- 3 tablespoons all-purpose flour
- 1/2 teaspoon salt

Pepper to taste

- 4 cups milk
- 2 cups (8 ounces) shredded Colby/Monterey Jack cheese

Seasoned salad croutons

Grated Parmesan cheese, optional

In a large saucepan, saute the onion in butter. Stir in the flour, salt and pepper until blended. Gradually add milk. Bring to a boil; cook and stir for 2 minutes or until thickened. Stir in Colby/Monterey Jack cheese until melted. Serve with croutons and Parmesan cheese if desired. **Yield:** 6 servings.

Broccoli Turkey Salad

(Pictured at left and on page 176)

Ready in 30 minutes or less

This medley of turkey, broccoli, pineapple and greens is especially good for a ladies' luncheon. —Joyana McShane, El Cajon, California

 Uses less fat, sugar or salt. Includes Nutritional Analysis and Diabetic Exchanges.

- 1 can (8 ounces) unsweetened pineapple chunks
- 2 cups torn salad greens
- 2 cups torn fresh spinach
- 2 cups broccoli florets
- 1 green pepper, julienned
- 1/2 cup thinly sliced red onion
- 2 cups cubed cooked turkey
- 1/4 cup olive *or* vegetable oil
- 2 tablespoons balsamic vinegar *or* red wine vinegar
- 1 tablespoon poppy seeds
- 2 teaspoons sugar
- 2 teaspoons Dijon mustard

Drain the pineapple, reserving 2 tablespoons juice; set aside (discard remaining juice or save for another use). In a large bowl, combine the greens, spinach, broccoli, green pepper, onion, turkey and pineapple. In a small bowl, combine oil, vinegar, poppy seeds, sugar, mustard and reserved pineapple juice; mix well. Pour over salad and toss to coat. Serve immediately. **Yield:** 10 servings.
Nutritional Analysis: One serving (1 cup) equals 111 calories, 7 g fat (1 g saturated fat), 17 mg cholesterol, 46 mg sodium, 7 g carbohydrate, 1 g fiber, 6 g protein. **Diabetic Exchanges:** 1 vegetable, 1 fat, 1/2 meat.

Giant Sandwich

(Pictured at left and on page 177)

Ready in 1 hour or less

This lovely layered loaf is definitely not your everyday sandwich. Piled high with a variety of fillings, the wedges are great for a special occasion. —Mildred Sherrer, Bay City, Texas

- 1 unsliced round loaf (1-1/2 pounds) rye bread
- 1 tablespoon prepared horseradish
- 1/4 pound thinly sliced deli roast beef
- 2 tablespoons mayonnaise
- 4 to 6 slices Swiss cheese
- 2 tablespoons prepared mustard
- 1/4 pound thinly sliced deli ham
- 6 bacon strips, cooked
- 6 slices process American cheese
- 1 medium tomato, thinly sliced
- 4 slices red onion, separated into rings
- 1 tablespoon butter *or* margarine, softened

Cut bread horizontally into six slices. Spread bottom slice with horseradish; top with roast beef. Place the next slice of bread over beef; spread with mayonnaise and top with Swiss cheese. Add next slice of bread; spread with mustard and top with ham. Add the next slice of bread; top with bacon and American cheese. Add next slice of bread; top with tomato and onion.

Spread butter on cut side of bread top; cover sandwich. Place on a baking sheet; loosely tent with foil. Bake at 400° for 12-14 minutes or until heated through. Carefully slice into wedges. **Yield:** 6-8 servings.

Lemon Chicken Spread

Ready in 15 minutes or less

I put a fresh face on chicken salad by adding lemon peel, green olives and mushrooms. There's just the right amount to make two satisfying sandwiches. —Violet Beard, Marshall, Illinois

- 1 cup cubed cooked chicken
- 1/2 cup chopped fresh mushrooms
- 1/3 cup chopped stuffed olives
- 1/4 cup minced fresh parsley
- 1/4 cup mayonnaise
- 2 teaspoons lemon juice
- 1-1/2 teaspoons grated lemon peel
- 1 to 1-1/4 teaspoons poultry seasoning
- 1/4 teaspoon salt
- 2 sandwich rolls *or* croissants

Lettuce leaves

In a blender or food processor, cover and process the chicken until minced. Transfer to a bowl; add the mushrooms, olives and parsley. In another bowl, combine the mayonnaise, lemon juice and peel, poultry seasoning and salt; add to the chicken mixture and mix well. Spread about 1/2 cup on each roll and top with lettuce. **Yield:** 2 servings.

Pasta Pizza Soup

Ready in 1 hour or less

A steaming bowl of this soup hits the spot on a cold rainy or snowy day, which we have in abundance.
—Linda Fox, Soldotna, Alaska

 Uses less fat, sugar or salt. Includes Nutritional Analysis and Diabetic Exchanges.

- 1 pound ground beef
- 4 ounces fresh mushrooms, sliced
- 1 medium onion, chopped
- 1 celery rib, thinly sliced
- 1 garlic clove, minced
- 4 cups water
- 1 can (14-1/2 ounces) Italian diced tomatoes, undrained
- 2 medium carrots, chopped
- 4 teaspoons beef bouillon granules
- 1 bay leaf
- 1-1/2 teaspoons dried oregano
- 1-1/2 cups cooked tricolor spiral pasta

In a large saucepan over medium heat, cook beef, mushrooms, onion, celery and garlic until meat is no longer pink and vegetables are tender; drain. Stir in water, tomatoes, carrots, bouillon, bay leaf and oregano. Bring to a boil. Reduce heat; cover and simmer for 20-25 minutes or until carrots are tender. Stir in pasta; heat through. Discard bay leaf. **Yield:** 8 servings (about 2 quarts).

Nutritional Analysis: One serving (prepared with low-sodium bouillon) equals 185 calories, 5 g fat (2 g saturated fat), 21 mg cholesterol, 164 mg sodium, 18 g carbohydrate, 2 g fiber, 15 g protein. **Diabetic Exchanges:** 1 starch, 1 meat, 1 vegetable.

Salsa Chicken Soup

(Pictured at right)

Ready in 30 minutes or less

You wouldn't guess that this quick-and-easy soup is low in fat. Since my husband loves spicy foods, I sometimes use medium or hot salsa in this recipe for extra zip.
—Becky Christman, Bridgeton, Missouri

 Uses less fat, sugar or salt. Includes Nutritional Analysis and Diabetic Exchanges.

- 1/2 pound boneless skinless chicken breasts, cubed
- 1 can (14-1/2 ounces) chicken broth
- 1-3/4 cups water
- 1 to 2 teaspoons chili powder
- 1 cup frozen corn
- 1 cup salsa

Shredded Monterey Jack *or* pepper-Jack cheese, optional

In a large saucepan, combine chicken, broth, water and chili powder. Bring to a boil. Reduce heat; cover and simmer for 5 minutes. Add corn; return to a boil. Reduce heat; simmer, uncovered, for 5 minutes or until chicken is no longer pink and corn is tender. Add salsa; heat through. Top with cheese if desired. **Yield:** 6 servings.

Nutritional Analysis: One 1-cup serving (calculated without cheese) equals 82 calories, 1 g fat (trace saturated fat), 22 mg cholesterol, 484 mg sodium, 9 g carbohydrate, 1 g fiber, 11 g protein. **Diabetic Exchange:** 1-1/2 lean meat.

South of the Border Salad

(Pictured at right)

Plan ahead...needs to chill

Several years ago, a co-worker gave me the recipe for this fast-to-fix salad. I frequently take it to potlucks when I'm short on time.
—Paula Ishii, Ralston, Nebraska

- 2 cans (15-1/4 ounces *each*) whole kernel corn, drained
- 2 cans (15 ounces *each*) black beans, rinsed and drained
- 1 can (10 ounces) diced tomatoes and green chilies, undrained
- 3/4 cup thinly sliced green onions
- 1/3 cup olive *or* vegetable oil
- 1/3 cup lime juice
- 1 tablespoon minced fresh cilantro *or* parsley
- 1 teaspoon salt
- 1 teaspoon ground cumin

In a large bowl, combine the corn, beans, tomatoes and onions. In a small bowl, combine the remaining ingredients; add to corn mixture and mix well. Cover and refrigerate for at least 2 hours. Serve with a slotted spoon. **Yield:** 8-10 servings.

Olive Chicken Roll-Ups

(Pictured at right)

Plan ahead...needs to chill

I serve these tasty handheld sandwiches with salsa on the side for dipping. Or slice them into pinwheels for appetizers.
—Lisa Hymson, Aurora, Colorado

- 1 package (8 ounces) cream cheese, softened
- 2 cans (4 ounces *each*) chopped green chilies, drained
- 1 can (2-1/4 ounces) chopped ripe olives, drained
- 1 jar (2 ounces) diced pimientos, drained
- 1/4 teaspoon garlic powder
- 1/4 teaspoon chili powder
- 1/4 teaspoon hot pepper sauce
- 8 flour tortillas (8 inches)
- 1-1/4 pounds deli smoked chicken

Salsa *or* picante sauce, optional

In a mixing bowl, beat cream cheese until smooth. Fold in chilies, olives, pimientos, garlic powder, chili powder and hot pepper sauce. Spread on one side of each tortilla; top with chicken and roll up tightly. Wrap in plastic wrap; refrigerate for at least 1 hour. Serve with salsa if desired. **Yield:** 8 servings.

South of the Border Salad
Salsa Chicken Soup
Olive Chicken Roll-Ups

Cukes and Carrots
Turkey Salad Croissants
Too-Easy Tortellini Soup

Turkey Salad Croissants

(Pictured at left)

Ready in 30 minutes or less

When I want to feed my family without heating up the kitchen, I turn to this tasty sandwich filling. I keep the creamy crunchy mixture on hand for lunches and after-school snacks. It's a great way to use up leftover turkey and make the most of garden-fresh vegetables. —Kim Due
Friend, Nebraska

2 cups diced cooked turkey
1/2 cup chopped celery
1/2 cup chopped cashews
1/2 cup mayonnaise *or* salad dressing
1/4 cup coarsely chopped radishes
2 tablespoons chopped green onions
2 tablespoons diced pimientos
1 tablespoon lemon juice
1 teaspoon dill weed
1 teaspoon seasoned salt
Lettuce leaves
6 croissants, split

In a bowl, combine first 10 ingredients. Place lettuce and 2/3 cup turkey salad on each croissant. **Yield:** 6 servings.

Too-Easy Tortellini Soup

(Pictured at left)

Ready in 30 minutes or less

I combine packaged tortellini and canned goods to quickly bring this hearty soup to the table. Basil and Parmesan cheese round out the flavor of this family favorite.
—Beth Daley, Chesterfield, Missouri

✓ Uses less fat, sugar or salt. Includes Nutritional Analysis and Diabetic Exchanges.

4 cups chicken broth
1 package (9 ounces) refrigerated cheese tortellini
1 can (15 ounces) white kidney *or* cannellini beans, rinsed and drained
1 can (14-1/2 ounces) Italian diced tomatoes, undrained
1-1/2 teaspoons dried basil
1 tablespoon red wine vinegar *or* cider vinegar
Shredded Parmesan cheese and coarsely ground pepper, optional

In a large saucepan, bring broth to a boil. Stir in tortellini. Reduce heat; simmer, uncovered, for 4 minutes, stirring occasionally. Stir in the beans, tomatoes and basil. Simmer for 4-6 minutes or until pasta is tender. Stir in the vinegar. Sprinkle with Parmesan cheese and pepper if desired. **Yield:** 6 servings.
Nutritional Analysis: One 1-cup serving (prepared with reduced-sodium broth; calculated without Parmesan cheese) equals 276 calories, 5 g fat (2 g saturated fat), 18 mg cholesterol, 457 mg sodium, 44 g carbohydrate, 1 g fiber, 14 g protein. **Diabetic Exchanges:** 2 starch, 1-1/2 lean meat, 1 fat.

Cukes and Carrots

(Pictured at left)

Plan ahead...needs to chill

Carrots and green peppers bring extra color and crunch to this refreshing cucumber salad. The sweet dressing is an ideal match for the crisp summer produce.
—Karla Hecht, Plymouth, Minnesota

5 medium cucumbers, thinly sliced
4 medium carrots, thinly sliced
1 medium onion, halved and thinly sliced
1 small green pepper, chopped
2 teaspoons canning salt
1-1/2 cups sugar
1/2 cup white vinegar

In a bowl, combine cucumbers, carrots, onion and green pepper. Sprinkle with salt; toss to coat. Cover and refrigerate for 2 hours. Combine sugar and vinegar; pour over vegetables. Cover and refrigerate for at least 1 hour. Serve with a slotted spoon. **Yield:** 12 servings.

Green Pepper Salad Dressing

Ready in 15 minutes or less

If you enjoy the flavor of green peppers, you'll love this salad dressing. Drizzle greens with the thick blend or serve it alongside a veggie tray. —Elizabeth Montgomery
Taylorville, Illinois

1 cup mayonnaise
3 tablespoons finely chopped green pepper
2 tablespoons finely chopped onion
2 tablespoons minced fresh parsley
1 tablespoon lemon juice
Torn salad greens

In a bowl, combine the first five ingredients. Cover and refrigerate until serving. Serve over salad greens. **Yield:** about 1-1/4 cups.

Honeydew Soup

Plan ahead...needs to chill

I keep my cool on hot days by whipping up this delicate cold soup. People are delighted with the flavor.
—Ruth Andrewson, Peck, Idaho

✓ Uses less fat, sugar or salt. Includes Nutritional Analysis and Diabetic Exchanges.

3 cups cubed honeydew
1/2 cup white grape juice
1 tablespoon sugar

In a blender, combine all ingredients; cover and process until smooth. Transfer to a bowl. Cover and refrigerate until chilled. **Yield:** 3 servings.
Nutritional Analysis: One serving (3/4 cup) equals 94 calories, trace fat (trace saturated fat), 0 cholesterol, 18 mg sodium, 24 g carbohydrate, 1 g fiber, 1 g protein. **Diabetic Exchange:** 1-1/2 fruit.

Toasted Chicken Sandwiches

Ready in 30 minutes or less

Pickle relish sparks the flavor of the chicken salad in these grilled sandwiches. They are especially good with the cheese sauce.
—*Ruth Peterson, Jenison, Michigan*

    1 cup cubed cooked chicken
1/2 cup finely chopped celery
1/4 cup mayonnaise
    2 to 3 tablespoons sweet pickle relish, drained
    2 teaspoons finely chopped onion
    1 teaspoon lemon juice
1/2 teaspoon salt, *divided*
1/8 teaspoon pepper
  12 bread slices, crusts removed
    1 egg
2/3 cup milk
    1 to 2 tablespoons butter *or* margarine
CHEESE SAUCE:
    8 ounces process cheese (Velveeta), cubed
1/3 cup milk

In a bowl, combine the chicken, celery, mayonnaise, relish, onion, lemon juice, 1/4 teaspoon salt and pepper. Spread over half of the bread; top with remaining bread. In a shallow bowl, whisk egg, milk and remaining salt. Dip both sides of sandwiches in egg mixture. In a large skillet or on a griddle, melt butter over medium heat; grill sandwiches on both sides until golden brown. Meanwhile, combine cheese sauce ingredients in a saucepan; cook and stir over low heat until cheese is melted. Serve as a dipping sauce with sandwiches. **Yield:** 6 servings.

Bean 'n' Corn Salad

(Pictured at right)

Plan ahead...needs to chill

I stir together this colorful medley of beans, peppers, corn and other vegetables, then marinate it overnight in a tasty sweet dressing. —*Glenda Parsonage Maple Creek, Saskatchewan*

    1 can (16 ounces) kidney beans, rinsed and drained
    1 can (14-1/2 ounces) cut green beans, drained
    1 can (14-1/2 ounces) wax beans, drained
    1 can (11 ounces) whole kernel corn, drained
    2 celery ribs, thinly sliced
    1 medium green pepper, chopped
1/2 cup chopped sweet red pepper
1/2 cup sliced ripe olives
1/2 cup sliced green onions, optional
    1 cup sugar
    1 cup white vinegar
    2 tablespoons vegetable oil
1/2 teaspoon ground mustard

1/4 teaspoon salt

In a large bowl, combine the first nine ingredients. In a jar with a tight-fitting lid, combine the sugar, vinegar, oil, mustard and salt; shake until sugar is dissolved. Pour over bean mixture and gently stir to coat. Cover and refrigerate overnight. Serve with a slotted spoon. **Yield:** 14 servings.

Shredded French Dip

(Pictured at right)

Plan ahead...uses a slow cooker

A chuck roast slow-simmered in a beefy broth is delicious when shredded and spooned onto rolls. I serve the cooking juices in individual cups for dipping.
—*Carla Kimball, Callaway, Nebraska*

    1 boneless beef chuck roast (3 pounds), trimmed
    1 can (10-1/2 ounces) condensed French onion soup, undiluted
    1 can (10-1/2 ounces) condensed beef consomme, undiluted
    1 can (10-1/2 ounces) condensed beef broth, undiluted
    1 teaspoon beef bouillon granules
    8 to 10 French *or* Italian rolls, split

Halve roast and place in a slow cooker. Combine the soup, consomme, broth and bouillon; pour over roast. Cover and cook on low for 6-8 hours or until meat is tender. Remove meat and shred with two forks. Serve on rolls. Skim fat from cooking juices and serve as a dipping sauce. **Yield:** 8-10 servings.

Creamy Monterey Jack Soup

(Pictured at right)

Ready in 30 minutes or less

This mild comforting soup can be made in a matter of minutes. Served as a first course, it upgrades any meal from so-so to wow!
—*Shannette Matlock Louisville, Kentucky*

2-1/2 cups water
    1 medium tomato, chopped
    1 can (4 ounces) chopped green chilies
    1 can (12 ounces) evaporated milk
    1 can (10-3/4 ounces) condensed cream of onion soup, undiluted
    1 can (10-3/4 ounces) condensed cream of potato soup, undiluted
1/8 teaspoon garlic salt
    8 ounces bulk Monterey Jack cheese, cut into 1-inch cubes

In a large saucepan, combine the water, tomato and chilies. Bring to a boil; boil for 5 minutes. Stir in milk, soups and garlic salt. Cook and stir over medium heat until heated through. Place cheese cubes in serving bowls; ladle hot soup over cheese. **Yield:** 6 servings.

Bean 'n' Corn Salad
Creamy Monterey Jack Soup
Shredded French Dip

Chunky Veggie Chowder
Hot Tortellini Salad
Cran-Orange Turkey Bagel

Cran-Orange Turkey Bagel

(Pictured at left)

Ready in 15 minutes or less

I adapted the recipe for this tasty turkey sandwich from a deli where I worked. To make it easier to eat, we often dip each bite into the cranberry mixture instead of spreading it inside. —Tanya Smeins, Washington, North Carolina

1 can (11 ounces) mandarin oranges, drained
1 can (16 ounces) whole-berry cranberry sauce
6 tablespoons cream cheese, softened
6 onion bagels *or* flavor of your choice, split and toasted
1 pound thinly sliced cooked turkey

In a bowl, mash mandarin oranges with a fork. Stir in cranberry sauce. Spread cream cheese over the bottom of each bagel; top with turkey and cran-orange sauce. Replace bagel tops. **Yield:** 6 servings.

Hot Tortellini Salad

(Pictured at left)

Ready in 30 minutes or less

Once you've cooked the tortellini, the rest of this salad is a breeze to finish in the microwave. Sour cream provides the mild coating over this memorable medley of pasta, ham and broccoli. —Catherine Allan, Twin Falls, Idaho

1 package (9 ounces) refrigerated cheese tortellini
2 cups fresh broccoli florets
4 to 5 green onions, sliced
2 tablespoons butter *or* margarine
6 ounces fully cooked ham, julienned
1/2 cup sour cream
1 teaspoon dried basil

Cook tortellini according to package directions. Meanwhile, in a 2-qt. microwave-safe bowl, combine the broccoli, onions and butter. Cover and microwave on high for 2-1/2 minutes; stir. Cook 2-1/2 minutes longer or until broccoli is tender.
Drain tortellini. Stir tortellini, ham, sour cream and basil into broccoli mixture. Cover and microwave on high for 1-2 minutes or until heated through. Let stand for 2 minutes before serving. **Yield:** 6-8 servings.
Editor's Note: This recipe was tested in an 850-watt microwave.

Chunky Veggie Chowder

(Pictured at left)

Ready in 1 hour or less

We enjoy this colorful chowder year-round. The light but flavorful soup is chock-full of vegetables and pleasantly seasoned with thyme. —Diane Molberg, Emerald Park, Saskatchewan

2 medium onions, finely chopped
2 garlic cloves, minced
2 tablespoons butter *or* stick margarine
3 medium carrots, chopped
2 celery ribs, sliced
2 medium potatoes, cubed
1 small zucchini, cubed
2 cans (10-1/2 ounces *each*) condensed chicken broth, undiluted
1/4 cup minced fresh parsley
3/4 teaspoon dried thyme
1 cup frozen peas
1 cup frozen corn
1/4 cup all-purpose flour
3 cups milk
Salt and pepper to taste

In a large saucepan or soup kettle, saute onions and garlic in butter until tender. Add the carrots, celery, potatoes, zucchini, broth, parsley and thyme. Bring to a boil. Reduce heat; cover and simmer until vegetables are tender, about 20 minutes.
Stir in peas and corn. In a bowl, combine flour, milk, salt if desired and pepper until smooth; gradually add to soup. Bring to a boil; cook and stir for 2 minutes or until thickened. **Yield:** 8 servings (2 quarts).
Nutritional Analysis: One 1-cup serving (prepared with fat-free milk and without salt) equals 176 calories, 5 g fat (2 g saturated fat), 11 mg cholesterol, 440 mg sodium, 29 g carbohydrate, 4 g fiber, 8 g protein. **Diabetic Exchanges:** 2 starch, 1 fat.

Chili Rellenos Burgers

Ready in 30 minutes or less

My husband loves hamburgers and Mexican food, so I combined the two to create this zesty sandwich. Garnish these dressed-up burgers with sliced avocados if you like. —Darlene Wilkinson, Quilcene, Washington

1 pound ground beef
1 medium onion, thinly sliced
1 teaspoon chili powder
1 teaspoon ground cumin
1/2 teaspoon salt
1/8 teaspoon pepper
1 can (4 ounces) whole green chilies, drained and halved
4 slices Colby-Monterey Jack cheese
1/2 cup salsa
2 tablespoons ketchup
4 sandwich buns, split
Sour cream

Shape beef into four patties. In a skillet over medium heat, brown patties on both sides. Top each with onion, chili powder, cumin, salt and pepper. Reduce heat; cover and simmer for 5 minutes or until meat is no longer pink. Top each patty with chilies and a slice of cheese. Cover and cook 3 minutes longer or until cheese is melted. In a small bowl, combine salsa and ketchup. Place burgers on buns; serve with the salsa mixture and sour cream. **Yield:** 4 servings.

Chapter 13

⏱ *Delectable Desserts*

AFTER-DINNER delights don't have to take a lot of time to prepare. Folks will think you fussed when you serve any of these impressive—yet easy-to-make—cakes, cookies, pies, desserts and more.

Each irresistible treat featured here looks and tastes special enough to serve weekend company. Yet they're so fast to fix you'll find yourself whipping them up for family and drop-in guests during the week.

In this chapter, you'll also find a mouth-watering array of take-along treats that are speedy solutions to last-minute bake sales and potlucks.

SPEEDY SWEETS. Clockwise from upper right: Fruity Angel Food Trifle (p. 192), Cherry Cheese Delight (p. 193) and Chocolate Raspberry Bars (p. 192).

Chocolate Chip Pumpkin Bread

Fruity Angel Food Trifle

(Pictured on page 191)

Plan ahead...needs to chill

This dessert showcases an attractive assortment of fresh and canned fruit. I refined the original recipe over time to suit our family's tastes.
—Louise Bouvier
Lafleche, Saskatchewan

4 cups cold milk
2 packages (3.4 ounces *each*) instant vanilla pudding mix
1 prepared angel food cake (8 inches)*
1 carton (8 ounces) frozen whipped topping, thawed
1 can (20 ounces) pineapple tidbits, drained
1 can (15 ounces) sliced pears, drained
1 pint strawberries, sliced
4 kiwifruit, peeled, halved and thinly sliced
1 cup fresh *or* frozen blueberries, thawed

In a mixing bowl, beat milk and pudding mix on low speed for 2 minutes; set aside. Split cake horizontally into thirds; place one layer in a 5-qt. serving bowl that is 9 in. in diameter. Top with a third of the pudding, whipped topping and fruit. Repeat layers twice. Cover and chill for at least 3 hours. **Yield:** 16-20 servings.

*Editor's Note: Before assembling trifle, check to make sure that the diameter of your serving bowl is large enough to accommodate the diameter of your cake. If the cake is too large, trim it to fit or cut into cubes.

Chocolate Chip Pumpkin Bread

(Pictured above)

A touch of cinnamon helps blend the chocolate and pumpkin flavors you'll find in this tender bread. And since the recipe makes two loaves, you can send one to a bake sale and keep one at home for your family to enjoy.
—Lora Stanley, Bennington, Kansas

3 cups all-purpose flour
2 teaspoons ground cinnamon
1 teaspoon salt
1 teaspoon baking soda
4 eggs
2 cups sugar
2 cups cooked *or* canned pumpkin
1-1/4 cups vegetable oil
1-1/2 cups semisweet chocolate chips

In a large bowl, combine the flour, cinnamon, salt and baking soda. In another bowl, beat the eggs, sugar, pumpkin and oil. Stir into dry ingredients just until moistened. Fold in chocolate chips.

Pour into two greased 8-in. x 4-in. x 2-in. loaf pans. Bake at 350° for 60-70 minutes or until a toothpick inserted near the center comes out clean. Cool for 10 minutes before removing from pans to wire racks. **Yield:** 2 loaves.

Chocolate Raspberry Bars

(Pictured on page 190)

Plan ahead...needs to chill

A boxed cake mix and raspberry jam simplify assembly of these sweet treats. The bars are very rich, so cut them into small pieces. —Diana Olmstead, Yelm, Washington

1 package (18-1/4 ounces) devil's food cake mix
1 egg
1/3 cup butter (no substitutes), softened
1 jar (12 ounces) seedless raspberry jam
TOPPING:
1 package (10 to 12 ounces) vanilla *or* white chips
1 package (8 ounces) cream cheese, softened
2 tablespoons milk
1/2 cup semisweet chocolate chips
2 tablespoons butter (no substitutes)

In a bowl, combine cake mix, egg and butter until crumbly. Press into a greased 15-in. x 10-in. x 1-in. baking pan. Bake at 350° for 8-10 minutes or until a toothpick inserted near the center comes out clean (crust will appear puffy and dry). Cool on a wire rack. Spread jam over the crust.

In a microwave or heavy saucepan, melt vanilla chips; stir until smooth. In a mixing bowl, beat cream cheese and milk until smooth. Add melted chips; mix well. Carefully spread over jam. Melt chocolate chips and butter; stir until smooth. Drizzle or pipe over the cream cheese layer. Refrigerate before cutting. **Yield:** about 6 dozen.

Cherry Cheese Delight

(Pictured on page 191)

Plan ahead...needs to chill

You couldn't ask for anything more than a nutty crust topped with a smooth cream cheese mixture and sweet cherries. This dessert can be made the night before.
—Kathy Branch, West Palm Beach, Florida

    1 cup all-purpose flour
    1 cup chopped pecans
  1/2 cup packed brown sugar
  1/2 cup butter *or* margarine, softened
FILLING:
    2 packages (8 ounces *each*) cream cheese, softened
  1/2 cup confectioners' sugar
    1 teaspoon vanilla extract
    1 carton (12 ounces) frozen whipped topping, thawed
    2 cans (21 ounces *each*) cherry pie filling

In a bowl, combine flour, pecans and brown sugar. With a fork, stir in butter until crumbly. Lightly pat into an ungreased 13-in. x 9-in. x 2-in. baking dish. Bake at 350° for 18-20 minutes or until golden brown. Cool completely.

For filling, in a mixing bowl, beat the cream cheese, confectioners' sugar and vanilla until smooth. Fold in whipped topping. Carefully spread over crust. Top with pie filling. Cover and refrigerate for at least 2 hours. **Yield:** 12-15 servings.

Coconut Caramel Oat Cookies

When I was a little girl, my grandma and I used to whip up this no-bake snack to munch on while playing rummy. I love to throw a batch together and remember those special times.   —Tammy Schroeder, Aitkin, Minnesota

  1/2 cup butter *or* margarine
  1/2 cup milk
    1 cup sugar
    1 teaspoon vanilla extract
  1/2 teaspoon salt
   25 caramels
    3 cups quick-cooking oats
    1 cup flaked coconut

In a heavy saucepan, bring butter and milk to a boil; add sugar, vanilla and salt. Cook for 1 minute. Add caramels and stir until melted, about 4 minutes. Stir in oats and coconut. Drop by heaping tablespoonfuls onto waxed paper. Let stand until set. **Yield:** 4-1/2 dozen.

Peanut Mallow Bars

(Pictured below)

Searching for the perfect combination of salty and sweet sensations? Well, look no further! Salted peanuts and rich caramel topping join marshmallow creme and brown sugar in these irresistible chewy bars. You won't be able to stop at just one!
—Claudia Ruiss
Massapequa, New York

    1 cup chopped salted peanuts
  3/4 cup all-purpose flour
  3/4 cup quick-cooking oats
  2/3 cup packed brown sugar
  1/2 teaspoon salt
  1/2 teaspoon baking soda
    1 egg, lightly beaten
  1/3 cup cold butter *or* margarine
TOPPING:
    1 jar (7 ounces) marshmallow creme
  2/3 cup caramel ice cream topping
1-3/4 cups salted peanuts

In a bowl, combine the first six ingredients; stir in the egg. Cut in butter until crumbly. Press into a greased 13-in. x 9-in. x 2-in. baking pan. Bake at 350° for 8-10 minutes or until lightly browned.

Spoon marshmallow creme over hot crust; carefully spread evenly. Drizzle with caramel topping; sprinkle with peanuts. Bake for 15-20 minutes or until lightly browned. Cool on a wire rack. Cut into bars. **Yield:** 3 dozen.

Peanut Mallow Bars

Blond Toffee Brownies

Whenever my co-worker brought these brownies to company bake sales, they sold in minutes. After getting the recipe from her, I was happy to discover how quickly they could be thrown together. I was even more excited when my family said that the thin chewy bars are the best they've ever tasted.
—Mary Williams
Lancaster, California

    1/2 cup butter *or* margarine, softened
      1 cup sugar
    1/2 cup packed brown sugar
      2 eggs
      1 teaspoon vanilla extract
  1-1/2 cups all-purpose flour
      2 teaspoons baking powder
    1/4 teaspoon salt
      1 cup English toffee bits *or* almond brickle chips

In a mixing bowl, cream butter and sugars. Add eggs, one at a time, beating well after each addition. Beat in vanilla. Combine the flour, baking powder and salt; gradually add to creamed mixture. Stir in toffee bits.

Spread evenly into a greased 13-in. x 9-in. x 2-in. baking pan. Bake at 350° for 35-40 minutes or until a toothpick inserted near the center comes out clean. Cool on a wire rack. Cut into bars. **Yield:** 1-1/2 dozen.

Cherry Trifle

(Pictured at right)

Plan ahead...needs to chill

I wanted to make a dessert that was light, refreshing and simple. The chocolate syrup in this tempting trifle is a sweet surprise, and everyone loves the topping of toasted coconut and almonds.
—Margo Seegrist
Shelton, Washington

  2-1/4 cups cold milk, *divided*
      1 package (3.4 ounces) instant vanilla pudding mix
      1 envelope whipped topping mix
    1/2 teaspoon vanilla extract
      1 prepared angel food cake (10 inches)
      2 tablespoons maraschino cherry juice
      1 can (21 ounces) cherry pie filling
    3/4 cup chocolate syrup
    1/2 cup flaked coconut, toasted
    1/4 cup sliced almonds, toasted

In a mixing bowl, combine 1-3/4 cups of milk and pudding mix. Beat on low speed for 2 minutes or until thickened. In another bowl, beat whipped topping mix, vanilla and remaining milk until stiff peaks form.

Cut cake into 1/2-in. cubes; place half in a 3-qt. glass bowl. Sprinkle with 1 tablespoon cherry juice. Top with half of the pie filling, half of the pudding and 1/4 cup of chocolate syrup. Repeat layers. Top with whipped topping and remaining syrup. Sprinkle with coconut and almonds. Cover and refrigerate for at least 4 hours. **Yield:** 12-15 servings.

Chocolate Mousse Pumpkin Pie

(Pictured at right)

Plan ahead...needs to chill

I combine canned pumpkin with two kinds of chocolate in this fluffy autumn delight that's perfect for special occasions. It's a tasty twist on traditional pumpkin pie.
—Kathy Peters, Omaha, Nebraska

      1 cup cooked *or* canned pumpkin
      2 cups miniature marshmallows
    1/2 cup milk chocolate chips
    1/2 cup miniature semisweet chocolate chips
      1 carton (12 ounces) frozen whipped topping, thawed
      1 graham cracker crust (9 inches)
Additional miniature semisweet chocolate chips, optional

In a large microwave-safe bowl, combine the pumpkin, marshmallows and chips. Microwave, uncovered, on high for 1-1/2 minutes; stir. Microwave 30-45 seconds longer or until marshmallows are melted and mixture is smooth, stirring every 15 seconds. Cool to room temperature, stirring several times.

Set aside about 1 tablespoon of whipped topping. Fold remaining topping into pumpkin mixture. Spoon into crust. Garnish with the reserved topping and miniature chips if desired. Refrigerate for at least 2 hours before slicing. **Yield:** 6-8 servings.

Editor's Note: This recipe was tested in an 850-watt microwave.

Rich Butter Cake

(Pictured at right)

I've been bringing this cake to family get-togethers and church meetings since the 1950s, and it draws rave reviews every time. The scrumptious standby, topped with cream cheese and nuts, can be prepared in a wink. Each bite is moist and rich, so no frosting is needed.
—Doris Schloeman, Naperville, Illinois

      1 package (16 ounces) pound cake mix
    1/2 cup butter *or* margarine, melted
      5 eggs
      2 cups confectioners' sugar, *divided*
      2 packages (one 8 ounces, one 3 ounces) cream cheese, softened
    1/2 teaspoon vanilla extract
      1 cup chopped walnuts

In a large mixing bowl, combine the dry cake mix, butter and 3 eggs; beat until smooth. Spread into a greased 13-in. x 9-in. x 2-in. baking pan. Set aside 2 tablespoons confectioners' sugar for topping. In a bowl, beat the cream cheese, vanilla, remaining confectioners' sugar and remaining eggs. Pour over batter. Sprinkle with walnuts.

Bake at 350° for 35-40 minutes or until cake begins to pull away from sides of pan. Cool on a wire rack. Dust with reserved confectioners' sugar. Store in the refrigerator. **Yield:** 12-15 servings.

Cherry Trifle
Chocolate Mousse Pumpkin Pie
Rich Butter Cake

Can't Leave Alone Bars

(Pictured below)

Convenient cake mix hurries along the preparation of these tasty bars. I bring these quick-and-easy treats to church meetings, potlucks and housewarming parties. I often make a double batch so we can enjoy some at home.

—Kimberly Biel, Java, South Dakota

    1 package (18-1/4 ounces) white cake mix
    2 eggs
 1/3 cup vegetable oil
    1 can (14 ounces) sweetened condensed milk
    1 cup (6 ounces) semisweet chocolate chips
 1/4 cup butter *or* margarine, cubed

In a bowl, combine the dry cake mix, eggs and oil. With floured hands, press two-thirds of the mixture into a greased 13-in. x 9-in. x 2-in. baking pan. Set remaining cake mixture aside.

In a microwave-safe bowl, combine the milk, chocolate chips and butter. Microwave, uncovered, on high for 45 seconds; stir. Microwave 45-60 seconds longer or until chips and butter are melted; stir until smooth. Pour over crust.

Drop teaspoonfuls of remaining cake mixture over top. Bake at 350° for 20-25 minutes or until lightly browned. Cool before cutting. **Yield:** 3 dozen.

Editor's Note: This recipe was tested in an 850-watt microwave.

Cocoa Munch Mix

(Pictured below)

This sweet snack is a nice change of pace from the typical cookies and brownies found at bake sales. Packed in resealable bags, it always goes fast. It's great for camping trips, too.   *—Amanda Denton, Barre, Vermont*

    4 cups Cheerios
    4 cups Chex
    1 cup slivered almonds
    2 tablespoons baking cocoa
    2 tablespoons sugar
 1/2 cup butter *or* margarine, melted
    1 cup raisins
    1 package (12 ounces) vanilla *or* white chips

In a large bowl, combine the cereals and almonds. In a small bowl, combine cocoa, sugar and butter. Pour over cereal mixture and toss to coat. Pour into a greased 13-in. x 9-in. x 2-in. baking pan. Bake at 250° for 1 hour, stirring every 15 minutes. Cool completely. Stir in raisins and chips. **Yield:** 10 servings.

Peanut Butter Oat Rounds

These irresistible peanut butter cookies are wonderful with a glass of milk. The addition of oats makes them hearty and nutritious.   *—Ann Pretty, St. Albert, Alberta*

Cocoa Munch Mix
Can't Leave Alone Bars

1 cup shortening
1 cup peanut butter*
1 cup sugar
1 cup packed brown sugar
2 eggs
2 cups all-purpose flour
1 cup quick-cooking oats
1-1/2 teaspoons baking soda
1/2 teaspoon salt

In a mixing bowl, cream shortening, peanut butter and sugars. Add eggs, one at a time, beating well after each addition. Combine dry ingredients; gradually add to creamed mixture. Roll into 1-in. balls. Place 3 in. apart on ungreased baking sheets. Flatten with a fork. Bake at 350° for 10-12 minutes or until bottoms are lightly browned. Remove to wire racks to cool. **Yield:** about 6-1/2 dozen.

Editor's Note: Reduced-fat or generic brands of peanut butter are not recommended for this recipe.

Marbled Orange Fudge

Honey Chip Granola Bars

Ready in 1 hour or less

A marshmallow, honey and peanut butter mixture is delicious over crunchy cereal, oats and nuts. —RosAnna Troyer, Millersburg, Ohio

1/4 cup butter *or* margarine
1/4 cup vegetable oil
1-1/2 pounds miniature marshmallows
1/4 cup honey
1/4 cup peanut butter*
5 cups old-fashioned oats
4-1/2 cups crisp rice cereal
1 cup graham cracker crumbs (about 16 squares)
1 cup flaked coconut
1 cup crushed peanuts
1/2 cup miniature chocolate chips

In a large saucepan, combine butter, oil and marshmallows. Cook and stir over low heat until mixture is melted and smooth. Remove from heat; stir in honey and peanut butter. Combine next five ingredients. Add to marshmallow mixture; mix well. Press into a greased 15-in. x 10-in. x 1-in. pan. Cool for 10-15 minutes. Sprinkle with chips; gently press into top. Cool before cutting. **Yield:** about 4 dozen.

Editor's Note: Reduced-fat or generic brands of peanut butter are not recommended for this recipe.

Making Peanut Butter Cookies

To make the crisscross pattern on peanut butter cookies, I use my round potato masher (first dipping it in sugar so the dough won't stick). —*Rosalie Bailey*
Darien, Wisconsin

Marbled Orange Fudge

(Pictured above)

Plan ahead...needs to chill

This decadent treat doesn't last long at our house. The soft fudge is guaranteed to get smiles because it has the familiar taste of frozen Creamsicles. Bright orange and marshmallow swirls make it the perfect take-along for autumn events and get-togethers. —Diane Wampler
Morristown, Tennessee

1-1/2 teaspoons plus 3/4 cup butter
(no substitutes), *divided*
3 cups sugar
3/4 cup whipping cream
1 package (10 to 12 ounces) vanilla *or* white chips
1 jar (7 ounces) marshmallow creme
3 teaspoons orange extract
12 drops yellow food coloring
5 drops red food coloring

Grease a 13-in. x 9-in. x 2-in. pan with 1-1/2 teaspoons butter. In a heavy saucepan, combine the sugar, cream and remaining butter. Cook and stir over low heat until sugar is dissolved. Bring to a boil; cook and stir for 4 minutes. Remove from the heat; stir in chips and marshmallow creme until smooth.

Remove 1 cup and set aside. Add orange extract and food colorings to remaining mixture; stir until blended. Pour into prepared pan. Drop the reserved marshmallow mixture by tablespoonfuls over top; cut through mixture with a knife to swirl. Cover and refrigerate until set. Cut into squares. **Yield:** about 2-1/2 pounds.

Ranch Snack Mix
Caramel Apple Cupcakes
S'more Sandwich Cookies
Frosted Peanut Butter Fingers

S'more Sandwich Cookies

(Pictured above)

Capture the taste of campfire s'mores in your kitchen. Graham cracker crumbs added to chocolate chip cookie dough bring out the flavor of the fireside favorite. Melting the cookies' marshmallow centers in the microwave makes them easy. —Abby Metzger, Larchwood, Iowa

  3/4 cup butter *or* margarine, softened
  1/2 cup sugar
  1/2 cup packed brown sugar
    1 egg
    2 tablespoons milk
    1 teaspoon vanilla extract
1-1/4 cups all-purpose flour
1-1/4 cups graham cracker crumbs (about 20 squares)
  1/2 teaspoon baking soda
  1/4 teaspoon salt
  1/8 teaspoon ground cinnamon
    2 cups (12 ounces) semisweet chocolate chips
  24 to 28 large marshmallows

In a mixing bowl, cream butter and sugars. Beat in egg, milk and vanilla. Combine the flour, graham cracker crumbs, baking soda, salt and cinnamon; gradually add to creamed mixture. Stir in chocolate chips.

Drop by tablespoonfuls 2 in. apart onto ungreased baking sheets. Bake at 375° for 8-10 minutes or until golden brown. Remove to wire racks to cool.

Place four cookies bottom side up on a microwave-safe plate; top each with a marshmallow. Microwave, uncovered, on high for 16-20 seconds or until marshmallows begin to puff (do not overcook). Top each with another cookie. Repeat. **Yield:** about 2 dozen.

Editor's Note: This recipe was tested in an 850-watt microwave.

Frosted Peanut Butter Fingers

(Pictured at left)

I first learned about these quick crowd-pleasers from a next-door neighbor when I sniffed the delightful aroma of a batch baking. Topped with extra peanut butter and chocolate frosting, the chewy bars became a family favorite that day when she brought us a plateful and shared the recipe. —Leah Gallington, Corona, California

      1 cup butter *or* margarine, softened
1-1/2 cups packed brown sugar
      1 cup sugar
2-1/2 cups creamy peanut butter,* *divided*
      1 egg
1-1/2 teaspoons vanilla extract
2-1/2 cups quick-cooking oats
      2 cups all-purpose flour
      1 teaspoon baking soda
  1/2 teaspoon salt
CHOCOLATE FROSTING:
      6 tablespoons butter *or* margarine, softened
      4 cups confectioners' sugar
  1/2 cup baking cocoa
      1 teaspoon vanilla extract
      6 to 8 tablespoons milk

In a mixing bowl, cream butter and sugars. Add 1 cup peanut butter, egg and vanilla; mix well. Combine oats, flour, baking soda and salt; add to the creamed mixture. Spread into a greased 15-in. x 10-in. x 1-in. baking pan.

Bake at 350° for 13-17 minutes or until golden brown. Cool slightly on a wire rack, about 12 minutes. Spread with remaining peanut butter. Cool completely.

In a mixing bowl, combine the butter, confectioners' sugar, cocoa, vanilla and enough milk to achieve spreading consistency. Spoon over peanut butter layer, then spread. Cut into bars. **Yield:** about 3 dozen.

*Editor's Note: Reduced-fat or generic brands of peanut butter are not recommended for this recipe.

Caramel Apple Cupcakes

(Pictured above left)

Bring these extra-special cupcakes to your next bake sale and watch how quickly they disappear—if your family doesn't gobble them up first! Kids will go for the fun appearance and tasty toppings while adults will appreciate the moist spiced cake underneath. —Diane Halferty, Corpus Christi, Texas

      1 package (18-1/4 ounces) spice *or* carrot cake mix
      2 cups chopped peeled tart apples
    20 caramels*
      3 tablespoons milk
      1 cup finely chopped pecans, toasted
    12 Popsicle sticks

Prepare cake batter according to package directions; fold in apples. Fill 12 greased or paper-lined jumbo muffin cups three-fourths full. Bake at 350° for 20 minutes or

until a toothpick comes out clean. Cool for 10 minutes before removing from pans to wire racks to cool completely.

In a saucepan, cook the caramels and milk over low heat until smooth. Spread over cupcakes. Sprinkle with pecans. Insert a wooden stick into the center of each cupcake. **Yield:** 1 dozen.

*Editor's Note: This recipe was tested with Hershey caramels.

Ranch Snack Mix

(Pictured at left)

Ready in 30 minutes or less

This is a wonderful fast-to-fix munchie. The recipe makes a generous 24 cups and doesn't involve any cooking. It's a cinch to package in individual snack bags, keeps its crunch and is a savory alternative to the cakes and pies usually offered at bake sales. —Linda Murphy, Pulaski, Wisconsin

      1 package (12 ounces) miniature pretzels
      2 packages (6 ounces *each*) Bugles
      1 can (10 ounces) salted cashews
      1 package (6 ounces) bite-size cheddar cheese fish crackers
      1 envelope ranch salad dressing mix
  3/4 cup vegetable oil

In two large bowls, combine the pretzels, Bugles, cashews and crackers. Sprinkle with dressing mix; toss gently to combine. Drizzle with oil; toss until well coated. Store in airtight containers. **Yield:** 6 quarts.

Cranberry Tart

Here's a fruity alternative to the abundance of chocolate the holidays bring. By adding a bit of citrus flavor to my golden-brown goody, it makes this tart so irresistible that it's likely to bring a smile to old Scrooge himself. —Norma Sockrider, Columbus, Nebraska

1-2/3 cups biscuit/baking mix
4-1/2 teaspoons sugar
  1/2 cup water
FILLING:
      1 to 1-1/4 cups sugar
      2 tablespoons biscuit/baking mix
2-1/2 cups fresh *or* frozen cranberries
  1/3 cup orange juice
      2 tablespoons butter *or* margarine

In a bowl, combine biscuit mix, sugar and water. With lightly floured hands, press mixture onto the bottom and up the sides of an ungreased 9-in. fluted tart pan with a removable bottom; set aside.

In a saucepan, combine sugar and biscuit mix. Add the cranberries, orange juice and butter. Cook and stir until mixture comes to a boil. Cook 1-2 minutes longer or until thickened and bubbly. Pour over crust. Bake at 375° for 30-35 minutes or until crust is golden and filling is bubbly. Cool on a wire rack. **Yield:** 8 servings.

Chocolate Bundt Cake
Soft Sugar Cookies
Creamy Lemonade Pie

Chocolate Bundt Cake

(Pictured at left)

Chocolate lovers will delight in this moist rich cake that's easy to prepare using handy mixes and canned frosting. I only make this dessert if I'm taking it somewhere. I don't want it sitting in my kitchen, where I might be tempted to eat it all!
—Nancy Baker
Boonville, Missouri

  1 package (18-1/4 ounces) yellow cake mix
  1 package (3.4 ounces) instant vanilla pudding
     mix
  1 cup (8 ounces) sour cream
  3 eggs
1/2 cup vegetable oil
1/2 cup water
  1 package (4 ounces) German sweet chocolate,
     grated
  1 cup (6 ounces) semisweet chocolate chips
1/2 cup chopped pecans
1/2 cup chocolate frosting, melted
Pecan halves

In a mixing bowl, combine cake and pudding mixes, sour cream, eggs, oil and water. Beat on low speed for 2 minutes. Fold in the grated chocolate, chocolate chips and pecans. Transfer to a greased and floured 10-in. fluted tube pan. Bake at 350° for 60-65 minutes or until a toothpick inserted near the center comes out clean. Cool for 10 minutes before removing from pan to a wire rack. Drizzle with frosting; garnish with pecan halves. **Yield:** 12-14 servings.

Soft Sugar Cookies

(Pictured at left)

These soft cookies are always a hit, so I often stir up a big batch. I usually add food coloring to the frosting to coordinate with the current holiday. —Coleen Walter
Bancroft, Michigan

  1 cup butter (no substitutes), softened
3/4 cup sugar
  2 eggs
  1 teaspoon vanilla extract
1/2 teaspoon almond extract
  2 cups all-purpose flour
  1 teaspoon cream of tartar
1/2 teaspoon baking soda
1/4 teaspoon salt
1/4 teaspoon ground nutmeg
FROSTING:
  3 cups confectioners' sugar
1/4 cup butter (no substitutes), softened
  1 teaspoon almond extract
  2 to 4 tablespoons hot water
Food coloring, optional

In a mixing bowl, cream butter and sugar. Beat in eggs, vanilla and almond extract. Combine the flour, cream of tartar, baking soda, salt and nutmeg; gradually add to creamed mixture. Drop by rounded teaspoonfuls 2 in. apart onto ungreased baking sheets. Bake at 350° for 8-10 minutes or until light brown. Remove to wire racks to cool.

For frosting, in a bowl, combine confectioners' sugar, butter, almond extract and enough water to achieve desired consistency. Tint with food coloring if desired. Frost the cookies. **Yield:** about 6 dozen.

Creamy Lemonade Pie

(Pictured at left and on cover)

Plan ahead...needs to chill

This luscious lemon pie looks quite elegant for an Easter dinner, yet it requires little effort. Guests will never suspect they're eating a quick-and-easy dessert.
—Carolyn Griffin, Macon, Georgia

  1 can (5 ounces) evaporated milk
  1 package (3.4 ounces) instant lemon pudding
     mix
  2 packages (8 ounces *each*) cream cheese,
     softened
3/4 cup lemonade concentrate
  1 graham cracker crust (9 inches)

In a mixing bowl, combine milk and pudding mix; beat on low speed for 2 minutes (mixture will be thick). In another mixing bowl, beat cream cheese until light and fluffy, about 3 minutes. Gradually beat in lemonade concentrate. Gradually beat in pudding mixture. Pour into crust. Cover and refrigerate for at least 4 hours. **Yield:** 6-8 servings.

Dandy Dessert Ideas

- I like to surprise my family once in a while with a special angel food cake. I use a box of angel food cake mix to make the batter. I divide it in half, then add 1/4 cup of baking cocoa to one portion. I pour each portion into an angel food cake pan and cut through the batters with a knife to swirl. Baked as directed, the cake has a lovely marbled look. —Donna Carper
South Jordan, Utah

- When I make chocolate frosting, I add about 1/4 cup of chocolate syrup as part of the liquid and use coffee instead of milk. I end up with a fudgy frosting that stays soft. —Sandy Olson
Big Lake, Minnesota

- I like to bake, but have encountered picky eaters as well as ones who are allergic to nuts. To keep everyone satisfied, I substitute Grape-Nuts cereal for the chopped nuts called for in my recipes. The cereal gives baked items the nice texture and crunch that you'd expect from nuts. —Tami Johnson
Eagan, Minnesota

- Looking for a great topping for ice cream, yogurt or pudding? Save the crumbs from the bottom of your cereal boxes. Store them in plastic bags to keep them crisp and delicious until you're ready to use them. —Susan Davis, Mullica Hill, New Jersey

Eggnog Pudding

(Pictured at right)

Plan ahead...needs to chill

Ring in the holidays with this creamy treat that pairs extra-thick pudding with crunchy cookie crumbs. The individual servings look so festive yet come together quite easily. —Anita Beaty, Mesa, Arizona

  12 Pirouette cookies *or* cookies of your choice
1/2 cup graham cracker crumbs (about 8
     squares)
   3 tablespoons butter *or* margarine, melted
   2 packages (8 ounces *each*) cream cheese,
     softened
   2 cups cold eggnog, *divided*
1-1/2 cups cold milk
   2 packages (3.4 ounces *each*) instant vanilla
     pudding mix
   2 to 3 teaspoons rum extract *or* vanilla extract
1/8 teaspoon ground nutmeg
Whipped topping

Crush four cookies; set remaining cookies aside for garnish. In a bowl, combine the crushed cookies, graham cracker crumbs and butter. Divide among eight serving dishes.

In a mixing bowl, beat cream cheese until smooth. Gradually beat in 1 cup eggnog. Add the milk, pudding mix, extract, nutmeg and remaining eggnog. Beat on low speed for 2 minutes. Spoon about 3/4 cup into each dish. Cover and refrigerate for 8 hours or overnight. Garnish with whipped topping and reserved cookies. **Yield:** 8 servings.

Editor's Note: This recipe was tested with Pepperidge Farm Pirouette cookies and commercially prepared eggnog.

Cherry Banana Cream Pie

(Pictured at right)

Plan ahead...needs to chill

The crunchy crust is spread with a rich butter layer, then topped with a fluffy filling flavored with banana, cherries and chocolate. Guests always tell me the pie reminds them of a banana split...and then ask for seconds. —Denise Elder, Hanover, Ontario

3/4 cup butter *or* margarine, softened, *divided*
   2 cups crushed vanilla wafers (about 60)
3/4 cup confectioners' sugar
FILLING:
   1 cup whipping cream
1/4 cup sugar
   2 tablespoons baking cocoa
   1 cup chopped walnuts
   1 large firm banana, thinly sliced
1/3 cup halved maraschino cherries
Whipped topping, chocolate curls and additional
   maraschino cherries

Melt 1/2 cup of butter; toss with wafer crumbs. Press into a 9-in. pie plate. In a small mixing bowl, cream the

remaining butter; beat in confectioners' sugar until combined. Spread over crust.

In another mixing bowl, beat the cream, sugar and cocoa until stiff peaks form. Fold in the walnuts, banana and maraschino cherries. Spoon into crust. Cover and refrigerate for 8 hours or overnight. Garnish with whipped topping, chocolate curls and cherries. **Yield:** 6-8 servings.

Pineapple Upside-Down Cake

(Pictured at right)

I need just a few easy ingredients to dress up a boxed mix and create this classic cake. It bakes up so moist and pretty, no one will believe it wasn't made from scratch. —Gloria Poyer, Oxford, New Jersey

   6 canned pineapple slices
   6 maraschino cherries
   1 cup chopped walnuts, *divided*
   1 package (18-1/4 ounces) white cake mix

Place pineapple slices in a greased and floured 10-in. tube pan. Place a cherry in the center of each slice. Sprinkle half of the walnuts around the pineapple. Prepare cake mix according to package directions; spoon batter over pineapple layer. Sprinkle with remaining nuts.

Bake at 350° for 40-45 minutes or until a toothpick inserted near the center comes out clean. Cool for 10 minutes before inverting onto a wire rack to cool completely. **Yield:** 10 servings.

Pistachio Cookie Dessert

Plan ahead...needs to freeze

With its smooth pistachio filling, this cool treat is a favorite refreshment at summer 4-H meetings. It's best made and frozen a day in advance. It will thaw as you head to a picnic or potluck. —Audrey Phillips, Gambier, Ohio

   1 quart vanilla ice cream
   1 package (20 ounces) chocolate cream-filled
     sandwich cookies
1/2 cup plus 2 tablespoons butter *or* margarine,
     melted
1-1/2 cups cold milk
   2 packages (3.4 ounces *each*) instant pistachio
     pudding mix
   1 carton (16 ounces) frozen whipped topping,
     thawed

Soften ice cream while preparing crust. Place cookies in a food processor or blender; cover and process until fine crumbs form. Stir in butter. Set aside 1 cup for topping. Press remaining crumb mixture into an ungreased 13-in. x 9-in. x 2-in. dish.

In a mixing bowl, beat milk and pudding mix on low speed for 2 minutes. Gradually add ice cream; mix well. Fold in whipped topping. Spread over crust. Sprinkle reserved crumb mixture over top, pressing down lightly. Cover and freeze for 4 hours or overnight. Remove from the freezer 20 minutes before cutting. **Yield:** 12-15 servings.

Pineapple Upside-Down Cake
Eggnog Pudding
Cherry Banana Cream Pie

Macadamia Chip Cookies

(Pictured below)

If you like cookies with a crunch, you'll love these golden treats. Crushed peanut brittle adds an unexpected kick to the vanilla chips and brown sugar that flavor the dough. It's hard to believe something this easy to make tastes so terrific.   —Dorothy Kollmeyer, Dupo, Illinois

    1 cup butter *or* margarine, softened
3/4 cup packed brown sugar
1/4 cup sugar
    2 eggs
    1 teaspoon vanilla extract
2-1/4 cups all-purpose flour
    1 package (3.4 ounces) instant vanilla pudding
       mix
    1 teaspoon baking soda
1/4 teaspoon salt
    1 package (10 to 12 ounces) vanilla *or* white
       chips
    2 jars (3-1/4 ounces *each*) macadamia nuts,
       chopped
1/2 cup finely crushed peanut brittle

In a mixing bowl, cream butter and sugars until smooth. Add eggs, one at a time, beating well after each addition. Beat in vanilla. Combine the flour, dry pudding mix, baking soda and salt; gradually add to creamed mixture and mix well. Stir in chips, nuts and peanut brittle.

Drop by rounded tablespoonfuls 2 in. apart onto greased baking sheets. Bake at 375° for 10-12 minutes or until golden brown. Remove to wire racks to cool. **Yield:** 5-1/2 dozen.

Macadamia Chip Cookies

Zucchini Chocolate Cake

Rely on shredded zucchini to make this one of the moistest cakes you've ever tried. I add walnuts and chocolate chips to guarantee each piece is met with a glass of milk and a smile.   —Grace Engle, Cortland, Ohio

1/2 cup butter *or* margarine, softened
1-1/2 cups sugar
    3 eggs
1/2 cup vegetable oil
    3 teaspoons vanilla extract
1-3/4 cups all-purpose flour
1/4 cup baking cocoa
    2 teaspoons baking soda
    1 teaspoon baking powder
1/2 teaspoon ground cinnamon
    2 cups shredded zucchini
    1 cup chopped walnuts, optional
1/2 cup semisweet chocolate chips

In a mixing bowl, cream butter and sugar. Add eggs, one at a time, beating well after each addition. Beat in oil and vanilla. Combine the flour, cocoa, baking soda, baking powder and cinnamon; gradually add to the creamed mixture. Fold in zucchini and walnuts if desired.

Spread into a greased 13-in. x 9-in. x 2-in. baking pan. Sprinkle with chocolate chips. Bake at 350° for 30-35 minutes or until a toothpick inserted near the center comes out clean. Cool on a wire rack. **Yield:** 12-15 servings.

Cherry Bars

(Pictured above right)

With their pretty color from cherry pie filling and subtle almond flavor, these fruit-filled bars are destined to become Christmas classics.   —Jane Kamp
Grand Rapids, Michigan

    1 cup butter *or* margarine, softened
    2 cups sugar
    4 eggs
    1 teaspoon vanilla extract
1/4 teaspoon almond extract
    3 cups all-purpose flour
    1 teaspoon salt
    2 cans (21 ounces *each*) cherry pie filling
GLAZE:
    1 cup confectioners' sugar
1/2 teaspoon vanilla extract
1/2 teaspoon almond extract
    2 to 3 tablespoons milk

In a large mixing bowl, cream butter and sugar. Add eggs, one at a time, beating well after each addition. Beat in the extracts. Combine flour and salt; add to the creamed mixture and mix until combined.

Spread 3 cups batter into a greased 15-in. x 10-in. x 1-in. baking pan. Spread with pie filling. Drop the remaining batter by teaspoonfuls over filling. Bake at 350° for 30-35 minutes or until a toothpick comes out clean. Cool on a wire rack. Combine the glaze ingredients; drizzle over bars. **Yield:** 5 dozen.

Almond Chocolate Biscotti
Cherry Bars

Almond Chocolate Biscotti

(Pictured above)

Boxed cake mix makes this biscotti easy to prepare, but the taste and appearance make it memorable. I've given neighbors these decadent chocolate-covered delights for the holidays. —Ginger Chatfield, Muscatine, Iowa

    1 package (18-1/4 ounces) chocolate cake mix
    1 cup all-purpose flour
1/2 cup butter *or* margarine, melted
1/4 cup chocolate syrup
    2 eggs
    1 teaspoon vanilla extract
1/2 teaspoon almond extract
1/2 cup slivered almonds
1/2 cup miniature semisweet chocolate chips
    1 package (10 to 12 ounces) vanilla *or* white
       chips
    2 tablespoons shortening

In a large mixing bowl, combine the dry cake mix, flour, butter, chocolate syrup, eggs and extracts; mix well. Stir in the almonds and miniature chocolate chips. Divide dough in half. On ungreased baking sheets, shape each portion into a 12-in. x 3-in. log. Bake at 350° for 30-35 minutes or until firm to the touch. Cool for 15 minutes. Transfer to a cutting board, carefully cut diagonally with a serrated knife into 1/2-in. slices. Place cut side down on ungreased baking sheets. Bake for 10-15 minutes or until firm. Remove to wire racks to cool.

In a small heavy saucepan over low heat, melt vanilla chips and shortening. Drizzle over biscotti; let stand until hardened. Store in an airtight container. **Yield:** about 3-1/2 dozen.

Coconut Shortbread

Plan ahead...needs to chill

My niece makes this shortbread for special occasions. My family enjoys the rich flavor of these cookies so much, I bake them all year long. To save time, I often divide this recipe into two tasks by making the dough one day and baking cookies the next. —Nancy Siefert
Wauwatosa, Wisconsin

    2 cups butter (no substitutes), softened
    1 cup sugar
    2 teaspoons vanilla extract
    4 cups all-purpose flour
1/2 cup flaked coconut
Confectioners' sugar

In a mixing bowl, cream butter, sugar and vanilla. Gradually add flour. Stir in coconut. Shape into two 8-in. rolls; wrap each in plastic wrap. Refrigerate for 1 hour or until firm. Unwrap and cut into 1/4-in. slices. Place 1 in. apart on ungreased baking sheets. Bake at 350° for 12-15 minutes or until edges are lightly browned. Dip both sides of cookies in confectioners' sugar while warm. Cool on wire racks. **Yield:** 5 dozen.

Mocha Angel Food Torte
Mint Chocolate Chip Pie
Berries 'n' Cream Brownies

Mocha Angel Food Torte

(Pictured at left)

Plan ahead...needs to chill

Chocolate, toffee and a hint of coffee make this torte a popular request. I use a few instant ingredients to give prepared angel food cake heavenly homespun flair.
—Hillary Brunn, Santa Rosa, California

1-1/3 cups cold milk
1 package (3.9 ounces) instant chocolate pudding mix
1 tablespoon instant coffee granules
1 cup whipping cream, whipped, *divided*
1 prepared angel food cake (10 inches)
2 Heath candy bars (1.4 ounces *each*), crushed

In a mixing bowl, combine milk, pudding mix and coffee; beat on low speed for 2 minutes or until thickened. Fold in half of the whipped cream.

Cut cake in half horizontally; place the bottom layer on a serving plate. Spread with half of the pudding mixture. Top with remaining cake.

Fold remaining whipped cream into remaining pudding mixture; spread over top and sides of cake. Sprinkle with crushed candy bars. Chill for 2 hours before serving. **Yield:** 10-12 servings.

Mint Chocolate Chip Pie

(Pictured at left)

Plan ahead...needs to chill

Your guests will be requesting the recipe after one bite of this fluffy and refreshing pie. It doesn't take much time to prepare, yet it tastes as though you spent hours in the kitchen.
—Laurie Bourgeois
New Bedford, Massachusetts

2 cups whipping cream
2 tablespoons confectioners' sugar
2 cups cold milk
1-1/2 teaspoons peppermint extract
5 to 6 drops green food coloring, optional
2 packages (3.4 ounces *each*) instant vanilla pudding mix
1 cup miniature semisweet chocolate chips
1 pastry shell (9 inches), baked

In a small mixing bowl, beat cream and sugar until soft peaks form. In a large mixing bowl, combine the milk, extract and food coloring if desired. Add pudding mixes; beat on low speed for 2 minutes or until thickened.

Fold in cream mixture and chocolate chips. Pour into pastry shell. Refrigerate for 3 hours or until set. **Yield:** 6-8 servings.

Berries 'n' Cream Brownies

(Pictured at left)

Plan ahead...needs to chill

If you like chocolate-covered strawberries, you'll love this sweet treat. It's an ideal ending to summer meals. A fudgy brownie, whipped topping and fresh fruit make this a no-fuss feast for the eyes as well as the taste buds.
—Anna Lapp, New Holland, Pennsylvania

1 package fudge brownie mix (13-inch x 9-inch pan size)
1 carton (8 ounces) frozen whipped topping, thawed
4 cups quartered fresh strawberries
1/3 cup chocolate hard-shell ice cream topping

Prepare and bake brownies according to package directions, using a greased 13-in. x 9-in. x 2-in. baking pan. Cool completely on a wire rack.

Spread whipped topping over brownies. Arrange strawberries cut side down over top. Drizzle with chocolate topping. Refrigerate for at least 30 minutes before serving. **Yield:** 12-15 servings.

Raspberry Rice Pudding

Ready in 15 minutes or less

We love this because it takes less time than baked rice pudding.
—Jennifer Eggebraaten, Hastings, Michigan

1-1/2 cups whipping cream
1/4 cup sugar
3/4 teaspoon vanilla extract
1-1/2 cups cold cooked rice
1/3 cup seedless raspberry jam
4 drops red food coloring, optional
1 cup fresh raspberries

In a mixing bowl, beat the cream, sugar and vanilla until soft peaks form. Stir in the rice, jam and food coloring if desired. Spoon into serving dishes. Garnish with raspberries. **Yield:** 4 servings.

Prebaking Pie Shells

TO KEEP pie crust from shrinking when it's prebaked, follow these suggestions:

1 Line the pastry shell with heavy-duty foil and fill it with 1-1/2 cups dried beans or rice. Bake at 450° for 8 minutes.

2 With oven mitts, carefully remove the foil and beans from the pie crust. Continue baking until crust is golden brown, about 5-6 minutes.

Crispy Pretzel Bars
Malted Milk Cookies

Malted Milk Cookies

(Pictured above)

My daughter substituted crushed malted milk balls in our favorite chocolate chip cookie recipe to create these crisp treats. They're so yummy fresh from the oven.
—Audrey Metzger, Larchwood, Iowa

    1 cup butter (no substitutes), softened
  3/4 cup packed brown sugar
  1/3 cup sugar
    1 egg
    2 teaspoons vanilla extract
2-1/4 cups all-purpose flour
    2 tablespoons instant chocolate drink mix
    1 teaspoon baking soda
  1/2 teaspoon salt
    2 cups malted milk balls, crushed

In a mixing bowl, cream the butter and sugars. Beat in egg and vanilla. Combine the flour, drink mix, baking soda and salt; gradually add to creamed mixture. Stir in malted milk balls. Shape into 1-1/2-in. balls. Place 2 in. apart on greased baking sheets. Bake at 375° for 10-12 minutes or until set. Cool for 1 minute before removing from pans to wire racks. **Yield:** about 3 dozen.

Crispy Pretzel Bars

(Pictured above)

Ready in 30 minutes or less

I often make a big batch of these peanut butter-flavored cereal bars on days that I don't want to heat up the kitchen. Kids especially love them, so they're great for picnics, potlucks and school bake sales.
—Jane Thompson, Eureka, Illinois

    1 cup sugar
    1 cup light corn syrup
  1/2 cup peanut butter
    5 cups crisp rice cereal
    2 cups pretzel sticks
    1 cup plain M&M's

In a large microwave-safe bowl, combine the sugar and corn syrup. Microwave on high for 3 minutes or until sugar is dissolved. Stir in peanut butter until blended. Add the cereal, pretzels and M&M's; stir until coated. Press into a greased 15-in. x 10-in. x 1-in. pan. Cut into bars. **Yield:** about 5 dozen.

Editor's Note: This recipe was tested in an 850-watt microwave.

Almond Poppy Seed Bars

These tender squares have a sweet frosting and generous sprinkling of poppy seeds throughout. The bars are a snap to whip up, plus they use ingredients I usually have on hand. —Pam Mroz, Rochester, Minnesota

        3 eggs
2-1/4 cups sugar
1-1/2 cups milk
        1 cup vegetable oil
1-1/2 teaspoons almond extract
1-1/2 teaspoons vanilla extract
1-1/2 teaspoons butter flavoring *or* additional
        vanilla extract
        3 cups all-purpose flour
4-1/2 teaspoons poppy seeds
1-1/2 teaspoons baking powder
1-1/2 teaspoons salt
FROSTING:
    1/3 cup butter *or* margarine, melted
        3 cups confectioners' sugar
        3 tablespoons milk

In a mixing bowl, beat the eggs, sugar, milk, oil, extracts and butter flavoring. Combine the flour, poppy seeds, baking powder and salt; add to the egg mixture and mix just until combined. Spread into a greased 15-in. x 10-in. x 1-in. baking pan. Bake at 350° for 20 minutes or until a toothpick inserted near the center comes out clean. Cool on a wire rack.

In a mixing bowl, combine the frosting ingredients; beat until smooth. Frost bars. **Yield:** about 5-1/2 dozen.

Chocolate Oat Scotchies

My mom found this recipe a long time ago, and it was a hit with our family. Each bite is packed with chocolate, butterscotch and peanut flavors. —Stephanie Helmke, Defiance, Ohio

    2/3 cup butter *or* margarine
        1 cup packed brown sugar
    1/4 cup corn syrup
    1/4 cup plus 2/3 cup chunky peanut butter,*
        divided
        1 teaspoon vanilla extract
        4 cups quick-cooking oats
        1 package (11-1/2 ounces) milk chocolate
        chips
    1/2 cup butterscotch chips
        1 cup salted peanuts

In a saucepan over low heat, melt the butter; stir in brown sugar and corn syrup until the sugar is dissolved. Stir in 1/4 cup peanut butter and vanilla until blended. Add the oats; mix well.

Press into a greased 13-in. x 9-in. x 2-in. baking pan. Bake at 375° for 12-15 minutes. Meanwhile, melt the chips and remaining peanut butter; stir in peanuts. Spread over crust. Refrigerate until cool; cut into bars. **Yield:** 6-1/2 dozen.

***Editor's Note:** Reduced-fat or generic brands of peanut butter are not recommended for this recipe.

Peanut Butter Candy Pie

(Pictured below)

Ready in 1 hour or less

It only takes a couple of ingredients and a few minutes to create two of these crispy colorful "pizzas". Whether sold as a whole pie or by the slice, the chocolate layer and coconut and peanut butter candy toppings will make it popular with children of all ages. —Laura Mahaffey, Annapolis, Maryland

    1/4 cup butter *or* margarine
        4 cups miniature marshmallows
        6 cups crisp rice cereal
      50 milk chocolate kisses *or* 1-1/3 cups milk
        chocolate chips
    1/2 cup flaked coconut
        2 cups Reese's Pieces

In a microwave-safe bowl, heat the butter and marshmallows on high for 1 minute; stir until marshmallows are melted. Add the cereal; mix well. Press onto the bottom and up the sides of two greased 9-in. pie plates.

In a microwave or heavy saucepan, melt chocolate kisses; stir until smooth. Spread over prepared crusts. Sprinkle with coconut and candy pieces; press down lightly. Let stand until chocolate is set. Cut into slices. **Yield:** 2 pies (8 slices each).

Editor's Note: This recipe was tested in an 850-watt microwave.

Peanut Butter Candy Pie

Hugs 'n' Kisses Brownie

(Pictured at right)

When I needed a dessert in a hurry, I dressed up a brownie mix with on-hand ingredients to come up with this impressive treat.
—Kristi Van Batavia
Kansas City, Missouri

    1 package fudge brownie mix (8-inch square
        pan size)
    1 egg
    1/4 cup vegetable oil
    1/4 cup water
1-1/2 cups vanilla *or* white chips, *divided*
   14 to 16 milk chocolate kisses
   14 to 16 striped chocolate kisses
1-1/2 teaspoons shortening

In a bowl, stir brownie mix, egg, oil and water until well blended. Fold in 1 cup vanilla chips. Pour into a greased 9-in. heart-shaped or round springform pan. Bake at 350° for 35-40 minutes or until a toothpick inserted 2 in. from the side of pan comes out clean.

Let stand for 10 minutes; alternate milk chocolate and striped kisses around edge of pan with points toward center. Melt shortening and remaining chips; stir until smooth. Drizzle over brownie. Cool completely. Remove sides of springform pan. **Yield:** 10-12 servings.

Banana Cream Dessert

(Pictured at right)

Plan ahead...needs to chill

I entertain often, so this crowd-pleasing dessert is frequently on the menu. When cleaning up the dishes, there's never a crumb left to scrape off.
—Evelyn Schmidt
Toms River, New Jersey

    3 cups graham cracker crumbs (about 48
        squares)
    1/2 cup butter *or* margarine, melted
3-1/2 cups cold milk
    2 packages (3.4 ounces *each*) instant vanilla
        pudding mix
    5 medium firm bananas, halved lengthwise
        and cut into 1/2-inch slices
    1 can (20 ounces) crushed pineapple, drained
    1 carton (20 ounces) frozen whipped topping,
        thawed
    1/3 cup chopped pecans, optional
    2 milk chocolate candy bars (1.55 ounces
        each), broken into squares
Maraschino cherries, optional

Combine cracker crumbs and butter. Press into an ungreased 13-in. x 9-in. x 2-in. dish. In a mixing bowl, beat milk and pudding mix on low speed for 2 minutes. Pour over crust; top with bananas and pineapple. Spread with whipped topping (dish will be full). Sprinkle with pecans if desired.

Chill for at least 4 hours before cutting. Garnish with candy bar pieces and cherries if desired. **Yield:** 16-20 servings.

Nutty White Fudge

(Pictured at right)

Plan ahead...needs to chill

Years ago, a friend gave me a batch of this soft fudge that's full of walnuts. It's great for bake sales or any time you need to satisfy a sweet tooth.
—Martha Boggs
Jackson, Kentucky

    1 package (3 ounces) cream cheese, softened
    1 tablespoon milk
    2 cups confectioners' sugar
    2 squares (1 ounce *each*) white baking
        chocolate, melted
    1/2 teaspoon vanilla extract
    1/8 teaspoon salt
    1 cup chopped walnuts

In a mixing bowl, beat the cream cheese and milk until smooth. Gradually add the sugar. Beat in melted chocolate. Add the vanilla and salt; mix well. Stir in the walnuts. Spread into a buttered 8-in. square pan. Chill for 4-5 hours before cutting. Store in the refrigerator. **Yield:** about 1 pound.

Pineapple Pretzel Fluff

Ready in 30 minutes or less

Looking for something different to bring to a potluck? Everyone goes crazy for this sweet and crunchy combination. Be sure to add the pretzel mixture right before serving to keep it crispy. —Beth Olby, Ashland, Wisconsin

    1 cup coarsely crushed pretzels
    1/2 cup butter *or* margarine, melted
    1 cup sugar, *divided*
    1 package (8 ounces) cream cheese, softened
    1 can (20 ounces) crushed pineapple, drained
    1 carton (12 ounces) frozen whipped topping,
        thawed

In a bowl, combine pretzels, butter and 1/2 cup sugar. Press into a 13-in. x 9-in. x 2-in. baking pan. Bake at 400° for 7 minutes. Cool. Meanwhile, in a mixing bowl, beat cream cheese and remaining sugar until creamy. Fold in pineapple and whipped topping; chill until serving. Break pretzel mixture into small pieces; stir into pineapple mixture. **Yield:** 6 servings.

Creative Cake Cutting

Cutting a decorated cake layer can sometimes create an unattractive presentation. To avoid the messy globs of frosting that collect on the knife, use dental floss to cut the cake

Just cut the floss to about 8 more inches than the widest part of the cake. Wrap one end around a finger of one hand and the other end around a finger of the other hand. Pull it taut, then pull the floss firmly straight down through the cake to slice it. It works wonderfully!
—Beckey Tibbets, Argyle, Texas

Hugs 'n' Kisses Brownie
Banana Cream Dessert
Nutty White Fudge

Orange Slice Cookies

(Pictured below)

Soft candy orange slices are a refreshing addition to these crispy vanilla chip cookies. To quickly cut the orange candy, use scissors, rinsing the blades with cold water occasionally to reduce sticking.
—Britt Strain
Idaho Falls, Idaho

> 1 cup candy orange slices
> 1-1/4 cups sugar, *divided*
> 1 cup butter *or* margarine, softened
> 1 cup shortening
> 1-1/2 cups packed brown sugar
> 2 eggs
> 2 teaspoons vanilla extract
> 4 cups all-purpose flour
> 2 teaspoons baking soda
> 1 teaspoon salt
> 1 package (12 ounces) vanilla *or* white chips
> 1 cup chopped pecans

Cut each orange slice into eight pieces. Roll in 1/4 cup sugar; set aside. In a mixing bowl, cream the butter, shortening, brown sugar and remaining sugar. Add eggs, one at a time, beating well after each addition. Beat in vanilla. Combine the flour, baking soda and salt; gradually add to creamed mixture. Stir in chips, pecans and orange slice pieces.

Roll into 1-in. balls. Place 2 in. apart on ungreased baking sheets. Bake at 375° for 10-12 minutes or until golden brown. Remove to wire racks to cool. **Yield:** about 10 dozen.

Graham Cracker Brownies

(Pictured below)

I enjoy making these brownies for last-minute bake sales and family gatherings alike. My grandmother first baked them nearly 50 years ago, and they're as popular today as they were then!
—Cathy Guffey
Towanda, Pennsylvania

> 2 cups graham cracker crumbs (about 32 squares)
> 1 cup (6 ounces) semisweet chocolate chips
> 1 teaspoon baking powder
> Pinch salt
> 1 can (14 ounces) sweetened condensed milk

In a bowl, combine all the ingredients. Spread into a greased 8-in. square baking pan. Bake at 350° for 30-35 minutes or until a toothpick inserted near the center comes out clean. Cool on a wire rack. **Yield:** 1-1/2 dozen.

Strawberry Jam Bars

I bake for a group of seniors every week, and this is one of the goodies they request most. I always keep the ingredients on hand for last-minute baking emergencies. Give these bars your own twist by replacing the strawberry jam with the fruit jam of your choice.
—Karen Mead, Pittsburgh, Pennsylvania

> 1/2 cup butter *or* margarine, softened
> 1/2 cup packed brown sugar

Orange Slice Cookies
Graham Cracker Brownies

Chips Galore Cookies
Crunchy Trail Mix

1 egg
1 package (18-1/4 ounces) white cake mix
1 cup finely crushed cornflakes
1 cup strawberry jam *or* preserves

In a mixing bowl, cream butter and brown sugar until smooth. Add egg; mix well. Gradually add dry cake mix and cornflakes. Set aside 1-1/2 cups for topping. Press remaining dough into a greased 13-in. x 9-in. x 2-in. baking pan. Carefully spread jam over crust. Sprinkle with reserved dough; gently press down. Bake at 350° for 30 minutes or until golden brown. Cool completely on a wire rack. Cut into bars. **Yield:** 2 dozen.

Crunchy Trail Mix

(Pictured above)

Ready in 15 minutes or less

Five ingredients make up this colorful crowd-pleaser that's crunchy, chewy and not too sweet. —Theresa Gingery
Holmesville, Nebraska

1 package (16 ounces) milk chocolate M&M's
1 package (10 ounces) peanut butter chips
1 can (3 ounces) chow mein noodles
1-1/2 cups raisins
1-1/4 cups peanuts

In a large bowl, combine all ingredients; mix well. Store in an airtight container. **Yield:** 8 cups.

Chips Galore Cookies

(Pictured above)

Chock-full of pecans, walnuts and three types of chips, these crisp treats will be such a hit with your family, they might not make it to the bake sale. —Shauna Stephens
San Diego, California

1 cup butter *or* margarine, softened
3/4 cup sugar
3/4 cup packed brown sugar
2 eggs
1 tablespoon almond extract
2-1/4 cups all-purpose flour
1 teaspoon baking soda
1/2 teaspoon salt
1-1/2 cups *each* semisweet chocolate chips, milk chocolate chips and vanilla *or* white chips
1-1/2 cups chopped pecans
1-1/2 cups chopped walnuts

In a mixing bowl, cream butter and sugars. Add eggs, one at a time, beating well after each addition. Beat in almond extract. Combine the flour, baking soda and salt; gradually add to creamed mixture. Combine chips and nuts; stir into dough. Cover and refrigerate for 1 hour or until easy to handle.

Drop by tablespoonfuls 2 in. apart onto greased baking sheets. Bake at 325° for 18-20 minutes or until golden brown. Remove to wire racks to cool. **Yield:** 9 dozen.

Chapter 14

⊙ *Fast, Delicious...and Nutritious*

LOOKING for fast-to-fix dishes that fit today's healthy lifestyle? If you're counting calories or trying to reduce fat, sugar or salt in your diet (and doing all this while keeping one eye on the clock), the lighter fare featured here should fit right in.

That's because these rapid recipes use less fat, sugar or salt and include Nutritional Analysis and Diabetic Exchanges.

Anyone on a special diet—and even those who aren't—will enjoy these delicious and nutritious dishes.

(All the quick good-for-you foods in this book are flagged with a red checkmark in the indexes beginning on page 334.)

GOOD-FOR-YOU FARE. Top to bottom: Cinnamon Nut Twists and Apricot Carrot Bread (both recipes on p. 228).

Chicken in Creamy Gravy
Lemon Linguine

7 g fat (1 g saturated fat), 72 mg cholesterol, 644 mg sodium, 18 g carbohydrate, 5 g fiber, 30 g protein. **Diabetic Exchanges:** 3 lean meat, 1 starch.

 All recipes in this chapter use less fat, sugar or salt and include Nutritional Analysis and Diabetic Exchanges.

Chicken in Creamy Gravy

(Pictured above)

Ready in 30 minutes or less

You only need a few ingredients and a few minutes to put together this tasty main dish. A burst of lemon in every bite makes it a well-received standby. —Jean Little
Charlotte, North Carolina

      4 boneless skinless chicken breast halves
         (1 pound)
      1 tablespoon canola oil
      1 can (10-3/4 ounces) reduced-fat reduced-
         sodium condensed cream of chicken and
         broccoli soup, undiluted
  1/4 cup fat-free milk
      2 teaspoons lemon juice
  1/8 teaspoon pepper
      4 lemon slices

In a nonstick skillet, cook chicken in oil until browned on both sides, about 10 minutes; drain. In a bowl, combine soup, milk, lemon juice and pepper. Pour over chicken. Top each chicken breast with a lemon slice. Reduce heat; cover and simmer until chicken juices run clear, about 5 minutes. **Yield:** 4 servings.

Nutritional Analysis: One serving equals 232 calories,

Lemon Linguine

(Pictured above)

Ready in 15 minutes or less

I coat pasta with a succulent blend of lemon and herbs, then sprinkle it with Parmesan cheese. Serve it as a versatile side dish...or dress it up with cooked chicken or ham for a delicious entree. —Ann Dockendorf
Clearwater, Minnesota

      8 ounces uncooked linguine
      3 tablespoons butter *or* stick margarine,
         melted
      1 tablespoon lemon juice
  1-1/2 teaspoons dried basil
  1/2 teaspoon garlic powder
  1/2 teaspoon salt-free lemon-pepper seasoning
  1/4 cup grated Parmesan cheese

In a saucepan, cook linguine in boiling water for 8-10 minutes or until tender. Meanwhile, in another saucepan, combine butter, lemon juice, basil, garlic powder and lemon-pepper; cook and stir until butter is melted. Drain linguine; add to butter mixture and toss to coat. Add Parmesan cheese and toss. **Yield:** 4 servings.

Nutritional Analysis: One serving (1 cup) equals 262

calories, 12 g fat (7 g saturated fat), 28 mg cholesterol, 306 mg sodium, 33 g carbohydrate, 2 g fiber, 9 g protein. **Diabetic Exchanges:** 2 starch, 1 lean meat, 1 fat.

Apricot Angel Dessert

Plan ahead...needs to chill

I top cubes of fluffy angel food cake with canned apricot halves and a yummy sauce. This light dessert is particularly good after a heavy meal. —Beverly King
Vulcan, Michigan

   1 loaf (14 ounces) angel food cake, cubed (about 8 cups)
   1 can (15-1/4 ounces) apricot halves, drained and diced
Sugar substitute equivalent to 1/2 cup sugar
   3 tablespoons cornstarch
   3 cups apricot nectar
   1 package (.3 ounce) sugar-free orange gelatin
   1 carton (8 ounces) reduced-fat frozen whipped topping, thawed

Place the cake cubes in an ungreased 13-in. x 9-in. x 2-in. dish; top with apricots. In a saucepan, combine the sugar substitute, cornstarch and apricot nectar until smooth. Bring to a boil; cook and stir for 2 minutes or until thickened. Remove from the heat. Stir in gelatin until dissolved. Pour over cake and apricots. Cover and chill for 3 hours or until gelatin is set. Spread with whipped topping. Refrigerate leftovers. **Yield:** 12 servings.

Nutritional Analysis: One serving equals 202 calories, 3 g fat (2 g saturated fat), 0 cholesterol, 187 mg sodium, 44 g carbohydrate, 1 g fiber, 3 g protein. **Diabetic Exchanges:** 2 fruit, 1 starch, 1/2 fat.

Raspberry Bran Muffins

Ready in 1 hour or less

Consider this recipe when you're looking to bring a healthy addition to the breakfast table. These wholesome not-too-sweet muffins have a golden brown crust. —Suzanne McKinley, Lyons, Georgia

   1 cup all-purpose flour
   1 cup wheat *or* oat bran
1/4 cup sugar
   3 teaspoons baking powder
1/4 teaspoon salt
1/4 cup egg substitute
   1 cup fat-free milk
1/4 cup canola oil
   1 cup fresh *or* frozen unsweetened raspberries*

In a bowl, combine the flour, bran, sugar, baking powder and salt. In another bowl, beat egg substitute, milk and oil; stir into dry ingredients just until moistened. Gently fold in raspberries.

Coat muffin cups with nonstick cooking spray or use paper liners; fill two-thirds full with batter. Bake at 400° for 20 minutes or until golden brown. Cool for 5 min-utes before removing from pan to a wire rack. **Yield:** 1 dozen.

Nutritional Analysis: One muffin equals 122 calories, 5 g fat (trace saturated fat), trace cholesterol, 127 mg sodium, 18 g carbohydrate, 3 g fiber, 3 g protein. **Diabetic Exchanges:** 1 starch, 1 fat.

*Editor's Note: If using frozen raspberries, do not thaw.

Italian Vegetable Soup

(Pictured below)

Ready in 30 minutes or less

One night when my husband and I needed a quick supper, I threw together this satisfying soup using only what we had on hand. It's a family favorite. —Margaret Glassic, Easton, Pennsylvania

   2 cans (14-1/2 ounces *each*) reduced-sodium chicken broth
   1 medium potato, peeled and cubed
   1 medium onion, chopped
   1 medium carrot, chopped
   1 celery rib, chopped
1/2 cup frozen peas
   1 bay leaf
   1 teaspoon Italian seasoning
1/8 teaspoon pepper
1/2 cup small shell pasta, cooked and drained
   1 can (14-1/2 ounces) diced tomatoes, undrained

In a large saucepan, combine the first nine ingredients. Bring to a boil. Reduce heat; cover and simmer for 15-20 minutes or until vegetables are crisp-tender. Add the pasta and tomatoes; heat through. Discard bay leaf before serving. **Yield:** 6 servings.

Nutritional Analysis: One serving (1 cup) equals 108 calories, 1 g fat (1 g saturated fat), 3 mg cholesterol, 224 mg sodium, 19 g carbohydrate, 3 g fiber, 5 g protein. **Diabetic Exchanges:** 1 starch, 1 vegetable.

Italian Vegetable Soup

Spinach Cheese Enchiladas

(Pictured below)

Ready in 1 hour or less

This tasty meatless dish is great because it's easy to prepare and low in fat. Plus, it travels well to potlucks.
—Carol Jackson, Eden Prairie, Minnesota

- 1 carton (15 ounces) reduced-fat ricotta cheese
- 1 package (10 ounces) frozen chopped spinach, thawed and drained
- 1 package (10 ounces) frozen corn, thawed and drained
- 2 cups (8 ounces) shredded part-skim mozzarella cheese, *divided*
- 1/4 cup egg substitute
- 10 fat-free flour tortillas (8 inches)
- 1 can (14-1/2 ounces) Italian diced tomatoes, undrained
- 1 can (8 ounces) tomato sauce
- 1 teaspoon dried basil
- 1/4 cup grated Parmesan cheese

In a bowl, combine ricotta, spinach, corn, 1 cup mozzarella and egg substitute. Spoon about 1/2 cup on each tortilla; roll up tightly. Place, seam side down, in a 13-in. x 9-in. x 2-in. baking dish coated with nonstick cooking spray. Combine tomatoes, tomato sauce and basil; spoon over tortillas. Sprinkle with Parmesan and remaining mozzarella. Bake, uncovered, at 375° for 35 minutes or until heated through. **Yield:** 10 servings.

Nutritional Analysis: One serving equals 334 calories, 12 g fat (6 g saturated fat), 26 mg cholesterol, 754 mg sodium, 40 g carbohydrate, 2 g fiber, 19 g protein. **Diabetic Exchanges:** 2 starch, 2 lean meat, 1 vegetable, 1 fat.

Tomato Cabbage Stir-Fry

Ready in 30 minutes or less

I've been serving this dill-seasoned side dish for more than 30 years. I fix it frequently in the summer using vegetables from our garden. —Agarita Vaughan, Fairbury, Illinois

- 4 cups shredded cabbage
- 2 cups diced fresh tomatoes
- 2 celery ribs, sliced
- 1 medium onion, chopped
- 1 medium green pepper, chopped
- 2 tablespoons stick margarine
- 1/2 teaspoon salt
- 1/2 teaspoon dill weed

Spinach Cheese Enchiladas

In a nonstick skillet, saute the cabbage, tomatoes, celery, onion and green pepper in margarine until vegetables are tender, about 20 minutes. Season with salt and dill. **Yield:** 6 servings.

Nutritional Analysis: One serving (2/3 cup) equals 76 calories, 4 g fat (1 g saturated fat), 0 cholesterol, 265 mg sodium, 10 g carbohydrate, 3 g fiber, 2 g protein. **Diabetic Exchanges:** 1-1/2 vegetable, 1 fat.

Light Cinnamon Coffee Cake

If you like cinnamon rolls but can't afford the preparation time or the fat and calories, this crumb-topped coffee cake is a satisfying substitute. We enjoy it a lot for breakfast.
—Becky Wagner
Friendsville, Maryland

- 1/2 cup fat-free milk
- 1/4 cup canola oil
- 1/4 cup egg substitute
- 3/4 cup all-purpose flour
- 3/4 cup whole wheat flour
- 1/2 cup sugar
- 2 teaspoons baking powder
- 1/2 teaspoon salt

TOPPING:
- 1/2 cup packed brown sugar
- 1/2 cup chopped walnuts
- 1 tablespoon all-purpose flour
- 1 teaspoon ground cinnamon
- 1 teaspoon stick margarine, melted

In a mixing bowl, beat milk, oil and egg substitute. Combine the dry ingredients; add to milk mixture and beat until smooth. Spoon into an 8-in. square baking pan coated with nonstick cooking spray. Combine the topping ingredients; sprinkle over batter. Bake at 375° for 25-28 minutes or until a toothpick inserted near the center comes out clean. Cool on a wire rack. **Yield:** 16 servings.

Nutritional Analysis: One serving equals 155 calories, 6 g fat (trace saturated fat), trace cholesterol, 118 mg sodium, 23 g carbohydrate, 1 g fiber, 3 g protein. **Diabetic Exchanges:** 1 fat, 1/2 starch.

Confetti Pork Chops

Pasta Crab Salad

Plan ahead...needs to chill

When it comes to cooking, I believe the simpler the better. A few years ago, a co-worker told me about this colorful, tasty and, most importantly, easy-to-prepare salad. It has been a favorite at our house ever since.
—Carol Blauw, Holland, Michigan

- 4-1/2 cups uncooked tricolor spiral pasta
- 1 package (16 ounces) imitation crabmeat, flaked
- 1/3 cup chopped celery, green pepper and onion
- 1/2 cup reduced-fat mayonnaise
- 1/2 cup reduced-fat ranch salad dressing
- 1 teaspoon dill weed

Cook pasta according to package directions; drain and rinse in cold water. Place in a large bowl; add the crab, celery, green pepper and onion. In a small bowl, combine the mayonnaise, salad dressing and dill. Pour over pasta mixture and toss to coat. Cover and refrigerate for at least 2 hours before serving. **Yield:** 10 servings.

Nutritional Analysis: One serving (1 cup) equals 242 calories, 7 g fat (1 g saturated fat), 15 mg cholesterol, 579 mg sodium, 33 g carbohydrate, 1 g fiber, 10 g protein. **Diabetic Exchanges:** 2 starch, 1 lean meat, 1/2 fat.

Fast Fruit

To quickly round out a meal, I defrost a package of frozen strawberries and add it to a jar of applesauce. This fruity combination makes an excellent side dish.
—Betty Pedigo, Green River, Wyoming

Confetti Pork Chops

(Pictured above)

Ready in 1 hour or less

When time is tight, I depend on this fast-to-fix pork chop dish flavored with marjoram. A helping of this casserole, with its bright blend of vegetables, looks beautiful over a bed of fluffy white rice.
—Joan Rose
Langley, British Columbia

- 1 large onion, halved and sliced
- 1/2 cup chopped green pepper
- 1/2 cup chopped sweet red pepper
- 1 tablespoon stick margarine
- 1 can (28 ounces) no-salt-added tomatoes, drained and chopped
- 1 cup frozen corn, thawed
- 1/2 teaspoon dried marjoram
- 4 boneless pork chops (1 pound), trimmed

Hot cooked rice, optional

In a large nonstick skillet, saute onion and peppers in margarine until tender. Stir in tomatoes, corn and marjoram; mix well. Cook 5 minutes longer or until heated through. Pour vegetable mixture into an ungreased 9-in. square baking dish; set aside.

In the same skillet, brown pork chops for 2-3 minutes on each side. Arrange over tomato mixture. Cover and bake at 350° for 15-20 minutes or until meat juices run clear. Serve over rice if desired. **Yield:** 4 servings.

Nutritional Analysis: One serving (calculated without rice) equals 279 calories, 9 g fat (3 g saturated fat), 63 mg cholesterol, 335 mg sodium, 25 g carbohydrate, 6 g fiber, 26 g protein. **Diabetic Exchanges:** 3 meat, 1 starch, 1 vegetable.

Fruit with Yogurt Sauce

Steamed Haddock Bundles

Ready in 30 minutes or less

Haddock fillets and corn are steamed inside packets made from cabbage leaves in this attractive entree.
—*Sophie Lis, East Peoria, Illinois*

4 large cabbage leaves
2 cups frozen corn, thawed
4 haddock fillets (3-1/2 ounces *each*)
4 teaspoons red wine vinegar *or* cider vinegar
1 tablespoon minced chives
1 tablespoon minced fresh parsley
2 teaspoons salt-free seasoning blend
1/2 teaspoon salt-free lemon-pepper seasoning

Cook cabbage leaves in boiling water for 3 minutes. Drain and rinse with cold water; pat dry. Place each cabbage leaf on a double layer of heavy-duty foil (about 15 in. x 12 in.). Place 1/2 cup corn on each leaf; top with a fish fillet. Sprinkle with vinegar. Combine seasonings; sprinkle over fillets.

Wrap cabbage leaves around fish; fold foil around cabbage and seal tightly. Place the packets on a baking sheet. Bake at 425° for 12-15 minutes or until the fish flakes easily with a fork. **Yield:** 4 servings.

Nutritional Analysis: One serving equals 165 calories, 1 g fat (trace saturated fat), 57 mg cholesterol, 81 mg sodium, 19 g carbohydrate, 2 g fiber, 22 g protein. **Diabetic Exchanges:** 3 very lean meat, 1 starch.

Fruit with Yogurt Sauce

(Pictured above)

Plan ahead...needs to chill

This citrus and spice sauce for fresh fruit is such a success that I had to share the recipe. It's terrific alongside fruit kabobs or tossed into a medley. —*Diane Hixon Niceville, Florida*

3/4 cup boiling water
1/4 cup raisins
1 carton (8 ounces) reduced-fat lemon yogurt
1/4 teaspoon ground ginger
1/8 to 1/4 teaspoon ground allspice
1/8 to 1/4 teaspoon ground cardamom
4 large firm bananas, cut into 1/2-inch slices
2 tablespoons lemon juice
2 medium cantaloupe, peeled, seeded and cubed
3 cups seeded cubed watermelon

Place the water and raisins in a bowl; let stand for 5 minutes. Meanwhile, combine the yogurt, ginger, allspice and cardamom in another bowl. Drain raisins; stir into yogurt mixture. Cover and refrigerate for at least 1 hour. Toss bananas in lemon juice. Alternately thread fruit on wooden skewers or place in a serving bowl. Serve with yogurt sauce. **Yield:** 8 servings.

Nutritional Analysis: One serving (with 2 tablespoons sauce) equals 170 calories, 1 g fat (trace saturated fat), 1 mg cholesterol, 47 mg sodium, 40 g carbohydrate, 3 g fiber, 4 g protein. **Diabetic Exchanges:** 1-1/2 fruit, 1 starch.

Chicken Salad Pockets

(Pictured on opposite page)

Plan ahead...needs to chill

A nicely seasoned dressing gives plenty of herb flavor to these fresh-tasting sandwiches. The colorful filling is a great way to use up leftover chicken. —*Donna Poole Marysville, Kansas*

2 cups cubed cooked chicken breast
1 medium cucumber, seeded and chopped
1 medium tomato, seeded and chopped
3 green onions, thinly sliced
1/4 cup lemon juice
3 tablespoons canola oil
2 garlic cloves, minced
1 teaspoon sugar
1/2 to 1 teaspoon dried basil
2 cups shredded red leaf lettuce *or* romaine
4 pita breads (6 inches), halved

In a bowl, combine the chicken, cucumber, tomato and onions. In a small bowl, combine lemon juice, oil, garlic, sugar and basil; mix well. Pour over chicken mixture and toss to coat. Cover and refrigerate for 2 hours. Just before serving, add lettuce and toss to coat. Spoon about 1/2 cup into each pita half. **Yield:** 4 servings.

Nutritional Analysis: One serving (2 filled pita halves) equals 406 calories, 14 g fat (2 g saturated fat), 60 mg cholesterol, 380 mg sodium, 41 g carbohydrate, 3 g fiber, 29 g protein. **Diabetic Exchanges:** 3 very lean meat, 2 vegetable, 2 starch, 2 fat.

Cauliflower Radish Salad

(Pictured below right)

Plan ahead...needs to chill

I love to cook, but with three young boys, I don't have a lot of time to spend in the kitchen. This crunchy blend is a snap to toss together.
—Janice Maynard
Sweetser, Indiana

 4 cups cauliflowerets
 1/2 cup sliced green onions
 1 can (8 ounces) sliced water chestnuts, drained and halved
 2/3 cup reduced-fat mayonnaise
 2 tablespoons lemon juice
 2 tablespoons ranch salad dressing mix
 1 cup thinly sliced radishes

In a bowl, combine the cauliflower, onions and water chestnuts. In a small bowl, combine the mayonnaise, lemon juice and salad dressing mix. Pour over vegetables; toss to coat. Cover and chill for at least 2 hours. Just before serving, stir in radishes. **Yield:** 8 servings.

Nutritional Analysis: One serving (3/4 cup) equals 103 calories, 7 g fat (1 g saturated fat), 7 mg cholesterol, 299 mg sodium, 10 g carbohydrate, 2 g fiber, 2 g protein. **Diabetic Exchanges:** 2 vegetable, 1 fat.

Dirt Pudding Cups

(Pictured at right)

Ready in 15 minutes or less

These darling little desserts are my daughter Crystal's favorite. At birthday parties, everyone loves the individual servings because each person gets a gummy worm.
—Linda Emery
Tuckerman, Arkansas

 2 cups cold fat-free milk
 1 package (1.4 ounces) sugar-free instant chocolate pudding mix
 1 carton (8 ounces) reduced-fat whipped topping
 1 package (16 ounces) reduced-fat chocolate cream-filled sandwich cookies, crushed
Gummy worms, optional

In a bowl, whisk milk and pudding mix for 2 minutes. Fold in whipped topping. Divide a third of the cookie crumbs and half of the pudding mixture among 10 dessert cups; repeat layers. Top with remaining crumbs. Garnish with gummy worms if de-

sired. **Yield:** 10 servings.

Nutritional Analysis: One 3/4-cup serving (calculated without gummy worms) equals 269 calories, 8 g fat (4 g saturated fat), 1 mg cholesterol, 406 mg sodium, 46 g carbohydrate, 2 g fiber, 5 g protein. **Diabetic Exchanges:** 2 starch, 1 lean meat, 1 fat.

Savvy Soups

- If you run out of instant potato flakes that you usually use for thickening soups or stews, try substituting dry mixed baby cereal instead. The cereal is similar in consistency to the potato flakes, tastes the same and provides more vitamins and minerals.
—Christi Ross, Mill Creek, Oklahoma

- If you're looking to reduce fat in soups and stews, make the recipe a day ahead of time and refrigerate overnight. Extra fat will float to the surface and harden, where it can easily be removed before you reheat the soup or stew. Cooking ahead also allows time for the flavors of the ingredients to blend and intensify.

Dirt Pudding Cups
Cauliflower Radish Salad
Chicken Salad Pockets

Radish Dip

(Pictured below)

Ready in 15 minutes or less

I put an unusual spin on yogurt dip by adding radishes. This creamy dip makes a zippy appetizer when served with cauliflower and broccoli florets or rye bread cubes.
—Donna Smith, Victor, New York

1 cup (8 ounces) fat-free plain yogurt
1 cup chopped radishes (about 13)
1/3 cup reduced-fat mayonnaise
1/4 teaspoon hot pepper sauce
1/8 teaspoon pepper
Raw vegetables

In a bowl, combine the first five ingredients; mix well. Cover and refrigerate until serving. Serve with vegetables. **Yield:** about 1-1/3 cups.

Nutritional Analysis: One serving (2 tablespoons) equals 29 calories, 1 g fat (trace saturated fat), 2 mg cholesterol, 53 mg sodium, 3 g carbohydrate, trace fiber, 1 g protein. **Diabetic Exchange:** 1 vegetable.

Garden Tuna Sandwiches

(Pictured below)

Ready in 15 minutes or less

This sandwich is perfect when you're having a few friends over for a light lunch. The garden-fresh taste comes from cucumber, green onions and carrot. *—Dani Ray*
Sherman Oaks, California

1 can (6 ounces) water-packed tuna, drained and flaked
2/3 cup chopped seeded peeled cucumber
1/2 cup shredded carrot
1/4 cup finely chopped green onions
1/4 cup fat-free mayonnaise
1/4 cup Dijon mustard
2 tablespoons fat-free sour cream
1 tablespoon lemon juice
Pepper to taste
8 slices whole wheat bread
4 lettuce leaves

In a bowl, combine the tuna, cucumber, carrot, onions, mayonnaise, mustard, sour cream, lemon juice and pep-

Radish Dip
Garden Tuna Sandwiches

per. Spread on four slices of bread; top with lettuce and remaining bread. **Yield:** 4 servings.

Nutritional Analysis: One sandwich equals 237 calories, 4 g fat (1 g saturated fat), 13 mg cholesterol, 936 mg sodium, 35 g carbohydrate, 5 g fiber, 18 g protein. **Diabetic Exchanges:** 2 starch, 1-1/2 meat, 1 vegetable.

Breakfast Bread Pudding

Ready in 15 minutes or less

This slightly sweet casserole for one is a fun alternative to typical breakfast entrees. It's a snap to prepare in the microwave on a busy morning. And it's yummy served warm or cold for dessert, too. —Anne Morrissey
Marshfield, Massachusetts

    1 slice bread, cut into 1/2-inch cubes
    1/4 cup diced peeled tart apple
    1 tablespoon raisins
    1/2 cup fat-free milk
    1/4 cup egg substitute
    1/2 teaspoon vanilla extract
Sugar substitute equivalent to 2 teaspoons sugar
    1/4 teaspoon apple pie spice

Place bread cubes, apple and raisins in a microwave-safe 2-cup bowl coated with nonstick cooking spray. In another bowl, whisk together the remaining ingredients; pour over bread mixture. Microwave, uncovered, on high for 3 minutes or until mixture puffs and bubbles around the edges. **Yield:** 1 serving.

Nutritional Analysis: One serving equals 233 calories, 4 g fat (1 g saturated fat), 3 mg cholesterol, 339 mg sodium, 34 g carbohydrate, 2 g fiber, 15 g protein. **Diabetic Exchanges:** 1 starch, 1 lean meat, 1 fruit, 1/2 milk.

Editor's Note: This recipe was tested in an 850-watt microwave.

Beef and Bean Macaroni

Ready in 1 hour or less

This hearty casserole with beans, beef and macaroni is a meal in itself. Since my husband, son and brother enjoy hunting, our freezer is stocked with venison, which I sometimes use in place of the ground beef. —Sally Norcutt
Chatham, Virginia

    1 pound lean ground beef
    1 package (7 ounces) elbow macaroni, cooked and drained
    2 cups (8 ounces) shredded reduced-fat cheddar cheese, *divided*
    1 can (16 ounces) kidney beans, rinsed and drained
    1 can (14-1/2 ounces) stewed tomatoes
    1 medium green pepper, diced
    1 medium onion, finely chopped
    1/4 teaspoon garlic powder
Crushed red pepper flakes and pepper to taste
    2 tablespoons grated Parmesan cheese

In a skillet over medium heat, cook the beef until no longer pink; drain. In a bowl, combine the macaroni, 1-1/2 cups cheddar cheese, beans, tomatoes, green pepper and onion. Stir in the beef, garlic powder, pepper flakes and pepper.

Spoon into a 13-in. x 9-in. x 2-in. baking dish coated with nonstick cooking spray. Sprinkle with Parmesan and remaining cheddar cheese. Cover and bake at 375° for 30 minutes or until heated through. **Yield:** 10 servings.

Nutritional Analysis: One serving (1 cup) equals 289 calories, 6 g fat (3 g saturated fat), 22 mg cholesterol, 289 mg sodium, 33 g carbohydrate, 6 g fiber, 24 g protein. **Diabetic Exchanges:** 2 starch, 2 meat, 1 vegetable.

Creamy Chicken Enchiladas

Ready in 1 hour or less

This casserole has so much zesty Mexican flavor that my husband doesn't even realize it's a low-fat dish. With its creamy sauce made from soup and cheeses, it tastes like a calorie-laden meal when it's not. —Shirley Meyer
New Prague, Minnesota

    1 small onion, chopped
    1 can (10-3/4 ounces) reduced-fat reduced-sodium condensed cream of chicken soup, undiluted
    1 can (10 ounces) diced tomatoes and green chilies, undrained
    1 cup (8 ounces) fat-free sour cream
    1 cup (4 ounces) shredded reduced-fat cheddar cheese, *divided*
    1 cup (4 ounces) shredded part-skim mozzarella cheese, *divided*
    6 fat-free flour tortillas (8-1/2 inches)
    2 cups cubed cooked chicken breast

In a skillet or saucepan coated with nonstick cooking spray, saute onion until tender. Remove from the heat. Add soup, tomatoes, sour cream, 3/4 cup cheddar cheese and 3/4 cup mozzarella cheese; mix well. Place 3 tablespoons on each tortilla; top with 1/3 cup chicken. Roll up tightly.

Place seam side down in a 13-in. x 9-in. x 2-in. baking dish coated with nonstick cooking spray. Top with remaining soup mixture; sprinkle with remaining cheeses. Bake, uncovered, at 350° for 20-25 minutes or until heated through. **Yield:** 6 servings.

Nutritional Analysis: One serving equals 362 calories, 10 g fat (5 g saturated fat), 66 mg cholesterol, 1,107 mg sodium, 37 g carbohydrate, 2 g fiber, 32 g protein. **Diabetic Exchanges:** 3 lean meat, 2 starch, 1 vegetable.

Simple Seasoning

I put salt and pepper into the same shaker. With my husband on a low sodium diet, I use a pinch-minute ratio. Since pepper is easily seen, I am not tempted to use too much salt when seasoning our food.
—Helen Anderson, Cantonment, Florida

Pear Bundt Cake
Bow Tie Chicken Supper

Bow Tie Chicken Supper

(Pictured above)

Ready in 30 minutes or less

My sister-in-law gave me a recipe for a healthy side dish, and I added chicken to it to make this colorful main course. It's wonderful with a salad and crusty bread.
—Nancy Daugherty, Cortland, Ohio

- 1 **pound boneless skinless chicken breasts, cut into 1/4-inch strips**
- 1 **tablespoon olive *or* canola oil**
- 1 **small sweet red pepper, julienned**
- 1 **small zucchini, cut into 1/4-inch slices**
- 1 **small onion, chopped**
- 2 **garlic cloves, minced**
- 1/2 **cup frozen peas, thawed**
- 1 **teaspoon Italian seasoning**
- 1/4 **teaspoon salt-free seasoning blend**
- 1 **cup bow tie pasta, cooked and drained**
- 2 **medium tomatoes, seeded and chopped**
- 1/4 **cup shredded Parmesan cheese**

In a large nonstick skillet, saute chicken in oil for 3-5 minutes or until no longer pink. Remove and keep warm. In the same skillet, stir-fry red pepper, zucchini, onion and garlic for 3-4 minutes or until vegetables are crisp-tender.

Add the peas and seasonings; stir-fry for 2 minutes. Add pasta and tomatoes; cook for 1 minute. Remove from the heat. Gently stir in chicken. Sprinkle with cheese. **Yield:** 4 servings.

Nutritional Analysis: One serving (1-1/2 cups) equals 256 calories, 7 g fat (2 g saturated fat), 71 mg cholesterol, 219 mg sodium, 15 g carbohydrate, 3 g fiber, 32 g protein. **Diabetic Exchanges:** 3 lean meat, 1 starch.

Pear Bundt Cake

(Pictured above)

Five simple ingredients are all it takes to fix this lovely light dessert. Tiny bits of pear provide sweetness to the moist slices.
—Veronica Ross
Columbia Heights, Minnesota

1 can (15-1/4 ounces) pears in light syrup
1 package (18-1/4 ounces) white cake mix
2 egg whites
1 egg
2 teaspoons confectioners' sugar

Drain pears, reserving the syrup; chop pears. Place pears and syrup in a mixing bowl; add dry cake mix, egg whites and egg. Beat on low speed for 30 seconds. Beat on high for 4 minutes.

Coat a 10-in. fluted tube pan with nonstick cooking spray and dust with flour. Add batter. Bake at 350° for 50-55 minutes or until a toothpick inserted near the center comes out clean. Cool for 10 minutes before removing from pan to a wire rack to cool completely. Dust with confectioners' sugar. **Yield:** 16 servings.

Nutritional Analysis: One slice equals 163 calories, 4 g fat (1 g saturated fat), 13 mg cholesterol, 230 mg sodium, 30 g carbohydrate, 1 g fiber, 2 g protein. **Diabetic Exchanges:** 1 starch, 1 fruit, 1 fat.

Low-Fat Brownies

Looking for sweets that won't add inches to your waist? These moist chewy brownies don't have much fat. And the recipe makes 2 dozen, so it's ideal for parties and potlucks.
—Anne Withers, Cortland, New York

1/2 cup egg substitute
1 can (14 ounces) fat-free sweetened
  condensed milk
1 teaspoon vanilla extract
1-1/3 cups all-purpose flour
1-1/4 cups sugar
3/4 cup baking cocoa
1 teaspoon baking powder
1/2 teaspoon salt

In a mixing bowl, beat egg substitute for 1 minute or until frothy and slightly thickened. Stir in milk and vanilla. Combine the flour, sugar, cocoa, baking powder and salt; add to the egg mixture and mix well.

Pour into a 13-in. x 9-in. x 2-in. baking pan coated with nonstick cooking spray. Bake at 350° for 18-22 minutes or until a toothpick inserted near the center comes out clean. Cool on a wire rack. **Yield:** 2 dozen.

Nutritional Analysis: One brownie equals 124 calories, 1 g fat (trace saturated fat), 1 mg cholesterol, 85 mg sodium, 27 g carbohydrate, 1 g fiber, 3 g protein. **Diabetic Exchange:** 1-1/2 starch.

Tortellini Nibblers

Ready in 1 hour or less

Looking for a unique appetizer idea? I pair cheese tortellini with a cool, creamy Parmesan sauce for dipping.
—Stephanie Krienitz, Plainfield, Illinois

1/2 cup fat-free milk
3 tablespoons nonfat dry milk powder
1-1/2 cups 1% cottage cheese
1/4 cup grated Parmesan cheese

1 tablespoon lemon juice
1-1/2 teaspoons minced fresh rosemary *or* 1/2
  teaspoon dried rosemary, crushed
1/4 teaspoon salt
1/8 teaspoon pepper
1 package (9 ounces) refrigerated cheese
  tortellini

In a blender or food processor, combine milk and milk powder until blended. Add cottage cheese, Parmesan cheese, lemon juice, rosemary, salt and pepper; cover and process until smooth. Cover and refrigerate for 30 minutes. Meanwhile, cook tortellini according to package directions; drain. Serve with Parmesan sauce for dipping. **Yield:** 20 appetizer servings.

Nutritional Analysis: One serving (4 tortellini with 2 tablespoons of sauce) equals 49 calories, 1 g fat (1 g saturated fat), 4 mg cholesterol, 168 mg sodium, 5 g carbohydrate, trace fiber, 4 g protein. **Diabetic Exchanges:** 1/2 starch, 1/2 meat.

Pineapple Cheese Spread

Ready in 1 hour or less

This satisfying snack is a real treat for my husband, who's watching his weight. Crushed pineapple adds a hint of sweetness to my low-fat version of a spread sold at a grocery store chain.
—Cindy Smith, Adel, Iowa

2 green onions, chopped
1/2 cup shredded reduced-fat cheddar cheese
1/2 cup shredded part-skim mozzarella cheese
1/4 cup unsweetened crushed pineapple
1/3 cup fat-free mayonnaise
Reduced-fat crackers

In a bowl, combine the first five ingredients; mix well. Cover and refrigerate for 30 minutes or until ready to serve. Serve with crackers. **Yield:** 1 cup.

Nutritional Analysis: One 1/4-cup serving (calculated without crackers) equals 100 calories, 5 g fat (3 g saturated fat), 16 mg cholesterol, 258 mg sodium, 7 g carbohydrate, trace fiber, 9 g protein. **Diabetic Exchanges:** 1 lean meat, 1 fat.

Eat Your Veggies!

- I often visit the supermarket salad bar after a busy day. I buy a head of lettuce and pick up the rest of the vegetable fixings already chopped and ready to go. This saves me a great deal of time and also encourages me and my family to eat more vegetables because I don't have to do all the chopping!
  —TerryAnn Moore, Oaklyn, New Jersey
- Fat-free canned chicken broth adds excellent flavor to most any vegetable. Use it instead of water when steaming or boiling vegetables. *—Marion Bruessel, Canyon Country, California*
- I add a small can of V-8 juice to vegetables to give extra flavor as well as more vitamins. *—Betty Brye, Milwaukee, Wisconsin*

1 salmon fillet (1 pound)
1-1/2 teaspoons dill weed, *divided*
1/2 cup reduced-fat plain yogurt
1/2 teaspoon sugar
1/2 teaspoon salt-free seasoning blend

Place the salmon in a 13-in. x 9-in. x 2-in. baking dish coated with nonstick cooking spray and sprinkle with 1/2 teaspoon dill. Cover and bake at 375° for 20-25 minutes or until the fish flakes easily with a fork. Meanwhile, in a small saucepan, combine the yogurt, sugar, seasoning blend and remaining dill. Cook and stir over low heat until heated through. Serve with the salmon. **Yield:** 4 servings.

Nutritional Analysis: One serving equals 227 calories, 12 g fat (3 g saturated fat), 77 mg cholesterol, 76 mg sodium, 3 g carbohydrate, 0 fiber, 24 g protein. **Diabetic Exchanges:** 2-1/2 lean meat, 2 fat.

Salmon with Dill Sauce

(Pictured below)

Ready in 30 minutes or less

This moist tender salmon is a savory treat draped with a smooth creamy dill sauce. When my daughter served this tempting main dish for dinner, I was surprised to learn how easy the recipe is. —Janet Painter
Three Springs, Pennsylvania

Raspberry Spinach Salad

(Pictured below)

Ready in 30 minutes or less

My family is always thrilled to see this lovely refreshing salad on the table. Its sweet raspberry dressing is the ideal topper for nutritious spinach, fresh berries and kiwi. Nuts and croutons provide a bit of crunch.
—Valerie Mitchell, Hudson, Ohio

3 tablespoons canola oil
2 tablespoons raspberry vinegar
2 tablespoons raspberry jam
1/8 teaspoon pepper
8 cups torn fresh spinach
2 cups fresh raspberries, *divided*
4 tablespoons slivered almonds, toasted, *divided*
1/2 cup thinly sliced onion
3 kiwifruit, peeled and sliced
1 cup fat-free seasoned salad croutons

In a jar with a tight-fitting lid, combine the oil, vinegar, jam and pepper; shake well. In a large salad bowl, gently combine spinach, 1 cup raspberries, 2 tablespoons almonds and onion. Top with kiwi, croutons and remaining berries and almonds. Drizzle with dressing; serve immediately. **Yield:** 7 servings.

Nutritional Analysis: One serving (1 cup) equals 164 calories, 9 g fat (1 g saturated fat), trace cholesterol, 101 mg sodium, 20 g carbohydrate, 5 g fiber, 4 g protein. **Diabetic Exchanges:** 2 fat, 1 vegetable, 1 fruit.

Salmon with Dill Sauce
Raspberry Spinach Salad

Vegetable Chicken Soup

I need to eat low-fat, and my husband loves a good hearty soup, so this recipe fills the bill for both of us. My relatives and friends rave about this soup. —Betty Kline
Panorama Village, Texas

3 quarts water
2 large carrots, sliced
1 cup chopped onion
3 celery ribs, sliced
2 cups broccoli florets
2 cups cauliflowerets
2 garlic cloves, minced
3 tablespoons chicken bouillon granules
3 tablespoons picante sauce
2-1/4 teaspoons minced fresh thyme *or* 3/4 teaspoon dried thyme
2-1/4 teaspoons minced fresh basil *or* 3/4 teaspoon dried basil
1 teaspoon minced fresh rosemary *or* 1/2 teaspoon dried rosemary, crushed
1/4 teaspoon cayenne pepper, optional
2 cups cubed cooked chicken breast
3-1/2 cups egg noodles, cooked and drained

In a large soup kettle, combine water, carrots, onion and celery. Bring to a boil. Reduce heat; cover and simmer for 20 minutes or until the vegetables are tender. Add broccoli, cauliflower, garlic, bouillon, picante sauce and seasonings. Cover and simmer for 20 minutes or until broccoli and cauliflower are tender. Add chicken and noodles. Cover and simmer for 5 minutes or until heated through. **Yield:** 12 servings (3 quarts).

Nutritional Analysis: One serving (1 cup) equals 133 calories, 2 g fat (trace saturated fat), 36 mg cholesterol, 935 mg sodium, 18 g carbohydrate, 2 g fiber, 11 g protein. **Diabetic Exchanges:** 1 starch, 1 lean meat.

Turkey Stir-Fry

Turkey Stir-Fry

(Pictured above)

Ready in 30 minutes or less

Ginger gives this speedy stir-fry a special taste. It's easy to prepare and even quicker when I use leftover turkey.
—Jackie Hannahs, Cadillac, Michigan

1 pound boneless skinless turkey breast, cut into 1/4-inch strips
2 tablespoons olive *or* canola oil, *divided*
1 medium sweet red pepper, sliced
1 cup broccoli florets
1/2 cup chopped onion
1 garlic clove, minced
1/4 teaspoon ground ginger *or* 1 teaspoon minced fresh gingerroot
2 teaspoons cornstarch
1/2 cup reduced-sodium chicken broth
1/4 cup white wine *or* additional reduced-sodium chicken broth
2 tablespoons reduced-sodium soy sauce
1 can (8 ounces) sliced water chestnuts, drained
1/4 teaspoon salt-free seasoning blend
5 cups hot cooked rice

In a large nonstick skillet or wok, stir-fry turkey in 1 tablespoon oil until no longer pink. Remove and keep warm. Stir-fry the red pepper, broccoli, onion, garlic and ginger in remaining oil for 3-4 minutes or until broccoli is crisp-tender.

In a small bowl, combine cornstarch, broth, wine or additional broth and soy sauce until smooth; stir into skillet. Bring to a boil; cook and stir for 1-2 minutes or until thickened. Add turkey, water chestnuts and seasoning blend; heat through. Serve over rice. **Yield:** 5 servings.

Nutritional Analysis: One serving (1 cup turkey mixture with 1 cup of rice) equals 393 calories, 7 g fat (1 g saturated fat), 76 mg cholesterol, 276 mg sodium, 47 g carbohydrate, 4 g fiber, 33 g protein. **Diabetic Exchanges:** 3 starch, 3 lean meat, 1 vegetable.

Cinnamon Nut Twists
Apricot Carrot Bread

Cinnamon Nut Twists

(Pictured above and on page 215)

Ready in 30 minutes or less

These tender treats are good with coffee. The golden twists have a pleasant cinnamon and nut filling and a hint of sweetness. —Mary Van Domelen, Appleton, Wisconsin

> 2 tubes (8 ounces *each*) refrigerated reduced-fat crescent rolls
> 2 tablespoons reduced-fat stick margarine
> 1/4 cup packed brown sugar
> 1 tablespoon ground cinnamon
> 1/3 cup finely chopped walnuts

Unroll both tubes of dough; press perforations and seams together to form two rectangles. Spread with margarine. Combine brown sugar and cinnamon; sprinkle over dough. Sprinkle with walnuts. Fold each rectangle in half, starting from a short side. Cut each into eight strips. Twist each strip and tie into a knot. Place on ungreased baking sheets. Bake at 375° for 10-12 minutes or until golden brown. Serve warm. **Yield:** 16 servings.

Nutritional Analysis: One piece equals 139 calories, 7 g fat (1 g saturated fat), 0 cholesterol, 251 mg sodium, 16 g carbohydrate, trace fiber, 2 g protein. **Diabetic Exchanges:** 1 starch, 1 fat.

Apricot Carrot Bread

(Pictured above and on page 214)

Since I am on a low-fat diet due to heart problems, I like slices of this sunny-looking quick bread.
—Geneva Cooper, Greeley, Colorado

> 1-3/4 cups all-purpose flour
> 1/2 cup sugar
> 1 teaspoon baking powder
> 1/4 teaspoon baking soda
> 1/4 teaspoon salt
> 1/2 cup finely shredded carrots
> 1/2 cup unsweetened applesauce
> 1/2 cup egg substitute
> 2 tablespoons canola oil
> 1/3 cup finely chopped dried apricots
> 1/2 cup confectioners' sugar
> 2 teaspoons water

In a bowl, combine the first five ingredients. In another bowl, combine the carrots, applesauce, egg substitute and oil; add to dry ingredients and stir until blended. Stir in apricots. Spoon into an 8-in. x 4-in. x 2-in. loaf pan coated with nonstick cooking spray. Bake at 350° for 45-50 minutes or until a toothpick inserted near the center comes out clean. Cool for 10 minutes before removing from pan to a wire rack to cool completely. Combine confectioners' sugar and water; drizzle over bread. **Yield:** 1 loaf (14 slices).

Nutritional Analysis: One slice equals 139 calories, 2 g fat (trace saturated fat), trace cholesterol, 99 mg sodium, 26 g carbohydrate, 1 g fiber, 3 g protein. **Diabetic Exchanges:** 1 starch, 1 fruit.

Frosted Spice Cake

This moist and flavorful cake pairs well with a variety of entrees. It's easy to add cinnamon to prepared vanilla frosting for the fast finishing touch. —Lorraine Darocha
Berkshire, Massachusetts

3 cups all-purpose flour
2 cups sugar
2 teaspoons baking soda
1 teaspoon salt
1-1/8 teaspoons ground cinnamon, *divided*
1/2 teaspoon ground cloves
1/2 teaspoon ground nutmeg
2 cups water
2/3 cup canola oil
2 tablespoons white vinegar
2 teaspoons vanilla extract
1 can (12 ounces) whipped vanilla frosting

In a mixing bowl, combine the flour, sugar, baking soda, salt, 1 teaspoon cinnamon, cloves and nutmeg. Combine the water, oil, vinegar and vanilla; add to dry ingredients and beat until smooth (batter will be thin). Pour into a 13-in. x 9-in. x 2-in. baking pan coated with nonstick cooking spray.

Bake at 350° for 25-30 minutes or until a toothpick inserted near the center comes out clean. Cool on a wire rack. Stir remaining cinnamon into frosting; spread over cake. **Yield:** 20 servings.

Nutritional Analysis: One piece equals 283 calories, 11 g fat (2 g saturated fat), 0 cholesterol, 261 mg sodium, 45 g carbohydrate, 1 g fiber, 2 g protein. **Diabetic Exchanges:** 2 starch, 2 fat, 1 fruit.

Editor's Note: This recipe contains no egg.

Giant Mushroom Burger

Ready in 30 minutes or less

I add mushrooms and onion to lean ground beef before forming it into one giant family-pleasing patty.
—Janice Delagrange, Mt. Airy, Maryland

1-1/2 pounds lean ground beef
1 can (4 ounces) mushroom stems and pieces, drained
1/4 cup egg substitute
1/2 cup chopped onion
1/4 cup ketchup
1 teaspoon Italian seasoning
1 teaspoon fennel seed, crushed
1/4 teaspoon pepper
1/4 teaspoon Worcestershire sauce

In a bowl, combine all ingredients. Pat into a 9-in. circle on a large sheet of waxed paper. Invert onto a greased wire grill basket; peel off waxed paper. Grill, covered, over medium heat for 20-25 minutes or until meat is no longer pink, turning once. Cut into six wedges. **Yield:** 6 servings.

Nutritional Analysis: One serving equals 224 calories, 11 g fat (4 g saturated fat), 41

mg cholesterol, 305 mg sodium, 6 g carbohydrate, 1 g fiber, 25 g protein. **Diabetic Exchanges:** 3 lean meat, 1 vegetable.

Steak Strips with Spaghetti

(Pictured below)

Ready in 1 hour or less

I've been serving this super skillet supper for many years. The flavorful beef dish is equally appealing when you substitute pork or veal. —*Iris Posey, Albany, Georgia*

1 medium onion, chopped
1/4 cup finely chopped green pepper
1 tablespoon butter *or stick margarine*
1 pound boneless beef sirloin steak, cut into strips
1 can (8 ounces) tomato sauce
1 cup water
1/4 teaspoon salt-free seasoning blend
1/4 teaspoon dried thyme
1/8 teaspoon pepper
1/2 cup shredded part-skim mozzarella cheese
6 cups hot cooked spaghetti

In a nonstick skillet, saute onion and green pepper in butter until tender; remove and set aside. In the same skillet, brown beef; drain. Add tomato sauce, water, seasoning blend, thyme, pepper and vegetables. Cover and simmer for 20-30 minutes or until meat is tender.

Remove from the heat. Sprinkle with cheese; cover and let stand for 5 minutes or until cheese is melted. Serve over spaghetti. **Yield:** 6 servings.

Nutritional Analysis: One serving (3/4 cup beef mixture with 1 cup spaghetti) equals 377 calories, 9 g fat (3 g saturated fat), 57 mg cholesterol, 335 mg sodium, 45 g carbohydrate, 3 g fiber, 27 g protein. **Diabetic Exchanges:** 3 lean meat, 2 starch, 1 fat.

Steak Strips with Spaghetti

Chapter 15

Centsible Foods—Fast and Frugal

OF COURSE you're looking for tasty recipes that don't keep you in the kitchen for hours. But you're likely also looking for savory dishes that are easy on the family budget.

Instead of relying on convenient yet costly carryout restaurant meals and store-bought packaged foods, look here for "centsible" express-eating alternatives that are as economical as they are appetizing.

Our test kitchen has figured the cost per serving for each delicious dish. So these fast and frugal recipes will result in prompt meals and a plumper pocketbook.

SWIFT 'N' THRIFTY. Clockwise from upper left: Moist Chocolate Cake (p. 235), Scalloped Potatoes and Veggies (p. 238), Broccoli Ham Puff Pancake (p. 240) and Tuna Salad Pepper Cups (p. 236).

In a Dutch oven or large saucepan, cook the beef, green peppers and onion over medium heat until meat is no longer pink; drain. Stir in the broth, soup, tomatoes and mushrooms. Bring to a boil. Reduce heat; cover and simmer for at least 30 minutes, stirring occasionally. Add rice; heat through. **Yield:** 10 servings (84¢ per serving).

Chili-ghetti

Ready in 30 minutes or less

I created this recipe when unexpected guests stopped over and I didn't have enough chili for everyone. The surprising supper became a family favorite.
—*Cindy Cuykendall*
Skaneateles, New York

    1 package (7 ounces) spaghetti
    1 pound ground beef
    1 small onion, chopped
    1 can (16 ounces) kidney beans,
      rinsed and drained
    1 can (14-1/2 ounces) diced
      tomatoes, undrained
    1 can (4 ounces) mushroom stems
      and pieces, drained
  1/3 cup water
    1 envelope chili seasoning
    2 tablespoons grated Parmesan
      cheese
  1/4 cup shredded mozzarella cheese

Cook spaghetti according to package directions. Meanwhile, in a large skillet, cook beef and onion over medium heat until meat is no longer pink; drain. Drain spaghetti; add to beef mixture. Stir in the beans, tomatoes, mushrooms, water, chili seasoning and Parmesan cheese. Cover and simmer for 10 minutes. Sprinkle with mozzarella cheese. **Yield:** 8 servings (68¢ per serving).

Editor's Note: The cost per serving in each recipe does not include optional ingredients such as garnishes. When there is a choice of two ingredients, the cost is figured with the first one listed.

Unstuffed Pepper Soup

(caption below photo)

Unstuffed Pepper Soup

(Pictured above)

Ready in 1 hour or less

One of my sisters gave me the recipe for this quick-and-easy soup that tastes just like stuffed green peppers. The thick hearty mixture is chock-full of good stuff. Plus, the aroma while it's cooking is wonderful. —*Evelyn Kara*
Brownsville, Pennsylvania

1-1/2 pounds ground beef
    3 large green peppers, chopped
    1 large onion, chopped
    2 cans (14-1/2 ounces *each*) beef broth
    2 cans (10-3/4 ounces *each*) condensed
      tomato soup, undiluted
    1 can (28 ounces) crushed tomatoes,
      undrained
    1 can (4 ounces) mushroom stems and pieces,
      drained
1-1/2 cups cooked rice

Baked Custard

This old-fashioned treat has a smooth custard filling and crunchy golden top. —*Melissa Bruce*
Crystal River, Florida

    2 cups milk
    4 eggs
  1/2 cup stick margarine, melted
    1 cup sugar
  1/2 cup all-purpose flour
    1 teaspoon vanilla extract
  1/4 teaspoon salt

In a blender, combine all ingredients. Cover and process until smooth. Pour into a greased 9-in. deep-dish pie plate. Bake at 350° for 50 minutes or until a knife inserted near the center comes out clean. Cool on a wire rack for 1 hour. Refrigerate until serving. **Yield:** 8 servings (12¢ per serving).

Crispy Mashed Potato Pancake

Ready in 15 minutes or less

Here's a tasty secret for using up leftover mashed potatoes. With just a few basic ingredients, I can fry up this delightful dish. —*Mary Schuster, Scottsdale, Arizona*

    2 cups cold mashed potatoes (prepared with
      milk and butter)
    1 egg, lightly beaten
    1 teaspoon Italian seasoning
    1/8 teaspoon garlic powder
    1 tablespoon olive *or* vegetable oil

Combine the potatoes, egg, Italian seasoning and garlic powder; mix well. In a small skillet, heat oil over medium-high heat. Add potato mixture; press with a spatula to flatten evenly. Cover and cook for 8 minutes or until bottom is crispy. Invert onto a serving plate. **Yield:** 3 servings (20¢ per serving).

Water Chestnut Pea Salad

Ready in 30 minutes or less

A local restaurant serves a pea salad that everyone raves over, so I came up with a similar version my family likes even better. My husband requests the well-dressed crunchy combination often during the summer. It doesn't cost a lot to make this chilled vegetable side dish. —*Maree Waggener Cheney, Washington*

    2 medium carrots, chopped
    1 package (16 ounces) frozen
      peas, thawed
    1 can (8 ounces) sliced water
      chestnuts, drained
    2 green onions, thinly sliced
    1/2 cup shredded mozzarella cheese
    1/2 cup prepared ranch salad
      dressing
    5 bacon strips, cooked and
      crumbled
    1/4 teaspoon pepper

Cook carrots in a small amount of water until crisp-tender; drain and rinse in cold water. Place in a serving bowl; add the peas, water chestnuts, onions and cheese. In a small bowl, combine salad dressing, bacon and pepper; mix well. Pour over salad and toss to coat. Chill until serving. **Yield:** 6 servings (70¢ per serving).

Spanish Noodles 'n' Ground Beef

(Pictured above right)

Ready in 30 minutes or less

Bacon adds flavor to this comforting stovetop supper my mom frequently made when we were growing up. Now I prepare it for my family. It disappears quickly and is budget-pleasing, too. —*Kelli Jones, Perris, California*

    1 pound ground beef
    1 small green pepper, chopped
    1 small onion, chopped
    3-1/4 cups uncooked medium egg noodles
    1 can (14-1/2 ounces) diced tomatoes,
      undrained
    1 cup water
    1/4 cup chili sauce
    1 teaspoon salt
    1/8 teaspoon pepper
    4 bacon strips, cooked and crumbled

In a large skillet over medium heat, cook the beef, green pepper and onion until meat is no longer pink; drain. Stir in the noodles, tomatoes, water, chili sauce, salt and pepper; mix well. Cover and cook over low heat for 15-20 minutes or until the noodles are tender, stirring frequently. Add the bacon. **Yield:** 5 servings (87¢ per serving).

Spanish Noodles 'n' Ground Beef

Easy Equivalents

Since I like to buy more economically sized packages rather than the smaller ones, I have a recipe card for "equivalents". For example, when a recipe calls for a 1-pound box of powdered sugar, I know it equals 3-3/4 cups. I jot down the equivalents of the ingredients I use most and keep the card in my recipe box.
—*Joyce Sprague, Colorado Springs, Colorado*

Tomato Corn Chowder

(Pictured below)

Ready in 1 hour or less

Five common ingredients are all you'll need to prepare this hearty full-flavored chowder. It's a terrific soup, particularly as the cooler season sets in. —Sue McMichael
Redding, California

 4 bacon strips, diced
 1 large onion, chopped
 2 cans (15-1/4 ounces *each*) whole kernel corn, undrained
 2 cans (14-1/2 ounces *each*) diced tomatoes, undrained
 4 medium potatoes, peeled and diced

In a large saucepan, cook bacon over medium heat until crisp. Remove to paper towels. Drain, reserving 1 tablespoon drippings. In the drippings, saute onion until tender. Add the corn, tomatoes and potatoes. Cook over medium heat for 25-30 minutes or until the potatoes are tender. Sprinkle with the bacon. **Yield:** 9 servings (55¢ per serving).

Zucchini Fries

Ready in 30 minutes or less

These flavorful fries are the first thing we make when the zucchini in our garden is ready. I fry several batches because our family of eight loves these crispy golden wedges. No one will know these fries are made with zucchini, not potatoes! —Debbie Brunssen, Randolph, Nebraska

 1 medium zucchini
 1/2 cup all-purpose flour
 1 teaspoon onion salt
 1 teaspoon dried oregano
 1/2 teaspoon garlic powder
 1 egg, lightly beaten
 1/3 cup milk
 1 teaspoon vegetable oil
 4 cups Corn Chex, crushed
Oil for deep-fat frying

Cut zucchini in half widthwise, then cut each half lengthwise into eight wedges; set aside. In a bowl, combine the flour, onion salt, oregano and garlic powder. Combine the egg, milk and oil; stir into the dry ingredients just until blended. Dip zucchini wedges in batter, then roll in crushed cereal.

In an electric skillet or deep-fat fryer, heat oil to 375°. Fry zucchini wedges, a few at a time, for 3-4 minutes or until golden brown. Drain on paper towels; keep warm. **Yield:** 4 servings (71¢ per serving).

Ground Beef Pie

Ready in 1 hour or less

This recipe for a beefed-up quiche doesn't require a prepared crust. The entree is easy to assemble. —Cleora Campbell, Bucyrus, Ohio

 1 pound ground beef
 1/2 teaspoon salt
 1/4 teaspoon pepper
 1 cup (4 ounces) shredded cheddar cheese
 2 eggs, beaten
 1-1/2 cups milk
 3/4 cup biscuit/baking mix

In a skillet, cook beef over medium heat until no longer pink; drain. Press into an ungreased 9-in. pie plate. Sprinkle with salt, pepper and cheese. In a bowl, combine the eggs, milk and biscuit mix just until combined. Pour over cheese. Bake at 400° for 35 minutes or until a toothpick inserted near the center comes out clean. **Yield:** 4 servings (82¢ per serving).

Spinach Crumb Casserole

Ready in 1 hour or less

Even people who say they don't like spinach ask for the recipe for this cheesy vegetable bake. It's a popular savory side dish for many occasions. —Dorothy Tobison
Coleman, Wisconsin

Tomato Corn Chowder

1 package (10 ounces) frozen
   chopped spinach, thawed
   and squeezed dry
2 eggs, beaten
1/2 cup milk
1/2 cup cubed process cheese
   (Velveeta)
1 tablespoon chopped onion
1/2 teaspoon salt
1 cup soft bread crumbs
4-1/2 teaspoons butter or
   margarine, melted

In a large bowl, combine the spinach, eggs, milk, cheese, onion and salt. Pour into a greased 1-qt. baking dish. Combine bread crumbs and butter; sprinkle over the top. Bake, uncovered, at 350° for 25-30 minutes or until a knife inserted near the center comes out clean. **Yield:** 4 servings (39¢ per serving).

Moist Chocolate Cake

(Pictured on page 230)

This proves you don't have to spend a lot to serve an elegant and delicious dessert. —Christa Hageman
Telford, Pennsylvania

2 cups sugar
1-3/4 cups all-purpose flour
3/4 cup baking cocoa
2 teaspoons baking soda
1 teaspoon baking powder
1 teaspoon salt
2 eggs
1 cup strong brewed coffee
1 cup buttermilk
1/2 cup vegetable oil
1 teaspoon vanilla extract
1 tablespoon confectioners' sugar

In a large mixing bowl, combine the first six ingredients. Add eggs, coffee, buttermilk, oil and vanilla; beat on medium speed for 2 minutes (batter will be thin). Pour into a greased and floured 10-in. fluted tube pan.

Bake at 350° for 45-50 minutes or until a toothpick inserted near the center comes out clean. Cool for 10 minutes before removing from pan to a wire rack to cool completely. Dust with confectioners' sugar. **Yield:** 12 servings (14¢ per serving).

Open-Faced Veggie Sandwiches

(Pictured above right)

Ready in 15 minutes or less

Since I'm a vegetarian, I love these broiled sandwiches. Even non-vegetarians like their fresh taste. The veggie-

Open-Faced Veggie Sandwiches

topped muffin halves make a great snack or quick lunch. Mix and match different vegetables to suit your family's taste. —Karen Mello, Fairhaven, Massachusetts

4 teaspoons spicy brown or horseradish
   mustard
4 English muffins, split
1/2 cup *each* chopped fresh broccoli, cauliflower
   and sweet red pepper
1 cup (4 ounces) shredded cheddar cheese

Spread mustard on cut sides of muffins. Top each with vegetables and cheese. Broil 4-6 in. from the heat for 3 minutes or until the cheese is melted. **Yield:** 4 servings (80¢ per serving).

Waste Not, Want Not

• I save the tiny broken bits of chips, pretzels and other savory packaged snacks, crush them and combine them in a jar. I use the mixture for topping casseroles and coating chicken and fish. —*Sandra Ayers
Aliquippa, Pennsylvannia*

• Wondering what to do with extra doughnuts, muffins or slices of coffee cake? Use them in place of some or all of the bread called for in a bread pudding recipe. You won't believe your family's reaction to this wonderfully revamped dessert.
—*Peggy Kinsel, Corpus Christi, Texas*

Ham Mushroom Pie

1 cup biscuit/baking mix
1/2 cup grated Parmesan cheese
1 tablespoon dill weed
1 teaspoon salt
1/8 teaspoon pepper
4 eggs, beaten
1/2 cup vegetable oil
3 cups chopped zucchini
1 large onion, chopped

In a bowl, combine biscuit mix, Parmesan cheese, dill, salt and pepper. Add eggs and oil; mix well. Stir in zucchini and onion until blended. Pour into a greased 1-1/2-qt. baking dish. Bake, uncovered, at 375° for 25-30 minutes or until golden brown. **Yield:** 5 servings (77¢ per serving).

Sauteed Cabbage

Ready in 30 minutes or less

Chopped onion, minced garlic and soy sauce add savory seasoning to this snappy side dish that pairs well with many meals. It's easy to stir-fry on the stovetop when time is short.
—Connie Moore, Medway, Ohio

1 tablespoon finely chopped onion
1 garlic clove, minced
1 tablespoon vegetable oil
5 cups chopped cabbage
1 tablespoon soy sauce
1/2 teaspoon sugar
1/8 teaspoon pepper

In a skillet or wok, saute onion and garlic in oil until tender. Add cabbage; cook and stir until crisp-tender, about 5 minutes. Reduce heat; add soy sauce, sugar and pepper. Cook and stir for 3-5 minutes or until cabbage is tender. **Yield:** 6 servings (10¢ per serving).

Ham Mushroom Pie

(Pictured above)

Ready in 1 hour or less

This brunch recipe was given to me by my grandmother, who loved making fast and delicious meals.
—Howie Wiener, Spring Hill, Florida

1 boneless ham steak (about 1 pound)
1 pastry shell (9 inches), baked
2/3 cup condensed cream of mushroom soup, undiluted
2/3 cup sour cream
3 eggs, lightly beaten
2 tablespoons minced chives
Dash pepper

Cut ham to fit the bottom of pastry shell; place in shell. In a bowl, combine the remaining ingredients; mix well. Pour over ham. Cover edges loosely with foil. Bake at 425° for 35-40 minutes or until a knife inserted near the center comes out clean. **Yield:** 6 servings (92¢ per serving).

Dilly Zucchini Casserole

Ready in 1 hour or less

Whenever I take this time-saving side-dish casserole to a potluck, I seldom bring any home, and folks often ask for the recipe. If I have fresh dill, I'll substitute a couple tablespoons for the dill weed. It's easy to assemble.
—Esther Kilborn, Bridgton, Maine

Tuna Salad Pepper Cups

(Pictured on page 230)

Ready in 15 minutes or less

I came up with this recipe on a hot summer day when I didn't feel like cooking. I frequently make it when friends come for lunch, and they all love it. Stuffed into a pretty pepper half, the fresh-tasting tuna mixture gets crunch from cucumber and green onions.
—Ellen Boucher
Denver, Colorado

2 large green peppers
2 cans (6 ounces *each*) tuna, drained
1 medium cucumber, chopped
2 green onions, chopped
1/2 cup mayonnaise
1/4 cup dill pickle relish

Cut green peppers in half lengthwise; remove seeds and membranes. In a bowl, combine tuna, cucumber, onions, mayonnaise and relish. Spoon into pepper cups. Serve immediately. **Yield:** 4 servings (87¢ per serving).

Norwegian Apple Cake

Ready in 1 hour or less

I bake this nutty apple cake that's pleasantly topped with a simple cinnamon-sugar mixture. Serve it with a dollop of whipped topping. —Lucia Johnson
Massena, New York

- 3/4 cup sugar
- 1/2 cup all-purpose flour
- 1 teaspoon baking powder
- 1/4 teaspoon salt
- 2 eggs, beaten
- 1/2 teaspoon vanilla extract
- 1 medium tart apple, peeled and chopped
- 1/2 cup chopped walnuts
- 1 tablespoon cinnamon-sugar, optional

In a bowl, combine the sugar, flour, baking powder and salt. Add eggs and vanilla; mix well. Stir in apple and walnuts. Spread into an ungreased 9-in. pie plate. Sprinkle with cinnamon-sugar if desired. Bake at 375° for 25-30 minutes or until a toothpick inserted near the center comes out clean. **Yield:** 8 servings (19¢ per serving).

Vegetable Beef Stew

(Pictured below)

Ready in 1 hour or less

Tasty vegetable chunks add color to this satisfying stew. I serve it with warm corn bread and a tossed salad for a delicious meal. —Bobbie Jo Yokley, Franklin, Kentucky

- 1-1/2 pounds beef bottom round roast, cut into 1/2-inch cubes
- 2 tablespoons vegetable oil
- 4 cups water
- 1 medium onion, diced
- 3 celery ribs, cut into 1-inch chunks
- 3 small carrots, cut into 1-inch chunks
- 3 medium potatoes, peeled and diced
- 2 tablespoons beef bouillon granules
- 1 cup frozen peas
- 3 tablespoons all-purpose flour
- 1/3 cup cold water

In a Dutch oven, brown beef in oil; drain. Add water, onion, celery, carrots, potatoes and bouillon. Bring to a boil. Reduce heat; cover and simmer for 25-30 minutes or until vegetables are tender. Stir in peas. Bring to a boil. Combine flour and water until smooth; add to beef mixture. Cook and stir for 2 minutes or until thickened and bubbly. **Yield:** 6 servings (95¢ per serving).

Vegetable Beef Stew

Cheeseburger Meat Loaf

(Pictured below)

I created this meat loaf one day when I wanted to make cheeseburgers—my husband's favorite—but it was too chilly to grill outside. I've served it numerous times since then, and it never fails to get rave reviews. Even your most finicky eater will enjoy this oven-baked main dish.
—Paula Sullivan, Barker, New York

- 1/2 cup ketchup, *divided*
- 1 egg
- 1/4 cup dry bread crumbs
- 1 teaspoon onion powder
- 1 pound lean ground beef
- 2 teaspoons prepared mustard
- 2 teaspoons dill pickle relish
- 6 slices process American cheese

In a bowl, combine 1/4 cup ketchup, egg, bread crumbs and onion powder. Crumble beef over mixture and mix well. On a large piece of waxed paper, pat the beef mixture into a 10-in. x 6-in. rectangle. Spread the remaining ketchup over meat to within 1/2 in. of long sides and 1-1/2 in. of short sides. Top with the mustard and relish.

Place four cheese slices on top; set remaining cheese aside. Roll up loaf, jelly-roll style, starting with a short side and pulling away waxed paper while rolling. Seal seams and ends well. Place loaf, seam side down, in a greased 11-in. x 7-in. x 2-in. baking pan.

Bake at 350° for 45 minutes or until meat is no longer pink and a meat thermometer reads 160°. Cut the reserved cheese slices in half diagonally; place on top of loaf. Return to the oven for 5 minutes or until cheese is melted. Let stand for 10 minutes before slicing. **Yield:** 6 servings (51¢ per serving).

Plantation Supper

Ready in 30 minutes or less

My husband loves this all-in-one casserole. We think it's even better the next day, although we rarely have any left over. It's inexpensive and family-pleasing.
—Linda Heller, Allison, Iowa

- 1-1/2 pounds ground beef
- 1 medium onion, chopped
- 1 can (15-1/4 ounces) whole kernel corn, drained
- 1 can (10-3/4 ounces) condensed cream of mushroom soup, undiluted
- 1 package (8 ounces) cream cheese, cubed
- 1 cup milk
- 1 teaspoon beef bouillon granules
- 1/4 teaspoon pepper
- 4-1/2 cups uncooked wide egg noodles

In a large skillet over medium heat, cook the beef and onion until meat is no longer pink; drain. Add the corn, soup, cream cheese, milk, bouillon and pepper. Cook and stir until the cheese is melted. Meanwhile, cook the noodles according to package directions; rinse and drain. Add to skillet; heat through. **Yield:** 8 servings (70¢ per serving).

Cheeseburger Meat Loaf

Scalloped Potatoes And Veggies

(Pictured on page 231)

Ready in 30 minutes or less

If you're like me, you're always searching for easy side dishes. This vegetable medley in a creamy cheese sauce couldn't be simpler.
—Linda Renberger, Derby, Kansas

- 2 large potatoes, peeled and sliced
- 1 cup sliced carrots
- 1 small onion, sliced
- 1/4 cup water
- 1 cup frozen peas
- 2 tablespoons all-purpose flour
- 1-1/2 teaspoons seasoned salt
- 1/4 teaspoon ground mustard
- 1/8 teaspoon pepper
- 1 cup milk
- 1/2 cup cubed process cheese product

In a 2-qt. microwave-safe dish, combine potatoes, carrots, onion and water. Cover and microwave on high for 7 minutes. Add peas; cook 4 minutes longer or until vegetables are tender.

Meanwhile, in a 1-qt. microwave-safe dish, combine the flour, seasoned salt, mustard, pepper and milk until smooth. Microwave, uncovered, on high for 4-5 minutes or until thickened and bubbly, stirring occasionally. Stir in cheese until melted. Drain vegetables; add cheese sauce and toss. **Yield:** 7 servings (24¢ per serving).

Editor's Note: This recipe was tested in an 850-watt microwave.

Saucy Beef Casserole

Ready in 1 hour or less

I rely on canned soups and crunchy chow mein noodles to flavor this hearty ground beef bake. My family gobbles it up. —Ferne Spielvogel
Fairwater, Wisconsin

> 1 pound ground beef
> 1 medium onion, chopped
> 1 can (10-3/4 ounces) condensed cream of chicken soup, undiluted
> 1 can (10-3/4 ounces) condensed vegetable soup, undiluted
> 3/4 cup chow mein noodles

In a skillet, cook the beef and onion over medium heat until meat is no longer pink; drain. Stir in the soups. Transfer to a greased 8-in. square baking dish. Cover and bake at 350° for 25-30 minutes or until heated through. Uncover; sprinkle with the chow mein noodles. Bake 5 minutes longer or until the noodles are crisp. **Yield:** 4 servings (94¢ per serving).

Peanut Butter Popcorn Bars

Ready in 30 minutes or less

If you're looking for a fun snack for kids, try these chewy popcorn treats that have a mild peanut butter taste. They're easy to stir up and can be pressed into a pan to form bars or shaped into balls. These are one of the first treats to disappear at potlucks.
—Kathy Oswald
Wauzeka, Wisconsin

> 10 cups popped popcorn
> 1/2 cup sugar
> 1/2 cup light corn syrup
> 1/2 cup creamy peanut butter
> 1/2 teaspoon vanilla extract

Place popcorn in a large bowl; set aside. In a saucepan over medium heat, bring sugar and corn syrup to a boil, stirring constantly. Boil for 1 minute. Remove from the heat.

Stir in peanut butter and vanilla; mix well. Pour over popcorn and mix until well coated. Press into a buttered 13-in. x 9-in. x 2-in. pan. Cool slightly before cutting. **Yield:** 2 dozen (4¢ per bar).

Apple Walnut Squares

Apple Walnut Squares

(Pictured above)

If you need a homespun snack or bake sale treat that can be assembled in a hurry, try these moist nutty bars. The squares are sweet, flavorful and loaded with chopped apple and nuts, and each bite captures the flavor of fall. Best of all, they won't break the bank. —Jennifer Dzubinski
San Antonio, Texas

> 1/2 cup butter, softened
> 1 cup sugar
> 1 egg
> 1 cup all-purpose flour
> 1/2 teaspoon baking powder
> 1/2 teaspoon baking soda
> 1/2 teaspoon ground cinnamon
> 1 medium tart apple, peeled and chopped
> 3/4 cup chopped walnuts

In a mixing bowl, cream the butter and sugar. Add the egg. Combine the flour, baking powder, baking soda and cinnamon; gradually add to the creamed mixture, beating just until combined. Stir in the apple and walnuts.

Pour into a greased 8-in. square baking dish. Bake at 350° for 35-40 minutes or until a toothpick inserted near the center comes out clean. Cool on a wire rack. **Yield:** 16 servings (15¢ per serving).

State Fair Subs

Carrot Burgers

Ready in 30 minutes or less

These carrot patties were a big hit with my children when they were growing up. Cornflakes provide the taste that kids find so appealing, while the low price makes them attractive to parents.
—Phyllis Moody
King William, Virginia

☑ Uses less fat, sugar or salt. Includes Nutritional Analysis and Diabetic Exchanges.

```
1-1/2 cups diced carrots
    2 cups crushed cornflakes
    2 eggs, beaten
  1/4 cup finely chopped celery
    1 tablespoon finely chopped onion
  1/2 teaspoon salt
  1/4 teaspoon sugar
  1/8 teaspoon pepper
    2 tablespoons vegetable oil
Hamburger buns, optional
```

Place carrots in a saucepan with a small amount of water. Bring to a boil; reduce heat. Cover and cook for 5 minutes or until tender; drain. In a bowl, combine carrots, cornflakes, eggs, celery, onion, salt, sugar and pepper; mix well. Form into six patties. Heat oil in a skillet over medium heat; cook patties for 3 minutes on each side or until browned. Serve on buns if desired. **Yield:** 6 servings (18¢ per serving).

Nutritional Analysis: One serving (prepared with nonstick cooking spray in place of oil; calculated without bun) equals 151 calories, 2 g fat (1 g saturated fat), 71 mg cholesterol, 565 mg sodium, 29 g carbohydrate, 1 g fiber, 5 g protein. **Diabetic Exchanges:** 2 vegetable, 1 starch, 1/2 fat.

State Fair Subs

(Pictured above)

Ready in 1 hour or less

My college roommate and I first ate these meaty sandwiches at the Iowa State Fair. After a little experimenting, we re-created the recipe. We ate the subs often because they were fast to fix between classes and didn't break our next-to-nothing grocery budget.
—Christi Ross
Mill Creek, Oklahoma

```
    1 loaf (1 pound) unsliced French bread
    2 eggs
  1/4 cup milk
  1/2 teaspoon pepper
  1/4 teaspoon salt
    1 pound bulk Italian sausage
1-1/2 cups chopped onion
    2 cups (8 ounces) shredded mozzarella cheese
```

Cut bread in half lengthwise; carefully hollow out top and bottom of loaf, leaving a 1-in. shell. Cube removed bread. In a large bowl, beat the eggs, milk, pepper and salt. Add bread cubes and toss to coat; set aside.

In a skillet over medium heat, cook sausage and onion until the meat is no longer pink; drain. Add to the bread mixture. Spoon filling into bread shells; sprinkle with cheese. Wrap each in foil. Bake at 400° for 20-25 minutes or until cheese is melted. Cut into serving-size slices. **Yield:** 6 servings (91¢ per serving).

Broccoli-Ham Puff Pancake

(Pictured on page 231)

Ready in 1 hour or less

You won't have to pay a pretty penny to prepare this special-looking Sunday supper. The golden brown puff pancake makes a tasty main dish for brunch, lunch or dinner when filled with a creamy ham and broccoli mixture.
—Edna Hoffman, Hebron, Indiana

```
  1/4 cup butter (no substitutes)
    1 cup all-purpose flour
    4 eggs
    1 cup milk
FILLING:
    3 tablespoons butter (no substitutes)
    3 tablespoons all-purpose flour
    1 cup plus 2 tablespoons milk
    1 package (16 ounces) frozen chopped
      broccoli, thawed
1-1/2 cups cubed fully cooked ham
  1/3 cup sour cream
1-1/2 teaspoons lemon juice
  1/8 teaspoon hot pepper sauce
```

Place butter in a 10-in. ovenproof skillet; place in a 425° oven for 3-4 minutes or until melted. In a mixing bowl, beat flour, eggs and milk until smooth. Pour into prepared skillet. Bake at 425° for 22-25 minutes or until puffed and golden brown.

Meanwhile, in a saucepan, melt butter. Stir in flour until smooth; gradually add milk. Bring to a boil; cook and stir for 2 minutes or until thickened. Reduce heat; add the remaining filling ingredients. Cook for 10 minutes or until heated through. Spoon into center of puff pancake. Cut into wedges; serve immediately. **Yield:** 6 servings (90¢ per serving).

Peas with Mushrooms

(Pictured below right)

Ready in 30 minutes or less

Crunchy water chestnuts give a nice contrast in texture to the tender peas in this snappy side dish. I prepare it often for company. —Judy Bennett, Vacaville, California

✓ Uses less fat, sugar or salt. Includes Nutritional Analysis and Diabetic Exchanges.

> 2 cups sliced fresh mushrooms
> 1/2 cup chopped onion
> 2 tablespoons butter
> 2 packages (16 ounces *each*) frozen peas, thawed
> 1 can (8 ounces) sliced water chestnuts, drained and halved
> 1/4 cup soy sauce

In a large saucepan, saute the mushrooms and onion in butter. Add the peas, water chestnuts and soy sauce. Cook until heated through, about 10 minutes. **Yield:** 8 servings (52¢ per serving).
Nutritional Analysis: One 3/4-cup serving (prepared with reduced-sodium soy sauce) equals 128 calories, 3 g fat (2 g saturated fat), 8 mg cholesterol, 478 mg sodium, 19 g carbohydrate, 8 g fiber, 7 g protein. **Diabetic Exchanges:** 1 starch, 1 vegetable.

Sauteed Apples

Ready in 30 minutes or less

Cinnamon and sugar coat warm apple slices in this change-of-pace side dish. It's priced right, so the sweetly seasoned specialty is fuss-free and frugal. —Shirley Heston, Pickerington, Ohio

> 5 medium Golden Delicious apples, peeled and thinly sliced
> 1/4 cup butter *or* margarine
> 1/4 cup water
> 1/2 cup sugar
> 1/2 teaspoon ground cinnamon

In a large skillet, saute apples in butter for 1 minute. Add water; bring to a boil. Sprinkle with sugar and cinnamon. Reduce heat; cover and simmer for 10-12 minutes or until apples are tender. **Yield:** 4 servings (56¢ per serving).

Tangy Meatballs Over Noodles

(Pictured below)

These moist meatballs are so easy to make, yet they taste fancy. The sweet and tangy sauce has surprising flavor from ginger and cloves. —Teri Lindquist, Gurnee, Illinois

> 1 egg, lightly beaten
> 1/3 cup milk
> 1/4 cup seasoned bread crumbs
> 1 tablespoon dried minced onion
> 1 teaspoon salt
> 1-1/2 pounds ground beef
> 2 cans (14-3/4 ounces *each*) beef gravy
> 1/2 cup packed brown sugar
> 1/4 cup cider vinegar
> 3/4 teaspoon ground ginger
> 1/4 teaspoon ground cloves
> 1 package (12 ounces) egg noodles

In a bowl, combine the first five ingredients. Crumble beef over mixture and mix well. Shape into 1-1/2-in. balls. Place 1 in. apart in greased 15-in. x 10-in. x 1-in. baking pans. Bake, uncovered, at 350° for 20 minutes.

With a slotted spoon, transfer meatballs to a greased 2-1/2-qt. baking dish. Combine gravy, brown sugar, vinegar, ginger and cloves; pour over meatballs. Cover and bake 30 minutes longer or until meat is no longer pink. Meanwhile, cook noodles according to package directions; drain. Serve with meatballs. **Yield:** 8 servings (40 meatballs) (78¢ per serving).

Peas with Mushrooms
Tangy Meatballs Over Noodles

Chapter 16

KIDS of all ages will jump at the chance to lend a hand with meal preparation when they see the fast, flavorful foods on the following pages.

From speedy snacks and hearty entrees to tasty side dishes and sweet desserts, younger children can mix and measure ingredients while older ones help you get a head start on dinner. (Toddlers can even help with "cleanup" by licking the bowl!)

Your kids are sure to enjoy the hands-on experience, and you'll appreciate the quality time spent together.

Best of all, the whole family will be pleased—and proud—to sit down to a delectable dinner they helped make.

KID APPEAL. Clockwise from the top. Kool-Aid Floats, S'more Tarts and Nutty Chicken Fingers (all recipes on p. 250).

Bacon Cheeseburger Rice

(Pictured below)

Ready in 30 minutes or less

My husband and I thought the original skillet dish lacked pizzazz, so we created this tastier version. I've had nieces and nephews request the recipe after their first bite.
—Joyce Whipps, West Des Moines, Iowa

    1 pound ground beef
1-3/4 cups water
  2/3 cup barbecue sauce
    1 tablespoon prepared mustard
    2 teaspoons dried minced onion
  1/2 teaspoon pepper
    2 cups uncooked instant rice
    1 cup (4 ounces) shredded cheddar cheese
  1/3 cup chopped dill pickles
    5 bacon strips, cooked and crumbled

In a large saucepan over medium heat, cook the beef until no longer pink; drain. Add water, barbecue sauce, mustard, onion and pepper. Bring to a boil; stir in the rice. Sprinkle with cheese. Reduce heat; cover and simmer for 5 minutes. Sprinkle with pickles and bacon. **Yield:** 4-6 servings.

Creamy Center Cupcakes

(Pictured below)

This recipe came from my mother, who made the cake from scratch when I was growing up. Sometimes she'd replace the smooth filling with homemade whipped cream, which was readily available on the farm.
—Caroline Anderson, Waupaca, Wisconsin

    1 package (18-1/4 ounces) devil's food cake mix
  3/4 cup shortening
  2/3 cup confectioners' sugar
    1 cup marshmallow creme
    1 teaspoon vanilla extract
    2 cans (16 ounces *each*) chocolate frosting

Prepare and bake cake according to package directions for cupcakes, using paper-lined muffin cups. Cool for 10 minutes before removing from pans to wire racks to cool completely. In a mixing bowl, cream shortening and sugar. Add marshmallow creme and vanilla; mix well. Insert a very small pastry tip into a pastry or plastic bag; fill with cream filling. Insert tip halfway into the center of each cupcake and fill with a small amount. Frost with chocolate frosting. **Yield:** 2 dozen.

Nutty Nanas

Ready in 15 minutes or less

While working on a recent cooking badge, my Girl Scout Cadette troop came up with this fun finger food. It's a yummy snack that's simple enough for young children to make. *—Diane Standridge, Sikeston, Missouri*

  1/4 cup sugar
    2 tablespoons half-and-half cream
    1 tablespoon mayonnaise *or* salad dressing
    2 cups salted peanuts, ground
    5 medium firm bananas, cut into thirds

In a shallow bowl, combine the sugar, cream and mayonnaise; mix well. Place peanuts in another shallow bowl. Dip each banana in mayonnaise mixture, then roll in peanuts. Serve immediately. **Yield:** 5 servings.

Bacon Cheeseburger Rice
Creamy Center Cupcakes

Greet the Day with Grins from the Griddle

IT'S EASY to get going in the morning when your breakfast plate is stacked with these fun flapjacks.

"Smiley Face Pancakes are a great way to start the day off with a smile," says Janette Garner of Carmel, Indiana.

"My husband, Kevin, sometimes prepares these pancakes on Saturday mornings," she states.

"Our children, Ryan, Jessie and Erin, look forward to helping him on these occasions," Janette notes. "They do most of the cooking—with Dad's supervision, of course."

The batter is easy for kids of all ages to stir up. Adding food coloring to small portions of the batter creates the bright facial features.

Youngsters are likely to have as much fun making the tender and tasty treats as they do eating them.

"Just top with your favorite fruit or syrup," Janette suggests.

Smiley Face Pancakes

Ready in 30 minutes or less

2 cups biscuit/baking mix
1-1/4 cups milk
1 egg, beaten
2 tablespoons sugar
2 tablespoons lemon juice
1 teaspoon vanilla extract
Red, green, yellow and blue
liquid *or* paste food coloring
Maple syrup, optional

In a bowl, combine the biscuit mix, milk, egg, sugar, lemon juice and vanilla; mix until smooth. Place 1 tablespoon of batter each in four bowls. Color one red, one green, one yellow and one blue. Drop remaining batter by 1/4 cupfuls onto a lightly greased hot griddle.

To create faces, paint colored batter on pancakes with a new small paintbrush. Cook until bubbles form on the top. Turn and cook until second side is golden. Serve with syrup if desired. **Yield:** about 1 dozen.

Smiley Face Pancakes

Broiled Sausage Sandwiches

Ready in 30 minutes or less

We've spiced up these open-faced sandwiches by adding jalapenos or extra cayenne from time to time. I've even spread the sausage mixture on a loaf of French bread for a potluck dinner. It was devoured in a hurry.
—Patricia Inman, Litchfield, Minnesota

1-1/2 pounds bulk Italian *or* pork sausage
1 medium onion, chopped
1 jar (14 ounces) pizza sauce
1 cup salsa
Dash cayenne pepper, optional
12 hamburger buns, split
1-1/2 cups (6 ounces) shredded mozzarella cheese

In a skillet over medium heat, cook sausage and onion until the meat is no longer pink; drain. Stir in pizza sauce, salsa and cayenne if desired; cook and stir for 5 minutes. Place buns, cut side up, on baking sheets. Broil 4 in. from the heat until lightly toasted.

Spread about 3 tablespoons sausage mixture over each bun half. Sprinkle with cheese. Broil for 2-3 minutes or until cheese is melted and lightly browned. **Yield:** 12 servings.

Spaghetti Mac
Kids' Breadsticks

2 cups uncooked elbow macaroni
1/2 pound ground beef
1 can (10-3/4 ounces) condensed tomato soup, undiluted
1 can (8 ounces) tomato sauce
1 teaspoon dried minced onion
1 teaspoon dried parsley flakes
1/2 teaspoon salt
1/2 teaspoon dried oregano
1/4 cup shredded Parmesan cheese

Cook macaroni according to package directions. Meanwhile, in a saucepan, cook beef over medium heat until no longer pink; drain. Stir in soup, tomato sauce, onion, parsley, salt and oregano; heat through. Drain macaroni; top with the beef mixture and sprinkle with cheese. **Yield:** 4 servings.

Oven-Shy Cookies

Ready in 30 minutes or less

There's no need to shy away from these sweet crispy snacks, because they're a snap to stir up on the stovetop. Our three children can't get enough of them.
—Charla Sackmann, Bangor, Wisconsin

1 package (1 pound) marshmallows
2 cups (12 ounces) semisweet chocolate chips
1/4 cup butter *or* margarine
3 cups crisp rice cereal
1 can (12 ounces) salted peanuts

In a saucepan over low heat, cook and stir marshmallows, chips and butter until marshmallows are melted and mixture is smooth. Remove from the heat. Stir in cereal and peanuts; mix well. Drop by rounded tablespoonfuls onto waxed paper; cool. **Yield:** about 6-1/2 dozen.

Kids' Breadsticks

(Pictured above)

Ready in 15 minutes or less

These cheesy breadsticks are simple to make because they start with convenient hot dog buns. I can whip up a batch in a matter of minutes...and they disappear just as quickly.   —Mary Miller, Fairfield, California

8 hot dog buns, split
6 tablespoons butter *or* margarine, melted
1 cup grated Parmesan cheese
2 to 3 tablespoons poppy *or* sesame seeds

Brush the cut sides of buns with butter. Place on ungreased baking sheets. Combine cheese and poppy or sesame seeds; sprinkle over buns. Bake at 450° for 7-9 minutes or until golden brown. **Yield:** 16 breadsticks.

Spaghetti Mac

(Pictured above)

Ready in 30 minutes or less

This hearty meal is my mother's creation and ranks among my kids' favorites. I often cook the sauce over the weekend and freeze it, then warm it in a jiffy after a busy day.
—Linda Sawin, Sterling, Massachusetts

Meal on a Bun

Ready in 15 minutes or less

Looking for a break from the usual peanut butter and jelly sandwich? This easy concoction is sure to be a hit with kids of all ages. I've replaced the jelly with a juicy slice of pineapple and topped it off with cheddar cheese.
—Lavina Taylor, Moline, Illinois

4 hamburger buns, split
1/2 cup peanut butter
1 can (8 ounces) pineapple slices, drained
4 slices cheddar cheese

Place buns, cut side up, on a baking sheet. Spread with peanut butter. Place a pineapple slice on each bun bottom and a cheese slice on each top. Bake at 350° for 5-7 minutes or until cheese is melted. Place cheese-topped buns over pineapple. **Yield:** 4 servings.

Tickle Their Taste Buds With Truck-Shaped Treats

WHEN MAKING crunchy Fire Truck Cookies, you'll probably want to call for help...from your kids. They'll be delighted to decorate the sweet snacks shared by Rhonda Walsh, day school director of a Baptist church in Cleveland, Tennessee.

But don't be alarmed. The tasty treats are easy to assemble for youngsters of all ages because there's no baking involved.

Rhonda's recipe calls for dressing up ordinary graham crackers with prepared frosting and store-bought goodies.

"Add red food coloring to a bowl of frosting and set out dishes filled with chocolate sandwich cookies, gumdrops and licorice," recommends Rhonda.

"Use a serrated knife to slice a corner off each cracker before giving them to the children," she notes. "Then let them get to work. They'll have as much fun frosting and decorating the treats as they will munching them."

Along with eight other day school teachers, Rhonda created the simple snacks as part of a fire safety program at the school. Activities also included a visit from local firefighters and Sparky the Dalmatian, a fire safety mascot.

With a serrated knife, cut the top left- or right-hand corner off of each graham cracker at a 45° angle. Tint frosting red; frost crackers. Place two sandwich cookies on each for wheels.

For each truck, cut licorice into two 2-1/2-in. pieces, five 1/2-in. pieces and two 1-1/2-in. pieces. Place the large pieces parallel to each other above wheels, with the small pieces between to form a ladder. Place the medium pieces at cut edge, forming a windshield. Add a gumdrop for light. **Yield:** 16 cookies.

Fire Truck Cookies

Fire Truck Cookies

16 whole graham crackers (4-3/4 inches x 2-1/2 inches)
1 cup vanilla frosting
Red paste *or* liquid food coloring
32 chocolate cream-filled sandwich cookies
Black shoestring licorice
16 red gumdrops

Beanie Wienies

Ready in 15 minutes or less

I create this kid-pleasing combo by blending hot dogs and canned pork and beans with extra seasonings. This dish is quick and easy to assemble. My family loves it.
—LaDonna Reed, Ponca City, Oklahoma

2 cans (15 ounces *each*) pork and beans
2 tablespoons brown sugar
2 teaspoons Worcestershire sauce
2 teaspoons prepared mustard
1/2 teaspoon onion powder
1 package (1 pound) hot dogs, halved lengthwise and cut into thirds

In a saucepan, combine the first five ingredients; mix well. Add hot dogs; bring to a boil. Reduce heat; cover and simmer for 3-4 minutes or until heated through. **Yield:** 6-8 servings.

Peanut Butter Bread
Chilly Peanut Butter Pie

Chilly Peanut Butter Pie

(Pictured above)

Plan ahead...needs to freeze

My 13-year-old requested this cool and creamy dessert instead of cake for her birthday. —Marietta Slater
Augusta, Kansas

> 1 carton (8 ounces) frozen whipped topping, thawed, *divided*
> 1 graham cracker crust (9 inches)
> 1/2 cup strawberry jelly *or* jam
> 1 cup cold milk
> 1 package (3.4 ounces) instant vanilla pudding mix
> 1/2 cup peanut butter

Spread 1 cup whipped topping over the bottom of the crust. Drop jelly by tablespoonfuls onto topping; spread carefully. In a bowl, whisk milk and pudding mix until thickened. Add peanut butter; mix well. Fold in the remaining whipped topping. Spread over jelly. Cover and freeze for 4 hours or until firm. Remove from the freezer 10 minutes before serving. **Yield:** 6-8 servings.

Peanut Butter Bread

(Pictured above)

Slices of this yummy loaf are great spread with grape jelly. Kids will ask for it along with a big glass of milk for an after-school snack. —Linda Muir
Big Lake, Minnesota

> 2 cups all-purpose flour
> 1/3 cup sugar
> 2 teaspoons baking powder
> 1 teaspoon salt
> 1 egg
> 1 cup milk
> 3/4 cup peanut butter*
> Grape jelly, optional

In a mixing bowl, combine the flour, sugar, baking powder and salt. Add egg, milk and peanut butter; stir just until combined. Pour into a greased 8-in. x 4-in. x 2-in. loaf pan. Bake at 350° for 50-60 minutes or until a toothpick inserted near the center comes out clean. Cool for 10 minutes before removing from pan to a wire rack. Serve with jelly if desired. **Yield:** 1 loaf.

*Editor's Note: Reduced-fat or generic brands of peanut butter are not recommended for this recipe.

Cheddar Mushroom Potatoes

When they were little, our children loved this creamy side dish. After an adult has sliced the potatoes, youngsters can do the rest. Overlapping the potatoes in the baking dish is half the fun.
—Jacqueline Thompson Graves, Lawrenceville, Georgia

> 4 medium potatoes, cut into
>   1/4-inch slices
> 1 cup (4 ounces) shredded cheddar cheese

1 can (10-3/4 ounces) condensed cream of
  mushroom soup, undiluted
1/2 teaspoon paprika
1/4 teaspoon pepper

Arrange potatoes in a greased shallow 2-qt. baking dish; sprinkle with cheese. In a bowl, combine soup, paprika and pepper; spread over cheese. Cover and bake at 400° for 45 minutes. Uncover; bake 10 minutes longer or until potatoes are tender. **Yield:** 4-6 servings.

Upside-Down Pizza

Ready in 1 hour or less

When everyone craves pizza and you have no time to prepare a homemade crust, try this easy upside-down version. —Karen Cook, Putnam Station, New York

1 pound ground beef
1 medium onion, chopped
1 jar (14 ounces) spaghetti sauce
2 cups (8 ounces) shredded mozzarella cheese
1 cup milk
2 eggs
1 teaspoon vegetable oil
1 cup all-purpose flour
1/2 teaspoon salt

In a large skillet, cook beef and onion over medium heat until the meat is no longer pink; drain. Add spaghetti sauce. Cover and simmer until heated through. Pour into a greased 13-in. x 9-in. x 2-in. baking dish. Sprinkle with cheese. In a blender, combine the milk, eggs, oil, flour and salt; cover and process until smooth. Pour over cheese. Bake, uncovered, at 400° for 25-30 minutes or until golden brown. **Yield:** 12 servings.

Seafood Satisfies Younger Set

HUNGRY KIDS will squirm with delight when they get a look at these remarkable smiley sea creatures perched on a bed of seaweed.

Kerry Tittle of Little Rock, Arkansas uses ordinary hot dogs and fast-to-fix ramen noodles to create Octopus and Seaweed for her four daughters, Tori, Whitney, Emily and Rebekah.

"Slice the hot dogs partway before cooking. When you drop them into boiling water, it will cause the strips to curl and create tentacles," she explains.

A little green food coloring transforms the plain noodles into a bed of seaweed for the octopus to rest on.

"To add to the ocean theme, we serve this with fish shapes we've cut out of slices of American cheese," Kerry says. "The kids love it!"

And you're "shore" to receive waves of compliments on the swell idea.

Octopus and Seaweed

Ready in 15 minutes or less

1 package (3 ounces) beef
  ramen noodles
4 hot dogs
5 drops liquid green food
  coloring, optional
Prepared mustard

In a saucepan, bring 1-1/2 cups water to a boil. Add the noodles and contents of seasoning packet. Boil for 3-4 minutes or until noodles are tender. Meanwhile, add 4 in. of water to a large saucepan; bring to a boil. Cut each hot dog lengthwise into eight strips to within 2 in. of one end. Drop into boiling water; cook until heated through. Add food coloring to noodles if desired. Drain if necessary. Place noodles on serving plates; top with a hot dog. Add eyes and mouth with dabs of mustard. **Yield:** 4 servings.

Octopus and Seaweed

Kool-Aid Floats
Nutty Chicken Fingers
S'more Tarts

Kool-Aid Floats

(Pictured above and on page 242)

Ready in 30 minutes or less

Youngsters love this refreshing punch. Sweet sherbet, fruity soft drink mix and orange juice concentrate make this beverage a popular way to beat the heat on summer days.
—Margaret Bossuot, Carthage, New York

- 3 envelopes unsweetened strawberry Kool-Aid
- 3 cups sugar
- 6 quarts cold water
- 1 can (12 ounces) frozen orange juice concentrate, thawed
- 1 liter ginger ale, chilled
- 1 quart raspberry *or* orange sherbet

In large pitchers, prepare Kool-Aid with sugar and water according to package directions. Stir in the orange juice concentrate. Just before serving, add the ginger ale. Pour into tall glasses. Add scoops of sherbet to glasses. **Yield:** 2 gallons.

Nutty Chicken Fingers

(Pictured above and on page 242)

Ready in 30 minutes or less

Watch the room light up with smiles when you bring this fun dish to the table. Our children love the crunchy nut coating on these chicken strips. And with only a handful of ingredients, preparation is a snap. —Beba Cates
Pearland, Texas

- 1/2 cup finely chopped pecans
- 1/3 cup crushed cornflakes
- 1 tablespoon dried parsley flakes
- 1/8 teaspoon garlic powder
- 1/8 teaspoon salt
- 2 tablespoons milk
- 3/4 pound boneless skinless chicken breasts, cut into 1-inch strips

In a shallow bowl, combine the first five ingredients. Place milk in another shallow bowl. Dip chicken in milk, then roll in pecan mixture. Place in a single layer in an ungreased 15-in. x 10-in. x 1-in. baking pan. Bake, uncovered, at 400° for 12-15 minutes or until juices run clear. **Yield:** about 2 dozen.

S'more Tarts

(Pictured above and on page 242)

Ready in 1 hour or less

Kids of all ages will quickly gobble up the individual graham cracker tarts filled with a fudgy brownie and golden marshmallows before asking, "Can I have s'more?"
—Trish Quinn, Cheyenne, Wyoming

- 1 package fudge brownie mix (13-inch x 9-inch pan size)
- 12 individual graham cracker shells
- 1-1/2 cups miniature marshmallows
- 1 cup milk chocolate chips

Prepare brownie batter according to package directions. Place graham cracker shells on a baking sheet and fill with brownie batter. Bake at 350° for 20-25 minutes or until a toothpick inserted in the center comes out with moist crumbs. Immediately sprinkle with marshmallows and chocolate chips. Bake 3-5 minutes longer or until marshmallows are puffed and golden brown. **Yield:** 1 dozen.

Cheeseburger Pancakes

Ready in 1 hour or less

This recipe combines the flavors of juicy cheeseburgers and freshly baked buns. Served with ketchup, a cheese sauce or cream of mushroom soup mixed with half-and-half, these "pancakes" are a hearty meal the whole family enjoys.
—Donna Wenzel, Monroe, Michigan

- 1 pound ground beef
- 1/2 cup chopped onion
- 1/2 cup chopped celery
- 1/4 cup chopped green pepper
- 1 can (10-3/4 ounces) condensed tomato soup, undiluted
- 1 teaspoon Worcestershire sauce
- 1/2 teaspoon celery seed
- 1/4 teaspoon salt
- 1/8 teaspoon pepper
- 1 cup (4 ounces) shredded cheddar cheese
- 2 cups all purpose flour
- 4 teaspoons baking powder
- 1 egg
- 1 cup milk

In a skillet, cook beef, onion, celery and green pepper until meat is no longer pink and vegetables are tender; drain. Stir in soup, Worcestershire sauce, celery seed, salt and pepper. Remove from heat; cool slightly. Stir in cheese. In a bowl, combine the flour and baking powder. Combine the egg and milk; stir into dry ingredients just until moistened. Add beef mixture; mix well. Pour batter by 1/4 cupfuls onto a lightly greased hot griddle. Cook for 4-6 minutes on each side or until golden brown. **Yield:** about 2 dozen.

Pizza Dogs

Ready in 15 minutes or less

I'm asked to make these special hot dogs whenever I come home from college. Dressed up with pizza sauce, pepperoni and melted cheese, these sandwiches are sure to be a hit at your house, too.
—Rachel Tollefson
Selby, South Dakota

- 1 jar (14 ounces) pizza sauce
- 15 slices pepperoni, chopped
- 1-1/2 cups (6 ounces) shredded mozzarella cheese
- 12 to 14 hot dog buns, split
- 12 to 14 hot dogs, cooked

In a saucepan, combine pizza sauce and pepperoni; heat through. Stir in the cheese until melted. Spoon about 2 tablespoons into each bun; top with a hot dog. **Yield:** 12-14 servings.

Youngsters Favor Fido

THE DOG DAYS of summer won't be the only time you'll invite this cool culinary canine to the dinner table. Since making him is a great way to involve children in food preparation, while encouraging them to eat more fruit, this pooch is likely to be welcome in your kitchen throughout the year.

"Not only does my daughter, Courtney, love this fruity nutritious salad, but it's something she can actually make herself," says Jenni Miller of Olathe, Kansas.

"Made from healthy dried and canned fruits, this cute dish doesn't require any baking or cooking," she adds. "It's an ideal snack for youngsters to assemble and eat."

Imagine the delight in your child's eyes as he or she puts this pear-fect pup together for the first time. Surely the delicious doggie will appear at your home time and again.

Puppy Dog Salad

Ready in 15 minutes or less

- 1 lettuce leaf
- 1 canned pear half
- 1 prune half
- 2 mandarin orange segments
- 1 red maraschino cherry
- 1 raisin

Place lettuce on a salad plate; place pear cut side down over lettuce. For ear, place the prune on the wide end of pear. Place orange segments along bottom for collar. Place cherry at the narrow end of pear for nose. Add raisin for the eye. **Yield:** 1 serving.

Puppy Dog Salad

Bacon Cheese Strips

(Pictured below)

Ready in 30 minutes or less

These cheesy strips are super for breakfast or as an appetizer. For years, they've been a hit with my family.
—Linn Morrison, Mesilla Park, New Mexico

  1/3 cup mayonnaise
    1 egg, beaten
  1/2 teaspoon Worcestershire sauce
  1/8 teaspoon ground mustard
    5 to 6 drops hot pepper sauce
Dash pepper
    1 cup (4 ounces) shredded cheddar cheese
    8 bacon strips, cooked and crumbled
    8 bread slices, crusts removed and toasted
Paprika, optional

In a bowl, combine the first seven ingredients; mix well. Stir in bacon. Spread over toast. Sprinkle with paprika if desired. Cut each slice of toast into three strips. Place on a baking sheet. Bake at 350° for 12-14 minutes or until cheese is melted. **Yield:** 2 dozen.

Pizza Omelet

(Pictured below)

Ready in 15 minutes or less

My son, Jeremy, has been helping around the kitchen since he was a toddler. One of his favorite recipes is this pizza-flavored omelet.
—Sandy Cork, Melvin, Michigan

    2 eggs
    2 tablespoons milk
    1 tablespoon butter *or* margarine
  1/4 cup pizza sauce
  10 slices pepperoni
  1/4 cup shredded mozzarella cheese
    1 tablespoon shredded Parmesan cheese

In a bowl, beat eggs and milk. In a skillet over medium heat, melt butter. Add egg mixture. As eggs set, lift edges, letting uncooked portion flow underneath. When eggs are completely set, remove from the heat. Spread pizza sauce over half of the eggs; top with the pepperoni and mozzarella cheese. Fold in half; sprinkle with Parmesan cheese. Serve immediately. **Yield:** 1 serving.

Apple Cartwheels

Plan ahead...needs to chill

The filling in these stuffed apples is an irresistible combination of peanut butter, honey, chocolate chips and raisins.
—Miriam Miller, Thorp, Wisconsin

  1/4 cup peanut butter
1-1/2 teaspoons honey
  1/2 cup miniature semisweet chocolate chips
    2 tablespoons raisins
    4 medium unpeeled Red Delicious apples, cored

In a bowl, combine peanut butter and honey; fold in the chocolate chips and raisins. Fill center of apples with peanut butter mixture; refrigerate for at least 1 hour. Cut into 1/4-in. rings. **Yield:** about 2 dozen.

Bacon Cheese Strips
Pizza Omelet

Snacks Teach Sweet Lessons

HUNGRY STUDENTS will eagerly dive into their homework when it involves these book-shaped bites. Young kids especially are bound to love making and munching the colorful Schoolbook Snacks.

The novel treats are easy to assemble with a few simple ingredients, including graham crackers, prepared frosting and shoestring licorice.

"The kids at our local elementary school enjoyed the sweet sandwich cookies at our fall open house," shares Diane Hunt of Camden, New Jersey.

Since they're so simple to whip up, they would also be a fun last-minute addition to a back-to-school party, youth get-together or graduation celebration.

Schoolbook Snacks

1 can (16 ounces) vanilla frosting
Red, yellow, green and blue food coloring
16 graham cracker squares
Black shoestring licorice
1 tube (4-1/4 ounces) black decorating icing

Place 1/4 cup of frosting each in four bowls; tint one red, one yellow, one green and one blue. Cover and set aside. With remaining frosting, frost half of the graham crackers; top with remaining crackers. Frost the top of two sandwiches with one color of frosting. Repeat with remaining colors.

Cut licorice into eight 2-1/2-in. strips. Place along one edge of each cracker. Insert writing tip into decorating icing tube; pipe a title on the front of each book. Place on wire racks to dry. **Yield:** 8 servings.

Schoolbook Snacks

Hot Dog Macaroni Bake

Ready in 1 hour or less

Looking for a main dish kids will like making and eating? I've served it quite often when time is short.
—Irene Delbaugh, York, Pennsylvania

4 hot dogs
1/4 cup chopped onion
2 tablespoons butter *or* margarine
4 cups cooked elbow macaroni
1 can (10-3/4 ounces) condensed tomato soup, undiluted
1/2 cup water
1 teaspoon prepared mustard
1/4 cup dry bread crumbs

Cut hot dogs in half lengthwise; cut into 1/2-in. slices. In a large skillet, brown hot dogs over medium-high heat. Reduce heat. Add onion and butter; cook until onion is tender. Stir in the macaroni, soup, water and mustard. Pour into a greased 11-in. x 7-in. x 2-in. baking dish. Sprinkle with bread crumbs. Bake, uncovered, at 350° for 25-30 minutes or until bubbly. **Yield:** 4 servings.

Making Cookies with Kids

LOOKING for some helpers during the holiday baking season? Why not recruit your children or grandchildren? Land O' Lakes shares timely tips that are sure to make baking holiday cookies with kids a memorable tradition in your home:

- Clear a large work space—kids need a big area to spread out their materials. Protect children's clothes with an apron or old T-shirt.
- Read through the recipe together first. Kids can help gather ingredients and utensils.
- Consider breaking up the cookie-baking tasks. Select a dough that can be prepared ahead and kept refrigerated. Then bake the cookies after school or on a Saturday afternoon.
- Boost creativity and fun by providing colorful icings, sprinkles and candies for decorating cookies.
- Help children develop good kitchen habits. Remind them to wash their hands before beginning, and have them help with cleanup.

Quick Tomato Soup
Hot Dog Roll-Ups

Quick Tomato Soup

(Pictured above)

Ready in 15 minutes or less

My family often requests my sweet home-made tomato soup on cold winter days. It's great with a sandwich and nearly as quick to fix as the canned variety.
—Jane Ward
Churchville, Maryland

1/4 cup butter *or* margarine
1/4 cup all-purpose flour
  1 teaspoon curry powder
1/4 teaspoon onion powder
  1 can (46 ounces) tomato juice
1/4 cup sugar
Oyster crackers, optional

In a large saucepan, melt butter. Stir in flour, curry powder and onion powder until smooth. Gradually add tomato juice and sugar. Cook, uncovered, until thickened and heated through, about 5 minutes. Serve with crackers if desired. **Yield:** 6 servings.

No-Cook Divinity

Looking for a no-bake recipe that satisfies your sweet tooth? This candy recipe is simple and yummy. It's the on-ly divinity I know that will turn out perfectly every time.
—Linda Huffman, Charleston, Arkansas

  1 package (7-1/2 ounces) white frosting mix
1/3 cup light corn syrup
  2 tablespoons boiling water
  1 teaspoon vanilla extract
  1 package (16 ounces) confectioners' sugar
    (3-3/4 cups)
  6 tablespoons hot water
  1 cup chopped nuts

In a large mixing bowl, combine the frosting mix, corn syrup, boiling water and vanilla. Beat on high speed for 5 minutes. Gradually add sugar, hot water and nuts; mix well. Drop by teaspoonfuls onto waxed paper. Let stand at room temperature overnight or until dry to the touch. Store in an airtight container. **Yield:** about 2 pounds.

Hot Dog Roll-Ups

(Pictured above)

Ready in 30 minutes or less

Not only do my grandchildren love these cheese-and-bacon filled hot dogs, but they enjoy helping put the meal together, too. It's the perfect solution to a last-minute lunch.
—Lyletta Searle, Morgan, Utah

8 hot dogs
1 block (4 ounces) cheddar cheese, cut into 8 strips
2 bacon strips, cooked and crumbled
1 tube (8 ounces) refrigerated crescent rolls

Cut a lengthwise slit in each hot dog; fill with a strip of cheese and about 1/2 teaspoon bacon. Separate crescent dough into eight triangles. Place a hot dog on wide end of each triangle; roll toward the point. Place cheese side up on an ungreased baking sheet. Bake at 375° for 12 minutes or until golden brown. **Yield:** 8 servings.

Sweet Potatoes on Pineapple Rings

Ready in 30 minutes or less

This side dish is easy to prepare, fun to serve and delicious to eat. It's a staple at my Thanksgiving dinner. I pop it in the oven and let it cook while I'm carving the turkey.
—Donna Gonda, North Canton, Ohio

2 cups mashed canned *or* cooked sweet potatoes (prepared without milk or butter)

1/2 cup packed brown sugar
3 tablespoons butter *or* margarine, melted
1/4 teaspoon salt
1/4 teaspoon ground cinnamon
1/4 teaspoon ground nutmeg
1 can (20 ounces) pineapple slices, drained
10 miniature marshmallows

In a large bowl, combine the sweet potatoes, brown sugar, butter, salt, cinnamon and nutmeg. Place pineapple slices in a greased 13-in. x 9-in. x 2-in. baking dish. Top each slice with 1/4 cup sweet potato mixture and a marshmallow. Bake, uncovered, at 400° for 10-15 minutes or until heated through. **Yield:** 10 servings.

Quick Cutting

Kitchen scissors are great for cutting pizza and pancakes, particularly if you need to cut them into bite-size pieces for young children.
—Romaine Becker
Wynot, Nebraska

Try This Tempting Timber

IN A FLAVORFUL SPIN on traditional French toast, slices of bread are coated with eggnog, fried to golden-brown perfection and arranged in a tree shape to create Big Pine French Toast.

Jan McCormick then includes pork sausage links and a dusting of decorative green sugar with her forest-inspired fare. "I love serving this on Christmas morning," she says from Rosemount, Minnesota.

Add a rising-sun orange slice and herb-garnish grass to this hearty hardwood and enjoy a taste of the great outdoors.

Big Pine French Toast

Ready in 30 minutes or less

2 cups eggnog*
8 slices day-old bread
8 pork sausage links
Green colored sugar
Confectioners' sugar
4 orange slices and fresh herbs, optional

Pour eggnog into a shallow bowl; dip both sides of bread in eggnog. In a nonstick skillet, cook bread over medium heat for 2 minutes on each side or until golden brown. Meanwhile, in another skillet, brown the sausage. Cut French toast diagonally; place four slices,

overlapping slightly, on each serving plate for the tree. Place two sausages at the bottom for the trunk. Sprinkle with sugars. If desired, add an orange slice for the sun and herbs for grass. **Yield:** 4 servings.

*Editor's Note: This recipe was tested with commercially prepared eggnog.

Big Pine French Toast

Chapter 17

Timeless Recipes with Kitchen Tools

WHEN time is ticking away, on-the-go cooks appreciate the convenience of slow cookers, grills and microwaves to get them out of the kitchen fast.

With just a little preparation, you can assemble all the ingredients for wonderful recipes in your slow cooker. Then simply put on the lid, switch on the pot...and go!

When it comes to putting a meal on the table in a hurry, grilling is "hot" no matter what the season.

Time-conscious cooks know the magic of a microwave. Now you can use yours for more than defrosting foods and reheating leftovers.

SAVORY AND SLOW-COOKED.
Ham with Cherry Sauce and Vegetable Medley (both recipes on p. 260).

Slow-Cooked Specialties

WHEN a full schedule keeps you away from the kitchen, put your slow cooker to work making a meal you and your family will love.

Savory Beef Fajitas

My family loves beef, and I love to use the slow cooker, so this dish pleases everyone. The meat comes out nice and tender to create these tempting fajitas.
—*Twila Burkholder, Middleburg, Pennsylvania*

☑ Uses less fat, sugar or salt. Includes Nutritional Analysis and Diabetic Exchanges.

  1 beef flank steak (2 pounds), thinly sliced
  1 cup tomato juice
  2 garlic cloves, minced
  1 tablespoon minced fresh cilantro *or* parsley
  1 teaspoon chili powder
  1 teaspoon ground cumin
1/2 teaspoon salt
1/2 teaspoon ground coriander
  1 medium onion, sliced
  1 medium green pepper, julienned
  1 medium sweet red pepper, julienned
  1 medium jalapeno, cut into thin strips*
12 flour tortillas (7 inches)
Sour cream, guacamole, salsa *or* shredded cheddar cheese, optional

Place beef in a slow cooker. Combine the next seven ingredients; pour over beef. Cover and cook on low for 6-7 hours. Add onion, peppers and jalapeno. Cover and cook 1 hour longer or until meat and vegetables are tender. Using a slotted spoon, place about 1/2 cup of meat-vegetable mixture on each tortilla. Add desired toppings. Roll up. **Yield:** 12 servings.

Nutritional Analysis: One serving (calculated without toppings) equals 225 calories, 7 g fat (3 g saturated fat), 39 mg cholesterol, 264 mg sodium, 19 g carbohydrate, 2 g fiber, 20 g protein. **Diabetic Exchanges:** 2 lean meat, 1 starch, 1 vegetable.

*Editor's Note: When cutting or seeding hot peppers, use rubber or plastic gloves to protect your hands. Avoid touching your face.

Slow-Cooked Meat Loaf

An old standby gets fun Mexican flair and an easy new preparation method in this recipe. The round loaf gets extra flavor when served with salsa. —*Julie Sterchi Harrisburg, Illinois*

  1 egg, beaten
1/3 cup taco sauce
  1 cup coarsely crushed corn chips
1/3 cup shredded Mexican-blend *or* cheddar cheese
  2 tablespoons taco seasoning
1/2 teaspoon salt, optional
  2 pounds lean ground beef
Additional taco sauce *or* salsa

In a large bowl, combine the first six ingredients. Crumble beef over mixture and mix well. Shape into a round loaf; place in a slow cooker. Cover and cook on low for 6-8 hours or until a meat thermometer reads 160°. Serve with taco sauce or salsa. **Yield:** 8 servings.

Casserole in the Cooker

For a complete meal-in-one, you'll savor this slow-cooked ham, broccoli and rice dish that has all the goodness of an oven-baked casserole. It's perfect for a Sunday afternoon dinner. —*Krista Harrison, Brazil, Indiana*

  1 package (16 ounces) frozen broccoli cuts, thawed and drained
  3 cups cubed fully cooked ham
  1 can (10-3/4 ounces) condensed cream of mushroom soup, undiluted
  1 jar (8 ounces) process cheese sauce
  1 cup milk
  1 cup uncooked instant rice
  1 celery rib, chopped
  1 small onion, chopped

In a slow cooker, combine broccoli and ham. Combine the soup, cheese sauce, milk, rice, celery and onion; stir into the broccoli mixture. Cover and cook on low for 4-5 hours or until rice is tender. **Yield:** 4 servings.

Meaty Spaghetti Sauce
(Pictured at right)

My family always enjoyed my homemade spaghetti sauce, but it's so time-consuming to make on the stovetop. My busy grown daughter adapted my recipe to take advantage of her slow cooker. The flavorful sauce still receives compliments. —*Arlene Sommers, Redmond, Washington*

☑ Uses less fat, sugar or salt. Includes Nutritional Analysis and Diabetic Exchanges.

  1 pound ground beef
  1 pound bulk Italian sausage
  1 medium green pepper, chopped
  1 medium onion, chopped
  8 garlic cloves, minced
  3 cans (14-1/2 ounces *each*) Italian diced tomatoes, drained
  2 cans (15 ounces *each*) tomato sauce
  2 cans (6 ounces *each*) tomato paste
1/3 cup sugar
  2 tablespoons Italian seasoning
  1 tablespoon dried basil

2 teaspoons dried marjoram
1 teaspoon salt
1/2 teaspoon pepper
Hot cooked spaghetti

In a large skillet over medium heat, cook beef and sausage until no longer pink; drain. Transfer to a 5-qt. slow cooker. Stir in green pepper, onion, garlic, tomatoes, tomato sauce, paste, sugar and seasonings; mix well. Cover and cook on low for 8 hours or until bubbly. Serve over spaghetti. **Yield:** 12 servings.

Nutritional Analysis: One serving (prepared with lean ground beef and Italian turkey sausage; calculated without spaghetti) equals 231 calories, 8 g fat (3 g saturated fat), 45 mg cholesterol, 1,188 mg sodium, 22 g carbohydrate, 3 g fiber, 17 g protein. **Diabetic Exchanges:** 2 starch, 2 meat, 1 vegetable.

Creamy Chicken Fettuccine

(Pictured below)

Convenient canned soup and process American cheese speed up the assembly of this creamy sauce loaded with chicken. —Melissa Cowser, Greenville, Texas

1-1/2 pounds boneless skinless chicken breasts, cut into cubes
1/2 teaspoon garlic powder
1/2 teaspoon onion powder
1/8 teaspoon pepper
1 can (10-3/4 ounces) condensed cream of chicken soup, undiluted
1 can (10-3/4 ounces) condensed cream of celery soup, undiluted

4 ounces process American cheese, cubed
1 can (2-1/4 ounces) sliced ripe olives, drained
1 jar (2 ounces) diced pimientos, drained, optional
1 package (16 ounces) spinach fettuccine *or* spaghetti
Thin breadsticks, optional

Place the chicken in a slow cooker; sprinkle with garlic powder, onion powder and pepper. Top with soups. Cover and cook on high for 3-4 hours or until chicken juices run clear. Stir in cheese, olives and pimientos if desired. Cover and cook until cheese is melted. Meanwhile, cook fettuccine according to package directions; drain. Serve with the chicken and breadsticks if desired. **Yield:** 6 servings.

Hot Chili Dip

I first made this zippy dip for my husband's birthday party. So many people asked for the recipe that I photocopied it to pass out. —Nikki Rosati
Franksville, Wisconsin

1 jar (24 ounces) salsa
1 can (15 ounces) chili with beans
2 cans (2-1/4 ounces *each*) sliced ripe olives, drained
12 ounces process American cheese, cubed
Tortilla chips

In a small slow cooker, combine the salsa, chili and olives. Stir in cheese. Cover and cook on low for 1-2 hours or until cheese is melted, stirring halfway through. Serve with chips. **Yield:** about 2 cups.

Meaty Spaghetti Sauce
Creamy Chicken Fettuccine

Ham with Cherry Sauce
Vegetable Medley

Ham with Cherry Sauce

(Pictured above and on page 256)

I often fix this delicious ham topped with a thick cherry sauce. It's such a favorite that I've served it at Easter dinners, church breakfasts and a friend's wedding brunch.
—Carol Lee Jones, Taylors, South Carolina

      1 boneless fully cooked ham (3 to 4 pounds)
  1/2 cup apple jelly
      2 teaspoons prepared mustard
  2/3 cup ginger ale, *divided*
      1 can (21 ounces) cherry pie filling
      2 tablespoons cornstarch

Score surface of ham, making diamond shapes 1/2 in. deep. In a small bowl, combine jelly, mustard and 1 tablespoon ginger ale; rub over scored surface of ham. Cut ham in half; place in a 5-qt. slow cooker. Cover and cook on low for 4-5 hours or until a meat thermometer reads 140° and ham is heated through. Baste with cooking juices toward end of cooking time.

For sauce, place the pie filling in a saucepan. Combine the cornstarch and remaining ginger ale; stir into pie filling until blended. Bring to a boil; cook and stir for 2 minutes or until thickened. Serve over sliced ham. **Yield:** 12-16 servings.

Vegetable Medley

(Pictured above and on page 257)

This is a wonderful side dish to make when garden vegetables are plentiful. The colorful combination is a great complement to any entree. —Terry Maly, Olathe, Kansas

✓ Uses less fat, sugar or salt. Includes Nutritional Analysis and Diabetic Exchanges.

      4 cups diced peeled potatoes
  1-1/2 cups frozen whole kernel corn
      4 medium tomatoes, seeded and diced
      1 cup sliced carrots
  1/2 cup chopped onion
  3/4 teaspoon salt
  1/2 teaspoon sugar
  1/2 teaspoon dill weed
  1/8 teaspoon pepper

In a slow cooker, combine all ingredients. Cover and cook on low for 5-6 hours or until vegetables are tender. **Yield:** 8 servings.

Nutritional Analysis: One 1-cup serving equals 116 calories, 1 g fat (trace saturated fat), 0 cholesterol, 243 mg sodium, 27 g carbohydrate, 4 g fiber, 3 g protein. **Diabetic Exchange:** 1-1/2 starch.

Pork and Cabbage Dinner

I put on this pork roast in the morning to avoid that evening dinner rush so common on busy weekdays. All I do is fix a side of family-favorite potatoes, and we can sit down to a satisfying supper. —Trina Hinkel
Minneapolis, Minnesota

       1 pound carrots
   1-1/2 cups water
       1 envelope onion soup mix
       2 garlic cloves, minced
     1/2 teaspoon celery seed
       1 boneless pork shoulder roast (4 to 6 pounds)
     1/2 teaspoon salt
     1/4 teaspoon pepper
   1-1/2 pounds cabbage, cut into 2-inch pieces

Cut carrots in half lengthwise and then into 2-in. pieces. Place in a 5-qt. slow cooker. Add water, soup mix, garlic and celery seed. Cut roast in half; place over carrot mixture. Sprinkle with salt and pepper. Cover and cook on high for 2 hours.

Reduce heat to low; cook for 4 hours. Add cabbage; cook 2 hours longer or until the cabbage is tender and a meat thermometer reads 160°. Remove meat and vegetables to a serving plate; keep warm. If desired, thicken pan drippings for gravy and serve with the roast. **Yield:** 8-10 servings.

Hominy Pork Soup

Tender pork and hominy make this chili-like soup different from the usual offerings. For a satisfying supper, I serve it with sliced green onions, shredded cheese, lime wedges and warm flour tortillas. I make this often because my family can't get enough of the Southwest flavors.
—Raquel Walkup, San Pedro, California

       1 pound pork chop suey meat, cut into
           1/2-inch cubes
       2 cans (15 ounces *each*) chili without beans
       1 can (15-1/2 ounces) hominy, drained
       1 can (8 ounces) tomato sauce
       1 medium onion, chopped
       1 bay leaf
       1 tablespoon chili powder
       1 teaspoon *each* dried basil, oregano and
           parsley flakes
       1 teaspoon ground cumin
   Warmed flour tortillas, shredded Monterey Jack
       cheese, sliced green onions and lime wedges,
       optional

In a slow cooker, combine the pork, chili, hominy, tomato sauce, onion and seasonings. Cover and cook on high for 4 hours or until meat is tender. Discard bay leaf. Serve with tortillas, cheese, green onions and lime wedges if desired. **Yield:** 7 servings.

Italian Bow Tie Supper

I appreciate the convenience of this meal—its flavor might remind you of ravioli. The recipe makes a lot, so I don't have to cook on the night we enjoy the leftovers.
—Joy Frey, Kelso, Missouri

   1-1/2 pounds ground beef
       1 medium onion, chopped
       1 garlic clove, minced
       2 cans (8 ounces *each*) tomato sauce
       1 can (14-1/2 ounces) stewed tomatoes,
           cut up
       1 teaspoon dried oregano
       1 teaspoon Italian seasoning
   Salt and pepper to taste
       1 package (16 ounces) bow tie pasta, cooked
           and drained
       1 package (10 ounces) frozen chopped
           spinach, thawed and well drained
   1-1/2 cups (6 ounces) shredded mozzarella
           cheese
     1/2 cup grated Parmesan cheese

In a skillet, cook the beef, onion and garlic over medium heat until meat is no longer pink; drain. Transfer to a slow cooker. Stir in the tomato sauce, tomatoes and seasonings. Cover and cook on low for 7-8 hours or until bubbly.

Increase heat to high; stir in the pasta, spinach, mozzarella and Parmesan cheese. Cover and cook for 10 minutes or until heated through and cheese is melted. **Yield:** 6 servings.

Chicken Stew Over Biscuits

A pleasant sauce coats this chicken and veggie dinner that's slow-cooked to tender perfection, then served over biscuits. When I first came up with this dish, my toddler couldn't get enough of it. —Kathy Garrett
Browns Mills, New Jersey

       2 envelopes chicken gravy mix
       2 cups water
     3/4 cup white wine *or* chicken broth
       2 garlic cloves, minced
       1 tablespoon minced fresh parsley
       1 to 2 teaspoons chicken bouillon granules
     1/2 teaspoon pepper
       5 medium carrots, cut into 1-inch chunks
       1 large onion, cut into eight wedges
       1 broiler/fryer chicken (3 to 4 pounds),
           cut up
       3 tablespoons all-purpose flour
     1/3 cup cold water
       1 tube (7-1/2 ounces) refrigerated buttermilk
           biscuits

In a slow cooker, combine gravy mix, water, wine or broth, garlic, parsley, bouillon and pepper until blended. Add the carrots, onion and chicken. Cover and cook on low for 7-8 hours.

Increase heat to high. In a small bowl, combine the flour and cold water until smooth; gradually stir into slow cooker. Cover and cook for 1 hour. Meanwhile, bake biscuits according to package directions. Place biscuits in soup bowls; top with stew. **Yield:** 4-6 servings.

Slow Cooker Chicken Dinner

I love using my slow cooker because it's so convenient. This meal-in-one, which includes juicy chicken and tasty veggies in a creamy sauce, is ready to eat when I get home from the office.
—Jenet Cattar
Neptune Beach, Florida

6 medium red potatoes, cut into chunks
4 medium carrots, cut into 1/2-inch pieces
4 boneless skinless chicken breast halves
1 can (10-3/4 ounces) condensed cream of chicken soup, undiluted
1 can (10-3/4 ounces) condensed cream of mushroom soup, undiluted
1/8 teaspoon garlic salt
2 to 4 tablespoons mashed potato flakes, optional

Place potatoes and carrots in a slow cooker. Top with chicken. Combine the soups and garlic salt; pour over chicken. Cover and cook on low for 8 hours. To thicken if desired, stir potato flakes into the gravy and cook 30 minutes longer. **Yield:** 4 servings.

Cheesy Potatoes

For a comforting side dish that feeds a crowd, try these saucy slow-cooked potatoes. A simple topping of buttered croutons covers the creamy combination.
—Melissa Marzolf, Marysville, Michigan

6 medium potatoes, peeled and cut into 1/4-inch strips
2 cups (8 ounces) shredded cheddar cheese
1 can (10-3/4 ounces) condensed cream of chicken soup, undiluted
1 small onion, chopped *or* 1 tablespoon dried minced onion
7 tablespoons butter *or* margarine, melted, *divided*
1 teaspoon salt
1 teaspoon pepper
1 cup (8 ounces) sour cream
2 cups seasoned stuffing cubes

Toss the potatoes and cheese; place in a 5-qt. slow cooker. Combine soup, onion, 4 tablespoons butter, salt and pepper; pour over potato mixture. Cover and cook

Tasty Toppers

I sprinkle all kinds of fun garnishes on bowls of soup. The following "souper" toppers are sure to get kids noticing soup: popcorn with a bit of grated Parmesan cheese, spoon-sized Shredded Wheat or Cheerios, mini pretzels, chow mein noodles, chopped peanuts or smoked almonds, cheese puffs or crushed barbecue potato chips. Or spoon salsa on a few taco chips and float them in your bowl.
—Mary Lou Pearce
Victoria, British Columbia

on low for 8-10 hours or until potatoes are tender. Stir in sour cream. Toss stuffing cubes and remaining butter; sprinkle over potatoes. **Yield:** 10-12 servings.

Mushroom Beef and Noodles

I've prepared this flavorful beef dish many times for family and friends. I've also shared the easy six-ingredient recipe with lots of cooks, and everyone thinks it's great.
—Virgil Killman, Mascoutah, Illinois

1 can (10-3/4 ounces) condensed golden mushroom soup, undiluted
1 can (10-3/4 ounces) condensed beefy mushroom soup, undiluted
1 can (10-3/4 ounces) condensed French onion soup, undiluted
1/4 cup seasoned bread crumbs
2 pounds beef stew meat, cut into 1/2-inch cubes
1 package (12 ounces) wide egg noodles

In a slow cooker, combine soups and bread crumbs; mix well. Stir in beef. Cover and cook on low for 8 hours or until meat is tender. Cook noodles according to package directions; drain. Serve with beef mixture. **Yield:** 6-8 servings.

Simmered Smoked Links

In this recipe, a tasty sweet-sour sauce glazes bite-size sausages. I frequently serve these effortless appetizers with toothpicks at parties or holiday get-togethers.
—Maxine Cenker, Weirton, West Virginia

2 packages (16 ounces *each*) miniature smoked sausage links
1 cup packed brown sugar
1/2 cup ketchup
1/4 cup prepared horseradish

Place sausages in a slow cooker. Combine brown sugar, ketchup and horseradish; pour over sausages. Cover and cook on low for 4 hours. **Yield:** 16-20 servings.

Beef 'n' Black Bean Soup

(Pictured above right)

I lead a busy life, so I'm always trying to come up with time-saving recipes. This zippy and colorful soup is one of my husband's favorites. It has been a hit at family gatherings, too. *—Vickie Gibson, Gardendale, Alabama*

☑ Uses less fat, sugar or salt. Includes Nutritional Analysis and Diabetic Exchanges.

1 pound ground beef
2 cans (14-1/2 ounces *each*) chicken broth
1 can (14-1/2 ounces) diced tomatoes, undrained
8 green onions, thinly sliced

Beef 'n' Black Bean Soup
Home-Style Ribs

3 medium carrots, thinly sliced
2 celery ribs, thinly sliced
2 garlic cloves, minced
1 tablespoon sugar
1-1/2 teaspoons dried basil
1/2 teaspoon salt
1/2 teaspoon dried oregano
1/2 teaspoon ground cumin
1/2 teaspoon chili powder
2 cans (15 ounces *each*) black beans, rinsed
  and drained
1-1/2 cups cooked rice

In a skillet over medium heat, cook beef until no longer pink; drain. Transfer to a slow cooker. Add the next 12 ingredients. Cover and cook on high for 1 hour. Reduce heat to low; cook for 4-5 hours or until vegetables are tender. Add the beans and rice; cook 1 hour longer or until heated through. **Yield:** 10 servings (2-1/2 quarts).

Nutritional Analysis: One 1 cup serving (prepared with lean ground beef) equals 213 calories, 5 g fat (2 g saturated fat), 17 mg cholesterol, 819 mg sodium, 25 g carbohydrate, 6 g fiber, 16 g protein. **Diabetic Exchanges:** 1-1/2 starch, 1-1/2 lean meat.

Home-Style Ribs

(Pictured above)

A dear friend gave me the recipe for these tender ribs simmered in a pleasant barbecue sauce. They're great to fix in the summer because you don't have to turn on the oven and heat up the kitchen.
—Roni Goodell
Spanish Fork, Utah

4 to 5 pounds boneless pork spareribs, cut
  into pieces
1 medium onion, thinly sliced
1 cup ketchup
1/2 to 1 cup water
1/4 cup packed brown sugar
1/4 cup cider vinegar
2 tablespoons Worcestershire sauce
2 teaspoons ground mustard
1-1/2 teaspoons salt
1 teaspoon paprika

Place half of the ribs in a slow cooker; top with half of the onion. Repeat layers. Combine the remaining ingredients; pour over all. Cover and cook on low for 8-9 hours or until ribs are tender. **Yield:** 6-8 servings.

Potato Chowder

(Pictured below)

One of the ladies in our church quilting group brought this savory potato soup to a meeting. It's easy to assemble in the morning, then cook all day. Cream cheese and a sprinkling of bacon provide richness.
—Anna Mayer, Ft. Branch, Indiana

✓ Uses less fat, sugar or salt. Includes Nutritional Analysis and Diabetic Exchanges.

    8 cups diced potatoes
  1/3 cup chopped onion
    3 cans (14-1/2 ounces *each*) chicken broth
    1 can (10-3/4 ounces) condensed cream of chicken soup, undiluted
  1/4 teaspoon pepper
    1 package (8 ounces) cream cheese, cubed
  1/2 pound sliced bacon, cooked and crumbled, optional
Snipped chives, optional

In a slow cooker, combine the first five ingredients. Cover and cook on low for 8-10 hours or until potatoes are tender. Add cream cheese; stir until blended. Garnish with bacon and chives if desired. **Yield:** 12 servings (3 quarts).

Nutritional Analysis: One 1-cup serving (prepared with reduced-fat cream of chicken soup and reduced-fat cream cheese; calculated without bacon) equals 148 calories, 4 g fat (2 g saturated fat), 13 mg cholesterol, 655 mg sodium, 22 g carbohydrate, 2 g fiber, 6 g protein. **Diabetic Exchanges:** 1-1/2 starch, 1/2 fat.

Shredded Beef Sandwiches

(Pictured below)

Our family loves these tasty shredded beef sandwiches with their mild barbecue flavor. The recipe makes a lot, so it's a nice choice for parties.
—Fran Frerichs
Gurley, Nebraska

    3 pounds beef stew meat, cut into 1-inch cubes
    3 medium green peppers, diced
    2 large onions, diced
    1 can (6 ounces) tomato paste
  1/2 cup packed brown sugar
  1/4 cup cider vinegar
    3 tablespoons chili powder
    2 teaspoons salt
    2 teaspoons Worcestershire sauce
    1 teaspoon ground mustard
   14 to 16 sandwich buns, split

In a slow cooker, combine the beef, green peppers and onions. In a small bowl, combine tomato paste, brown sugar, vinegar, chili powder, salt, Worcestershire sauce

Potato Chowder
Shredded Beef Sandwiches

and mustard. Stir into meat mixture. Cover and cook on high for 7-8 hours or until meat is tender.

Skim fat from cooking juices. Shred beef, using two forks. With a slotted spoon, place about 1/2 cup beef mixture on each bun. **Yield:** 14-16 servings.

Hamburger Vegetable Soup

I work full time and have a family of four. We sit down to a home-cooked meal just about every night, many times thanks to my slow cooker. This hearty soup is often on the menu. —*Theresa Jackson, Cicero, New York*

✓ Uses less fat, sugar or salt. Includes Nutritional Analysis and Diabetic Exchanges.

- 1 pound ground beef
- 1 medium onion, chopped
- 2 garlic cloves, minced
- 4 cups V8 juice
- 1 can (14-1/2 ounces) stewed tomatoes
- 2 cups coleslaw mix
- 2 cups frozen green beans
- 2 cups frozen corn
- 2 tablespoons Worcestershire sauce
- 1 teaspoon dried basil
- 1/2 teaspoon salt
- 1/4 teaspoon pepper

In a saucepan, cook beef, onion and garlic over medium heat until meat is no longer pink; drain. In a slow cooker, combine the remaining ingredients. Stir in beef mixture. Cover and cook on low for 8-9 hours or until the vegetables are tender. **Yield:** 10 servings.

Nutritional Analysis: One 1-cup serving (prepared with lean ground beef) equals 159 calories, 4 g fat (2 g saturated fat), 17 mg cholesterol, 511 mg sodium, 19 g carbohydrate, 3 g fiber, 12 g protein. **Diabetic Exchanges:** 1 starch, 1 lean meat, 1 vegetable.

Tangy Tender Chicken

Brown sugar, garlic and ginger provide the traditional sweet-sour flavor in this chicken medley. The aroma is heavenly after working outside all day. —*Milton Schutz, Pandora, Ohio*

- 1 pound baby carrots
- 1 medium green pepper, cut into 1/2-inch strips
- 1 medium onion, cut into wedges
- 6 boneless skinless chicken breast halves
- 1 can (20 ounces) pineapple chunks
- 1/3 cup packed brown sugar
- 1 tablespoon soy sauce
- 2 teaspoons chicken bouillon granules
- 1/2 teaspoon salt
- 1/2 teaspoon ground ginger
- 1/4 teaspoon garlic powder
- 3 tablespoons cornstarch
- 1/4 cup cold water
Hot cooked rice

In a slow cooker, layer carrots, green pepper and onion. Top with the chicken. Drain pineapple, reserving juice. Place pineapple over chicken. Add brown sugar, soy sauce, bouillon, salt, ginger and garlic powder to pineapple juice; pour over pineapple. Cover and cook on low for 8-9 hours.

Combine cornstarch and water until smooth; gradually stir into cooking juices. Cook 30 minutes longer or until sauce is thickened, stirring once. Serve over rice. **Yield:** 4-6 servings.

Hearty Pork 'n' Beans

This sweet chunky mixture tastes great as a main dish with French bread or corn bread. It's also a good side dish to serve at a barbecue or potluck. —*Janice Toms, Saline, Louisiana*

- 1 pound ground beef
- 1 medium green pepper, chopped
- 1 small onion, chopped
- 1 package (16 ounces) smoked sausage, halved lengthwise and thinly sliced
- 1 can (16 ounces) pork and beans, undrained
- 1 can (15-1/4 ounces) lima beans, rinsed and drained
- 1 can (15 ounces) pinto beans, rinsed and drained
- 1 cup ketchup
- 1/2 cup packed brown sugar
- 1 teaspoon salt
- 1/2 teaspoon garlic powder
- 1/4 teaspoon pepper

In a skillet, cook beef, green pepper and onion over medium heat until meat is no longer pink; drain. In a slow cooker, combine the remaining ingredients. Stir in beef mixture. Cover and cook on high for 4-5 hours or until heated through. **Yield:** 8 main-dish servings or 12 side-dish servings.

Ham and Hash Browns

You just can't beat the slow cooker for convenience...I use mine two or three times a week all year-round. Here's a new way to prepare an old-fashioned favorite but without the fuss. —*Marlene Muckenhirn, Delano, Minnesota*

- 1 package (28 ounces) frozen O'Brien hash brown potatoes
- 2 cups cubed fully cooked ham
- 1 jar (2 ounces) diced pimientos, drained
- 1 can (10-3/4 ounces) condensed cheddar cheese soup, undiluted
- 3/4 cup milk
- 1/4 teaspoon pepper

In a slow cooker, combine potatoes, ham and pimientos. In a bowl, combine soup, milk and pepper; pour over potato mixture. Cover and cook on low for 7-8 hours or until potatoes are tender. **Yield:** 4 servings.

Autumn Beef Stew
Apple-Nut Bread Pudding

Autumn Beef Stew

(Pictured above)

Chock-full of tender beef, hearty potatoes and colorful carrots, this down-home dinner is a staple. —*Margaret Shauer*
Great Bend, Kansas

✓ Uses less fat, sugar or salt. Includes Nutritional Analysis and Diabetic Exchanges.

- 12 small red potatoes, halved
- 1 pound carrots, cut into 1-inch pieces
- 1 large onion, cut into wedges
- 2 pounds lean beef stew meat, cut into 1-inch cubes
- 1/3 cup butter *or* stick margarine
- 1 tablespoon all-purpose flour
- 1 cup water
- 1 teaspoon salt
- 1 teaspoon dried parsley flakes
- 1/2 teaspoon celery seed
- 1/2 teaspoon dried thyme
- 1/8 teaspoon pepper

Place potatoes, carrots and onion in a 5-qt. slow cooker. In a large skillet, brown beef in butter. Transfer beef to slow cooker with a slotted spoon.

Stir flour into the pan drippings until blended; cook and stir until browned. Gradually add water. Bring to a boil; cook and stir for 2 minutes or until thickened. Add

salt, parsley, celery seed, thyme and pepper; pour over beef. Cover and cook on low for 8-9 hours or until meat and vegetables are tender. **Yield:** 8 servings.

Nutritional Analysis: One serving (1 cup) equals 366 calories, 16 g fat (8 g saturated fat), 91 mg cholesterol, 436 mg sodium, 34 g carbohydrate, 5 g fiber, 27 g protein. **Diabetic Exchanges:** 3 meat, 2 starch.

Apple-Nut Bread Pudding

(Pictured above)

Traditional bread pudding gives way to autumn's influences in this comforting dessert. —*Lori Fox*
Menomonee Falls, Wisconsin

- 8 slices raisin bread, cubed
- 2 medium tart apples, peeled and sliced
- 1 cup chopped pecans, toasted
- 1 cup sugar
- 1 teaspoon ground cinnamon
- 1/2 teaspoon ground nutmeg
- 3 eggs, lightly beaten
- 2 cups half-and-half cream
- 1/4 cup apple juice
- 1/4 cup butter *or* margarine, melted
Vanilla ice cream

Place bread cubes, apples and pecans in a greased slow cooker. In a bowl, combine sugar, cinnamon and nutmeg. Add eggs, cream, apple juice and butter; mix well. Pour over bread mixture. Cover and cook on low for 3-4 hours or until a knife inserted in center comes out clean. Serve with ice cream. **Yield:** 6-8 servings.

Hearty Pasta Tomato Soup

I adapted the original recipe for this flavorful soup so I could make it in the slow cooker. Italian sausage and vegetables add a tasty twist to traditional tomato soup.
—Lydia Kroese, Plymouth, Minnesota

    1 pound bulk Italian sausage
    6 cups beef broth
    1 can (28 ounces) stewed tomatoes
    1 can (15 ounces) tomato sauce
    2 cups sliced zucchini
    1 large onion, chopped
    1 cup sliced carrots
    1 cup sliced fresh mushrooms
    1 medium green pepper, chopped
  1/4 cup minced fresh parsley
    2 teaspoons sugar
    1 teaspoon dried oregano
    1 teaspoon dried basil
    1 garlic clove, minced
    2 cups frozen cheese tortellini
Grated Parmesan cheese, optional

In a skillet, cook the sausage over medium heat until no longer pink; drain. Transfer to a 5-qt. slow cooker; add the next 13 ingredients. Cover and cook on high for 3-4 hours or until the vegetables are tender. Cook tortellini according to package directions; drain. Stir into slow cooker; cover and cook 30 minutes longer. Serve with Parmesan cheese if desired. **Yield:** 14 servings (about 3-1/2 quarts).

Flank Steak Roll-Up

I roll stuffing mix and mushrooms into flank steak before simmering it in an easy gravy. —Sheryl Johnson
Las Vegas, Nevada

    1 can (4 ounces) mushroom stems and pieces, undrained
    2 tablespoons butter *or* margarine, melted
    1 package (6 ounces) seasoned stuffing mix
    1 beef flank steak (1-3/4 pounds)
    1 envelope brown gravy mix
  1/4 cup chopped green onions
  1/4 cup dry red wine *or* beef broth

In a bowl, toss the mushrooms, butter and dry stuffing mix. Spread over steak to within 1 in. of edges. Roll up jelly-roll style, starting with a long side; tie with kitchen string. Place in a slow cooker. Prepare gravy mix according to package directions; add onions and wine or broth. Pour over meat. Cover and cook on low for 8-10 hours. Remove meat to a serving platter and keep warm. Strain cooking juices and thicken if desired. Remove string from roll-up; slice and serve with gravy. **Yield:** 6 servings.

Creamy Chicken and Beef

I relied on this dish often when our children lived at home. Since it cooked while I was at work, the only thing left to do was prepare noodles and fix a salad.
—Jane Thocher, Hart, Michigan

    6 bacon strips
    1 package (2-1/2 ounces) thinly sliced dried beef
    6 boneless skinless chicken breast halves
  1/4 cup all-purpose flour
    1 can (10-3/4 ounces) condensed cream of mushroom soup, undiluted
  1/4 cup sour cream
Hot cooked noodles

In a skillet, partially cook bacon over medium heat. Drain on paper towels. Place beef in a greased slow cooker. Fold chicken pieces in half and wrap a bacon strip around each; place over the beef. Combine the flour, soup and sour cream until blended; spread over chicken. Cover and cook on low for 8-9 hours or until chicken juices run clear. Serve over noodles. **Yield:** 6 servings.

Buffalo Chicken Wing Soup

My husband and I love buffalo chicken wings, so we created a soup with the same zippy flavor. It's very popular with guests. —Pat Farmer, Falconer, New York

    6 cups milk
    3 cans (10-3/4 ounces *each*) condensed cream of chicken soup, undiluted
    3 cups shredded cooked chicken (about 1 pound)
    1 cup (8 ounces) sour cream
  1/4 to 1/2 cup hot pepper sauce

Combine all ingredients in a slow cooker. Cover and cook on low for 4-5 hours. **Yield:** 8 servings (2 quarts).

Pepper Beef Goulash

No one will ever guess an envelope of sloppy joe seasoning is the secret behind this great goulash. —Peggy Key
Grant, Alabama

  1/2 cup water
    1 can (6 ounces) tomato paste
    2 tablespoons cider vinegar
    1 envelope sloppy joe seasoning
    2 to 2-1/4 pounds beef stew meat (3/4-inch cubes)
    1 celery rib, cut into 1/2-inch slices
    1 medium green pepper, cut into 1/2-inch chunks
Hot cooked noodles

In a slow cooker, combine the water, tomato paste, vinegar and sloppy joe seasoning. Stir in the beef, celery and green pepper. Cover and cook on high for 4-5 hours. Serve over noodles. **Yield:** 4-5 servings.

Pork 'n' Pepper Tortillas

I season a pork roast with onions, garlic and spices and cook it slowly until tender. Then I shred the flavorful meat and wrap it along with colorful peppers in warm tortillas. —Rita Hahnbaum, Muscatine, Iowa

    1 bone-in pork shoulder roast (3 to 4 pounds)
    1 cup boiling water
    2 teaspoons beef bouillon granules
    3 garlic cloves, minced
    1 tablespoon dried basil
    1 tablespoon dried oregano
    1 teaspoon ground cumin
    1 teaspoon pepper
    1 teaspoon dried tarragon
    1 teaspoon white pepper
    2 medium onions, sliced
    1 *each* large green, sweet red and yellow
      pepper, sliced
    1 tablespoon butter *or* margarine
   12 to 14 flour tortillas (7 inches), warmed
Shredded lettuce, chopped ripe olives, sliced
   jalapeno peppers and sour cream, optional

Cut roast into quarters; place in a 5-qt. slow cooker. Combine water, bouillon, garlic and seasonings; pour over roast. Top with onions. Cover and cook on high for 1 hour. Reduce heat to low. Cook for 7-8 hours or until pork is very tender.

When cool enough to handle, remove meat from bone. Shred meat and return to slow cooker; heat through. Meanwhile, in a skillet, saute peppers in butter until tender. Using a slotted spoon, place about 1/2 cup pork and onion mixture down the center of each tortilla; top with peppers. Add lettuce, olives, jalapenos and sour cream if desired. Fold sides of tortilla over filling; serve immediately. **Yield:** 12-14 servings.

Egg Noodle Lasagna

The perfect take-along for charity events and church potlucks, this comforting crowd-pleaser is sure to warm tummies on the coldest of winter nights.
                   —Mary Oberlin, Selinsgrove, Pennsylvania

6-1/2 cups uncooked wide egg noodles
    3 tablespoons butter *or* margarine
1-1/2 pounds ground beef
2-1/4 cups spaghetti sauce
    6 ounces process cheese (Velveeta), cubed
    3 cups (12 ounces) shredded mozzarella
      cheese

Cook noodles according to package directions; drain. Add butter and toss to coat. In a skillet, cook beef over medium heat until no longer pink; drain. Spread a fourth of the spaghetti sauce in an ungreased 5-qt. slow cooker. Layer with a third of the noodles, a third of the beef, a third of the remaining sauce and a third of the cheeses. Repeat layers twice.

Cover and cook on low for 4 hours or until the cheese is melted and the lasagna is heated through. **Yield:** 12-16 servings.

Apple Chicken Stew

Every fall we buy cider to use in this sensational slow-cooked stew. —Carol Mathias, Lincoln, Nebraska

    4 medium potatoes, cubed
    4 medium carrots, cut into 1/4-inch slices
    1 medium red onion, halved and sliced
    1 celery rib, thinly sliced
1-1/2 teaspoons salt
  3/4 teaspoon dried thyme
  1/2 teaspoon pepper
  1/4 to 1/2 teaspoon caraway seeds
    2 pounds boneless skinless chicken breasts,
      cubed
    2 tablespoons olive *or* vegetable oil
    1 large tart apple, peeled and cubed
1-1/4 cups apple cider *or* juice
    1 tablespoon cider vinegar
    1 bay leaf
Minced fresh parsley

In a slow cooker, layer potatoes, carrots, onion and celery. Combine salt, thyme, pepper and caraway; sprinkle half over vegetables. In a skillet, saute chicken in oil until browned; transfer to slow cooker. Top with apple. Combine apple cider and vinegar; pour over chicken and apple. Sprinkle with remaining salt mixture. Top with bay leaf. Cover and cook on high for 4-5 hours or until vegetables are tender and chicken juices run clear. Discard bay leaf. Stir before serving. Sprinkle with parsley. **Yield:** 6-8 servings.

Crock o' Brats

Slices of bratwurst take center stage alongside potatoes, sauerkraut, apple and onion in this hearty dish.
                   —Maryellen Boettcher, Fairchild, Wisconsin

    5 bratwurst links (about 1-1/4 pounds),
      cut into 1-inch pieces
    5 medium potatoes, peeled and cubed
    1 can (27 ounces) sauerkraut, rinsed and well
      drained
    1 medium tart apple, chopped
    1 small onion, chopped
  1/4 cup packed brown sugar
  1/2 teaspoon salt

In a large skillet, brown bratwurst on all sides. In a 5-qt. slow cooker, combine the remaining ingredients. Stir in bratwurst and pan drippings. Cover and cook on high for 4-6 hours or until potatoes and apple are tender. **Yield:** 6 servings.

Slow-Cooked Chicken

Place a cut-up broiler/fryer, 2 cups water and a chicken bouillon cube in a slow cooker; cook on low 8 hours. Debone the chicken; store meat in 1-cup amounts in the freezer. —Carol Hamilton, Lenoir, North Carolina

Saucy Apricot Chicken

(Pictured below)

The tangy glaze is just as wonderful with ham or turkey. Leftovers reheat nicely in the microwave. —Dee Gray Kokomo, Indiana

   6 boneless skinless chicken breast halves (about 1-1/2 pounds)
   2 jars (12 ounces *each*) apricot preserves
   1 envelope onion soup mix
Hot cooked rice

Place chicken in a slow cooker. Combine the preserves and soup mix; spoon over chicken. Cover and cook on low for 4-5 hours or until tender. Serve over rice. **Yield:** 6 servings.

Potato Minestrone

(Pictured below)

I only have to slice some bread and prepare a salad to serve with this soup. For a thicker consistency, mash half of the garbanzo beans before adding to the slow cooker.
—Paula Zsiray, Logan, Utah

✓ Uses less fat, sugar or salt. Includes Nutritional Analysis and Diabetic Exchanges.

   2 cans (14-1/2 ounces *each*) chicken broth
   1 can (28 ounces) crushed tomatoes
   1 can (16 ounces) kidney beans, rinsed and drained
   1 can (15 ounces) garbanzo beans *or* chickpeas, rinsed and drained
   1 can (14-1/2 ounces) beef broth
   2 cups frozen cubed hash brown potatoes, thawed
   1 tablespoon dried minced onion
   1 tablespoon dried parsley flakes
   1 teaspoon salt
   1 teaspoon dried oregano
  1/2 teaspoon garlic powder
  1/2 teaspoon dried basil
  1/2 teaspoon dried marjoram
   1 package (10 ounces) frozen chopped spinach, thawed and drained
   2 cups frozen peas and carrots, thawed

In a slow cooker, combine the first 13 ingredients. Cover and cook on low for 8 hours. Stir in the spinach, peas and carrots; heat through. **Yield:** 12 servings (about 3 quarts).

Nutritional Analysis: One serving (1 cup) equals 172 calories, 2 g fat (trace saturated fat), 1 mg cholesterol, 943 mg sodium, 31 g carbohydrate, 8 g fiber, 9 g protein. **Diabetic Exchange:** 2 starch.

Potato Minestrone
Saucy Apricot Chicken

Great Grilling Recipes

WANT to spend a lot less time in the kitchen? Step outdoors anytime of year and fix a meal on the grill. It's easy to cook up an entire menu at once...plus there's less mess and cleanup.

Kielbasa Apple Kabobs

(Pictured below)

Ready in 30 minutes or less

I rely on sausage to make these colorful kabobs different from most. The meaty chunks are skewered with tart apples and colorful peppers, then basted with a mild sweet glaze. —Edna Hoffman, Hebron, Indiana

✓ Uses less fat, sugar or salt. Includes Nutritional Analysis and Diabetic Exchanges.

- 1/4 cup sugar
- 1 tablespoon cornstarch
- 3/4 cup cranberry juice
- 2 tablespoons cider vinegar
- 2 teaspoons soy sauce
- 1 pound fully cooked kielbasa *or* Polish sausage, cut into 1-1/2-inch pieces
- 2 medium tart apples, cut into wedges
- 1 medium sweet red pepper, cut into 1-inch pieces
- 1 medium green pepper, cut into 1-inch pieces

In a saucepan, combine sugar and cornstarch. Stir in cranberry juice, vinegar and soy sauce. Bring to a boil; cook and stir for 1-2 minutes or until thickened. On metal or soaked wooden skewers, alternately thread sausage, apples and peppers. Grill, uncovered, over indirect heat for 8 minutes or until heated through, turning and brushing with glaze occasionally. **Yield:** 8 servings.

Nutritional Analysis: One serving (prepared with reduced-fat turkey sausage) equals 168 calories, 6 g fat (2 g saturated fat), 47 mg cholesterol, 455 mg sodium, 19 g carbohydrate, 2 g fiber, 10 g protein. **Diabetic Exchanges:** 1 meat, 1 vegetable, 1 fruit.

Grilled Ham Slices

Plan ahead...needs to marinate

A simply spiced marinade gives mild sweet flavor to these tender grilled ham slices. It's very good served with scrambled eggs for brunch. We round out the meal with melon balls and buttered toast. —Rita Deere
Evansville, Indiana

- 2 fully cooked ham slices (about 1 pound *each*)
- 1 cup pineapple juice
- 1 cup sherry *or* apple juice
- 1/4 cup butter *or* margarine, melted
- 1 tablespoon ground mustard
- 1/4 teaspoon ground cloves

Place ham in a large resealable plastic bag. In a bowl, combine the remaining ingredients; mix well. Remove 1/2 cup for basting; cover and refrigerate. Pour remain-

Kielbasa Apple Kabobs

ing marinade over ham; seal bag and turn to coat. Refrigerate for 8 hours or overnight.

Drain and discard marinade. Grill ham, uncovered, over medium-hot heat for 3-4 minutes on each side, basting frequently with the reserved marinade. **Yield:** 6 servings.

Skewered Ginger Beef

Plan ahead…needs to marinate

I marinate and skewer several servings of this dish, freezing extras for future events. Not only do these tender slices of beef make a quick and easy dinner, but they make impressive appetizers, too. —Jean Gaines *Russellville, Kentucky*

✓ Uses less fat, sugar or salt. Includes Nutritional Analysis and Diabetic Exchanges.

- 1 cup sugar
- 1 cup soy sauce
- 1/2 cup vegetable *or* canola oil
- 1 bunch green onions, sliced
- 6 garlic cloves, minced
- 1/4 cup sesame seeds, toasted
- 3/4 teaspoon ground ginger *or* 2 teaspoons grated fresh gingerroot
- 2 teaspoons pepper
- 2 pounds beef sirloin steak, cut into 1/4-inch strips

In a large resealable plastic bag, combine the first eight ingredients; add steak. Seal bag and turn to coat; refrigerate for 8 hours or overnight. Drain and discard marinade. Thread steak onto metal or soaked wooden skewers. Grill, covered, over indirect medium heat for 15 minutes or until meat reaches desired doneness, turning occasionally. **Yield:** 8 servings.

Nutritional Analysis: One serving (prepared with reduced-sodium soy sauce) equals 297 calories, 12 g fat (4 g saturated fat), 101 mg cholesterol, 378 mg sodium, 7 g carbohydrate, trace fiber, 35 g protein. **Diabetic Exchanges:** 3-1/2 lean meat, 1-1/2 fat, 1/2 starch.

Breakfast on the Grill

Ready in 30 minutes or less

I thought having breakfast in our backyard would be a nice way to christen our new patio, so I came up with this combination to cook on the grill. It's a fun idea for camping, too. —Shirley Ellul, Redford, Michigan

- 1 can (8 ounces) pineapple chunks
- 1/3 cup sugar
- 1-1/2 teaspoons ground cinnamon
- 3 cups cubed French bread (1-inch cubes)
- 1/4 cup butter *or* margarine, melted
- 8 slices Canadian bacon, quartered

Drain the pineapple, reserving 2 tablespoons juice; set aside. In a bowl, combine sugar and cinnamon. Dip

bread cubes in butter, then in cinnamon-sugar. Place bread, bacon and pineapple on a large piece of greased heavy-duty foil (about 28 in. x 18 in.). Drizzle with reserved juice.

Fold foil around bread mixture and seal tightly. Grill, uncovered, over medium heat for 4-5 minutes on each side or until heated through. **Yield:** 4 servings.

Horseradish Burgers

Ready in 1 hour or less

My husband and I love to grill burgers year-round. This variation with a creamy and flavorful filling is a hit with our family and friends. —Chris Anderson *Morton, Illinois*

- 2 pounds ground beef
- 2 tablespoons steak sauce
- 3/4 teaspoon seasoned salt
- 1 package (3 ounces) cream cheese, softened
- 1 to 2 tablespoons prepared horseradish
- 1 teaspoon prepared mustard
- 8 hamburger buns, split

In a bowl, combine beef, steak sauce and seasoned salt; mix well. Shape into 16 patties. In a small bowl, combine cream cheese, horseradish and mustard. Spoon about 1 tablespoonful into the center of half of the patties; top with remaining patties. Press edges to seal.

Grill, uncovered, over medium-hot heat for 10 minutes on each side or until meat is no longer pink. Serve on buns. **Yield:** 8 servings.

Threading Skewers

TO PREVENT the food on skewers from spinning around as you turn them on the grill, try piercing the foods with two parallel skewers rather than one.

Placing just one type of food on each skewer, rather than alternating foods, will make it easier to cook each item to the desired doneness without over- or under-cooking other items.

Crispy Catfish
Grilled Squash Medley

Crispy Catfish

(Pictured above)

Ready in 15 minutes or less

Grilling is my family's favorite way to fix meals. Because my husband savors well-prepared meals, this recipe quickly became one of his most requested.
—Rhonda Dietz, Garden City, Kansas

3/4 cup finely crushed saltines (about 22 crackers)
1 teaspoon seasoned salt
1/2 teaspoon celery salt
1/2 teaspoon garlic salt
4 catfish fillets (about 8 ounces *each*)
1/3 cup butter *or* margarine, melted

In a shallow dish, combine the first four ingredients. Pat fillets dry; dip in butter, then coat with crumb mixture. Coat grill rack with nonstick cooking spray before starting grill. Grill fillets, covered, over medium-hot heat for 10 minutes or until fish flakes easily with a fork, carefully turning once. **Yield:** 4 servings.

Grilled Squash Medley

(Pictured above)

Ready in 30 minutes or less

This colorful combination of yellow summer squash, carrot, onion and zucchini makes a great addition to any menu, regardless of the main entree. —Kathleen Ruggio Oswego, New York

✓ Uses less fat, sugar or salt. Includes Nutritional Analysis and Diabetic Exchanges.

1 small zucchini, julienned
1 small yellow summer squash, julienned
1 small carrot, julienned
1 small onion, chopped
2 tablespoons butter *or* margarine
Salt, pepper and garlic powder to taste
2 tablespoons grated Parmesan cheese
2 tablespoons shredded mozzarella cheese

Place the vegetables in order listed on a double layer of heavy-duty foil (about 18 in. x 15 in.). Dot with butter; season with salt, pepper and garlic powder. Fold foil around vegetables and seal tightly. Grill, covered, over medium heat for 14-16 minutes or until vegetables are tender, turning once. Sprinkle with cheeses. Serve immediately. **Yield:** 4 servings.

Nutritional Analysis: One 3/4-cup serving (prepared with part-skim mozzarella and without salt) equals 106 calories, 7 g fat (5 g saturated fat), 20 mg cholesterol, 145 mg sodium, 7 g carbohydrate, 2 g fiber, 4 g protein. **Diabetic Exchanges:** 1 vegetable, 1 fat, 1/2 starch.

All Seasons Marinade

Ready in 15 minutes or less

This mixture is so versatile, it can be used to marinate just about anything. I like to mix up a batch and keep it in the fridge. —Joan Hallford, North Richland Hills, Texas

3/4 cup soy sauce
1/2 cup vegetable oil
1/2 cup red wine vinegar *or* cider vinegar
1/3 cup lemon juice
1/4 cup Worcestershire sauce
2 tablespoons ground mustard

2 tablespoons minced fresh parsley
1-1/2 teaspoons pepper
1 teaspoon salt
2 garlic cloves, minced

In a jar with a tight-fitting lid, combine all of the ingredients; shake well. Cover and refrigerate until ready to use. Use as a marinade for beef, pork, chicken or shrimp. **Yield:** 2 cups.

Summer Beef Skewers

(Pictured below right)

Plan ahead...needs to marinate

The marinade that seasons these skewers has a robust flavor that friends and family love. They're a breeze to marinate ahead of time, then assemble before grilling.
—Cheryl Arnold, Lake Zurich, Illinois

✓ Uses less fat, sugar or salt. Includes Nutritional Analysis and Diabetic Exchanges.

    1 cup pineapple juice
    1 cup red wine *or* beef broth
    1/2 cup soy sauce
    1/2 cup Worcestershire sauce
    1 medium onion, chopped
    1 teaspoon dried thyme
    1 teaspoon dried rosemary, crushed
    1/2 teaspoon pepper
    3/4 pound cherry tomatoes
    1/2 pound whole fresh
        mushrooms
    3 small zucchini, cut into
        1/2-inch slices
    2 small yellow summer
        squash, cut into
        1/2-inch slices
    2 pounds sirloin tip
        steak, cut into
        1-1/4-inch cubes
Hot cooked rice, optional

In a bowl, combine first eight ingredients and mix well. Pour 1 cup into a large resealable plastic bag; add vegetables. Pour remaining marinade into another resealable bag; add beef. Seal bags and turn to coat; refrigerate for 4-6 hours or overnight, turning occasionally.

Drain and discard marinade from beef. Drain and reserve marinade from vegetables. On metal or soaked wooden skewers, alternately thread beef, tomatoes, mushrooms, zucchini and summer squash.

Grill, uncovered, over medium heat for 3 minutes on each side. Baste with reserved marinade. Continue turning and basting for 8-10 minutes or until meat reaches desired doneness (for rare, a meat thermometer should read 140°; medium, 160°; well-done, 170°). Serve kabobs over rice if desired. **Yield:** 8 servings.

Nutritional Analysis: One serving (prepared with wine and reduced-sodium soy sauce; calculated without rice) equals 266 calories, 13 g fat (5 g saturated fat), 74 mg cholesterol, 459 mg sodium, 9 g carbohydrate, 1 g fiber, 24 g protein. **Diabetic Exchanges:** 3 lean meat, 1-1/2 fat, 1 vegetable.

Grilled Onion Potatoes

When we were growing up, my mother often fixed these potatoes when we grilled outdoors. The tasty treatment requires just a few ingredients.
—Janet Gioia
Broadalbin, New York

    5 medium baking potatoes
    1 small onion, sliced
Salt and pepper to taste
    1 bottle (8 ounces) zesty Italian salad dressing

Cut each potato into five slices. Place onion between slices and sprinkle with salt and pepper. Reassemble each potato; place on a double layer of heavy-duty foil (about 12 in. square). Pour 2-4 tablespoons of salad dressing over each potato. Wrap foil around potatoes and seal tightly. Grill, covered, over medium heat for 50-60 minutes or until the potatoes are tender. **Yield:** 5 servings.

Summer Beef Skewers

Orange Chicken and Veggies

(Pictured below)

Plan ahead...needs to marinate

A mild maple marinade seasons the chicken, vegetables and fruit in this summery supper. —*Violet Klause Onoway, Alberta*

✓ Uses less fat, sugar or salt. Includes Nutritional Analysis and Diabetic Exchanges.

1 can (6 ounces) frozen orange juice concentrate, thawed
3/4 cup maple syrup
4 teaspoons canola oil
3/4 teaspoon curry powder
1/4 teaspoon cayenne pepper
6 boneless skinless chicken breast halves (1-1/2 pounds)
2 medium sweet red peppers, halved and seeded
1 medium green pepper, halved and seeded
3 medium zucchini, halved lengthwise
1 fresh pineapple, peeled and cut into 1/2-inch slices
2 unpeeled medium oranges, cut into 1/2-inch slices

In a bowl, combine the orange juice concentrate, syrup, oil, curry and cayenne. Place chicken in a large resealable plastic bag; add half of the marinade. Seal bag and turn to coat. Place the peppers, zucchini, pineapple and oranges in another resealable bag; add remaining marinade. Seal bag and turn to coat. Refrigerate chicken and vegetables for 8 hours or overnight, turning occasionally.

Drain chicken, discarding marinade. Drain vegetables and fruits, reserving marinade for basting. Grill the chicken, vegetables and fruits, uncovered, over medium heat for 3 minutes on each side. Baste with reserved marinade. Continue turning and basting 6-8 minutes longer or until chicken juices run clear, vegetables are tender and fruits are golden brown. **Yield:** 6 servings.

Nutritional Analysis: One serving (1 chicken breast with 3/4 cup vegetable mixture) equals 320 calories, 5 g fat (1 g saturated fat), 73 mg cholesterol, 71 mg sodium, 40 g carbohydrate, 4 g fiber, 29 g protein. **Diabetic Exchanges:** 3-1/2 very lean meat, 2 vegetable, 2 fruit, 1/2 fat.

Eggplant Mexicano

Ready in 15 minutes or less

We had an overabundance of eggplant some years ago when this recipe caught my eye. My husband and I think it's delicious. —*Alyce de Roos, Sarnia, Ontario*

1/2 cup vegetable oil
1 teaspoon garlic powder
1 teaspoon dried oregano
1 medium eggplant, peeled and cut into 1/2-inch slices
2/3 cup salsa, warmed
1/2 cup shredded Monterey Jack cheese

In a bowl, combine the oil, garlic powder and oregano; brush over both sides of eggplant. Grill, uncovered, over indirect medium heat for 2 minutes on each side or until tender. To serve, spoon a small amount of salsa into center of each; sprinkle with cheese. **Yield:** 6 servings.

Orange Chicken and Veggies

Barbecued Olive Bread

Ready in 30 minutes or less

We cook on the grill all year long, so this zesty olive-topped bread accompanies everything from pork to beef to chicken. It also makes a tempting appetizer.
—Patricia Gasper
Peoria, Illinois

  1 can (4-1/2 ounces) chopped ripe olives, drained
1/2 cup chopped stuffed olives
3/4 cup shredded Colby/Monterey Jack cheese
3/4 cup grated Parmesan cheese, *divided*
1/4 cup butter *or* margarine, melted
  1 tablespoon olive *or* vegetable oil
  2 garlic cloves, minced
  3 drops hot pepper sauce
  2 cups biscuit/baking mix
2/3 cup milk
  2 tablespoons minced fresh parsley
Paprika

In a bowl, combine the olives, Colby/Monterey Jack cheese, 1/2 cup Parmesan cheese, butter, oil, garlic and hot pepper sauce; set aside. In another bowl, combine biscuit mix, milk, 2 tablespoons Parmesan cheese and parsley just until moistened. Press into two greased 9-in. disposable aluminum pie pans. Top with olive mixture; sprinkle with paprika and remaining Parmesan.

Grill bread, covered, over indirect heat for 8-10 minutes or until bottom crust is golden brown when edge of bread is lifted with a spatula. **Yield:** 2 loaves (6-8 servings each).

Sausage Bread Kabobs

Ready in 1 hour or less

This fun pizza on a skewer is amazingly easy to assemble. Served with a tossed salad, it has become a favorite of family and friends.
—Darby Barbazon
Lilburn, Georgia

  2 pounds Italian sausage links
1/2 pound French bread, cut into 1-inch cubes
1/4 cup olive *or* vegetable oil
1/8 to 1/4 teaspoon pepper
  1 jar (16 ounces) spaghetti sauce, *divided*
  1 tablespoon minced fresh basil *or* parsley

Pierce sausages with a fork. Grill, covered, over medium heat for 10-12 minutes or until no longer pink, turning occasionally. Remove from the grill; cut into 2-in. pieces.

Green Chili Chicken Sandwiches

On metal or soaked wooden skewers, alternate sausage pieces with two bread cubes. Combine oil, pepper and half of the spaghetti sauce; brush over kabobs. Grill 5 minutes more or until sausage is heated through and bread is toasted. Sprinkle with basil. Heat remaining spaghetti sauce; serve with kabobs. **Yield:** 8-10 servings.

Green Chili Chicken Sandwiches

(Pictured above)

Ready in 1 hour or less

I enjoyed a sandwich similar to this in a restaurant and decided to try making it at home. The spicy chicken is a quick-and-easy alternative to hamburgers when entertaining outdoors.
—Paula Morigeau
Hot Springs, Montana

  4 boneless skinless chicken breast halves
2/3 cup soy sauce
1/4 cup cider vinegar
  2 tablespoons sugar
  2 teaspoons vegetable oil
  1 can (4 ounces) whole green chilies, drained and sliced lengthwise
  4 slices Pepper Jack *or* Monterey Jack cheese
  4 kaiser *or* sandwich rolls, split

Pound chicken to flatten; place in a large resealable plastic bag. In a bowl, combine the soy sauce, vinegar, sugar and oil; mix well. Set aside 1/4 cup for basting. Pour the remaining marinade over chicken; seal bag and turn to coat. Refrigerate for 30 minutes.

Drain and discard marinade. Grill chicken, uncovered, over medium heat for 3 minutes. Turn and baste with reserved marinade; grill 3 minutes longer or until juices run clear. Top each with a green chili and cheese slice; cover and grill for 2 minutes or until cheese is melted. Serve on rolls. **Yield:** 4 servings.

Banana Boats

Ready in 30 minutes or less

When I was a church youth leader, I introduced many young campers to this scrumptious treat. It's wonderful because each person can add their choice of yummy toppings to this warm dessert that tastes almost like a banana split.
—Sandy Vanderhoff, Waldron, Arkansas

4 medium unpeeled ripe bananas
2 tablespoons flaked coconut
2 tablespoons chopped maraschino cherries
2 tablespoons raisins
2 tablespoons peanut butter chips
1/2 cup miniature marshmallows

Cut banana peels lengthwise about 1/2 in. deep and to within 1/2 in. of each end. Open peel to form a pocket. Combine coconut and cherries; spoon into pockets of two bananas. Combine raisins and peanut butter chips; fill remaining bananas. Divide marshmallows between bananas. Wrap each in an 18-in. x 12-in. piece of heavy-duty foil. Grill, uncovered, over medium heat for 10-15 minutes or until marshmallows are melted and golden brown. **Yield:** 4 servings.

Colorful Grilled Veggies

(Pictured below)

Ready in 30 minutes or less

I put this combination together one day when trying to serve a side dish other than mushrooms in butter. Everyone loves this pleasantly seasoned medley and asks for the recipe. *—Susan Jesson, Oro Station, Ontario*

✓ Uses less fat, sugar or salt. Includes Nutritional Analysis and Diabetic Exchanges.

10 cherry tomatoes, halved
2 celery ribs, thinly sliced
1 medium green pepper, sliced
1 medium sweet red pepper, sliced
1 medium red onion, sliced and separated into rings
1 cup sliced fresh mushrooms
1 tablespoon red wine vinegar *or* cider vinegar
1 tablespoon olive *or* canola oil
1 teaspoon lemon juice
1 garlic clove, minced
1 teaspoon dried basil
1/2 teaspoon salt
1/2 teaspoon pepper

Divide the vegetables between two pieces of heavy-duty foil (about 18 in. square). In a small bowl, combine the remaining ingredients; drizzle over vegetables. Fold foil around vegetables and seal tightly. Grill, covered, over medium heat for 10-15 minutes or until the vegetables are crisp-tender. **Yield:** 6 servings.
Nutritional Analysis: One serving (3/4 cup) equals 51 calories, 3 g fat (trace saturated fat), 0 cholesterol, 212 mg sodium, 7 g carbohydrate, 2 g fiber, 1 g protein. **Diabetic Exchange:** 2 vegetable.

Seasoned Flank Steak

(Pictured below)

Plan ahead…needs to marinate

I always keep a flank steak in the freezer for unexpected company. This recipe has often saved me when our son appears on the doorstep. The easy four-ingredient marinade provides delicious flavor.
—Betty Graham
Sun City, California

1/4 cup vegetable oil
2 tablespoons water
1 to 2 tablespoons lemon-pepper seasoning
1 to 2 teaspoons seasoned salt
1 beef flank steak (about 1-1/2 pounds)

In a large resealable plastic bag, combine the first four ingredients; add steak. Seal bag and turn to coat; refrigerate for 1-2 hours, turning occasionally.
Grill steak, uncovered, over medium-hot heat for 6-12 minutes or until meat reaches desired doneness (for rare, a meat thermometer should read 140°; medium, 160°; well-done, 170°). **Yield:** 6 servings.

Colorful Grilled Veggies
Seasoned Flank Steak

Microwave Magic

TRY THESE made-in-minutes recipes and you'll never again use your "zapper" just for heating up coffee or warming leftovers. This marvelous kitchen tool is wonderful for preparing main meals, side dishes, snacks, desserts and more!

Editor's Note: All of these recipes were tested in an 850-watt microwave.

Raisin Pecan Oatmeal

Ready in 30 minutes or less

My mom often made us this warm and comforting breakfast when we were growing up. Now I like to make this treat on busy mornings or when we have overnight guests.
—Anna Kenagy, Carlsbad, New Mexico

    1/2 cup butter *or* margarine, softened
      1 cup sugar
      2 eggs
      1 teaspoon vanilla extract
      3 cups quick-cooking oats
      2 teaspoons baking powder
      1 teaspoon salt
    1/2 teaspoon ground cinnamon
      1 cup milk
    1/2 cup raisins
    1/2 cup chopped pecans
Additional milk

In a mixing bowl, cream butter and sugar. Add eggs and vanilla; mix well. Combine the oats, baking powder, salt and cinnamon; add to the creamed mixture alternately with milk. Stir in the raisins and pecans. Pour into a greased 3-qt. microwave-safe dish. Cover and microwave on high for 4 minutes; stir. Cook at 50% power for 6 minutes or until oats are tender. Serve warm with additional milk. **Yield:** 6-8 servings.

Chocolate Mallow Nut Bars

Ready in 1 hour or less

I've depended on this recipe for years when I need a sweet treat in a hurry. The speedy squares are easy to make and taste like a candy bar. *—Eleanor Mielke Mitchell, South Dakota*

      1 cup semisweet chocolate chips
      1 cup butterscotch chips
    1/2 cup peanut butter

    1/4 cup butter *or* margarine
  2-1/2 cups miniature marshmallows
      1 cup salted peanuts

In a microwave-safe bowl, combine the chips, peanut butter and butter. Cover and microwave on high for 1 minute; stir until smooth. Add marshmallows and peanuts; stir until well coated. Spread into a greased 13-in. x 9-in. x 2-in. pan. Cover and chill for 30 minutes or until firm. Cut into squares. **Yield:** 4 dozen.

Refried Bean Wraps

Ready in 15 minutes or less

We fall back on this speedy recipe when our cupboards are getting bare and time is short. It's simple, nutritious and filling. *—Arlene Stamy, Hasty, Colorado*

      1 can (16 ounces) refried beans
      1 can (16 ounces) refried beans and green
          chilies
      1 can (10 ounces) diced tomatoes and green
          chilies, undrained
      1 can (4-1/4 ounces) chopped ripe olives,
          drained
     12 flour tortillas (7 inches)
  1-1/2 cups (6 ounces) shredded cheddar cheese
Salsa and sour cream

In a bowl, combine the beans, tomatoes and olives; mix well. Spread about 1/3 cupful over each tortilla; sprinkle with 2 tablespoons of cheese. Fold sides and ends over filling and roll up. Arrange in a circle on a microwave-safe 12-in. round plate.

Cover with waxed paper. Microwave on high for 8 minutes or until heated through. Serve with salsa and sour cream. **Yield:** 1 dozen.

Microwave Marvels

- I use my microwave to cook fresh corn on the cob. Simply place one to five ears with husks intact in a casserole dish and cover it. (No water is needed if you leave the husks on.) Cook them for 3-4 minutes per ear, depending on the wattage of your microwave.
  After cooking, rinse the cobs with warm water, and the corn silk falls off easily as the husks are removed. Corn is so delicious this way that I wouldn't cook it using any other method. *—Flora Metz Jackson, Tennessee*

- To quickly crisp up stale cereal, potato chips, crackers or other snacks, I put them on a microwave-safe plate and zap them in the microwave for 30-45 seconds. Then I let them stand a minute or so until they're crisp. *—Colette Ruzinski, Greenfield, Wisconsin*

- To make potato salad in a hurry, I bake potatoes in the microwave and mash them with a potato masher. I add chopped onions, eggs and celery, then finish with my family's favorite dressing and seasonings.
  —Joyce Wilson, Somerset, Kentucky

Pineapple Veggie Chicken

Pineapple Veggie Chicken

(Pictured above)

Ready in 30 minutes or less

Our family enjoys this medley of tender chicken, sweet pineapple, colorful peppers and crisp snow peas.
　　　　　　　—Lori Hunter, Poca, West Virginia

✓ Uses less fat, sugar or salt. Includes Nutritional Analysis and Diabetic Exchanges.

　1 pound boneless skinless chicken breasts, cut
　　into 1/2-inch strips
　1 small green pepper, cut into 1-inch pieces
　1 small sweet red pepper, cut into 1-inch
　　pieces
　1 celery rib, thinly sliced
　1 medium onion, cut into eighths
　1 cup fresh *or* frozen snow peas, thawed
　1 jar (12 ounces) mushroom gravy
　2 to 3 tablespoons soy sauce
1/4 teaspoon ground ginger
　1 can (8 ounces) unsweetened pineapple
　　chunks, drained
Hot cooked rice, optional

Place chicken in a 2-qt. microwave-safe dish. Cover and microwave on high for 4-5 minutes or until no longer pink, stirring twice. Drain; remove chicken and set aside. In the same dish, combine the peppers, celery, onion and peas. Cover and microwave on high for 4-5 minutes or until vegetables are crisp-tender, stirring once.

Combine gravy, soy sauce and ginger; stir into the vegetables. Add pineapple and chicken. Cover and microwave on high for 4-5 minutes or until heated through, stirring twice. Serve over rice if desired. **Yield:** 4 servings.

Nutritional Analysis: One serving (prepared with fat-free gravy and 2 tablespoons reduced-sodium soy sauce; calculated without rice) equals 223 calories, 3 g fat (1 g saturated fat), 63 mg cholesterol, 819 mg sodium, 22 g carbohydrate, 3 g fiber, 26 g protein. **Diabetic Exchanges:** 3 very lean meat, 1-1/2 vegetable, 1 fruit.

After-School Treats

Ready in 1 hour or less

These delicious no-bake bars satisfy my craving for chocolate and are much easier to whip up than brownies or cookies from scratch. Requiring just five ingredients, they're especially handy for a bake sale or after-school treat.
　　　　　　　—Andrea Neilson, East Dundee, Illinois

　2 cups (12 ounces) semisweet chocolate chips
1/4 cup butter-flavored shortening
　5 cups crisp rice cereal
　1 package (10 ounces) Milk Duds
　1 tablespoon water

In a large microwave-safe bowl, combine chocolate chips and shortening. Cover and microwave on high until chocolate is melted, about 2 minutes; stir until well blended. Stir in cereal until well coated.

In another microwave-safe bowl, combine Milk Duds and water. Cover and microwave on high for 1 minute or until mixture is pourable; mix well. Stir into cereal mixture. Spread into a buttered 13-in. x 9-in. x 2-in. pan. Cover and refrigerate for 30 minutes or until firm. Cut into bars. **Yield:** 2 dozen.

Beef Tortilla Casserole

Ready in 30 minutes or less

I take advantage of my microwave to fix this moist and meaty main dish. Its mild taco flavor is complemented by sour cream and two kinds of cheese. —Patty Burchett
Louisville, Kentucky

      2 pounds ground beef
      1 medium onion, chopped
      1 bottle (8 ounces) taco sauce
      6 corn tortillas (6 inches), halved and cut into
         1-inch strips
      2 cups (16 ounces) sour cream
      1 cup (4 ounces) shredded cheddar cheese
      1 cup (4 ounces) shredded mozzarella cheese

Crumble beef into a large microwave-safe dish. Stir in onion. Microwave, uncovered, on high for 8-9 minutes or until meat is no longer pink, stirring and draining every 2 minutes. Stir in taco sauce and tortillas. In a greased 2-1/2-qt. microwave-safe dish, layer half of the beef mixture, sour cream and cheeses. Repeat layers. Cover and cook at 70% power for 10-11 minutes or until heated through. Let stand for 2-4 minutes before serving. **Yield:** 6-8 servings.

Speedy Salisbury Steak

(Pictured below right)

Ready in 30 minutes or less

Ground beef patties get fast family appeal when covered in a tasty gravy with nice chunks of mushrooms. This is great served over rice or mashed potatoes. It also freezes well. —Cindy Stephenson, Houston, Texas

      1 egg, beaten
   1/2 cup soft bread crumbs
   1/4 cup chopped onion
      2 teaspoons
         Worcestershire sauce
   1/2 teaspoon garlic
         powder
      1 pound ground beef
GRAVY:
      2 tablespoons
         all-purpose flour
      1 can (14-1/2 ounces)
         beef broth
   1/4 cup ketchup
      1 tablespoon
         Worcestershire sauce
   1/4 teaspoon dried basil
      1 jar (4-1/2 ounces)
         sliced mushrooms,
         drained
Mashed potatoes

In a bowl, combine the first five ingredients. Crumble beef over mixture and mix well. Shape into four patties; place in a shal-

low 2-qt. microwave-safe dish. Cover and microwave at 70% power for 6 minutes. Meanwhile, in a bowl, combine flour and broth until smooth. Stir in the ketchup, Worcestershire sauce, basil and mushrooms.

Turn patties; drain. Pour gravy over patties. Cover and microwave at 70% power for 6-8 minutes. Gently stir gravy; cover and let stand for 5 minutes. Serve over mashed potatoes. **Yield:** 4 servings.

Zippy Broccoli

(Pictured below)

Ready in 15 minutes or less

I changed the original recipe for this side dish to use hot pepper sauce instead of red pepper flakes. The zesty seasonings really punch up the flavor. —Bryan Forster
Clayton, Ontario

☑ Uses less fat, sugar or salt. Includes Nutritional Analysis and Diabetic Exchanges.

      7 cups fresh *or* frozen broccoli florets
   1/4 cup water
      2 tablespoons olive *or* vegetable oil
      1 tablespoon lemon juice
      2 garlic cloves, minced
      1 teaspoon salt
      1 teaspoon hot pepper sauce

Place broccoli and water in a microwave-safe bowl; cover and cook on high for 5-7 minutes or until crisp-tender. Meanwhile, combine remaining ingredients. Drain broccoli. Drizzle with lemon juice mixture; toss to coat. **Yield:** 8 servings.

Nutritional Analysis: One serving equals 49 calories, 4 g fat (trace saturated fat), 0 cholesterol, 326 mg sodium, 4 g carbohydrate, 2 g fiber, 2 g protein. **Diabetic Exchanges:** 1 vegetable, 1/2 fat.

Speedy Salisbury Steak
Zippy Broccoli

Cheesy Chicken

(Pictured below)

Ready in 30 minutes or less

This tender chicken with its cheesy crumb coating is one of my husband's favorites. It's always a hit with company, too, because it comes out juicy and great-tasting every time. —Joan Ergle, Woodstock, Georgia

    5 tablespoons butter *or* margarine, melted,
       divided
    1 cup crushed cheese-flavored snack crackers
 1/4 teaspoon pepper
    4 boneless skinless chicken breast halves
 1/2 cup sour cream

Place 1 tablespoon of butter in an 11-in. x 7-in. x 2-in. microwave-safe dish; set aside. Combine cracker crumbs and pepper. Dip chicken in remaining butter, then spread with sour cream. Roll in the crumb mixture. Place in prepared dish. Cover loosely and microwave on high for 6-7 minutes or until chicken juices run clear. Let stand for 5-10 minutes before serving. **Yield:** 4 servings.

Microwave Rice Pilaf

(Pictured below)

Ready in 30 minutes or less

I cook this speedy side dish to complement most any meal. It's just the right amount for my husband and me. But it's easy to double for a larger family. —Norma Jean Koelmel, Shattuc, Illinois

 1/4 cup *each* chopped onion, celery and green
       pepper
    1 tablespoon butter *or* margarine
 1/2 cup hot water
    1 jar (4-1/2 ounces) sliced mushrooms,
       drained
 1/3 cup uncooked instant rice
 1-1/2 teaspoons chicken bouillon granules

In a 1-qt. microwave-safe dish, combine the onion, celery, green pepper and butter. Microwave, uncovered, on high for 3-5 minutes or until vegetables are crisp-tender. Stir in the remaining ingredients. Cook on high for 12-14 minutes or until rice is tender. **Yield:** 2 servings.

One-Dish Spaghetti

Ready in 1 hour or less

I rely on this made-in-minutes main dish quite often. You don't even have to precook the spaghetti. Served with a green salad and garlic bread, it makes a quick-and-easy supper. —Trudie Reed, Orange, California

    1 pound ground beef
    1 large onion, chopped
    1 to 2 garlic cloves, minced
    2 cans (8 ounces *each*) tomato sauce
 1-1/2 cups water
 1/2 teaspoon salt
 1/2 teaspoon dried oregano
    4 ounces uncooked spaghetti, broken into
       thirds
Grated Parmesan cheese

Microwave Rice Pilaf
Cheesy Chicken

Taco Tidbits
Party Crab Dip

In a 2-1/2-qt. microwave-safe dish, combine beef, onion and garlic. Cover and microwave on high for 2-1/2 minutes; stir to crumble meat. Cook 1-1/2 to 2-1/2 minutes longer or until meat is no longer pink; drain. Add the tomato sauce, water, salt and oregano; mix well. Cover and microwave on high for 4 minutes.

Add the spaghetti and mix well. Cover and cook on high for 14-16 minutes, stirring twice. Let stand for 5-10 minutes. Serve with the Parmesan cheese. **Yield:** 4 servings.

In a microwave-safe bowl, combine the cornstarch and the wine or broth until smooth. Add cream cheese. Cover and microwave on high for 1 minute; stir. Microwave 1 to 1-1/2 minutes longer or until smooth and slightly thickened. Stir in the crab, cream, parsley and Worcestershire sauce. Cover and microwave on high for 1 minute; stir. Add cheddar cheese; heat 1 minute longer. Stir until the cheese is melted. Sprinkle with seafood seasoning if desired. Serve with crackers and vegetables. **Yield:** about 3 cups.

Party Crab Dip

(Pictured above)

Ready in 15 minutes or less

Nothing shaves time from party preparations like a no-fuss appetizer. This rich and flavorful seafood spread is the perfect example. I suggest serving it with crackers or toasted bread rounds. —Kimberly McGuire, Dunlap, Illinois

   1 teaspoon cornstarch
1/2 cup white wine *or* chicken broth
   1 package (8 ounces) cream cheese, cubed
   2 cans (6 ounces *each*) crabmeat, drained, flaked and cartilage removed
   2 tablespoons half-and-half cream
   2 tablespoons minced fresh parsley
   1 tablespoon Worcestershire sauce
   1 cup (4 ounces) shredded cheddar cheese
Seafood seasoning *or* paprika, optional
Crackers *and/or* raw vegetables

Taco Tidbits

(Pictured above)

This four-ingredient combination is a great change of pace from typical snack mixes. And it's a good thing the crispy treat is so simple to throw together.
—Sharon Mensing, Greenfield, Iowa

   6 tablespoons butter *or* margarine
   2 to 3 tablespoons taco seasoning
   8 cups Corn Chex
1/4 cup grated Parmesan cheese

Place butter in an 11-in. x 7-in. x 2-in. microwave-safe dish. Cover and microwave on high for 60-70 seconds or until melted. Add taco seasoning. Stir in the cereal until evenly coated. Microwave on high for 1 minute; stir. Heat 1 to 1-1/2 minutes longer; stir. Sprinkle with Parmesan cheese; microwave for 1 minute. Stir; heat 1 minute longer. Cool. **Yield:** 8 cups.

Sweet-and-Sour Meat Loaf

Sweet-and-Sour Meat Loaf

(Pictured above)

Ready in 1 hour or less

I combined a few great-tasting meat loaf recipes to create this flavorful family favorite. My husband loves it, and because it's made in the microwave, it's ideal for busy nights.
—*Deb Thompson, Lincoln, Nebraska*

☑ Uses less fat, sugar or salt. Includes Nutritional Analysis and Diabetic Exchanges.

  1 egg
  5 tablespoons ketchup, *divided*
  2 tablespoons prepared mustard
1/2 cup dry bread crumbs
  2 tablespoons onion soup mix
1/4 teaspoon salt
1/4 teaspoon pepper
  1 pound ground beef
1/4 cup sugar
  2 tablespoons brown sugar
  2 tablespoons cider vinegar

In a bowl, lightly beat the egg. Add 2 tablespoons of ketchup, mustard, bread crumbs, dry soup mix, salt and pepper. Crumble beef over mixture and mix well. Shape into an oval loaf.

Place in a shallow 1-qt. microwave-safe dish; cover with waxed paper. Microwave on high for 11-12 minutes or until meat is no longer pink, rotating a half turn once; drain.

In a small bowl, combine the sugars, vinegar and remaining ketchup; drizzle over meat loaf. Cover and microwave on high for 3-5 minutes. Let stand for 10 minutes before slicing. **Yield:** 4 servings.

Nutritional Analysis: One serving (prepared with lean ground beef) equals 375 calories, 13 g fat (5 g saturated fat), 94 mg cholesterol, 960 mg sodium, 38 g carbohydrate, 1 g fiber, 27 g protein. **Diabetic Exchanges:** 3 lean meat, 2-1/2 starch.

Nutty Brownies

Ready in 1 hour or less

I often whip up these tasty treats when unexpected guests stop by. They always receive favorable comments. They also make a fast dessert to take along to a picnic. Making chocolaty homemade brownies has never been easier!
—*Neva Mathes, Pella, Iowa*

  1 cup sugar
  2 eggs
  1 teaspoon vanilla extract
1/2 cup butter *or* margarine, melted
3/4 cup all-purpose flour
1/3 cup baking cocoa
1/2 teaspoon salt
  1 cup chopped nuts
Confectioners' sugar, optional

In a mixing bowl, combine the sugar, eggs and vanilla; mix well. Add butter; mix well. Combine the flour, cocoa and salt; add to butter mixture just until combined. Stir in nuts. Spread into a greased microwave-safe 8-in. square dish.

Microwave, uncovered, on high for 6-7 minutes or until top appears dry and springs back when lightly touched, rotating a quarter turn every 2 minutes. Dust with confectioners' sugar if desired. **Yield:** about 1-1/2 dozen.

Microwave French Onion Soup

Ready in 1 hour or less

Enjoy the taste and comfort of this classic soup through the convenience of microwave cooking. It's a recipe that I turn to time and again.   —Mina Dyck, Boissevain, Manitoba

    3 cups boiling water
    1 can (14-1/2 ounces) beef broth
    3 tablespoons butter *or* margarine
    2 teaspoons beef bouillon granules
    1 teaspoon Worcestershire sauce
  1/8 teaspoon salt
  1/8 teaspoon pepper
    3 cups thinly sliced onions
    2 cups seasoned croutons
1-1/3 cups shredded mozzarella cheese

In a 3-qt. microwave-safe dish, combine the first eight ingredients. Cover and microwave at 50% power for 25-30 minutes or until onions are tender. Ladle hot soup into four microwave-safe bowls. Top with croutons and cheese. Cover with waxed paper; microwave on high for 1 minute or until cheese is melted. Serve immediately. **Yield:** 4 servings.

Italian Orange Roughy

(Pictured below)

Ready in 1 hour or less

My family loves this moist and tender fish swimming in a flavorful sauce. It's easy to marinate first, then cook quickly in the microwave.   —Alice Mashek Schaumburg, Illinois

✓ Uses less fat, sugar or salt. Includes Nutritional Analysis and Diabetic Exchanges.

    1 pound orange roughy fillets
  1/2 cup tomato juice
    2 tablespoons white vinegar
    1 envelope Italian salad dressing mix
  1/4 cup chopped green onions
  1/4 cup chopped green pepper

Place fish fillets in a shallow 2-qt. microwave-safe dish, positioning the thickest portion of fish toward the outside edges. Combine tomato juice, vinegar and salad dressing mix; pour over fish. Cover and refrigerate for 30 minutes.

Sprinkle with onions and green pepper. Cover and microwave on high for 3 minutes. Turn fillets over; cook 2-4 minutes longer or until fish flakes easily with a fork. Let stand, covered, for 2 minutes. **Yield:** 4 servings.

Nutritional Analysis: One serving equals 110 calories, 1 g fat (trace saturated fat), 23 mg cholesterol, 760 mg sodium, 9 g carbohydrate, trace fiber, 17 g protein. **Diabetic Exchanges:** 2 very lean meat, 1/2 starch.

Dessert Pears

Ready in 30 minutes or less

I use a touch of vanilla to turn fruit and berry flavors into a delightful dessert. This four-ingredient treat is a pear-fect way to top off dinner without spending lots of time in the kitchen.   —Terri Casteel, Fairfax, Virginia

✓ Uses less fat, sugar or salt. Includes Nutritional Analysis and Diabetic Exchanges.

    4 medium pears, peeled, cored and halved
  1/4 cup cranberry juice
  1/4 cup strawberry preserves
  1/2 teaspoon vanilla extract

Place pears in a 9-in. square microwave-safe dish. Combine the cranberry juice, preserves and vanilla; pour over pears. Cover with waxed paper; microwave on high for 7-9 minutes or until pears are tender. **Yield:** 4 servings.

Nutritional Analysis: One serving (prepared with reduced-sugar preserves) equals 132 calories, 1 g fat (trace g saturated fat), 0 cholesterol, trace sodium, 33 g carbohydrate, 4 g fiber, 1 g protein. **Diabetic Exchange:** 2 fruit.

Italian Orange Roughy

THE theme-related recipes on the following pages are tops for taste and time-saving.

Give foods a fresh taste when you cook with oranges, apples, dried cranberries and pecans.

Asparagus and mushrooms are versatile vegetables that add life to snacks, salads, entrees and more.

Bring old-fashioned flavor to your table with dairy delicious buttermilk and ice cream.

Mouth-watering recipes prove that basic ingredients like ground beef and noodles are anything but boring.

And if recipes that serve two people are music to your ears, tune in to our timely menus.

COLD CONFECTIONS. Clockwise from upper left: Scoops of Ice Cream Pie, Pineapple Cherry Ice Cream and Caramel Chocolate Sauce (all recipes on p. 291).

Sunny Citrus

THE NATURALLY sweet tang of oranges makes for timeless treats you can count on around the clock.

Mandarin Beef Stir-Fry

(Pictured below right)

Ready in 1 hour or less

Crispy veggies contrast nicely with the tender beef and juicy oranges. —Anne Drouin, Dunnville, Ontario

  1 cup orange juice
1/2 cup soy sauce
  2 tablespoons Worcestershire sauce
  1 teaspoon garlic powder
1/4 teaspoon ground ginger
  1 pound beef round steak, cut into thin strips
  2 cups fresh *or* frozen snow peas
  1 medium onion, cut into wedges
  1 medium green pepper, julienned
  1 cup sliced fresh mushrooms
  2 tablespoons vegetable oil
  1 can (11 ounces) mandarin oranges, drained
  2 tablespoons cornstarch
Hot cooked rice

In a large bowl, combine the first five ingredients; remove half and set aside. Add beef to remaining marinade; cover and refrigerate for 15 minutes. In a large skillet or wok, stir-fry vegetables in oil for 2 minutes; remove and keep warm. Drain and discard marinade. In the same skillet, stir-fry beef until no longer pink. Add the oranges and reserved vegetables. Combine the cornstarch and reserved marinade until smooth; add to skillet. Bring to a boil; cook and stir for 2 minutes or until thickened. Serve over rice. **Yield:** 6 servings.

Orange Brownies

(Pictured at right)

Chocolate and orange go together deliciously in these moist fudgy brownies. And pecans add a pleasant crunch.
—Rosella Peters, Gull Lake, Saskatchewan

1/2 cup butter *or* margarine
1/4 cup baking cocoa
  2 eggs
  1 cup sugar
3/4 cup all-purpose flour
1/2 cup chopped pecans
  2 tablespoons orange juice concentrate
  1 tablespoon grated orange peel
1/8 teaspoon salt
FROSTING:
1-1/2 cups confectioners' sugar

  3 tablespoons butter *or* margarine, softened
  2 tablespoons orange juice concentrate
  1 tablespoon grated orange peel, optional

In a small saucepan, melt butter. Stir in cocoa until smooth. Remove from the heat. In a bowl, beat eggs until frothy. Without stirring, add the sugar, flour, pecans, orange juice concentrate, peel and salt. Pour cocoa mixture over the top; mix well. Transfer to a greased 8-in. square baking pan. Bake at 350° for 28-32 minutes or until edges begin to pull away from sides of pan. Cool completely on a wire rack. For frosting, combine confectioners' sugar, butter and orange juice concentrate; mix well. Spread over the brownies. Cut into bars; garnish with orange peel if desired. **Yield:** 16 servings.

Orange Pecan Muffins

Ready in 1 hour or less

You'll agree these naturally sweet and nutty muffins are a "must" for managing the mid-morning munchies.
—Julia Livingston, Frostproof, Florida

1/2 cup butter *or* margarine, softened
  1 cup sugar
  2 eggs
  1 cup (8 ounces) plain yogurt
  2 cups all-purpose flour
  1 teaspoon baking soda
3/4 cup chopped pecans, toasted
  1 teaspoon grated orange peel
TOPPING:
1/4 cup orange juice
  1 tablespoon sugar

In a mixing bowl, cream butter and sugar. Beat in eggs and yogurt. Combine flour and baking soda; stir into creamed mixture just until moistened. Fold in pecans and orange peel. Fill paper-lined muffin cups three-fourths full. Bake at 375° for 18-20 minutes or until a toothpick comes out clean. Brush orange juice over hot muffins; sprinkle with sugar. Cool for 5 minutes before removing to a wire rack. **Yield:** about 1 dozen.

Orange Brownies
Mandarin Beef Stir-Fry

Apple Ham Hotcakes
Buttermilk Peach Slush

Buttermilk Is Dairy Delightful

IN Great-Grandma's day, buttermilk was the tart liquid left over from the arm-aching process of churning cream into butter. Luckily, with today's commercial version of buttermilk, you can whip up the following cream-of-the-crop recipes in no time.

Editor's Note: If you don't happen to have buttermilk on hand, try this easy substitute. For each cup of buttermilk, place 1 tablespoon of lemon juice or white vinegar in a measuring cup. Add enough milk to measure 1 cup total liquid; stir vigorously. Let the mixture stand for 5 minutes before using.

Apple Ham Hotcakes

(Pictured above)

Ready in 30 minutes or less

Hearty ham, sweet applesauce and a hint of caraway flavor these light buttermilk pancakes. They're so delicious, I often serve them hot off the griddle without syrup.
—Kelly Thornberry, La Porte, Indiana

- 1 cup all-purpose flour
- 1 tablespoon baking powder
- 1 tablespoon brown sugar
- 1/2 teaspoon baking soda
- 1/2 teaspoon salt
- 1/2 teaspoon caraway seeds, crushed, optional
- 1 egg
- 1 cup buttermilk
- 3/4 cup chunky applesauce

- 2 tablespoons butter *or* margarine, melted
- 3/4 cup diced fully cooked ham
- Warm maple syrup, optional

In a bowl, combine the first six ingredients. In a small bowl, beat egg, buttermilk, applesauce and butter; stir into dry ingredients just until moistened. Fold in ham. Pour batter by 1/4 cupfuls onto a lightly greased hot griddle; turn when bubbles form on top of pancakes. Cook until second side is golden brown. Serve with syrup if desired. **Yield:** 15 pancakes.

Buttermilk Peach Slush

(Pictured at left)

Ready in 15 minutes or less

This refreshing drink is a breeze to make and brings a cool taste of summer to any season. Our house is surrounded by fruit orchards, so I've tried this recipe with peaches, apricots and pears. —Darlene Markel, Mt. Hood, Oregon

☑ Uses less fat, sugar or salt. Includes Nutritional Analysis and Diabetic Exchanges.

- 3/4 cup apricot nectar
- 1/2 cup buttermilk
- 2 tablespoons lime juice
- 2 cups unsweetened sliced peaches
- 2 to 4 tablespoons sugar
- 5 ice cubes

In a blender, combine all of the ingredients. Cover and process until smooth. Pour into glasses; serve immediately. **Yield:** 4 servings.
Nutritional Analysis: One serving (prepared with 1% buttermilk and 2 tablespoons sugar) equals 103 calories, trace fat (trace saturated fat), 2 mg cholesterol, 34 mg sodium, 25 g carbohydrate, 2 g fiber, 2 g protein. **Diabetic Exchange:** 1-1/2 fruit.

Plum Quick Bread

Friends and family will rush to get another slice of this quick bread. Plum and cinnamon make a mouth-watering combination. —Deb Thierwechter, Clayton, Delaware

- 3 eggs
- 2 jars (6 ounces *each*) plum *or* plum with apples baby food
- 1 cup vegetable oil
- 1 cup buttermilk
- 2-1/2 cups all-purpose flour
- 2 cups sugar
- 2 teaspoons baking soda
- 1 teaspoon ground cinnamon
- 1/2 teaspoon salt

In a mixing bowl, combine the eggs, baby food, oil and buttermilk. Combine dry ingredients, add to the egg mixture and beat just until moistened. Transfer to two greased 9 in. x 5 in. x 3-in. loaf pans. Bake at 350° for 60-65 minutes or until a toothpick inserted near the center comes out clean. Cool for 10 minutes before removing from pans to wire racks. **Yield:** 2 loaves.

Asparagus Puff Pizza

Asparagus Potato Soup

Ready in 30 minutes or less

Hearty bowls featuring potatoes and asparagus get a special touch when topped with bacon and cheddar cheese.
—*Sherry McKellar, Spanish Fork, Utah*

- 2 cups diced peeled potatoes
- 1/2 pound fresh asparagus, chopped
- 1/2 cup chopped onion
- 2 celery ribs, chopped
- 1 tablespoon chicken bouillon granules
- 4 cups water
- 1/4 cup butter *or* margarine
- 1/2 cup all-purpose flour
- 1 cup whipping cream
- 1/2 cup milk
- 1/2 teaspoon salt
- Dash pepper
- 12 bacon strips, cooked and crumbled
- 3/4 cup shredded cheddar cheese

In a large saucepan or soup kettle, combine the potatoes, asparagus, onion, celery, bouillon and water. Bring to a boil. Reduce heat; cover and simmer for 15 minutes or until vegetables are tender. Stir in the butter. In a bowl, combine flour, cream, milk, salt and pepper until smooth; add to the vegetable mixture. Bring to a boil; cook and stir for 2 minutes or until thickened. Garnish with bacon and cheese. **Yield:** 6-7 servings.

Spring Means Asparagus

LET YOUR COOKING reflect nature's green hues by incorporating asparagus into your mealtime menu.

Asparagus Puff Pizza

(Pictured above)

Ready in 30 minutes or less

You can prepare this homemade pizza in less time than it takes to bake a frozen one. It relies on a prebaked crust, so it's ready in a jiffy. For extra flavor, season the asparagus with garlic salt, basil and thyme before arranging in a pretty sunburst pattern.
—*Norma Shouse Zephyrhills, Florida*

- 2 pounds fresh asparagus, cut into 2-inch pieces
- 1 prebaked Italian bread shell crust (1 pound)
- 1/2 cup mayonnaise
- 2 tablespoons grated Parmesan cheese
- 1/4 teaspoon ground mustard
- 3 egg whites

Place asparagus in a steamer basket over 1 in. of boiling water in a saucepan; cover and steam until crisp-tender, about 4 minutes. Drain on paper towel. Place crust on an ungreased 12-in. pizza pan; arrange asparagus on top. In a bowl, combine mayonnaise, cheese and mustard; mix well. In a small mixing bowl, beat egg whites until stiff peaks form. Fold into mayonnaise mixture; spread over asparagus. Bake at 450° for 12-13 minutes or until golden brown. Cut into wedges; serve warm. Refrigerate leftovers. **Yield:** 8 servings.

Asparagus Crab Au Gratin

Ready in 1 hour or less

This rich casserole is so easy that I fix it often. The compliments are unending.
—*Nancy Thibodeau Overgaard, Arizona*

- 1 package (10 ounces) frozen asparagus cuts, thawed and drained
- 1 can (6 ounces) crabmeat, drained, flaked and cartilage removed *or* 1 cup flaked imitation crabmeat
- 1/2 cup shredded cheddar cheese
- 4 tablespoons butter *or* margarine, *divided*
- 2 tablespoons all-purpose flour
- 1 cup milk
- 1/2 teaspoon ground mustard
- 1/2 teaspoon salt
- 1/8 teaspoon pepper
- 2 teaspoons lemon juice
- 1 cup soft bread crumbs

Place asparagus in a greased 1-qt. baking dish. Top with crab and sprinkle with cheese; set aside. In a saucepan, melt 2 tablespoons butter. Stir in flour until smooth. Whisk in milk, mustard, salt and pepper. Bring to a boil over medium heat; cook and stir for 2 minutes or until thickened.

Remove from the heat; stir in lemon juice. Pour over asparagus. Melt remaining butter; toss with bread crumbs. Sprinkle over top. Bake, uncovered, at 350° for 30 minutes or until heated through. **Yield:** 4 servings.

Mmmushrooms!

LOOKING for an ingredient to jazz up your meals? Consider the garden-fresh taste of mushrooms.

Mushroom Pimiento Salad

(Pictured below)

Plan ahead...needs to marinate

Green onions and celery blend with pimientos and mushrooms in a simple dressing.
—Sally Hook
Houston, Texas

>   1 pound fresh mushrooms, quartered
>   2 cups sliced celery
>   2 jars (2 ounces *each*) diced pimientos, drained
>   3 hard-cooked egg whites, chopped
>   3 tablespoons sliced green onions
> 3/4 cup vegetable oil
> 1/4 cup red wine vinegar *or* cider vinegar
> 1/4 cup sugar
>   1 garlic clove, minced
>   1 teaspoon celery seed
> 1/2 teaspoon salt
> 1/4 teaspoon pepper
> 1/4 teaspoon dried marjoram
>
> Lettuce leaves

In a bowl, combine the mushrooms, celery, pimientos, egg whites and onions. In a blender or food processor, combine the oil, vinegar, sugar, garlic and seasonings; cover and process until blended. Drizzle over vegetables and toss to coat. Cover and refrigerate for 1 hour. Serve in a lettuce-lined bowl. **Yield:** 10 servings.

Hot Mushroom Dip

(Pictured below left)

I've whipped up this thick hearty dip for many potluck dinners.
—Ellen Derflinger, Jefferson, Maryland

>   4 bacon strips, diced
> 1/2 pound fresh mushrooms, chopped
>   1 medium onion, finely chopped
>   1 garlic clove, minced
>   2 tablespoons all-purpose flour
> 1/4 teaspoon salt
> 1/8 teaspoon pepper
>   1 package (8 ounces) cream cheese, cubed
> 1/2 cup sour cream
>   2 teaspoons Worcestershire sauce
>   1 teaspoon soy sauce
>
> Assorted raw vegetables *or* crackers

In a skillet, cook bacon over medium heat until crisp. Remove bacon to paper towels. Drain, reserving 2 tablespoons drippings. In the drippings, saute mushrooms, onion and garlic until tender. Add flour, salt and pepper; cook and stir for 1 minute or until thickened. Reduce heat. Add next four ingredients; cook and stir until cheese melts. Stir in bacon. Serve warm with vegetables or crackers. **Yield:** 2 cups.

Philly Cheesesteak Pizza

This pizza is an ideal busy weeknight recipe. I add mushrooms to this combination of my husband's favorite foods.
—Anne Zirkle, South Riding, Virginia

>   1 prebaked Italian bread shell crust (16 ounces)
>   1 medium onion, thinly sliced and separated into rings
>   1 small sweet red pepper, cut into 1/8-inch strips
>   2 garlic cloves, minced
>   1 tablespoon olive *or* vegetable oil
> 1/2 pound thinly sliced deli roast beef, cut into 1/4-inch strips
>   1 jar (6 ounces) sliced mushrooms, drained
>   1 teaspoon dried oregano
>   1 teaspoon dried basil
> 1/4 teaspoon salt
> 1/4 teaspoon pepper
>   1 cup (4 ounces) shredded mozzarella cheese
> 1/2 cup shredded Parmesan cheese

Place crust on a 14-in. pizza pan; set aside. In a skillet, saute the onion, red pepper and garlic in oil for 3-5 minutes or until crisp-tender. Add beef and mushrooms; cook and stir for 3-5 minutes or until heated through. Drain. Stir in the seasonings. Spread meat mixture over crust to within 1/2 in. of edge. Combine the cheeses; sprinkle over pizza. Bake at 350° for 15 minutes or until the crust is golden and the cheese is melted. **Yield:** 4-6 servings.

Hot Mushroom Dip
Mushroom Pimiento Salad

Popular Pecans

ALTHOUGH pecans are primarily grown in the South, their down-home flavor is a welcome addition to main dishes and desserts prepared by cooks from across the country.

Toffee Pecan Bars

(Pictured below)

Plan ahead...needs to chill

Curl up with a hot cup of coffee and one of these treats. The golden topping and flaky crust give way to the heart-warming taste of old-fashioned pecan pie.
—Dianna Croskey, Gibsonia, Pennsylvania

    2 cups all-purpose flour
1/2 cup confectioners' sugar
    1 cup cold butter *or* margarine
    1 egg
    1 can (14 ounces) sweetened condensed milk
    1 teaspoon vanilla extract
    1 package English toffee bits (10 ounces) *or* almond brickle chips (7-1/2 ounces)
    1 cup chopped pecans

In a bowl, combine the flour and sugar; cut in butter until the mixture is crumbly. Press into a greased 13-in. x 9-in. x 2-in. baking pan. Bake at 350° for 15 minutes. In a bowl, combine the egg, milk and vanilla; mix well. Fold in toffee bits and pecans. Spoon over crust. Bake for 25 minutes or until golden brown. Chill until firm before cutting. **Yield:** 3 dozen.

Buttermilk Pecan Chicken

(Pictured below left)

Ready in 1 hour or less

My family enjoys chicken and always asks me to bake it this way. Sometimes I like to give this dish kid appeal by cutting the chicken into strips before coating with the nut mixture. —*Julie Jahn, Decatur, Indiana*

    1 cup ground pecans
1/4 cup sesame seeds, optional
    1 tablespoon paprika
    2 teaspoons salt
1/8 teaspoon pepper
    1 cup all-purpose flour
1/2 cup buttermilk
    6 boneless skinless chicken breast halves
    2 tablespoons butter *or* margarine, melted
18 pecan halves

In a shallow bowl, combine the pecans, sesame seeds if desired, paprika, salt and pepper. Place flour and buttermilk in separate shallow bowls. Coat chicken with flour, dip in buttermilk, then coat with pecan mixture. Place in a greased 13-in. x 9-in. x 2-in. baking dish. Drizzle with butter. Top each with three pecan halves. Bake, uncovered, at 375° for 30-35 minutes or until juices run clear. **Yield:** 6 servings.

Toffee Pecan Bars
Buttermilk Pecan Chicken

Cherry Pecan Bread

I've used this recipe for nearly 30 years, and it's always a success. Not only is it easy to prepare, but it freezes well, so I usually have an extra loaf on hand.
—Mary Weeks
Central, South Carolina

1/2 cup butter *or* margarine, softened
    1 cup sugar
    2 eggs
    1 cup buttermilk
    2 cups all-purpose flour
    1 teaspoon baking soda
3/4 teaspoon salt
    1 jar (10 ounces) maraschino cherries, drained and chopped
    1 cup chopped pecans

In a mixing bowl, cream butter and sugar. Add eggs and buttermilk. Combine the flour, baking soda and salt; add to creamed mixture just until blended. Fold in the cherries and pecans. Transfer to a greased 9-in. x 5-in. x 3-in. loaf pan. Bake at 350° for 55-65 minutes or until a toothpick inserted near the center comes out clean. Cool for 10 minutes before removing from pan to a wire rack. **Yield:** 1 loaf.

Scoops of Ice Cream Pie
Pineapple Cherry Ice Cream
Caramel Chocolate Sauce

upon standing). Refrigerate leftovers. **Yield:** 2 cups.

  *Editor's Note: This recipe was tested with Hershey caramels in an 850-watt microwave.

Scoops of Ice Cream Pie

(Pictured at left and on page 284)

Plan ahead...needs to freeze

My kitchen is a popular spot when I serve up this deluxe dessert on hot summer days. Garnished with raspberries, each slice features smooth vanilla ice cream piled on a nutty chocolate crust. Eliminate last-minute fuss by preparing and freezing this pretty pie ahead of time. —Beverly Gottfried Candler, North Carolina

> 2 pints vanilla ice cream, *divided*
> 1 cup chocolate wafer crumbs (about 16 wafers)
> 1/2 cup chopped almonds
> 1/4 cup butter *or* margarine, melted
> Fresh raspberries
> Fresh mint, optional

Soften 1 pint of ice cream. Combine the cookie crumbs, nuts and butter. Press onto the bottom and up the sides of a 9-in. pie plate. Spread with the softened ice cream. Cover and freeze until firm. Scoop remaining ice cream into small balls; pile into crust. Cover and freeze for up to 2 months.

Remove from the freezer 10 minutes before serving. Arrange raspberries between scoops. Garnish with mint if desired. **Yield:** 6-8 servings.

Pineapple Cherry Ice Cream

(Pictured above left and on page 285)

Plan ahead...needs to freeze

This fruity treat has been an all-time favorite with my family for years. Use an ice cream freezer to make this colorful crowd-pleaser, which is sure to be a success no matter what time of year it's served. —Johanna Gimmeson Powell, Wyoming

> 2-1/2 cups sugar
> 1 package (6 ounces) cherry gelatin
> 2 cups boiling water
> 4 cups milk
> 4 cups whipping cream
> 1 can (20 ounces) crushed pineapple, drained
> 1/3 cup lemon juice

In a bowl, dissolve sugar and gelatin in boiling water. Refrigerate for 1 hour or until cool. Stir in the milk, cream, pineapple and lemon juice; mix well. Fill cylinder of ice cream freezer two-thirds full; freeze according to manufacturer's directions. Refrigerate remaining mixture until ready to freeze. **Yield:** 3 quarts.

An At-Home Ice Cream Parlor

AMERICA'S first ice cream parlor opened in 1776, and our love of the dairy dessert hasn't waned since. A special serving from an ice cream stand or parlor still seems to ease life's little problems, so why not enjoy that cool comfort at home?

  Whether smothered in chocolate sauce, scooped into a pie shell or blended with fruit, ice cream is sure to help you leave your troubles behind.

Caramel Chocolate Sauce

(Pictured above and on page 284)

Ready in 15 minutes or less

This quick fix takes ice cream toppings to new heights. Melted caramels give the rich fudge-like sauce extra appeal. —June Smith, Byron Center, Michigan

> 30 caramels*
> 1 cup (6 ounces) semisweet chocolate chips
> 1 can (5 ounces) evaporated milk
> 1/2 cup butter (no substitutes)
> Ice cream

In a 1-qt. microwave-safe bowl, combine the caramels, chocolate chips, milk and butter. Microwave, uncovered, on high for 2 minutes; stir. Heat 1-2 minutes longer or until the caramels are almost melted; stir until smooth. Serve warm if desired over ice cream (sauce will thicken

Autumn Apples

NO MATTER how you slice them, apples are an inviting addition to all kinds of dishes.

Citrus-Apple Tossed Salad

(Pictured at right)

Ready in 30 minutes or less

This crisp fruit salad bursts with flavor. A light dressing lets the fresh taste of the ingredients shine through.
—Dorothy Swanson, St. Louis, Missouri

 Uses less fat, sugar or salt. Includes Nutritional Analysis and Diabetic Exchanges.

      8 cups torn salad greens
      3 medium navel oranges, peeled and sectioned
      2 medium red apples, thinly sliced
      1 medium pink grapefruit, peeled and sectioned
      1 medium cucumber, thinly sliced
      1 celery rib, chopped
HONEY LEMON DRESSING:
  1/3 to 1/2 cup canola oil
  1/3 cup lemon juice
  1/4 cup snipped chives
      1 tablespoon honey
  1/2 teaspoon paprika
  1/4 teaspoon salt
  1/2 cup cubed cream cheese, optional
Seasoned salad croutons, optional

In a salad bowl, combine the first six ingredients. In a jar with a tight-fitting lid, combine the oil, lemon juice, chives, honey, paprika and salt; shake well. Pour over salad and toss to coat. Sprinkle with cream cheese and croutons if desired. **Yield:** 12 servings.

Nutritional Analysis: One 1-cup serving (prepared with 1/3 cup oil and without cream cheese and croutons) equals 105 calories, 6 g fat (trace saturated fat), 0 cholesterol, 62 mg sodium, 13 g carbohydrate, 3 g fiber, 1 g protein. **Diabetic Exchanges:** 1 fruit, 1 fat.

Cream Cheese Apple Muffins

(Pictured above right)

My husband likes to take these muffins to work for his morning snack.   —Marcia Hill, Byron Center, Michigan

      1 package (3 ounces) cream cheese, softened
  3/4 cup sugar
      2 eggs
  1/2 cup milk
  1/4 cup butter *or* margarine, melted
      1 tablespoon lemon juice

Citrus-Apple Tossed Salad
Cream Cheese Apple Muffins

      1 teaspoon vanilla extract
  1-1/2 cups all-purpose flour
  1-1/2 teaspoons baking powder
  1/2 teaspoon baking soda
  1/2 teaspoon salt
      1 cup diced peeled tart apples
  1/2 cup bran flakes
TOPPING:
  1-1/2 teaspoons sugar
      1 teaspoon ground cinnamon

In a mixing bowl, combine the first seven ingredients; beat until smooth. Combine dry ingredients; stir into cream cheese mixture just until moistened. Fold in apples and bran flakes. Fill greased or paper-lined muffin cups two-thirds full. Combine topping ingredients; sprinkle over batter. Bake at 375° for 20-25 minutes or until a toothpick comes out clean. Cool for 5 minutes before removing from pan to a wire rack. **Yield:** 1 dozen.

Simple Apple Dumplings

Ready in 1 hour or less

Crescent rolls make these delicious dumplings a time-saving treat.   —Jean Killen, Loretto, Tennessee

      1 tube (8 ounces) refrigerated crescent rolls
      2 medium apples, peeled and quartered
      1 cup sugar
      1 cup orange juice
  1/2 cup butter *or* margarine
  1/2 teaspoon apple pie spice

Unroll crescent dough and separate into eight triangles. Roll up one apple wedge in each triangle; pinch edges to seal. Place in a greased 8-in. square baking dish. In a small saucepan, bring sugar, orange juice and butter to a boil. Pour over dumplings (dumplings will float to the top). Sprinkle with apple pie spice. Bake, uncovered, at 350° for 20-25 minutes or until golden brown. Serve warm. **Yield:** 8 servings.

It Takes Two

THESE recipes show you how to transform common ingredients—ground beef and noodles—into mouth-watering meals.

Hamburger Macaroni Skillet

(Pictured below right)

Ready in 1 hour or less

This flavorful meal is great for busy nights because it's a snap to prepare. —Teresa Ray, Lewisburg, Tennessee

1-1/2 pounds ground beef
1-1/2 to 2 teaspoons garlic powder
    2 cups uncooked elbow macaroni
    2 cans (10-3/4 ounces *each*) condensed tomato with roasted garlic and herbs soup, undiluted
1-3/4 cups water
    2 cups frozen mixed vegetables

In a large skillet, cook beef and garlic powder over medium heat until meat is no longer pink; drain. Stir in the macaroni, soup, water and vegetables. Bring to a boil. Reduce heat; simmer, uncovered, for 20 minutes or until macaroni is tender. **Yield:** 6-8 servings.

Ground Beef Noodle Soup

Ready in 1 hour or less

This is a terrific-tasting fast soup to make any day of the week. —Judy Brander, Two Harbors, Minnesota

1-1/2 pounds ground beef
  1/2 cup *each* chopped onion, celery and carrot
    7 cups water
    1 envelope au jus mix
    2 tablespoons beef bouillon granules
    2 bay leaves
  1/8 teaspoon pepper
1-1/2 cups uncooked egg noodles

In a large saucepan or Dutch oven, cook beef, onion, celery and carrot over medium heat until meat is no longer pink and vegetables are tender; drain. Add water, au jus mix, bouillon, bay leaves and pepper; bring to a boil. Stir in the noodles. Boil, uncovered, for 15 minutes or until noodles are tender, stirring occasionally. Discard bay leaves. **Yield:** 8 servings (2 quarts).

Swift Spaghetti

Ready in 30 minutes or less

I add dry onion soup mix to the water when cooking my spaghetti, then I stir in a nicely seasoned meat sauce. —Louise Miller, Westminster, Maryland

5-1/2 cups water
    1 package (7 ounces) spaghetti
    1 envelope onion soup mix
    1 pound ground beef
    1 can (8 ounces) tomato sauce
    1 can (6 ounces) tomato paste
    1 tablespoon dried parsley flakes
    1 teaspoon dried oregano
  1/2 teaspoon dried basil
  1/4 to 1/2 teaspoon garlic powder

In a large saucepan, bring water to a boil. Add spaghetti and dry soup mix. Cook for 12-15 minutes or until spaghetti is tender (do not drain). Meanwhile, in a skillet, cook beef over medium heat until no longer pink; drain. Stir in the tomato sauce, tomato paste, parsley, oregano, basil and garlic powder. Add to the spaghetti mixture; heat through. **Yield:** 4-6 servings.

Cheesy Beef 'n' Noodles

Ready in 1 hour or less

Shredded cheese, diced tomatoes and whole kernel corn jazz up ground beef in this satisfying skillet supper. —Nikki Detwiler, Lancaster, Ohio

    1 pound ground beef
    4 cups uncooked wide egg noodles
    1 can (28 ounces) diced tomatoes, undrained
  1/2 cup water
  1/4 cup diced celery
  1/4 cup whole kernel corn
    1 envelope onion soup mix
    1 garlic clove, minced
    1 cup (4 ounces) shredded process cheese (Velveeta)

In a large skillet, cook beef over medium heat until no longer pink; drain. Add noodles, tomatoes, water, celery, corn, dry soup mix and garlic. Bring to a boil. Reduce heat; cover and simmer for 20 minutes or until noodles are tender. Remove from the heat; sprinkle with cheese. Cover and let stand for 5 minutes or until cheese is melted. **Yield:** 4-6 servings.

Hamburger Macaroni Skillet

Crowd-Pleasing Dried Cranberries

IF you're looking for a fun change of pace from other dried fruits, try dried cranberries. The raisin-like morsels burst with flavor that's sweet and tart. Plus, their chewy texture adds interest to all kinds of foods, from baked goods to fresh-tasting salads to holiday candies. So try one of the following recipes that makes the most of these bright berries.

Cranberry Buttermilk Scones

(Pictured below)

Ready in 30 minutes or less

I bake these light, fluffy scones that are loaded with dried cranberries and topped with cinnamon-sugar. I take them to breakfast meetings, serve them at brunches, and share them with neighbors and friends. —Loraine Meyer Bend, Oregon

    3 cups all-purpose flour
  1/3 cup plus 2 tablespoons sugar, *divided*
2-1/2 teaspoons baking powder
  3/4 teaspoon salt
  1/2 teaspoon baking soda
  3/4 cup cold butter *or* margarine
    1 cup buttermilk
    1 cup dried cranberries
    1 teaspoon grated orange peel
    1 tablespoon milk
  1/4 teaspoon ground cinnamon

In a bowl, combine the flour, 1/3 cup sugar, baking powder, salt and baking soda; cut in butter. Stir in the buttermilk just until combined. Fold in the cranberries and orange peel. Turn onto a floured surface; divide dough in half. Shape each portion into a ball and pat into a 6-in. circle. Cut each circle into six wedges. Place on a lightly greased baking sheet. Brush with milk. Combine the cinnamon and remaining sugar; sprinkle over scones. Bake at 400° for 15-20 minutes or until golden brown. **Yield:** 1 dozen.

Holiday Tossed Salad

(Pictured below left)

Ready in 30 minutes or less

Since you use packaged greens, it takes just a few moments to put together all the ingredients for this salad.
—Carol Dilcher, Emmaus, Pennsylvania

    1 package (10 ounces) Italian-blend salad greens
    1 package (5 ounces) spring mix salad greens
    2 cans (11 ounces *each*) mandarin oranges, drained
1-1/2 cups dried cranberries
    1 medium red apple, cored and chopped
    1 cup chopped walnuts
  1/3 cup shredded cheddar cheese
    1 bottle (8 ounces) raspberry vinaigrette

In a large salad bowl, toss the greens, oranges, cranberries, apple, walnuts and cheese. Drizzle with vinaigrette just before serving; toss to coat. **Yield:** 12 servings.

Cranberry Clusters

Ready in 1 hour or less

I need just three ingredients to stir up these chewy, crunchy treats that make a nice addition to a candy tray. I sometimes use white chocolate in place of semisweet and replace the cashews with macadamia nuts. —Kari Caven Post Falls, Idaho

    2 cups (12 ounces) semisweet chocolate chips
  2/3 cup dried cranberries
  2/3 cup cashews

In a microwave or saucepan, melt the chocolate chips; stir in the cranberries and cashews. Drop by teaspoonfuls onto a waxed paper-lined baking sheet. Let stand until set. **Yield:** about 2 dozen.

**Cranberry Buttermilk Scones
Holiday Tossed Salad**

Dinner Duets

FOR FOLKS cooking for one or two people, speedy suppers that feed a crowd are not always in harmony with their lifestyle.

So our test kitchen came up with six recipes for six main dishes that serve two people. (These recipes are great for singles, too. Just wrap the extras so you can enjoy a home-cooked meal the next day.)

Stuffed Steak Rolls

(Pictured below)

Ready in 1 hour or less

These hearty beef rolls don't require a lot of fuss—they just look like they do. Use a boxed stuffing mix or leftover stuffing for the filling, then top with a tasty sauce full of onion and green pepper. Serve with vegetables and a dessert of your choice.

    1 small green pepper, cut into 1-inch pieces
    1 small onion, sliced and separated into rings
    1 garlic clove, minced
    1 tablespoon vegetable oil
  3/4 cup prepared stuffing
    2 tablespoons grated Parmesan cheese
    2 beef cube steaks (about 3/4 pound)
  1/2 cup hot water
  1/2 teaspoon beef bouillon granules
  1/3 cup chili sauce

In a skillet, saute green pepper, onion and garlic in oil until crisp-tender; remove with a slotted spoon and set aside. Combine stuffing and cheese; spoon onto the center of steaks. Roll up and tuck in ends; secure with toothpicks. In the same skillet, cook steak rolls until browned. In a bowl, combine water and bouillon; stir in chili sauce

and reserved vegetable mixture. Pour over the steak rolls. Cover and simmer for 25-30 minutes or until meat is no longer pink, occasionally spooning sauce over rolls. Remove toothpicks. **Yield:** 2 servings.

Herb-Roasted Game Hens

Herb-Roasted Game Hens

(Pictured above)

These golden Cornish hens are seasoned with basil, sage and thyme for plenty of flavor. They're simple to prepare yet make any occasion seem special. For a fast finish, serve corn bread stuffing and chunky cinnamon applesauce…or roasted cubed potatoes with peppers and carrots plus instant chocolate pudding for dessert.

    2 Cornish game hens (20 ounces *each*)
    2 tablespoons butter *or* margarine, melted
    2 garlic cloves, minced
    1 teaspoon dried basil
  1/2 teaspoon salt
  1/2 teaspoon rubbed sage
  1/2 teaspoon dried thyme
  1/4 teaspoon lemon-pepper seasoning

Place hens, breast side up, on a rack in a shallow roasting pan. In a small bowl, combine the remaining ingredients. Brush over hens. Bake, uncovered, at 350° for 50-60 minutes or until juices run clear. **Yield:** 2 servings.

Stuffed Steak Rolls

Knead a Few Biscuits?

When making just a few biscuits from a mix, I use a large flat dinner plate to knead the dough. The "dusting" flour stays on the plate, and cleanup is easy.

—*Betty Mgrditchian, Englewood, Florida*

Veggie Turkey Roll-Ups

Alfredo Shrimp Shells

(Pictured below)

Ready in 1 hour or less

Prepared Alfredo sauce streamlines the preparation of the tasty stuffed shells. They're filled with shrimp, mushrooms and green onion. For a fast finish, complete the meal with Caesar salad and crusty French bread. Or serve sauteed zucchini followed by cubed cantaloupe and watermelon for dessert.

> 1/2 cup chopped fresh mushrooms
> 1 teaspoon butter *or* margarine
> 1 green onion, sliced
> 1 package (5 ounces) frozen cooked salad shrimp, thawed
> 2 tablespoons plus 1/2 cup Alfredo sauce, *divided*
> 6 jumbo pasta shells, cooked and drained
> Lemon wedges and fresh parsley

In a skillet, saute mushrooms in butter until almost tender. Add onion; cook until tender. Stir in the shrimp and 2 tablespoons Alfredo sauce. Pour 1/4 cup of the remaining sauce into a greased 8-in. square baking dish.

Fill each pasta shell with 2 tablespoons shrimp mixture; place in baking dish. Top with the remaining Alfredo sauce. Cover and bake at 350° for 20-25 minutes or until bubbly. Serve with lemon wedges and parsley. **Yield:** 2 servings.

Veggie Turkey Roll-Ups

(Pictured above)

Ready in 30 minutes or less

Colorful veggies are wrapped inside tender turkey breast slices to create these fresh-tasting bundles. Serve with rice pilaf and angel food cake topped with fresh fruit. Or accompany with parsley potatoes and purchased chocolate chip cheesecake for dessert.

> 1/4 cup *each* julienned sweet red pepper, carrot, yellow summer squash and zucchini
> 4 uncooked turkey breast slices
> 2 tablespoons all-purpose flour
> 1/8 teaspoon paprika
> 1 tablespoon vegetable oil
> 1/4 cup water
> 3 tablespoons lemon juice
> 4-1/2 teaspoons white wine *or* additional water
> 2-1/4 teaspoons chicken bouillon granules
> 1/2 teaspoon dried basil

Combine the red pepper, carrot, summer squash and zucchini; spoon down the center of each turkey slice. Roll up and secure ends with toothpicks. In a shallow bowl, combine flour and paprika; roll turkey in mixture until coated. In a skillet over medium heat, cook roll-ups in oil until golden brown. In a bowl, combine the remaining ingredients; pour over turkey. Cover and simmer for 3 minutes or until meat juices run clear and the vegetables are crisp-tender. Discard toothpicks from roll-ups; serve with the pan drippings. **Yield:** 2 servings.

Alfredo Shrimp Shells

Cheese Steak Subs

Ginger Pork Chops

(Pictured below)

A pleasant combination of honey, soy sauce and ginger glazes these tender pork chops and makes them seem special. Serve with buttered green beans and instant mashed potatoes. Or complete the meal with peas and scalloped potatoes from a boxed mix.

- 2 bone-in pork loin chops (3/4 inch thick)
- 1 teaspoon cornstarch
- 2 tablespoons soy sauce
- 1/4 cup honey
- 1 garlic clove, minced

Dash ground ginger *or* 3/4 teaspoon grated fresh gingerroot
- 1 tablespoon sliced green onion

Broil pork chops 3-4 in. from the heat for 5-6 minutes on each side or until no longer pink. Meanwhile, in a small saucepan, combine cornstarch and soy sauce until smooth. Stir in the honey, garlic and ginger. Bring to a boil; cook and stir for 1 minute or until thickened. Drizzle over the pork chops. Sprinkle with green onion. **Yield:** 2 servings.

Cheese Steak Subs

(Pictured above)

Thin slices of roast beef are topped with peppers, onions and cheese to create this satisfying stacked sandwich. It's quick to fix, flavorful and sure to please even the biggest appetite. Accompany it with deli potato salad and brownies...or serve frozen french fries and store-bought sugar cookies for dessert.

- 1/2 cup julienned sweet red pepper
- 1/2 cup julienned green pepper
- 1/2 cup sliced onion
- 1/2 teaspoon vegetable oil
- 2 slices mozzarella cheese
- 4 ounces thinly sliced deli roast beef
- 2 submarine sandwich buns, split

In a skillet, saute peppers and onion in oil until tender. Cut cheese slices in half. Place beef and cheese on bottom of each bun. Broil 4 in. from heat for 1-2 minutes or until cheese melts. Top with pepper mixture and bun tops. **Yield:** 2 servings.

Ginger Pork Chops

Chapter 19

298

NO TIME for entertaining? Think again! An elaborate meal can have time-easing elements that make hosting a get-together a snap—and a lot more fun— for the hostess.

Here, fellow busy cooks share an assortment of favorite, fast-to-fix recipes they like to prepare for company.

Our test kitchen combined some of these timely dishes to create five complete menus that will keep your kitchen time to a minimum and that will easily impress family and friends.

Plus, you'll see how to add special touches to your table with easy and inexpensive garnishes, table decorations and napkin folds.

GREAT FOR GUESTS. Clockwise from upper right: Mandarin-Cashew Tossed Salad (p. 310), Hearty Twice-Baked Potatoes (p. 313), Strawberry Banana Crepes (p. 312) and Orange Glazed Cornish Hens (p. 310). (See page 319 for table topper ideas.)

Mouth-Watering Mexican Meal

DURING the cooler months, add a little spice to your everyday menus. Invite a few friends over for a casual dinner party that features these south-of-the-border selections. Your guests are sure to warm up to the Mexican flavors in this festive meal. (Turn to page 314 for simple decoratiNg ideas.)

Chili Cheese Tart

(Not pictured)

Ready in 1 hour or less

When I fix this flavorful appetizer, I have to keep an eye out for sneaky fingers. My family just can't resist sampling the cheesy wedges. These hearty starters are delicious topped with salsa and sour cream. —Rachel Nash
Pascagoula, Mississippi

    1 package (15 ounces) refrigerated pie pastry
      (2 sheets)
    1 can (4 ounces) chopped green chilies,
      drained
    1 cup (4 ounces) shredded cheddar cheese
    1 cup (4 ounces) shredded Monterey Jack
      cheese
    1/4 teaspoon chili powder
Salsa and sour cream

Place one sheet of pie pastry on an ungreased pizza pan or baking sheet. Sprinkle the chilies and cheeses over pastry to within 1/2 in. of edges. Top with the remaining pastry; seal edges (see page 314) and prick top with a fork.

Sprinkle with chili powder. Bake at 450° for 10-15 minutes or until golden brown. Cool for 10 minutes before cutting into wedges. Serve with salsa and sour cream. **Yield:** 10-14 servings.

Southwest Stuffed Chicken

Ready in 1 hour or less

Our daughter served these tender chicken rolls to us a long time ago, and we've enjoyed them often since then. A zippy cheese filling gives them special flavor while a golden coating enhances their appearance. —Alcy Thorne
Los Molinos, California

    6 boneless skinless chicken breast halves
      (about 1-1/2 pounds)
    6 ounces Monterey Jack cheese, cut into
      2-inch x 1/2-inch sticks
    2 cans (4 ounces *each*) chopped green chilies,
      drained
    1/2 cup dry bread crumbs
    1/4 cup grated Parmesan cheese
    1 tablespoon chili powder
    1/2 teaspoon salt
    1/4 teaspoon ground cumin
    3/4 cup all-purpose flour
    1/2 cup butter *or* margarine, melted

Flatten chicken to 1/8-in. thickness. Place a cheese stick down the middle of each; top with chilies. Roll up and tuck in ends. Secure with a toothpick. In a shallow bowl, combine the bread crumbs, Parmesan cheese, chili powder, salt and cumin. Coat chicken with flour, then dip in butter and roll in crumb mixture.

Place roll-ups, seam side down, in a greased 13-in. x 9-in. x 2-in. baking dish. Bake, uncovered, at 400° for 25 minutes or until chicken juices run clear. Discard toothpicks. **Yield:** 6 servings.

Spanish Rice

Ready in 15 minutes or less

Instant rice and convenient canned goods simplify the stovetop preparation of this tangy side dish. Its traditional taste makes it a perfect accompaniment to a Mexican-style entree. —Flo Burtnett
Gage, Oklahoma

    1 cup chopped onion
    1/2 cup chopped green pepper
    1 tablespoon vegetable oil
    1 cup uncooked instant rice
    1 can (14-1/2 ounces) stewed tomatoes
    3/4 cup tomato juice
    1/2 teaspoon prepared mustard

In a skillet, saute the onion and green pepper in oil until tender. Add the remaining ingredients and mix well. Bring to a boil; reduce heat. Simmer, uncovered, for 5 minutes or until rice is tender and liquid is absorbed. **Yield:** 6 servings.

Burnt Custard

Plan ahead...needs to chill

The recipe for this smooth-as-silk custard came from a local restaurant years ago. With most of the prep work done ahead of time, it's easy to just broil until the topping is golden brown, then serve. It looks pretty in individual cups. —Heidi Main, Anchorage, Alaska

    2 cups whipping cream
    4 egg yolks
    1/2 cup plus 6 teaspoons sugar, *divided*
    3 teaspoons vanilla extract

In a saucepan, heat cream over medium-low until almost simmering; remove from the heat. In a mixing bowl, beat egg yolks and 1/2 cup sugar until thick and lemon-colored. Gradually beat in cream; add vanilla. Pour into six ungreased 6-oz. custard cups. Place cups in a 13-in. x 9-in. x 2-in. baking pan. Fill pan with boiling water to a depth of 1 in.

Bake at 350° for 45 minutes or until custard center is almost set. Remove cups from pan to a wire rack; cool for 15 minutes. Refrigerate for at least 2 hours or until chilled. Sprinkle with remaining sugar. Broil 4-6 in. from the heat for 2 minutes or until golden brown. Serve immediately. **Yield:** 6 servings.

A Taste of Italy

PASTA is always pleasing, especially when it features a creamy, cheesy filling. Caesar salad, fresh-baked rolls and a rich chocolate dessert round out the meal. (For tips on filling manicotti shells and for making the centerpiece, turn to page 315.)

Special Cheese Manicotti

Shredded zucchini and Italian salad dressing give such yummy flavor to the cheese filling in this pasta bake. It's perfect for a small gathering. —Lisa Otis, Drain, Oregon

    1 package (8 ounces) manicotti shells
2-1/2 cups (10 ounces) shredded mozzarella
        cheese, *divided*
  1/2 cup grated Parmesan cheese
    3 tablespoons minced fresh parsley
  1/4 teaspoon salt
  1/4 teaspoon pepper
  1/8 teaspoon ground nutmeg
    1 egg, lightly beaten
  3/4 cup sour cream
  1/3 cup prepared Italian salad dressing
  1/2 cup shredded zucchini
    1 jar (14 ounces) spaghetti sauce

Cook manicotti according to package directions; rinse in cold water and drain. In a large bowl, combine 2 cups mozzarella cheese, Parmesan cheese, parsley, salt, pepper and nutmeg. Stir in the egg, sour cream, salad dressing and zucchini. Carefully stuff manicotti; place in a greased 13-in. x 9-in. x 2-in. baking dish. Pour spaghetti sauce over top. Bake, uncovered, at 350° for 35 minutes. Sprinkle with remaining mozzarella. Bake 5 minutes longer or until heated through. **Yield:** 7 servings.

Rosemary Potato Rolls

Plan ahead...uses bread machine

I sprinkle sesame seeds, poppy seeds or rosemary over these pretty golden rolls. The dough is easily made in the bread machine. —Mary Dixson, Decatur, Alabama

    1 cup plus 2 tablespoons water (70° to 80°)
    2 tablespoons olive *or* vegetable oil
  1/2 cup mashed potato flakes
    2 tablespoons nonfat dry milk powder
    1 tablespoon sugar
    1 teaspoon dried rosemary, crushed
    1 to 1-1/2 teaspoons salt
    3 cups bread flour
2-1/4 teaspoons active dry yeast
    1 egg, lightly beaten
Sesame seeds, poppy seeds *or* additional crushed
    rosemary

In bread machine pan, place the first nine ingredients in the order suggested by the manufacturer. Select the dough setting (check dough after 5 minutes of mixing; add 1 to 2 tablespoons of water or flour if needed). When cycle is completed, turn dough onto a lightly floured surface. Punch down; let stand for 10 minutes.
   Divide dough into 12 portions. Shape each into a

10-in. rope. Holding one end of rope, loosely form into a coil. Tuck end under; pinch to seal. Place 2 in. apart on a greased baking sheet. Cover and let rise in a warm place until doubled, about 30 minutes. Brush tops with egg. Sprinkle with sesame or poppy seeds or rosemary. Bake at 375° for 13-16 minutes or until golden brown. Remove from pan to a wire rack. **Yield:** 1 dozen.

Pepperoni Caesar Salad

Ready in 15 minutes or less

Here's my recipe to make the best-tasting Caesar salad ever. Pepperoni slices add a spicy spin to this classic. —Dorothy Smith, El Dorado, Arkansas

  1/3 cup olive *or* vegetable oil
    2 tablespoons red wine vinegar *or* cider
        vinegar
    2 tablespoons mayonnaise
    2 garlic cloves, minced
  1/2 teaspoon Dijon mustard
  1/4 teaspoon Worcestershire sauce
  1/4 teaspoon pepper
    8 cups torn romaine
    1 cup halved thinly sliced pepperoni
1-1/2 cups Caesar salad croutons
  1/4 cup shredded Parmesan cheese

In a small bowl, combine the oil, vinegar, mayonnaise, garlic, mustard, Worcestershire sauce and pepper; set aside. In a large salad bowl, combine romaine and pepperoni. Drizzle with dressing; sprinkle with croutons and Parmesan. Serve immediately. **Yield:** 8 servings.

Almond Chocolate Torte

Plan ahead...needs to chill

This no-bake chocolate dessert has a tasty almond crust and smooth fluffy filling that's almost like a mousse. —Rhonda Lanterman, Terrace, British Columbia

  2/3 cup sliced almonds, toasted
    8 squares (1 ounce *each*) semisweet chocolate
    2 packages (8 ounces *each*) cream cheese,
        softened
    1 cup sugar
    1 envelope unflavored gelatin
  1/4 cup cold water
    2 cups whipping cream, whipped

Set aside 1 tablespoon almonds for garnish. Chop remaining almonds; sprinkle into a greased 9-in. springform pan. In a microwave or heavy saucepan, melt chocolate; stir until smooth. Cool slightly. In a mixing bowl, beat cream cheese and sugar.
   In a small saucepan, sprinkle gelatin over cold water; let stand for 1 minute. Cook and stir over low heat until gelatin is completely dissolved. Beat into cream cheese mixture. Add melted chocolate; beat until blended. Fold in the whipped cream. Pour into prepared pan. Sprinkle with reserved almonds. Cover and refrigerate for at least 3 hours. **Yield:** 10-12 servings.

Patio Party

HEAD TO the great outdoors and take advantage of your grill to fix this flavorful feast. The fresh flavors of this menu make it perfect for spring and summer. (You'll find ideas for adding special touches to your table on page 316.)

Teriyaki Pork Tenderloin

Plan ahead...needs to marinate

I'm always looking for easy recipes, and this one fits the bill perfectly. It marinates for several hours, then grills in mere minutes. I've made this pleasantly seasoned pork several times for company and received many compliments.
—*Debora Brown, St. Leonard, Maryland*

    1/2 cup soy sauce
    1/4 cup olive *or* vegetable oil
      4 teaspoons brown sugar
      2 teaspoons ground ginger
      1 teaspoon pepper
      2 garlic cloves, minced
      4 pork tenderloins (3/4 to 1 pound *each*)
Coarsely ground pepper, optional

In a large resealable plastic bag, combine the first six ingredients; add pork. Seal bag and turn to coat; refrigerate for 4 hours, turning occasionally.

Drain and discard marinade. Grill the tenderloins, covered, over indirect medium heat for 8-9 minutes on each side or until meat juices run clear and a meat thermometer reads 160°. Sprinkle with pepper if desired. **Yield:** 8 servings.

Pesto-Corn Grilled Peppers

Ready in 30 minutes or less

We grill almost daily and enjoy using fresh produce from our garden. This summery side dish of colorful pepper halves filled with a basil-seasoned corn mixture is my husband's favorite. As soon as company arrives, I place the peppers on the grill and assemble the corn and pesto mixture. —*Rachael Marrier, Star Prairie, Wisconsin*

    1/2 cup plus 2 teaspoons olive *or* vegetable oil,
        divided
    3/4 cup grated Parmesan cheese
      2 cups tightly packed fresh basil
      2 tablespoons sunflower kernels *or* walnuts
      4 garlic cloves
    1/2 cup finely chopped sweet red pepper
      4 cups whole kernel corn
      4 medium sweet red, yellow *or* green peppers
    1/4 cup shredded Parmesan cheese, optional

For pesto, combine 1/2 cup of oil, grated Parmesan cheese, basil, sunflower kernels and garlic in a blender or food processor; cover and process until blended. In a skillet, saute red pepper in remaining oil until tender. Add corn and pesto; heat through.

Halve peppers lengthwise; remove seeds. Place, cut side down, on grill over medium heat; cover and cook for 8 minutes. Turn; fill with corn mixture. Grill 4-6

minutes longer or until tender. Sprinkle with shredded Parmesan cheese if desired. **Yield:** 8 servings.

Sweet-Sour Broccoli Salad

Plan ahead...needs to chill

This refreshing medley is a good way to get broccoli into your meals. Just three simple ingredients create the tangy-sweet dressing that coats this crunchy combination. For a twist, toss in some cauliflower as well.
—*Bea Ramirez, Kansas City, Kansas*

      4 cups broccoli florets
      1 cup peanuts
      1 cup raisins
    1/2 cup chopped onion
      1 cup mayonnaise
      2 tablespoons cider vinegar
      2 tablespoons sugar

In a bowl, combine broccoli, peanuts, raisins and onion. In a small bowl, combine mayonnaise, vinegar and sugar. Pour over vegetables; toss to coat. Cover and refrigerate for at least 2 hours. **Yield:** 8 servings.

Blueberry Swirl Cheesecake

Plan ahead...needs to chill

I rely on convenient canned blueberry pie filling and a prepared graham cracker crust to assemble this pretty pie. Slices are delightful when draped with extra pie filling.
—*Suzanne McKinley, Lyons, Georgia*

      2 packages (8 ounces *each*) cream cheese,
        softened
    1/2 cup sugar
    1/4 teaspoon vanilla extract
      2 eggs
      1 graham cracker crust (9 inches)
      1 can (21 ounces) blueberry pie filling, *divided*

In a mixing bowl, beat cream cheese, sugar and vanilla until smooth. Add eggs, beating just until combined. Pour into crust. Drop 1/2 cup of pie filling by heaping teaspoonfuls onto the cream cheese mixture; cut through with a knife to swirl the pie filling (see below).

Bake at 350° for 35-40 minutes or until center is almost set. Cool on a wire rack. Chill for 2 hours. Top with remaining pie filling. **Yield:** 8 servings.

Creating a Swirled Cheesecake

Spoon small amounts of pie filling in a random pattern onto cheesecake filling.

Cut through cheesecake filling with a knife to swirl in pie filling. Be careful not to draw the blade through the filling too often or they'll blend and you'll lose your pretty pattern.

Casual Summer Menu

SUMMER is a perfect time to host an informal get-together with family and friends. This special supper starts with a make-ahead salad and dessert, while the stuffed sandwich and beverage can be prepared in minutes. (Turn to page 317 for tips on sugaring the rims of glasses and other table topper hints.)

Ham and Swiss Stromboli

Ready in 1 hour or less

This pretty swirled sandwich loaf is fast, easy and versatile. Fill it with anything your family likes. Try sliced pepperoni and provolone cheese, or anchovies and ripe olives if you're feeling adventurous. —Pat Raport
Gainesville, Florida

      1 tube (11 ounces) refrigerated French bread
      6 ounces thinly sliced deli ham
      6 green onions, sliced
      8 bacon strips, cooked and crumbled
1-1/2 cups (6 ounces) shredded Swiss cheese

Unroll dough on a greased baking sheet. Place ham over dough to within 1/2 in. of edges; sprinkle evenly with onions, bacon and cheese. Roll up jelly-roll style, starting with a long side. Pinch seams to seal and tuck ends under. Place seam side down on baking sheet.

With a sharp knife, cut several 1/4-in.-deep slits on top of loaf. Bake at 350° for 26-30 minutes or until golden brown. Cool slightly before slicing. Serve warm. **Yield:** 6-8 servings.

Zucchini Tomato Toss

Plan ahead...needs to chill

A co-worker shared this flavorful medley of tomatoes and zucchini with me many years ago. It's a wonderful way to use up garden produce in the summer. —Jan Clark
Salt Lake City, Utah

      4 cups thinly sliced zucchini
      2 medium tomatoes, cut into wedges
  1/4 cup thinly sliced green onions
  3/4 cup white wine vinegar *or* cider vinegar
  2/3 cup vegetable oil
      1 garlic clove, minced
      2 tablespoons sugar
      1 teaspoon salt
      1 teaspoon dried basil
Dash to 1/8 teaspoon pepper

In a serving bowl, combine the zucchini, tomatoes and onions. In a jar with a tight-fitting lid, combine the remaining ingredients; shake well. Pour over the zucchini mixture and toss gently to coat. Cover and refrigerate for at least 2 hours. Serve with a slotted spoon. **Yield:** 8 servings.

Special Lemonade

Ready in 1 hour or less

This refreshing beverage is a little different from your run-of-the-mill lemonade. The recipe comes from a charm-ing tearoom in a historic home that my mother and I enjoy visiting. When guests arrive, I greet them with cool glasses of this beverage. —Erin Schneider
St. Peters, Missouri

      2 medium lemons
1-1/2 cups sugar
      2 cups milk
      3 cups chilled club soda
      2 to 3 drops yellow food coloring, optional
Additional sugar, optional

Remove ends from lemons and discard. Remove the lemon peel with a knife; set aside. Quarter the lemons; squeeze the juice into a bowl. Remove and discard white membrane. Place the peel and pulp in a blender or food processor; cover and process until coarsely chopped. Add the peel mixture and sugar to lemon juice; mix well. Let stand for 30 minutes.

Stir in the milk. Strain the lemon mixture; add the club soda and food coloring if desired. Serve immediately in sugar-rimmed glasses if desired (see page 317). **Yield:** 8 servings.

Mini Apricot Cheesecakes

Ready in 1 hour or less

I rely on vanilla wafers to create the no-fuss crusts for these darling individual desserts. For a different look and taste, vary the kind of preserves that tops these tempting treats. Guests are sure to help themselves to "just one more". —Carol Twardzik, Spy Hill, Saskatchewan

  24 vanilla wafers
      2 packages (8 ounces *each*) cream cheese, softened
  3/4 cup sugar
      2 eggs
      1 tablespoon lemon juice
      1 teaspoon vanilla extract
      1 cup apricot preserves

Place wafers flat side down in paper- or foil-lined muffin cups; set aside. In a mixing bowl, beat cream cheese and sugar until smooth. Add the eggs, lemon juice and vanilla; beat well. Fill muffin cups three-fourths full. Place on a baking sheet.

Bake at 375° for 17-20 minutes or until top is set. Cool on a wire rack for 20 minutes. Top each cheesecake with 2 teaspoons preserves. Refrigerate until serving. **Yield:** 2 dozen.

In a Jam?

If you don't have the apricot preserves called for in the Mini Apricot Cheesecakes recipe above, you can substitute a different flavor preserve or jam.

There are a few slight differences between preserves and jams. Preserves are made with whole fruit or coarse pieces, sugar and usually pectin. Jams are made with mashed fruits, sugar and sometimes have added pectin.

A Harvest of
Fall Flavors

CAPTURE the spirit of autumn with a menu that's rich in the season's tastes, scents and sights. (See page 318 for ways to liven up your table.)

Creamy Wild Rice Soup

I make this comforting soup year-round…and after a few spoonfuls, you'll likely do the same. —Angie Schramm
Yankton, South Dakota

        4 cups water
    1/2 teaspoon salt
    1/2 cup uncooked wild rice
        3 tablespoons chopped green onions
    1/4 cup shredded carrot
        3 tablespoons chopped pecans
        6 tablespoons butter *or* margarine
    1/3 cup all-purpose flour
        2 cans (14-1/2 ounces *each*) chicken broth
    1/2 cup diced fully cooked ham
    1/4 teaspoon pepper
        1 cup half-and-half cream
Green onion strips, optional

In a large saucepan, bring water and salt to a boil. Add rice. Reduce heat; cover and simmer for 50-55 minutes or until tender. Remove from the heat. Let stand for 10 minutes; drain and set aside.

In a soup kettle or Dutch oven, saute the onions, carrot and pecans in butter for 1-2 minutes. Stir in flour until blended. Gradually add broth. Bring to a boil; cook and stir for 2 minutes or until thickened. Reduce heat. Add the ham, pepper and wild rice. Cover and simmer for 5 minutes or until carrots are tender. Reduce heat. Add cream; heat through (do not boil). Garnish with green onion strips if desired. **Yield:** 8 servings.

Chicken with Mushroom Sauce

Ready in 1 hour or less

This is a fast but special treatment for chicken. Chicken breasts are browned to juicy perfection, then topped with a buttery sauce. —Patsy Jenkins, Tallahassee, Florida

        8 bone-in chicken breast halves
        2 tablespoons olive *or* vegetable oil
        2 cups sliced fresh mushrooms
        2 green onions, chopped
        1 cup white wine *or* chicken broth
        3 tablespoons butter *or* margarine
    1/2 teaspoon salt
    1/4 teaspoon pepper
        1 tablespoon cornstarch
        2 tablespoons cold water

In a large skillet, brown chicken in oil. Cover and cook until juices run clear, about 20 minutes. Remove chicken; keep warm. In the same skillet, saute mushrooms and onions until tender. Stir in wine or broth, butter, salt and pepper. In a small bowl, combine cornstarch and water until smooth; add to skillet. Bring to a boil; cook and stir for 2 minutes or until thickened. Return chicken to skillet; heat through. **Yield:** 8 servings.

Lemon Broccoli

Ready in 15 minutes or less

Add a hint of citrus to your vegetables with an attractive side dish. Ideal with most any entree, this time-saving specialty dresses up broccoli, pimientos and onions with a dash of lemon. —Tonya Farmer, Iowa City, Iowa

        3 pounds fresh broccoli, cut into florets
    1/4 cup butter *or* margarine
        2 tablespoons diced onion
        2 tablespoons diced pimientos
        3 to 4 teaspoons lemon juice
        2 teaspoons grated lemon peel
    1/2 teaspoon seasoned salt
Dash pepper

Add 1 in. of water to a large saucepan; add broccoli. Bring to a boil. Reduce heat; cover and simmer for 5-8 minutes or until crisp-tender. Meanwhile, melt butter; stir in remaining ingredients. Drain broccoli; add butter mixture and toss to coat. **Yield:** 8 servings.

Pumpkin Orange Cake

This moist make-ahead spice cake with its flavorful orange frosting is popular at family gatherings. It's simple to prepare. —Shirley Glaab, Hattiesburg, Mississippi

    1/2 cup butter *or* margarine, softened
  1-1/4 cups sugar
        2 eggs
        1 cup cooked *or* canned pumpkin
    1/2 cup orange juice
    1/4 cup milk
        1 tablespoon grated orange peel
        2 cups all-purpose flour
        3 teaspoons baking powder
        1 teaspoon ground cinnamon
    1/2 teaspoon baking soda
    1/2 teaspoon salt
    1/2 teaspoon ground ginger
    1/2 teaspoon ground allspice
    1/2 cup chopped walnuts
ORANGE FROSTING:
    1/3 cup butter *or* margarine, softened
        3 cups confectioners' sugar
        3 tablespoons milk
        2 teaspoons orange juice
  4-1/2 teaspoons grated orange peel
Candied orange peel, optional

In a mixing bowl, cream butter and sugar. Add eggs, one at a time, beating well after each addition. In another mixing bowl, beat pumpkin, orange juice, milk and orange peel. Combine dry ingredients; add to creamed mixture alternately with pumpkin mixture. Fold in nuts.

Pour into a greased 13-in. x 9-in. x 2-in. baking pan. Bake at 350° for 30 minutes or until a toothpick comes out clean. Cool on a wire rack.

For frosting, combine butter and confectioners' sugar in a mixing bowl. Beat in the milk, orange juice and peel. Frost cake. Garnish with candied peel if desired (see p. 318). **Yield:** 12 servings.

Mom's Oven-Barbecued Ribs

4 Cornish game hens (22 ounces *each*)
1/4 cup butter *or* margarine, melted
1 teaspoon salt
1/2 teaspoon pepper
3/4 cup orange juice
1/2 cup packed brown sugar
1/2 cup Madeira wine, sherry *or* chicken broth
2 tablespoons lemon juice
1 teaspoon ground mustard
1/4 teaspoon ground allspice

Tie legs of each hen together; turn wing tips under backs. Place on a greased rack in a roasting pan. Brush with butter; sprinkle with salt and pepper. Bake, uncovered, at 350° for 1 hour.

In a saucepan, combine the remaining ingredients; bring to a boil. Reduce heat; simmer, uncovered, for 15 minutes. Spoon over hens. Bake 15 minutes longer or until a meat thermometer reads 180°. **Yield:** 4 servings.

Mandarin-Cashew Tossed Salad

(Pictured on page 299)

Ready in 30 minutes or less

Mandarin oranges and chopped red onion add a touch of color to mixed greens and sweet roasted cashews in this refreshing salad. You're sure to be handing out the recipe once friends and family get a taste of the tangy honey dressing. —Sheri Shaffer, Northfield, Ohio

5 cups torn red leaf lettuce
5 cups torn iceberg lettuce
3 cups torn Boston lettuce
2 cans (11 ounces *each*) mandarin oranges, well drained
3/4 cup chopped green pepper
1 celery rib, thinly sliced
1/4 cup chopped red onion
HONEY LIME DRESSING:
1/4 cup vegetable oil
1/4 cup honey
1/2 teaspoon ground mustard
1/2 teaspoon grated lime peel
1/4 teaspoon paprika
1/8 teaspoon salt
Dash white pepper
1 cup honey roasted cashews

In a large salad bowl, combine the lettuces, oranges, green pepper, celery and onion. In a small bowl, combine oil, honey, mustard, lime peel, paprika, salt and pepper; mix well. Drizzle over salad. Add cashews; toss to coat. Serve immediately. **Yield:** 10-12 servings.

Mom's Oven-Barbecued Ribs

(Pictured above)

My mom made these tender ribs for special Sunday suppers when we were growing up. A few common ingredients are all you need to make the zesty sauce that coats them. My family's eyes light up when I bring a plate of these ribs to the table, and company never suspects how easy they are to prepare. —Yvonne White, Williamson, New York

3 to 4 pounds country-style pork ribs
1-1/2 cups water
1 cup ketchup
1/3 cup Worcestershire sauce
1 teaspoon salt
1 teaspoon chili powder
1/2 teaspoon onion powder
1/8 teaspoon hot pepper sauce

Place ribs in a greased roasting pan. Bake, uncovered, at 350° for 45 minutes. Meanwhile, in a saucepan, combine the remaining ingredients. Bring to a boil; cook for 1 minute. Drain ribs. Spoon sauce over ribs. Cover and bake for 1-1/2 hours. Uncover; bake 30 minutes longer, basting once. **Yield:** 4-6 servings.

Orange-Glazed Cornish Hens

(Pictured on page 298)

This is a wonderfully elegant entree to serve at a cozy dinner party for four. Your guests will think you spent hours in the kitchen preparing the tender golden-brown hens and perfecting the full-flavored basting sauce.
—Laurie Bartley, Lake Hiawatha, New Jersey

Special Scallops and Chicken

Ready in 1 hour or less

I make this main course when I want to wow company. It tastes heavenly, and guests always love it. We enjoy the subtle flavor of tarragon in the creamy sauce.
—Sheila Vail, Long Beach, California

1/2 cup all-purpose flour
1/2 teaspoon salt
1/2 teaspoon pepper
  6 boneless skinless chicken breast halves
1/2 pound bay scallops
1/4 cup olive *or* vegetable oil
1-1/2 cups sliced fresh mushrooms
  1 medium onion, chopped
1/4 cup white wine *or* chicken broth
  2 teaspoons cornstarch
1/2 cup whipping cream
  1 teaspoon dried tarragon
1/2 cup shredded Swiss cheese

In a large resealable plastic bag, combine the flour, salt and pepper. Add chicken and scallops in batches; shake to coat. In a large skillet, saute chicken and scallops in oil until lightly browned. Transfer to a greased 13-in. x 9-in. x 2-in. baking dish.

In the pan drippings, saute mushrooms and onion. Add wine or broth. Bring to a boil; cook until liquid is reduced to 2 tablespoons. Combine cornstarch, cream and tarragon until blended; add to skillet. Bring to a boil; cook and stir for 1 minute or until thickened. Spoon over chicken and scallops. Sprinkle with cheese. Bake, uncovered, at 375° for 18-20 minutes or until chicken juices run clear. **Yield:** 6 servings.

Caramel Pear Crumble

Ready in 1 hour or less

This is the first recipe I turn to after my mother shares juicy pears from her orchard. The down-home flavor of the not-too-sweet dessert is a welcomed alternative to apple crisp. Its crumbly topping and hint of caramel keep friends asking for more. —Karen Ann Bland, Gove, Kansas

1-1/4 cups all-purpose flour
  1 cup quick-cooking oats
  1 cup packed brown sugar
  1 teaspoon ground cinnamon
1/2 cup butter *or* margarine, melted
 20 caramels*
  1 tablespoon milk
  3 medium pears, peeled and sliced
Whipped topping and additional cinnamon, optional

In a bowl, combine the flour, oats, brown sugar and cinnamon. Stir in butter (mixture will be crumbly); set aside 1 cup. Press the remaining mixture into an ungreased 9-in. square baking dish.

In a small saucepan over low heat, cook and stir caramels and milk until caramels are melted and mixture is smooth. Remove from the heat. Arrange pears over crust; spoon caramel mixture over pears. Sprinkle with the reserved crumb mixture.

Bake at 350° for 30-35 minutes or until the pears are tender and top is golden brown. Serve warm. Garnish with whipped topping and cinnamon if desired. **Yield:** 6-9 servings.

***Editor's Note:** This recipe was tested with Hershey caramels.*

Maple-Mocha Brownie Torte

(Pictured below)

This impressive-looking dessert is at the top of my list of speedy standbys. It's simple to make because it starts with a boxed brownie mix. Then the nutty brownie layers are dressed up with a fluffy frosting that has a rich creamy texture and irresistible maple taste. —Amy Flory
Cleveland, Georgia

  1 package brownie mix (13-inch x 9-inch pan size)
1/2 cup chopped walnuts
  2 cups whipping cream
  2 teaspoons instant coffee granules
1/2 cup packed brown sugar
1-1/2 teaspoons maple flavoring
  1 teaspoon vanilla extract
Chocolate curls *or* additional walnuts, optional

Prepare batter for brownie mix according to package directions for cake-like brownies. Stir in walnuts. Pour into two greased 9-in. round baking pans. Bake at 350° for 20-22 minutes or until a toothpick inserted 2 in. from the edge comes out clean. Cool for 10 minutes before removing from pans to wire racks to cool completely.

In a bowl, beat cream and coffee granules until stiff peaks form. Gradually beat in brown sugar, maple flavoring and vanilla. Spread 1-1/2 cups over one brownie layer; top with second layer. Spread remaining cream mixture over top and sides of torte. Garnish with chocolate curls or walnuts if desired. Store in the refrigerator. **Yield:** 12 servings.

Maple-Mocha Brownie Torte

Sausage Wonton Stars

(Pictured below)

Ready in 30 minutes or less

These fancy-looking appetizers are ideal when entertaining large groups. The cute crunchy cups are stuffed with a cheesy pork sausage filling that kids of all ages enjoy. We keep a few in the freezer so we can easily reheat them for late-night snacking.
—Mary Thomas
North Lewisburg, Ohio

  1 package (12 ounces) wonton wrappers
  1 pound bulk pork sausage
  2 cups (8 ounces) shredded Colby cheese
1/2 medium green pepper, chopped
1/2 medium sweet red pepper, chopped
  2 bunches green onions, sliced
1/2 cup ranch salad dressing

Lightly press wonton wrappers onto the bottom and up the sides of greased miniature muffin cups. Bake at 350° for 5 minutes or until edges are browned.

In a large skillet, cook sausage over medium heat until no longer pink; drain. Stir in the cheese, peppers, onions and salad dressing. Spoon a rounded tablespoonful into each wonton cup. Bake for 6-7 minutes or until heated through. **Yield:** about 4 dozen.

Cheesy O'Brien Egg Scramble

Ready in 1 hour or less

This breakfast bake is a snap to prepare. It's perfect for a brunch buffet or when out-of-town guests stay the night.

Sausage Wonton Stars

Full of bacon, cheese, hash browns and eggs, the all-in-one dish is a hearty crowd-pleaser.
—Margaret Edmondson, Red Oak, Iowa

  1 package (28 ounces) frozen O'Brien hash brown potatoes
1/2 teaspoon garlic salt
1/4 teaspoon pepper
  1 can (10-3/4 ounces) condensed cheddar cheese soup, undiluted
  1 pound sliced bacon, cooked and crumbled
12 eggs, lightly beaten
  2 tablespoons butter *or* margarine
  2 cups (8 ounces) shredded cheddar cheese

In a large skillet, prepare hash browns according to package directions. Sprinkle with garlic salt and pepper. Transfer to a greased 2-1/2-qt. baking dish. Top with soup. Set aside 1/2 cup of bacon; sprinkle remaining bacon over soup.

In another skillet, scramble eggs in butter until nearly set. Spoon over bacon. Sprinkle with cheese and reserved bacon. Bake, uncovered, at 350° for 20-25 minutes or until cheese is melted. **Yield:** 10-12 servings.

Orange-Nut Sweet Potatoes

Ready in 30 minutes or less

When my siblings and I were young, my mom created this recipe in hopes that we would eat more vegetables. It worked! The citrus sauce went so well with the tender sweet potatoes that the dish became a family favorite.
—Kathleen Wright, Richmond, Kentucky

  2 pounds sweet potatoes, peeled and cubed
2/3 cup sugar
4-1/2 teaspoons cornstarch
  1 teaspoon salt
  1 cup orange juice
  2 tablespoons butter *or* margarine
1/2 teaspoon grated orange peel
1/4 cup chopped walnuts

Place the sweet potatoes in a large saucepan; cover with water. Bring to a boil. Reduce heat; cover and simmer for 6-8 minutes or until tender. Meanwhile, in a small saucepan, combine the sugar, cornstarch and salt. Gradually stir in orange juice. Bring to a boil; cook and stir for 2 minutes or until thickened. Add butter and orange peel; stir until butter is melted.

Drain sweet potatoes; place in a serving dish. Add orange juice mixture and gently stir to coat. Sprinkle with walnuts. **Yield:** 6 servings.

Strawberry Banana Crepes

(Pictured on page 298)

These sweet sensations are as fast to make as they are fabulous. You can cook the crepes the night before, refrigerate them with waxed paper in between, then warm them in the morning before filling.
—Shelly Soule
Las Vegas, Nevada

        1 cup all-purpose flour
        1 tablespoon sugar
    1/2 teaspoon ground cinnamon
1-1/2 cups milk
        2 eggs
        1 to 2 tablespoons butter *or* margarine
FILLING:
        1 package (8 ounces) cream cheese,
        softened
        1 carton (8 ounces) frozen whipped
        topping, thawed
    1/2 cup confectioners' sugar
TOPPING:
        2 cups sliced fresh strawberries
        2 medium firm bananas, sliced
    1/4 cup sugar, optional

In a mixing bowl, combine the flour, sugar, cinnamon, milk and eggs; mix well. Cover and refrigerate for 1 hour.

In an 8-in. nonstick skillet, melt 1 teaspoon butter. Stir batter; pour about 2 tablespoons into the center of skillet. Lift and tilt pan to evenly coat bottom. Cook until top appears dry; turn and cook 15-20 seconds longer. Remove to a wire rack. Repeat with remaining batter, adding butter to skillet as needed. When cool, stack crepes with waxed paper or paper towels in between.

In a mixing bowl, combine the filling ingredients. Spread 2 rounded tablespoonfuls on each crepe; roll up. Combine topping ingredients; spoon over crepes. **Yield:** 18 crepes.

Feta Bruschetta

Hearty Twice-Baked Potatoes

(Pictured on page 299)

Everyone raves about these extra-special spuds that are perfect for meat-and-potato lovers. The creamy, nicely seasoned potatoes are a great accompaniment to grilled chicken, but hearty enough to serve as a comforting meal on their own. —*Rebecca Williams, Alapaha, Georgia*

        8 large baking potatoes
    1/2 pound bulk pork sausage
    1/4 cup butter *or* margarine, softened
        2 cups (8 ounces) shredded cheddar cheese
1-1/2 cups diced fully cooked ham
        6 bacon strips, cooked and crumbled
        1 cup (8 ounces) sour cream
    1/2 cup Italian salad dressing
Salt and pepper to taste

Scrub and pierce potatoes. Bake at 400° for 40-60 minutes or microwave, uncovered, on high for 12-14 minutes or until tender. Meanwhile, in a skillet, cook the sausage over medium heat until no longer pink; drain.

When potatoes are cool enough to handle, cut in half lengthwise; scoop out pulp, leaving a 1/4 in. shell. In a large mixing bowl, mash the pulp with butter. Stir in the sausage, cheese, ham, bacon, sour cream, salad dressing, salt and pepper.

Spoon into potato shells. Place on two ungreased baking sheets. Bake at 400° for 30 minutes or until golden brown. **Yield:** 16 servings.

Feta Bruschetta

(Pictured above)

Ready in 30 minutes or less

You won't believe the compliments you'll receive when you greet guests with these warm appetizers. Each crispy bite offers the savory tastes of feta cheese, tomatoes, basil and garlic. They're terrific for holiday parties or most any gathering. —*Stacey Rinehart, Eugene, Oregon*

    1/4 cup butter *or* margarine, melted
    1/4 cup olive *or* vegetable oil
    10 slices French bread (1 inch thick)
        1 package (4 ounces) crumbled feta cheese
        2 to 3 garlic cloves, minced
        1 tablespoon minced fresh basil *or* 1 teaspoon
        dried basil
        1 large tomato, seeded and chopped

In a bowl, combine butter and oil; brush onto both sides of bread. Place on a baking sheet. Bake at 350° for 8-10 minutes or until lightly browned on top.

Combine the feta cheese, garlic and basil and sprinkle over the toast. Top with tomato. Bake 8-10 minutes longer or until heated through. Serve warm. **Yield:** 10 appetizers.

Table Toppers

WHEN company's coming, take a little extra time to dress up your table. Our kitchen staff came up with these inexpensive ideas for attractive table toppers, neat napkin folds and fancy food presentation.

Peppers Perk Up Your Table

A COLLECTION of fresh produce, such as colorful peppers, makes an effortless arrangement for your dinner table.

To start, choose an appropriate container to hold your arrangement. Try a shallow woven basket (shown in the photo below), or a clear glass bowl that will let the vegetables' bright colors show through.

The size of the container will depend on the size and number of items you plan to put into it.

Fill the container with an assortment of appealing peppers whose colors will complement your menu and dishware.

Visit your grocer's produce section to choose from green, red, yellow and orange sweet peppers as well as different sizes and colors of hot peppers.

Place the larger sweet peppers in the container first, arranging them in a fashion that highlights their bright shades and different shapes. Then tuck smaller hot peppers around edges of the container and into any gaps between the sweet peppers.

Once dinner is over, you can refrigerate the peppers and use them later in the week.

Sealing Edges of Pastry Crust

A WARM and winning appetizer, like the Chili Cheese Tart (recipe on page 301), is a terrific way to begin a memorable meal. The spicy wedges are just the thing to whet your appetite.

This recipe calls for a technique that gives the tart a finished edge while sealing it to keep the cheese from melting out.

To seal the pastry crusts together, press a fork down along the edge and pull it

back to seal the edge. Repeat this step around the entire edge of pastry.

This technique can be used when making potpies, fruit turnovers and pasties. When you're in a hurry, you can also finish off the edges of a double-crust pie this way.

Dressed-Up Dessert Dishes

MOST ANY dessert will dazzle guests when served on plates you've dressed up with bright tissue paper to coordinate with your table. It's easy to do by sandwiching the scraps of colorful paper between pairs of clear plates.

To assemble each decorated dish, you'll need two clear glass dessert plates. The plates should stack rather snugly, so the paper in between is pressed firmly in place.

If you don't have glass plates, clear plastic disposable plates will work instead for desserts served either chilled or at room temperature.

1 First, cut tissue paper into a few 1- to 2-inch strips. Then cut the strips into different sized squares, rectangles or diamonds. Place the pieces of tissue in a pleasing pattern on top of one plate.

2 Gently place the second plate on top of the first one, being careful to avoid moving the scraps of tissue.

Then use these doubled dishes to serve individual cups of Burnt Custard (recipe on page 301) as shown in the photo at left or

whatever dessert is on your menu.

What's nice about this idea is that you can adapt it to use whatever you have on hand.

Instead of tissue paper, you could sandwich bright fabric scraps or colorful paper napkins trimmed to the size of the plate. Or create pretty patterns by sandwiching fresh ferns and flowers that flatten easily.

Jazzy Napkin Fold

GIVE a sleek look to an ordinary napkin with this simple fold that accentuates diagonal lines. It's easy to do when you start with a square cloth napkin that coordinates with your dishes.

1 Fold the napkin in quarters to form a square. Pick up the open point of the top layer of cloth and fold it down in about 1- to 1-1/2- inch folds until it reaches the outside corners.

2 Next, repeat folds with the point of the second layer, stopping just before you reach the previous fold.

3 With napkin placed squarely in front of you and diagonal folds intact, fold napkin in thirds, tucking sides underneath. Smooth folds and place a completed napkin on center of plate at each setting.

Put the Squeeze on Pasta

PUTTING a tasty filling into pasta, like the Special Cheese Manicotti on page 303, can sometimes be tedious if you use a spoon to stuff the tube-shaped noodles. To save time and effort, use this simple technique that easily squeezes the filling just where you want it.

Place the filling in a heavy-duty resealable plastic bag. Cut a 1/2-inch hole in one corner. Holding a noodle in one hand, pipe the filling into one end; turn the noodle around and fill the other end. Place noodles in the baking dish. Repeat with the remaining noodles.

This method also comes in handy when filling jumbo pasta shells. It's a great way to pipe mashed potatoes on a shepherd's pie or whipped cream into cream puffs.

Charming Spring Centerpiece

LEND a breath of spring to your table by topping it with bright blooms arranged in a cute sprinkling can like the one pictured above.

Start with a small watering can about 4-1/2 to 5 inches tall. If the container is strictly decorative, place a plastic liner inside to prevent water leaks.

You'll also need sticky floral tape to create a grid that will help hold your flowers in place.

Then select flowers and greenery. We selected yellow daisies, red mini gerbera daisies, yellow freesia, white monte casino and jasmine for the greenery.

1. Fill sprinkling can or liner three-fourths of the way with water. Place strips of tape parallel to one another across top of container. Repeat with more tape, this time placing strips perpendicular to first set.

The distance between the strips depends on the size and sturdiness of the flower stems. Place strips closer together for smaller stems or droopier flowers.

2. Insert larger flowers, like the daisies in our arrangement, into the individual squares created by the tape grid. Space them out to spread the color.

3. Now tuck smaller flowers and greenery into the squares to fill out the arrangement and cover the green tape. Display the centerpiece on your table and gather compliments on its charming appearance.

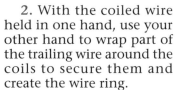

2. With the coiled wire held in one hand, use your other hand to wrap part of the trailing wire around the coils to secure them and create the wire ring.

3. Once you're comfortable they're secure, thread a bead onto the free end of wire. When it reaches the ring, pull the wire taut and around the ring to hold the bead in place. Wrap the wire once around the ring and add the next bead.

Continue until beads are positioned evenly and secured around the entire ring. Then trim or wrap any extra wire before placing completed ring over the top of votive holder (as shown in photo at left).

Shiny Wire Bead Napkin Rings

SEARCHING for napkin rings to match your dishes or linens, but just can't find the right ones? Then fashion your own out of bright brass wire.

1. We started with some 16-gauge brass wire we bought at a hardware store. We shaped it into an attractive design with curlicue ends, then brightened up the ends with colorful craft beads. (We used the same plastic beads featured on the votive holder.)

For each napkin ring, cut an 18- to 20-inch length of wire with wire cutters. Wrap the wire three times around a 1-1/4-inch wooden dowel, leaving about a 1/2-inch space between wraps. Bring both free ends of the wire to the same side of the dowel.

2. Starting with one end of the wire, use a needle-nose or long-nose pliers to begin bending the tip into a small circle. Before the tip is bent in a complete circle, consider adding a bead to it. (Feel free to leave off the bead if you find bending the wire with the bead in place is too tricky.)

Continue using the pliers to bend the wire into a larger curlicue. If you're having difficulty manipulating the wire while it's wrapped around the dowel, remove the dowel and then try.

Repeat the curlicue at the other end of the wire. Then simply remove your new napkin ring from the dowel and slide it around a cloth napkin (as shown in the photo at top left).

Creative Candle Holder

WITH JUST two common craft items—wire and plastic beads—you can create a decorative ring that will dress up a plain votive holder in minutes.

1. First, choose a round glass candle holder that has a smaller top opening than its outside diameter. (The wire ring may slide down tapered or straight-sided candle holders.)

You'll also need a spool of 28-gauge gold-colored crafting or beading wire and an assortment of 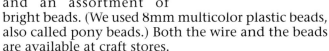 bright beads. (We used 8mm multicolor plastic beads, also called pony beads.) Both the wire and the beads are available at craft stores.

To create coils the proper size, wrap wire around an aluminum can or glass jar (like the applesauce jar we used here) that's a little larger than the top rim of your votive holder.

Wrap the jar about 20 times, being sure not to wrap the wire too tightly or it will be difficult to remove.

Add an additional 20 inches to the end of the wire before cutting it. Then hold the coils together while carefully removing them from the jar.

Bordered Napkin Fold

IT REQUIRES just a few uncomplicated moves to create this casual napkin fold that jazzes up individual place settings in a jiffy.

To begin, you'll want to choose a square cloth napkin. Those edged with lovely lace, pretty piping, bold borders or frilly fringes are good candidates for this fold because it highlights their attractive trim.

First, fold the napkin in half diagonally to form a triangle.

1 Bring the two outside points of the triangle to the center to meet the open point. This will form a square.

2 Next, bring the two outside points that were formed with the previous fold together to meet each other in the center.

Smooth the creases and brush fringes into place if necessary. Place folded napkin on a plate.

Fresh Produce Grouping

SHOW OFF a bounty of summer veggies and fruit with this colorful centerpiece that's a breeze to assemble. It's a fun accompaniment to the special summer menu featured on pages 306-307.

First, you will want to choose three different sized flowerpots. At a local garden center, we picked up terra-cotta pots that measure 3-1/2 inches, 4 inches and 5 inches in diameter.

You can arrange the pots on a 12-inch serving platter that coordinates with your dinner plates like we did. Or place them on a terra-cotta garden saucer.

Now, fill the pots with produce. We spotlighted some of the ingredients called for in the recipes on page 307, but feel free to use items that complement your menu.

If you have a green thumb, you can pick the vegetables for this grouping from your backyard garden. If not, just buy extra at the grocery store or farmer's market.

Be sure to get enough to not only fill the pots but to tuck around them on the serving platter. We needed a total of a dozen mini zucchini, a pint of cherry tomatoes (about 20) and five small lemons.

Once the fruit and vegetables are in place, feel free to tuck greenery or fresh herbs around the pots to fill out the arrangement. We used lemon leaves as shown in the photo at right.

Add a Sweet Touch to Glasses

TRY THIS simply sweet technique that gives a lovely frosted look to refreshing glasses of Special Lemonade (recipe on page 307). Dipping the rims in sugar gives each sip an extra touch of sweetness.

1. To make the sugar cling to the rims, you'll want to moisten them with fresh lemon juice first. To do that, cut a thick slice of lemon into quarters. Make a slit in one of these pieces, then place the rim of a glass into the slit. Rub the lemon piece around the entire rim of glass until it's moistened.

2. Put a small amount of granulated sugar into a shallow dish or saucer. Dip the moistened rim of the glass into the sugar, completely coating the rim. Gently tap the glass to remove any excess sugar.

Pour the lemonade into your frosty-topped glasses and enjoy!

Appealing Orange Garnishes

ADD a sugary sight to any of your after-dinner delights by garnishing them with these easy-to-fix candied orange peels.

After washing and drying an orange, use a vegetable peeler to remove the peel. On a cutting board, cut away any white membrane and slice the peel into thin strips, about 1 to 2 inches long.

1. Mix 1-1/2 cups each of sugar and water in a saucepan and bring to a boil, stirring constantly. Add the orange peel; reduce the heat and simmer for 10 minutes. Remove from the heat and transfer peel to a sieve to drain.

2. Put a small amount of granulated sugar in a resealable bag and add a few of the orange peel strips. Shake until evenly coated. Remove the peel and place on waxed paper to dry.

Then use these edible embellishments to garnish pieces of Pumpkin Orange Cake (photo and recipe on pages 308-309) or most any fruit dessert.

Leaf Place Settings

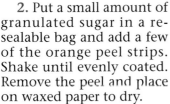

IT'S A BREEZE to bring a splash of color to your table with colorful leaves.

Dinner plates wreathed in fall foliage and place markers made from single leaves (as shown in the photo below right) make distinctive accompaniments to the harvest menu featured on pages 308-309.

First, you need to gather some brilliant red, orange and gold leaves from your backyard. Leaves that have just fallen and have not had time to curl and dry will work best. Or buy silk leaves at a craft store like we did.

For each place setting, arrange the leaves on your table in a circle with the stems inward. Make the circle large enough so the leaves will peek out from beneath the dinner plate, but small enough so the plate will hold them in place. As you complete each circle, set a plate on it, rearranging the leaves if needed.

To create place markers, write the name of each guest on a leaf. We used a silver metallic marker on a silk leaf.

Then place the markers on top of the plates or tuck them into raffia tied around each cloth napkin.

Making a Squash Vase

WHETHER harvested yourself or purchased from the grocery store, a butternut squash adds a unique twist to your centerpiece.

To start, select an unblemished butternut squash that's not too ripe. Try to find one that will stand upright. If you can't, use a knife to cut a thin slice off the bottom to even it out.

1 Cut off the top of the squash about 2 inches below the stem. If the squash's interior is solid in this area, use your knife to remove the flesh to reach the seed-filled interior.

2 With a small spoon or melon baller, hollow out the squash, removing seeds, membranes and any excess flesh. Leave about a 3/4-inch thickness of flesh around the entire shell.

3 Fill vase with water and place it on a saucer to protect the surface of your table. Create an arrangement with your favorite blooms or ones that coordinate with your table linens and dinnerware.

Once your centerpiece is complete, simply place it on your table and enjoy the inviting color it brings (see photo below).

Pretty Pepper Poinsettias

RED PEPPER poinsettias make a colorful accompaniment to a special entree, as shown with the Orange-Glazed Cornish Hens (photo on page 298).

You'll need one sweet red pepper and one green onion for each poinsettia. On a cutting board, slice off the stem and top 2 inches of the pepper. Discard this portion as well as the pepper's seeds, core and any white membrane.

1. Place the pepper cut side down. Carefully make an upside-down V shaped cut about 1-1/2 inches long in the pepper. Discard small piece of pepper. Repeat this step, beginning each V where the previous one ended, four more times or until you have worked your way around the pepper. Turn pepper over and, if necessary, trim petals so they are uniform.

2. Trim the root end of a green onion. Gently insert one blade of a clean pair of small scissors into the root end, placing the tip of the blade above the circular center of the onion. Make a V-shaped cut about 1/2 inch long. Repeat these cuts around the center of the onion. Bend the cut edges away from the onion's circular center and soak in cold water until sides curl slightly. Trim the green end to make onion about 1-1/2 inches long. Break a toothpick in half. Discard one half and insert the other into the non-curly end of the onion, leaving some of the toothpick visible. Gently place the onion in the center of the pepper flower, pushing the exposed toothpick into the pepper.

Candles Make Spirits Bright

MAKE your evening memorable with candles you stylized and grouped on a plate as a centerpiece (see photo at left). The only materials you need are pillar candles and sturdy pins or tacks with decorative heads. Pins with colored, metallic or pearlized heads can be found at fabric and craft stores and also in the sewing or craft departments of department and discount stores. Look for heavier pins that aren't likely to bend or break when being pushed into the candle.

We used nickel-plated steel pins with gold heads and 1/2-inch brass upholstery tacks with rounded heads.

Once you've chosen a design, carefully insert the pins into the candle. If the pins are difficult to push in all the way, you might need to use a thimble.

Heavenly Place Markers

COMPLETE with precious halos and billowing wings, cute paper angels can be personalized for place markers (as shown in the photo above left) or simply as charming decorations. Fold a white 6-inch paper plate in half. Use a scissors to make a 1-1/4-inch cut along the fold toward the plate's center.

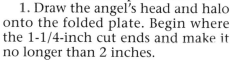

1. Draw the angel's head and halo onto the folded plate. Begin where the 1-1/4-inch cut ends and make it no longer than 2 inches.

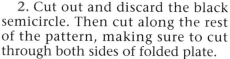

2. Cut out and discard the black semicircle. Then cut along the rest of the pattern, making sure to cut through both sides of folded plate.

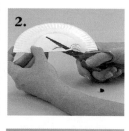

3. Unfold the plate. Follow the cut on the left side of the angel down and around the halo and head. At the point where the cut stops, cut a 1-1/2-inch horizontal slit toward the plate's left edge. Then, starting at the opposite edge of the plate, cut another 1-1/2-inch slit toward the center of the plate, making these slits as closely in line with one another as possible.

4. Turn the plate over and gently bend the two large halves of the plate toward you, overlapping the wing in your left hand over the wing in your right. Continue until slits meet and can be inserted into one another. Adjust wings until the bottoms are even. Turn the angel to face you and fold the halo forward to hover over the angel's head.

To create a place marker, write the name of a dinner guest on the angel's body with a fine-tip marker. To use the paper angel as a decoration, leave it as is or spray-paint it like the one we painted gold in the photo on page 299.

Chapter 20

DURING the week, most folks barely have an extra moment to sit and relax, much less spend time cooking.

But on those more leisurely weekends, when you do have a few minutes to spare, why not head to the kitchen for a refresher on common cooking techniques or for a chance to tackle a little more challenging recipes?

Whether you need to review the basics for selecting, storing and serving "spuds", preserving fresh herbs and preparing various cuts of beef, or you'd like to try your hand at stirring up rich sauces, decorating eye-catching cakes and baking impressive souffles, these easy-to-follow recipes and helpful hints will sharpen your culinary skills.

FALL FOR SOUFFLES. Cheese Souffles (p. 333).

Savory Sauces

Au Gratin Potatoes
Creamed Carrots

A CREAMY SAUCE can be a busy cook's best friend. It doesn't require a lot of ingredients, yet it can transform ordinary items into dressed-up dishes.

While there are many different kinds of sauces, we'll focus on white sauce and hollandaise sauce. Once you've mastered these basic sauces, you can experiment with endless flavor variations (see box on opposite page).

A white sauce is one of the most useful sauces, because it can complement a main-dish meat, dress up a vegetable side dish, add creaminess to a casserole or turn leftovers into a comforting potpie.

White sauce typically starts with a roux, a smooth mixture of equal parts butter and flour.

To make a roux, melt butter in a heavy saucepan. Then whisk flour into it to make a smooth paste. (See how-to photos at right.) Using a whisk is important so the flour doesn't sink to the bottom of the pan and burn.

Once the roux is smooth, a liquid—traditionally milk—is added. Use the whisk again to blend the mixture, then bring it to a boil. Once the mixture cooks for 2 minutes, it's ready to use.

The thickness of white sauce depends on the proportion of flour and butter to liquid. It's easy to vary it to suit your family's preferences.

In general, use the following amounts of flour and butter for each cup of liquid: 1 tablespoon each for a thin sauce, 2 tablespoons each for a medium sauce, 3 tablespoons each for a thick sauce and 4 tablespoons each for a heavy sauce.

Unlike white sauce, hollandaise sauce uses warmed egg yolks as a thickener instead of flour. Cooks often find this lemony butter sauce tricky to make, because the egg yolks can curdle or the sauce can fail to thicken.

To avoid these pitfalls, it's best to heat the egg yolks slowly over low heat. Heating them too quickly will make them granular; using too high of a heat will cook them like scrambled eggs.

Since egg yolks can only absorb a little butter at a time, it's important to gradually add it in small amounts, or the sauce will not thicken. The butter must be completely incorporated into the yolks before more butter is added.

If too much butter is added at one time and the sauce won't thicken, it can usually be saved. Rinse out a mixing bowl with hot water to warm it. Add a teaspoon of lemon juice and a tablespoon of the sauce to the bowl. Whisk briefly until the mixture blends and thickens.

Then whisk in the remaining sauce—2 teaspoons at a time. It's important to beat each addition until thickened before adding the next.

If a finished sauce starts to separate, a tablespoon of cold water beaten into it will often save it.

Making a White Sauce

1 To start a white sauce, whisk flour into melted butter over medium heat until mixture becomes smooth.

2 Gradually whisk milk into the mixture until blended. Bring mixture to a boil; cook and stir for 2 minutes.

Basic White Sauce

For years I have used this smooth sauce to make many dishes, including the two on the opposite page. The recipe can easily be doubled or tripled. —Lois Gelzer
Oak Bluffs, Massachusetts

- **2 tablespoons butter *or* margarine**
- **2 tablespoons all-purpose flour**
- **Salt and pepper to taste**
- **1 cup milk**

In a saucepan over medium heat, melt butter. Whisk in the flour, salt and pepper until smooth. Gradually add milk. Bring to a boil; cook and stir for 2 minutes or until thickened. Use immediately or refrigerate. **Yield:** 1 cup.

Au Gratin Potatoes

(Pictured on opposite page)

This is one of my favorite ways to fix potatoes. Slices are coated in a cheesy sauce and topped with golden crumbs.
—Lois Gelzer

2 cups Basic White Sauce (recipe on opposite page)
1-1/4 cups shredded cheddar cheese
1-1/2 teaspoons salt
1/4 teaspoon pepper
6 medium potatoes, peeled, cooked and cut into 1/4-inch slices
1/2 cup soft bread crumbs
2 tablespoons butter *or* margarine, melted

In a saucepan, prepare a double recipe of the white sauce. Stir in cheese, salt and pepper; cook and stir until cheese is melted. Gently stir in the potatoes until coated. Transfer to a greased 2-qt. baking dish. Toss bread crumbs and butter; sprinkle over potatoes. Cover and bake at 350° for 20 minutes. Uncover; bake 10 minutes longer or until crumb topping is golden brown. **Yield:** 8 servings.

Creamed Carrots

(Pictured on opposite page)

I use my white sauce in this comforting treatment. My grandmother handed down the recipe for these attractive carrot coins.
—Lois Gezler

8 medium carrots (1 pound), cut into 1/4-inch slices
1/4 cup chopped onion
1 cup Basic White Sauce (recipe on opposite page)
2 tablespoons butter *or* margarine
2 tablespoons minced fresh parsley
1/2 teaspoon salt
1/4 teaspoon pepper

In a saucepan, bring 1 in. of water to a boil. Place carrots and onion in a steamer basket over the boiling water; cover and steam for 8-10 minutes or until crisp-tender. Remove basket; drain liquid and return vegetables to the pan. Add white sauce, butter, parsley, salt and pepper; heat through. **Yield:** 4 servings.

Hollandaise Sauce

(Pictured at right)

This traditional sauce, shared by our test kitchen, adds an elegant touch to fresh steamed asparagus. The rich lemony mixture is the typical sauce for eggs Benedict and is also delicious served over broccoli.

Basic White Sauce Taste Twists

ONCE you've accomplished making a basic white sauce, there's no limit to the flavorful variations you can create. Here are a few suggestions compiled by our test kitchen:

Cheese Sauce: Stir 1/2 to 3/4 cup shredded cheddar cheese into 1 cup of white sauce. Heat just until cheese is melted.

Curry Sauce: Stir 1/2 teaspoon curry powder and a pinch of ground ginger into 1 cup of white sauce.

Mornay Sauce: Stir 1/4 cup shredded Swiss cheese, Parmesan cheese or a combination of both and a pinch of ground nutmeg into 1 cup of white sauce.

Mustard Sauce: Stir 1 tablespoon Dijon mustard into 1 cup of white sauce.

Brown Sauce: Follow recipe for a white sauce except substitute beef broth for the milk. For richer color, add a dash of browning sauce.

Veloute Sauce: French for "velvety", this sauce substitutes a light-colored stock such as chicken, turkey or fish broth for the milk.

3 egg yolks
1/4 cup water
2 tablespoons lemon juice
1/2 cup cold butter (no substitutes)
1/8 teaspoon salt
1/8 teaspoon paprika
Dash pepper

In a small saucepan, whisk together egg yolks, water and lemon juice. Cook and stir over low heat until mixture bubbles around edges and reaches 160°, about 20 minutes. Cut cold butter into eight pieces; add to yolk mixture, one piece at a time, whisking after each addition until melted. Stir in salt, paprika and pepper. Serve immediately. **Yield:** 1 cup.

Hollandaise Sauce

Beef Basics

BEFORE the meat industry made an effort to standardize the names of meat cuts, there was some confusion. A specific cut of meat might have more than one name, or be called different names in different regions of the country. Occasionally, the same name would describe different cuts of meat.

By reading the label these days, you should be able to learn the kind of meat (such as beef), the area of the animal the meat comes from (such as the loin) and the common retail cut (such as boneless top loin steak). See chart on opposite page for retail names, along with other names the cut may be called.

Knowing where the cut comes from on the animal can give an indication of the tenderness of the beef. For example, a cut such as a pot roast from the chuck portion comes from a heavily exercised area of the animal, so it will be less tender. See illustration above right.

In general, words like "chuck", "round" and "flank" connote a less tender cut. The terms "loin" and "rib" typically suggest a tender cut. Less tender cuts are sometimes made into ground beef or beef stew meat or are tenderized into cube steaks.

The United States Department of Agriculture grades the quality of beef by giving it three designations: prime, choice and select. Grades are determined by the amount of marbling (the flecks of fat within the meat), the meat's texture, its color and its appearance.

Prime meat, which is usually available only in fine restaurants, has the most marbling. Select meat has the least marbling, while choice is in between. Less marbling means less fat, therefore select has fewer calories. However, it may not be as tender, juicy or flavorful as choice or prime cuts.

Choose packages that are cool to the touch, have little or no excess liquid and have no punctures.

And always check the "sell-by" date.

While almost any meat can be prepared with any cooking method, cooks will find the results more satisfying when the appropriate method is used. The "right" method is determined by the tenderness of the beef cut.

Tender cuts are better prepared by dry heat methods such as roasting, broiling, outdoor grilling, pan-broiling, pan-frying and stir-frying.

These methods are suggested for tender cuts of meat from the rib, loin, round and flank regions of the animal. Examples are rib roasts, rib eye steaks, T-bone steaks, tenderloin and top loin steaks, sirloin steaks and top round steaks.

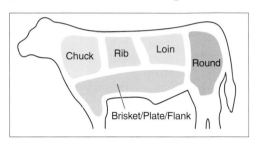

On the other hand, less tender cuts are better prepared by moist heat methods such as braising and cooking in liquid. Slowly cooking the meat with steam or hot liquid softens the connective tissues for a more tender product.

These methods are recommended for less tender cuts of meat from the chuck, round, brisket, plate and flank regions. Examples are arm steaks, blade pot roasts, short ribs, stew meat and brisket.

Some cuts from the same part of the animal, such as the round and flank, can be prepared different ways. For example, round and flank steak can be braised (a moist cooking method) or pan-fried (a dry heat cooking method) with good results.

Grilled Flank Steak

(Pictured below)

Plan ahead…needs to marinate

Mustard and soy sauce really add flavor to this juicy flank steak. With a potato dish and green salad, this is a favorite meal for family and friends.
—*Kristin Roberts*
Colorado Springs, Colorado

> 1/2 cup soy sauce
> 1/4 cup red wine *or* beef broth
> 2 green onions, sliced
> 3 tablespoons lemon juice
> 3 tablespoons vegetable oil
> 2 tablespoons Worcestershire sauce
> 1 to 2 garlic cloves, minced
> 1 beef flank steak (1-1/2 pounds)
> 2 tablespoons prepared mustard

In a large resealable plastic bag, combine first seven ingredients; mix

Grilled Flank Steak
Beef with Sweet Peppers

well. Add beef; seal bag and turn to coat. Refrigerate several hours or overnight, turning once. Drain and discard marinade. Brush both sides of meat with mustard. Grill, covered, over medium-hot heat for 5-10 minutes on each side (for rare, a meat thermometer should read 140°, medium, 160°; well-done, 170°). Slice thinly across the grain. **Yield:** 6 servings.

Seasoned Rib Roast

Beef with Sweet Peppers

(Pictured on opposite page)

Ready in 1 hour or less

Strips of beef chuck roast are simmered to a tasty tenderness in this dish. —Kim Shea, Wethersfield, Connecticut

- 1 boneless beef chuck roast (2 pounds), cut into 1/4-inch strips
- 2 tablespoons olive *or* vegetable oil
- 1 large onion, cut into wedges
- 1 medium green pepper, julienned
- 1 medium sweet red pepper, julienned
- 3 garlic cloves, minced
- 2 tablespoons butter *or* margarine
- 1 can (14-1/2 ounces) stewed tomatoes
- 1 tablespoon dried basil
- 1 teaspoon sugar
- 1/2 to 1 teaspoon garlic salt
- 1/4 teaspoon pepper
- Hot cooked rice

In a large skillet, cook beef in oil until browned, about 4 minutes; drain. Remove and set aside. In the same skillet, saute onion, peppers and garlic in butter until crisp-tender. Add tomatoes and seasonings; mix well. Return meat to pan; bring to a boil. Reduce heat; cover and simmer for 35-40 minutes or until meat is tender. Serve over rice. **Yield:** 6 servings.

Seasoned Rib Roast

(Pictured above)

This is a very special and savory way to prepare a boneless beef rib roast. Gravy made from the drippings is exceptionally tasty. —Evelyn Gebhardt Kasilof, Alaska

- 1-1/2 teaspoons lemon-pepper seasoning
- 1-1/2 teaspoons paprika
- 3/4 teaspoon garlic salt
- 1/2 teaspoon dried rosemary, crushed
- 1/4 teaspoon cayenne pepper
- 1 boneless beef rib roast (3 to 4 pounds)

In a small bowl, combine the seasonings; rub over roast. Place roast, fat side up, on a rack in a shallow roasting pan. Bake, uncovered, at 350° for 1-3/4 to 2-1/2 hours or until meat reaches desired doneness (for rare, a meat thermometer should read 140°; medium, 160°; well-done, 170°). Remove to a warm serving platter. Let stand for 10-15 minutes before carving. **Yield:** 6-8 servings.

Location	Retail Name	Also Known As
Chuck	Arm Steak	Round Bone Steak Swiss Steak
Chuck	Top Blade Pot Roast	Top Chuck Roast 7-Bone Roast
Chuck	Short Ribs	Barbecue Ribs Braising Ribs
Rib	Back Ribs	Beef Riblit Rib Bones
Rib	Rib Eye Roast	Delmonico Roast Roll Roast
Loin	Tenderloin Steak	Fillet Mignon Fillet Steak
Loin	Boneless Top Loin Steak	Boneless Club Steak New York Strip Steak Kansas City Steak Strip Steak Ambassador Steak
Round	Top Round Steak	Top Round London Broil Short Cut Steak
Round	Tip Roast	Tip Sirloin Roast Knuckle Roast
Flank	Flank Steak	Flank Steak Fillet London Broil Jiffy Steak
Plate	Skirt Steak	Fajita Meat Philadelphia Steak
Brisket	Whole Boneless Brisket	Fresh Beef Brisket

Frosted Cakes

Cupcakes with Whipped Cream Frosting

IT'S EASY to create impressive cakes once you're familiar with the equipment and techniques.

If you plan to do a lot of cake decorating, you may want to consider buying a pastry bag made of sturdy plastic or canvas that can be washed and reused.

Disposable plastic pastry bags are available as well as parchment triangles that can be rolled into cones to create one-use bags. (Even an ordinary plastic sandwich bag can be used—snip a small hole in the corner of a bag and insert tip through the inside.)

If you only plan to decorate an occasional birthday cake, you may want to buy a few individual tips. But if you plan to decorate all kinds of desserts, you may want to consider a decorating set that includes a nice selection of basic tips.

Most metal tips are marked with a universal tip number, which allows you to follow patterns and achieve the same results each time. A particular style of tip may come in several sizes. For example, leaf tips are generally numbered 65 to 70. Each of those tips will make a different sized leaf.

You can find both pastry bags and decorating tips in the housewares section of many department stores and at cooking stores, or you can order them from cooking catalogs or through the Internet. Many stores—including large grocery stores—stock plastic tips for the novice decorator.

One tool that's particularly handy when decorating cakes is a two-piece coupler. It allows you to switch decorating tips without changing pastry bags when using the same color frosting.

To use a coupler, place the large part of the coupler inside the pastry bag. (See illustration above right.) Trim the top of the bag if necessary in order to let the coupler extend about 1/4 inch outside the bag. Place the coupler ring over the tip and screw both parts of the coupler together.

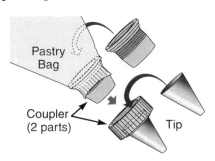

To change tips and continue using the same color frosting, simply unscrew the coupler ring, switch decorating tips and screw on the ring with the new tip.

Our test kitchen shares two frosting recipes here. If you're short on time, you can even use prepared canned frosting.

For most cakes, you'll want to tint some of the frosting. There are three kinds of food colorings you can use: liquid, paste and soft concentrated gel.

To make the desired color, begin with a single drop of liquid food coloring or a small amount of paste or gel and mix it into the frosting thoroughly before adding more. Use concentrated gel or paste coloring if you're trying to create a very dark or rich shade.

Once you've tinted the frosting, spoon it into a folded-down pastry bag with tip until it's no more than two-thirds full. Twist or fold the bottom of the bag to keep the frosting from coming out.

To eliminate air bubbles in the bag, squeeze out a small amount of frosting before starting. Then, as you decorate, continue to twist or roll down the bag to keep steady pressure on the frosting.

As a beginner, or to regain your confidence, you may want to review the common techniques illustrated on the opposite page. Simply use one color of frosting to practice on a sheet of waxed paper. When you're comfortable with the techniques, you can scrape the frosting off the waxed paper and reuse it.

Cupcakes with Whipped Cream Frosting

(Pictured above left)

While not as sweet as buttercream, this frosting made with whipping cream is smooth and creamy.

> 1 package (18-1/4 ounces) cake mix
> 1-1/4 teaspoons unflavored gelatin
> 5 teaspoons cold water
> 1-1/4 cups whipping cream
> 5 tablespoons confectioners' sugar
> 1/4 teaspoon vanilla extract
> Red and yellow food coloring

Prepare and bake cake mix according to package directions for cupcakes. Cool on wire racks. In a saucepan, sprinkle gelatin over water; let stand for 1 minute to soften. Cook and stir over low heat until gelatin is dissolved. Remove from the heat; cool. In a mixing bowl, beat cream until soft peaks form. Add sugar, vanilla and gelatin mixture; beat until well combined.

Set aside 1 cup for decorating. Spread remaining frosting over tops of cupcakes. Divide reserved frosting in half; tint one portion pink and the other yellow. Use a toothpick to outline shape of heart, flower or sunburst on tops of cupcakes. Use medium star tip to pipe pink or yellow stars along outline. Fill in shape with piped stars as desired. **Yield:** *2 dozen.*

Cake with Buttercream Decorating Frosting

(Pictured below)

This sweet creamy frosting made with real butter is easy to blend together and holds its shape nicely.

> 1 package (18-1/4 ounces) cake mix
> 1 cup butter (no substitutes), softened
> 1 cup shortening
> 3 pounds confectioners' sugar (12 cups)
> 1 tablespoon vanilla extract
> 1/4 teaspoon salt
> 3/4 to 1 cup milk
> Blue, yellow and green gel, paste *or* liquid food coloring

Prepare and bake cake mix according to package directions for two 9-in. layers. Cool on wire racks. In a mixing bowl, cream the butter and shortening. Beat in sugar, vanilla, salt and enough milk to achieve spreading consistency. Place 1/4 cup frosting each in three small bowls; tint one blue, one yellow and one green. Set aside 2-1/4 cups of remaining frosting for basket weave decoration and shell border. Spread remaining frosting between layers and over top and sides of cake.

To decorate, place reserved white frosting in pastry bag. Use medium basket weave tip to decorate sides of cake using basket weave pattern (see diagrams at right). Change to medium star tip to pipe shell border along bottom and top edges of cake.

For writing, use medium round tip and blue frosting to pipe desired greeting off-center on top of cake. Use medium round tip to pipe green vines around writing. Switch to medium leaf tip to pipe green leaves along vines. Use small flower tip to pipe yellow and blue flowers along vines. Leftover frosting can be frozen for up to 3 months. **Yield:** 10-12 servings (7 cups frosting).

Editor's Note: Use of a coupler will allow you to easily change tips for different designs.

Cake with Buttercream Decorating Frosting

Techniques for Tips

TO CREATE the patterns shown on the cake and cupcakes on these pages, use the suggested metal or plastic cake decorating tips to follow the techniques below. Unless otherwise noted, hold pastry bag at a 45° angle.

Basket Weave Pattern: With serrated side of basket weave tip facing up, pipe a vertical line of frosting. Squeeze out a short horizontal bar over the top of the vertical line. Add additional bars, each about a tip width apart, to cover line. Make another vertical line of frosting to the right of first one, a tip width apart, overlapping ends of horizontal bars. Repeat the procedure of covering lines with bars by gently tucking tip under line first to create a basket weave effect.

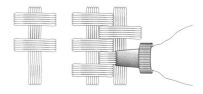

Shell Border: Using a star tip, squeeze bag and slightly lift tip as frosting builds and fans out. Relax pressure as you lower tip to make the tail. Stop pressure completely and pull tip away. Work from left to right, resting the head of one shell on the tail of the previous shell.

Writing, Printing, Vines: Using a round tip, touch the surface lightly, squeezing frosting out evenly as you go. Release pressure and touch the cake surface to stop each line, letter or vine.

Leaves: Using a leaf tip, lightly touch tip to surface, squeezing bag and holding tip in place to let frosting fan out to create wide base of leaf. Relax and stop pressure as you pull tip away from leaf and draw it to a point.

Top view

Drop Flowers or Stars: Using a flower or star tip, hold the bag at a 90° angle with tip just above the surface. Squeeze bag and hold tip in place as flower or star is formed; stop pressure and pull tip up. Increase or decrease pressure to slightly change the size.

Fresh Summer Herbs

FRAGRANT flavorful herbs enhance all kinds of foods, from main and side dishes to salads, soups, sauces and more.

If you have a green thumb, you likely have herbs planted in your garden, growing in containers on your patio or sprouting from pots on a sunny windowsill. To enjoy herbs at the peak of their flavor, you should pick them when they're healthy and vigorous.

If herbs aren't harvested soon enough, and the plants form flowers, the flavor in the leaves can diminish and become bitter. Picking leaves regularly will encourage the plants to continue growing.

When harvesting herbs, most plants should be trimmed above leaf buds, where the plant branches out. But woody herbs, like rosemary, should be cut at the point at which new branches grow off a central stem. (The central stem should not be cut, because this will slow new growth.)

Not a gardener? Summer is a great time to buy fresh herbs at your grocery store or a farmer's market. When selecting harvested herbs, pick firm stalks with leaves that are not wilted or bruised.

If you have a choice between fresh whole leaves or chopped herbs, choose whole leaves. They keep their flavor longer than chopped herbs.

If you're not going to use them right away, you can store unwashed herbs for up to 1 week. Place bunches of herbs with their stems in a vase of water in the refrigerator. (Be sure to keep the leaves out of the water.)

Pack loose leaves in perforated plastic bags in the refrigerator. Place a dry paper towel at the bottom of the bag to absorb excess moisture, which can promote decay.

Clean the herbs once you're ready to use them. Place them in a sink or large bowl of cool water that has salt added to it. (The salt will drive away insects without damaging the herbs.) Gently swish the herbs in the water, remove them and dry in a salad spinner, or place on paper towels and pat dry.

Remove leaves from herb stems, like thyme, by holding the top of the stem and running your fingers down the stem in the opposite direction of leaf growth. Herbs with larger leaves, like basil, should be snipped from the stems.

To use in recipes, chop herbs by placing them in a small bowl and using the tips of kitchen scissors to snip them.

For longer storage, consider freezing or drying herbs once they're cleaned.

Herbs can be frozen for up to 4 months. Freeze whole herbs on a tray for about 3 hours, then crumble them, put in freezer containers or heavy-duty resealable bags and return to the freezer. This way, you can remove a desired amount a spoonful at a time.

Another way to freeze herbs is to make them into herb ice cubes. Put chopped herbs in an ice cube tray and cover with water or broth. Once frozen, the cubes can be stored in plastic containers. They're particularly good for adding directly to sauces and soups.

If you prefer, air-dry your herbs instead. Tie them together in little bunches by the stems, then hang upside down in a well-ventilated place with low humidity. You can also spread herbs loosely on paper or a clean cloth stretched over a wire rack or screen.

Stored in a tightly closed container in a cool dark place, dried whole herbs can be kept for 1 year, while dried crushed herbs can be kept for 6 months.

To substitute dried herbs when fresh herbs are called for in a recipe, use 1 teaspoon of crumbled dried leaves for every tablespoon of finely chopped fresh herbs.

Freeze chopped fresh herbs in freezer containers or bags; any amount needed can be used directly from the freezer.

Place chopped fresh herbs in an ice cube tray and cover with water or broth. Use herb cubes without thawing.

Tie the stems of small bundles of fresh herbs and hang them upside down to dry in a well-ventilated area.

Tarragon Cheese Loaf

(Pictured at right)

Ready in 1 hour or less

The distinctive taste of tarragon seasons this savory layered bread.
—*Sheryl Hurd-House, Fenton, Michigan*

- 1 unsliced round bread (1 pound)
- 1/4 cup butter *or* margarine, softened
- 2 tablespoons minced fresh tarragon
- 1 cup (4 ounces) shredded Monterey Jack cheese
- 2 cups shredded Parmesan cheese

Slice bread horizontally into thirds; remove top section and set aside. Spread butter over the bottom and middle sections; sprinkle with the tarragon and cheeses. Re-assemble loaf; tightly wrap in foil. Bake at 350° for 25 minutes or until cheese begins to melt. Let stand for 5 minutes. Cut into wedges. **Yield:** 8-10 servings.

Tarragon Cheese Loaf
Herbed Tortilla Rounds
Chicken with Herb Sauce

Herbed Tortilla Rounds

(Pictured above right)

Plan ahead…needs to chill

Take this flavorful summer appetizer to parties, church potlucks or anytime you want a snack.
—*Margaret Slocum, Ridgefield, Washington*

- 1 package (8 ounces) cream cheese, softened
- 2 tablespoons butter *or* margarine, softened
- 1 to 2 tablespoons minced chives

- 1 to 2 tablespoons minced fresh parsley
- 1/2 teaspoon garlic powder
- 1/4 teaspoon dill weed
- 1/8 teaspoon dried thyme
- Pepper to taste
- 5 flour tortillas (6 inches)

In a small mixing bowl, beat cream cheese and butter. Add seasonings; mix well. Spread evenly over tortillas. Roll up tightly and wrap in plastic wrap. Refrigerate until firm. Unwrap; cut into 3/4-in. slices. **Yield:** about 2-1/2 dozen.

Chicken with Herb Sauce

(Pictured above)

Ready in 30 minutes or less

My grandmother gave me the recipe for these moist golden chicken breasts topped with a tangy butter sauce.
—*Irene Cooney, Manheim, Pennsylvania*

- 4 boneless skinless chicken breast halves
- 1/2 teaspoon salt
- 1/4 teaspoon pepper
- 2 tablespoons butter *or* margarine, *divided*
- 2 tablespoons olive *or* vegetable oil, *divided*
- 1/2 cup chicken broth
- 2 tablespoons minced chives
- 2 tablespoons minced fresh parsley
- 2 teaspoons lime juice
- 1 teaspoon minced fresh basil
- 1 teaspoon Dijon mustard

Place the chicken breasts between two sheets of waxed paper; flatten evenly with a mallet. Sprinkle both sides with salt and pepper. In a large skillet, heat 1 tablespoon each of butter and oil; brown chicken over medium-high heat for about 6 minutes on each side or until juices run clear. Remove and keep warm. Stir broth, chives, parsley, lime juice, basil, mustard and remaining butter and oil into drippings; cook and stir until butter is melted. Serve over chicken. **Yield:** 4 servings.

Common Herbs and Their Uses

Basil: Licorice-like flavor is good in tomato, pasta, meat and vegetable dishes as well as dips, soups and salads; a traditional ingredient in pesto.

Chives: Mild onion flavor complements many savory dishes; often snipped and sprinkled as garnish.

Mint: Refreshing addition to desserts, fruit dishes and beverages; makes a pretty garnish.

Oregano: Peppery flavor is common in pizza and pasta sauces; often used to season meats, soups, stews and chili.

Parsley: Peps up salads, sauces and soups; also a popular garnish.

Rosemary: Somewhat piney flavor is popular with roasted meats; also complements cheese and tomato-based sauces.

Sage: Camphor-like flavor is good with pork and other meat dishes plus soups.

Tarragon: Mild licorice-like flavor seasons chicken, fish, egg and cheese recipes as well as salad dressings and creamy sauces.

Thyme: Rich earthy taste complements stuffing, soups, stews, beef, chicken, fish and vegetables.

Potato Pointers

WHETHER a potato is baked, fried, boiled, mashed or steamed, its down-home comfort can't be beat.

The versatility of the potato makes it stand out, but it also has a long shelf life, is low in cost and offers a wealth of vitamins and minerals.

While there are some 100 different varieties of potatoes, most fall into one of five types: russet, white, round, red and sweet.

Russet: Often called Idahos, russets are oblong thick-skinned potatoes. They are perfect for baking and mashing because their texture is light and fluffy. Due to their crumbly flesh, russets do not hold their shape when cooked, so they are not suggested for salads or casseroles. They are, however,

great for frying because they stay crispy on the outside, soft on the inside and don't absorb as much oil as other potatoes.

White: White potatoes are similar in shape to russets. Even though they can be baked, they are known as boilers because they hold their shape so well when cooked this way. They are often used in casseroles, soups and stews. White potatoes are also referred to as long whites.

Round: Sometimes called Irish potatoes, round potatoes are similar to whites but have thinner and smoother skin. Rounds are also ideal for boiling and for dishes where they are cut because they, too, hold their shape.

Red: Red potatoes are popular for boiling and steaming. They have a thin skin, but the skin's red pigment makes the potato a colorful choice for salads.

New potatoes, also known as early or immature potatoes, are simply smaller versions of their full-grown counterparts. They are fresh from a garden and have never been stored. Available in both red and white, they taste best when boiled or steamed.

Sweet: The sweet potato is a high-energy food that is chock-full of vitamins and minerals. When used in recipes, sweet potatoes are interchangeable with yams. They can be boiled, baked or candied.

The type of potato you choose should be based on how you're going to prepare it. Begin by selecting those that are firm and heavy for their size.

Avoid any that are shriveled or have cuts, blemishes, decay or green discoloration under the skin.

When buying sweet potatoes, look for a medium-size, thick potato that tapers toward the ends. Sweet potatoes with darker skins tend to be sweeter and moister than others. Don't buy sweet potatoes with large knots or blemishes.

It's best to store all potatoes in a cool, dry, dark and well-ventilated place—not a refrigerator. Keeping potatoes in a basket, net or paper bag is better than storing them in a plastic bag. If plastic bags are used, they should be perforated so the potatoes can breathe.

Before using a potato, scrub it with a vegetable brush and rinse it in water. Remove the potato's eyes or sprouts with a paring knife. If you aren't going to prepare peeled or cut potatoes immediately, cover them with cold water to prevent them from darkening.

Then choose one of the flavorful reader recipes that follow…or try one of the common cooking methods listed in the box below.

Pointers for Preparing Potatoes

WHEN it comes to cooking potatoes, there are several simple ways to achieve tasty results. Regardless of the cooking method you choose, avoid using aluminum or iron pots as they can turn tubers gray. And while you can peel the potatoes first, try leaving the skins on for a nutritious change of pace.

Boiling

Cut large potatoes into pieces. Place the pieces in a saucepan and cover with water. Cover and bring to a boil. Boil for 15-30 minutes or until the potatoes are tender; drain well. (If you boil russets, it's recommended that you peel them first as their skins will likely come off during boiling.)

Steaming

Place potato pieces in a steamer basket over 1 inch of boiling water in a pan. Cover and steam until tender, 15-30 minutes.

Baking

Pierce whole potatoes several times with a fork. Bake directly on an oven rack or on a baking sheet at 375° for 45-60 minutes or until potato feels soft when gently squeezed. Russet potatoes bake the best. If a soft-skinned potato is preferred, wrap it in foil or rub it with oil before baking.

Microwaving

Pierce whole potatoes and microwave on high for 8-10 minutes or until tender. Place quartered potatoes in a microwave-safe dish. Cover and cook on high until tender, about 9-12 minutes; stir halfway through.

Sweet Potatoes

Place whole potatoes in a large pan and cover with water. Cover and boil gently until potatoes can easily be pierced with a fork, about 30-45 minutes; drain. (Sweet potatoes peel easier after they have been cooked and are cool enough to handle.)

Sweet potatoes can be baked in the oven like russets; however, their juices may escape while baking. Be sure to put them on a baking sheet or place foil beneath them.

Grilled Vegetable Medley

(Pictured below)

Ready in 1 hour or less

This hearty potato dish is a no-fuss favorite. And because everything is wrapped in foil and cooked on the grill, cleanup is a snap. —Susan Hase, Larsen, Wisconsin

- 12 small red potatoes, halved
- 1 medium sweet potato, peeled and cut into chunks
- 4 tablespoons butter *or* margarine, melted, *divided*
- 4 to 6 garlic cloves, minced, *divided*
- 2 tablespoons minced fresh parsley, *divided*
- 1-1/2 teaspoons salt, *divided*
- 1/2 teaspoon lemon-pepper seasoning, *divided*
- 3/4 pound whole fresh mushrooms
- 1 large onion, sliced
- 1 medium green pepper, cut into 1/4-inch slices
- 1 small zucchini, cut into chunks
- 1 medium yellow summer squash, cut into chunks
- 1 cup (4 ounces) shredded mozzarella *or* Swiss cheese

Sour cream, optional

Place potatoes and sweet potato on an 18-in. x 15-in. piece of heavy-duty foil. Drizzle with half of the butter; sprinkle with half of the garlic, parsley, salt and lemon-pepper. Seal packet tightly. Grill, covered, over indirect medium-hot heat for 20 minutes on each side.

Meanwhile, place mushrooms, onion, green pepper, zucchini and summer squash on a 20-in. x 18-in. piece of heavy-duty foil. Drizzle with remaining butter; sprinkle with remaining seasonings. Seal packet tightly. Grill, covered, over medium-hot heat for 10 minutes on each side or until the vegetables are crisp-tender.

Combine the contents of both packets in a serving

bowl; sprinkle with cheese. Serve with sour cream if desired. **Yield:** 8-10 servings.

Herbed Mashed Potatoes

(Pictured below left)

Ready in 1 hour or less

I add rosemary, garlic and lemon peel to this rich potato side dish. —Sandi Pichon, Slidell, Louisiana

✓ Uses less fat, sugar or salt. Includes Nutritional Analysis and Diabetic Exchanges.

- 4 large potatoes, peeled and cubed
- 1/3 cup chopped onion
- 1 garlic clove, minced
- 1 tablespoon butter *or* margarine
- 3/4 cup sour cream
- 1 teaspoon dill weed
- 1/4 to 1 teaspoon salt
- 1/2 teaspoon minced fresh rosemary
- 1/2 teaspoon grated lemon peel
- 1/4 teaspoon crushed red pepper flakes, optional

Paprika, optional

Place potatoes in a saucepan and cover with water; cover and bring to a boil over medium-high heat. Cook for 15-20 minutes or until tender. In a skillet, saute onion and garlic in butter until tender. Drain and mash the potatoes; add onion mixture, sour cream, dill, salt, rosemary, lemon peel and red pepper flakes if desired.

Spoon into a greased 1-1/2-qt. baking dish. Sprinkle with paprika if desired. Cover and bake at 350° for 25 minutes or until heated through. **Yield:** 6 servings.

Nutritional Analysis: One 3/4-cup serving (prepared with reduced-fat sour cream and 1/4 teaspoon salt) equals 160 calories, 5 g fat (3 g saturated fat), 15 mg cholesterol, 145 mg sodium, 25 g carbohydrate, 2 g fiber, 5 g protein. **Diabetic Exchanges:** 1-1/2 starch, 1 fat.

Crab Potato Salad

Plan ahead...needs to chill

This recipe has been in my husband's family for 100 years. I've replaced the canned crab with imitation crab. —Clarice Schweitzer, Sun City, Arizona

- 4 to 6 medium potatoes, peeled and cubed
- 2 packages (8 ounces *each*) imitation crabmeat, chopped
- 1 cup finely chopped onion
- 1/2 to 3/4 teaspoon salt
- 1/2 teaspoon pepper
- 1/4 teaspoon dill weed
- 3 cups mayonnaise

Place potatoes in a saucepan and cover with water; cover and bring to a boil over medium-high heat. Cook for 15-20 minutes or until tender. Drain and cool. In a large bowl, combine the potatoes, crab, onion, salt, pepper and dill. Add mayonnaise; toss to coat. Refrigerate for 2-3 hours before serving. **Yield:** 10-12 servings.

Grilled Vegetable Medley
Herbed Mashed Potatoes

Special Souffles

EVERYDAY EGGS go from ordinary to extraordinary when you serve them in a sensational souffle. The thought of preparing a traditional souffle can be intimidating. But, it doesn't have to be, once you learn some secrets.

Souffle comes from a French word that means "to blow or puff up" and describes the dish created when a custard base made with egg yolks is lightened with beaten egg whites and baked. Since the puffed-up results fall shortly after being removed from the oven, a souffle should be served immediately.

It can be sweet or savory depending on additional ingredients, so consider one for your next brunch, as a scrumptious side dish or delectable dessert.

Properly preparing the batter is one of the keys to stirring up a standout souffle. The batter has two components—a base and egg white foam.

The base provides the souffle's substance and flavor. It is usually a thick cooked cream sauce or puree that is combined with egg yolks.

To create the batter, egg white foam is then gently folded into the base. Souffles puff up when baked due to the air trapped in the egg white foam.

We've compiled the following tips that will help you prepare an egg-cellent souffle batter:

• When separating eggs, make sure no yolks get into the egg whites, or they won't whip properly.

• To separate several eggs, work over a small bowl, and transfer the whites to a larger bowl a few at a time. That way, if you accidentally break an egg yolk into the whites, you don't ruin all of the whites you've separated.

• When whipping the egg whites, glass mixing bowls are better than plastic ones, which tend to retain grease.

• Be sure that the beaters and bowl are dry before they touch the whites. Water prevents whites from whipping properly.

• Egg whites should be brought to room temperature before beating. Warm egg whites, expand more than cold ones and will give you better volume.

• When beaten, the whites should be just firm enough to form and hold a peak when the beaters are lifted. This is known as stiff peaks.

• When folding the egg whites into the egg yolk base, pile the beaten whites on top of the base. Don't pour the base on top of the whites as that will press the air out of them. Then use a rubber spatula to gently cut down through the ingredients, move the spatula across the bottom of the bowl and bring up the base mixture. Repeat this circular motion just until the mixture is combined.

Once the batter is done, it's time to pour it into a dish and bake it. Souffle dishes should have straight sides, which allow the batter to "climb" up the sides while baking. Individual souffles can be made in custard cups or ramekins.

If you'd like to cut down on last-minute details when making a souffle for company, you can prepare the batter in advance. Combine the mixture and spoon it into the dish as directed in the recipe. Then cover it with plastic wrap and refrigerate it for up to 2 hours before baking.

Be sure your oven temperature is accurate. A high baking temperature helps form a skin on top of the souffle, which keeps it moist inside. An oven that is even 25° off can affect the end result.

Place souffles on the middle rack of the oven. If a souffle is baked on the lowest rack, the bottom of the souffle may burn. If the rack is too high, the top of the souffle may burn before the inside is baked...or the souffle may even rise and burn onto the top of the oven or heating elements.

Only keep the oven door open for an instant when you put in the souffle.

It's also recommended that you open the door as few times as possible during baking and carefully close it to prevent the souffle from collapsing. (Banging the door shut could cause it to fall.)

But how can you check for doneness without opening the oven door? First view the souffle through your oven window. If the souffle looks risen and browned on top, it should be firm enough not to fall.

Then open the door and touch the top of the souffle lightly with your hand. If it feels firm, it should be done.

To double-check for doneness, insert a wooden or metal skewer or sharp knife at a 45° angle through the souffle into the center. It should come out clean. A properly cooked souffle should be firmly set around the outside, but still moist and creamy in the center, not overly dry.

A souffle will stay puffed up for at least 1 to 2 minutes after being removed from the oven. It's common and to be expected that it will collapse shortly after, so present this distinctive dish immediately. Your guests are sure to fall for it!

Chocolate Souffle

Chocolate Souffle

(Pictured below left)

I serve this rich chocolate dessert when entertaining. The sumptuous souffle has a light, airy texture, yet its center is moist and almost fudge-like.
—Linda Blaska, Dunwoody, Georgia

    1/2 cup sugar
      2 tablespoons cornstarch
    1/4 teaspoon salt
    3/4 cup milk
      2 squares (1 ounce *each*) unsweetened chocolate
      3 tablespoons butter *or* margarine
      4 eggs, *separated*
      1 teaspoon vanilla extract
    1/4 teaspoon cream of tartar
Confectioners' sugar, optional

In a saucepan, combine the sugar, cornstarch and salt. Add milk. Bring to a boil; cook and stir for 2 minutes or until thickened. Add the chocolate and butter; cook until chocolate and butter are melted and smooth. Remove from the heat. Add 1/3 cup chocolate mixture to the egg yolks; return all to the pan, stirring constantly. Stir in vanilla; cool slightly.

In a mixing bowl, beat egg whites until foamy. Add cream of tartar; beat until stiff peaks form. Fold into chocolate mixture. Pour into a greased 2-qt. souffle dish. Bake at 350° for 45-50 minutes or until a knife inserted near center comes out clean. Dust with confectioners' sugar if desired. Serve immediately. **Yield:** 8-10 servings.

Cheese Souffles

(Pictured above right and on page 320)

Ready in 1 hour or less

I think it's a shame that souffles are often overlooked. These individual souffles are elegant for brunch.
—Dennis Blankenbaker, Greenfield, Indiana

      3 tablespoons butter *or* margarine
      3 tablespoons all-purpose flour
    1/4 teaspoon ground mustard
Dash cayenne pepper
      1 cup milk
      1 cup (4 ounces) shredded cheddar *or* Swiss cheese
      4 eggs, *separated*

In a saucepan, melt butter. Stir in flour, mustard and cayenne until smooth; gradually add milk. Bring to a boil; cook and stir for 1-2 minutes or until thickened. Reduce heat; stir in cheese until melted. Remove from the heat. Stir a small amount of hot mixture into egg yolks; return all to the pan, stirring constantly. Cool slightly. In a mixing bowl, beat egg whites until stiff peaks form. Fold into egg yolk mixture. Pour into four greased 10-oz. souffle dishes or custard cups. Bake at 350° for 20 minutes or until a knife inserted near center comes out clean. Serve immediately. **Yield:** 4 servings.

Cheese Souffles

Carrot Souffle

This festive flavorful side dish is perfect for company. I have made souffles for years using other vegetables, but carrots remain our family's favorite. —Mrs. Travis Baker
Litchfield, Illinois

    2-1/4 cups sliced carrots
      3 tablespoons butter *or* margarine
      3 tablespoons all-purpose flour
    1/2 teaspoon salt
Dash hot pepper sauce *or* 1/8 teaspoon pepper
    3/4 cup milk
      4 egg yolks
      6 egg whites
    1/2 teaspoon cream of tartar

Place 1 in. of water in a saucepan; add carrots. Bring to a boil. Reduce heat; cover and simmer for 8-10 minutes or until tender. Drain. Place carrots in a food processor or blender; cover and process until pureed. Measure 1 cup and set aside.

For white sauce, melt the butter in a saucepan. Stir in flour, salt and pepper sauce until smooth. Gradually add milk. Bring to a boil; cook and stir for 2 minutes or until thickened. Remove from the heat; set aside.

In a small mixing bowl, beat egg yolks until thick and lemon-colored. Add 1/3 cup white sauce; mix well. Return all to the pan, stirring constantly. Cook and stir for 1-2 minutes. Stir in the pureed carrots; mix well. Cool completely, about 30 minutes.

In another mixing bowl, beat the egg whites until foamy. Add cream of tartar; beat until stiff peaks form. Gently fold a third of the egg whites into carrot mixture. Fold in the remaining egg whites. Pour into a greased 2-qt. souffle dish. Bake at 350° for 40-45 minutes or until top is golden brown and puffy. Serve immediately. **Yield:** 6 servings.

General Recipe Index

*This handy index lists every recipe by food category, major ingredient
and/or cooking method, so you can easily locate recipes to suit your needs.*

✓ Recipe includes Nutritional Analysis and Diabetic Exchanges

✓ Recipe includes Nutritional Analysis and Diabetic Exchanges

✓ *Recipe includes Nutritional Analysis and Diabetic Exchanges*

✓ Recipe includes Nutritional Analysis and Diabetic Exchanges

✓ Recipe includes Nutritional Analysis and Diabetic Exchanges

✓ Recipe includes Nutritional Analysis and Diabetic Exchanges

✓ Recipe includes Nutritional Analysis and Diabetic Exchanges

✓ Recipe includes Nutritional Analysis and Diabetic Exchanges

✓ Recipe includes Nutritional Analysis and Diabetic Exchanges

✓ *Recipe includes Nutritional Analysis and Diabetic Exchanges*

✓ Recipe includes Nutritional Analysis and Diabetic Exchanges

✓ *Recipe includes Nutritional Analysis and Diabetic Exchanges*

✓ Recipe includes Nutritional Analysis and Diabetic Exchanges

✓ Recipe includes Nutritional Analysis and Diabetic Exchanges

Alphabetical Index

*This handy index lists every recipe in alphabetical order
so you can easily find your favorite recipes.*

✓ Recipe includes Nutritional Analysis and Diabetic Exchanges

✓ *Recipe includes Nutritional Analysis and Diabetic Exchanges*

✓ *Recipe includes Nutritional Analysis and Diabetic Exchanges*

✓ Recipe includes Nutritional Analysis and Diabetic Exchanges

✓ *Recipe includes Nutritional Analysis and Diabetic Exchanges*